Praise for *Killing the Dream*

"Posner's *Killing the Dream* is the most comprehensive and definitive story of the King assassination to date. In many ways Mr. Posner has done for the murder of Dr. King what he did in his best-known previous work *Case Closed*, which slammed down the lid on the numerous conspiracy theories on the assassination of President John F. Kennedy. Mr. Posner's new book covers all the questions that have been raised about Mr. Ray as Dr. King's killer. One finishes this book reassured that no dark secrets remain. . . . A fine and timely book."
—Richard Bernstein, *The New York Times*

"*Killing the Dream*, a heavily researched and well-written examination of the facts by author Gerald Posner, strives to lay the question to rest, much to the chagrin of the cadre of conspiracy buffs. Posner succeeds."
—CNN Interactive Book Reviews

"For 30 years, suspicion has hung over the murder of the Rev. Martin Luther King, Jr. Members of King's family are among the many who doubt that Ray had anything to do with it. King's son Dexter said on ABC last year—with others in the family nodding in assent—that they did not believe Ray pulled the trigger or even knew the murder was about to take place. Posner has taken on the task of liberating everyone from surmises. . . . First-rate."
—*The Washington Post Book World*

"Combining fresh reporting with a careful review of investigations, and using the common sense that is a scarce commodity in this field, Posner does for the King assassination what he did for the JFK killing in his 1994 book, *Case Closed*. He doesn't merely uphold the official version of the King killing, he marches forward to expose the alternative theories as frauds." —*USA Today*

"Here Posner demolishes Ray's shifting claims and alibis by reconstructing his activities in the months prior to King's death. Posner's convincing conclusion: Ray, a small-time loser, most likely killed King on his own." —*People*

"With *Killing the Dream*, Posner has written a superb book: a model of investigation, meticulous in its discovery and presentation of evidence, unbiased in its exploration of every claim. And it is a wonderfully readable book, as gripping as a first-rate detective story."
—Anthony Lewis, *The New York Times Book Review*

"Writing in the clear, forceful manner of a reporter in total command of his facts, Posner has produced what will, conspiracy theorists to the contrary, almost surely turn out to be the definitive account of a landmark event."
—*The Philadelphia Inquirer*

"As with its predecessor, the true persuasiveness of *Killing the Dream* lies not so much in its debunking of alternative theories as in its vivid, believable portrait of the assassin. . . . Posner's work confirms what the Kings, of all people, should have realized long before now. In championing Ray's cause, they are embracing a killer."
—*The Cleveland Plain Dealer*

"If *Killing the Dream* shares the copious research and good storytelling of the author's Kennedy investigation, this book promises to be one of the notable books of the year. After all of the recent sensational theorizing, King's death deserves Posner's calm and able sleuthing."
—*Library Journal*

"A rational, meticulously researched road map to help wade through Ray's endlessly evolving claims of innocence. Posner cuts through years of legal posturing and myth-making and places the focus back where it belongs: on James Earl Ray. . . . What results is an impressive study of a hardened, violent criminal. Well-researched journalism, thoroughly sourced with on-the-record interviews . . . full of fresh insights."
—*The Oakland Tribune*

"With Dexter King and his mother claiming a government conspiracy in the death of the reverend to anyone who will listen to them, this study, by a relentless investigator, will prove popular."
—*Booklist*

"The definitive study of the King assassination . . . sparks immediate interest from its opening account of the last days of the famed civil-rights leader and his involvement in labor turmoil in Memphis. Posner's careful analysis overpowers the various flawed and unsupported theories offered over the years. He pronounces this case closed—and his readers likely will, too."
—*The Seattle Times*

"A new book on the King killing is timed just right . . . Posner's *Case Closed* went on to become a best-seller as it convinced numerous doubters that Lee Harvey Oswald really acted alone, period. This is Posner's encore."
—*Newsday*

"Posner discounts the theory that King's murder was plotted by anyone except Ray. In the process, he paints such a detailed portrait of Ray and his pathetically criminal family that by the end, the reader is interested in Ray the human being."
—*San Francisco Chronicle*

Killing the
Dream

ALSO BY GERALD POSNER

Mengele: The Complete Story

Warlords of Crime:
Chinese Secret Societies—The New Mafia

The Bio-Assassins

Hitler's Children

Case Closed: Lee Harvey Oswald and
the Assassination of JFK

Citizen Perot: His Life and Times

Killing the Dream

James Earl Ray and the
Assassination of
Martin Luther King, Jr.

GERALD POSNER

A HARVEST BOOK
HARCOURT BRACE & COMPANY
San Diego   New York   London

Grateful acknowledgment is made to Hobby-Catto Properties, L.L.C., for permission to reprint
excerpts from "I Had Been in Trouble Most of My Life, in Jail Most of It" by William Bradford Huie
(*Look*, November 12, 1968, pp. 96–113) and "I Got Involved Gradually and I Didn't Know Anybody Was to Be Murdered" by William Bradford Huie (*Look*, November 26, 1968, pp. 67–99).
Reprinted with permission from Hobby-Catto Properties, L.L.C.

First published by Random House in 1998

Library of Congress Cataloging-in-Publication Data
Posner, Gerald L.
Killing the dream: James Earl Ray and the assassination of Martin
Luther King, Jr./ Gerald Posner.—1st Harvest ed.
        p.   cm.
Originally published: New York: Random House, 1998.
Includes bibliographical references and index.
ISBN 0-15-600651-0 (pbk.)
1. King, Martin Luther, Jr., 1929–1968–Assassination. 2. Ray,
James Earl, 1928– . I. Title.
[E185.97.K5P67   1999]
364.15'24'092—dc21   98-52845

Printed in the United States of America
First Harvest edition 1999
A C E D B

To my wife, Trisha, my eternal partner

Contents

PART TWO

The Assassin

PART THREE

The Search for Truth

PART I

The Assassination

1

"I Am a Man"

I Am A Man." Those were the simple words on the signs carried by many of more than 1,300 striking Memphis sanitation workers—nearly all black— during the spring of 1968.[1] Trouble had been brewing for years. Among the lowest paid of city employees, with no medical insurance, workers' compensation, or overtime pay, the sanitation workers had unsuccessfully tried twice before to get the city to recognize their union.[2] The slide toward a strike had begun on February 1, 1968, when two workers seeking shelter during a torrential rainstorm hid inside the rear of a garbage truck. They were crushed to death when a switch was accidentally thrown. The city refused to compensate the victims' families, and other workers were infuriated. That tragedy was compounded a few days later when, in the midst of another storm, twenty-two black sewer workers were sent home without pay. The white supervisors who had ordered them home went to work after the weather cleared and were paid for a full day. Following a formal protest, the black employees received only two hours' pay. That prompted a work stoppage on Lincoln's birthday, Monday, February 12. The demands were straightforward: All garbage and sewer workers wanted a new contract that guaranteed a fifty-cent-an-hour increase and the right to have their union dues deducted directly from their paychecks.

The strike would have had a different history if Memphis had not had Henry Loeb III as mayor. The forty-five-year-old Loeb, who was six-five with a booming voice, had been elected only five weeks earlier. He was an heir to one of the city's wealthiest Jewish families, and had converted to Episcopalianism just after being sworn in. An opinionated and stubborn man, Loeb, while not a racist, had a plantation view of blacks—he would see they were taken care of since he knew what was best for them. That attitude ensured that in the recent election, forty-nine of every fifty blacks voted against him.

Now threatened with the sanitation strike, Loeb adopted a hard position. Since a strike of municipal workers was illegal, he refused to negotiate unless they returned to work, and in no case would he allow a paycheck deduction to the union, since that meant he would be the first major Southern mayor to recognize a black municipal union.

The day after the sanitation workers walked off their jobs, officials of the national union began arriving to lend their support. Loeb announced midweek that if workers did not return to work the following day, he would fire them. On Thursday, only four days after the walkout started, Loeb began hiring scabs, and with a police escort they made limited attempts at picking up garbage.

The racial overtones were evident from the start. The bulk of workers were black, and most white Memphians had little sympathy for their cause. Initially, the only support came from the National Association for the Advancement of Colored People (NAACP) and local black pastors, led by James M. Lawson. Many of the strikers were members of Lawson's Centenary Methodist Church. Lawson himself was a friend of Dr. Martin Luther King, Jr., having met him shortly after the successful 1956 Montgomery bus boycott. Thirty-nine years old, he had served three years as a missionary in India, where he became a follower of Ghandi's principles of nonviolence, and had spent thirteen months in prison for refusing to fight in the Korean War. Lawson, together with the Reverend H. Ralph Jackson, called for a meeting between Loeb and the Memphis Ministers Association. Loeb refused to talk to them.

On Friday, February 23, more than a thousand strikers and supporters crammed a meeting of the city council's Public Works Committee. The rumor was that the committee had decided to recognize the union and approve the paycheck deduction, but, once the meeting started, the city council dodged the issue and threw the strike, as an "administrative matter," back to Loeb. The reaction was swift and furious, with strike leaders calling for an impromptu march down Main Street to Mason Temple, strike headquarters. It was the first defiant black march in Memphis history. The police shoved the men to the right side of the street, four abreast. After several blocks trouble started. A police car came too close to the crowd and ran over a woman's foot. In a moment, young black men were rocking the squad car. Riot police, clad in blue helmets and gas masks, then swarmed into the crowds, indiscriminately macing and clubbing protestors.[3]

The violent police reaction converted the strike from the single issue of better conditions for the sanitation workers into a symbolic racial battle for better treatment of the city's black community. "It showed many people," recalled Lawson, "beyond the shadow of a doubt, that we were in a real struggle."[4] That night, strike leaders met and elected a strategy committee, Community On the Move for Equality (COME). Lawson was chairman, Jackson vice chairman, and Jesse Epps, an international union representative, an adviser. The next day, COME presented a five-point program to all 150 of the city's black ministers and their congregations. The program included fund-raising campaigns and rallies in churches, a boycott of all downtown businesses as well as companies with the Loeb name, and two daily marches through downtown Memphis, the first for strikers, families, and supporters, and the second for students.

When the police had attacked and maced the Memphis demonstrators, Martin Luther King, Jr., was in Miami, at a ministers' retreat sponsored by the Ford Foundation. One of those attending was the Reverend Samuel "Billy" Kyles, a tall, thin, charismatic pastor of Memphis's Monumental Baptist Church. Kyles, in his early thirties, was a prominent Memphis pastor who, together with Lawson and Jackson, helped form public opinion in much of the city's black community.

"The Miami police begged Martin not to leave the hotel because there were so many threats against him," recalls Kyles.* "So we stayed inside. And we got around to talking about the threats. 'You just kind of live with it,' he said. 'I don't walk around every day scared, but I was really scared twice.' Once was when the three civil rights workers were killed in Mississippi.[5] At a church rally there, Ralph [Abernathy] and Martin were praying, and Martin said, 'Oh Lord, the killers of these boys may be hearing us right now.' And a big sheriff who was standing there to guard Martin said, 'Damn right!' The second time was when he had marched in Cicero, Illinois, back in 1966. He had never encountered that type of hatred, even in the South. People lined the streets hurling insults and threats at him. And when he walked along a street with trees, he said, 'From those trees, I expected any moment to get shot.' "[6]

When Kyles called home, he learned about the police attack on the demonstrators. His own seven-year-old daughter was among those maced. Later that day, "I mentioned it off-handedly to Martin, that they had a march in Memphis and had been attacked. Maybe you have to come down and help us out. 'I may do that,' he said."[7]

By coincidence, a few days after Kyles had spoken to King, Lawson proposed that prominent national figures be invited weekly to rally the strikers and their

---

* In this book, whenever a person is quoted in the present tense, it reflects an interview conducted by the author. The past tense indicates all other sources.

supporters. Memphis newspapers and television had given the strike minimum coverage. Lawson hoped to force their hand by transforming the strike into a national issue.[8] Among those considered was Roy Wilkins, head of the NAACP, Whitney Young of the National Urban League, Bayard Rustin of the A. Philip Randolph Institute, and Dr. King. Wilkins and Rustin, the first approached, agreed to speak in Memphis on March 14. When King was invited, he was hesitant, saying that his doctors had recently told him to get more rest. "All of his staff was against Martin coming," recalls Kyles. "He was way behind schedule for the preparation for the [Poor People's] march on Washington [scheduled for April 22]."[9]

Most of King's energies were going toward the Poor People's Campaign. His announcement the previous November that he wanted "waves of the nation's poor and disinherited" to descend on Washington, D.C., and stay there until the government responded with reforms had already caused many whites to fear that the summer would be racked by major civil disturbances.

However, the sanitation strike seemed a clear-cut issue of right or wrong, and King and his staff relented, finally shifting a March 18 meeting of his Southern Christian Leadership Conference (SCLC) executive committee from Jackson, Mississippi, to Memphis.[10]

The strike, meanwhile, remained at a standstill.[11] On Monday, March 18, King arrived shortly after 7:00 P.M. Lawson and Epps picked him up at the airport. He was tired, but the sight of a packed auditorium—15,000 people at Mason Temple—revitalized him. There were people standing in the rafters, in the back, and on the sides. "You fellows must really have something going on here," he told Lawson.[12] A huge white banner—NOT BY MIGHT, NOT BY POWER, SAITH THE LORD OF HOSTS, BUT BY MY SPIRIT—was draped behind the podium. King, a rousing orator who was best before large crowds, was in rare form that night. Time and again, he had the crowd on its feet. By the end of his talk, the three shiny garbage cans on the stage near him had over $5,000 in contributions for the strikers.

"Martin, we are having daily marches," Lawson said to King on the podium. "Why don't you come back and lead a big march? You see how they receive you. It would be terrific!"[13]

Lawson had approached King at the right moment. Reveling in the excitement of the tumultuous reception he had just received, King checked with two of his closest advisers, Andrew Young and Ralph Abernathy, both of whom agreed it was worth returning. "He said it was like the old days," says Kyles. "It really energized him."[14] King pulled out his appointment book and checked for an open date. The crowd fell silent as they saw him back at the microphone. "I want to tell you that I am coming back to Memphis on Friday. I want all of you to stay home from work that day. I want a tremendous work stoppage, and all of you, your families and children, will join me, and I will lead you in a march through the center of Memphis."[15] That announcement prompted a thunderous response from the crowd.*[16]

During the following days, the union leaders and ministers prepared for the day Memphis would be shut down. King's entry into the sanitation strike exacerbated the division between blacks and whites. Many whites thought King was an interloper who had latched on to the strike as a way of burnishing his own image. They resented his involvement. Blacks, on the other hand, welcomed it. "We never viewed him as an outsider," says Kyles. "We didn't need Martin Luther King to come and tell us to be free, we just needed him to come and help us be free."[17]

On March 21, the day before King's return, a freak storm hit the area. It began snowing about 4:00 P.M. Snow is rare in Memphis, and almost unheard of in March. "I looked at it with curiosity," recalled Lawson. "I really thought the stuff would stop, it won't last, it's too wet."[18] It snowed, however, through the night, and by dawn a foot was on the ground, on the way to seventeen inches, the second-largest snowstorm in Memphis history. Lawson telephoned King, who was scheduled to take a flight into the city by 9:00 A.M. Everything was canceled, but they agreed on a new date, Thursday, March 28.[19] Many white Memphians, however, greeted the snowstorm's arrival with relief. "Our prayers were answered," says the wife of the city's then police homicide chief.[20] Yet the tension among whites only temporarily lessened, since a new work stoppage was only six days away.

On Wednesday, March 27, around 1:30 P.M., a middle-aged man—slim, with dark brown hair, a thin nose, thick black-framed glasses, manicured nails, and a complexion so pale it appeared he was seldom in the sun—walked into the Gun Rack, a Birmingham, Alabama, store some 240 miles from Memphis.[21] "I would like to see your .243-caliber rifles."[22] His voice had a slightly high pitch, but was soft, hard to hear. Clyde Manasco, the clerk, thought he recognized him and that he had been in the shop before, always alone. He was the man with all the questions: What was the most accurate rifle? How much would a bullet drop at one hundred yards? At two hundred? What rifle provided the flat-

---

* James Earl Ray's latest attorney, William Pepper, contends in his book *Orders to Kill* that "a team of federal agents conducted electronic surveillance on Dr. King in his suite at the Holiday Inn Rivermont Hotel on the evening of March 18." Pepper cites a source "who must remain nameless." The problem, however, is that King actually spent the night of March 18 at his regular motel, the black-run Lorraine.

test and longest trajectory? What scope was the best, affording excellent sighting with no distortion? He had even inquired about a Browning automatic
.264 that had been written up in gun magazines but not yet shipped to stores.[23]

On other occasions, Manasco, as well as the owner, Quinton Davis, had
given the customer some booklets—one on Redfield scopes and another on
Winchester guns—as well as referred him to books that contained manufac-
turers' technical specifications.[24] The questions did not strike Davis as odd,
since he assumed the customer might be interested in doing his own hand re-
loading of ammo. At other times, Davis had taken guns off the rack and offered
them to him, but the customer never handled them. Instead he just looked and
studied.[25]

Whenever Davis or Manasco talked to him, the man stared back. Both later
recalled his unusual light blue eyes. Davis thought he might be a Southerner,
and while he talked intelligently and was always neatly dressed in a sports
jacket, he somehow seemed "under a strain or slightly mentally disturbed."[26]

When the man walked through the front door that Wednesday, Manasco
sighed. The Gun Rack did not get many customers as difficult as him. Most
knew what they wanted. But this time, Manasco had a feeling the man with the
questions might be, as he later put it, "about ready to buy a gun."[27]

Manasco informed him he did not have any Remington .243s in stock, and
instead tried to interest him in a Remington .30-06. "No, it's too expensive,"
the man said. Instead, he asked Manasco for a ballistics chart, but since he
could not take it with him, he studied it for a few minutes before leaving. At the
curb, he got into a white Mustang and drove off. The employees at the Gun
Rack never saw him again.

2

The Riot

By Thursday, March 28, the freak snowstorm seemed a distant memory. The weather had turned hot. It was already in the low eighties by 8:00 A.M., when a large crowd of marchers gathered at Clayborn Temple. A contingent of Invaders was already there. They were a gang of college-age radicals who carried the mantle of black activism, but the police suspected this was a cover for petty crimes. Recently, with the advent of the sanitation strike, the Invaders had taken the community's most militant stands.

King was supposed to arrive at 9:00, but his plane from New York was late. "People were restless," remembers the Reverend Billy Kyles. "And some of the Invaders started working the crowd. 'We don't need anything peaceful,' they said. I knew there was trouble brewing and felt we'd better start the march without King. But Jim Lawson overruled me and said we should wait for King. I knew that was a mistake."[1] King's car did not arrive until nearly 11:00 A.M.

"We had planned to go inside and 'work-shop' the people in the theory and techniques of non-violence," recalled Abernathy.[2] Young men crowded around the car, initially making it impossible for King to step outside. Bernard Lee, one of King's aides, recognized them as Invaders. "They're a bunch of troublemakers who are trying to horn in on the march," he said. Lawson worked his way through the crowd. "The only way we'll get away from them is to get out and start the march," he said.[3] So King and the others got out of the car. King

linked arms with Abernathy and Bishop Julian Smith of the Methodist Episco-
pal Church, and they started off, singing "We Shall Overcome." Riot police remained out of sight so they would not incite the crowd.[4] It was a few minutes
after 11:00.

"I stayed in the back to give some direction," says Kyles. "Before everyone
had even left the church, young thugs had ripped the sticks off their placards to
use as clubs."[5]

"After a few blocks," recalled Abernathy, "we heard what sounded like gun-
shots, though we later learned it was the smashing of glass windows. The Invaders had used the cover of our march to commit acts of violence."[6]

"I heard a police walkie-talkie," says Kyles. " 'The Negroes are looting the
stores. Permission to break up the march.' Then a slight pause. 'Permission
granted.' The police just rioted. They made no attempt to find out who were ri-
oters, looters, or peaceful demonstrators."[7]

The melee that followed quickly eroded into bedlam, with police—some
having removed their badges and identification numbers—chasing any black
demonstrator they could find. Young rabble-rousers continued shattering store
windows and grabbing whatever merchandise they could carry, while those
who had come to march legitimately in support of the strikers fled in panic.
Lawson excitedly told King that for his own safety he had to leave immediately.[8]
A line of state troopers was gathering in front of King and his aides, effectively
hemming them in. But then a Pontiac driven by a black woman pulled up to the
nearest corner, and King, Lee, and Abernathy pushed their way to the car and
pleaded to be allowed inside.[9] Recognizing them, she let them into the car and
the police moved aside, allowing them to pass. As the car approached the Mississippi River, the group saw two policemen and pulled over to seek help.

"Where are you trying to go?" one of the policemen asked.

"The Peabody Hotel." Union officials had rented a room for them there.

"Forget it. There's pandemonium at the Peabody."

"What about the Lorraine?" That was the black-owned motel at which
King and his entourage normally stayed.

"Pandemonium there. As a matter of fact, we've declared a curfew. We're
going to clear the streets. Follow us."[10]

The police took King and his aides to the Rivermont Holiday Inn, a luxury
hotel on the river.* It was only there, when King turned on the television and saw
live coverage of the riot, that he realized how serious the situation was. The po-

---

* The FBI tried to use King's stay at the Rivermont to embarrass him. The Bureau had
long conducted a relentless and at times illegal surveillance campaign against King. It
later tried to get a "cooperative news source" to publicize the fact that "there was a first-
class Negro hotel in Memphis, the Hotel Lorraine, but King chose to hide out in a white

lice had shot and killed a sixteen-year-old Invader. Scores were hurt, including five shot and one stabbed. Three hundred were arrested.[11] Every window in a two-block stretch of historic Beale Street was smashed. By mid-afternoon, after a series of pitched street battles between riot police armed with tear gas and black students showering them with bricks and bottles, Governor Buford Ellington ordered four thousand National Guardsmen into the city, complete with armored personnel carriers. More than a hundred fires broke out in downtown Memphis, many the result of arson. Mayor Loeb instituted a strict 7:00 P.M. to 5:00 A.M. curfew; police allowed people on the streets only to go to or from work.[12]

"This is terrible," King said, wringing his hands and shaking his head in disbelief. "Now we will never get anybody to believe in nonviolence."

"It's not our fault, Martin," said Abernathy, trying hard to reassure himself as much as King. "Those young men—"

"It doesn't matter who did it," King shouted. "We'll get the blame."[13] He was as despondent as Abernathy had ever seen him. "He was extremely depressed," agrees Kyles, who visited him later at the hotel.[14]

What worried King and his aides was that the violence in Memphis could be a deathblow to his Poor People's Campaign. "Maybe we just have to admit that the day of violence is here," King remarked to Abernathy, "and maybe we have to just give up and let violence take its course. The nation won't listen to our voice—maybe it'll heed the voice of violence."[15]

There was already finger-pointing among King's aides as to why they had even allowed him to march for the strikers. "If we made a mistake, it was in going to Memphis at all," declared King's chief aide, Andrew Young.[16]

By the time Lawson visited King at the Rivermont later that night, King was resting in bed. He was scheduled to leave the next morning, but already he wanted to return soon to lead another demonstration. "If we don't have a peaceful march in Memphis, no Washington," King said. "No Memphis, no Washington."[17] Lawson and King decided to hold a press conference the following morning, where they would announce their intent to have a new march. King agreed to pull some of his aides off the Poor People's Campaign and send them to Memphis to conduct nonviolence workshops before he returned.[18]

King did not get to sleep until nearly 4:00 A.M. The next morning he met with some of the Invaders who arrived to offer their apologies. The press conference started near noon. Abernathy later said that it was "perhaps his finest performance with the press."[19] He was witty, precise, and honest about the

---

owned and operated Holiday Inn" [MLK FBI file 100-106670, section 94]. The following day, the Memphis *Commercial Appeal* had a cartoon depicting a petrified King fleeing the scene with the caption "Chicken-a-la-King."

problems in the previous day's march. He told the reporters he hoped to return in "three or four days" for another demonstration.

About the time King was holding his press conference in Memphis, a man walked into the Long-Lewis hardware store in Bessemer, Alabama, some ten miles outside Birmingham. The store's manager, Mike Kopp, remembered him as a young white man, dressed in a dark brown suit, a blue and yellow pin-striped shirt, and a green tie. He had dark hair, a thin nose, manicured nails, and thick horn-rimmed glasses.[20]

"Do you handle high-powered rifles?" the stranger asked.

Kopp said yes, and offered to show him a .30-30.

"That wouldn't be powerful enough." The man had a soft voice, but pro-nounced each word clearly. There was no noticeable accent.[21]

Instead, the customer asked about a .243, .308, and .30-06. He wanted to know the prices of each as well as how many inches the bullet might drop at 600 yards. He also inquired about 6.5mm ammunition that might fit a Japa-nese rifle. At one point, Kopp took a Browning off the rack, and the customer opened and closed the bolt action.[22]

The customer also asked about scopes and how long it would take Kopp to mount one. When informed that it would take two days—Kopp sent his rifles to Birmingham for mounting scopes—the man asked for names of other local stores that might carry high-powered rifles.

As he was leaving, the customer stopped near a large mounted moose head. "That's a nice trophy. I once tried to bring one down, but I missed."[23] To Kopp, the man seemed "weak," and with his pale, almost sickly, complexion, not the outdoors type. He looked around some more. "I might come back here," he said, as he walked out the door.

Three hours later, at Aeromarine Supply Company, across the road from Birmingham's municipal airport, John DeShazo, a twenty-five-year-old gun enthusiast, was leaning across a counter waiting for his friend, Don Wood, the owner's son, to return from lunch. Aeromarine Supply, a sprawling, single-story warehouse-style building, had one of the largest gun selections in the South. DeShazo thought the man who walked in, in a wrinkled brown suit and thick horn-rims, seemed out of place in the store. He could have been a sales-man.[24]

He meekly approached one of the clerks, Hugh Baker, and asked to exam-ine a Remington Gamemaster .243 rifle. By the way he handled it, DeShazo concluded that he did not know much about guns. Then the customer asked to examine a Browning .243 safari-grade rifle and a Remington .30-30 caliber. "Have you got a scope for this?" the man asked, pointing to the Remington

.243. He quickly settled on a premier Redfield 2×7 scope. After discussing price for a moment, Baker told the man that if he could wait, the store would mount and calibrate the scope. He agreed.[25]

As he watched the entire transaction, DeShazo became aggravated. He is the type of person, DeShazo thought, who buys a rifle, kills his wife, and then gives all weapons a bad name.[26] He has no business buying a rifle.

DeShazo walked up to him. Although the man was not visibly drunk, he smelled of alcohol. "You've really got quite a gun there—you'll have to learn how to use it."[27] The man gave a crooked smile, almost a smirk. As DeShazo recalled, the man said that his brother, or perhaps brother-in-law, had invited him to go deer hunting in Wisconsin. He walked away from DeShazo and started filling in the store's purchase form, giving his name as Harvey Lowmeyer and his address as 1907 South Eleventh Street in Birmingham. He paid the $248.59 bill in cash.[28]

As he was ready to leave, his salesman explained to him that the original box for the Remington could no longer be used since the scope made it too large to fit inside, so instead the store fashioned a makeshift container from a large Browning gun box. The man left with the Remington box as well.

About 5:00 P.M. that same day, Lowmeyer telephoned Aeromarine and reached Don Wood. "He stated that he had had a conversation with his brother," recalled Wood, "and decided that the gun he had purchased was not the gun he wanted, and he requested whether he could exchange it for a Remington, Model 760, .30-06 caliber."[29] Wood said yes, but that it would cost another five dollars. That was all right, said Lowmeyer. When could he come in? Since the store was closing, Wood suggested the following day, Saturday, March 30.

Lowmeyer was at Aeromarine when it opened at 9:00 A.M.

"Why don't you want the .243?" asked Wood. "It's big enough to bring down any deer in Alabama."

"I want to hunt bigger game in Wisconsin," Lowmeyer quietly said.*[30]

---

* The bolt of the .243 rifle was covered with hardened gun grease, and Lowmeyer evidently had trouble loading the weapon, so he decided to swap it for a different gun (CA, 4/5/93/Ct. Proceeding File). While the .243 was a good gun for hunting varmints and small deer, the pump-action Remington Gamemaster Model 760 .30-06-caliber rifle was a much more powerful weapon. Remington described it as "the fastest hand-operated big game rifle made." The .30-06 bullets weigh nearly twice as much as the .243 ammo, travel 2,670 feet at 100 yards, and drop less than .01 of an inch in that distance. As opposed to a military, fully jacketed bullet designed to cut through flesh, giving the victim a chance of survival if no major organ is struck, a soft-point bullet expands on impact and is deliberately designed to rip flesh or organs with explosive violence. The rules of the Geneva Convention on ground warfare prohibit the use of soft-nosed slugs. The .30-06 bullet, hitting with an impact of over 2,000 pounds of energy, is strong enough to stop a charging rhinoceros at 100 yards, or to kill a man as far away as 1,500 yards. King was slain from a distance of 66 yards.

Wood told him to return by 3:00 P.M., when he would have transferred the Redfield scope to the new gun. Lowmeyer came back in mid-afternoon and exchanged the box of .243 ammunition he had bought the earlier day for twenty rounds of Remington-Peters .30-06 Springfield high-velocity, 150-grain, softpoint Core-Lokt cartridges. Thanking Wood, Lowmeyer took his new package, got into a white Mustang parked outside, and drove away.

3

"Nobody's Going to Kill You, Martin"

Martin Luther King, Jr., and his entourage arrived back in Atlanta around 5:00 P.M. on Friday, March 29. He and his wife, Coretta, spent the evening at the home of Ralph and Juanita Abernathy. "He didn't talk about the movement that night," recalled Abernathy. "Instead he talked about the times before the Montgomery bus boycott when we were all younger and hadn't taken on the burdens of the black people. He remembered people long forgotten, did some of his imitations, and told a few stories."[1] After dinner, the two men retired to the family room, where they collapsed onto two matching loveseats, exhausted from the two days in Memphis. They slept there undisturbed until the following morning when Abernathy's son came for breakfast.

On Saturday, March 30, the SCLC staff held its regular meeting at the Ebenezer Baptist Church. The chief topic was the Poor People's Campaign, but a return to Memphis was also debated. Andrew Young, James Bevel, and Jesse Jackson presented objections to Memphis. King, who arrived late, listened uncomfortably to the griping. Abernathy noticed that King seemed particularly restless and downhearted. When he finally spoke, King said it was necessary to make another trip to Memphis. But his top aides were opposed, fearful that any further diversion of resources to Memphis would inalterably harm the march on Washington. Cancel Washington, if Memphis must be done, was the common sentiment.[2] King chastised them for their disunity, and halfway through the meeting he stood up, took a set of car keys from Abernathy, and walked out.[3]

Abernathy followed him into the hallway. When he asked King if he was all right, King tried to reassure him, but Abernathy later recalled having a "deep sense of foreboding. He seemed preoccupied and depressed."[4] Jesse Jackson had stepped out of the meeting to see if there was a problem. When King saw him, he snapped, "Jesse, it may be necessary for you to carve your own individual niche in society. But don't you bother me." Jackson was stunned. King walked outside and drove away. When Abernathy returned to the meeting, he impressed upon the staff how much strain King was under, and that they needed to come together to make it easier for him. It was not the right time for conflict and division within the ranks.

Within an hour, a new timetable had been set. King would keep a long-scheduled preaching commitment at National Cathedral in Washington on Sunday, March 31. That same day Andrew Young, Hosea Williams, and James Bevel would travel to Memphis and start the nonviolence workshops. Jackson and the rest of the SCLC staff would arrive on Monday, April 1. Finally, on Tuesday, the second, King, Abernathy, and Bernard Lee would travel to Memphis. The new march was tentatively set for Friday, April 5.

Now Abernathy called King and pleaded with him to return to the meeting. King took several hours to get there.[5] He listened impassively as the staff informed him of its decisions. "He was still in a strange mood," recalled Abernathy.[6]

On Sunday morning, King and Andrew Young flew to Washington, and after King's sermon they met with reporters to stress that the Poor People's Campaign was still on target. He also reiterated his opposition to Lyndon Johnson's reelection campaign. Later, they met with Michigan congressman John Conyers and Gary, Indiana, mayor Richard Hatcher to discuss a possible "commission of inquiry" to examine the positions of all 1968 presidential candidates as they related to blacks. That evening, King's spirits were noticeably buoyed by Lyndon Johnson's unexpected announcement that he would not seek reelection.[7]

King returned to Atlanta on Sunday evening. On Monday, while his staffers met with the Invaders and ministers in Memphis, King rested, saw no one in the organization, and tried to regain his physical and mental balance. It was on April 1 that the SCLC publicly announced that King would return to Memphis.

The next day, King finally called Abernathy.

"Where are you?" Abernathy asked. "Where have you been?"

"Around," replied King. "Don't worry about it. We can go tomorrow."

"But we're due today."

"Please, let's not go till tomorrow."

Although Abernathy worried that the others "would be disappointed and even angry," he heard the "plaintive quality" in King's voice and relented.[8] The following day, April 3, when they finally boarded a plane for the flight to Memphis, it remained at the gate for an unusually long time. The pilot finally announced that a bomb threat had delayed them, but every piece of luggage had been checked, and they were now cleared for takeoff.

King laughed. "Well, it looks like they won't kill me this flight, not after telling me all that."

"Nobody's going to kill you, Martin," said Abernathy.[9]

King just looked out the plane's window, staring at the runway. Abernathy thought he noticed a tight smile.

On Monday, April 1, the day the SCLC made the official announcement that King would return to Memphis, Annie Estelle Peters, the manager at the Piedmont Laundry in Atlanta, was on duty. Shortly after 10:00 A.M., a white man came in with some clothing. He was pale, thin, with dark hair, and sported horn-rimmed glasses. He placed four undershirts, three pairs of briefs, a pair of socks, and a washcloth on the counter. He also gave her a suit jacket, a separate pair of dress trousers, and a tie for dry cleaning.

"Can I have your name, please?" she asked.

"Eric Galt." He spelled it for her.[10]

Her customer seemed so neatly dressed, and yet he was in the middle of Atlanta's small but intense hippie district. With his neatly combed hair, suit, and crisp shirt, he seemed anything but a hippie.

A decaying green-and-white rooming house around the corner from the laundry served as Galt's Atlanta address. Like Peters, Jimmie Garner, the manager, thought his neatly dressed middle-aged tenant did not fit with the rest of his young "flower-power" roomers. Galt had arrived two days earlier, paid cash for his $10.50-a-week room, and was a quiet boarder who kept to himself.[11] At the rear of the rooming house, in a tiny gravel-covered lot, he parked his pale yellow Mustang (so light that everyone later remembered it as white). It bore an Alabama license plate and had two Mexican tourist visa stickers stamped October 1967 on the windshield. Neighbors later recalled it because they were aggravated that Galt parked the car diagonally across three parallel parking spaces.

On Wednesday, April 3, Galt drove along U.S. Highway 78 toward Birmingham. At some point, he pulled off the highway and stopped near a secluded spot. Getting out of his car, he opened the trunk and retrieved the Browning box that contained his new rifle. Although Aeromarine had bore-sighted the scope for accuracy, he wanted to get a feeling for the gun. He set the Redfield scope to its maximum magnification, seven power. He fired about two dozen shots at trees, rocks, leaves, whatever seemed a good target. With the scope, items a hundred yards away seemed virtually in front of him. Satisfied with his new Remington, Galt carefully placed it back into the Mustang's trunk.[12] After he passed through Birmingham, he stayed on Highway 78. Memphis was only 250 miles away.

4

"I've Been to the Mountaintop"

Dr. King arrived in Memphis early Wednesday afternoon and was met by Solomon Jones, a driver for a local funeral home that provided a white Cadillac as a makeshift limousine. A Memphis police security detail of four men, headed by chief of detectives Don Smith, was also there.[1] Two other detectives later joined the group.[2] Jones took King and Abernathy to their usual lodging, the black-owned Lorraine Motel.*[3] From there they went to a strategy meeting at Lawson's church, where they learned that Memphis city lawyers had successfully obtained a temporary injunction prohibiting King and the strikers from staging any protest for ten days. "Martin fell silent again," recalled Abernathy. "Nothing was going right."[4]

Abernathy and King returned to the Lorraine to rest. They had landed in Memphis just ahead of a fierce storm, and by late afternoon the wind was

---

* King's checking into the Lorraine has been a source of controversy, as some have suggested that he seldom stayed there and somehow had been maneuvered to that motel since it might make him an easier target. In 1993, twenty-five years after the assassination, former King aide Hosea Williams testified in an HBO mock trial of James Earl Ray that he didn't remember King ever staying at the Lorraine before the final trip to Memphis. "Hosea did not know about the Lorraine because he never had come to Memphis except one time before," the Reverend Billy Kyles told the author. "Martin always stayed there. It was the one place he wanted to be at, and they treated him special.

whipping around the balcony and the rain pelted the windows, punctuated by
thunder and lightning. Through the miserable weather, at least six Memphis
attorneys who had heard about the injunction traveled to the Lorraine to offer
their assistance to King. King decided the lawyers, led by Lucius Burch, a
prominent Memphian, should go to court the following morning to seek
changes to the order. He warned Burch, however, that he was ready to march
even if the injunction was in place.

After dinner, Ralph Abernathy left alone to speak at Mason Temple. King
was tired, and with the violent weather—"as bad a rain and wind as we'd seen
in months," recalled Abernathy—the men decided it was best for King to rest
while Abernathy rallied the crowd.* There were about two thousand people at
Mason Temple, a modest gathering compared to the crowd that had packed
the grand, vaulted hall two weeks earlier for King. But they had ventured out
in the terrible weather and were clearly disappointed when they did not see
King. Abernathy called him and pleaded that he come over. King agreed, and
when he finally arrived, Abernathy took the podium and gave a heartfelt
thirty-minute introduction. Starting with King's birth, he lionized almost
every part of his life. It was an unusual departure for Abernathy, and later he
could not explain why he had suddenly chosen that moment to deliver what

---

306 was his room, the hotel's best." Ralph Abernathy told the House Select Committee
on Assassinations, "We just felt a part of the Lorraine. . . . We always stayed there, and
we always stayed in that room, 306. This was the King-Abernathy suite."

Ray's lawyer William Pepper also asserted that King's room at the Lorraine was
changed at the last second from 202 on the ground floor to 306 on the second floor,
which afforded an assassin, placed across the road in the rooming house, a clear view.
"Upon our arrival . . . someone else was in the room [306] and . . . the next day they
were moved out and we were put in our usual room," testified Abernathy. Walter Bailey,
the Lorraine's owner, said that his records showed that King had stayed at the hotel
more than thirteen times, and 306 was always his room. The delay in moving him there
on April 3 was, as Abernathy had recalled, because someone else initially occupied it.

* By the time Abernathy had left, the police security detail was also gone. That has, of
course, caused considerable speculation as to whether it was part of a coordinated plot
to leave King vulnerable to an assassination attempt. However, the police detail was actually pulled away because King and his staff did not relish the police presence around
them. Considering that the police had rioted and injured scores of black demonstrators
only a week earlier, the image of the civil rights leader being surrounded by policemen
was one he disliked and did not want in Memphis. Not only did King not wish to appear
scared, but also he and his aides were not sure whether the police were there to protect
him or to spy on him. When they returned from Lawson's church to the Lorraine, King
and his staff tried unsuccessfully to lose the police security detail. After that, security detail chief Smith called and received permission from headquarters to be removed from
the scene. (HSCA Rpt., pp. 547–49.)

essentially became a eulogy. When he finished, one of the other ministers leaned over to him. "We thought you weren't going to make a speech. Didn't you know that they came to hear Martin?" Abernathy chuckled. "I don't know, it just happened."[5]

King started slowly. He paid tribute to Abernathy as "the best friend I have in the world." Recounting an attempt on his life ten years earlier in a Harlem department store, when a deranged woman had stabbed him in the chest with a letter opener, King said the blade had struck so close to his heart that if he had sneezed he would have died. "And I want to say tonight, I want to say I am happy I didn't sneeze." Jim Lawson, who had walked to the back of the hall, listened to the speech, and when King talked about his brush with death, "I said to myself, 'I've never heard him do that in public in quite that way.'"[6]

His voice rising, King continued to list all the great episodes in the civil rights movement of the previous decade that he would have missed had he died. Then he spoke about the bomb threat on the plane earlier that morning.

"And then I got into Memphis. And some began to say the threats, or talk about the threats that were out. What would happen to me from some of our sick white brothers? Well, I don't know what will happen now. We've got some difficult days ahead. But it doesn't really matter with me now." He paused, and when he started again his voice rose. "Because I've been to the mountaintop." The crowd was applauding frenetically. The storm—pelting rain and thunder—could be heard outside.

"And I don't mind. Like anybody, I would like to live a long life. Longevity has its place. But I'm not concerned about that now. I just want to do God's will. And He's allowed me to go up to the mountain. And I've looked over. And I've *seen*"—he lingered on the word—"the Promised Land. I may not get there with you. But I want you to know tonight, that we, as a people"—his words were rushed now, and forceful—"will get to the Promised Land. And I'm happy, tonight. I'm not worried about anything. I'm not fearing any man. Mine eyes have seen the glory of the coming of the Lord."[7]

King was drenched in sweat, and as he moved back to his seat he almost collapsed into Ralph Abernathy's arms. Some thought he was so swept by emotion that he was in tears. Young and Abernathy, who had heard variations of the speech many times, could not remember when King had seemed so involved in it, the passion of his words rousing the audience into a tumultuous cheer. "I heard him hit high notes before," said Abernathy, "but never any higher."[8] "It was remarkable," agreed Lawson.[9] "I never heard Martin talk about death publicly like that," says Kyles. "That speech was a cleansing of his own fear of death. He purged himself of any foreboding he might have had about dying."[10]

The same day King made his "mountaintop" speech, Eric Galt finished his seven-hour drive from Atlanta and arrived in Memphis. He had stopped earlier in the day at a Rexall drugstore in Whitehaven, Tennessee, and purchased a Gillette shaving kit.[11] The salesclerk later remembered him because he was wearing what appeared to be an expensive dark suit.[12] Later, he stopped to get a haircut.[13]

Around 7:15 P.M., the Mustang with the Alabama license plate pulled into the New Rebel Motel at 3466 Lamar Avenue. Lamar was the continuation of Highway 78, just within the city limits. The storm was in full force, shaking the windows and rattling the doors of the fully exposed one-story motel. The desk clerk, Henrietta Hagemaster, greeted the single male customer looking for a room for the night. He filled out the registration slip as Eric S. Galt, listed his Mustang and its Alabama license number, and signed the card. She put him in Room 34.

Ivan Webb replaced Hagemaster at 10:00 P.M. As part of his overnight duties, he patrolled the motel's grounds hourly as a security check.[14] He noticed the Mustang parked in front of Room 34. Although the curtains were drawn shut, it was evident the room was brightly lit. During his 4:00 A.M. security walk, the room still had its lights on. Whoever is in there, thought Webb, is not getting much sleep tonight.[15]

5

Mrs. Brewer's Rooming House

Long before King awoke on Thursday, April 4, Andrew Young and Jim Lawson headed to federal court to assist the effort to get the temporary injunction against the march either lifted or modified. King was finally up in time to go to the Lorraine's grill with Abernathy, where they had their favorite meal, fried catfish. After lunch, King convened a meeting with his aides in his motel room, to discuss the best ways to neutralize the Invaders. "Some of the younger staff members were nervous," recalled Abernathy. "Martin was impatient with them. 'There was no more reason to be frightened now than in the past,' he said. 'I'd rather be dead than afraid,' he said contemptuously, as much to himself as to the rest of us."[1]

King's brother, Alfred Daniel (A.D.), had arrived unexpectedly the night before. After the staff meeting ended, King joined A.D. in his first-floor room and the two called Mama King and spoke to her for nearly an hour.[2] Later, King complained that he had not heard all day from Young and was anxious to know what had happened in court. Around 4:30, Young appeared, but before he could even announce that the judge was willing to issue a modified order the following Monday, King "started fussing in a kind of joking way about 'why don't you call and let me know what's going on? We're sitting here all day long waiting to hear from you and you didn't call.' "[3] Then King picked up a pillow and threw it at Young, who quickly threw it back. In a moment, half a dozen men were scrambling around the room, laughing hysterically and hurling pillows at one another. It lasted only a few minutes until they all collapsed from exhaustion. "Occasionally, he would get in those kinds of hilarious moods," recalled Young.

Around 5:30, King returned to Room 306 with Abernathy. He watched the evening news and some of his aides wandered in and out, chatting with him about minor matters. With his tie loosened, King lay across the large bed and seemed more relaxed than he had in days.

Half a block away, at 484 South Main Street, a law enforcement team was ensconced in Fire Station No. 2. The newly constructed one-story building, of light brick with large glass windows, was to the left of the motel and about 150 feet away. There, when King was in town, law enforcement watched him. For this April visit, because of the recent violence and the possibility of more, surveillance on King had been increased. Not only were Memphis police officers there observing with binoculars focused through small cutouts in newspapers pasted over the windows, but FBI agents were also on the scene, and even several military intelligence officers wandered in occasionally.[4] King and his aides expected there were informants around them, and constant police surveillance wherever they traveled. J. Edgar Hoover had publicly declared war on King years earlier, obsessed with what he thought were King's pro-Communist connections, as well as his sex life. For several years, the FBI had conducted a campaign, sometimes illegal, of harassment, interference, infiltration, and steady surveillance of King and the SCLC. The Johnson administration had drafted military intelligence—against the desires of some leading officers—to assist in monitoring the civil unrest and antiwar activities that were building powerfully in the late 1960s.[5]

The Memphis police officers most responsible for surveillance on April 4 were black: a detective, Ed Redditt, and a patrolman, W. B. Richmond. Both knew most of the black personalities in the city. They recorded the names of people and the times they visited King as well as the license numbers of cars that came to the hotel. If King left the Lorraine, they were to follow him and report on his activities. The Memphis police, the FBI, and military intelligence all deny that they had any electronic surveillance on King at the Lorraine, although since it would have been illegal, none of them would be expected to admit it even if they had.*

---

* On April 4, Memphis Police Tactical (TACT) Units, which had been formed after the March 28 violence, were pulled back five blocks from the immediate vicinity around the

Across the street from the Lorraine Motel was a retaining wall and a slope over-grown with weeds and trees leading up to the rear of two adjacent two-story brick buildings. A covered passageway connected the two buildings. They fronted on South Main Street, the next block over from the motel. The ground floor had stores—a bar and grill, and a jukebox repair and record shop. The second floors had been converted into separate wings of a single rooming house. It was in a commercial area largely populated with vagrants and winos, and on the border of Memphis's black community. Pawnshops were the area's mainstays. Between 3:00 and 3:30 P.M. on April 4, there was a knock on the door of Room 2, which served as the building's office. The manager, Mrs. Bessie Brewer, a heavyset woman in her thirties with her hair in curlers, dressed in jeans and a man's wrinkled checked shirt, opened the door as far as the chain would permit. Standing there was a trim white man who appeared to be in his early thirties. He had dark hair, blue eyes, and a thin nose and wore a dark suit that seemed much too nice for the neighborhood. What first struck her was his unusual smile, a cross between a "sneer" and a "smirk."[6] She did not think he "fit in" with her tenants, and he unnerved her.[7]

Lorraine. Some charge that was a lessening of security that made King an easier target. However, the TACT squads were not there to protect King, but instead to ensure there was no repeat of the recent rioting, firebombing, and looting. They were an obvious reminder to King that the Memphis police did not intend to tolerate any further civil disturbance. So it is not surprising to learn that when the House Select Committee on Assassinations investigated the issue of the TACT squad removal, it discovered that the request to move the units away from the motel actually came from an unidentified member of King's party.

That same afternoon, Detective Redditt was removed from his surveillance post when a threat was made on his life. That threat later turned out to be bogus. Although a black police officer replaced Redditt, since the assassination Redditt has given numerous interviews in which he contended that his removal was evidence that King's security had been deliberately stripped away. However, when the Select Committee grilled Redditt, he admitted that his job was to surveil King, not protect him. Moreover, he acknowledged that it was "absolutely false" when he had implied he was part of a security detail. He apologized for his earlier statements. The committee concluded that Redditt had "knowingly allowed the nature of his job on the day of the assassination to be misrepresented and exploited by advocates of conspiracy theories" and that his conduct "was reprehensible" (HSCA Rpt., pp. 549–55).

Finally, two black firemen were also transferred from the fire station the day before the assassination. Conspiracists have charged that their removal was to facilitate the assassin's escape the following day. Actually, it was Detective Redditt who requested they be transferred, since he thought they were so sympathetic to King and the strikers that they might interfere with his surveillance operation (HSCA Rpt., p. 556).

"Do you have a room for rent?" he asked.

"Yes. Do you want one by the week or by the month?"

"By the week."[8]

She then unfastened the chain and led the stranger to Room 8. When she opened the door, he looked inside without actually entering.

"Well, I don't need the stove and refrigerator since I won't be doing any cooking. I was thinking more of a sleeping room."

She led him to the other wing, which had the only available sleeping room. She removed the padlock on the door. There was no door handle, but instead a wire coat hanger had been pushed through the opening and served as a handle. The room was small, with a single window with tattered green and gold floral curtains. The window looked out onto the alleyway between the two wings, but also provided a view of part of the Lorraine. He looked at the stained bed with a thin mattress laid haphazardly over the open springs. In front of the boarded fireplace was a portable gas heater. A naked lightbulb dangling from the cracked ceiling illuminated a ripped red sofa with a greasy pillow. A strong odor of disinfectant permeated the room. The last tenant, an elderly man, had died there a few weeks earlier. "I'll take it. Where is the bathroom?" he asked.

Brewer pointed out the communal bathroom at the end of the long, narrow hallway. A hand-lettered sign—TOILET & BATH—was tacked on the door.

Suddenly the door of the room next to them opened. Forty-six-year-old Charlie Stephens, an unemployed tuberculosis patient, peered into the hallway. He stared for a moment at the new tenant.[9] Stephens had a wrench in his hand. "I've got the tank working," he said to Bessie Brewer. "All right, Charlie," she said as he returned to his room. "He usually drinks," Brewer said to Willard, pointing toward Stephens's room.[10] What she did not tell her new tenant—though it probably would have pleased him—was that his other neighbors were mostly either drunks or invalids. In his wing, where the new boarder had settled into Room 5B, there was Stephens in Room 6B, who besides having a drinking problem also had to care for a bedridden wife; in Room 1B was Jessie Ledbetter, a deaf-mute; Rooms 2B and 3B were vacant; in Room 4B was Willie Anschutz, the only tenant who was actually employed (at the Duvall Transfer Company).[11] In the adjoining wing, besides Brewer and her husband, Room 3 had Bertie Reeves, an elderly man who was hard of hearing and had poor eyesight; Room 4 had Harold Vance, an older man who had been on a two-day drunk; Room 5 had T. L. Messer, a man of eighty who was almost deaf and suffered from senility; Room 7 had Frank Marley, an elderly man who usually was so drunk that he seldom came out of his room; Room 9 had Harold Carter, whose weakness was cheap wine; Room 10 had Leonard Eaton, in his early sixties and a longtime resident of the rooming house who was often passed out in his room from too much alcohol.

Bessie Brewer took the new tenant back to her office. He gave his name as John Willard, and when told the rent was $8.50 per week, he paid her with a twenty-dollar bill. He left her office without asking her about the padlock, which most people rented so they could lock the door when they were out. She did not see him again.

About half an hour after Willard had checked into the rooming house, he showed up several blocks away at the York Arms Company.

"Could I help you?" asked Ralph Carpenter, a salesman.

"I need a pair of field glasses," Willard said.

Carpenter was low on binoculars. "All I have is a pair selling for two hundred dollars and another around ninety."

"That's a little expensive," said Willard, turning to go.

"Wait a minute," said Carpenter. He went to the display window and retrieved a pair of Bushnell binoculars priced at $39.95. Willard raised them to his eyes and seemed to like them.

"Are there instructions in the box?"

The question seemed odd to Carpenter, since it was hard to imagine an easier device to use than binoculars. "You really don't need instructions, you just need to place them to your eyes and adjust the eye pieces."[12] Willard agreed to take them, paid the $41.55 (including tax) in cash, and quickly left.*

Willard drove back to the rooming house, but he had lost his previous parking place at the curb directly in front of Jim's Grill. Instead, he had to park a few car lengths beyond the rooming-house entrance. He turned off the motor but did not immediately get out of the car.†

Across the street from the rooming house was the Seabrook Wallpaper Company. Elizabeth Copeland, a customer service representative, finished work at 4:30 and was waiting for her husband to pick her up. As she was looking out the front showroom window for her husband's car, she saw the Mustang drive up and park across the street. The driver sat inside as though he were waiting for someone or something.[13] Another woman, Frances Thompson, was waiting for her daughter to pick her up. She also saw the Mustang pull up about 4:30.[14]

---

* If the tenants at the rooming house left a lot to be desired as witnesses, the FBI and Memphis police did not have much more help from Ralph Carpenter, who ended up in a mental institution a couple of months after the assassination (MURKIN 4442–4500, section 57, p. 133).

† Some witnesses saw a Mustang parked directly in front of Jim's Grill, while others saw it some fifty to sixty feet just past the Canipe Amusement Company. That led to a conspiracy theory that there were two Mustangs. However, not all the witnesses, especially those in Jim's Grill, are precise or accurate about the time they saw the car. What the witnesses are describing, undoubtedly, is that Willard moved the car from Jim's to get the binoculars, and then had to park further away when he returned.

Thompson called out to one of her coworkers, Peggy Hurley, that her husband had arrived for her. When Hurley came to the window, she shook her head. "No, it's not Charlie—we've got a Falcon. That's a Mustang." It was about 4:45 P.M.[15] When Peggy Hurley's husband arrived just a few minutes later, he also saw the Mustang and a lone white man sitting in the driver's seat.[16] Fifteen minutes later, two men entering Jim's Grill saw the Mustang, but it was empty.[17]

No one saw Willard reenter the rooming house. Stephens heard someone in Room 5B walking around, and sometimes the door opened and footsteps headed to the bathroom at the far end of the hallway.[18] Stephens was aware that the tenant in 5B was spending a lot of time in the bathroom, but he heard the toilet flush only once. He later estimated that the person probably stayed in the bathroom for a total of twenty to thirty minutes. Willie Anschutz twice tried to use the bathroom to pour out some water he had used to wash dishes, but each time it was occupied. Anschutz knocked on Stephens's door and angrily inquired about who was keeping the bathroom occupied. "The new tenant," said Stephens, nodding with his head to the empty Room 5B.[19]

Across the street at the Lorraine, King and his staff were having their raucous pillow fight. King had less than an hour to live.

6

The Assassination

I n his second-floor room, Dr. King was getting ready to leave for the Reverend Billy Kyles's new home for dinner. Standing in the bathroom in his trousers and an undershirt, he began applying a powerful depilatory to his face. It was made by mixing water with Magic Shave Powder—which had a horrible odor, akin to rotten eggs—into a thick mud. Because of his sensitive skin, it was the only way King could shave. He applied it using a spatula and in a few minutes, when it dried into a claylike mask, used the spatula to scrape it off. "Under similar circumstances most men would have grown a beard," said Abernathy, "but Martin was meticulous about this particular procedure, and it was one reason he was always late."[1] On this day, Abernathy was with him, and he sought King's advice about the difficulty he was having in arranging for a revival-week speaker in Atlanta who would not conflict with the Poor People's march on Washington.[2]

There was a knock on the door shortly after 5:30. It was Billy Kyles.[3] King was still dressing, while Abernathy sat on the edge of the bed. They started teasing Kyles about the upcoming meal. Unknown to Kyles, King had already had Abernathy call Mrs. Kyles to learn about the night's menu: roast beef, pigs' feet, candied yams, chitlins, and vegetables.

"All right now, Billy, I don't want you fooling me," said Abernathy. "Are we going to have some real soul food? Now if we go over there and get some filet mignon or T-bone, you're going to flunk."

"We don't want no filet mignon," chimed in King. "Yeah, now we don't want you to be like that preacher's house we went to in Atlanta. Had a great big house, we went over there for dinner and had some ham. A ham bone."

"Yeah, there wasn't no meat on it," agreed Abernathy.

"Yeah, we had Kool-Aid and it wasn't even sweet," said King. "And if that's the kind of dinner we're going to, we'll stay here."

"We're going to have soul food," said Kyles. "Now just get ready, let's go." They were supposed to be there by 6:00, but King, true to form, was running late.

"I know your wife, she's so pretty," King said. "Are you sure she can *really* cook soul food?"[4]

King had trouble buttoning the top of his shirt, and the other men teased him about getting fat. As he fussed with his tie, the three changed the subject. "It was just preacher talk," recalls Kyles, "like people talk baseball talk, or barbershop talk."[5]

It was approaching 6:00 P.M. Darkness would arrive in less than half an hour.[6] King finished splashing some sweet-smelling cologne over his face and neck to mask the odor of the Magic Shave Powder and walked outside onto the balcony that ran along the front of the motel. Having seen King put on cologne, Abernathy went to his room to do the same. In the courtyard below was the white Cadillac loaned to King by the local funeral home. Its driver, Solomon Jones, Jr., stood nearby. SCLC general counsel Chauncey Eskridge and aides Andrew Young, James Bevel, Jesse Jackson, and Hosea Williams were milling around the car. Kyles stood near King on the balcony. King leaned over the edge of the three-foot-high railing and began talking to some of those in the courtyard. He told Eskridge to invite Jackson to dinner with them. Jackson walked closer to the balcony with another man. "Doc, this is Ben Branch. Ben used to live in Memphis. He plays in our band." King told Jackson to get ready to leave and chided him, "You know the whole band can't go to dinner with us."

King leaned a little farther over the balcony. "Ben," he said, "I want you to sing for me tonight. I want you to do that song 'Precious Lord.' Sing it real pretty."

Branch nodded enthusiastically. "I sure will, Doc."

Solomon Jones yelled out that King should put on a topcoat since it might be chilly later. "O.K.," King replied, and he started to straighten up. Kyles had turned to walk down to get his car. He had taken about five steps when he heard a loud report and spun around to see King's body, in profile, lying in a growing pool of blood on the balcony. "Oh, my God, Martin's been shot!" someone screamed. "Hit the ground," someone else yelled. Those in the courtyard instinctively took cover near the limousine. Abernathy looked out his door upon hearing the noise and saw King crumpled on the balcony, then bolted outside and gathered his friend in his arms, patting his head.

"I looked down at Martin's face," Abernathy recalled. "His eyes wobbled, then for an instant he focused on me. 'Martin, it's all right. Don't worry. This is Ralph. This is Ralph.' "*[7]

King had been struck in the lower right jaw by a single .30-06 bullet. It was a fatal shot. Because of the angle at which King was standing, the bullet smashed his jawbone, pierced his neck, tearing major blood vessels and nerves, including the jugular vein, and then severed the spinal cord before coming to rest in his shoulder blade against the skin.[8]

Pandemonium erupted at the Lorraine, with King's aides and friends, other guests, and reporters all scurrying about trying desperately to find out what had happened. Most thought the shot had come from across the street, in the vicinity of the rooming house.[†] Solomon Jones had jumped into the car and

---

* Among the first to reach King's body was Marrell McCollough, a Memphis police undercover officer. A former Army officer, he grabbed a towel and tried to slow the flow of blood. The fact that he was an undercover agent who was close to the King entourage has since raised much consternation. McCollough subsequently went to work for the CIA, where he was still employed as of 1998. The House Select Committee extensively investigated his role and found that while he supplied surveillance information to the police, who in turn provided it to the FBI and other intelligence agencies, he performed only that role and had no hand in inciting violence during the March 28 riots. The committee also determined he had no contact with King or his schedule on the day of the assassination. McCollough, despite repeated requests through the CIA's Office of Information and Privacy, refuses to be interviewed.

† Witnesses who provided statements soon after the assassination included Bernard Lee, a secretary and bodyguard to King, who knew from his Army experience that the sound was from a high-caliber rifle and thought it came from the buildings, including the rooming house, across the street from the motel (MURKIN ME, Sub. D, section 1, pp. 29–30); Marrell McCollough knew the sound was a gunshot and almost immediately looked west to the rooming house (MURKIN ME, Sub. D, section 1, pp. 58–59); Chauncey Eskridge thought the sound was a firecracker, but once he realized it was gunfire, thought it originated from the rooming house area (MURKIN ME, Sub. D, section 1, p. 113); the Reverend Billy Kyles believed it was likely a rifle shot and looked west to the buildings that included the rooming house (MURKIN ME, Sub. D, section 1, p. 178), as did Jesse Jackson and Ben Branch (HSCA Rpt., p. 377).

There were those who thought the shot originated elsewhere. Ralph Abernathy, who was in his motel room at the time, thought the shot came from directly outside his door (MURKIN ME, Sub. D, section 1, p. 104). To Andrew Young, King's top aide, the sound was a firecracker and it came from the bushes above the retaining wall across the street from the motel (MURKIN ME, Sub. D, section 1, p. 106); Solomon Jones, the driver assigned to King by the funeral parlor, told the police it sounded like a firecracker, and that after he ran around the area to see if he could spot anything unusual, he saw something or someone moving quickly through the bushes across the street—which has

was driving it frantically back and forth across the parking lot as though doing so might exorcise what had just happened. Kyles was pounding the bed in a motel room as he tried to get an ambulance. Others were gathering around King on the balcony, trying in vain to see some flicker of life in their fallen leader.

Just before the shot was fired, W. B. Richmond was the policeman on duty responsible for watching King through the peephole that had been cut into the newspapers covering the fire station windows. A fireman, George Loenneke, came into the locker room to get a pack of cigarettes. He asked Richmond if he could look through the peephole for a moment. As he put his eye to the window, he saw King on the balcony, leaning on the railing, looking down and talking to someone in the parking lot. Then there was the crack of a rifle. "He's been shot," yelled Loenneke. He ran back into the main part of the fire station, screaming the news.[9]

There had been no contingency plan in case of trouble at the Lorraine or an attack on King. Richmond ran from his observation post to a telephone several

---

raised the specter over the years that an assassin was hiding in the foliage (Memphis's version of Dealey Plaza's infamous Grassy Knoll) (MURKIN ME, Sub. D, section 1, pp. 148–49). However, Jones admitted, in a sworn statement to the House Select Committee on Assassinations, that he saw the object only for a brief time. He did not see a head or arms; he assumed the object was human simply because he could offer no other explanation, but he could not tell whether it was black or white, or male or female. In addition, Jones stated that at the moment of the assassination both Bernard Lee and Andrew Young "reached and got me on each shoulder and pulled me to the ground." He stated further that by the time he got up off the ground, policemen had "almost" arrived at the Lorraine Motel from a nearby firehouse. The Select Committee believed that the movement Jones perceived actually "occurred several moments after the shot. If it was, in fact, a person it may have been a law enforcement officer responding to the shot" (HSCA Rpt., p. 377). Rev. Kyles, who knew that Jones had a criminal record and a reputation for embellishing stories, told the FBI that Jones was standing behind a brick retaining wall that surrounded the motel's swimming pool and that he could not even see to the west side of the street where there was foliage (MURKIN ME, Sub. D, section 1, p. 178). Others who looked directly into the bushes did not see anything like Jones described.

Finally, Harold "Cornbread" Carter gave an August 1968 interview in which he said he had been drinking wine in the bushes across the street from the motel when he heard the rifle shot. Next he saw someone run through the foliage carrying a gun. The problem is that Carter, who lived at the rooming house where the shot originated, told the FBI and Memphis police immediately after the shooting that he was in his room when he heard the shot and he stayed inside until the police arrived about fifteen minutes later. He did not see anything unusual before or after the shot (MURKIN 2322, section 20, p. 47).

feet away and placed a call to the intelligence section at police headquarters to inform them of the shooting. Simultaneously, all the other police officers and firemen responded instinctively, immediately rushing out of the station and toward the Lorraine. Most dropped over an eight-foot retaining wall at the rear of the fire station in their rush to the crime scene.[10] However, that meant they ran away from South Main Street, the road on which the rooming house fronted, and from which any shooter would emerge. That was fortuitous for the assassin, who could not have known when he picked his perch at the rooming house that the neighboring fire station was teeming with police.

At the rooming house, the rifle shot startled most tenants. Willie Anschutz was watching television when he heard a sound that he thought was a gunshot. He walked to his door and, as he opened it, saw a man moving quickly toward him. As he passed Anschutz's door, the man—who was carrying something long and wrapped in a blanket in one hand—held his free hand and arm over his face, preventing Anschutz from getting a good look at him. Anschutz felt it might be the new tenant from Room 5B, but he was not certain. "I thought I heard a shot," Anschutz said. "Yeah, it was a shot," the man muttered as he rushed by.[11] Anschutz, who thought the shot came either from the bathroom or Room 5B, glanced quickly at the bundle in the man's arm. It looked like a gun. Meanwhile, Charlie Stephens, who had heard a gunshot that sounded like it came from the bathroom that adjoined his room, opened his door and glanced down the hallway. He saw a man leaving the vicinity of the bathroom, carrying a three-foot-long package wrapped in what appeared to be newspaper. It was possibly the new tenant in 5B, but since he saw him only from the rear, he based that hunch on the man's general build, dark hair, and dark suit. Stephens watched as the stranger hurried down the hallway and turned left to leave the building.*[12]

A moment after Stephens and Anschutz saw the stranger flee the rooming house with a bundle in his arms, Guy Canipe, the owner of the Canipe Amusement Company, located on the ground floor at the front of the rooming house,

---

* There has been much controversy over the years as to whether Charlie Stephens had been drinking that day, especially since he later developed into the state's key eyewitness against Ray. Even if sober, his testimony was not that compelling, as the best he could say for the prosecution was that the man leaving the scene of the crime looked like the 5B tenant by build, hair, and clothes. However, the author spoke to ex–Memphis homicide detective Roy Davis. "I took the written statement from Stephens at the police station within a couple of hours of the shooting. He was not real drunk, but he was not sober even then. I distinctly remember that he said he could not identify the man. I would not like to rely on him as my only witness." (Interview June 16, 1997.)

heard a thud outside. He looked to the front of the store and immediately saw a white man in a dark suit walking south on the sidewalk—the direction in which Willard would have had to go to retrieve his Mustang. After hesitating a moment, Canipe walked outside, looked in both directions, and saw a white compact car, with only the driver inside, speed away from the curb. Two customers had been in the store, and one of them, Bernell Finley, was peering out the door behind him, and later identified the car that screeched away as a Mustang.[13]

Willard's escape in the Mustang preceded the arrival on South Main of two officers from TACT 10 by a matter of seconds. The two approached the rooming house from opposite directions after having first gone toward the Lorraine. Canipe saw one of them, Lieutenant J. E. Ghormley, walking rapidly toward him, a revolver drawn. Within a couple of minutes, more police had arrived. Their interest quickly focused on the package that had caused the thud against the front of the store. It was a long bundle consisting of an old green blanket wrapped around a large pasteboard box. From the top of that box the tip of a gun barrel was evident. A zippered bag was also inside the blanket.[14] The murderer had gotten away, but he had left the murder weapon behind.

7

The Hunt

Martin Luther King was rushed to St. Joseph's Hospital, where a team of doctors made a final, futile effort to revive him. In the meantime, the Memphis police poured over the rooming house and the surrounding neighborhood. When the chief of homicide, N. E. Zachary, went inside Room 5B, he put his head through the window and could see the Lorraine just two hundred feet away.[1] It was evident that someone had used the room to monitor the motel, waiting for King to come outside: A dresser had been pushed away from the window and replaced by a straight-back chair; a strap from a pair of binoculars was on the floor; the window was three-quarters open and the curtains pushed wide. However, to use the window, the viewer had to lean partially outside. Room 5B, therefore, was not an ideal sniper's nest.

The bathroom, down the hall, was the best spot for a clear shot. Even there, the shooter would have had to stand in the large cast-iron tub, located directly under the window. The window was open, and a small mesh screen had been pushed outside into the backyard. Scuff marks were in the tub, and there was what looked like a partial palm print on the wall. Zachary also noticed a very tiny indentation on the windowsill, as though the shooter had rested his rifle there when making the shot.[2]

How had the assassin managed to get away when police were on the scene within minutes? The shooting had taken place at approximately 6:01 P.M. Although the police surveillance team at the fire station knew about it immediately, it was not until 6:03, after receiving confirmation, that the dispatcher put the news on the air.[3] Patrol cars and units from a wide area then headed toward the Lorraine. It took five minutes after the shooting before the dispatcher ordered the two-block area around the motel and the rooming house sealed off.[4] By 6:08 there was a description of the suspect as a young, well-dressed white male, and two minutes later, the late-model white Mustang was broadcast as a possible getaway car.[5] By the time of the Mustang report, the shooter was likely in another state. From the rooming house, Arkansas was only six to seven minutes away to the west, and to the south, the Mississippi state line was about fifteen minutes away. The Memphis police dispatcher did broadcast a "Signal Q" to have all the downtown lights changed to red in the hope of slowing the fleeing assassin, but no all-points bulletin was issued to the neighboring states of Arkansas, Mississippi, Alabama, or Georgia. Also, contrary to Memphis police procedures, roadblocks were not set up at major arteries leading out of the city. The dispatcher later explained these serious lapses by claiming they were "attributable to the massive confusion and huge volume of radio traffic which erupted immediately following the assassination of Dr. King and which caused me to overlook the function of these duties."[6] This meant that once the assassin crossed the state line, nobody would be looking for him or his car.*[7]

---

* At 6:36, the dispatcher reported a white Mustang driving north at a high rate of speed. For the next twelve minutes, the dispatcher received transmissions from a person who claimed to be broadcasting from a CB radio while giving hot pursuit to the fleeing Mustang. At one point, the CB broadcaster even yelled, "He's shooting at me—he's hit my windshield!" Police cars were diverted to this chase. Finally, the police realized the broadcasts were coming from a fixed location, not from a moving car. The broadcaster had led police cars at least six miles out of their way to the northeast corner of the city, when a logical escape route for the assassin would have been in the opposite direction. Was it part of a plot, a phony broadcast by a coconspirator to help the shooter leave the city? The problem with that hypothesis is the time of the hoax. It started thirty-five minutes after the shooting, at a time when the assassin would have already been safely in Arkansas or Mississippi, even if he had encountered heavy traffic. The broadcast would have done no good at that late stage. Moreover, the broadcaster used Channel 17, one of the lesser-used CB frequencies, not the best means of penetrating the police network. The Memphis police investigated and concluded that they had found the prankster, an eighteen-year-old high school student and CB enthusiast. However, while the House Select Committee questioned the accuracy of that conclusion, it did agree after an extensive investigation of the issue that the broadcast was not linked to a conspiracy in the assassination (MURKIN ME, Sub. D, section 2, pp. 116–19; HSCA Rpt., pp. 502–6).

And even within Memphis confines, less than half of the police cars and nearly a third of the force did not respond to any of the dispatcher broadcasts to engage in the hunt for the assassin. Police department officials later maintained it was necessary to keep the TACT units on alert for any rioting and looting that might occur following news of the assassination.*

The police at the scene began to interview witnesses, sweep the premises for fingerprints, and search the neighborhood for other evidence. However, the key to the crime was the covered bundle found in front of Canipe's store. It contained not only the Remington rifle purchased six days earlier in Birmingham, but also the binoculars bought the day of the assassination, nine .30-06 bullets, some clothing, a section of *The Commercial Appeal* reporting that King was at the Lorraine, a transistor radio, and an assortment of toiletries in a fifteen-by-twenty-inch blue plastic overnight bag.

Although murder is a state crime, the FBI had been brought in almost immediately on the supposition that the shooter may have crossed a state line. Within the next few days, as the country mourned or flared in anger over Dr. King's violent death, more than 3,500 FBI agents were assigned to track down the assassin. It was the largest manhunt in the Bureau's history. Cartha De-Loach, the FBI's assistant director and Hoover's trusted friend, was so confident of success that he bet Attorney General Ramsey Clark a bottle of sherry that the murderer would be caught within twenty-four hours.[8]

DeLoach lost his bet—but not for lack of trying. The FBI followed hundreds of leads in more than a dozen countries. The very next day, it traced the gun to Aeromarine Supply in Birmingham and had the name and description of the buyer, Harvey Lowmeyer. By April 11, one week after the shooting, the Bureau had traced a laundry mark on the T-shirt and shorts abandoned at the scene to the Home Service Laundry in Los Angeles, eighteen hundred miles away. Fortunately, the machine that had processed the number on the shorts had been used only between March 4 and March 18. The manager, Lucy Pinela, checked her records, it showed the number—02B-6—had been assigned to a Mr. Eric S. Galt. He had been bringing in his laundry since January 15.[9] Agents also traced a pair of flat-nose duckbill pliers found at the crime scene to Rompage Hardware, located only two blocks from the laundry.[10] Was the Galt who had been in Los Angeles for at least three months the same person as the Lowmeyer who had bought

---

* More than a hundred American cities were hit with riots in the aftermath of the King assassination. Some 50,000 Army and Air Guardsmen assisted local law enforcement during the week to ten days that the violence continued. Twenty thousand regular Army troops backed up the Guardsmen. Two of the cities struck worst were the nation's capital, with 11 dead, 1,200 injured, 7,600 arrested, and 1,200 fires; and nearby Baltimore, with 6 dead, 700 injured, 5,800 arrested, and 1,000 small businesses destroyed.

the gun in Birmingham? The same man as the Willard who rented Room 5B the day of the assassination in Memphis? The physical descriptions indicated to the Bureau that it might be looking for one suspect using several aliases.

The same day that the laundry and pliers were traced to Los Angeles, another break brought the FBI closer to the assassin. For six days, a white Mustang had been parked in the rear of an eight-hundred-unit low-cost housing project, Capitol Homes, in Atlanta. It had been noticed immediately because it seemed too expensive a sports car for the neighborhood. Several residents had actually seen the car arrive, and all described the man who drove it as trim, white, about thirty-five years old, wearing a dark suit and white shirt. Every day the car remained it became more of a topic of discussion within the housing project. On April 10, Mrs. John Riley called the local FBI office and told an agent about the suspicious auto. The agent, one of dozens whose only job was to field the flood of incoming tips, suggested she call the Atlanta police, which she did. Two policemen came by that night and looked the car over carefully. The next day, April 11, FBI agents swarmed into the area and towed the car away.[11] A quick check revealed it was registered to an Eric Starvo Galt, 2608 South Highland Avenue, Birmingham. His 1967 application for an Alabama license showed he was five-eleven, thirty-six years old, and had brown hair and blue eyes, similar to the description given by the witnesses who had dealt with Harvey Lowmeyer when he bought a rifle, and to John Willard when he rented Room 5B in Memphis.[12]

While the name Galt meant nothing to the Atlanta police, it filled in a significant part of the puzzle for the FBI. The day before the car was found, two agents were canvassing all the hotels in the Memphis area for anyone resembling a white man with a white Mustang. At the New Rebel Motel they discovered that an Eric S. Galt, of 2608 South Highland Avenue, Birmingham, had been there the night of April 3 and checked out early on April 4. That meant that Galt, whose clothes had been found in Memphis at the scene of the crime, was now at least known to have been in Memphis the day of the murder.

The car was also examined exhaustively—trunk, interior, ashtray, wheel hubs, paint scrapings, and the like—and all the physical evidence flown to Washington for further study by the FBI lab.[13] Mexican tourist visa stickers showed the car had been south of the border the previous fall.

In Birmingham, the FBI also produced some solid information about the mysterious Mr. Galt. The address listed on the car registration led the police to a run-down rooming house and its manager, Peter Cherpes. He remembered Galt as a seaman who stayed there from August to October 1967.[14] A check of the Mustang's previous owner turned up a Birmingham businessman, William Paisley, who had sold the car to Eric S. Galt for $1,995 in cash in August 1967.[15]

Meanwhile, a sticker pasted inside the Mustang's left front door showed that it had been serviced at a Los Angeles garage in February. The garage's records listed Galt's local address as 1535 North Serrano Avenue. The landlady remembered him staying there from mid-November 1967 until January 21, 1968. She also recalled him as a quiet tenant who had no visitors and drove a white Mustang.[16] Post office records showed that in January, when he left the Serrano apartment, Galt moved just a few blocks away to a seedy residential hotel, the St. Francis.[17] He checked out of the St. Francis on March 17, the day King had been in Los Angeles, and gave his forwarding address as general post office delivery, Atlanta, Georgia.[18] There his trail was lost.

Although the FBI questioned hundreds of Galts in the United States, none had the middle name Starvo, and none had traveled as had the man who was suspected of killing Dr. King. A check of social security and IRS records turned up nothing.

While the field hunt was filling in a picture of Eric Galt's movements, the lab investigation in Washington found that fibers in the Mustang's trunk and floor mats, as well as from a sweatshirt and jacket found abandoned in the car, matched fibers from the sheets and pillows in Room 5B at the Memphis rooming house. Hair found in the Mustang was similar to hair found on a brush in the bundle thrown away at Canipe's store.[19] The FBI now knew that whoever was in Room 5B was also the person who abandoned the Mustang in Atlanta the day after the murder. A handwriting comparison soon confirmed that Lowmeyer's signature on the gun receipt at Aeromarine Supply on March 29 was written by the same man who signed the name Eric S. Galt at the New Rebel Motel in Memphis on April 3.

By mid-April, the FBI had learned a good deal more from interviewing people who knew Galt at his Los Angeles apartments: He had visited New Orleans the previous December, might have had a racial altercation at a local bar, and was a supporter of Alabama governor George Wallace for president. More significant, it turned out, someone remembered Galt talking about taking dance lessons. Agents scoured the area and finally discovered that he had taken a course at National Dance Studio in Long Beach.[20] There, one of the teachers recalled him talking about bartending school. Soon the agents located the International School of Bartending on Sunset Boulevard.[21] The school's manager, Tomas Lau, had a photograph of Galt at the graduation ceremony. Galt was standing uncomfortably in a tight bartender's jacket and crooked bow tie, with his eyes closed, holding his graduation certificate. Twelve hours later, Donald Wood, of Aeromarine Supply in Birmingham, picked that photo out of an eight-picture lineup, positively identifying him as Lowmeyer. The FBI now knew it had the first photo of its suspect.

In the meantime, the FBI had examined all money orders recently purchased in the Los Angeles area, and found one an Eric Galt had made payable
to the Locksmithing Institute of Little Falls, New Jersey. He had begun the correspondence course in locksmithing techniques from Montreal, Canada, and
the last lesson had been sent to him at 113 Fourteenth Street, a cheap rooming
house in the middle of Atlanta's small hippie district.[22] At first the Bureau
watched the apartment, then sent in two agents disguised as hippies to rent an
adjoining room, and finally broke into Galt's room. There, along with John
Birch Society pamphlets and a box of Nabisco crackers, they found a map of
Atlanta. Not only did it have four circles drawn in pencil—near Dr. King's
home, the SCLC headquarters, the Ebenezer Baptist Church, and the Capitol
Homes housing project (where the Mustang had been abandoned)—but it also
produced a clear left thumbprint.

When the rooming-house manager, Jimmie Garner, picked out the bartending photo of Galt as his tenant, the FBI knew the print in Atlanta belonged
to the same Galt whose photo they had from Los Angeles.[23] Although the Bureau had lifted twenty-six prints from the evidence in Memphis, only three
were clear—one on the rifle, one on the Redfield scope, and the other on the
binoculars. Other prints on the beer can, newspaper, and aftershave were similar but blurred.[24] Now the Bureau had prints to go with its photo.

On April 17, the bartending graduation photo of Eric Starvo Galt was publicly released. Attorney General Clark announced that Eric S. Galt was wanted
for a conspiracy, together with "an individual he alleged to be his brother," to
"injure, oppress, threaten, or intimidate" Dr. King.*[25]

On that same day, FBI fingerprint experts began matching prints at 9:00
A.M. The Bureau had narrowed the search to white men under fifty years of
age, but that still left 53,000 sets of prints.[26] It could take two months working
day and night to get a match, assuming that Galt had his prints on file with the
government.

Several FBI teams worked in shifts around the clock. Forty-eight hours
later, shortly past 9:00 A.M. on April 19, they reached the seven-hundredth
card and got lucky with a match. The name on the card was James Earl Ray, a
forty-year-old ex-convict who was a four-time loser. From the age of twenty-
four, Ray had spent twelve of his next sixteen years behind bars, mostly for robberies. He had escaped from Missouri State Penitentiary in April 1967, in the
midst of serving a twenty-year sentence. Although he did not seem to fit the

---

*   The original charge included Galt's brother, since the owner of Aeromarine Supply,
the Birmingham gun store where the murder weapon was purchased, remembered that
the buyer had swapped the first rifle, a .243 caliber, for a .30-06, because his brother
had told him he had bought the wrong gun.

mold of a murderer, there was no doubt that Ray was Galt. Later that day, April 19, the FBI made a public announcement, and this time provided mug shots of Ray over a ten-year span.[27] Two hundred thousand wanted posters were soon distributed around the country, and thirty thousand were printed in Spanish for distribution in Mexico.[28]

When the FBI approached Ray's two living brothers, John and Jerry, both ex-convicts, they refused to provide any help in finding James. Agents who interviewed John Ray noted that he was "initially uncooperative and told them, 'What's all the excitement about? He only killed a nigger. If he had killed a white man, you wouldn't be here. King should have been killed ten years ago."[29] Jerry, meanwhile, told a friend that he would "tell the FBI only enough to keep them off my back." Asked by the same friend if James had killed King, Jerry said, "This is his business. I didn't ask him. If I was in his position and had eighteen years to serve and someone offered me a lot of money to kill someone I didn't like anyhow, and get me out of the country, I'd do it."*[30]

---

* John Ray, who has described himself as a "mild segregationist," later told the House Select Committee that this statement was not reflective of his general view toward King in 1968. He testified, "I probably was drunk, if I did say that." However, in a letter he wrote from prison to author George McMillan in June 1972, John said, "The common man . . . knows that King was not a saint as these try to picture him. There are millions of Rays in the United States with the same background and beliefs, who know that King was not only a rat but with his beaded eyes and pin ears looked like one."

As for Jerry Ray, when asked about the accuracy of his statement, he said, "It might have been true. I can't remember exactly what I said, but I have told other people. I said if he done it there had to be a lot of money involved because he wouldn't do it for hatred or just because he didn't like somebody, because this is not his line of work."

8

"I Feel So Trapped"

When the FBI put Ray on the most-wanted list on April 19 and broadcast his picture internationally on television on the twenty-first, most people assumed the hunt would soon be over. But days and then weeks passed, and public frustration and speculation mounted. The FBI was accused of incompetence or even abetting the fugitive's escape. A common notion was that Ray had probably been killed by coconspirators.[1] Author Truman Capote reflected that conclusion when he confidently announced on *The Tonight Show*, "James Earl Ray is dead. He has been dead for at least a month."[2] More than a dozen corpses—bodies that matched Ray in age and height—found in the United States and Mexico had their fingerprints and teeth compared to Ray's records.[3] Each time, the police had to wait for pathology reports before knowing whether the hunt was still on. All the while, hundreds of leads on a living Ray continued to pour into the FBI: He had boarded a yacht in Key West and was now living in Cuba; he had been flown by the CIA to South America; he had driven his Mustang up a ramp into the rear of a large moving truck and was now sheltered by a secret KKK underground gang.[4]

Rumors of a conspiracy grew daily. The nation's black community was convinced of it, fueled by statements from Ralph Abernathy, who also spoke on behalf of Coretta King, Jesse Jackson, and other civil rights leaders.[5] By mid-April, just weeks after the murder, the Kennedy Assassination Inquiry Committee, a group of hardcore JFK conspiracy buffs, announced that the King suspect looked like one of three unidentified tramps photographed at Dealey Plaza after the JFK assassination.[6] Louis Lomax, a prominent black journalist, began working on a syndicated series that would place Ray doing the hit for a wealthy New Orleans industrialist, and the FBI protecting him after the murder. White hate groups promoted the idea that King had been killed as a result of internecine rivalries within the SCLC, or at the very least by black militants who resented his popularity and nonviolent message.

The FBI, with the help of Canadian and Mexican authorities, searched for Ray both north and south of the border. Ray had visited both Mexico and Canada in 1967, so the Bureau knew either was likely. The Royal Canadian Mounted Police, under Superintendent Charles Sweeney, established a task force of a dozen officers in early May. At the External Affairs Passport Division Office in the capital, Ottawa, they slowly worked through 264,000 passport applications made since Ray had escaped from Missouri State Penitentiary back on April 23, 1967.[7]

On May 20, a twenty-eight-year-old Canadian policeman suddenly stopped and stared at a photo. There was the same thin nose, the slightly protruding left ear, the dark hair, the sallow complexion. But the man in the passport application, a Ramon George Sneyd, sported thick, black horn-rimmed glasses. None of the photos circulated of Ray showed him wearing glasses. "This looks like him if he wore glasses," the policeman announced.[8] The rest of the officers examined the photo, but most did not think it looked like Ray. Nevertheless, it was put aside along with eleven other "possibles."

As breaks in cases go, the Sneyd passport application was a lucky one. There was a real Ramon Sneyd, and he was a police officer in Toronto.* One call to the real Sneyd revealed that he had never applied for a passport, although somebody claiming to be from the Passport Division had called him around May 1 asking if he had lost a passport. "You've got the wrong Mr. Sneyd," he told the stranger. The Mounties sent a copy of the passport application to Washington, where FBI handwriting experts confirmed that the *S* and *G* of the signed Ramon George Sneyd matched the capital *S* and *G* of Eric S. Galt.[9]

That prompted an alert to Canadian customs and immigration authorities. The Toronto address Ray had given on the Sneyd passport application was a

---

* Not only was Sneyd a real person, but living within a few miles of him in the same Toronto neighborhood was an Eric S. Galt, a businessman; John Willard was an insurance appraiser who lived in the same area; a man bearing another name that would soon come into the case, Paul Bridgman, an educator, also lived there. Except for Willard, the other men bore a general resemblance to Ray, which has raised the charge that Ray's aliases were given to him as part of a sophisticated conspiracy to kill King. See Chapters 20 and 27 for a further discussion of those aliases.

rooming house at 962 Dundas Street, run by Mrs. Sun Fung Loo. Soon they discovered that Ray, using the alias Paul Bridgman, had arrived in Toronto no later than April 8, only four days after King's murder, and had stayed at a rooming house on Ossington Avenue. The real Paul Bridgman was a thirty-five-year-old consultant at the Toronto Board of Education.

The Mounties then traced Ray's path to a travel agency—the Kennedy Travel Bureau—and learned that there, using his Sneyd alias, he had bought an excursion-fare ticket to London and had left on May 6. While the Toronto–London portion of the ticket had been used, the return to Toronto had not. Ray could still be in Europe. Since the FBI had located letters from Ray inquiring about immigrating to white-run Rhodesia, it was also possible he might be there, and getting extradition for the murderer of Martin Luther King from a country that practiced aggressive race politics would not be easy.[10]

June 8, 1968, was a surprisingly warm day for London and the last vestiges of fog had burned off by midmorning. The conversation that dominated the city—whether among picture-snapping tourists strolling by Buckingham Palace or bare-chested soccer players in Regents Park—was the assassination of Senator Robert Kennedy only two days earlier in Los Angeles. Much of the London commentary centered on how America's predisposition for violence had unalterably changed its political and social climate. Just two months earlier a single bullet had shattered Martin Luther King's face while he leaned over a balcony railing at a Memphis motel. In the Kennedy murder, the assassin—a twenty-four-year-old Palestinian named Sirhan Sirhan—was grabbed at the scene. It highlighted even more the failure of the FBI to find James Earl Ray.

Around 11:30 A.M., at Heathrow Airport's Terminal Two, an unassuming middle-aged man strolled through the frenetic crowds to the passport desk.[11] The traveler wore a knee-length beige raincoat over a dark sports jacket and gray trousers. He calmly pulled a blue Canadian passport—in the name of Ramon George Sneyd—from a billfold in his jacket pocket and handed it to a young immigration officer. His destination was Brussels.

Everything seemed in order. The passport had been issued just three weeks earlier at the Canadian Embassy in Lisbon, Portugal.[12] The photo—of a neatly dressed, bespectacled man—matched the traveler.

"May I see the other one?" the immigration officer suddenly asked. When Ray had closed his billfold, the officer had noticed a second passport.[13] Ray seemed unfazed. The second passport was a canceled one, identical to the first except it had been issued in Ottawa in late April under the name Ramon George Sneya.[14]

"Why are the names different?"

Ray said that he had misspelled his own name in Canada, but had not had time to fix it before leaving on his trip. In Lisbon, he visited the Canadian Embassy, where he had his old passport canceled and was issued a new one. While he spoke, a second policeman at the passport desk, Detective Sergeant Philip Birch, stared at him intently. "My first impression of him was that he was an academic," recalls Birch, "almost an absent-minded professorial air about him, and that he was slightly nervous. I did not attach any significance to that, since so many passengers are nervous about flying."[15]

Part of Birch's duties included checking all the passengers against the "Watch For and Detain" booklet. He immediately saw an "All Ports Warning"—issued only two days earlier—that Ramon George Sneyd was wanted by Scotland Yard for "serious offences."[16] He now took both passports.

"I say, old fellow, would you mind stepping over here for a moment? I'd like to have a word with you."[17] When Ray protested that he had a flight to catch, Birch assured him he would not miss it. With another policeman in tow, they walked the long distance across the sprawling terminal to an administrative office.[18]

Once inside, Birch asked, "Would you mind if I searched you?"

Ray stood and raised his arms from his sides. Birch quickly found a Japanese-made .38 revolver in Ray's right trouser pocket.[19] The handle was wrapped with black electrician's tape, the kind professional gunmen use to reduce the slipperiness of smooth-handled revolvers or to strap a gun to a lower leg in the hope of avoiding detection if searched. Birch opened the barrel and spun it. It had five bullets. The safety catch was on.[20]

"Why are you carrying this gun?"

Ray's eyes darted down and away. "Well, I am going to Africa. I thought I might need it." A crooked smile crossed his face. "You know how things are there."[21]

Birch assumed he was lying. If he was worried about conditions in Africa, there was no reason to travel with a loaded pistol in London. "I have reason to believe you have committed an arrestable offense," Birch said softly while handing the pistol to another policeman. Ray seemed unconcerned. Birch continued the search. Among other items, he found a one-way ticket to Brussels, the unused return portion of a ticket between London and Toronto, and a certified birth certificate in the name of Ramon George Sneyd.[22]

Soon, two of Scotland Yard's top investigators—Detective Chief Superintendent Thomas Butler, who had cracked the Great Train Robbery of 1963, and Chief Inspector Kenneth Thompson of the Interpol office—arrived.[23]

"We are police officers," said Butler in a formal, clipped tone. "I understand you have in your possession two passports in the names Sneya and Sneyd. What is your name?"

"I can't understand why I am here," Ray protested. His voice rose slightly, a tone of nervousness having broken his calm detachment. "My name is Sneyd."

Butler held up the passports. "Both passports show that you are a Canadian citizen born in Toronto on October 8, 1932. Are these details correct?"

Ray seemed impatient. "Yes, of course they are."

"This .38 revolver with five rounds of ammunition in its chambers was found in your hip pocket when you were first seen. Is it your gun?"

"Yes, it is mine."

"Would you like to tell us why you are carrying a gun at all?"

"I am going to Brussels."

"Why should you want to take a gun to Brussels?"

Again, Ray's eyes darted to the floor. His words were now a bit rushed. "Well, I am really thinking of going on to Rhodesia and things aren't too good there right now."

Butler stared at him for a moment before proceeding. "You have to have a firearms certificate to possess a gun and even ammunition in this country. Have you a firearms certificate issued by the competent authority?"

Ray shook his head. "No. No, I haven't any certificate for it."

Now Butler raised his voice ever so slightly. "I must inform you, Mr. Sneyd, that you are under arrest for possession of a gun without a permit. I must also caution you that anything you say may be held against you."[24]

The other police surrounded Ray and spirited him from Heathrow to London's Cannon Row jail, a five-story redbrick-and-granite cell block located at Scotland Yard. There he was fingerprinted and placed in a large empty cell, with an armed guard posted nearby.[25] If Ray was nervous, he gave no indication of it. Shortly before 5:00 P.M., Butler and Thompson entered his cell. Again, Butler did the talking.

"As a result of inquiries made since you were detained, we have very good reason to believe that you are not a Canadian citizen, but an American."

Ray was quiet for a moment, and then nodded his head while muttering, "Oh well, yes, I am."

Butler ignored him and continued. "I now believe your name is not Sneyd but James Earl Ray, also known as Eric Starvo Galt and other names, and that you are wanted at present in the United States for serious criminal offenses, including murder in which a firearm was used." His words, enunciated clearly and loudly, reverberated in the small concrete cell.

Suddenly Ray seemed scared. His body stiffened and his face drained of what little color it had. He staggered backward and then crumpled onto a nearby bench, burying his head in his hands. "Oh God," he stammered. Then after a moment of silence he spoke again, seemingly more to himself than to anyone else in the cell. "I feel so trapped."

"I should caution you again," Butler interrupted, "anything you say may be held against you."

Ray did not lift his head. He stared straight at the floor.

"Yes," he said weakly. "I shouldn't say anything more now. I can't think right."*[26]

The sixty-five-day hunt for the man charged as Martin Luther King's assassin had ended.

---

* Ray, who evidently considered his actions to show weakness and fear, later emphatically denied ever making such a statement or acting with such dejection. However, both Butler and Thompson were consistent in their recollections, which were first recorded in official statements only two days after the arrest. Thompson's notes of the encounter record that Ray "was obviously engaged in some mental struggle, and when we left the cell, he again dropped his head in his hands." Butler testified about the incident, under oath, at Ray's extradition proceedings only weeks after the arrest. There is little reason to doubt it did not happen as the two British officers described.

9

Story for Sale

The British solicitor appointed to represent Ray, Michael Eugene, met his client for the first time on June 10, 1968, two days after his arrest. Ray gave his trademark weak handshake, looked at the floor most of the time, and seemed to answer the initial volley of questions with grunts. Then suddenly he leaned forward, tapped his fingers on the table, and pointedly declared, "Look, they have got me mixed up with some guy called James Earl Ray. My name is Ramon George Sneyd. I don't know this Ray guy and they are trying to say that he is me. I've never met the guy in my life and I don't know anything about this. They are just trying to pin something on me that I didn't do."[1]

A few minutes later, Ray told Eugene that he wanted him to contact his brother, Jerry Ray, in Chicago. Eugene did not say anything, but wondered if his client realized that by giving his brother's surname he had exposed his real identity. Next, Ray instructed Eugene to call a lawyer in Birmingham, Alabama, Arthur Hanes. When Eugene asked if he knew him, Ray said no, "but I know he'll represent me and look after my interests back in the States." One other lawyer, J. B. Stoner, the fanatical counsel for the virulently anti-Semitic and racist National States Rights Party, had offered his services free of charge.[2] But at that early stage, Ray seemed interested only in the premium names in the legal profession. As backups to Hanes, he told Eugene to contact F. Lee Bailey in Boston and Melvin Belli in San Francisco.

Did he have any money to pay these top-ranked attorneys? asked Eugene.

"I'm not worried about their fees," Ray announced. "Even if it takes a hundred thousand dollars, I can raise it. They'll be taken care of."[3]

Before Eugene left, Ray, who had turned talkative, also expressed his anger over a press report that claimed he had spoken to Assistant Attorney General Fred Vinson, Jr., who had flown to London the previous day. "There's been a pack of lies printed about Vinson seeing me. . . . I saw nobody. I have never seen anybody. . . . I want to make this quite clear so the people back home won't think that I've seen anybody." This emphatic side of Ray was remarkably different from the quiet, monosyllabic man Eugene had first encountered. He seemed eager to convince Eugene that he had not even thought of cooperating with the police or talking about the crime.

Arthur Hanes was a good choice by Ray. The fifty-one-year-old former FBI agent had been mayor of Birmingham in 1963 when King had his civil rights campaign there.[4] It was under the Hanes administration that police commissioner "Bull" O'Connor had turned police dogs and fire hoses on the marchers. Hanes had compounded the incident by bitterly denouncing King.[5] A right-wing segregationist, his biggest courtroom victory was the acquittal of four Klan members accused of killing Viola Liuzzo, a white housewife from Detroit who had been shot to death while driving a car with a young black SCLC volunteer between Selma and Montgomery.

Ray knew about Hanes's career—"I do read the papers quite a bit," he once said—and was impressed by the Liuzzo acquittal.[6] Hanes worked with his son, Art junior, then twenty-seven (he later became a state judge in Alabama).

Besides asking Eugene to call, Ray also wrote to Hanes, still using his Sneyd alias, requesting representation.[7] By Monday, June 17, Hanes was leaning toward taking the case. He arranged for expedited passports for himself and Art junior so they could fly to London.[8] From his initial review of the facts, Hanes thought it likely that Ray was a hired assassin whose motivation was money. His possible suspects for the paymaster were colored by his political views, and patently illogical: black militants, backed perhaps by Castro or even Chinese Communists. But Hanes was also innovative. He had previously heard the rumors that J. Edgar Hoover had tape-recorded some of King's extramarital liaisons, and he contemplated getting those, playing them in a trial, and arguing to the jury that a jealous husband may have had a better motive for killing King than James Earl Ray.[9]

On the eve of his departure for London, Hanes received a telephone call from William Bradford Huie, a well-known contemporary author who had written extensively about the South, the Ku Klux Klan, and civil rights, including the bestsellers *The Revolt of Mamie Stover* and *The Execution of Private Slovik*. King had written the introduction for another of Huie's books, *Three Lives for*

Mississippi, which was about the 1964 murder of the civil rights activists Andrew Goodman, Michael Schwerner, and James Chaney. Huie also believed in checkbook journalism—"there is no substitute for money," he once boasted. Huie had paid KKK informers for *Three Lives*. When he wrote a book about the 1955 murder of fourteen-year-old Emmett Till in Mississippi, he paid $4,000 to two Klansmen who had been acquitted at trial, and with the legal impunity granted them by their acquittal, they boasted to Huie about how they killed the youngster for whistling at a white woman.[10]

Huie had an interesting offer for Hanes. "The only way we are going to know what happened in the King assassination," he contended, "is for someone like me to make a deal with your client to tell me all he can about his involvement and who helped him." Huie wanted exclusive access to Ray and the right to publish his story after the trial. In return, he would strike a financial deal with Hanes and Ray. Hanes was interested. He was about to spend his own money on the upcoming trip to England, but he told Huie he was not going "to chase around the world and defend that boy" unless there was money to pay the bill.*[11] Huie made Hanes a proposition: He was willing to spend up to $40,000 of his own money investigating the story if Hanes, after meeting with Ray, thought "the prospects are good."[12]

Hanes was not able to give Huie a quick answer, however, because he was not allowed to see Ray on his first trip to London, which lasted four days.[13] The magistrate had not yet decided the extradition matter, so Hanes was considered to have no standing in British courts.

Meanwhile, the Justice Department and Memphis prosecutors were aggressively working to get Ray extradited back to Tennessee. The U.S. government had to convince the British there was probable cause that Ray was the assassin.[14] And Ray could be tried for no other crime in the United States than that for which he was extradited.† A team of prosecutors from the district attorney

---

*   In 1978, George Wilson, a former Midwestern leader of the United Klans of America (UKA), told the House Select Committee on Assassinations that the UKA had contributed $10,000 to Hanes for his Ray representation, under the pretense of Hanes's legal representation of a group of North Carolina Klansmen. Two sources independently confirmed Wilson's charge. Beyond financial assistance, the Klan also evidently offered additional help to Hanes. The committee received information that Robert Shelton, the UKA's imperial wizard, had arranged with Hanes to review the jury list in Ray's trial in order to identify sympathetic jurors. Hanes vigorously denied receiving financial or other assistance from the UKA for his defense of Ray.

†   This technicality could have caused havoc once Ray returned to the United States if the defense had been clever enough to exploit it. The government presented a case at the extradition hearing that Ray was the sole shooter who murdered King on April 4, 1968.

general's office in Memphis coordinated the extradition effort with the Justice Department and the FBI.

In mid-June, the Justice Department submitted to the British courts a skeletal outline of its case against Ray, including affidavits of witnesses and experts ranging from FBI agent George Bonebrake, who said he had identified Ray's prints on the rifle, scope, and binoculars found at the murder scene, to Donald Wood, the Aeromarine Supply worker who sold Ray the rifle.[15] The government's presentation also revealed one of the early problems with the prosecution's evidence. FBI ballistics expert Robert Frazier—who had handled the ballistics on Oswald's Mannlicher-Carcano for the JFK assassination—submitted an affidavit that said the murder bullet was identical to the other bullets found in the bundle at the scene, but that "because of distortion due to mutilation and insufficient marks of value, I could draw no conclusion as to whether or not the submitted bullet was fired from the submitted rifle."[16]

During the extradition proceedings, Ray made weekly trips to court from his prison, first at Cannon Row, and then at the Wandsworth maximum-security facility. British law prohibited a prisoner from being held without charge for longer than seven days at a time, so at his weekly visits, the magistrate would remand him back to prison for another seven-day stretch. On each of those trips from prison to court, Ray was accompanied by the same policeman, Alexander Eist, a sergeant on Scotland Yard's Flying Squad, an elite group of policemen assigned to high-profile and difficult cases. Eist had also been with Ray for nine hours on his first morning in a British jail. There, and on each of the seven jail transfer trips, as well as whenever Ray was in a detention cell at the courthouse or in the court itself, Eist was handcuffed to him.[17] "Initially, he didn't want to say anything to anybody," recalled Eist. On the first day, Ray only glared at him, and it was uncomfortable. "But I suppose [because of] my constant contact with him, he began to look on me as somebody he could talk to."[18] Eist helped Ray by getting him eating utensils—they were at first prohibited, since authorities feared he might try suicide—and performed other small favors, such as giving him magazines. Ray appreciated Eist's efforts and slowly the two developed a rapport, rare for Ray with anyone. Yet even then the

---

If, upon his return, Ray had admitted his involvement, but instead claimed it was a conspiracy of which he was only the provider of the weapon or the getaway driver, the prosecutors could not have tried him. When CBS's Dan Rather asked Ray in 1977 if he "knowingly had anything to do with the shooting of Dr. King," Ray did not give a direct answer, but instead fell back on the technicality of his extradition, telling Rather, "I think that is a new question because when I was extradited . . . the thing they could try me on would be doing the actual shooting . . . aiding and abetting and conspiracy or that stuff, they wouldn't be able to charge against that under the treaty terms."

conversations were mostly one-way, with Ray doing the talking. Eist noticed that if he asked Ray a specific question, Ray would "refuse to say any more, and then sit there and stare at me." Instead, Eist found it best to bring up a subject, and then Ray would conduct a monologue. Once Ray started, Eist said, sometimes "you had a job to stop him talking."

Ray once began by listing the differences between the British and American justice systems. Then he told Eist about the time he served at the Missouri State Penitentiary, and at another point said he kept himself in money as a fugitive by "small robberies."[19] "The only person that he ever mentioned to me at any time was a brother," testified Eist, but he did not name him. The conversations that Eist remembered best were those nearer the end of their time together, when they got around to discussing blacks. Ray called them "niggers" and "he told me that he tried to get into Africa at some stage—he said to kill some more of them . . . he didn't go into a great deal of conversation about that because apparently he had been unsuccessful in whatever he tried to do. He did, in fact, mention the Foreign Legion."[20] Eist had the feeling that Ray considered himself a hero of sorts for the King murder. "He was continually asking me how he would hit the headlines in the newspapers, and he kept wanting news of publicity." When Eist told him that his arrest and the King case had not made a major impact in Britain, Ray told him, "You haven't seen anything yet."

Finally, King's murder came slowly into their talks. Ray was convinced that he could make real money from the notoriety of the case, and he was not worried since he believed that all he could be charged with was conspiracy—"I will only get one to ten, or one to twelve years for that," he confidently predicted. "It was at this time," Eist recalled, "that he said there was no way that they would actually be able to pin the murder on him except that he had thrown the gun away; that was the mistake he had made. I recall he said to me he had seen a policeman or police vehicle and panicked and thrown the gun away, and his fingerprints would obviously be found on this weapon."[21] Eist also remembered that Ray "had never ever shown any regret."*

---

* For years after the extradition hearings, no American or British authority ever asked Eist if he had had conversations with Ray. Yet Eist had told acquaintances, including a London reporter, about them. In 1976, he met an American Air Force major stationed in Great Britain and related the same story he had told others for nearly a decade. The major told Eist he should contact the FBI, since there was an effort to have a new investigation into the case under way in Congress. Eist did so and as a result testified under oath to the House Select Committee on Assassinations on its opening day of public hearings, November 9, 1978. His testimony caught Ray and his then attorney Mark Lane by surprise. Lane responded by trying to attack Eist personally, charging that he had been placed on trial for accepting bribes and had also been

While Ray was talking to Eist, the British magistrate was reviewing the affidavits and submissions from the United States. On June 27, Ray appeared in court for the brief extradition hearing dressed in a blue-checked suit with a blue open-necked shirt. He chewed gum, occasionally scratched the back of his neck, and seemed unperturbed by the proceedings. Michael Eugene, his appointed solicitor, argued strenuously that the crime was "political" and was therefore exempt from extradition.[22] When Ray was called to testify, the court clerk asked him for his religion so the appropriate Bible could be used. Ray replied softly that he did not have any religion. On the stand, he denied that he knew King, bore a grudge against him, or killed him.[23]

Five days later, Magistrate Frank Milton ruled there was sufficient evidence to extradite Ray back to the States to stand trial for murdering King.

Once the order was in, Hanes returned to London and announced that Ray would not appeal the decision. He saw Ray for half an hour on July 5, and again for thirty minutes the following day. They sat in a tiny interview room, separated by a glass partition covered with wire mesh. A guard stood directly behind Ray. Ray's British solicitor was with Hanes.[24] Ray implored Hanes to sue *Life* magazine because of a story it had printed portraying him as a childhood bully who developed into a lone assassin. But Hanes was not interested in talking about civil suits until he was first certain that he, and he alone, would represent Ray. Hanes firmly announced that he would not represent Ray if J. B. Stoner of the National States Rights Party joined the defense team. Ray agreed. Hanes then turned to his major reason for the meeting, that he and his son would defend Ray so long as Ray agreed to tell his complete story for publication after the trial. With Michael Eugene as a witness, Ray—still using the alias "R. G. Sneyd"—signed a one-page document granting Hanes a broad power of attorney; the right to act on Ray's behalf as exclusive agent and attorney for contracts, negotiations, and the sale of entertainment rights; and most important, the transfer to Hanes of a 40 percent interest in Ray's share of any agreement eventually reached with author Huie.[25]

Reporters were waiting for Hanes when he left the courthouse. He announced that he had agreed to take the case and then was asked how his fee and expenses would be paid. He did not mention the agreement in his suit

---

dismissed from the police because he was suspected of being involved in jewel robberies throughout England. Lane was wrong. In fact, Eist had been charged in one case involving a false alibi, but it later turned out that his name had mistakenly appeared on the original arrest record as the officer in charge of that case. Once the error was discovered, the case against him was dismissed and the government paid his defense costs. When Eist retired much later, it was actually for medical reasons, not for suspicion of criminal behavior.

pocket. "He assured me he can take care of my fee," Hanes said disingenuously. "He had indicated he may be able to raise the money from his family. He ain't going to pay me with love, I can tell you that."*[26]

When he returned to Birmingham, Hanes met with Huie and shared his first impressions of Ray. "He's cagey, like an old con. He doesn't look you straight in the eye, sort of hangs his head and grins out of the side of his mouth. He's incapable of trusting any man on earth. He's definitely not like any Negro killer I've ever known. I don't think he hates Negroes. I don't think he has strong feelings about anything. If he didn't kill King for money, I can't see that he had any motive. . . . I told him we had to have the truth, and had to sell it."†[27]

Huie was now confident that Ray was worth the gamble of a formal contract. His lawyer had already drafted an agreement, and he and Hanes signed it in on July 8, 1968. Ray executed it on August 1 when he returned to the States. It guaranteed Ray and Hanes an equal split of 60 percent of any money earned by Huie on the case, whether for books, magazines, television, or film.‡

However, since Hanes was then incurring expenses, and Ray had no money, the lawyer and defendant wanted some money up front from Huie. So Huie, against the advice of both his literary agent and his lawyer, signed yet another

---

* Ray's brothers, John and Jerry, had set up a "defense fund" for him. They held a press conference in Memphis and asked for contributions. It soon closed, since so little money came in. However, they were inundated with hundreds of letters of support, good wishes, and congratulations for James.

† Hanes was not the only one who reached an early conclusion that if Ray did it, it was likely for money. John Ray, after James's capture, said, "if my brother did kill King, he did it for a lot of money. He didn't do anything if it wasn't for money. . . . If he does have to stand trial, I would like to see him get the same sentence as the guy who killed Rockwell." John C. Patler, the assassin of American Nazi Party leader George Lincoln Rockwell, received a twenty-year sentence.

‡ Since Hanes had already obtained 40 percent of Ray's 30 percent, it meant that Hanes was really earning 42 percent of the entire project, while Ray was left with 18 percent. However, in early September, without Huie's knowledge, Ray and Hanes modified their own agreement so that instead of Hanes permanently deducting 40 percent of Ray's share, Ray would give him all his early share until Hanes had received $20,000 plus expenses. That meant that after Hanes collected that $20,000 fee, Ray would again have his full 30 percent of the overall deal. Clearly, Ray was willing to give all his immediate money to Hanes on the possibility that his story would bring in enormous profits, and then, with a full 30 percent share, he would collect far more in the future. "Had I been consulted," said Huie, "I would not have agreed to any change in the original two-party agreement between Mr. Hanes and Ray. Because I wanted Ray and his brothers to get the money at once and develop an appetite for more, so that I would be in a stronger position to compel Ray to tell me the truth."

agreement with them, in which he agreed to pay Ray and Hanes $40,000 over several months, as a nonrefundable loan against any money eventually earned by selling Ray's story.*[28]

The problem with such an agreement was that it created an inherent conflict of interest from the very beginning among lawyer, client, and journalist. Ray's sole interest was in being acquitted of the charge of killing King. The truth was secondary to beating the rap, as it would have been for any four-time loser who had spent most of his adult life in prison. Part of Hanes's interest— obtaining an acquittal—coincided with Ray's, but he also wanted to ensure that Ray's story was profitably exploited. There were also ethical considerations for Hanes. For instance, after the British magistrate had ordered Ray extradited, Hanes advised Ray not to appeal. However, under the terms of the contract with Huie, the cash payments from Huie would not start until Ray returned to the United States. Could that have affected Hanes's decision as to whether his client's best interest would have been served by appealing the extradition ruling? Would future decisions, such as the question of whether Ray should testify at his own trial, be influenced by the fact that if Ray's story was to be sold in a book or film it might be more valuable if he had not already told it on the witness stand?[†] And Huie claimed he wanted only the truth, which might well have been different from what was necessary for the defense to craft an acquittal, or even to get a hung jury.[29]

This arrangement encouraged Ray to develop a dramatic tale that was commercially profitable. Merely contending "I didn't do it" would not entice many people to buy a book or watch a movie. The better the story, the more money he might make.

Hanes and Huie were eager to hear his story, but British prison officials would not permit a private interview.[30] So they had to wait for Ray's return to the United States. At midnight on July 18, in a secret transfer dubbed Operation Landing, Ray boarded a C-135 U.S. Air Force jet. It normally carried 125 people, but that night it had only 6 passengers: Ray, a physician, and four FBI agents.[31] Hanes's request to accompany his client had been rejected.[32] Ray remained strapped into an aisle seat near the rear, except for the one time he went

---

*   The agreement was structured so that Huie paid Ray $10,000 upon signing a book contract, $5,000 one month after Ray was transferred to jail in the States, and then $5,000 a month after that until the total of $40,000 was paid.

†   In a subsequent lawsuit that Ray filed against Hanes, Huie, the lawyer Percy Foreman, and others (Ray v. Foreman), the court concluded that Ray was a voluntary and intelligent party to the agreements and there was no evidence to support Ray's contention that the conflicts of interest compromised the way his case was litigated. The fee arrangement negotiated by Hanes, however, was in apparent violation of the American Bar Association's code of professional responsibility.

to the bathroom, accompanied by two of the agents. The group arrived at Millington Naval Air Base, eighteen miles from Memphis, at 4:00 A.M. The purpose of the midnight flight was so that Ray could leave London under cover of darkness and arrive in Memphis the same way, which made it easier to keep the press away and monitor security.[33] If there was a conspiracy, there might be those who would try to silence him. Even with no conspiracy, there was real fear of a KKK or white supremacist attack to set him free, or black militants trying to avenge King's death.[34] No one wanted a repeat of Jack Ruby's murder of Lee Oswald.

Shelby County sheriff William Morris, Jr., greeted Ray, who stood naked in the aisle of the plane, his head cast down. He had been stripped of his clothes in preparation for a quick physical exam before being turned over to the sheriff. His skin was a sickly white.[35]

Morris spoke. "James Earl Ray, alias Harvey Lowmeyer, alias John Willard, alias Eric Starvo Galt, alias Paul Bridgman, alias Ramon George Sneyd, will you please step forward three paces?"

Ray did so. The accompanying doctor listened to his heart, took his blood pressure, and after a few minutes nodded to Morris, who then read Ray his rights. A deputy opened a small case and removed a pair of dark green pants, a green plaid shirt, and sandals. After Ray had put them on, a bulletproof vest was slipped over him, and then his hands were manacled to a leather harness. Ray did not say a word as Morris and his deputies virtually carried him down the plane's steps and lifted him into an armored vehicle borrowed from the Jackson, Mississippi, police. The armored car was led by two squad cars of guards carrying submachine guns, and followed by another three squad cars, two with sheriff's deputies and the third with federal marshals.[36]

A half-hour later Ray was back in an American prison for the first time in over a year. An editorial in *The New York Times* welcomed his return to the United States, since now the truth about King's murder might be discovered. "The meager evidence offered in the extradition case—all the United States has to show is 'probable cause' that Ray was the assassin, not proof—is hardly enough to persuade anyone that the killer acted alone. If and when James Earl Ray goes on trial in Tennessee, the United States and the world will want to see any evidence throwing light on whether there was a conspiracy to kill King or whether it was the work of one vengeful or unbalanced man."[37]

10

Enter Raoul

C ell Block A in Memphis's Criminal Courts building, which served as
death row, had been specially converted for Ray's arrival. The security
precautions were extraordinary. There were six individual cells, each with a
single bunk, a toilet, and a washbasin. All were empty so that Ray could be randomly transferred, never spending two consecutive nights in the same cell. His
food came from the prison mess and no one there knew which portion went to
him. When taken into the prison yard, not only did two guards escort him, but
also he was allowed only into a small corner hidden from any outside view. And
at least two guards were always with him in the cell block. The entire section
was brilliantly lit with large standing lights that were never turned off, forcing
Ray often to put a pillow over his head to sleep.[1] Microphones hung conspicu-
ously from the ceiling. Cameras in the corners transmitted images monitored
by the guards outside the bars. Sheriff Morris had a speaker and monitor installed in his office, two floors below Ray. Cameras even monitored Ray when
he used the toilet and showered.[2]

When Arthur Hanes, Sr. and Jr., visited, they were assured by the prosecutors that the microphones were turned off, but they took no chances. They lay
with Ray on their backs on the cell's cement floor, their heads close together,
whispering softly. Still, Hanes senior worried that if the television cameras
filmed them, someone could read their lips. Hanes also ran the shower in the

background in the hope it would drown out their conversations in case the ceiling microphones were on.*

At their first meeting, Hanes looked at Ray and said, "All right, Jimmy, let's start talking. From your breakout on April 23, 1967, to June 8 when they picked you up in London."[3]

Ray began to relate an astonishing story. The Haneses had to pass everything to Huie, since Judge W. Preston Battle, the jurist who had been assigned the case, rejected Huie's request to meet personally with Ray. Eventually, Ray also sent Huie handwritten letters and notes, including even crude hand-drawn maps of places he had visited as a fugitive. Because of their cumulative size these writings were dubbed "the 20,000 Words."

Huie had agreed to wait to publish until after the verdict, but instead signed a deal with *Look* magazine to tell Ray's story before the trial.[†] The first of three installments ran in the November 12, 1968, issue, and was titled "The Story of James Earl Ray and the Conspiracy to Kill Martin Luther King." It followed Ray from his escape from the Missouri State Penitentiary for four months through his stay in Montreal, Canada, in August 1967 and often quoted from Ray's letters to Huie. It also introduced his creative alibi.[‡]

Ray described how, in the seventh year of a twenty-year sentence, he escaped from his maximum-security jail in Missouri by scaling a twenty-three-foot wall. He then spent three months at menial jobs, maintaining a low profile in Chicago, Alton, and Quincy, Illinois.

In mid-July, Ray drove to Montreal, where he hoped to get seaman's papers and a job on a ship so that he could leave North America. As a result, he "spent his days and evenings with 'the boats' " along the waterfront, Huie wrote. "He frequented Neptune Tavern, 121 West Commissioners Street. . . . On his third or fourth night in the Neptune, Ray says he 'sort of let the word get around that he had had a little trouble down in the States, that he was looking for ID and capital, and just might be available for activities that didn't involve too much

---

*   In September, the Haneses filed a motion before the trial judge on the Ray case, asking for the "inhumane" conditions to be improved, and also to be allowed to have private conversations with their client.

†   Huie said Ray agreed to the early publication so long as Huie stopped his narrative at March 23, 1968, eleven days before the assassination. That installment was still set for publication after the trial. The early articles earned Huie a contempt citation, since the court had placed a ban on pretrial publicity, but Judge Battle died before he ever punished Huie.

‡   Ray's version, as originally given to Huie, is presented here without any comment or correction. It is discussed in detail in Chapters 19 through 26. Any quotations in this chapter refer to one of three Huie installments in *Look*.

risk.' This resulted in a contact. A man whom Ray calls Raoul and describes to me as being a blond Latin about 35, and whom Ray took to be a seaman, showed interest in him. They began cautious verbal exploration, with Raoul hinting that if Ray was willing to assist certain projects, Raoul might be able to provide Ray ID and capital. Ray says this exploration continued during 'at least eight meetings' over a period of three weeks."[4]

Although Raoul had promised the possibility of a passport or work on a ship, "Ray's next action was one that I have found to be typical of him," wrote Huie. "He never puts all his eggs in one basket." Ray tried to get a Canadian passport on his own by meeting a Canadian woman who might vouch that she had known him for at least two years, a requirement he mistakenly thought was necessary for a passport. After buying a fashionable new wardrobe, Ray set out for a premier Canadian resort—Gray Rocks Inn—where he did meet a woman and had a brief affair. But when he eventually discovered that she was employed by the Canadian government, he dropped the idea of asking her for help on the passport and instead returned to Raoul.

From August 8 to the 18th, Ray says he talked at least five more times with Raoul at the Neptune Tavern. And Raoul made him this proposition:

1. That Ray would meet Raoul in the railroad station at Windsor at 3 p.m. on Monday, August 21.
2. That Ray would make several trips across the border from Windsor to Detroit for Raoul, using both the bridge and tunnel border crossings, carrying packages concealed in the old red Plymouth.
3. That Ray would then sell the Plymouth and go by train or bus to Birmingham, Ala. There, Ray would lie low, take no risks, pull no hold ups, accumulate a little ID, and wait for instructions by general delivery mail.
4. That Raoul would pay 'living expenses' and also come to Birmingham and buy Ray a 'suitable car.'
5. That after a few weeks or months, after a little joint activity, Raoul would pay Ray $12,000 and give him a passport and 'other ID' and help him go 'anywhere in the world.'
6. That Ray would ask no questions. . . . Raoul did, however, reveal to Ray that he [Raoul] had spent some of his time in New Orleans, and he gave Ray a New Orleans telephone number.[5]

Ray told Huie "I didn't know what to do." On the one hand, if he accepted Raoul's offer he had to return to the States, where he risked being sent back to the Missouri State Penitentiary. On the other hand, "I was running out of capital again, and I didn't want to risk another hold-up in Canada. I couldn't get on a ship. I couldn't get I.D." So, Ray said, he accepted Raoul's offer.

In the second installment in *Look*—"I Got Involved Gradually, and I Didn't Know Anybody Was to Be Murdered"—Huie began by informing the reader that he had done his own extensive investigation. He had personally traveled to Chicago, Montreal, Ottawa, Los Angeles, and Birmingham and Selma, Alabama. As a result of that reporting, Huie concluded:

"That the plot to murder Martin Luther King, Jr., existed as early as August 15, 1967, eight months prior to the murder on April 4, 1968.

"That Ray was drawn unknowingly into this plot in Montreal on August 18, 1967, and thereafter moved as directed by the plotters.

"That as late as March 23, 1968, less than two weeks before the murder with which he is charged, Ray did not know that the plot included the murder or that it was aimed in any way at Dr. King."[6]

In this article, Huie described in great detail how Ray, over seven months, made various trips at Raoul's direction. At different times he lived in Birmingham, Mexico, and then Los Angeles. He did some smuggling for Raoul, and in return Raoul periodically gave him money, totaling $8,200.

On March 15, 1968, Ray received the directive from Raoul for which he had been waiting. "He was wanted in Selma and Birmingham, Ala.," wrote Huie. Ray drove through New Orleans and spent the night of Friday, March 22, in Selma. The next day he left for Atlanta.

Huie wrote in his own summary to this second article: "The outline of the plot to murder Dr. King now begins to become visible to me. It may not be visible to my readers because, until Ray has been tried, I cannot reveal all that I have found to be true. But from what I know, from what I have learned from Ray, and from my investigative research, [the plot's ringleaders were] calculating men who wanted to use King's murder to trigger violent conflict between white and Negro citizens." King was to be murdered during the 1968 election year, and it was to be done "not while he was living quietly at his home in Atlanta, but at some dramatic moment," preferably in Birmingham, Montgomery, or Selma, "since these cities were milestones in his career as an advocate of racial change." Moreover, Huie wrote, King "was to be murdered by a white man, or white men, who would be described as 'Southerners' and racists." And finally, "there was no necessity, after the murder, for the murderer or murderers to be murdered to prevent a trial or trials—because a trial or trials could yield extra dividends of hatred and violence."

The editors of *Look* closed the November 26 issue by promising that "in a future issue, William Bradford Huie plans to tell in detail the personal story that may not be developed at the trial—the activities of James Earl Ray between March 23 and the day that he was arrested in London."

11

Hiding the Truth

Huie's first two articles caused an uproar. It was the first time the public learned what Ray had consistently been telling his attorneys since their first meeting in Memphis. Although Huie had not yet written about the key days just before the assassination, it was clear that he and the Haneses thought Ray was a pawn in a sophisticated plot to kill Dr. King. Not only did the stories introduce a conspirator by name, but they were also filled with new details about Ray's fugitive year leading up to the assassination. The FBI even learned new information about the places Ray had been and the people he had been in touch with before King's murder.[1]

The stories had great impact because of their timing. They added to the growing perception that while Ray may have been involved in King's death, likely as the triggerman, conspirators were still free.* Huie's second installment, concluding that Ray was an unwitting part of the King conspiracy, was on the newsstands on Monday, November 11, just before the trial was to begin.

---

* Ray himself added to that perception. In Cell Block A, he developed a talkative relationship with Dr. McCarthy DeMere, an energetic man who had been General George Patton's medical aide during World War II. Once DeMere asked Ray, "Did you really do it?" "Well, let's put it this way: I wasn't in it by myself." John Ray, James's brother, reported to the *St. Louis Post-Dispatch* that James had told him the same thing before he pleaded guilty.

Judge Preston Battle, a sixty-year-old recovered alcoholic, who had issued a pretrial order restricting publicity and barred any reporter from having personal access to Ray, was infuriated. He immediately issued a new order prohibiting all potential witnesses listed by the prosecution or defense from reading any news accounts of the case.[*2]

Thirty-six hours before the start of the trial, Ray stunned the court by dismissing Hanes as his attorney. Battle had to postpone the trial. Behind the scenes, there had been friction between attorney and client—Ray was angry that the information Hanes had passed to Huie had inadvertently helped the FBI.[3] In late September, Hanes had announced in open court that he might withdraw as Ray's lawyer, and in early October, J. B. Stoner, the racist counsel for the National States Rights Party—the one person whom Hanes had told Ray he would not tolerate as part of the defense team—had visited Ray, at Ray's invitation.[4] Moreover, James's brother Jerry had met with Huie and was convinced that Huie did not want James to take the witness stand at his trial since it would hurt the upcoming book's commercial success. Hanes was also against Ray taking the stand. When they met in early November, Jerry warned James that Hanes and Huie were selling him out.[5] But the real reason for the dissension between Ray and Hanes was that Ray's brothers had long been convinced there was a better attorney: the celebrated Houston lawyer Percy Foreman.[6] When Jerry and John Ray finally met Foreman, Jerry recalled, he would "tell me about all these other cases he won. Then he says this would be the easiest case he ever had. . . . He said, 'They have no actual evidence. I've got guys out before where they had evidence against them but they don't have evidence against James.' "[†7]

The sixty-five-year-old Foreman at first seemed the perfect choice for Ray. At six-four and 250 pounds, he was not only one of the country's most physically imposing attorneys, but certainly among its most flamboyant. More important, he boasted that in hundreds of cases, he had lost only one client to the death penalty.[8]

---

* A panel of seven Memphis lawyers had been appointed to advise Judge Battle on questions of pretrial publicity. Arthur Hanes, Sr., two Memphis newspaper reporters, and a private investigator had already been held in contempt of court for giving interviews or, in the case of the journalists, writing stories that contained interviews banned under the pretrial order. After the publication of the Look article, the panel recommended that Huie be held in contempt, as well as FBI fingerprint expert George Bonebrake, who had given a lecture at a police school, attended by some reporters, in which he discussed the prints found on the rifle at the murder scene.

† Jerry Ray had contacted Foreman and asked him to visit James in jail. Foreman later told CBS's Dan Rather that James himself had written a letter asking for his help. But Foreman could never produce a copy of such a letter, and Ray always denied writing it.

But Foreman turned out to be a terrible choice, and Ray should have recognized the signs of trouble at their first jail meeting on November 9, the day before Ray fired Hanes. "He got down to business pretty quick," recalled Ray. But "business" did not mean the King assassination. Foreman told Ray that his initial impression was that Ray would "probably barbecue" and that to defend him his fee would be $150,000, appeals and all. "And then he started discussing a retainer fee," recalled Ray, "and he asked me about the Mustang and this rifle." Ray signed over any ownership interest he had in the car and rifle to Foreman.*

Ray also said that Foreman "had these various contracts with him, the ones with Mr. Bradford Huie and Arthur Hanes."[9] Foreman told Ray he did not like the agreements signed by Huie and Hanes and that they were not good for Ray. He did not tell Ray, however, that he had already called Huie and okayed the contracts. "Now, you know, of course, that I'm depending on you for my fee," Foreman told Huie over the phone. "So tote that bale, boy! Get to work!"[10] Two weeks after he met Ray, and had officially become his counsel of record, Foreman met Huie in Fort Worth.† Foreman was blunt. "I like the idea of owning 60% of one of your books while you own only 40%. So you get Hanes out and let me in, then goddamn it, get to work and write us a good book and make us a good movie and make us some money."[11]

At that meeting, Foreman told Huie he was convinced that Ray murdered King. Whether there was a conspiracy or not did not matter to him—he only had to worry about his client.[12]

Since Foreman had concluded early on that Ray had fired the shot, he showed little enthusiasm for investigating the case to discover a viable defense. Foreman visited the Haneses in Birmingham near the end of November. "We offered him everything we had," recalled Arthur Hanes, Sr., "but he took nothing with him." Arthur junior agreed. "He wasn't interested in the case. He wanted to drink some Scotch, eat some dinner, and talk about his famous cases. He also told us about how he made speeches all over the country."[13]

Foreman saw Ray only a few times in November, sometimes taking notes, and only once in December, when Foreman came down with pneumonia. On December 18, Foreman brought in public defenders Hugh Stanton, Sr., and

---

* Renfro Hays, the chief investigator for the Haneses, later filed suit claiming he was entitled to the car and rifle, but it was dismissed. Hays, one of the most colorful characters in Memphis during the late 1960s, was a private investigator who had a reputation for doing anything for his clients, even concocting evidence. He was single-handedly responsible for much of the early false information about the case that is still in circulation. See Chapter 28 for further discussion.

† In sworn testimony in a lawsuit brought against him by Ray, Foreman said he never met Huie until late January 1969. But that is clearly wrong, as Huie places the meeting on November 27, 1968, and made contemporaneous notes about it.

Hugh Stanton, Jr., to help on the defense. He told Ray it was necessary to save money.* He did not see Ray again until the third week of January.[14] After the guilty plea, Foreman claimed he could not find any of his files or notes on the case. He said that although he had not hired a professional investigator, he had used the volunteer services of eight senior law students from Memphis State University.[†15] Yet Foreman could not remember any of their names and was vague about their duties and the scope of their investigation. Foreman's student investigators apparently never conducted a single interview, and at least one has indicated that the group did no investigation for him.[16] Foreman never obtained such basic items as the FBI's ballistics report, the complete extradition proceedings, or even the affidavit of the state's chief witness, Charles Stephens.[17] He was never able to provide a list of witnesses he interviewed. Although he claimed to have spent seventy-five hours in consultations with Ray, the Shelby County logs reveal that he visited no more than twenty hours. The House Select Committee on Assassinations concluded this was "an inordinately small amount of time with his client for a case of such magnitude."[18] One of the few things he did was show Ray some photos of three tramps arrested at Dealey Plaza on the day of President John F. Kennedy's murder, to find out if any of them looked like Raoul.[19] One, the tallest, was similar, said Ray.

The Select Committee understandably concluded that "Foreman did not conduct a thorough and independent investigation into the death of Dr. Martin Luther King, Jr., on behalf of Ray."[20]

If Foreman was lackadaisical in Ray's defense, he was certainly energetic in protecting his own financial interests. On January 29, 1969, Foreman, Huie, Hanes, and Ray signed a new agreement, in which Hanes returned all his rights to Ray.[21] Then, five days later, Foreman signed a separate agreement with Ray in which Ray assigned all his income under the agreements to Foreman.[‡22] Huie was dismayed when he learned of that agreement "because with

---

* Stanton was also assigned to represent Charles Stephens, the state's chief witness against Ray, when the prosecutor tried to put Stephens in protective custody, fearful he might leave town. Years later, Ray unsuccessfully tried to obtain a new trial by contending that Judge Battle committed reversible error by appointing Stanton to represent two clients, in the same case, with potentially different interests.

† Before the trial, Foreman told a Memphis newspaper that he would be his own investigator and he would not have any assistants, as do many other lawyers.

‡ When asked about his questionable deal with Ray, Foreman claimed he took the assignment of all of Ray's interest in the literary agreement because he was trying to protect Ray in case Mrs. King sued in a civil suit. The House Select Committee on Assassinations examined Foreman's contention, and rejected it. The contracts involved an unconditional transfer of Ray's interest, with no provision for a return of the money in case no civil suit was filed, or if it was filed and Ray prevailed.

it went my last hope of ever being able to exert financial leverage on Ray."[23] When Huie wrote two more checks to Ray, for $5,000 each, Foreman had Ray endorse those checks to him.[24] He told Ray that he needed cash to hire a prominent Nashville attorney, John J. Hooker, Sr., as cocounsel. When Ray asked why he needed another lawyer, Foreman told him that Hooker's son was going to be Tennessee's next governor, and that even if Ray went to prison, he would be pardoned in two to three years.[25] (John J. Hooker, Jr., ran for governor and lost in both 1966 and 1970.)

Another time, according to Ray, Foreman advised his client to consider selling some pictures to *Life* magazine or giving an interview to author George McMillan, for which McMillan would pay at least $5,000. "I just told him there is no point in getting involved with any more writers," recalled Ray. "If we have to associate a writer we will just stay with Huie."[26]

On February 13, Foreman visited Ray and for the first time raised the possibility that Ray should plead guilty. Foreman presented Ray a letter for his signature, in which Ray agreed to let him negotiate a plea with the prosecution. Unknown to Ray, Foreman had unofficially been talking to prosecutors about a plea for several weeks. In the letter he gave Ray, Foreman concluded, "In my opinion there is little more than a ninety-nine percent chance of your receiving a death penalty verdict if your case goes to trial. Furthermore, there is a hundred percent chance of a guilty verdict. . . . If I am able to save your life by negotiation with the attorney general and the court, I will consider it one of the great accomplishments of my career in the court room."[27] Foreman had a small file of papers given him by Huie, covering the basic police reports in the case and some information about Ray's previous crimes.[28] Waving that file and citing adverse pretrial publicity, Foreman told Ray that the jury would be stacked with blacks and business leaders ready to send him to death. He dismissed Ray's contention that the evidence was circumstantial and that at most he would be convicted of "some sort of aiding and abetting."[29] "He was kind of loud on signing this paper," remembered Ray. "I know one time I had to kind of keep him down because they have guards and microphones."[*][30]

---

* Not only did Foreman come to an early and unshakable conclusion that Ray was guilty, but at least part of his conclusion was evidently based on incorrect information. For instance, Foreman later wrote in *Look* (April 1969) that Ray had left behind fingerprints and a palmprint in the bathroom of the rooming house because "he wanted to escape, but he didn't want to lose credit." Foreman later claimed that Ray told him that he left his fingerprints on the rifle because "he wanted the boys back at Jefferson City [Missouri State Penitentiary] to know that he had done it." Ray adamantly denies telling Foreman that, and it is unlikely that he would ever have made such an admission to Foreman, who did little to inspire any real trust in the four months he represented Ray.

Foreman even visited Ray's family in St. Louis to try to persuade them to pressure James into considering a plea. Although they did not agree, Foreman told Ray they had endorsed the idea of a plea. On February 18, after more pressure from Foreman, Ray relented and signed a letter agreement that officially allowed Foreman to negotiate a plea bargain.[31] During the last week of February, Foreman brought Ray a prosecutor's draft of stipulations concerning facts in the case to which they wanted Ray to agree. The stipulations were detailed, and Ray was to admit to being the sole shooter in King's murder. For ten to twelve days, Foreman and Ray fought over them. Ray was particularly incensed by a stipulation that he had worked on behalf of George Wallace's presidential campaign.[32] Foreman's deal was simple: If Ray pleaded guilty, he would receive a ninety-nine-year sentence and avoid the death penalty. The stipulations would become his admissions. Ray knew that if he went to trial and was convicted, he could draw either the death penalty or life in prison. What Foreman may not have told him was that if he were given a life sentence from a trial, he would be eligible for parole in thirteen years, but if he accepted the ninety-nine-year sentence, he would not be eligible for parole until forty-five years had passed. Also, it is not clear if Ray knew that no one had been executed in Tennessee in seven years, and Shelby County, where he was to be tried, was not an easy jurisdiction for prosecutors to win the death penalty.

In the midst of the plea discussions, Ray was distracted by a request from Jerry for money. He needed $500, and Ray asked Foreman to loan his brother the money. Around this time Ray began to feel that if he forced Foreman to trial, Foreman might "have faked the case," or done less than his best to ensure it turned out as he predicted.[33] When Foreman visited on Sunday, March 9, Ray asked him to withdraw from the case. "I thought," said Ray, "that I had to dismiss Foreman and go to trial with the public defender, and I was worried about that. . . . The only other possibility was in some manner to defend myself, but that's a pretty bad thing to defend yourself."[34]

Foreman refused to withdraw. Instead, he presented Ray with a new letter agreement he had drafted. In it, he was willing to cap the income he would earn from Ray's literary share at $165,000, with everything beyond that going to Ray. Moreover, he was willing to give Jerry Ray the $500 and add it to the $165,000. "But I would not make any other advances," Foreman wrote, "just this one five hundred dollars. And this advance, also, is contingent upon the plea of guilty and sentence going through on March 10, 1969, without any unseemly conduct on your part in the court." In a separate letter Foreman had prepared, he said he would hold any income earned from Huie above $165,000 in trust for Ray, and he reiterated that he would do this so long as "the plea is entered and the sentence accepted and no embarrassing circumstances take place in the court room."[35]

Unknown to Ray at the time, Foreman had told Huie a few weeks earlier that he was confident he could persuade Ray to plead guilty. On March 17, Huie and Cowles Communications (the owner of *Look*) entered into an agreement whereby Huie agreed to finish a 6,000-word article on why Ray murdered King and Hanes and Foreman would be paid to contribute 1,000-word articles to the same issue. The agreement said, "James Earl Ray is expected to plead guilty, on or about March 10, 1969."[36]

Ray relented on March 9 and countersigned both Foreman letters. He had already agreed to the prosecution's forty-six stipulations. Ray says he naively thought that if he pleaded guilty he could get rid of Foreman, and "later on I would try to engage other counsel and open the case up on exculpatory evidence."[37]

The following day was Ray's forty-first birthday. The official start of the trial was four weeks away. But three days earlier, Battle had ordered a special hearing, telling reporters to be present for "a development in the Ray case." Dressed in a dark blue suit with a white shirt and a narrow navy tie, his hair slicked back, Ray walked into the packed criminal courtroom shortly after 9:00 A.M. As always, the casual observer would think he seemed more a bank clerk than an assassin, though his face was drained of what little color it normally had.

He almost seemed to shuffle. He cast his head down and stared straight at the floor, not even glancing at his two brothers, sitting uncomfortably in dark suits, nervously wringing their hands in their laps. Once in his chair, Ray looked straight ahead, almost as though he feared that if he looked around the room he might meet somebody's eyes.

Percy Foreman hovered by Ray. The prosecutors, District Attorney General Phil Canale and his assistants, Robert Dwyer and James Beasley, huddled only feet away near their mock-ups of the murder scene and boxes of documents. Thirty-eight reporters crowded the right side of the courtroom. They were quiet, straining to see any reaction from Ray. Celebrity authors with book contracts already signed, such as Clay Blair, George McMillan, and Gerold Frank— who had with him his engraved invitation to the victory party for defendant Clay Shaw in yet a different trial for a different assassination—were in the rear. Although three seats of the forty-two set aside for spectators had been reserved for King family members, none were present.

Judge Battle, solemn-faced, walked into the courtroom at exactly 9:46 A.M. The bailiff rose and called the court to order.

"All right," said Battle, his neatly combed hair offsetting a flushed, plump face, "I believe the only matter we have pending before us is the matter of James Earl Ray."

There had been rumors over the weekend that Ray might use this occasion to fire Foreman. Others said that Ray was about to make a sensational disclosure, or even that Foreman had found a fatal flaw in the prosecution case and would move for a dismissal. But the most persistent gossip—reported in newspapers over the weekend as "unconfirmed reports from Memphis"—was that Ray had agreed to plead guilty.[38] That was the hardest to believe, however, certainly not in a case in which the specter of Raoul hung heavily over the proceedings. Reporters and prosecutors were constantly debating whether there was such a person, and if so, what role he had played in killing King. Oswald may have yelled at reporters that he was a "patsy," but Ray had presented a detailed story to back up his claim—one that was hard to dispute. And the most important part of that story, centering on the two weeks leading up to the assassination, had yet to be published by Huie. James Bevel, one of Dr. King's former aides, had already announced that he thought Ray was innocent, and even tried unsuccessfully to join the defense team (the judge barred him since he was not a lawyer).[39]

Even aside from the Raoul story, journalists had raised substantive questions about the state's case: the chief eyewitness was a drunk, none of Ray's fingerprints were found inside the rooming house, and reports of a professional gunman at a different position continued to circulate. There were local witnesses who claimed to have heard a mob-associated produce dealer tell someone over the phone, an hour before the assassination, "Kill the son-of-a-bitch, shoot him on the balcony." And what of the phony citizen's band radio report that led the police in the wrong direction after the assassination? Could it all be coincidence?

Ray had escaped from a maximum-security prison a year before the assassination—how did he get out and stay free? There were reports he spent extravagantly while on the run—was the money payment for a plot to kill King? Moreover, how did Ray, the country boy from a poor white trash background, a petty criminal, suddenly transform into an accomplished assassin who not only managed to get his prey, but almost got away with it? During his criminal career, Ray was a thief, not a murderer—how could he so coolly stalk his target, pick a perfect sniper's nest, and then dispatch a single shot as effectively as any professional hit man, without guidance from others? How did a man with an eighth-grade education somehow manage unaided to escape the murder scene, flee to Canada, develop false passports, then move to London, Lisbon, and back to London before a break in the investigation finally led to his arrest after two months, just as he was about to board a plane for Brussels?

"May it please the court," Foreman began in his deep, resounding voice, "in this case we have prepared, and the defendant and I have signed, and Mr. Hugh Stanton, Sr. and Jr., will now sign, a petition for waiver of trial and request for acceptance of a plea of guilty." Reporters started scribbling furiously as Foreman handed the petition to Judge Battle. People started talking to one another in the back rows.*

"James Earl Ray, stand," said Battle. Ray rose awkwardly, one shoulder dipped as though he were afraid someone was about to strike him. He loosely clasped his hands behind his back. His feet were planted slightly apart.

"Have you a lawyer to explain all your rights to you, and do you understand them?"

"Yes, sir," Ray replied so softly that only a few people heard him. His voice sounded almost feminine.

Battle then asked Ray detailed questions about the plea, whether he understood it, if it was voluntary, and if he knew that by making it he was losing his right to trial and appeal. After some fifteen minutes, Battle reached the critical question.

"Are you pleading guilty of murder in the first degree in this case because you killed Dr. Martin Luther King under such circumstances that it would make you legally guilty of murder in the first degree under the law as explained to you by your lawyers?"

"Yes, legally, yes," was the barely audible reply. Not a simple *yes*, but rather *legally yes*, as if Ray somehow knew that being part of a conspiracy to murder made him legally guilty of that murder. Reporters noted the distinction and were surprised that Battle did not pursue his slight equivocation.

The chief prosecutor, Phil Canale, then rose before the court and summarized the state's evidence. He concluded, "We have no proof other than that Dr. King was killed by James Earl Ray and James Earl Ray alone." But it somehow rang hollow. The plea meant Ray would not take the stand, would not be cross-examined, and would tell nothing. There was a sense of palpable disappointment, of growing suspicion in the courtroom gallery.

Foreman followed and endorsed the state's case against his client, confirming that he accepted the conclusion of Attorney General Ramsey Clark that there was no conspiracy to kill King. Then Judge Battle was given the detailed stipulations to which Ray had agreed, in writing, to each of the elements of the state's case.

As Foreman returned to his chair, Ray suddenly stood up. Foreman thought he was going to say something to him, but became concerned when he saw

---

* It should have been clear to seasoned courtroom reporters in Tennessee that the hearing was to accept a guilty plea since a jury was in place on the right side of the court. The trial was not due to start for another several weeks, and there had been no jury selection. However, under Tennessee's unusual criminal procedure rules, if a guilty plea is offered in a murder case, the first twelve people that qualify from the jury roll are impaneled to listen to summaries from the prosecution and defense, and then to rubber-stamp the plea and the agreed-upon sentence.

that Ray's gaze was focused instead on Judge Battle. His eyes wide, Foreman froze, because this was not part of the carefully written script. Ray rocked slightly on his feet. Reporters nudged one another that Ray was about to speak. A hush settled over the courtroom.

"Your Honor, I would like to say something too, if I may."

Everyone in the spectators' gallery leaned forward to hear the soft-spoken Ray.

Judge Battle was noncommittal. "All right."

"I don't want to change anything I have said but I don't want to add anything on to it, either." Ray paused for a moment as if catching his breath. "The only thing I have to say is, I don't exactly accept the theories of Mr. Clark."

Battle looked confused. The prosecutors grimaced. Foreman seemed exasperated, and interjected, "Ramsey Clark."

"And Mr. Hoover," added Ray, seemingly gaining a bit of confidence, his words now distinct and clear.

Battle leaned forward. "Mr. who?"

"Mr. J. Edgar Hoover," announced Ray. "The only thing I say, I am not—I agree to all these stipulations. I am not trying to change anything. I don't want to add something on to it."

Rocking in his chair, Battle seemed uncomfortable. "You don't agree with these theories?" he asked somewhat incredulously. The courtroom was now utterly silent, everyone looking at Ray.

"I mean Mr. Canale, Mr. Clark, and Mr. J. Edgar Hoover. I mean on the conspiracy thing." Those were exactly the words no one wanted to hear, especially from Ray. He forged ahead determinedly. "I don't want to add something on to it that I haven't agreed to in the past."

Foreman, who after months of representing Ray had grown accustomed to his roundabout way of talking, again interpreted for the court. "I think that what he is saying is that he doesn't think that Ramsey Clark's right or J. Edgar Hoover is right. . . . You are not required to agree or withdraw or anything else, Jim." Foreman moved near Ray and almost forced him back into his seat. He was not about to let Ray ruin the carefully crafted plea arrangement by suddenly talking about conspiracy.

There was an uncomfortable silence in the courtroom as Judge Battle considered what to do next. The defendant in one of the nation's most searing political murders had just interrupted his guilty plea to inform the court that he did not agree with the statements of the prosecutors, the attorney general, and the FBI director that he had acted alone and that there was no conspiracy in the case. Ray had opened Pandora's box. Should Battle quiz him about collaborators? About Raoul?

Battle suddenly grabbed the sheet from which he had been reading before Ray interrupted him, and waved it. He had decided to give Ray a final chance to finish the plea without any further drama. "There is nothing in these answers to these questions I asked you—in other words, you change none of these."

"No sir, no sir," Ray said.

"I think the main question here I want to ask you is this: Are you pleading guilty to murder in the first degree in this case because you killed Dr. Martin Luther King under such circumstances that would make you legally guilty of murder in the first degree under the law as explained to you by your lawyer?"

Ray nodded his head up and down. "Yes, sir, make me guilty on that."

"Your answers are still the same?"

"Yes, sir."

"All right, sir, that is all."

Foreman and the prosecutors were visibly relieved. Many reporters were disturbed, however, that Battle had not aggressively pursued Ray's interruption about a conspiracy.

On the way out of the courtroom, a reporter asked a smiling Percy Foreman if Ray had ever admitted to any conspiracy behind the King assassination. "I don't give a goddamn if there was a conspiracy or not," Foreman said sharply. "No. I never asked him that."

Coretta Scott King issued a statement within hours of Ray's plea restating her belief that Ray had not killed her husband on his own, and urging the government to "continue until all who are responsible for this crime have been apprehended."*[40]

The day following the plea, the *New York Times* editorial page, expressing a sentiment that was widely held, charged that "the aborted trial of James Earl Ray for the assassination of Dr. Martin Luther King Jr. is a shocking breach of

---

* The prosecutors, before accepting the plea, had asked for the approval of Attorney General Ramsey Clark, Tennessee governor Buford Ellington, and Coretta Scott King and her family. Any of the three could have vetoed the plea, but all accepted it. The prosecutors who worked out the plea agreement, however, were not fully convinced that Ray had acted alone. James Beasley told the author, "By the time of the plea, I knew Ray was the triggerman and did all he had to to kill King. Whether someone had paid him $25,000 to do it, I didn't know. But it didn't make any difference as to whether Ray was the killer for the charge we had." Judge Battle, before his death, also expressed doubts that Ray had acted alone, but said he concurred in the plea agreement because "I was convinced then and am convinced now that the trial would have muddied our understanding of the substantial evidence which established Ray as the killer." Maybe Battle should have been more aggressive in acting on his doubts. In Los Angeles, in the trial of Sirhan Sirhan, the defense and prosecution were close to a plea arrangement similar to that in the Ray case. There, however, Judge Herbert Walker stopped it and forced a trial.

faith with the American people. . . . By no means, legal or pragmatic, should the doors of the courtroom and the jail be slammed shut on the facts, the motives and the doubts of this horrible murder. And yet that is exactly what has just occurred with stunning suddenness in a Memphis courthouse. . . . Nothing but outrage and suspicion can follow the handling of this long-delayed and instantly snuffed-out trial. . . . In the ghetto and in the world outside the ghetto, the question still cries for answer: Was there a conspiracy to kill Dr. King and who was in it?"

Within hours of leaving the courthouse, Ray told one of the guards transferring him back to prison that he was sorry he had pleaded guilty. He was innocent, but Foreman had strong-armed him into accepting the plea.*[41] For the next three days, he worked on drafting a letter to Judge Battle. He sent it on March 13, and in it he stated that Foreman no longer represented him and asked for "a post conviction hearing in the very near future." On March 26, Ray sent off another letter to Battle officially asking for "a reversal of the 99-year sentence" and the appointment of a public defender. Battle received the second letter when he returned from a brief vacation on March 31. At 5:00 P.M., James Beasley, the assistant district attorney general, walked by the door, saw a light on, and knocked. When there was no answer, he pushed the door open and found Battle dead of a heart attack, slumped over Ray's latest letter. A few days later, J. B. Stoner, the racist mouthpiece for the National States Rights Party, got his longtime wish and became Ray's attorney of record.

———————

Since his first letter to Judge Battle within seventy-two hours of his guilty plea, Ray has never stopped proclaiming his innocence and asserting that the elusive Raoul was the key to unlocking what really happened in the assassination. Ray's immediate repudiation of his guilty plea started speculation that the plea was part of an elaborate plot to silence Ray and protect his coconspirators. He has done nothing to quell that speculation. Rather, he has used a succession of attorneys to pursue every conceivable opportunity to win a new trial. Among many actions, he brought a federal habeas corpus proceeding in the mid-1970s that many thought would lead to a trial but ultimately did not; appeared before the House Select Committee on Assassinations in the late 1970s; and

———————

*   Ray also later claimed that his harsh prison conditions had worn him down and were a contributing factor in his decision to plead guilty. However, Dr. McCarthy De-Mere, who was Ray's physician while in jail in Memphis, reported that Ray seemed to thrive in his solitary jail wing. Not only did his health remain excellent, but he gained weight while there and slept well after adjusting to the constant brightness. Ray's only ailments were occasional nosebleeds and headaches, which were treated with aspirin. DeMere likened Ray's prison surroundings to a good motel suite.

even as late as 1997 had new life infused into his effort when the family of Martin Luther King met with Ray, endorsed his innocence, and joined with those calling for a trial.

Also, by 1997, with Ray's health failing from cirrhosis of the liver, the defense team's investigators were certain they had made a major breakthrough by finally tracking down a man they believed was Raoul, supposedly living in upstate New York. This came not long after another apparent break when Loyd Jowers, the owner of Jim's Grill, which had been located on the ground floor of the Memphis rooming house from which the shot was fired, admitted that he was involved in the plot to kill King, but that he would not disclose the details unless he was granted immunity. These developments forced the district attorney general in Memphis to open up its old files and conduct a new inquiry into whether more than one person was behind King's murder.

Thirty years after the assassination, the question of who killed Martin Luther King remains unsettled for many people. Finding the answers seemed impossible when prosecutors accepted a 1969 guilty plea rather than demand a trial. Instead of resolving the uneasiness over the case, the guilty plea actually seemed the ultimate cover-up, as though someone had the power to force Ray, through money or fear, to remain silent.

Much of the information that would have surfaced in a trial—Ray's background, his past crimes, his prison escape, his year as a fugitive leading up to the murder, the actual assassination, his story of Raoul, his escape to Europe— is examined in the coming pages. Ray clearly knows precisely what happened in Memphis in April 1968, but he has persistently failed to reveal the truth. But by investigating Ray's life, those with whom he associated, what motivated him, and how he came to cross paths with Dr. King in Memphis in April 1968, it is possible to discover what most likely happened in the assassination, even though Ray refuses to disclose it.

PART II

The Assassin

12

Little Dixie

James Earl Ray was born on March 10, 1928, in a two-room basement apartment a few doors from the largest whorehouse in one of the poorest and roughest neighborhoods in the blue-collar town of Alton, Illinois.*[1] He was the first child of George and Lucille Ray, who had married two years earlier.[2] His father's side of the family had a nearly one-hundred-year unbroken history of violence and run-ins with the law. Ned Ray, hanged for being part of the notorious Plummer gang, which killed over a hundred men in a series of brutal mid-1800s robberies, was likely James's great-grandfather.† James's paternal grandfather was an alcoholic itinerant bootlegger and sometime bar-

---

* Most who conclude that Ray was a patsy fail to study him in order to discover whether he was capable of such a crime. For instance, Harold Weisberg completely omits Ray's biography in his 530-page book; theorist Mark Lane, who was one of Ray's attorneys in the 1970s, does not even mention Ray in the first half of his book; Ray's latest attorney, William Pepper, also wrote a book, but in over five hundred pages he devoted less than a page and a quarter to Ray's background.

† Poor rural families like the Rays do not normally keep family trees, diaries, letters, or written records, but Ray's father was the keeper of the family's oral history. He told author George McMillan that Ned Ray was "probably" his grandfather, that the history of Ned Ray "sounds right, just like what my old man used to tell me about his father."

tender who barely scraped together a living for his family.[3] Ray's own father did little better.[4] George, nicknamed "Speedy" as a joke because he spoke so slowly that people thought he had an impediment, tried and failed at a series of straight jobs ranging from mechanic to beer-joint boxer to brakeman for a regional railway.[5] However, the easy money from crime also beckoned him, and he considered it a "right" to lie to and deceive others if it was done to support a family.[6] He also viewed crime as an honorable profession. "Now, if there's anything I hate it's petty larceny," he said. "I can't stand the fella that will steal just this and that. Now, when a man holds up a bank, that's a different thing. The fella that holds up a bank is trying to make good, he's trying to make something of himself."[7]

Speedy Ray used a dozen different surnames, usually just a variation of Ray but often with an *n* added—Ryan, Raines, or Raynes—as well as often using a different first name.[8] When arrested in 1921, he gave his name as George Ray, but on his marriage certificate he was James Gerald Ray, and years later, when he was pursued for failure to deliver a certificate of title, he was Jerry Rayns.* It was one way to get a new start in the river towns to which he moved, without any reminders of the failures he left behind. As a young man, he shuffled around the country trying his hand at menial jobs and petty crimes. When he was twenty-one, he was arrested for his first felony—breaking and entering—and given a ten-year sentence in the Iowa State Penitentiary at Fort Madison.[9] He was paroled in June 1923, two years before his marriage.†

Speedy's brother, Earl—for whom James was given his middle name—was the meanest of the Rays, especially when he drank. A carnival boxer, he was first brought into court at ten for stealing and "associating with immoral persons." By eleven he was declared a delinquent and packed off to an institution. With almost a dozen arrests, Earl spent most of his adult life in prison (he was in the state penitentiary at Menard for a rape conviction when James was born), and on the few occasions he was out, he subjected his family to acts of brutality—from regular fistfights with Speedy to throwing acid into the face of one of his wives.[10] "Earl was never any good for anything. You couldn't hurt Earl," recalled Speedy, who once feared that Earl was mad enough to burn

---

*   Jerry Ray, James's younger brother, was given so many different names by his father that he later told the FBI, "I was about twenty years old before I knew my name."

†   James Earl Ray is often not the best source of information about his own family. In his book *Who Killed Martin Luther King, Jr.?*, he writes that his father was sentenced to prison in 1925, four years after it actually happened, and then says he escaped from prison, when in fact he was paroled.

down the Rays' house. "He didn't have no feeling. But I never did care enough about him to kill him."*[11]

James's mother, Lucille Maher—known as Ceal—was a quiet and introverted woman from a hardworking, if somewhat troubled, family. Her father, John, a glass blower in a local factory, was a drunk who abandoned the family while Ceal was a youngster.[12] Mary, her mother, was a devout Irish Roman Catholic who worked tirelessly as a steam presser at local cleaners to care for her two children. It was Mary who rented the basement apartment in which James was born in 1928. Speedy had so little money that the family would have otherwise ended up in a single room in an even worse slum in St. Louis.

A year and a half after James's birth, the Rays drifted to Bowling Green, Missouri, another lean blue-collar town farther up the river.[13] For the next five years of James's life, his father tried hard to make it in the straight world. "I never used no other names all that time, just my own right name," he later boasted.[14] But he only managed to keep the family in grinding poverty. He had a job wrecking cars for nearly a year before he was fired in 1931. Mary Maher helped support Speedy and her daughter by cashing in two small life insurance policies and working at a second job.[15] But Speedy resented his reliance on Maher and frequently fought with her in front of Ceal and James. He also vented his anger at the wealthy, politicians, gangsters, and even blacks, whom he considered different and inferior—"they just lay around and fuck all the time," he complained.[16]

In February 1935, Speedy was arrested in Alton for forgery. When he was free on bond, he decided to move, even though it meant pulling James out of the first grade at St. Mary's Elementary School. Mary Maher spent nearly $1,000 for some sixty acres of infertile land on the edge of Ewing, Missouri, a little country town of 350 people. In August, Speedy, then thirty-five, and Ceal, twenty-six, moved there—"on the lam," as James later said—with their children.[17] For his life in Ewing, Speedy took a new name, Jerry Raynes. There were now four children: James Earl; Marjorie, born in 1930; John Larry, born in 1931; and Gerald William, called Jerry, born a month before the move to Ewing. Five more were to come.

On the property was an abandoned house. Ravaged by harsh winters and blistering summers, it had a rusted tin roof that allowed rain to pour inside, and its sides had split wooden boards through which the wind whipped. There

---

*   Speedy and Earl also had a younger sister, Mabel, who married a Quincy man, Frank Fuller. James Earl Ray later described Frank as making "a living in the rackets, collecting cash from slot machines owned by the local mob."

was no electricity or plumbing.[18] But it was the Rays' new home, and after their failures and close brushes with the law, the promise of a hard life in Ewing did not seem intolerable. "We did not have elaborate lives," was James's understated way of later summarizing their plight.[19] "We didn't live," his brother Jerry recalled frankly. "We survived."*[20]

The new town of Ewing fit with Speedy's disillusioned and angry temperament. James later described the area as "the riverboat country of Tom and Huck and Nigger Jim and the jumpin' frog of Calaveras Country."[21] Actually, Lewis County, in which Ewing sat, was originally settled by Southerners from Kentucky, Tennessee, and Virginia. However, since the area was not good for farming, it attracted only the poorest whites, who were enticed by the almost giveaway land prices. In this barren patch of Missouri, generations of families eked out a marginal existence. Although they supported the South during the Civil War, they were too poor to own slaves, and were instead looked down upon by urban whites as poor white trash. This setting of poverty among transplanted Southerners—in a population of nearly twelve thousand in 1933, only thirty-eight people earned enough money to file income tax returns—was a perfect breeding ground for the Ku Klux Klan, which flourished in Lewis County during the 1920s and early 1930s.[22] Not a single black lived in the town.† "No nigger's ever spent the night in Ewing," was a frequently heard boast to new visitors.[23] And Ewing, nicknamed "Little Dixie" by a local newspaper, was as physically backward as its racial attitudes.[24] When the Rays arrived, there was still no sewage system, doctor, bank, library, or movie house. There were no paved streets. Only two of the town's houses had electricity or flush toilets.[25] The highlight of the year was a small traveling fair that stopped by each summer.

Speedy's timing in moving to Ewing could hardly have been worse. He had decided to try farming on his new land, but arrived on the heels of the Great Depression, at a time when even die-hard locals were abandoning agriculture. His property was quite brushy, with lots of timber, and the soil was thin and poor for planting. The following year, 1936, brought a severe drought. In 1937, the federal government loaned money to local farmers just so they could feed their livestock.[26] In addition to his fitful start in farming, Speedy also bought a battered 1931 Chevrolet truck for $2.50, painted his name on the

---

* James is extremely sensitive to his family's early conditions and its image of having come from a "Tobacco Road" background, and often tries hard to downplay the depth of their poverty.

† Even as of 1970 the town had not had a black resident. "The only time we ever saw a nigger," recalled one old-timer, "was when they was building the highway. But they kept them in a special camp."

door, and declared himself in the "hauling business."[27] That second business actually brought the Rays a bit of hope, for despite the poor times, people needed help in moving livestock. Although most did not have money to pay Speedy, they bartered and he ended up with extra goods, including another two decrepit trucks that sat rusting behind his house. But eventually Speedy was too lazy to make his work pay the family's way. "He ain't worked more than a month his whole life," his son Jerry would later remark.[28] Even when he tried briefly working on a WPA rock crushing and gravel project, he could almost never get up early enough to catch the truck when it came by in the morning.[29]

The family's stifling poverty made Speedy increasingly bitter. He resented the breaks that he felt others received and bemoaned his own unmitigated streak of bad fortune.[30] His failure to provide for his family shattered any remnant of self-esteem. Within a year of settling in Ewing, he no longer made a pretense at working, but instead spent his time in Cason's pool hall, behind the local barbershop. Even there, wearing his trademark denim coveralls and a cap, he often complained and argued with others. Each evening he would go to sleep no later than 9:00 P.M., demanding that the children remain absolutely quiet so as not to disturb him, and then he would not get up until noon.[31] He dropped from 127 to 112 pounds (on a five-seven frame) and started suffering severe headaches.[32] "I told the kids they wasn't no use working," he later said. "I told 'em they'd never have anything if they worked."[33]

All of this took a toll on Ray's mother. Although the Rays' house was within walking distance of the town, Ceal seldom went there, and nobody visited her at the farm. In the eight years the Rays lived in Ewing, Ceal never once set foot in a neighbor's house.[34] On the few occasions when she ventured into town, people noticed that she looked destitute and unkempt, with her children in rags, clinging to her, and an air of utter despair about her.[35] She was ashamed of the circumstances in which the Rays now found themselves.[36] "Ceal hated the farm," admitted Speedy.[37] She tried to run off once, but Speedy chased after her and pleaded with her on the dirt road leading away from their farm. She returned. "Where would Ceal go if she did want to leave Ewing," her youngest son, John, later asked in a letter. "Those days persons did not run to Judges to get there problems solved. Especial for our family. The Law always hound, persecute the Ray's for over a century, and they still haven't let up."*

---

* John made those comments in a 1973 letter written to author George McMillan from the federal penitentiary at Marion, Illinois, where he was serving eighteen years for driving the getaway car in a bank robbery. The writings of all the Ray children are filled with misspellings and grammatical errors. In this book, they are cited verbatim, complete with the original errors.

All of the unpleasantness also had a profound effect on the children, especially the oldest, James. When his parents argued, he often stopped it by flying into his own rage. That anger, and the grudges he held, set him apart from his siblings.*[38] His parents did not try to control his rage but rather viewed it admiringly as a sign of masculinity and courage. They were convinced that James was smarter than either of them and the brightest of all the children (he later tested with an average 108 IQ), and that he was "always different."[39] However, by the age of seven, James had developed no close friends beyond his family. He spent much time with his father, proudly wearing one of his father's tattered jackets, which flapped around his knees, and was often seen riding in the truck to town, where he spent entire days with Speedy at the pool hall.[40] "He was quiet, not like any boy I ever saw before," recounted one of the other men who played pool there. "He made so little rumpus, I thought he must have a complex or something. He just sat there watching."[41] "He was just a man when he was a kid," concluded Speedy.[42]

The start of school in the fall of 1935 held the promise to expand this quiet youngster's world, but it actually had the opposite effect. The school, Ewing Consolidated, one of the few brick buildings in town, consisted of three basement classrooms. All students from the first through third grades were in Room 1, those from the fourth through sixth grades were in Room 2, and the students in the seventh and eighth grades were in Room 3.[43] This meant that a student would have the same teacher for three years. When James entered the school, under the name Jimmy Rayns, he was one of only three students in the first grade and his teacher was Miss Madeline "Tots" McGhee, a strict disciplinarian and spinster from one of Ewing's "prominent" families.[44] She took an almost instant dislike to the painfully shy youngster. She later remembered that when he reported for school his hair was uncombed and he wore torn pants, a dirty shirt, and a man's suit jacket spotted with grease.[45] He was barefoot and sometimes smelled of urine.[46] He had picked up his father's habits with strangers, looking warily at anyone who came near him, and looking away, or casting his eyes to the floor, if someone tried hard to make eye contact. Quiet, he occasionally smiled, but never seemed comfortable.[47] Although many of the nearly fifty children in the school were from poor families, Tots considered James to be at the very bottom. He found no warmth in her to replace the affection missing at home, no help in his studies, no advice that there were possibilities in the straight world with which to rise above poverty.

The Ewing school system not only failed to help James Earl Ray, but it set him back. The other students ridiculed the way he dressed, and at recess he was often

---

* "We all took after Ceal by not holding a grudge," wrote John. "Jimmy and the old man was different. They would hold a grudge the rest of there lives."

in fights.[48] "He fought as if he would never stop," recalled one, "flailing away at whoever was around him, tears streaming down his cheeks."[49] "He was constantly being picked on by the older fellows in the school," recalled another student, Robert Brown. "Jimmy was sort of weak and they picked on him to see him get mad. He was also mistreated by his teachers. We would all do mean things and get by with them. Jimmy, though, always seemed to get caught."[50]

The Ewing school also reinforced some of the negative lessons he was receiving from Speedy about race. Racial segregation was taught and enforced. When the basketball team from nearby Quincy came to play, it was warned to leave its black players at home—and it did.*[51]

James, not surprisingly, hated school and flunked the first grade.[52] Absenteeism was high among many of the students, especially during the harsh winters. James, who walked a mile and a quarter through beanfields, the town's backstreets, and the local cemetery to reach school, stayed at home when the rough winters arrived. He sometimes rode with his father on deliveries or stayed with him at the pool hall, and his education suffered. "The old man also wanted to keep us out of school to do work around the house," recalled Jerry.[53] James missed 48 of the 190 school days his first year, and though he missed 47 days the following year, he managed to pass. In third grade, his fourth and last year with Tots, he was again absent a third of the time. Her disgust for him was quite open by then. In a section of his report card where the teacher jotted remarks about the student, Tots's feelings about James were evident. Under "Attitude toward regulations," she wrote, "Violates all of them"; "Was the child honest?" prompted her to write, "Needs watching"; "Was he courteous?" brought, "Seldom, if ever polite"; and for "Appearance," she wrote, "Repulsive."[54] The tension at the school was unsettling for James. By the time he finished the third grade, he was suffering from recurring nightmares, including one in which he was losing his eyesight. He had other problems, including bed-wetting, stuttering, and at times such fitful sleep, with jerking and twitching, that a local doctor decided he had had an epileptic seizure.†[55]

---

* One student a few years ahead of James, Merle Wenneker, later commented about the school's and town's racial biases, "I suppose we had them but did not know it. As no Negros [sic] attended the school we were not acquainted with the problem. We referred to black people as nigger but not in a derrogatory [sic] way. . . . As a matter of fact I believe if we had any prejudices it was maybe toward the Jewish people—because we had a Jewish family."

† The nightmares were evidently so powerful that he remembered them for thirty years, because that is when he told a prison psychiatrist about them. They were probably the cause of Ray's sleep disturbances. The diagnosis of epilepsy was almost certainly wrong, since Ray never showed any further symptoms.

James's difficulty at school, however, paled in comparison to a personal tragedy the family suffered. In the spring of 1937, Speedy arrived home late one afternoon and placed a bag of groceries on the rear porch. Marjorie, then six, found a box of matches in the bag. A moment later the family heard piercing screams and saw Marjorie run into the house, her dress in flames, the fire enveloping her head. She was dead by the next morning. The child's death momentarily fostered a streak of kindness toward the Rays. School was let out and the students marched the short distance to the cemetery for her burial.[56] The town's one Catholic priest performed the service, although the Rays, "nominal Catholics" as James described them, had never been to mass.*[57]

Marjorie's death pushed Ceal into a depression. The relatively quick birth of two more daughters—Melba in 1938 and Carol in 1941—did not alleviate her melancholy; the added burden actually greatly accelerated her drinking, which she started in earnest shortly after Marjorie's death.[58]

The death of his sister pushed James even closer to his brothers, a bond evident even to outsiders.[59] James's sister Carol was convinced that except for his two brothers, he did not care about the rest of the family.[60] Speedy later recalled that "it seemed like he always wanted to look out for them [Jerry and John], like he was their father or something like that. He always told Jerry . . . he'd take care of him."[61] But slowly, over the next few years, he also started forming his first acquaintances outside the family. In 1939, when James was eleven, he was often seen with three other boys, Robey and Charlie Peacock, poor kids who lived on an adjacent farm, and Gerald Hobbs, who lived with the Peacocks after his mother died. They entertained themselves with everything from playing marbles to fishing, billiards, and shooting squirrels and rabbits with a BB gun.[62]

There are reports that these youngsters were tough and mean.[63] Some described them as bullies.[64] *Life* magazine classified James as "an unmanageable bully" and "uneducated school bully."[†] However, while he undoubtedly did have his share of fights, and once stole the class lunch money, it seems as

---

* Ray has never exhibited much sentiment or emotion. For instance, in his own books, he spends many pages on some of his favorite topics, such as how thoroughly he enjoyed the challenge of trying to escape from prison. As for things more personal, such as his sister's death, he covers it in a single perfunctory sentence (and gets her age wrong as well): "Marjorie was killed at age eight when her clothing caught fire as she was playing with matches."

† Jerry Ray was evidently eager to cash in on his brother's notoriety immediately after the assassination. He seemed more concerned about his fee than what the coverage of his brother would be, something other family members resented. For instance, *Life* drew one of the harshest portraits ever published of James, but Jerry was willing to cooperate fully so long as they paid him $150, which the magazine did.

though he was not one of the town's meanest kids.*[65] Speedy admitted that
James "had a little mischief in him, that's all," but he also showed kindness to
some—for example, when a friend came down with polio, it was James who
carried his books.[66] "If Jimmy was by himself, he was OK," recalled one student. "He didn't have the push."[67]

James may have struck up the new acquaintances in the hope that other
students would stop picking on him. If so, it largely worked, as others began
leaving young Ray alone. But it was still difficult for him to form any close
friendships. "Jimmy wasn't the kind to be telling his troubles to anybody, especially outside the family," recalled his brother Jerry. "Anyway, he was much
closer to us at home than he was to those boys."[68] John commented years later
that no one in the family had "many friends. But we don't want none, having
friends is the quickest way winding up on the end of a rope."[69]

If James was close to any of the three, it was Charlie Peacock. The two spent
afternoons playing together, usually around the Peacock house. Charlie was a
Boy Scout and James became interested in joining. He did show up at a couple
of Scout meetings but could not afford the fifty cents for the manual. "He
wasn't the kind of boy to be forward," remembered Jerry Ball, the local scout-
master. "He was kind of withdrawn. He stayed in the back row."[70] The budding
friendship with Charlie Peacock faltered.

In 1940, when James was twelve, the Rays began slowly cannibalizing their
decrepit house, pulling it apart plank by plank in order to use it as firewood. It
gradually disintegrated until they needed a new home.[71] Speedy's solution was
to truck in a one-room shack. Ceal hung a sheet from the ceiling to partition it,
and the two adults and five children lived there without any privacy. John and
Jerry slept in the same bed, while James slept on the floor.[72]

Yet those difficult years in Ewing evidently strengthened the special bond
among the Rays. They had shared the same mean existence and were proud
of surviving it without owing anything to outsiders. They trusted and relied
only on one another. Even much later, after jail had kept them apart for years,
there was a unique attachment. "We are closer than we seem," said Jerry. "It's
just the way you're raised. If you've been brought up kind of rough, you appreciate it."[73]

---

* In an interesting prelude to his way of dealing with many of his future problems
with the law, young James adamantly denied being responsible for the theft. This despite
the fact that a teacher saw him leave an empty classroom, and thinking something
amiss by the look on his face, checked to find the lunch money gone. She then pursued
James, who took off running, leading her on a chase to the pool hall, where he got away.
But his mother, Ceal, discovered the canister and most of the money—$1.50—buried
under their farmhouse. Ashamed, she returned it and made James admit his responsibility.

But the years in Ewing had also left scars, and it showed in the children's sometimes erratic behavior. One night Jerry, the family joker, became so infuriated at his father's incessant teasing that he burned the privy to the ground.[74] John, quieter than Jerry, suffered from a speech impediment that made it sound as if he swallowed his words. And one day in the school lunchroom, Jimmy stuck a knife into John's ear over a fight for a piece of meat.[75] Speedy and Ceal were either oblivious or indifferent to these signs of trouble. There was no guidance in the Ray household, no family member to whom any of the children could look for inspiration, no encouragement to do well at school or to make friends, and no role model who showed it was possible to work honestly and diligently to pull oneself out of poverty.

In the first week of school in 1942, James played in a game of scrub football. He was evidently so eager to excel that he broke his leg while trying to bust the ball through a line of much larger boys. Virgil Graves, the eighth-grade teacher, took him to the hospital in nearby Quincy and noticed that no matter how much pain the boy had, he lay still without saying a word.[76] But after the cast was set and James started healing, a strange thing happened—the boy known for mostly keeping to himself began visiting Graves. A small and energetic man, who was also a part-time minister, Graves thought James was a "somewhat disturbed child" who was going through some undefined personal crisis.[77] He was puzzled by the contrast between his "rebellion against authority" and the "sensitive" side he discovered.[78] "I can't remember a single incident," Graves later recalled, "in where [sic] Jimmy showed a malicious or wanton heart."[79]

Everyone knew that James Earl Ray was one of a handful of children at the school who could not afford even the five cents that hot lunches cost. Every week, he apologetically approached Graves, explaining he did not have any money and asking if he could still eat at the cafeteria (even those without money were always let in). Self-conscious about his tattered appearance, he once asked, "Are you ashamed of me?"[80] And Graves found that the youngster he taught in eighth grade showed great interest in history and current affairs. Under Graves's influence, when other students left at recess James often remained indoors listening to news over the school's only radio. It was apparently here that he developed an interest in politics, and he showed it by defiantly arguing with the rest of his family. "Jimmy was about the only Republican in Ewing," his brother John recalled. "The Old Man and Ceal was strong for FDR, just like everybody else was in Ewing. Jimmy used to argue them up and down. He was very strong for Wilkie. But mostly he was against Roosevelt. Jimmy said Roosevelt wasn't doing anything but throwing off propaganda on Hitler. He kept saying all that stuff Roosevelt was saying about

Hitler wasn't true at all."[81] "Jimmy was always interested in politics," said Jerry.[82]

Whatever interest James had in politics, it was not in evidence on his trips to Quincy, where Speedy's parents lived and where Uncle Earl stayed whenever he was out of jail.[83] He had hitchhiked the twenty miles on weekends and during the summer for several years, but in 1943, he began to visit more often.[84] A town of 45,000, split largely into Irish and German immigrants, Quincy had been Illinois's second-largest city in the mid-1800s, a bustling river port. By the time Ray visited, however, it had long since lost its river trade to competing railways and was economically and socially stagnant, marked by a suicide rate twice the national average.[85] It was a politically conservative town with a small, segregated black community, a place where blacks could not go to a downtown movie until 1964.[86] James's grandparents lived in the northern section of the city among the so-called river people, Quincy's lowest social class. James said that the "biggest industries [there] were whoring and gambling."[87] Sometimes he accompanied his uncle Frank Fuller on his rounds of collecting cash from mob-run gambling dens.[88] But most of the time, James ran with Uncle Earl, who took him on nightly barroom excursions that mixed heavy drinking with mean-spirited brawling. By early morning, they often wound up at a whorehouse run by a madam called Big Marie.[89] It was there that Earl bought James his first girl.[90] James used to run errands for Big Marie while Earl stayed with one of the girls. Once James hid near one of the open windows on the first floor and tried to steal wallets from johns who were busy with the prostitutes. His first attempt ended with the john chasing but failing to catch him. Ray dropped the wallet along the way. Big Marie suspected he was the thief and banned him.

According to Speedy, this was the period when James was "always hustling, trying to make money."[91] His first "arrest" was at fourteen when he was with his brother John, who was eleven. "We was going down the street," John later wrote in a letter to author George McMillan, "and we pick up a stack of newspapers that a truck had toss off. The Alton cops arrest us, him on one corner me on the other Selling these paper. I was scared of the police, and Jimmy was getting tough with them, I'm trying to shut him up. They took us over and Lock up in Jail. I got scared and Started hollering for Mom. Mom Jump on the police For having us Lock in a cell." The boys were released with a warning.[92]

This was also when James met Walter Rife, a contemporary who lived in the small Illinois town of Kellerville but often visited his brother in Quincy.[93] Rife came from a large, poverty-stricken family, and the two quickly formed a young thieves' friendship.[94] According to Rife, the two never planned any thefts, but "we would just be walking around the streets and one of us would say, 'Let's go in there.' "[95] Although Rife said it was only "boy stuff," he admitted that Ray broke into houses and stole goods that Uncle Earl helped him fence.[96] He also frequently robbed drunks and "would obtain money any way that a thief could."[97] Sometimes fifteen-year-old Ray used his extra cash at local whorehouses. "He'd just take any prostitute, didn't care whether he ever saw that same girl again," recalled Rife. "When he talked about women it was in the most contemptuous way. 'All those fucking whores,' he would say."[98] Rife never saw him with a girlfriend. "We'd meet girls," recalled Rife. "He just couldn't talk to them. He was shy. I'd get him a date and we'd go on an excursion boat and his girl would be gone off with another guy before the boat got halfway on the trip."[99]

To James, the flophouses and all-night bars packed with prostitutes and pimps, illicit gambling, bar fighting, and low-level hoodlums, seemed normal. "The vices in Quincy were considered commercial rather than abnormal," he would write years later.[100]

In late 1943, however, James's wild run suddenly ended. "I lost my guide to the Quincy underworld when Earl was jailed for assault," he later lamented.[101] Earl's imprisonment greatly upset James. "Jimmy worshipped Earl," recalled Walter Rife.[102]

Shortly before Earl was imprisoned, he had visited Ewing. At a carnival, a strongman welcomed all comers to several rounds of boxing. Earl, quite drunk, was still standing at the end of three rounds. Then the barker challenged Speedy to enter the ring, and he did take his shirt off as if he were going to fight. His three sons—James, John, and Jerry—were there. As John later recalled, Speedy had often told the boys that he "could hit harder than Gene Tunney . . . drive his fist through a concrete wall. . . . He had so much power in his arm he scared he break his wrist if he hit at his maximum."[103] The boys were crushed when Speedy finally refused to enter the ring. While Earl had the courage James admired, his father's backing out of the carnival fight was a last straw in a long series of events that led James to lose respect for him both as a father and as a man. From that point, for the rest of his life, when asked if he had a father—whether by employees, the Army, the police, or prison authorities—James said he was dead.*

In May 1944, sixteen-year-old James Earl Ray, filled with his immature but absolutist view of world politics, quit the eighth grade and returned to his birthplace, Alton. There he moved in with his maternal grandmother, Mary

---

* James's brothers did the same. For instance, when the FBI interviewed Jerry Ray after the King assassination, in his first interview he said his father had died in 1951. The next day, the FBI located his father, but Jerry still denied that his father was alive, swearing instead that the man found by the FBI was only his stepfather.

Maher. Shortly after James moved, his father decided to leave Ewing for nearby Galesburg. The Rays, who had a seventh child born a few months earlier—Franklin Dennis Ray—moved out quietly, leaving only one unpaid bill: a twelve-dollar balance on Marjorie's funeral. Her grave was abandoned as an unmarked mound, overgrown with weeds, in a corner of the Queen of Peace cemetery.

13

"Hitler Politics"

James Earl Ray's move to Alton temporarily took him away from his father's bitterness and anger, his mother's increasing drunkenness, and the family's stifling poverty. Although he preferred Quincy, his uncle Earl's imprisonment meant he had lost his mentor there. Alton at least offered the comfort of his grandmother, who was always willing to help the family. Now that her first grandchild was setting forth on his own, she readily offered a room in her Broadway rooming house, and promised to help him find work.

Ray, who had decided to try his hand at a straight job, believed his parents when they told him he was the smartest in the family and that he could amount to something. Now was his chance to prove that to himself and to them.

Mom Maher helped Ray almost immediately land a job at the International Shoe Company tannery in nearby East Hartford. He worked in the dye department, earning seventy-seven cents an hour, and commuted the ten miles to work by streetcar. War production meant that many factories were at full capacity, and Ray accumulated plenty of overtime. Diligent about saving his money, he talked about opening his own gas station. Mom Maher was impressed with his serious approach to work as well as his personal discipline. He did not drink, smoke, or chase women. "Never went out . . . never ran around," Maher later said. "As far as girls he was backwards. He was bashful with girls.

No pals of men, either. Just stayed home. He's quiet and easy. Always comes in with a smile on his face."[1]

For a while Ray spent time with Maher's son, his uncle Willie. They went to football games, played pool, and joined in pick-up baseball games at a local park.* But soon Ray left Willie behind when he found a new friend at work, Henry Stumm, an older, ethnic German. The two became, according to factory shop steward Eric Duncan, "bosom buddies . . . together all the time."[2] Stumm, who was single (and some coworkers thought gay), was a German nationalist who publicly professed unpopular wartime admiration for Hitler and the Nazi party.[†3] His views were a combustible mixture to Ray's already reactionary political beliefs. According to George "Boob" Roberts, the owner of a local restaurant where the two men sat huddled for hours, they used to talk "Hitler politics."[4] Shop steward Duncan said Ray admired Stumm, who "went around the shop calling Germany the Fatherland."[5] Mom Maher recalled that Ray told her Stumm carried a picture of Hitler, whom he claimed he knew personally.[6] Willie Maher later confirmed to the FBI that James had a relationship with an "individual who had pro-Nazi leaning and Ray became anti-Negro and anti-Jewish as [a] result."[‡7]

"What appealed to Jimmy in the first place about Hitler," recalled Jerry Ray, "was that he would make the U.S. an all-white country, no Jews or Negroes. He would be a strong leader who would just do what was right and that was it. Not try to please everybody like Roosevelt [did]. If Hitler could win it would be a dif-

---

* Speedy later put much of the blame for James's problems on Willie Maher, claiming he had "a goddamn old filthy mind. . . . That Bill done him [James] more harm than anybody on earth." Whatever went on with Willie and young Ray, years later James finally beat him up one night, saying, "I've been wanting to whip your ass for twenty years."

† After the King assassination, Stumm initially denied even knowing Ray and emphatically claimed he was pro-American and had never been a Nazi sympathizer. However, Stumm's pro-Hitler leanings were well known during the war, both at the factory and in the town where he lived. Willie Maher said that Stumm thought "Hitler was all right" and that his sentiments were so blatant that he and Ray had joked about it. Meanwhile, Ray conveniently omits Stumm in both his books. In the 20,000 Words he wrote about his life for author William Bradford Huie, Ray recalled only three of his coworkers, again leaving out Stumm.

‡ Maher made that admission about Stumm to the FBI about two weeks after the assassination. Over ten years later, he tried to downplay the Stumm-Ray relationship when he was interviewed by the House Select Committee on Assassinations. He also told the Select Committee investigators that he had never heard Ray utter an antiblack remark. However, there is no reason to doubt that his contemporaneous statements to the Bureau in the immediate aftermath of King's murder are correct, and that his backpedaling in 1978 was a belated attempt to help his nephew.

ferent world. Jimmy didn't think Hitler would kill Jews and blacks, just put
them in their own country someplace. Jimmy thought Hitler was going to suc-
ceed and still thinks he would have succeeded if the Japs hadn't attacked Pearl
Harbor."[8] One of James's sisters concluded, "There no doubt about it. Jimmy
liked Germany better than he did the United States."[9] James's mother, Ceal, was
petrified that his beliefs might get him killed.[10]

Ray, pleased at having found a political ally in a coworker, was also satisfied
with his new job. When he visited home he told his brother John to "stay out of
trouble—it's easier working—you can make more than you can steal."[11] By
December 1945, he had stockpiled $1,180 in his new account at the Alton
Bank & Trust Company, more money than his father had saved in a lifetime.
But Ray's experiment with straight life ended abruptly that same month when
he was fired due to the suspension of the factory's military shoe production.
Even years later, Ray mused that if he had not been let go, "possibly, I would still
be working for International Shoe."[12]

Jobless only weeks before the Christmas holidays, he was crushed. For several weeks he tried in vain to find work, but it was a bad time to be unemployed,
as most manufacturing plants were trimming their staffs and older workers
with seniority had the first claim on jobs. Then, on February 19, 1946, two
months after he was fired, Ray impulsively visited an Army recruiting office in
East St. Louis and enlisted.* He was seventeen years old. When asked for his
preference of a duty station, he requested Germany.[13] When he visited home
and told Ceal he was entering the Army, she sobbed.[14] "She took it bad when
Jimmy went into the army," recalled Speedy.[15]

Ray was sent to Camp Crowder, Missouri, for basic infantry training. There
he qualified with a rifle on the practice range as a marksman.† On leave at

---

*   Ray, in his two published books that are part autobiography and partly his defense in
the assassination, makes numerous factual errors about his own life. Most of them are
insignificant—such as the date of his Army enlistment, which he has as a month
later—but cumulatively the errors indicate a sloppiness about details and an imprecise
recall that must be considered when Ray later recounts, with great specificity, his alleged meetings in the year leading up to the assassination with the person he calls
Raoul.

†   Marksman is the lowest of three military rankings, below sharpshooter and expert.
Ray has tried to downplay his marksmanship medal. In 1993, he "testified" in a televised mock trial of his case, "You have to qualify as a marksman or they will keep you
out on the rifle range for six months until you do," he contended. When asked on cross-
examination how long he had had to stay on the range before he qualified, Ray admitted, "I qualified as a marksman when I first went out there." While Ray's proficiency
with a rifle does not necessarily indicate whether he could make an assassin's shot, even
an easy one, over twenty years later, it is a factor to be weighed. However, Mark Lane,

home, his enthusiasm for the Army was high, and he boasted that he would quickly become a captain.[16] By July 1946, five months after enlisting, he was shipped to occupied Germany. "I think he went over there," recalled Jerry Ray, "with the idea in his head that he would work to support the Nazi party, even though the war was over."[17] Ray's uncle Willie Maher agreed that James's "sole motive for enlisting in the U.S. Army was to go to Germany and perhaps study Hitler's racist techniques."[18]

Ray was initially assigned to drive refrigerated trucks in the Quartermaster Corps in Nuremberg. He had difficulty, however, in maneuvering the large trucks—"I couldn't drive," he later wrote—and became the butt of jokes.[19] In December 1946, Ray was transferred as a driver to the 382nd Military Police Battalion in Bremerhaven, northern Germany.[20] That assignment was fortuitous for him since Bremerhaven—a city of 100,000—was a regional center for a booming black market. More than two-thirds of the city had been destroyed by Allied bombing raids.[21] There were few streetlights and no public transportation, and the sewage system was badly damaged.[22] Americans had to travel in pairs to avoid a group of ex–German soldiers dubbed "werewolves," who robbed and beat, sometimes killing, GIs.[23] Ray, however, was still sympathetic to the Germans and later wrote that while "heavily populated residential areas were reduced to rubble, many if not most of the German military compounds I saw were untouched." He charged that the Allies had spared the military targets in order to use them after the war—"I wasn't surprised to learn this. Life had already taught me that governments need human blood to live."[24]

Bremerhaven had all the vice and seediness of Quincy, but now Ray was part of the unit that was supposed to prevent crime. The temptation to profit from the black-market trade, however, was just too great. The market's currency was cigarettes.[25] Although strictly prohibited by the Army, soldiers actively traded cigarettes for jewelry, cameras, radios, and even art.[26] For Ray, who had learned from Uncle Earl how to fence goods, it was simple, and soon he asked his family to steadily supply him with cigarettes.[27] In return, he sent money home. "We never lived so well as we did when Jimmy was in the army," said Jerry Ray. "He sent money home nearly every month."[28]

Another of Bremerhaven's postwar industries was prostitution.[29] Ray frequented the local dives, and his Army record reflects the consequences: Among the twelve illnesses for which he was treated while stationed in Germany, he had acute gonorrhea twice, syphilis once, and pubic lice another time.[30] But

---

Harold Weisberg, Joachim Joesten, and William Pepper, in their eagerness to diminish Ray's proficiency with a rifle and therefore his likelihood of being a successful assassin, omit from their books any discussion of his military rifle training.

while he took advantage of the local prostitutes, he also despised them. They sold themselves even to black soldiers.[31] These were not the proud Germans of whom Stumm had boasted. Nor did Ray find redeemable qualities in the other Germans he encountered. While he arrived expecting to find a noble people and the remnants of a heroic Reich, instead he watched scornfully as Germans pleaded to work as maids, drivers, and cooks for American officers, ran in gangs that robbed GIs, or spent their days hustling for pennies in the black market. Another soldier, who served in the city at the same time as Ray, later wrote, "The wreckage was human as well. I couldn't and still can't get over the fact of people going through garbage, or throwing a cigarette butt away and young kids running for it, of sleeping with a woman for a pack of cigarettes or kids waiting on railroad tracks for GI's to come through and hope they'd throw out some of their K-rations."[32]

Ray was also distressed by the war crimes trials of top Nazi leaders. "He got discouraged after he saw the Nuremberg trials," recalled Jerry. "That was the turning point. He saw what happened to the Nazis and gave up hope."[33]

His disillusionment caused problems.* Throughout late 1947 and early 1948, Ray had begun drinking. According to his brother John, this was also when he started experimenting with drugs, most likely amphetamines—he had "not seemed right since," John later said.[34] By April 1948 he was transferred from the more prestigious Military Police to the regular infantry, Company B in Frankfurt, which he disliked—"Everyone kicks you around there," he later said.[35] Ray was unhappy and "asked to get out."[36] The Army denied his request. In October 1948, he was charged with being drunk in quarters.[37] Three days later he escaped and was briefly AWOL before he was captured and taken back to the stockade.[†38] In November, despite his not-guilty plea, a court-martial tribunal demoted him from private first class to buck private, sentenced him to three months hard labor, and ordered that his $45-a-month pay be forfeited for four months.[39] To Ray, it was a hard comedown and left him bitter. Ironically, he served his time at the Military Post Stockade at Nuremberg,

---

* Jerry Ray told author George McMillan that this was also the period when James and a friend attacked a group of black GIs in an alley and worked them over. Soon afterward, according to Jerry, Ray was involved in a riotous barracks-room brawl that started when he aired some of his political views. Both of those stories, reprinted by McMillan, are false and were invented by Jerry Ray.

† Ray always has a more exculpatory, albeit incorrect, version of almost every incident in which he has gotten into trouble. Regarding his military problems, he claims he was originally arrested only for having missed one of his guard shifts since he was "ill." Then, while confined to quarters, says that he merely "hitch-hiked into Nuremberg. While there, a sweep by the MPs caught me and several other soldiers who were where they weren't supposed to be."

across the street from the Palace of Justice, where some of Nazi Germany's top leaders had been tried and executed for war crimes.*

In December, Ray's sentence was commuted and he was shipped back to the States.[40] According to his brother John, the journey home further infuriated him. "What really burn Jimmy and the rest of soldiers coming back from Germany was the orders that all married couple ride first class and singles ride second," John recalled. "They almost had a riot on ship when white soldiers who did the fighting had to ride second. The Black soldiers who were the kitchen workers had all married German girls and rode first class. The Blacks would parade around on the deck with a white gal on his arm, getting the best service."[41]

The Army had given up on Ray. He was given a general discharge (neither honorable nor dishonorable) two days before Christmas "for ineptness and lack of adaptability for military service."[42] The action was only days before Ray's regular enlistment duty would have expired. That enraged him. "This was a slap in the face," he later wrote. "If the Army had wanted, it could have let me stay a soldier another 48 hours and muster out with a standard honorable discharge."[43] He never forgot that slight, never told his family why he was dismissed, and always told prospective employers that he was honorably discharged.[44]

When Ray returned to the States, he discovered that his family, now resettled in the heart of Quincy, had accelerated their downward spiral of poverty and misery. An eighth child, Suzan Ray, had been born in 1947.[†] Ceal was now fat and bloated from the cheap wine she drank. When a juvenile probation court officer visited the house and opened a closet, "nothing fell out but wine

---

* Ray continued to exhibit his anti–U.S. government leanings, even years later. As late as 1987, when he wrote his first book, *Tennessee Waltz*, he not only implied that the Allies had merely invented the category of war crimes in order to prosecute German military and civil leaders, but he also bitterly complained about a "cruel deportation project" in which Soviet defectors and deserters who had come west were returned to the Soviets. "How many Americans know their government was instrumental in snuffing out so many friendly lives? Not many, because government agencies use official mechanisms to suppress and conceal facts which, if widely known, might jeopardize their policies."

† Records show that Suzan was placed into the Catholic Children's Home in Alton when she was six, and stayed there for seven years. Then she remained a ward of the court until 1965. When she was officially discharged from supervision, she moved to Chicago and became a go-go dancer at the Bourbon Street Club, a job she quit when she married shortly before the assassination. Ashamed of her family and background, however, when questioned by the FBI after King's murder, she claimed the Rays had abandoned her when she was one, and that after eight years in a children's home, she was taken by foster parents. She also claimed never to have met James and said she would not recognize him if she saw him. Ray, in his two books, does not mention her.

bottles—dozens of wine bottles."[45] Twice arrested for public drunkenness, Ceal was increasingly unable to care for the children.[46] The youngest ones were largely neglected and the older ones were mostly uncontrollable. Melba, then ten, showed severe emotional problems. She had tested with a subnormal IQ, and was often seen riding her bike near the courthouse, screaming obscenities at passersby.[47] Speedy had also started drinking heavily. Although he handled his liquor better than his wife did, it meant that Ceal now had a partner for her all-day binges.[48]

"Very often they would both be drunk . . . four or five nights a week," recalled Jerry Ray, then thirteen. "They would have awful fights, hit each other. That's why we older children stayed out all the time. I wouldn't come home until one o'clock, [then I would] go straight to sleep, sneak in without their hearing me, the stairs I used were on the outside of the house. And John would be gone two or three days at a time, robbing. The younger kids had to stay home and suffer."[49] By this time, neighbors had started complaining about the fights and squalor at the Ray apartment. Probation officers assigned to Quincy's court system began visiting the family. "When we went down there the children were throwing garbage out the windows. . . . They were filthy and covered with lice," recalled one officer.[50] Ceal was warned that if conditions did not improve, the courts might take away her children.

When James Earl Ray discovered his family's disarray, he did not stay very long. "He was ashamed of the way we lived," said Jerry. "He had got away from the stuff of sleeping on the floor."[51] The only good side effect of James's brief visit was that Ceal and Speedy stopped fighting while he was there. "They didn't dare," recalled Jerry. "They were afraid to. He was too violent."[52]

When he left his parents, Ray tried to find Uncle Earl, but discovered that he was back in prison in Menard. This time he had hurled a bottle of carbolic acid at his wife, severely burning her face, mouth, and arms.[53]

Instead, James returned to the relative calm of his grandmother's boardinghouse in Alton. With some $1,400 in the bank, and extra cash from his black-market dealings, he had high hopes.[54] He told his aunt Mabel that the GI bill would allow him to finish high school and then go to college.[55] Financing the purchase of a two-year-old Mercury, he talked about opening a furniture store, a gas station, a nightclub, or even a high-class whorehouse.[56] None of these ideas ever got past the planning stage—a bank rejected his one serious effort to borrow money for a bar.[57] Meanwhile, he spent freely, giving money to his parents in Quincy and buying gifts for his siblings. But as his savings dwindled, he briefly contemplated returning to Germany, where he thought there were greater opportunities.[58] However, whatever Ray was doing at this time, he had evidently not returned to the thefts to which he had become accustomed prior to enlisting in the Army. His only brush with the law was an arrest by Alton police for reckless driving, for which he was fined $45.

Not everyone in the family thought James was the same since leaving the Army. The most extreme view was expressed by his uncle Willie Maher, who now recognized problems in his introverted nephew, a sullenness not evident beforehand. "I knew the boy was badly in need of psychiatric attention upon his release from military service. . . . I should have helped more than I didn't."[59]

By June, six months after his Army discharge, his money had dried up, except for an education allowance from the Veterans Administration.*[60] He moved to Chicago, less than two hundred miles away, in the hope it might be easier to find a job. Ray later wrote only that he took some high school classes there until the "cold wind started coming in off Lake Michigan in September [and] I decided I wanted to live in a more hospitable climate."[61] Actually, Ray landed work within weeks of his arrival, as a rubber mold operator for the Dryden Rubber Company.[†] Still painfully shy with girls and without any friends in the new city, he spent much of his time in pool hall dives, going to movies, or in his cheap rooming house reading detective novels. When he was dismissed in early September, he was penniless. His Mercury was repossessed. At twenty-one, he was nowhere near the expectations he had set for himself when he left the family three years earlier. Instead, he gave up on Chicago and headed west by riding railroad boxcars.[62]

In three weeks, he had only reached Colorado. "I was hanging around waiting for a California-bound train when a migrant labor recruiter offered me a job," recalled Ray.[63] Needing money, he accepted. While most of the Mexican laborers were trucked daily to the fields, he and a few others stayed behind at

---

* FBI files reveal that when Ray applied in April for his veteran's benefits at the local Quincy office he listed his occupation as "Student, American Television School, St. Louis, MO." Actually, there was only an enrollment office in St. Louis, but the school was in Chicago. It does not appear that Ray attended any classes in Chicago after he moved there that summer.

† Part of the difficulty in recounting full details of Ray's experiences at his various jobs is the absence of records from the companies for which he worked. For instance, at Dryden, when FBI agents approached company officials after King's assassination, they discovered that the company had no personnel records for the period Ray was employed there, since its policy was to destroy them after seven years. Many of the employees who had been there almost twenty years before had left. The few remaining had no recall of a person who worked there only a few months, two decades earlier. Each of the other places at which Ray was employed presented similar problems in trying to reconstruct his work history.

the migrant camp to build more housing for workers.[64] Each night, according to Ray, "the place went crazy, everybody staying up until two or three in the morning drinking and fighting."[65] Some of the Mexican workers had brought along girlfriends or wives. While the men worked in the fields each day, Ray claimed that he and some of the other men left behind had sex with the women. Within a couple of days, Ray said there was animosity because he was a "gringo" and since he did not care "to lay awake at nights looking out for possessive boy friends with shanks, I decided to move on."[66] Collecting a week's wages, he walked into the nearest town and caught a freight train heading southwest. A few days later, sitting atop a boxcar, he arrived in Los Angeles.[67]

Ray had enough money to rent a room in a run-down flophouse on lower Broadway. At night he continued "a habit I'd started in the Army" by drinking in "a nearby honky-tonk."[68] His first run-in with the law happened in less than a week. On the night of October 7, 1949, Lee Strayhorn, the assistant manager of a seedy downtown cafeteria, the Forum, entered his business office on the third floor. When he switched on the light, he saw Ray partially hidden behind the safe. Before Strayhorn could do anything, Ray grabbed a chair and threw it at him, then ran to a rear window, climbed through, and fled down the fire escape.[69] A typewriter, evidently already carried outside by Ray, was resting outside the window. Strayhorn leaned out and screamed for help. A parking lot attendant lurched at the running Ray and grabbed him for a moment, but Ray broke free and sprinted around the corner.[70]

Unfortunately for Ray, his Army discharge papers and a bank passbook flew from his shirt pocket when the parking lot attendant tried to tackle him. But since there was no Los Angeles address for him, the matter would probably have been forgotten had Ray not been foolish enough to reappear at the same corner four days later. The parking attendant recognized him and called the police, who arrested him.* At the downtown booking station, both the parking attendant and Strayhorn positively identified Ray as the perpetrator.

This burglary arrest was the first on Ray's rap sheet, and is significant because it reveals a certain pattern that would reappear in his subsequent crimes: While there was a degree of ineptness to many of them, and some violence (usually with Ray as the victim), they demonstrated a remarkable, if misplaced, self-confidence on Ray's part that he could always concoct a story after his arrest that would set him free. On the occasion of his first adult arrest, Ray typically pleaded not guilty, denied everything, and told a rather remarkable story that placed him at the scene but only as an innocent victim of circum-

---

*   On the arrest report, under "Distinctive Characteristics," the police listed "talks slow like a southerner" and "slim."

stance.* At the time he was arrested, he told the police "I never was in the building and I don't even know where it is. I've only been in town three or four days. Someone stole my identification papers."[71] A few days later, his story had changed in a handwritten statement given to the police: "I had left a theatre on Broadway approximately 30 minutes before I entered the restaurant. I did not enter the building to commit a theft. I was stopped for a few seconds after I entered the building by an employee, I guess, as some people went out as I came in. He grabbed ahold of me and told me to leave the building, which I did. After I got down the street about half a block he started hollering for the police. About a week later I was arrested. I don't know anything about a typewriter or whether there was one in the building."[72] Ray challenged the police to produce fingerprints from the crime scene. Years later, in his first book, he modified his defense by saying that he actually had been at his favorite bar that night, and "I either drank too much or the hostess slipped a goof-ball in my drink. All I recall is some character shaking me awake from dozing in a hallway. There was a brief argument as to why I had entered the building, and then I departed somewhat hastily while the other party commenced hollering for the police."[73]

The probation report is filled with Ray's fanciful version of his life. He told the probation officer that his only living relatives were his mother and uncle since his father had died in 1956, that he had completed one year of high school, and that while he could not remember the name or address of the rooming house at which he was staying in Los Angeles, he was there to arrange for a construction job in Guam. According to Ray, he was a wayward Catholic who went to the movies several times weekly, read magazines and "common ordinary books," liked to play baseball, and dated many girls. Denying that he was anything more than a social drinker, he did admit, however, "to an occasional excessive use of intoxicants."[74] The probation officer, emphasizing the obvious, concluded: "He does not appear to be completely truthful in discussing his crime."

The brief trial was held on December 9, 1949. Ray was convicted of second-degree robbery and sentenced to eight months in the county jail and two years probation, on the condition that when released he either find a full-time job or return to Illinois. During the sentencing, the judge also admonished him about his fondness for alcohol: "I want you to stay out of drinking places and not indulge in the use of alcoholic liquor or frequent or go to places where it is the principal item of sale."[75]

---

* One of Ray's future lawyers, Robert Hill, told author George McMillan that "Ray has an automatic eraser in his mind—if he thought that bookshelf wasn't there, he would will it away. It's not there for him. He can rearrange reality to suit himself."

In March 1950, Ray's application for a "good time" early release was approved, and after serving only ninety days, he walked out of the Los Angeles County Jail by the end of the month. The five-ten Ray was nearly twenty pounds lighter, but his brief stint in prison had not turned him away from crime.[76] He recalled that since he had virtually no money, "I passed the first day out of jail looking for a place to burglarize for nourishment and enough money to carry out the court's mandate to 'get out of Dodge City.' "[77] He went to a Chinese restaurant and used his last loose change to buy a bowl of chili. While there he noticed an exhaust fan—large enough for a man to squeeze between the blades—over the rear door. That night, Ray returned and "in my lighter condition, thanks to jail, I had no problem maneuvering between the blades of the exhaust fan."[78] He left with a bag full of rolls of silver dollars and some groceries. "The only potential obstacle I encountered in the place," he later wrote, "was a sleeping dog that probably ended up in the Chinaman's 'Special' the next day."*[79] He had had enough of Southern California. That night, Ray caught a freight train headed for Las Vegas. It was the start of his journey home.

---

* In his first book, *Tennessee Waltz*, Ray sometimes used expressions that were derogatory to various races, such as "wetback" for Mexicans and "Chinaman" for Chinese. He also was quite political, on subjects ranging from Allied war crimes trials to alleged government cover-ups of dirty programs. By 1992, when his second book, *Who Killed Dr. Martin Luther King?*, was published, he dropped the ethnic slurs and political overtones. None appears in the second, "politically correct," version.

14

The Red Top Caper

Ray hitchhiked and rode freight trains east, but by April 18, he had reached only Marion, Iowa. When the train stopped there, a deputy sheriff, Harlan Snyder, searched the cars looking for hobos and spotted Ray crouched inside. Snyder frisked him and found one of the silver-dollar rolls from the Chinese restaurant heist. Snyder arrested Ray for vagrancy and suspicion of robbery and booked him into the nearby Cedar Rapids county jail.[1] Ray told the police that he had been honorably discharged from the Army and, equally untrue, that he was just returning from Los Angeles where he had worked as a drill press operator for Brynes Sheet Metal Company. As for the coins, Ray claimed he had won them in Las Vegas by gambling with a man he called Bill Holland.[2] According to Ray, while he knew that Holland lived in Salt Lake City, he could not describe him. The police found no evidence that any such man existed—Ray had apparently invented the character. But in the three weeks he was in custody, the police failed to link the coin roll to any reported robberies in the cities Ray had visited.

Although this was only his second jail stint, he adapted better to confinement. He put on the weight he had lost in Los Angeles, and actually so enjoyed the view of the Iowa River from his cell that he "was thinking of sticking around until the weather improved before making any noises about getting sprung."[3] But after the police inquiries came back negative, he was released on

May 8 and given a four-month suspended sentence for vagrancy.[4] Deputy Snyder drove him directly from the courthouse to the bus station, bought him a one-way ticket to Chicago, and waited until the bus pulled away from the station with Ray aboard.[5]

In late May Ray returned to Quincy. When he checked in with his family, he found it had further deteriorated. Garbage was piled inside the apartment, and Ceal and Speedy were still often drunk. John, recently turned nineteen, had robbed a service station the previous December. He was convicted of two counts of second-degree burglary and was now serving a two- to five-year sentence in the Indiana State Reformatory at Pendleton. Jerry, at fourteen, had fallen in with, as he put it, "some fellas my own age there in Quincy [and] began to roll drunks, snatch purses, and the next thing I knew I was on the way to jail."[6] He was committed that January to the Illinois State Training School for Boys at St. Charles, Uncle Earl's alma mater. Psychological tests administered to him there showed he "functioned between low, average and dull in intelligence."[7] Jerry took part in a prison riot and got another eighteen months tacked on to his robbery sentence. He was put on parole in 1951, but he violated it in less than a month with a grand larceny conviction and was sentenced to the tougher juvenile penitentiary at Sheridan, Illinois.[8] As for eleven-year-old Melba, her emotional problems had worsened. A now familiar character in Quincy, she shuffled along the streets, stooped sharply over, her eyes darting everywhere but almost always cast downward. The other two middle children—Carol, nine, and Franklin, six—were erratically attending the local St. Boniface school under the name Ryan.

Probation officers still monitored the Rays. On one visit it was reported that the children "ran wild in the streets. They urinated out of the windows and shouted obscenities at people passing by."[9] Astonishingly, later that year Ceal would be pregnant with her ninth child, Max.

Ray worked briefly at the Quincy Compressor Company, but he moved back to Chicago that summer. It marked the start of nearly two years of relative stability. Although he lived in run-down rooming houses, Ray had only two addresses during that time. "I generally stayed inside the law," he later wrote.[10]

In July he took a ninety-cent-an-hour assembly-line job at a plastics company, Neo Products, but left the following month for higher-paying work in the envelope-manufacturing department of Arvey Corporation.[11] That fall, Ray, who wanted to earn a high school diploma, enrolled at the Academy for Young Adults, a block from the Cook County courthouse. He soon bought a black 1949 Buick.

When his paternal aunt, Mabel Fuller, visited, she was pleased at how settled he seemed. Ray, typically exaggerating, boasted that he was attending Northwestern University.[12] He was dating a girl, also a factory worker, for the first time anyone in the family could remember.* Mabel met her and thought she looked liked a young Ceal.[13] Ray's landlady told Mabel that her nephew was a clean, quiet boarder who never caused problems. Mabel returned to Quincy convinced that Ray was finally on the road to self-respect and success.

It was difficult, however, for Ray to be patient with his new lifestyle. The work was hard and the pay little. The easier and faster money to be made in crime was always a lure. And there was no one close to him who could serve as a role model in the straight world. For reasons still not clear, after ten months at Arvey, Ray suddenly did not show up for work on June 15, 1951. Ten days later he wrote to say he had resigned. He went to Mom Maher's Quincy house for a two-month stay, any apparent relationship with a girlfriend over.[†] He also stopped attending classes at the Academy for Young Adults, short of the requirements to earn his much-wanted high school diploma. On July 23, he was stopped by Alton police for driving a car without license plates, city identification, or a driver's license.[14] Three days later he was arrested for "investigation," charged with vagrancy, and given a ninety-day sentence.[15]

In September, Ray returned to Chicago and found another job, assembly-line work at a manufacturing company, Borg-Ericson.[16] While he was there, the news from his family in Quincy worsened. Speedy finally abandoned Ceal and the children. In March 1952, he took what little money the family had saved and moved in with another woman, assumed the name Gerry Rayns, and went to work at a furniture factory.

Ray's Borg-Ericson job lasted only eight months. On the night of May 6, 1952, wearing a sports shirt and dark slacks, Ray hailed a Red Top taxi at 1:00 A.M. and told the heavyset driver, Lewis Knox, to take him to 67 Cedar Street, a dark, quiet, tree-lined street. Cars were parked on both sides, so the taxi rolled

---

* In a 1970 interview with author George McMillan, Ray's sister Carol insisted that he had had girlfriends, although she could not recall any names. McMillan's notes of the interview indicate that Carol was extremely sensitive to the implication that Ray might be homosexual. Ray was often ambiguous about his sexuality. His father worried that James's one friend in Chicago, the German Stumm, was "queer." Later, in prison, statements from fellow prisoners indicate that while Ray was not a homosexual predator, he enjoyed receiving fellatio from other men, and was known to pay for it. However, Walter Rife, who later spent two weeks with Ray on the road, saw no evidence Ray was gay. "I know he wasn't no freak," said Rife. "We slept in the car together many nights and he never went for me." Yet years later, one of Ray's own attorneys, Robert Hill, told author McMillan that he wondered whether Ray was gay since he thought Ray was "sexually attracted" to him. Arthur Hanes, Sr., was convinced Ray was a "limp wrist."

† In his two books, Ray does not even mention this girlfriend. Instead, he describes his entire period in Chicago by writing, "I lived alone on Fullerton Avenue. My social life included occasional visits to the local bars. Once in a while I caught a Cubs game."

to a stop in the middle of the road. Ray then suddenly drew a pistol and shoved it against the back of the driver's head, demanding both money and the taxi itself. Ray intended to steal the car and use it as the getaway vehicle in the robbery of a bookie operation. While Ray was hijacking the taxi, an accomplice was waiting near the target in Ray's own Buick.[17]

Unfortunately for Ray, at that very moment a thirty-two-year-old production manager for a local advertising agency, Robert Everhart, was walking to his own car. He glanced up in time to see the glint of a gun barrel and froze. Next, Everhart watched as the driver suddenly got out of the taxi and walked rapidly away. Then he saw the gun-toting passenger scramble over the rear seat and put himself behind the wheel as though he intended to drive away.

But the cabbie had evidently taken the keys, and suddenly a frustrated Ray leaped from the taxi and sprinted down the street. Everhart, who came from an indigent working background (his mother had scrubbed floors at night to support the family) was infuriated that Ray had tried to "rob a poor cab driver who has to work like hell for his money."[18] So he took off after Ray, who by now had scampered through a construction site and then down an alley. "When I made it to the Buick, my partner took off in the opposite direction," Ray recalled.[19] He continued running.

"He could run like hell," Everhart recalled.[20] Everhart decided to outfox Ray by doubling back, thereby hoping to catch him as he exited the alley. As he sped around the corner, Everhart almost ran directly into an unmarked police car. He excitedly told the officers about the robbery and jumped into the patrol car's backseat.

"He can't get out of that alley," one of the policemen said. "It's a dead end."

The cruiser pulled to the front of the alley, turned off its lights, and parked to block the exit. Both policemen stepped outside, their revolvers drawn. In a moment, Ray came tearing around the corner at full speed, heading directly toward them. "Stop!" the police yelled in unison. Ray reversed and raced toward a small fence that separated the alley from the backyard of a row house. One of the officers, George Green, fired a warning shot, but Ray ignored it and jumped the fence. He cut through the backyard and either tripped or dived through the basement window of the house, landing on his head and causing a large gash. When the two policemen arrived, Ray, slightly dazed, was climbing the staircase to flee.[21] Green ordered him to stop, and when Ray again did not, Green shot him. The bullet passed through his right forearm and grazed his left arm as it exited.[22] Ray then crumpled onto the staircase, bleeding from both his cut head and his bullet wounds.

The police dragged him by his armpits out of the house and back to their patrol car. As they propped him against a brick wall and called for a police wagon, Ray stared at Everhart. "What are you going to get out of this?"

"I hadn't even thought of that," Everhart later said.[23]

Ray's luck finally improved. An inebriated woman left a nearby bar, and seeing the police and the bleeding Ray, she started accusing the police of beating their prisoner. She was so strident that the police tried to calm her, and instead of patting down Ray, they merely handcuffed him and placed him in the backseat of their patrol car as they waited for the wagon. While he was in that car, "I managed to wrestle the revolver out of my pocket and shove it under the seats." Ray was smart enough to know that simple act would "reduce the charge against me from armed to unarmed robbery."[24]

He was taken to Cook County Hospital, where his head was partially shaved and his wound stitched.[25] While lying on his stomach on the operating table, with his arms outstretched, a police photographer took a photo of him. His head and both arms covered in bandages, he was taken to the police station, where he was booked for armed robbery. Everhart came along and picked Ray out of a lineup, although since he was the only one covered with bandages, it would have been impossible to miss him.

Jerry Ray, who was then on parole and working at a riding stable in suburban Chicago, read about the crime in the newspaper. He was not surprised that he had to discover it in the paper, since "Jimmy didn't tell nobody nothing."[26] Jerry sent a clipping to his mother. "A few days later I couldn't believe it," Jerry recalled. "Ceal was walking down the gravel road, she had walk all the way from Le Grange. It must have been six or seven miles. I told her I could of borrow my employer's car and pick her up, she said she didn't want to bother me. They was a few cabins behind a tavern for rent, no lights. I got her a room there. Ceal look very sad that time sitting on side of the bed white and wore out, with her head down trying to keep from crying. The next day she went into Chicago and saw Jimmy. I found out later she was broke, had to work as a dishwasher to pay her way home. After that, Ceal didn't have nothing else to live for."[27] Ceal's life had been unraveling for a long time. She had placed so many of her hopes on James, her first child. He had seemed to get out of the house before the worst of the trouble had started. After Marjorie's death, he was her favorite. But seeing him in prison in Chicago shattered whatever fantasy she had conjured for him. He had not escaped the Ray background after all. Heartbroken, Ceal returned to the rest of her family in Quincy.

As for Ray, while the police did find $11.50 that he had stolen from the taxi driver, they could not find the gun.[28] Ray pleaded not guilty and swore he never had a weapon and that Everhart and the taxi driver were mistaken about seeing one. On June 2, 1952, he pleaded guilty to simple robbery. In the presentencing investigation, Ray told the probation officer that he had been honorably discharged from the Army, had never been in "serious" trouble with the law before, and promised that if he received probation he would "get a job and never become involved with the law again."[29] On June 4, he was sentenced to one to two years in a state penitentiary.*

Joliet, famous for the Chicago gangsters it housed in the 1920s, was the "reception center" for the Illinois prison system. There, Ray was issued his prison uniforms and given medical and mental aptitude tests. He scored 111 on an Army Alpha test, a "superior" rating.[30] On another test, to determine academic achievement, he finished slightly above a typical second-year high school student, with his strongest subjects being history, geography, and reading, and his worst spelling and grammar. The psychologist who interviewed him to determine where he should be placed in the prison system found Ray to be of "superior intelligence" and "without psychotic or intellectual defect." However, he also thought he was an "unstable personality—[a] questionably improvable offender—problematic prognosis."[31] Ray told the psychologist that he was one of three children, and that his father had been a railroad brakeman and a "good provider" until his death by heart attack in 1947. He also claimed to have finished fifteen months of high school and to have been honorably discharged from the Army. "Apparently he was somewhat of a solitary person," the psychologist noted in his report, "but said he had occasional dates. He denies any persistent drinking, although admitting occasional alcoholic excess."[32] The report concluded that Ray was "seemingly a person who has some drive, but has not been able to settle down to just what he wants," the recommendation was that Ray be given one of the best assignments in the state prison system: placement at a medium-security prison in Pontiac, where prisoners with a possibility of improvement served their time.

In early July, he was transferred to Pontiac. There he was assigned to the main cell block and worked in the kitchen. With 1,300 prisoners, it was radically different from the small, transient county jails where he had previously done his time. "Big houses" such as Joliet and Pontiac have a certain order and hierarchy imposed by the prisoners. Although Ray was technically a newcomer to prison life—called a "fish" by other prisoners—he knew from Uncle Earl how to behave like a veteran prisoner. He was quiet, stayed to himself, and kept out of trouble. Ray made no friends and had no visitors, and wrote only to Ceal and Jerry.[33] One official later said, "The best men you know the least. Ray was one of those."†[34]

---

* In *Tennessee Waltz*, Ray wrote, "In retrospect, I really see no reason for this caper. I had a job at the time, and didn't have a goofball or alcohol habit to support. Further, even if the undertaking had been successful, it still would have been meaningless, because a couple thousand dollars would not have appreciably improved my financial status for long. Such robberies as this I believe merely reflects a lack of self-discipline."

† Ray kept so much to himself that when inmates who had served time with him were interviewed after the King assassination, almost none could recall him.

Soon he was moved to the "honor farm" just south of the main building. It was a much sought-after transfer by inmates, although Ray described it as "a monastery, minus the prayers and psalms."[35] There were only one hundred men on the farm, with ten to a dormitory. During the day, prisoners were free to walk around in a wide area. Ray again worked in the kitchen, but he soon landed a soft job in the warden's and officers' quarters. The psychologist who handled his case later remarked, "He knew how to conform, there's no doubt about that."[36]

A six-month progress report on Ray noted that he was "good" in his "attitude toward his work" and "his ability to get along with officers and other inmates" but "only fair as far as proficiency, initiative, progress and ability to work in the free community were concerned."[37] After nearly a year at Pontiac, he was finally eligible for parole. For another progress report, prepared to determine whether parole should be granted, Ray's case was discussed at staff meetings and he submitted to one long and one short interview. The report is telling in several areas. It concluded that Ray's "traumatic" service in the Army had left him "highly unsettled," but that "he does not care to tell, or cannot verbalize" exactly what went wrong for him in the service.[38] The report concluded, "He seems to be rather solitary and unhappy. . . . It is difficult for us to make an adequate prediction in this case. In view of the two known instances of impulsive delinquent behavior connected with drinking, the lack of any indication of change or progress here, and the age at which this pattern was continuing, we would judge that he would eventually repeat this behavior, especially if discouraged. . . . The prognosis seems to be problematic to doubtful."[39]

Parole was denied. Six months later, a "Release Progress Report" summarized not only how Ray had served his time, but also forecast the outlook for his future. According to prison officials, he had a "clean card," a rare accomplishment for a first-timer.[40] It concluded, however, "His future plans are indefinite. . . . Inmate's delinquencies seem due to impulsive behavior, especially when drinking. There is a relationship to inmate's tendency to be easily discouraged, and this tendency still exists. . . . The prognosis is doubtful."[41]

On March 12, 1954, after serving twenty-two months, Ray was finally freed. Two days earlier he had turned twenty-six. He was given his release papers, $25, a one-way bus ticket home to Quincy, 130 miles away, and a turnout suit—a dark-colored outfit made by prisoners—to be worn until he could get some regular clothes. Ray stopped in Quincy for a few days, and then went to Mom Maher's house in Alton, where he learned how thoroughly the rest of his family had disintegrated. Since John, now twenty-three, had been released from reform school a year earlier, he had burglarized a tavern, stolen a car, and tried to escape from jail.[42] In June 1953—under the name John Ryan—he had pleaded guilty to the theft of the twelve-year-old jalopy worth only a couple of hundred dollars. Nevertheless, because of his earlier run-in with the law, he was given a tough sentence of five to ten years in Menard.[43] There he joined Uncle Earl.[44] Jerry, now eighteen, had become the extroverted clown in the Ray family, but was still just a step behind John and James. On February 1, 1954, Jerry and three friends snatched a purse from an elderly lady and knocked her down. Jerry's share of the proceeds was only $20, but when he was arrested, the charge was burglary. He pleaded guilty to the lesser charge of grand larceny and sought probation, but it was denied because of his previous record. At his February 24 trial, Jerry was given a harsh two- to five-year sentence at Menard.[45] He entered the prison as Gerald Ryan, and there joined his brother John and his uncle Earl.* For John and Jerry, it was fortunate that their uncle was at the same jail: He broke them into prison life and taught them how to do their time without causing any problems.

As for the rest of the children, they had finally been taken away forcibly from Ceal. In a futile last attempt to keep them, Ceal had visited Robert Hunter, the county and juvenile judge responsible for her family's case. But not only did he already know the horrific conditions at home and that Ceal was "a lush," but also on that day her clothes smelled and her hair was so filthy that it stood almost straight up. Hunter thought she was the "most slovenly woman" he had ever seen.[46] When he rejected her heartfelt pleas, she became, according to Hunter, "a wild gal," screaming and cursing. He had her removed and issued the order to take the children. On the day the court officials arrived, they had to pry the youngest child, Max, from Ceal's arms as she wailed and sobbed.[47]

Max turned out to be retarded and was placed in a special home in Alton.[48] Suzan and Franklin were wards of the court in a Catholic home in Springfield, Illinois.[49] Melba was put into a special school in Ohio for emotionally disturbed children. "I knew she had gone when she said she had seen Jesus," remembered Jerry.[50] After she had pulled her hair out by the roots, broke the lights, and turned on the water and flooded her room, she was locked into a padded cell, which she managed to set on fire.[51] Soon she was committed to the state mental hospital at Jacksonville, Illinois, where she would stay until she was twenty.[52] As for Ceal, Ray learned she had moved in with her mother immediately after the children were taken, but that was short-lived. She had returned to Quincy,

---

* Of all his sons, Speedy expressed contempt only for Jerry, sometimes calling him "nigger" because of his dark complexion. Speedy later told author George McMillan that Jerry was "never any good," and that he was a "clown that lets whores insult him and take all his money." He ridiculed Jerry's writing to a lonely hearts' club in the hope of marrying a wealthy woman, and he concluded that Jerry was stupid, too slow-witted even to be a boxer.

where she was a regular at local taverns, and had been arrested for assault and battery and larceny.[53] There were reports that she had turned to prostitution, and later a judge would hear testimony that one evening, "when she was unable to find any dates [she] had brought in her fourteen-year-old daughter, Carol, and attempted to obtain prostitution dates for her," although years later Carol averred, "I never bedded with anybody."[54] Carol, described by neighbors as "a very rough and wild individual," was also placed in a foster home.*[55]

That spring and summer of 1954, Ray stayed mostly in Alton. He did some work for his uncle Willie Maher, who was then a part-time painting contractor. He also pumped gas, a comedown from when he boasted to Mom Maher that he would own a service station. Ray was back to his regular but controlled drinking in local taverns, where he often watched television for hours, fascinated with Senator Joseph McCarthy's hearings on Communist influence in government. Still fancying himself wise in politics, he became a strong McCarthy booster.[56]

But again, Ray found that his legitimate jobs did not bring enough money, and he decided to rob a dry cleaner in the adjacent town of East Alton. Around 4:00 A.M. on the night of Saturday, August 27, in the midst of a heavy rainstorm, two security guards were patrolling a row of shops. They saw that one of the side windowpanes to National Cleaners was broken, indicating a possible forced entry. Calling for police backup, they also roused the owner of the cleaners to come and open the store. While they waited, they fanned out in the nearby area and found a single car they did not recognize. Thinking it might belong to the burglar, one of the security men disconnected the car's distributor so it could not be started. Finally, when the store's owner arrived, they entered. Inside, they saw a man at the rear window, incredibly coming back into the store. Although they shouted for him to stop, the solitary figure jumped back out the window and took off running. When the two security guards ran around the rear, they saw that the burglar's shoes were still there, having gotten stuck in the thick, soggy mud outside the store. Then, after a few moments, they saw him run and jump over a low fence, and though they gave chase, he got away. When they returned to the strange car on which they had earlier disconnected the distributor, they found a pair of wet brown work gloves had been thrown on the front seat. The thief had evidently run back to the car but had been unable to start it. Searching the car, they quickly found a registration card in the name of James Earl Ray.

At dawn the next day, an Alton policeman found Ray walking along the railway tracks wearing a gray gas-station uniform, his stocking feet bruised

---

* Years later, Carol said, "I don't hate my Mother for giving me away. Nobody's perfect. Court records don't tell everything."

and bleeding. Despite his protestations of innocence, he was taken to the police station and booked for the theft of $28 from the cleaners.[57] "He was very quiet," recalled Alton police chief Harold Riggins. "When he was lying, he'd duck-jerk his head several inches to the side like he was expecting you to slug him or something. He wouldn't look you in the eye."[58] Andrew Biro, one of the security guards involved in the chase, remembered, "He was a real bulldog type. He denied his guilt and never changed his story once. When you asked him a question, he'd pretend he wasn't listening."[59] Ray, as usual, denied everything: The shoes, which were his size, were not his. He did not know how his car had gotten there. He was just out for a long walk when stopped by the police, he said.*

His bail was posted by a local nightclub owner, Dominic Tadaro, who charged Ray a steep interest.[60] The Alton police suspected Ray of a number of other petty crimes, ranging from stripping parked cars to filling half-pint bottles with cheap wine to sell to winos when the liquor stores were closed, and had decided to make his life miserable. "He was the most reluctant, sarcastic, overbearing liar I ever saw," said Chief Riggins.[61] Before his trial could begin, Ray was arrested two weeks later for vagrancy. Again, Tadaro posted his bail. This time Ray skipped town and moved back to Quincy.

"In Quincy I was scraping by, trying to stay even on my monthly payments to Tadaro," Ray later wrote. "I had to steal to make ends meets, living in cheap hotels. In the course of hanging around the usual joints, I met Walter Rife, a petty thief and part-time pimp. Uncle Earl, who was then out of jail, tried to warn me off the acquaintance, but I ignored him."[62] Ray fails to mention, of course, that he had known Rife as a teenager in Quincy. Rife had had his own problems since the two had last seen each other: He had deserted the Army in 1947, was captured and sentenced to Fort Leavenworth, and then escaped. He was subsequently rearrested and convicted of forgery. When he ran into Ray, he had recently been released from Menard, where he had spent time with Jerry and John Ray.[63]

As their friendship rekindled, the two spent much time together. They became close enough for Rife to learn things about Ray that few outsiders ever discovered.† He found that Ray was a loner with a flash temper, but he was dependable in a pinch.[64] While he never heard Ray talk of his mother or father ("I always figured they was dead"), Ray constantly spoke of Uncle Earl. "There was a little hero worship in there somewhere or other," said Rife. "He approved of

---

*   In the presentencing report for a subsequent 1955 crime, Ray admitted that he had burglarized the cleaners, but denied stealing anything.

†   Although Rife saw a frank side of Ray, even he later admitted, "There will always be a mystery in James's life, until he decides to tell it himself."

anything his uncle did."[65] Ray was somebody who thought not about the future, but only about "the next day. . . . I think he's just spent his whole life trying to make a living without working. He's just a thief."[66] But he added that Ray was "capable of killing, as we all are."[67]

Rife also saw that Ray had developed an "immense" dislike for blacks. "There was nothing particular he had against them, nothing they had done to him. He said once they ought to be put out of the country. Once he said, 'Well, we ought to kill them, kill them all.' . . . He was unreasonable in his hatred for niggers. He hated to see them breathe. If you pressed it, he'd get violent in a conversation about it. He hated them! I never did know why."[68] When Rife and Ray visited bars, Ray "would get a little hot about it if a Negro came in. But I'd say, well, leave him alone. He'd say, that's what we've been doing all along, leaving them alone, that's the trouble."[69] Rife, however, did not find Ray's racial attitudes surprising. He later told author George McMillan that "if you talk to 85 people out of 100, they'll tell you the same thing. . . . I took it for granted, I knew what he [Ray] was talking about."*[70]

But what they talked about the most was how to make a score that would allow them to escape from the poverty-stricken existence they hated but continued to eke out. By early 1955, Ray, with Rife's help, was on his way to becoming a three-time loser.

---

* Ray has often been asked whether he is a racist, but instead of simply saying no, has attempted to finesse the issue, leaving the distinct impression that he holds many of the same prejudices as his siblings and others who were raised in the same poor, working-class, white neighborhoods. When asked by *Playboy* in 1977 how he felt about blacks, Ray contended that there were "cultural differences" among the races, and added, "Well, they're just here and I'm here. I don't really have no really strong feelings one way or the other. I guess they're looking out for their interests as everyone else is. And, of course, I'm trying to look out for mine. But I don't see no conflict there." Yet even his brother Jerry admitted to the FBI that James "was not particularly fond of Negroes." More than two dozen inmates who served with him described, in detail, his animosity toward blacks. However, typical of defenders of Ray, conspiracy theorist Harold Weisberg, writes, "Most of those who knew him say Ray showed no signs of special feelings against Negroes."

15

"A Menace to Society"

Kellerville, Illinois, the town where Walter Rife grew up, was so small that its post office was simply a shed next to a general store. It sold less than $1,000 worth of stamps a year. But Rife assured Ray that it would be a surefire target, filled with a rich cache of postal money orders—issued by the government and easy to cash with little identification.

On the night of March 7, 1955, three days before Ray's twenty-seventh birthday, Ray and Rife bought a phony driver's license for seventy-five cents in a bar in St. Louis.[1] They then drove to Kellerville and entered the closed post office through a boarded window, netting sixty-six money orders as well as the stamps needed to validate them. The two, flush with success, set off for sixteen days on a seven-state odyssey through Memphis, as far south as Miami (where they bought a new car), as far west as New Orleans, and then north through a gambler's hangout in Hot Springs, Arkansas, on the way to visit some acquaintances in Kansas City.[2]

"The trip was Jimmy's idea," recalled Rife. Ray did most of the driving, but "he couldn't drive worth a shit" and "he wouldn't talk too much," said Rife.[3] The two stopped at dozens of small country stores along the way, buying cigarettes, luggage, watches, clothes, a radio, and a camera.[4] Rife cashed most of the $1,805 in money orders they used during their spree.[5] "Half the time they'd never ask me for identification," he later boasted.[6] Rife also felt that Ray was a liability when he used the money orders. "He was a lousy forger. He'd walk into a store and just look guilty. He was heat personified."[7]

Meanwhile, federal postal inspectors hunted for the thieves by tracking the serial numbers of the stolen money orders. As they were presented to the government for payment, a computer rejected them as stolen and pinpointed where they had been presented. But Ray and Rife kept moving, and the inspectors were invariably a day behind.

The two thieves stayed within speed limits to avoid attracting any police, and Ray initially kept his daily drinking to two shots of Walker's Deluxe Bourbon and Coke. They sometimes pulled quick thefts. In Tampa they got lucky picking wallets and netted $1,700 in less than an hour.[8] At night they often visited whorehouses, and they stayed, at Ray's insistence, in the cheapest flophouses.[9] But while Ray was generally frugal, Rife noticed that "after a couple of drinks he really began to throw his money around." He was eager to spend money on clothes and enjoyed primping in front of mirrors, spending a lot of time to ensure his hair was perfectly styled in the then fashionable pompadour.

There was also an impulsive side to Ray. When he and Rife were in Miami, Ray dickered at length with a used-car salesman over a 1949 Lincoln. The two were only dollars apart when suddenly Ray shocked Rife by agreeing to throw in his old car to cinch the deal. "I don't know what possessed him to do that," said Rife. "Ordinarily he was so chintzy."[10]

Rife also discovered that Ray, while not looking for trouble, had a sharp temper and would not back away from any fight. "He was a mean, nasty fighter," recalled Rife. "He fought to win, no matter what it took, a club, knife or gun. I never saw him lose a fight."[11] Occasionally Ray would decide the fight was not worth the effort, as when Rife got into a wild scuffle with a transvestite at a Florida gay bar at which the two had stopped to buy more phony identification.[12] But at a bar in Kansas City, Rife saw that Ray could sometimes become violent with little or no provocation. "Somebody at a bar said something to him, nothing serious, like move your glass down. And Ray said, 'Oh, forget about it,' and he didn't look mad, and he just walked out the front door as if he was forgetting about it. But he went around the place and came in the back door, walked up behind this fella and stuck a knife in him. The fella fell off the stool, and we just walked right out of there."*[13]

---

* Ray has never spoken about the knifing incident, although when asked by *Playboy* in 1977 if he had ever stabbed anyone, he replied noncommittally, "I can't remember ever stabbing anyone. Of course, I've been in a few fights." Without an exact location or time, it has not been possible to locate a police report about the Kansas City incident, assuming the victim even filed one. However, if Rife's recollection of the event is accurate, it is significant, since many of Ray's strongest defenders point to his supposed lack of violence prior to the King assassination as evidence that he did not have the disposition to

On March 21, the two were caught in a springtime snowstorm in Kansas City. Ray decided to kill some time by buying clothes at Askins, a local men's clothing store. He was fitted for a new suit, said he would pick it up later, and paid with a $75 money order.[14] The manager was suspicious and called postal inspectors after Ray left. But before the inspectors arrived at Ray's hotel, he had checked out, and he never returned to the store for the suit. Meanwhile, Rife had also become careless at a store only two blocks from Askins. He bought a $58 typewriter and paid with a $75 money order. The store's owner was suspicious because Rife "didn't seem the kind to buy a typewriter."[15] The owner noted the model of Rife's car and jotted down its license number as he drove away. He also telephoned postal inspectors, but again they were too late to arrest the pair.[16]

Two days later, as a blizzard further blanketed the region, Ray impulsively decided to visit Hannibal, Missouri. Rife argued with him, but Ray prevailed. "I don't know why he wanted to go to Hannibal," said Rife. "He always wanted to go to Hannibal. But he didn't know anyone there. We'd go there and sit in a bar. But he was like that."[17]

As they neared Hannibal, a Missouri highway patrolman spotted the wanted license plate and called for backup. Ray and Rife were pulled over just south of Hannibal, together with Katherine Buskirk, an eighteen-year-old Quincy girl Rife had picked up earlier that day. Thirty-four of the stolen money orders were found, all stamped with the validating machine, which was hidden under the car's dash.[18] For the first time in his growing criminal career, Ray surrendered without trying to escape. At the station, when they asked him for his occupation, Ray smirked and said, "Lover."*[19]

Both Rife and Ray knew that robbery of a federal post office carried serious penalties, and as a result they had already planned a defense if they were caught. Rife claimed that he had merely bought the money orders and validating stamp for $20 from a Quincy wino named Willard J. McBride.[20] It was, he said, just a coincidence that the post office McBride supposedly robbed happened to be in Rife's hometown. Ray and Rife then asserted that they had bought identification papers for a dollar from an unidentified man in a St. Louis

---

carry out that murder. "His criminal record is all one way, entirely non-violent," contends Harold Weisberg. If Ray, however, had the capability to stab someone because he did not like the way that person spoke to him, it could indicate a streak of violence that was part of Ray's underlying personality. Ray's family members are split over whether he had such a violent streak. His uncle Willie Maher thought Ray would only shoot someone if he were "hopped up."

*   When booked, Rife gave his name as Vernon Elmo Rife, one of his many aliases. After King's assassination, until the FBI determined that Walter Terry Rife was actually the person arrested with Ray, Rife's alias caused confusion and anxiety, since at first the FBI thought it could not find one of Ray's former accomplices.

bar.* Actually, McBride was a fictitious person the two had invented, and they had used the name in passing several of the money orders.[†21] Their gambit worked. No one had seen them rob the post office and there was no physical evidence to tie them to the scene. On March 28, the two were booked only for passing stolen money orders.

When they appeared in federal court in Kansas City just eight days after their arrest, they were pleased to plead guilty to the reduced charge.[22] Rife, who had a more serious criminal record than Ray, received a lenient sentence of thirty-six months at Leavenworth Penitentiary in Kansas. Ray was startled to receive forty-five months and upset that his sentence was harsher than Rife's. He later speculated that it was due to his refusal to cooperate in the presentencing report—"I tried to protect myself and my family as best I could."[23] What Ray did not know was that the probation officer who prepared the report, Edward B. Murray, recommended that Ray be given a harsh sentence. Again, Ray had lied repeatedly, saying that he was an only child, and that both his parents were deceased, and he offered a weak defense for each of his previous arrests. But Murray was not fooled. His presentencing report concluded, "Defendant shows absolutely no remorse at this time. He anticipates receiving a substantial sentence for the instant offense. In writer's opinion he is a confirmed criminal and a menace to society when in the free world."[24]

The two convicts arrived at Leavenworth on July 7, 1955. Ray still simmered about the disparity in sentencing. Six weeks later, he wrote to the trial judge asking for a nine-month reduction in his time. "I recd 45 months, my codefendant recd 36. We both plea guilty to the charge of forgery," Ray wrote. But the judge rejected his petition and the sentence stood.

Leavenworth was one of the country's most famous prisons when Ray entered. "That's where they separate the men from the boys," said Rife. "They

---

* At the time, the two seemed to present a coordinated story. However, more than twenty years later, Ray tried to put all the blame on Rife. He wrote that when he ran into Rife in Quincy, Rife told him he had broken into the Kellerville post office and stolen the money orders. According to Ray, Rife "made me an offer: if I'd drive him to Florida, where he could forge and cash the paper, he'd pay me for transportation. Then we'd part company." In his first book, Ray put the blame solely on Rife for passing the stolen money orders, but in his second book, he said Rife passed "most" of them. Actually, Ray passed twelve of the twenty-seven money orders presented by the two during their spree.

† When Rife was interviewed by the FBI after the King assassination, he admitted that McBride was a concoction. While Rife would not confess to the burglary of the post office to the FBI, he did admit that "he and Ray obtained the money orders in Adams County, Illinois. He said that the Post Office at Kellerville, Illinois, is located in Adams County, Illinois . . . and that neither Ray nor Rife obtained the money orders outside of Adams County."

treat you like a man. It's a tough place, full of big-time people."[25] Ray, in his own book, says that while his "fellow prisoners were bank robbers, drug traffickers, mobsters, Communists . . . and bent labor leaders. . . . Leavenworth is just another jail."[26] Serving time no longer involved any trauma for him. He was now comfortable in jails, finding an order in the institutionalized environment that did not exist in the more chaotic and less predictable outside world. By this time Ray found prison life "like a small city. . . . like life on the outside. You have a place to live, a place to eat, a job to do, rules to follow, and people you have to get along with. . . . Anything you can get on the outside, you can get in prison."[27] He also had accepted a maxim that helped him become accepted by most other inmates: "Informants are about the lowest life form in the prison food chain."[28]

Prison authorities found he had almost no interest in rehabilitation. "This man has no trade nor skills, is not interested in Vocational Training or Self-Improvement programs," concluded an interim Leavenworth report. "His only interests are to work in the culinary department."[29] After initially being placed in the fire department, Ray worked in the bakery but was quickly removed "for not being dependable."[30] Another report, written a year after Ray arrived, again showed no promise of rehabilitation. "He apparently lacks foresight, or is afraid of the future, as he absolutely refuses to look forward. He claims that he can do his time better if he doesn't think . . . and apparently is enjoying his present situation."[31]

While prison officials thought Ray made no progress, he was doing all the right things as far as his fellow convicts were concerned. Working out in the exercise yard with weights, he pumped himself up by nearly twenty pounds.* He took typing and English classes, two prerequisites for becoming an effective jailhouse lawyer. And he also joined a Spanish class, useful since he "wanted to get out of the United States entirely" upon his eventual release.[32] "I'd say Leavenworth did Jimmy Ray more good than anything that ever happened to him," commented his cohort Walter Rife, who saw him almost daily at the prison. "Leavenworth is where he grew up."[33] Of course, "growing up" meant something different to a career criminal such as Rife than it would to most people.†

---

* Ray, always a bit of a hypochondriac, looked fit, but continued to complain to prison doctors about a wide range of ailments, from headaches to chronic difficulty in breathing due to allergies. Although he was often at the infirmary, his records note that he refused any rectal tests or examination of his genitals, an action that some psychologists have interpreted to fit with Ray's possible repression or fear of latent homosexuality.

† Author Clay Blair, Jr., presents Ray as a "reticent, awkward hillbilly" during his time at Leavenworth. Blair concludes that "Ray was rejected by his peers. He withdrew into his shell, as usual, bottling up who knows what rage and anger." But available prison records reveal that Ray's adjustment was actually untroubled, and he left other prisoners alone, and they did the same with him.

Again, as in Pontiac, Ray did not have a single visitor, but he did write to Jerry and John, who were incarcerated for much of the same period.[34] The brothers' common fate—prison—bonded them more strongly to one another.

There was only one incident that blemished Ray's prison record. On September 12, 1957, he was approved for the prison's honor farm, a much sought-after transfer since it meant less work and greatly enhanced freedom. However, he rejected it. According to a later prison progress report, Ray had refused the move "due to the fact that he did not feel he could live in an Honor Farm Dormitory because they are integrated."*[35] Except for the honor farm, Leavenworth was a racially segregated prison, with blacks fed and housed in separate dormitories.[36] Ray, then twenty-nine years old, had never lived or worked near a black person. He was not about to start.

By April 1958, Ray was ready for a conditional release, whereby he would be transferred to Kansas City and required to check in daily with a parole officer. On April 15, Ray was set free and given $100, another turnout suit, and a dollar for the bus ticket to Kansas City.[37]

---

* Although several dozen family members, associates, and prison inmates of Ray's have spoken about his racial biases and feelings about blacks, the honor farm incident is important since it is one of the few recorded events that demonstrates the depth of Ray's feelings about blacks. Twenty years later, Ray told *Playboy* in an interview that he had refused to go to the farm since the prison handed out extra time for marijuana possession, and since blacks were there, he assumed they used marijuana and he might get in trouble by just being there. Thirty-six years after the event, in a televised trial of his case on HBO, Ray went even further in defending his rejection of the transfer: "There was a possibility that I could get ten years for drugs since some of the blacks out there used marijuana." According to Ray, while the whites in the prison made "homemade liquor" the blacks and Mexicans used marijuana. The author could find no evidence that any white inmate at Leavenworth ever had his sentence increased because a black inmate had used or left marijuana nearby. As for the contemporaneous prison documents that demonstrate Ray refused the transfer because the farm was integrated, Ray contended that "these records have been falsified for years."

16

A Professional Criminal

I t was Ray's bad fortune on arriving in Kansas City to discover that his parole officer was Edward Murray, the same person who had written his harsh presentencing report three years earlier. "Neither of us showed much enthusiasm for renewing the acquaintance," Ray recalled.[1] Murray was strict and required Ray to give daily updates of his efforts to find work. Instead, Ray decided that if he stayed in Kansas City, "I'd be right back in Leavenworth."[2] Under the rules of his conditional release, it was possible for him to transfer to the jurisdiction where his family lived if the probation officer in that area was willing to add him to his caseload.

The remnants of the Ray family had begun migrating to St. Louis, mostly settling into a dirt-poor riverbank area called Soulard, similar to the crime-stricken river wards in Quincy.[3] Speedy had been there since he abandoned the family, working in odd jobs and drinking less than when he was with Ceal. Mom Maher, who had lived most of her life in Quincy, had moved there and bought a run-down boardinghouse. She eventually persuaded Ceal to move in with her. Some of the children taken by the courts had returned: Carol was living with Speedy; Melba, released from the state mental hospital, was with her mother and grandmother, as was Franklin, who was released from the Catholic children's home when he turned fourteen in 1958. John and Jerry Ray would also move to St. Louis when they were released from Menard. Ray decided that St. Louis was also where he wanted to be.[4]

After a few weeks in Kansas City, he used what money he had left to buy a pair of large metal clips and a few feet of heavy-duty electrical wire. He fashioned a makeshift hot-wire and stole a car to drive the 130 miles to St. Louis.[5] Five miles outside St. Louis the car broke down, and Ray walked the rest of the way to Mom Maher's boardinghouse. It was the first time he had seen his mother since she visited him in jail in Chicago six years earlier, and he was startled at how she had deteriorated. Ray, who had intended to stay at his grandmother's rooming house, decided the atmosphere was too depressing. Instead, since he was broke, he asked Ceal for some money. "She lent me a little cash," he recalled, "and I moved into an apartment house on Mississippi Street, not far from where the winos hung out."[6]

Ray checked in with a local parole officer, who then authorized the transfer of his case file to St. Louis.[7] According to Ray, during this time he worked part-time as a baker and then a cook. Actually, he went to the bakers' union but could not find any work, and then landed a job as a cook's helper at the nearby Glen Echo Country Club, a position he held for a single day before he was fired.[8] Unable to hold a steady job, and in close proximity to the city's winos, he reverted to a business he had dabbled in when living in Alton: "At the end of the week," he recalled, "I'd stock up on fifths of muscatel, hold them until the package stores closed, and then on Sunday offer my wares at inflated prices."[9] This was profitable enough to carry him through the end of his conditional prison release in December 1958.[10]

A few nights before Christmas, Ray drove to Madison, Illinois, to visit, in his words, "a long line of bars, whorehouses, and gambling joints."[11] At one of the bars, he got involved in a backroom dice game and quickly lost $200, all his savings. Ray went to his car, retrieved his pistol, and then robbed the bar and dice room. "It was a case of crook robbing crooks," he later said.[12] Ray not only got back his money, but also had the bartender empty the night's receipts into a sack, nabbing another $1,300. He then raced in his car across the Mississippi to St. Louis to escape the professional gamblers he had just robbed. Deciding to leave town until things cooled down, he drove south and briefly stopped in New Orleans to inquire at a local school about obtaining merchant seaman's papers, something that he had decided would be worthwhile. Ray thought seaman's papers were "a kind of passport to migrate to a foreign country."[13] But the New Orleans school for apprentice seamen was closed over the Christmas holidays, so he moved on, first to Brownsville, Texas, and then across the border into Matamoros, Mexico. At Leavenworth, Ray had listened as other convicts boasted of the time they spent in either Mexico or Canada when they had run from the law. This was now his first opportunity to judge how easy it was to leave the United States. In Matamoros he obtained a Mexican tourist visa and during the next several weeks he drove from Mexico City to Veracruz to Acapulco. Ray later told a fellow convict, Cecil Lillibridge, that he made some money by smuggling into the country small appliances that had a high tariff in Mexico. In the port town of Campeche, he sold the goods to a local smuggler.[14] He told another convict, James Owens, that he had a fight with a man in Mexico City and had to strike him on the head with his pistol.[15] Ray spoke about no other problems, said he made himself understood with pidgin Spanish, and enjoyed the cheap prices and readily available liquor and prostitutes. In each port, he inquired about obtaining seaman's papers, but could find nothing.[16]

"By February 1959 I was back in St. Louis, bootlegging to the Sunday winos," Ray remembered.[17] One of his main customers was a middle-aged drunk nicknamed Dirty John, who was soon picked up for robbing a local businessman at gunpoint. The car Dirty John was driving had previously belonged to Ray, prompting the St. Louis police to burst into Mom Maher's rooming house, guns drawn, looking for James. When Ray heard the police were searching for him, he again left St. Louis until the heat died down, this time heading for Canada, the other safe haven he had learned about at Leavenworth.[18] He spent nearly three months there, living under the alias O'Connor and renting a room near Ste. Catherine Street in Montreal's Latin Quarter.[19] "It was a familiar setting," said Ray. "An old town at the side of a river, full of gamblers, prostitutes, and bunco artists."[20]

Ray did not hold a regular job there, and perhaps pulled small robberies to keep himself in money. While he was in Canada, his uncle Earl, who helped steep him in crime, died of an apparent heart attack at the age of fifty-four.[21] He was found under a railroad bridge in upstate New York, but Ray did not learn of his death until he returned to the States.

By early summer, Ray was back in St. Louis.[22] He soon visited both John and Jerry in prison at Menard. Jerry remembered, "He was in a good mood then. We talked and laughed and planned a reunion."[23] It was the first time James had seen both brothers in nearly nine years.

While Ray has portrayed his only source of income during this time as the selling of wine to drunks on Sundays, he actually was involved in a several-months' spree of successful robberies. His accomplice was John Eugene Gawron, a fifty-eight-year-old heavy-drinking ex-con who had spent most of his adult life behind bars. Ray does not even mention him in his two autobiographies.

When Gawron was paroled in 1954, he had moved to Quincy and met Ray's mother. Sent back to jail in 1956 for a burglary, he escaped from Menard in 1959 and returned to Mom Maher and Ceal's St. Louis rooming house.[24] There he met James, and he later boasted that he taught Ray how to be a top-notch burglar, introducing him to tools used by professional thieves. The older Gawron thought of himself as Ray's tutor, and although he liked the way James dressed in expensive and flashy clothes, he also tried to improve his dealings with women. It was to no avail; as Gawron later recounted, Ray was so shy with women that he would often lisp or stutter when introduced to one. Gawron quickly discovered, as others had before him, that Ray preferred prostitutes in brief encounters at third-rate motels.[25] Although Gawron may not have had much success improving Ray's love life, he did help his pocketbook. During the summer of 1959, Gawron and Ray pulled approximately twelve successful burglaries.*[26]

Near the end of June, Ray, introducing himself as Jim O'Connor, met two other men who would soon be his accomplices. One was Joseph Elmer "Blackie" Austin, then fifty-seven. Austin had just been released from Illinois State Penitentiary at Menard after serving thirty-three of the last thirty-four years behind bars, most of them for the 1927 murder of a man in an armed robbery.[27] His accomplice in that robbery had been hanged for the crime. Some who knew Austin kept their distance from him because they thought he was slightly deranged (when tried for a subsequent crime, he was judged mentally incapable of assisting in his own defense).[28] But Ray took a liking to him.[†]

The second person Ray met was James Owens, a chubby, five-three, forty-one-year-old ex-convict with eight previous arrests for robbery and burglary. He had also recently been released from Menard.[29] Both men were staying at the St. Louis Rescue Mission, a remodeled pink stucco theater that served as a skid-row halfway house for winos and ex-cons. Unknown to its director, the Reverend James Wyninger, who was a former Tennessee bootlegger, the mission was a point of contact for the lowest elements in the St. Louis underworld.[‡]

Convicts just released from prison, as Austin and Owens were, are careful in sizing up other ex-cons, determining which, if any, they can trust. Both liked

---

* One of the most common misconceptions about Ray is that he was a hapless criminal. That conclusion is mistakenly drawn by casual observers who focus only on Ray's arrests. However, between those arrests, Ray sustained himself with dozens of successful crimes. His run of burglaries with Gawron was only one such period during which he stayed in crime but free of the law. Jerry Ray later estimated that James probably pulled a robbery every two to three weeks when he was out of jail. As for Gawron, who became so friendly with the Ray family that many of them referred to him as Uncle Jack, he did not have the same luck with James's relatives. In 1961, he was arrested with John Ray and Albert Pepper, Carol's husband.

† Curiously, Ray omits any mention of Austin in both of his books.

‡ Occasionally, convicts stayed incognito at the mission after local robberies. While Rev. Wyninger was unaware of the misuse of his mission, a subsequent investigation uncovered many of the excesses, and convicts were banned.

Ray. They judged him a quiet loner, a moderate drinker of bourbon highballs who enjoyed bluegrass and country music and "never pried or bragged."[30] Owens viewed Ray as a "thinker and a reader," interested in a wide range of magazines and books, especially detective novels.[31] Ray, who also read the two major St. Louis daily newspapers, seemed smart to the other two, and they later commented on how Ray was the type who "plans every angle before he makes a move."[32] They also discovered that while Ray had little interest in women ("they were something to use and forget"), he was a gun enthusiast, particularly about pistols and handguns.[33] Sometimes he went to secluded locations to target shoot, and according to Owens, he was "an excellent shot"—on one occasion when the two went shooting, Ray shot at a can and kept it bouncing by firing at it and hitting it repeatedly before it stopped rolling.*[34]

Since Ray was unemployed but nevertheless appeared "well-heeled," Owens and Austin figured that he was a professional thief. They classified him as a "pistol man" for future jobs.[35] When they saw Ray frequently in Gawron's company, they correctly assumed that Gawron was Ray's partner. But soon Austin, Owens, and Ray worked together to pull off even larger jobs.

On July 11, 1959, at a few minutes after 9:00 A.M., Austin, wearing a broad-brimmed brown hat and large sunglasses, pointed a nickel-plated revolver at the manager of a Kroger supermarket in St. Louis and demanded that he open the safe. His accomplice was a younger man, also with dark glasses, along with a white straw hat pulled low over his brow. The two thieves fled with $1,200, but not before they were caught on the store's fixed-focus camera, normally used to identify check cashers.[36] In front of the store, the two men jumped into a waiting car with a driver already inside, and the vehicle screeched away.[37] That car was later involved in a crash and abandoned, but since it was stolen it did not lead the police to the robbers. However, the pictures snapped during the crime were useful. Two witnesses and the store manager pored over mug shots at police headquarters. It did not take them long to identify Joseph Austin as the stick-up man, and soon all three also picked Ray as his accomplice.[38] The police issued arrest warrants for both men, but they managed to stay free.†

---

* Owens's observations about Ray's interest and talent with guns, reported here for the first time, are potentially important because many of Ray's staunchest defenders contend that there was no evidence Ray ever fired a gun after he left the Army in 1948.

† Ray evidently viewed his robbery of a supermarket as a move up in his criminal career. In a 1977 *Playboy* interview, when Ray was asked if he thought there was "much chance for success in liquor-store robberies," he replied, "That type of robbery is nonsense. You don't get any money, plus you get just as much time as if you rob something substantial." The interviewer then asked, "What do you consider substantial?" "Well, a supermarket," Ray replied. "That's really a corporation's money and they're probably gougin' it out of somebody else, anyway. Better to rob them than an individual."

Almost a month later, on a blisteringly hot August 7, Austin and Ray reappeared, this time at an I.G.A. food market in Alton, its safe filled in anticipation of cashing weekly paychecks for regular customers.[39] About 9:30 A.M. the two walked through the front door, Austin looking gaunt while Ray again wore a straw hat pulled low over his forehead. Ray asked for the manager, and then both pulled out pistols and demanded money. After clearing the cash registers, Ray ordered that the safe be emptied. When the employees responded slowly, he started screaming, running up and down the aisles like a "wild man," according to one witness, until he located the quivering owner.[40] He dragged the owner back toward the safe. Meanwhile, unknown to the thieves, when the robbery began the butcher had crouched behind the meat counter and quietly telephoned the police.

After they cleared the safe, the thieves ran from the store, grabbing more money from the cash registers as they left. Their total take was nearly $1,000.*[41] They jumped into a blue 1950 Buick. The store's owner, Vincent Hromadka, kept a .22-caliber automatic rifle behind the counter. He fired half a dozen shots at the fleeing getaway car, none of them hitting their target.[42] Ray, who was driving, slammed on the gas pedal, and as the car screeched from the parking lot the left front door suddenly swung open and he nearly fell out.

An armed robbery in Alton was a fairly rare event, and the small police force responded with an emergency alert. One police cruiser set off down Alby Street, along which the getaway car had sped away, and after several minutes the officers were astonished to see the car heading back into town. Suddenly the getaway car careened out of control, smashed into the backyard of a nearby house, and slammed into a tree. Both robbers leaped from the car and ran into an adjoining thicket.

The police found $342 in cash scattered inside the car, another $100 on the ground outside, two sets of license plates, and two fully loaded .38 revolvers.[43] Twelve policemen set out on foot to search the three-mile-square thicket. After a while, one of them, exhausted from the search, returned and sat in his patrol car. Meanwhile, a crowd had gathered to watch. An older man walked slowly from the direction of the woods and mingled with the crowd. The policeman thought something about him did not seem right. It turned out to be Joseph Austin. There was no sign of his accomplice.

When the police took Austin to the station, he quickly confessed to the crime. Three witnesses picked him from a lineup. But Austin initially refused to give up his accomplice, saying only that his name was Jack Sims. The three wit-

---

* Jerry Ray later told author George McMillan that one of the things he most admired about James was that "he's got steel nerves—he just walks in like its an every day thing, get the money, and walks out."

nesses could not make a positive identification of Austin's accomplice because
of the sunglasses and hat he wore during the robbery. Although the Edwardsville grand jury would indict Austin and Ray for the robbery that October, neither man ever stood trial. Austin was returned to Menard on a parole
violation and became sick with tuberculosis. Ray melted into St. Louis's sleazy
riverfront district. Having had his largest payday ever for the I.G.A. robbery, he
felt more confident about his advancement to armed robbery. He did not know
that he had left $15,000 behind in another of the store's safes.

Without Austin as an accomplice, Ray now turned to James Owens. On October 9, the two went on an all-night partying binge.[44] The following morning,
"at the tail-end of a drunk," according to Owens, they discovered they were
broke. That is when they decided to rob a nearby Kroger supermarket they had
cased the previous day.[45] Ray produced two revolvers.[46]

Around 8:45 A.M. on October 10, Ray and Owens entered the Kroger store
in St. Louis, their guns drawn. Owens stayed at the front of the store as a look-
out. Ray, again wearing dark glasses and a large hat, walked directly to the
manager's office and demanded the money in the safe.[47] The manager told Ray
that he could not open it without a second key and then paged someone whom
he knew was too busy to come to the office. After waiting several minutes, Ray
became nervous and ran to the front of the store, and he and Owens emptied
the cash register of $120.[48] They then sprinted to a 1950 black Ford they had
stolen earlier that morning.[49] This time, $18,000 was left in the safe.

As the two sped away, the Kroger manager ran outside and jotted down the
license number.[50] A customer, Robert Culis, jumped into his own car to follow
the two robbers. He stayed a block behind and watched as the Ford stopped next
to a new green-and-white Plymouth and one of the thieves stepped out and
drove off in the second car. He jotted down the license number of the second car
and returned to Kroger, where that information was relayed to the police.[51]

Fifteen minutes later, two policemen noticed the Plymouth parked in front
of a cheap rooming house at 2023 Park. They called for backup, and two detectives arrived almost at the moment when James Owens left and started to
enter the Plymouth. He was immediately arrested and placed in one of the patrol cars.[52] The uniformed police covered the rooming house's front and rear
exits, and the detectives went to the second floor. Suddenly Ray came out of the
bathroom. One of the detectives identified himself and told Ray to stop. Instead,
Ray ran to the rear sun porch. He stopped in his tracks when he saw another
policeman in the backyard. Ray cursed, turned, and ran back inside, almost directly into the arms of Detective Harry Conners. Ray grabbed Conners and
gave him a bear hug as if he were trying to squeeze the air out of him. Conners
broke the hold and fired a shot over Ray's head. Ray charged him again, and
this time Conners smashed him over the head with the butt of his gun. Dazed,

Ray still managed to stumble into an adjoining room. Conners followed and fired another shot, which finally caused Ray to stop.[53]

"I guess you want me for that Kroger store stickup?" Ray asked him.[54]

When the police searched Ray they found $81.63, which he told them was his share of the loot. In his room they discovered two pistols hidden under the dresser, one a nickel-plated .38-caliber revolver and the other a Belgian 7.65-caliber automatic. Both were fully loaded.[55] The police also found a brown felt hat and green jacket, similar to those the thief had used in the Kroger robbery.

Ray was taken to City Hospital, where his head wound was stitched closed, a scene reminiscent of the followup to his taxi fiasco in Chicago seven years earlier. From there he was taken to police headquarters, where he told them that he was a baker and a Catholic and had finished two years of high school, and that his father was dead.[56] But when he was quizzed about the robbery, he refused to give any statement and denied making an earlier admission to the arresting officers.[57] Owens, however, did confess. He said that he had planned the robbery with Ray; that Ray had provided him with a pistol; that they had cased the supermarket before the robbery, and that he and Ray had split the money at the rooming house. Owens then picked Ray at the station as his accomplice.[58] Later, Ray was positively identified by six witnesses from the Kroger robbery.[59] The police also brought in two employees from the I.G.A. food market that Ray had robbed in August. Both identified him as one of the robbers.[60] According to a later prison commitment report on the robbery, "the police officers reported he sat there with a silly grin on his face and said, 'I cannot deny it and I won't admit it.'"[61] Later, he finally signed a statement acknowledging his role in the Kroger robbery.[62]

Ray and Owens were charged with first-degree robbery with a deadly weapon of the Kroger store. Ray was also charged with resisting arrest, and his bail was set at $10,000 and his trial scheduled for December 15.* On that day, Earl Riley, an elderly deputy sheriff, showed up to escort Ray through an underground tunnel that connected the city jail with the courthouse. Ray was handcuffed for the short walk. When they arrived at the courthouse, Riley led Ray to a cell behind the courtroom. He had unlocked one of the handcuffs when Ray suddenly grabbed Riley, shoved him violently into a row of benches, and then kicked him in the gut before running from the cell and jumping into the open elevator. Before the doors closed, Riley recovered and ran over to grab the door. Ray tried in vain to push him away. By this time, an armed guard

---

* While he was in jail, he was treated by a prison physician, Dr. Dowd, for an ailment. There are no records of the treatment, but the jail's warden, William Borger, later said it was for treatment of a venereal disease. Ray denied this and instead insisted he had a kidney infection.

down the hallway saw the commotion and ran over with his gun drawn. Ray stopped, turned to the wall, and covered his face with his hands. Ray's court appearance was canceled that morning and several guards returned him to his cell.[63]

Having failed in his impetuous escape attempt, Ray next demanded a jury trial and directed the strategy of his case, even insisting that he take the stand, although that meant the prosecutor could then enter Ray's criminal past into the record. As Ray's crimes had become more ambitious, his sense of his own ability to defend himself grew proportionately. His court-appointed lawyer, Richard Schreiber, later said, "He pretty well ran his own trial. He came on hard, like a jailhouse lawyer. He was very persistent."[64]

The prosecution's case seemed strong, with six witnesses, the physical evidence found at the rooming house, and most important, Owen's and Ray's signed confessions. In his defense, Ray presented a single witness who claimed, in contradiction to one of the policemen, that when Ray ran out of the bathroom the door had been closed, not open. No one understood what that was supposed to signify.

When Ray took the stand he denied everything, repudiating his signed statement. He now said he had had nothing to do with the robbery, that the evidence seized at the rooming house was not his, and that the police had violated his constitutional rights. He even stunned his attorney by voluntarily denying that he had offered a $200 bribe to one of the detectives to perjure himself by claiming he had not found two pistols in Ray's room. Until Ray mentioned this issue of possible witness tampering, the jury had never heard of it. "He didn't make a lot of sense," recalled Schreiber. "He rambled and got kind of wild."[65]

The jury took twenty minutes to find Ray guilty as charged. His strategy of running his own trial had backfired. Owens, who pleaded guilty to the robbery charge, was sentenced to seven years.[66] Ray drew twenty years in the state penitentiary.

Three months later, on St. Patrick's Day, 1960, James Earl Ray was ready to be transferred. He was a four-time loser who had just turned thirty-two a week earlier. His brothers John and Jerry were only a few weeks away from being released from Menard. But he would miss them. Ray was transferred, in a heavily guarded railcar with forty other prisoners, to his new home, the Missouri State Penitentiary, one of the toughest prisons in the United States.

17

"A Natural Hustler"

Missouri State Penitentiary, opened in 1836, was the only prison in Missouri for nearly one hundred years. A collection of Gothic-inspired limestone buildings perched on a bluff overlooking the Missouri River at Jefferson City, surrounded by massive walls and sixteen gun turrets, it was once dubbed "square foot for square foot the bloodiest 47 acres in America."[1] Prisoners called the imposing structure, which housed the state's only active gas chamber, either Jeff City or MSP.[2] When Ray arrived in the spring of 1960, it had over 2,000 prisoners, nearly double the number for which it was built.[3] It also had a reputation among many convicts as one of the worst places to serve time. A riot in 1954 had left five inmates dead, seven buildings burned completely, and a score of guards injured. A former Marine colonel, James D. Carter, who was brought in to run the prison after the riots, found the complex so unmanageable that he later told the Missouri legislature it was the "roughest damn prison in the country" and that his recommendation for improvement was simply to abandon it.[4]

Following the 1954 riots, violence among prisoners worsened each year for a decade.[5] Once, in 1963, three inmates were murdered within twenty-four hours, prompting an investigation by the Missouri Legislative Committee on Prisons. Its study covered 1961–63—near the beginning of Ray's term there—and concluded that the prison was "a medieval twilight zone."[6] The study documented nearly 500 acts of violence during the two years it dealt with, including 145 stabbings, 134 assaults with clubs or bats, and even 11 cases of attacks with acid or lye.[7] Seven inmates died; others lost eyes or limbs or sustained other permanent injuries.[8] The psychiatric ward was run by a man who had been booted from the Army for emotional instability. When committee members visited the hospital, they saw horrific conditions, ranging from "thousand of bugs scampering about" to medical experiments conducted on prisoners in return for sixty days "good time" off their sentences.[9] Near the end of the legislative investigation, the warden, E. V. Nash, had killed himself with a pistol while a Christmas party was in full swing just outside his office.

An official prison history summarizes some of the problems that exacerbated the violence: "gambling; debts; sexual affairs; grudges; decline in the age of the prisoners; an atrocious physical plant that made it almost impossible to control the population; low morale among guards who were unarmed in a giant prison where one inmate testified, 'Every Tom, Dick and Harry has got a knife.' "[10] The legislative investigation discovered that guards—largely composed of farmers, bellhops, taxi drivers, and clerks who were "underpaid, undertrained, [and] uncertain of advancement"—mostly moonlighted to earn an adequate living.[11]

It is not surprising that in this decaying atmosphere the prisoners largely ran Jeff City. Inmates were forced to pay other inmates for medical treatment (Ray paid $40 for some dental work). Some acted as "switchmen" and "lever men" with the right to open cells and allow inmates to transfer from one cell to another, usually for sex. For a price, prisoners could even "marry." Guards often bought their own safety with favors and gifts.*

An elite group of inmates ran the prison when Ray arrived. Jeff City was essentially segregated into two prisons: seven and eight blacks were crammed into cells designed for three in the so-called A Hall.[12] The dining halls were segregated and blacks were not allowed into the television room.[†13] The white

---

*   Much has been written about the conditions at Jeff City during the 1960s, including the time Ray was incarcerated. To ensure those reports were accurate and not exaggerated, the author submitted one of the most damning descriptions, that presented by George McMillan in his book *The Making of an Assassin*, to Tim Kniest, the current public information officer for the Missouri Department of Corrections. Instead of taking issue with the brutal portrayal of Jeff City, Kniest, who spoke with those in the department who had worked there during the 1960s, confirmed the accuracy of the harsh portrait.

†   In June 1964, prison authorities tried to integrate the prison. Within a few days, a group of blacks was attacked by a dozen white inmates. One black convict was stabbed to death and three seriously injured. Jerry Ray initially boasted to author George McMillan that James was one of the attackers. But when confronted with prison records that showed that James was assigned to a different section of the prison when the attack happened, Jerry admitted he was wrong. However, several prisoners later told the FBI that Ray was "associated" with, or knew, the attackers.

prison was run by an inmate, Jimmy Bradley, who lived in a cell with uphol-stered furniture, draperies, and a TV set. The warden had his picture taken with Bradley, his arm draped around the convict's shoulders.[14] Ray later wrote that when he first entered the prison, "immediately I saw that Jeff City had a live-and-let-live attitude. In the rec area, you could get into a poker game or buy and rent magazines or books of any kind."[15]

Ray was held in isolation his first thirty days while prison officials decided where to place him. They finally assigned him to K Hall and a job in the dry-cleaning plant.[16] He had been there only nine months when he received word that his mother had died at a city hospital in St. Louis from complications of cirrhosis of the liver—the same ailment that would afflict Ray some twenty-six years later. She was fifty-one years old. Except for James, the entire Ray family had gathered at Ceal's bedside the night she died. In August 1961, within months of Ceal's death, Speedy remarried (it lasted two years, until his new wife sued successfully for divorce on the grounds that he was an alcoholic).[17] Ray never discussed his family with his fellow inmates. None of them learned of his mother's death.*

During his early months in prison, Ray focused on how to escape. "My job in the dry cleaning plant offered a reasonable opportunity for such an under-taking," he later said. "That and my 20-year sentence were all the encourage-ment I needed to plan an escape."†[18]

Ray was one of only seven inmates in the dry-cleaning plant. A head count was done nightly at 8:00 P.M. To Ray, that meant that during the fall and win-ter hours he had "about two hours of weak light in which to pull off an escape before I'd be missed."[19] One evening in November 1961, when the small crew left work at six o'clock, Ray hid behind boxes in the rear of the workroom.[20] He then fashioned a makeshift ladder from the oak shelves on which supplies were kept. Once he had assembled a ladder almost twelve feet long, he dragged it be-

---

* In his two published books, Ray refers a few times to his parents, but never mentions his mother by name, and does not even mention her death.

† Ray, who makes numerous mistakes in recounting his past, wrote in *Who Killed Mar-tin Luther King?* that he tried his first escape after serving seven months at the prison. Actually, he did not make his first attempt until eighteen months had passed. As Ray noted, not every prisoner thinks of escaping. "For a lot of prisoners, the idea of trying to escape is frightening, and they want nothing to do with it. For others, the outside wall is a challenge they can't resist. It isn't a matter of choice or heroism or bravery—they don't have a choice. They have to try." Ray's willingness to try to escape is rare among prisoners. In one study by a penologist, inmates ranked escape attempts as the second-worst infraction of more than twenty listed, even outranking forcible sodomy. Even at Jeff City, there were only six to eight attempts a year, most by inmates with very long sentences who had nothing to lose if caught.

hind him "toward the clothing shop 50 feet away."[21] The guard who was supposed to be watching the pathway did not see him. Once at the clothing plant,
Ray pulled the ladder along a narrow passage that put him within twenty feet
of the wall. When he scurried to the wall, the ladder in tow, another watchtower guard failed to spot him. Ray placed the ladder against the fourteen-foot
wall and began climbing. He was halfway to the top when the ladder collapsed
and he slammed into the ground. Astonishingly, none of the watchtower
guards heard the commotion.[22] Ray quietly gathered the broken pieces and
hurriedly returned to the cleaning plant to implement a backup plan. Using
pipe from the metal racks on which the prison's dry cleaning was hung, he
quickly screwed together another makeshift ladder.[23] He returned—again unseen—to the same section of wall that he had tried to scale fifteen minutes earlier. "This time I made it two-thirds of the way to the top before my ladder gave
way," Ray remembered. "I landed in a heap, and a section of pipe crashed onto
my head."[24] Ray thought the tower guard did not notice him, but the ruckus finally attracted attention. When he returned to the cleaning plant, guards arrested him.

Ray's bungled attempt did not increase his prison sentence, but he did lose
his "good time" and he was put into long-term segregation, a harsh section on
the upper floor of E Hall.[25] There, with only a straw-filled mattress and a blanket, he spent six months. The few windows were so loose that the winter cold
kept many prisoners pinned under their mattress and blanket. According to
Ray, his neighboring cells were filled with "head cases, who would harass the
guards, provoking them into shooting tear gas into the offending parties'
cells."[26] The gas would spread throughout the cell block, forcing Ray to lie on
the floor and try to suck in fresh air from the cracks next to the cell's plumbing.

When he was returned to the general prison population in May 1962, the
first thing he noticed was that "a large spotlight atop the clothing plant was
aimed at the stretch of wall I'd tried to scale."[27] He was assigned to the "spud
room," peeling potatoes. That area was considered one of the worst in the
prison, staffed usually by sex offenders—"not exactly my cup of tea," said
Ray.[28] So he refused to work, which prompted another ten days in solitary confinement, with only a single meal daily. This time, upon his release, Ray better
understood how Jeff City worked—he slipped $10 to one of the convict clerks,
who allowed him to pick his own job.[29] He selected the bakery, where he remained for the next three years.

Ray had decided to adapt to prison life at Jeff City. He has described his time
there as innocuous and without incident, similar to his stretch at Leavenworth. But there is a jumble of conflicting statements from fellow prisoners
about how Ray spent those years, and the truth of Ray's assertions is key to understanding what kind of person he was.[30]

The few inmates who knew him from Leavenworth found Ray bitter at Jeff City, complaining he had been framed on his robbery charge and that the arresting police had concocted evidence against him.[31] But to others, who had never met him before, James earned the same reputation he had at his earlier prisons—as a quiet man who enjoyed country-and-western music and liked being alone. He made no real friends.[32] "Anyone who says they knew Jim Ray real well are liars," the Jeff City barber later said.[33] Ray continued to be interested in baseball, and was a reader, devouring the James Bond series and going through a broad range of periodicals from newspapers to *Time* and *Argosy* to the *National Enquirer.*[34] He also read travel books.[35]

His time at Jeff City, however, was anything but uneventful. Did Ray apparently decide that if he was going to do time in a place where prisoners ran a host of illegal rackets, he should profit from them? Since he had dealt successfully in the black market when in the Army, and had learned from his uncle Earl how to fence stolen goods, wasn't he a natural to become one of the prison's "merchants," who smuggled contraband—such as drugs, alcohol, cigarettes, pornography, and so on—into the prison?*

"Personally, I think a man is born to be a hustler," said Jerry Ray, "like he's born to be a baseball player. Not everybody's got it in them to be a hustler. I haven't. . . . A lazy person can't be a hustler. There would be ten or twelve of them in Jeff City, but most of them got too well known, had to go out of business at one time or another. Like, many of those hustlers live good and show off. . . . Then the heat gets on you, and the guards don't want to fool with you. But Jimmy was so quiet. Mostly, there'd be a shakedown only if somebody was under suspicion, and Jimmy didn't do anything to make them suspicious of him. He just wanted to make money, didn't put on no show. He was a natural hustler."[36]

James, according to Jerry, started trading such commissary goods as steaks, candies, and soups from the bakery and kitchen where he worked.[37] By 1963, he had graduated to dabbling in the prison's most profitable trade: drugs. To deal in dope, a merchant had to have the aid of a guard, who served both as a

---

* After King's assassination, Missouri corrections commissioner Fred Wilkinson insisted that Ray was "just a nothing here. If James Earl Ray had amounted to a hill of beans here, I would have had a card on him in this pack of Big Shots and Bad Actors. And Ray isn't in here." However, Wilkinson's sweeping statement that Ray was a "nothing" at Jeff City because he was not in the three-by-five-inch index card file of troublemakers is misleading, since that file included only prisoners who were identified as violent troublemakers, usually those involved in fights or assaults. Ray certainly did not fall into that category. The only disciplinary mark against him at Jeff City was for a 1965 violation for carrying contraband—five packs of cigarettes, one jar of Maxwell House instant coffee, one pack of razor blades, and one can of Campbell's soup—into the prison hospital.

local protector and as a conduit to send money out of the prison.[38] "That's the key to being a merchant," said Jerry, "the guard's trust. . . . You have to be close-mouthed. Jimmy talked to a lot of people but he didn't have no friends. They could shake him down and nobody could break him. Nobody could make Jimmy talk."[39] Even James himself later said that the reason Jeff City officials could not control the internal drug traffic was "because the guards, like other prison officials, didn't share [any] enthusiasm. Prison administrators seem to appreciate the way drugs serve to divert prisoners from their more dangerous propensities."[40]

When Ray did deal in drugs, it evidently was amphetamines. According to Jerry, a guard brought some of the dope to James, who then sold it to prisoners. Ray also bought his own supply from other inmates. Then he gave cash to the guard, who took his share before sending it by mail, usually to Jerry Ray and sometimes to John.[41] When Jerry received the money, he wrote "OK" on a piece of paper and mailed it back to the guard.[42] Jerry considered that money as "Jimmy's account" and was supposed to hold it for his brother.*

"He was a peddler at Jeff City, all right," said Raymond Curtis, a fellow inmate who had served time with Ray at two previous jails including Leavenworth.[43] Curtis confirmed Jerry's account of Ray's prison dealing, saying that it started with stolen goods from the kitchen—one dollar a dozen for eggs to several dollars for steaks, butter, even gallons of homemade beer or "potato water"—and graduated to drugs. Curtis, who pinpointed Ray's main source of contraband as another inmate in the commissary, admitted that he sometimes hid Ray's stash of pills when there was a prison shakedown.[44] "A fella like Ray would end up paying about seven hundred fifty dollars a pound [for amphetamines]. With pills you make more. You buy a thousand for fifty cents apiece, and sell them for a dollar apiece."[45] Also, Curtis said Ray was one of only a handful of dealers who sold small baggies containing a mixture of powdered sugar and speed, at prices ranging from $50 to $75 per bag, depending on the demand.[46]

Others confirmed Curtis's account. Cecil Lillibridge, one of Ray's cellmates, said that Ray sold amphetamines during his entire term at Jeff City.[47] James Owens, who robbed the Kroger supermarket with Ray in 1959, was also jailed at the prison. He became aware that Ray was dealing speed when he saw other prisoners pay Ray for their purchases.[48] Inmates Paul Lail and Kenneth Lee Wade confirmed not only that Ray peddled dope but also that he was directly

---

* Jerry said his sister Carol had initially set up an account under her printing business that was supposed to handle the money James sent out of Jeff City, but there was never more than a few hundred dollars in it, and the account did not work as well as the letter system from the guard, so the Rays abandoned that idea. After that account was closed, Jerry claims that Carol was not involved in any of James's prison money.

connected to the prison's main suppliers.[49] Richard Menard, who knew Ray for four years at Jeff City, said Ray told him he had a brother in St. Louis who helped supply his drugs (both John and Jerry lived near St. Louis for different periods of Ray's imprisonment).[50] Ray averaged $200 monthly from his dope sales, estimated Menard, although depending on the supply, there might be no sales in some months and $1,000 in business in others.[51] Even John Ray, who told the FBI that his brother first started using drugs while in the Army, admitted that when James finally escaped from Jeff City in 1967, he had money stashed away from selling amphetamines.[52]

Besides drugs, Ray also dealt in other contraband. Billy Miles, who worked in the bakery with Ray, did not know about his drug dealing, but did operate a small prison bookmaking operation with him.[53] William Turner, the first black guard to have general jurisdiction over the Jeff City recreation yard, also did not know about Ray's drug trade, but knew he dealt in cigarettes for cash and sometimes loaned books and "girlie magazines" for money.*[54]

Ray's contraband business must have been profitable. Author George McMillan, and Phil Canale, the chief Memphis prosecutor on the King assassination, later estimated that Ray smuggled nearly $7,000 out of prison in the five years he was a merchant.[55] When asked in a 1977 interview if he had made "a substantial amount of money from dope peddling in prison," Ray did not directly deny his involvement, but he downplayed it—"I've never been any type of *big* operator in drugs in Missouri. [emphasis added]"[56]

While the actual amount is not verifiable, it may not be as much as speculated.[†] The reason is that Ray evidently broke the cardinal rule of drug dealers—he began using the drugs he sold. He partially denies it: "I've never used any kind of, what you call hard narcotics. That's cocaine, heroin. Of course, everybody in the penitentiary, at one time or another, take tranquilizers, something of that nature."[57] However, it was impossible to keep such a secret in the close prison confines.

Jimmy Carpenter, who was close to Ray at Jeff City, said that Ray was a drug user and that he often came to Carpenter's cell and offered him dope.[58] Inmates

---

* Some inmates claim that Ray resorted to violence to protect his business. According to Julius Block, another inmate, Ray stabbed a competitor while a cohort held the victim. Ray did not kill him, and prison officials never learned that Ray was the perpetrator. Another prisoner said Ray arranged for two men to beat a convict who had failed to pay for amphetamines.

† If Ray was making huge profits, it is unlikely that his family would have continued sending him money orders while he was in prison. Jeff City officials maintained a list. Ray received thirty-five, most from Jerry and John Ray, totaling $526.25. Those helped supplement his official $2.00 per month salary for his food-services job. He also sent several hundred dollars out of prison in money orders, most of it—$260—to Jerry.

Walter Nolan and Harry Sero also knew Ray was an amphetamine abuser, and Frank Guinan said he was addicted to "bennies."[59] Jimmy Bradley, who lived near Ray in K Hall, was one of several inmates who claimed Ray mainlined amphetamines, sometimes with two to three shots daily, but that he had difficulty because of his small veins.[60] Orlan Eugene Rose, who knew Ray at both Leavenworth and Jeff City, recalled that Ray shot amphetamines whenever he could get them, paying between two and five dollars a shot.[61] The chief cook, Lewis Raymond Dowda, worked with Ray in the culinary section. He remembered that Ray not only sold dope, but also had a $35- to $40-a-week habit.[62] Ray kept his user's kit, a nose dropper with a needle with which he could shoot an amphetamine solution, in his cell.[63] Inmates noticed that Ray was often nervous and slept little, and his weight fluctuated frequently and rapidly within a ten- to fifteen-pound range, further evidence of amphetamine use.*[64]

Ray often complained of headaches and stomach problems, and he became a regular at the infirmary.[65] Even in his own book *Tennessee Waltz*, Ray observed that when a prisoner did too much speed, he would be taken to the fifth floor of the prison hospital and the "doctor would hold his patient there three or four days, or until he dried out, then return him to the prison population."[66] James Richardson, who was on death row in Jeff City, worked in the hospital. He recalled that Ray was not only one of the "cowboys" involved with petty thievery and gangsterism, but also used whatever type of medication he could obtain.[67]

Some prisoners thought he developed into a hypochondriac, as he started complaining of symptoms, imagined or real, and reading medical literature in the prison library.[68] Cecil Lillibridge said Ray took six to seven pills daily, imagining that he had a "cranial depression" and a "rapid palpitation of the heart."[69] Carl Craig also recalled that Ray always complained about stomach trouble, so much so that he stopped smoking.[70] He used a fellow inmate's watch with a second hand to time his pulse. Anxious that he might one day develop arthritis, Ray even got pills from an inmate to treat the disease.[71] He told another prisoner that he lifted weights to combat a heart problem he imagined he had.[72] Insomnia led him to fret about "serious nervous troubles such as severe depression or even suicidal tendencies."[73] Jerry admitted that by his last year in prison, James complained frequently in his letters "about more and more headaches."[74] In mid-1965, Ray wrote to his local congressman pleading

---

*   When Ray was eventually arrested in June 1968 at Heathrow, the police found a hypodermic syringe in the room he had last occupied in London. They were not certain if it belonged to him or a previous boarder. However, prior to his extradition back to the United States, the authorities were so concerned about the quick evidence they discovered from former inmates about Ray's amphetamine abuse that they feared he had used an alcohol method to allow an amphetamine solution to soak into his clothing, and that he might be able to later retrieve it. As a precaution, Ray was issued a new suit of clothing.

"that the state legislature appropriate funds to pay the Doctors." He had, he said, "contacted some kind of illness which has caused me to be admitted to the hospital three times."[75] Ray complained that he had not yet seen a doctor despite several requests for examinations, and also claimed that Jerry had written to one of the prison doctors and offered to pay for the exam.[76]

Amphetamine abuse could produce many of the physical symptoms of which Ray complained, and might also induce a level of paranoia and fear that might exacerbate any tendency toward hypochondria.

Besides Ray's dope dealing and abuse, the last contentious issue about his years at Jeff City is whether or not he was an avowed bigot.[77] "There are no nigger lovers in prison," Jerry Ray once defiantly said.[78] James evidently agreed. John Ray said that James was "crazy about niggers"—and not in a good way.*[79] When a black guard, William Turner, was placed in his cell block, Ray told another inmate "that's one Nigger that should be dead."[80] James Brown, a fellow inmate who knew Ray for two years, recalled that after John Kennedy was shot, Ray said, "That is one nigger-loving S.O.B. that got shot."[81] Glen Buckley remembered that Ray "hated Negroes."[82] Inmate Harry Sero said Ray had a great dislike for blacks.[83] Ray once got into a fight with a black inmate after a group of blacks had refused to work when a guard called them "boys."[84] When Jeff City's intramural sports were finally integrated, Ray refused to attend since blacks comprised a majority on the teams.[85] He often talked of moving to other countries when he got out of prison, and Australia was high on the list because Ray thought there were no blacks there.[86] James's brother John later told the FBI that during his prison visits, James spoke highly of the government of Rhodesia, then one of two segregationist African countries.[87]

Cecil Lillibridge said that although Ray never expressed any particular hatred toward Martin Luther King—he simply disliked blacks in general. However, Lillibridge, who described Ray as a reader of weekly newsmagazines whose main ambition was to make a "score of $20,000 to $30,000 and hide out in Mexico," overheard Ray refer to King as "Martin Luther Coon" and witnessed his agitation about the publicity received by King, H. Rap Brown, and Stokely Carmichael.[88] Sometimes Ray even talked to Lillibridge about whether a splinter group might offer money for the murder of Brown or Carmichael, but he never mentioned King in that way.[89]

Harry Sero actually put the idea of killing King for money to Ray—he once speculated, in front of Ray and other inmates, that if King attempted economic boycotts, it would be worth a lot for businessmen to have him killed.[90] Others recalled that Ray himself sometimes talked about the possibility of killing King

---

* William Bradford Huie said John told him that in 1969, but before the House Select Committee in 1978 John claimed, "I don't recall making that statement."

for money.* Lewis Dowda, who worked with Ray, was an avowed racist who said that Ray "definitely hated Negroes." Dowda also claimed that Ray had boasted that he would kill King if the price were right.[91] Fellow inmate James Brown claimed that Ray cursed and became considerably aggravated whenever he read newspaper articles about King and his civil rights work. Ray boasted to Brown that when he got out of Jeff City, he could get $10,000 to kill King.[92] Ray made the boast, according to Brown, on several occasions to other prisoners, including Johnny Valenti, an inmate with mob connections. Valenti denied even knowing Ray after the assassination.[93]

Thomas Britton knew Ray from his cell block and recalled him as "money crazy" and a "day dreamer" who was usually "solemn faced . . . never laughed or enjoyed a good story."[94] Ray once told him "there are more ways of making money than robbing banks."[95] When Britton asked what he meant, Ray said there was a "businessman's association" that was offering up to $100,000 for King to be killed. "King is five years past due," Ray told Britton. When Britton asked Ray what the businessman's group was, Ray said, "I don't know but I will find out."[†96]

---

* That would not have surprised Jerry Ray. When he first learned that his brother might be involved in the assassination, his reaction was, "I knew there had to be a lot of money involved in it before he would get involved in anything like that" (HSCA Rpt. p. 432).

† In addition to the above inmates who heard Ray make threats against King, another convict, Ray Curtis, said that Ray told him as early as 1963 that there was a bounty on King and that he intended to collect it. Except for Sero and Curtis, none of the above inmates knew one another, and they gave their statements independently to the FBI within days of one another. There are questions, however, about Curtis's version, and that is why he is omitted from the main body of the text. After King's assassination, Curtis sold a story to *Jet* magazine in which he said the Ku Klux Klan had offered a $100,000 bounty on King. Moreover, according to Curtis, Ray was agitated after Oswald killed JFK, and often critiqued that assassination while also talking about killing King himself. Curtis said that whenever King appeared on the television at Jeff City, Ray got very agitated and said, "Somebody's gotta get him." Mark Lane, the conspiracy buff and lawyer who represented Ray in the 1970s, claimed to have unmasked Curtis as a liar when the Jeff City warden told him there were no television sets in the cell blocks until 1970, three years after Ray escaped. However, Ray himself has confirmed that there were TVs at Jeff City while he was there, and that he primarily watched sports and the news. While the television issue does not discredit Curtis, the author discovered that he substantially contradicted himself in interviews with the FBI as early as 1968, as well as with House Select Committee investigators in 1977. He refused to give sworn testimony to either. It is also troubling that he tried to profit from his information. Therefore, while Curtis's statements regarding Ray's desire to kill King are discounted, elsewhere in this chapter his observations regarding Ray and possible drug dealing while at Jeff City are cited. Curtis did know Ray for an extended time, and he was not only an admitted drug dealer himself but also an avid user while at Jeff City. As opposed to his statements about Ray and King, his observations regarding Ray and his role with drugs are consistent and confirmed by other inmates.

It is surprising that the normally close-mouthed Ray would openly threaten King if he thought that one day he might undertake such an assignment. He may not, however, have been serious about the threats. His braggadocio could have resulted from an amphetamine binge, as the drug tends to produce aggressive and boisterous behavior. Also, the boasts might have been merely the venting of white anger. Fearful whites like Ray unleashed their frustration over social progress and the sweep of black power on King, who had become the embodiment of the civil rights movement. While Ray's threats may not have been unusual in prison, or even serious on his part, there is the more daunting question of whether that idle chatter brought him to the attention of some group that wanted the civil rights leader dead.*

Prison officials denied the existence of a Ku Klux Klan chapter, but there was a loosely organized alliance of white supremacists. A Jeff City equivalent had a standing offer for King's death.[97] A few of these prisoners wore white sheets over their heads and killed a black inmate when the warden tried to integrate in 1964.[98] A $100,000 offer from the White Knights of the Mississippi Ku Klux Klan had evidently filtered into the prison system.[99] A few inmates claimed to know of a Cooley's Organization, supposedly a Jeff City protection and enforcement group that had put forth a King bounty of up to $100,000.[100]

In its 1976–79 investigation into the John Kennedy and Martin Luther King murders, the House Select Committee on Assassinations discovered yet another group that may have wanted King dead and may have crossed paths with Ray at Jeff City. In late 1966 or early 1967, Russell G. Byers, a low-level St. Louis hoodlum, was supposedly offered money to kill King.[†101] According to Byers, who

---

* In this section, the author focuses only on groups or individuals that wanted King dead about whom Ray may have heard. For instance, when the author reviewed the FBI's files on Martin Luther King, there were literally dozens of threats on King's life, and standing bounties usually between $10,000 and $50,000, for most of the 1960s. Such right-wing groups as the Minutemen, the National Socialist White People's Party, the American Nazi Party, various branches of the KKK, segregationist parties, and the like all seemed to target King at one point or another. The threats—such as a bomb scare for King's February 1968 visit to Miami—kept coming into the FBI even in the weeks preceding King's death in Memphis. As a result of the volume of threats, the Bureau has been justifiably criticized for not informing the King staff of the dangers. The difficulty, however, for historians is in figuring out not who wanted King dead—that list is extensive—but rather who wanted him dead *and* had some contact with Ray.

† Byers had unwittingly told this to an informant in 1973, and the informant had passed it along to the FBI. The information was ignored until years later during an FBI file review in an unrelated investigation. It was brought to the HSCA's attention in March 1978. The two special agents who had handled the informant were then interviewed by the FBI and admitted they had failed to follow up on the lead when it came to their attention and therefore the trail of evidence had cooled.

was granted immunity by the Select Committee, he was approached by John Kauffmann, a local real estate and motel developer with some underworld connections, and asked if he wanted to earn up to $50,000.[102] When Byers showed interest, Kauffmann drove with him to the home of John Sutherland, a wealthy lawyer and segregationist who lived in nearby Imperial, Missouri. According to Byers, the three men met in Sutherland's study. The room was filled with Confederate memorabilia, and Sutherland himself was wearing a Confederate colonel's hat.[103] After a brief conversation, Sutherland offered Byers $50,000 to kill, or arrange to kill, Martin Luther King. Sutherland told Byers the money was coming from a wealthy, secret Southern organization he would not name.[104] Byers was not interested and when he left the house with Kauffmann, he turned down the offer.[105]

By the time Byers testified before the Select Committee, both Kauffmann and Sutherland were dead. Yet, in an extensive effort to investigate the story, the committee interviewed dozens of associates of the three men, and also reviewed local, state, and federal files about them. Although the deaths of the principals made the investigation a difficult one, the committee discovered corroborating evidence, including two attorneys that confirmed Byers had told them about Sutherland's offer.[106] The committee finally concluded, "The Byers allegation was essentially truthful."[107]

Did Ray learn of Sutherland's $50,000 offer, or could Ray's idle threats against King have reached Sutherland?

Kauffmann, the go-between for Sutherland and a potential assassin, was convicted of the manufacture and sale of amphetamines—more than one million pills to undercover agents—in 1967.[108] Testimony at his narcotics trial revealed that one of Kauffmann's accomplices smuggled some of the amphetamine supply into Jeff City, where Ray was dealing in and using the very same drug.[109]

Inside the prison was John Paul Spica, Byers's brother-in-law, who was incarcerated there from 1963 to 1973 for a contract murder. During part of his sentence, he was in the same cell block as Ray.[110] Byers visited Spica regularly at Jeff City.[111] Spica worked in the hospital for the prison doctor, Hugh Maxey. It was there that Ray, according to other inmates, kept checking himself in to try and get all types of drugs.[112] Ray also pushed a food cart in the hospital in late 1966 and early 1967, the same time the Sutherland offer was made.[113] "One of the prisoners I got to know while working in the hospital was a St. Louis guy named John Paul Spica," Ray later wrote, "who was doing life for conspiracy to commit murder. He was said to have heavy mob connections."[114]

In addition to Spica, Dr. Maxey was a close friend of John Kauffmann's.[115] Maxey supplied inmates, under a work release program, to Kauffmann, and there were even allegations—unproven by the Select Committee investigation—

that Maxey had been involved with Kauffmann in the distribution of ampheta-mines at Jeff City.[116] Prison records reveal that Maxey had contact with Ray.[117] Maxey, if he was informed of the standing bounty by Kauffmann, did not neces-sarily have to pass the information directly to Ray, but merely placing it into the prison population at Jeff City would have been enough to circulate it.*

Not surprisingly, all of the people who might have informed Ray of the King bounty, or informed Sutherland of Ray's possible interest in the job, denied any complicity. When interviewed by the Select Committee, Dr. Maxey, then in his eighties and of failing health, claimed he never knew about the bounty on King, much less discussed it with Ray.[118] As for John Paul Spica, he said he had never learned of any King bounty before the assassination.†[119]

Despite the denials, Ray may have learned of the offer. Another Jeff City in-mate, Donald Lee Mitchell, worked with Ray in the commissary. In 1966, shortly before Mitchell was released from the prison, Ray told him that some friends in St. Louis had arranged for him to collect $50,000 for killing King, and that if Mitchell wanted, he could join the plot and also pocket $50,000. Ray assured him they would not get caught, and even if they did, a good lawyer would get them off since "who in the South like niggers?"[120] Mitchell told that to the FBI only five months after King's murder.

The Sutherland offer was not then publicly known. Both the city and the amount offered were correct, a strong indication that Ray may have plugged into the pipeline offering a bounty on Martin Luther King.

---

* There is also the possibility that information between Sutherland and Ray was ex-changed, after Ray's 1967 escape, by one of his brothers, John or Jerry. This is discussed at length in Chapter 23.

† In the fall of 1979, whatever possibility existed of learning more from Spica ended when he tried starting his Cadillac in the St. Louis suburb of Richmond. A trip-wired bomb ripped off his legs and he was dead before an ambulance arrived. The murder re-mains unsolved.

18

Breakout

At the close of 1965, Ray's time at Jeff City was evaluated in a "Pre-Parole Progress Report." It concluded he was an excellent worker in the bakery and noted he had only one contraband violation on his record. Under "Family Relations," it stated, "His brother, Jerry, corresponds regularly and visits occasionally. He sometimes hears from his brother, John."[1] As for postrelease plans, Ray indicated he wanted to live with one of his brothers. The associate warden who prepared the report, Carl White, noted that Ray "denies use of narcotics" and concluded that while he seemed "well-established" in prison, "prognosis for making a successful adjustment in society is considered marginal at best."[2]

Ray had a parole hearing scheduled next for 1967 (his application for early parole three years before had been denied).[3] The long-standing appeal of his 1959 robbery conviction was still pending in the courts.* However, at the start of 1966, Ray decided not to count on either of those possibilities to set him free. "Three and a half years had elapsed since my last escape attempt," he later wrote, "too long, I decided."[4] In preparation, he arranged a transfer from the

---

* In 1962, Ray had acted as his own attorney in appealing his conviction to the Missouri Supreme Court. His petition was denied. But Ray, who was indigent, then had a lawyer appointed and the appeals process started again.

bakery to K Hall's clean-up crew, allowing him to roam outside his cell until as late as 9:00 P.M.[5] But after a few months he asked for another transfer, this time to J Hall, since he had discovered that any escape from K Hall involved a thirty-foot drop from the windows to the ground. "I began collecting tools," he later wrote, "hacksaw blades and a long pole with a hook at the end used to open hard-to-reach casement windows—and watching for my chance."[6]

His chance came the day after his thirty-eighth birthday, March 11, 1966.* It was a Friday night, when movies were shown at the prison; since, as Ray said, "the darkness was an excellent cover in which to exact revenge." Most of the prison guards were assigned to the movie hall.[7] While the film ran, Ray placed a dummy in his bunk and returned to a scaffold that his work crew had used to clean the higher windows at the rear of J Hall.[8] There, he used a hacksaw to cut through a small wire screen and squeezed through, trailing a fourteen-foot pole.[9] He was now in a covered passageway that linked several buildings. Crawling nearly 140 feet, he finally reached the edge of the administration building, the nearest to the outside wall. He planned to use the pole, with a hook fastened to its end, to snag the roof gutter, pull himself to the top of the roof, and then drop down outside the wall, landing on the road in front of the prison.

"Everything went smoothly," Ray recounted, "until the gutter gave way. I fell about 15 feet, injuring my right arm."[10] No guards heard the commotion. Looking around, he spotted a small shack on the roof where he had fallen. It contained a generator. The door was padlocked, but he yanked the air-vent slats away, crawled inside, and then replaced the vents so as not to attract attention. He waited until after midnight and then slipped out to try again scaling the wall. He was surrounded by guards before he ever reached it. They took him to the hospital for his injured arm.[†]

Typically, criminal charges were not brought against a prisoner for an escape attempt; instead, the usual punishment was six months in solitary, followed by six months in restricted segregation. But the warden, Harold Swenson, decided to make an example of Ray, and the district attorney formally charged him with attempted escape, an offense that could have added several years to his sentence. Ray pleaded not guilty and demanded a trial. Charles Quigley, a local attorney, was appointed to defend him.[11]

---

* Ray's inability to get the facts right about his own life persist at almost every stage. In his book *Who Killed Martin Luther King?* he places the escape in the wrong year, 1965. He does, however, get the year right in his first book, *Tennessee Waltz*.

† When Ray was captured, he was carrying a bag stuffed with assorted pills. He omits this from his own three-page version of his escape in *Who Killed Martin Luther King?*

"He turned out to have some creative ideas," Ray recalled. "He suggested to the judge that I might not have been in possession of all my faculties when I allegedly tried to escape."[12] To determine whether Ray was competent to stand trial, the judge transferred him in September 1966 to the Missouri Hospital for the Criminally Insane in nearby Fulton. According to Ray, on his first day there he peered through the metal mesh on the bottom of his cell door and watched as attendants gave "a severe ass-kicking" to another inmate who had arrived with him.[13] The next morning, as he lined up with other patients to have his first interview with a psychiatrist, he passed a glass-paneled door through which he saw a patient receiving electroshock treatment. "Although this type of treatment is not uncommon in mental asylums," Ray later wrote, "seeing someone flopping around on a table with wires attached to his head can have an unsettling effect on one. Needless to say, when it came my turn to be interviewed by the Chief Bug Doctor, I no longer had an interest in being treated for a mental ailment."[14]

Ray "came clean with the shrink" and confessed he was just there to try and beat his charge of attempted escape. The psychiatrist told him to stay out of trouble and "to mind my own business."[15] After two months a report was issued that found Ray competent to stand trial. It also showed that he tested with a 105 IQ, and that while he exhibited "no evidence of a psychosis," he was a "sociopathic personality, antisocial type with anxiety and depressive features."[16]

Six weeks after he was returned to Jeff City, Ray was examined by a prison psychiatrist, Henry Guhleman, for the upcoming parole hearing, which was still scheduled despite Ray's escape attempts. In his report, Guhleman said, "Ray is an interesting and rather complicated individual."[17] Ray lied to Guhleman about his education (two years of high school), his military service (private first class and an honorable discharge), his love life (he lived briefly with different women), and his father (deceased). But he also seemed eager to talk about other matters, especially his recent physical ailments. He told Guhleman that during the past year he had suffered from pain in the "solar plexes," tachycardia (rapid heartbeat), and severe "intracranial tension" (head pain). When Guhleman commented that Ray was using complex medical terms, James said he had been reading medical literature as he feared he might have cancer or heart trouble.[18] Ray trusted Guhleman enough to tell him about his nightmares at the age of ten. He also described nervous habits he had recently acquired—when he felt anxious or afraid, he would put a glass of water on the table in front of him and move it back and forth until he felt better. To Guhleman, Ray's "problem revolves around what appears to be an increasingly severe obsessive compulsive trend. . . . This is not psychotic in nature but severely neurotic."[19] Guhleman put Ray on Librium, an antidepressant and muscle relaxant. He also recommended against probation: "It is felt that he is in need of psychiatric help and that should any serious parole consideration be given, some type of psychiatric help should be considered."[20] Parole was denied.*

While undergoing his examination by Guhleman, Ray had asked for a new kitchen job but was assigned to pushing the food cart in the hospital ward. Since he now fretted that he had mononucleosis, he was actually happy to be in the hospital, where he could obtain a high-protein diet and "conserve my energies."[21] He also immediately noticed that "there was considerable trafficking in goof balls and other illicit drugs through the hospital."[22] This is the assignment, in late 1966 and early 1967, that put Ray in the same prison section with Dr. Hugh Maxey and the inmate John Paul Spica, men who may well have known about the St. Louis offer of a $50,000 bounty on Martin Luther King.

After several months there, Ray was transferred back to the bakery. Other inmates noticed that he now read books about Mexico and even borrowed a Spanish dictionary from a fellow prisoner.[23] Unknown to them, he was planning a new escape. There was talk among Jeff City inmates about the countries that were the easiest in which to obtain new identities and were also safe as hideouts.[24] George Edmundson, an inmate who had been on the FBI's Top Ten list, was well known for having obtained a Canadian passport while on the run. He told the FBI that it was "very easy" to get one, and that the procedure was known to probably "every fugitive" in the United States.[25] According to Edmundson, all that was necessary was a guarantor, a baptismal or birth certificate, and a $5 fee. "Guarantors" were available among the "floaters, prostitutes and hustlers" in the Rue Notre Dame area of Montreal.[26]

Ray had read an article about Lowell Birrell, a New York securities operator indicted for fraud, who had fled successfully to Brazil after obtaining a Canadian passport.[27] With another inmate, Ray discussed a newspaper article in which an Italian criminal escaped from the United States to Italy after obtaining a Canadian passport, which the article said was simple to get.[28] In conversations with other prisoners, Ray indicated he was aware of how to use baptismal records, newspaper archives, and city records to obtain certified copies of birth certificates.[29] At other times, he focused on Mexico as a good place to "hide out" or "cool off," but other inmates argued with him, contending it would be easier for a white American to blend into Canada.[30] However,

---

* It is important to decode the technical language of both the Fulton and Guhleman reports. Those were completed by prison psychiatrists, accustomed to examining antisocial individuals often beset with extreme mental problems. For those psychiatrists to conclude that Ray was not psychotic merely means he was not outright crazy within the meaning of Missouri State Code 552.010, and that he could still function within the prison system. However, the diagnoses that he was a "sociopathic personality" and "severely neurotic" mean he was acutely sick as to how he related to the rest of society.

Ray did not abandon the idea of escaping to Mexico, indicating he had thought of trying to darken his eyes, and he once claimed to have experimented with staining his skin with a "walnut dye."[31]

Ray planned his escape for early May, but fearing that a guard might have stumbled on to the plot, he moved the date to late April.[32] On April 21, he bought a Channel Master transistor radio from the inmate canteen.*

On Saturday, April 22, 1967, the day before Ray implemented what would be a successful jail break, he was visited by his brother John.[33] Prison records reveal that John visited James eleven times at Jeff City, including the April 22 meeting. Jerry visited on five separate occasions.[34] It is probable that at that meeting John and James not only discussed the next day's escape, but that John also provided James some last-minute assistance. When James fled Jeff City, he had a social security number (318-24-7098) in the name of John L. Rayns, a number and alias previously used by John.†[35] Nothing less would be expected of brothers so close that after the assassination John told a local newspaper, "James would do anything for us [John and Jerry], and we for him."[36]

However, despite the evidence, John has never admitted to even visiting James the day before his successful escape. His denials and obfuscation provide a fine example of the Ray family at its dissembling best, gathering its defenses to ensure that no member provides useful information about another to law enforcement. It is also useful in judging the credibility of John's and Jerry's later denials of assisting James while he was a fugitive or in the period leading up to the King assassination.

Two weeks after the assassination, John told the FBI that he had not seen his brother in four years, and that before that visit, he had not seen him in fifteen years.‡[37] A few days later, he changed his story slightly and admitted to two or three visits to Jeff City, but still denied seeing James the day before the escape.[38] When confronted with the prison records by the House Select Committee on Assassinations, John unconvincingly claimed, "I do not have no recollection of that."[39] When the committee produced an interview with James in

---

* When inmates purchased radios from the canteen, their prisoner numbers were etched onto the side of the small portables. Ray's number, 00416, was put there when he bought it.

† James incredibly claimed in his letters to author William Bradford Huie that he remembered the number from a time he used it once in 1951. Yet he had evidently never used the name or alias in the intervening years before his escape. Given Ray's poor recall of many events in his life, it is almost certain that his claim of remembering the nine-digit number for sixteen years is a lie.

‡ Jerry Ray was not much more truthful than John. Despite his five visits to James in Jeff City, and having seen James after his escape in 1967, Jerry originally told the FBI that he had last seen James in 1964 (MURKIN 3334–3335, section 35).

which he had acknowledged that "one of my brothers visited a couple of days before I escaped. . . . I believe it was John," a visibly flustered John said, "I don't deny it, no, I just said I don't recall it."[40] At another point he suddenly claimed that maybe Jerry had visited James at the prison and used his name, but Jerry shot that one down, telling the committee, "I positively didn't visit him." John got so flummoxed in maintaining his denials that he even once claimed he was not certain if he ever knew that James had escaped from Jeff City. "I can't recall being aware [of James's escape]," said John. "It's possible, but I can't recall of being aware. I can't remember him escaping."[41]

One of James's former accomplices, Walter Rife, was imprisoned with John at Leavenworth after the King assassination. There, John confided in Rife that he had assisted James by picking him up on a highway outside the prison.[42] When confronted with that statement, John did not directly deny it, but rather accused Rife of "being a more or less a certified liar."[43] It is not surprising that the Select Committee's final report concluded that John's "responses were inherently incredible, excellent examples of the obstructionist posture [he] assumed throughout the investigation."*[44]

While John persistently tried to keep the truth from investigators, James also lied about the escape for nearly a decade. In 1968, he wrote to author William Bradford Huie and maintained that he had escaped from Jeff City by merely scaling the wall—he was adamant that he did not have the aid of family members or other prisoners.[45] Huie, despite some suspicions that Ray was lying in order to protect those who had helped him, published that version in *Look* in November 1968.[46] Prison officials were skeptical that Ray had managed to scale a twenty-three-foot wall in broad daylight without being spotted. Finally, in Ray's eighth interview with House Select Committee investigators in December 1977, he revealed that two inmates, whom he refused to identify, did assist in his escape.[47]

What actually happened was that on Sunday, April 23, Ray was working in a section of the bakery responsible for packing bread loaves into a three-by-four-foot metal box with a hinged lid.[†] A truck would arrive, pick up the box,

---

*   John himself may have inadvertently given the best indication of his own involvement when he wrote a letter to George McMillan in 1973 in which he said that James had been given identification and access to a car upon his escape—"the person who went and help him, also is doing time now in a federal prison for a charge that I expect is a frame-up." At the time he wrote the letter, John was in a federal penitentiary for a bank robbery conviction, one he always contended was an FBI frame-up. Later, John admitted to the assassinations committee in executive session that he was talking about himself when he wrote the letter, but he claimed he had fabricated the story of assistance.

†   Ray escaped only four days before the Missouri Supreme Court was to hear the long-standing appeal of his 1959 robbery conviction. Evidently, he had little faith in obtaining a reversal or he might have waited for the court's decision before trying to escape.

and then take it to the prison's honor farm.[48] It was a daily routine, and depending on the needs at the farm, up to one hundred loaves were put inside.[49] Ray's plan was to have an accomplice place him inside the box and then cover him with enough bread so it would pass through the normal checks. Once outside the prison gates, when the truck slowed at an intersection, Ray would jump from the rear.

The planning for this escape was thorough and demonstrates how Ray had matured in his seven years at Jeff City—the impetuous and inept prisoner had transformed into a patient and calculating one. To ensure that the guard did not touch him if he reached into the loaves of bread, Ray had fashioned a false bottom and ventilated the sides of the box so he could easily breathe.[50] Worrying that his prison uniform—dark green pants with a large black stripe down the leg—would quickly identify him as a fugitive, he managed to get a pair of plain black pants from a member of the prison band.[51] Finally, he connived with several inmates to arrange that if he was successful, a well-known informant would be slipped the word that Ray had *not* made it out and that instead he was still hiding somewhere inside Jeff City. The hope was that such a ruse would keep the guards searching within the walls, thereby giving Ray the chance to get a decent distance away.

"At about eight o'clock on the morning of April 23, 1967 I entered the kitchen," Ray wrote. "I normally took breakfast there rather than in the dining room, although I didn't start work until eleven o'clock. After cleaning up about a dozen eggs (I didn't know where my next meal was coming from), I waited for my accomplice's pre-arranged signal indicated the coast was clear to enter the bread storage room."[52] Ray carried a sack containing twenty candy bars, a comb, a razor and blades, a small mirror, soap, and his recently purchased radio.[53] Since prisoners were allowed to shower and shave in the kitchen's bathroom, the sack did not attract attention.

Everything was ready. Ray climbed into the bread box and covered himself with the false bottom, and the loaves were then stacked on top of him.

Normally the box was checked by both the driver and a guard at the prison's security tunnel. Because it was a Sunday, the regular driver and guard were off.[54] Although the relief driver, Alfred Burkhardt, thought it strange that the box was already sitting on the loading dock when he arrived, he allowed two inmates to load it into the rear of the truck without searching to ensure it contained only bread.[55] At the tunnel, the relief guard lifted the cover, saw the loaves neatly packed, and waved Burkhardt through.[56] As the truck left the prison compound, Ray pushed away the bread, pulled himself out of the box, and hurriedly changed from his prison uniform into the black pants. By the time he finished, the truck had passed through all the stoplights it would encounter between the prison and the honor farm. Ray feared he would either have to jump from the truck at 45 miles per hour or be captured at the farm.

"Fortunately," he later wrote, "my dilemma was resolved when the truck stopped briefly at the gravel road that led to the farm in order to let some on-coming cars pass. I leapt to the ground. Not wanting to look like a desperado, I casually waved toward the driver when I straightened up, as if I'd just been a civilian hitching a ride. Whether the wave worked or he didn't see me, he roared on toward the farm."[57]

When the truck arrived at the honor farm, only thirty loaves were found in-side, all so smashed that they had to be fed to the chickens.*[58] Ray's ploy—let-ting officials at Jeff City get word from an informant that he was hiding out inside—worked. Warden Swenson had guards search for him for two days within the prison's labyrinth.[59] Inmates were forbidden to take food out of the eating area because officials thought they might be taking it to Ray.[60]

The prison bureaucracy was slow and inefficient in acting on a successful escape. Finally, on April 25, a flyer was issued with a routine reward listed for a prisoner of no notoriety—$50. The notice listed three possible contacts: John Ray of 1918 Park Avenue, St. Louis (an address of his father's junk store, sold several years earlier); Mary Maher, James's grandmother, who had died three years earlier; and Jerry Ray, with a correct address in Wheeling, Illinois. The fingerprints attached to the notice were the wrong ones.[†] The photograph of Ray—a thin man with a crew cut and a sour expression—bore little resem-blance to him. Officials were so slow to search Ray's cell to check for possible clues that it had already been emptied by inmates who had learned of the es-cape.[61] But Ray did not need the inefficiency of Jeff City's officials to complete his getaway. By the time the $50 reward was posted for his capture, James Earl Ray was well on his way to freedom and the comfort of his family.

---

*   As a result of Ray's escape, Jeff City changed the size of its bread boxes so that they were too small to hide anyone. Many inmates refused to believe that Ray had escaped in-side the box, and a commonly told story was that he had arranged to "buy" a guard's uniform and simply walked out the prison's front door.

†   Some researchers have focused on the error of the wrong fingerprints to charge that Ray was released from prison with the help of either the CIA or FBI, with the long-range intent that he play a decoy role in the plot to kill King. German writer Joachim Joesten, in his self-published book *The Greatest Police Fraud Ever: The James Earl Ray Hoax*, is typical when he writes, "Ray did not escape from prison, he was surrepti-tiously let out with the consent of the Warden who went so far as to circulate to police authorities a false set of fingerprints designed to foil any chance recapture of the 'fugi-tive.'" Actually, the error was detected by fingerprint experts in Kansas City only two weeks after Ray's escape, and Warden Swenson immediately ordered corrected ones re-sent.

19

Indian Trail

O nce outside the prison, thinking the police would expect him to head immediately for St. Louis, where his brothers lived, Ray instead started walking west toward Kansas City.[1] Listening to his radio for news that never arrived about his escape, he walked for six days.[2] He ate candy bars, drank spring water, broke into a trailer once to steal some food, and suffered from badly swollen and blistered feet.[3] Finally, deciding "the heat is off now," he rode a freight train toward his brothers, where "I call a friend [former crime partner Jack Gawron] who takes me to a small town [Edwardsville] out of East St. Louis where I catch the bus to Chicago."[4] "I didn't see any of my relatives," Ray contended.*[5]

On April 30, one week after his escape, Ray checked into a $12-a-week rooming house in Chicago and registered under the alias John Larry Rayns, the name he had gotten from his brother.†[6] Mrs. Donnelly, the co-owner, remem-

---

* Ray gave the House Select Committee a second, conflicting version of his arrival in East St. Louis, saying that he had tried to reach Gawron but he was not home, forcing Ray to take a ten-mile taxi ride to the bus station. However, Ray knew nothing about the taxi route or the approximate fare, indicating that his first version, in which Gawron gave him a ride, was correct.

† In the case of the rooming house's owners, the Donnellys, author William Bradford Huie found them, as he did many others in the case, based on the notes and descriptions

bered Ray "had foot trouble when he came here. He could hardly walk for several days."[7] She and her husband said Ray was nice, quiet, and tidy.[8] On May 3, he saw an advertisement in the *Chicago Tribune* offering a $94-a-week job as a dishwasher at a local restaurant, the Indian Trail. Located just north of Chicago in the affluent suburb of Winnetka, the Indian Trail was a large family-style restaurant, a local institution for about thirty-five years. It was also convenient to Jerry, who lived and worked as a $113-per-week night handyman at the Sportsman Country Club less than ten miles away.*[9]

Ray arrived on May 4, gave his alias John L. Rayns, and landed the dishwasher job. Three days later he began work in the rear of the enormous kitchen. Of seventy-eight employees, twenty-seven were black and four Filipino, and none of them recalled any animosity from James. They remembered him fondly as an industrious, quiet, and polite person.[10] The owners, in a report on his work habits, concluded that he was "a reliable man of excellent potential for food service industry."[11] After a few days, he was promoted to "food server," and his pay jumped to $117.50.

Gertrude Struve Paulus, one of the owners, had helped Ray when he first arrived by showing him how to bind his injured feet to relieve the pain. Paulus had lived in Germany as a youngster and spoke with Ray about Bremerhaven. But she found him reticent. "He seemed lonely and shy," she recalled. "And once or twice I kidded him about the girls. But he didn't like it. He was not a man who liked the girls. I recognized that in him."[12] But Ray's apparent lack of interest in women was actually part of his new self-discipline, something he had evidently learned while at Jeff City. "There's nothing strange about me not looking for a woman in Chicago," he said, "I had waited seven years so I could wait a few weeks longer. A woman is a risk for a fugitive. She might report you to the police. And a woman costs money, and I was trying to accumulate capi-

---

Ray provided to him as part of their postassassination exclusive writing deal. Huie had the advantage of locating those witnesses before even the FBI had talked to them, and in many instances, as with the Donnellys, they did not even realize that the man they had known was James Earl Ray, the accused assassin of Martin Luther King. All were shocked when Huie informed them of Ray's real identity and the crime for which he had been arrested. But he invariably did so after the interviews, thereby ensuring his advantage that most of his interviewees were not biased by what they subsequently learned about Ray or heard about the assassination.

* FBI interviews with the country club's owner, locker room manager, and other employees reveal that Jerry had a reputation as a harmless man who was not that bright. While there, he married a waitress, Gjirdis Anna D. Olsen, and she had a child from her previous husband while they were together. They were divorced eighteen months after their marriage. Olsen was also somebody that the club management thought was slow-witted.

tal as fast as I could without risking a holdup."[13] Ray boasted to Huie that while he was in Chicago, "I wasn't taking dope, staying drunk, and hunting prostitutes."[14]

Henry Johnson, a cook's helper, often drove Ray to the bus stop after work, and remembered him as a shy man who avoided personal questions and almost always seemed to be reading a newspaper. While Ray was employed at the Indian Trail he would likely have read the *Chicago Tribune*'s coverage of Martin Luther King's early May criticism of General Westmoreland, the June 12 story that the Supreme Court had upheld King's 1963 conviction for violating an Alabama injunction, and the June 18 challenge by King that the black movement for equality had entered a more difficult phase that will "cost the nation something."

By his own account, Ray had roughly $300 when he escaped from Jeff City. His willingness to work at the Indian Trail suggests that his brothers had not yet returned to him any money he had sent them from prison for safekeeping. For a man who had refused to move to an integrated honor farm at Leavenworth, the mixed-race kitchen could not have been pleasant. Moreover, the work was hard, the pay little, and there is nothing in Ray's past to indicate that if he had enough money he would have stuck with such menial work.

Ray initially stayed away from his family because he mistakenly believed that the authorities were conducting a painstaking search for him and probably watching them.[15] That was because he had an inflated view of how important a fugitive he was. The same newfound self-discipline that kept him from going with any women in the weeks after his escape also meant that he would not risk contacting his family until he was satisfied that the FBI was not monitoring them.

After a week of freedom, he called Jerry and asked "if the police were around surveilling."*[16] Another week passed and the two brothers had a quick drink at a local bar.[17] It gave James more confidence that the FBI might not be following his family, but still he kept his distance and, therefore, a low profile. "Usually I drank two cans of beer every night in my room," he re-

---

*   To the Select Committee, James admitted to at least three, and maybe four, meetings with Jerry. However, a decade earlier he had lied to author William Bradford Huie by claiming he had not seen any of his relatives when he returned home. He was, of course, protecting them at the time, since the statute of limitations on harboring a fugitive had not yet expired. "My reason for not seeing any relatives is that criminal charges can be filed against a relative or anyone for harboring a fugitive if the police can prove it."

called. "I read *The Chicago Tribune,* listened to the transistor radio, and some-times read murder mysteries or books about Canada and Latin America. Nat-urally, most of my thinking was about how to live outside the U.S."[18] Also, Ray frequented a local bar on Diversey Street. While he had returned to mod-erate drinking, there is no evidence that he had resumed his amphetamine binges.

As the weeks passed with no sign of the FBI or local police, the brothers began relaxing. At the Indian Trail, none of the employees remembered James receiving any telephone calls until his last week, when he got three or four. Some employees thought he seemed excited by those calls, while others thought he appeared disturbed and distracted.[19] Two of the restaurant's own-ers, Harvey and Clara Klingeman, remembered that the male voice on the other end of the telephone identified himself as James's brother.[20] This was also the time when some visitors arrived at the restaurant's rear door and waited to talk to James outside.*[21] Jerry admits that he was one of James's visitors at the Indian Trail.[22] James also visited Jerry for drinks near the country club where Jerry worked.[23]

It was around this time—five to six weeks after the escape—that the three brothers may have held a meeting first reported by author George McMillan. According to Jerry Ray, the three gathered at Chicago's Atlantic, a historic hotel that had degenerated into a crumbling skid-row haven by 1967.† It was the first time in twenty years that the brothers were all out of jail at the same time. They settled into separate rooms under false names and paid cash so the hotel's records could not confirm the visit. The next morning they met and dis-cussed several possibilities to get some money, said Jerry, including kidnapping then-governor Otto Kerner or Jack Brickhouse, a local star broadcaster, or even a wealthy member of the country club where Jerry worked. They also toyed

---

* The FBI played tape recordings of voices, presumably Jerry and John Ray, for the restaurant owners and employees. But no one could identify them. There was a similar failure to recognize any photographs the FBI brought in an attempt to determine who Ray's visitors were.

† In the version Jerry Ray gave McMillan, he said the meeting took place on April 24, the day after James's escape. There had been an initial misunderstanding about where John was supposed to meet James—some forty miles outside the prison—but eventually James called, John picked him up, and the two drove to Chicago. However, that is clearly wrong. James had just started his six-day walk west from prison. The injury to his feet that came from so much walking was confirmed by witnesses both at his rooming house and at the Indian Trail restaurant where he worked. Also, James's fear that the author-ities were watching his family would have prevented him from arranging such an early rendezvous.

with the idea of going into the porn business—something James showed great interest in—but they could not agree on anything.*[24]

Then James surprised both of them. "I'm going to kill that nigger King," he calmly said. "That's something that's been on my mind. That's something I've been working on." Jerry thought the job far too dangerous and ambitious—he says he flatly told James he would not help him. John also opted out: "That's crazy! You can count me out of that deal. There ain't no money in killin' a nigger. I'm going back to St. Louis."[25] If James knew of a bounty on King, he evidently did not share it with his brothers at that time.

Before they departed, John and Jerry made an accounting to James of the money he had sent from prison. The amount is not certain. In Jerry's first version, James received $4,600, and $1,500 was held in reserve in case of any emergency.[26] At other times, he gave James $2,200, then $1,200, and even once said it was only $110.[27] Subsequently, James's only noticeable expenditure was $100 for a 1960 Chrysler.[28] Whatever the amount, James felt secure enough to leave the Indian Trail, which he did on June 25.†[29]

John and James have since denied there was such a meeting, but Jerry's reaction when confronted by House Select Committee investigators suggests otherwise. Normally, when asked about things he had told author George McMillan, Jerry claimed that either they were false or spoken in jest, or that McMillan had concocted them. However, when quizzed about this critical meeting where James expressed interest in killing King, Jerry surprisingly did not initially deny it. Instead, he invoked his Fifth Amendment right against self-incrimination. Although the Select Committee had granted him immunity in order to compel his testimony, he was not exempt from a perjury prosecution.[30] "I don't remember," Jerry said, visibly nervous. "I am going to have to invoke

---

*   In 1963, James's younger brother Franklin died at the age of eighteen in a car crash near Quincy. Also killed in the crash was eighteen-year-old Virginia May Johnson. U.S. postal inspectors had found nude photographs they believed were of Johnson and traced them to a ring that sold explicit photos of young girls, operating out of 1913 Hickory Street in St. Louis, the boardinghouse owned by Mom Maher. Postal inspectors raided the house but found nothing, although they suspected that the porn ring was composed of John Ray and his younger brother Franklin. Interviews with other family members were not productive. "It was a close-mouthed family," commented postal inspector H. M. McLaughlin, "all protecting each other." After the deaths of Franklin Ray and Virginia Johnson, the investigation stalled, and no charges were ever filed.

†   Ray had received eight paychecks totaling $813.66, and his net income after withholding taxes was $664.34. His expenses were low during that period, with his $12-a-week rent being his biggest one, probably leaving him between $500 and $550, apart from any monies his brothers may have given him.

the Fifth Amendment on all this stuff because I can't remember all this stuff and this has been going on since 1968 with McMillan."[31] Later, when pressed, Jerry claimed, "I am saying I don't remember saying anything like that."[32] Eventually, he followed the lead of James and John and denied that the meeting took place.

Three days after James left the Indian Trail, he wrote a letter to the restaurant's owners informing them that he had quit because "I have been offered a job on a ship so will take it." Ray asked them to send his last check to his brother Jerry.[33]

Ray left Chicago for Quincy, where he spent the next three weeks unemployed and traveling to his childhood haunts of Quincy, Alton, and East St. Louis. He stayed in a series of cheap motels, usually costing $1.50 per night.[34] As might be expected, he has not been very forthcoming in identifying the people he saw while there. He told Huie in 1968, "I can't give anyone information that would lead to the prosecution of anyone else. I think you can understand that in short I don't want to burn any bridges and I think I owe something to those who have helped me in the past."[35]

One of his former inmates at Jeff City, James Carpenter, ran into him in St. Louis in early May, and over a beer Ray mentioned that he needed a gun in case he had to pull a robbery. Carpenter was unable to help.[36] James saw an old friend, Ted Crawley, who owned a local Quincy tavern, and Jerry said that it was there that James arranged to get a pistol.[37] James later admitted to obtaining a .38-caliber revolver during this time, but claimed he had gotten one free from his friend Jack Gawron.*[38]

As he felt safer, he more openly visited his family, at least Jerry, occasionally seeing him at two of Jerry's local hangouts, the Northbrook Bar and the Cypress Tavern.[39] The one person Ray evidently did not run into was James Owens, his accomplice on the Kroger robbery that finally landed him in Jeff City with a twenty-year sentence. His brother John said that if Ray had found Owens, he would have killed him on sight since he blamed him for the Kroger arrest.[40]

However, despite the ease with which he moved around these river towns he knew so well, Ray had no intention of staying there very long. He was determined to leave the country, and had taken the advice of other prisoners to try Canada first. While at the Indian Trail, he had written to the Canadian con-

---

* When Ray identified Gawron before the House Select Committee, Gawron had not only died, but had also testified in another case against Ray's brother, John. It is likely that James used his name as a cover for whoever really provided him the pistol. Gawron, shortly after the assassination, denied to the FBI that he had seen Ray, since he feared being charged with harboring a fugitive.

sul asking how he might emigrate to Canada.[41] When he left Mrs. Donnelly's rooming house in Chicago, he had told her that "he had to go to Canada on business."[42]

While James was in East St. Louis on July 13, nearly three weeks after he quit his Indian Trail job, the Bank of Alton—twenty miles away—was robbed of $27,230 by two shotgun-wielding, masked gunmen.[43] Besides James, John and Jerry were also in the area that day. It was Jerry's day off from his country club job. John was suspected of being involved in five similar local bank robberies in a two-year span, all with a similar modus operandi.*[44] Did the three Ray brothers pull that heist? The FBI—trying to establish where Ray had obtained the funds he used while a fugitive—investigated the Alton robbery, as well as other unsolved cases, in the immediate aftermath of the assassination. In addition to the Ray brothers, at least fifteen other people were considered suspects at some point.[45] The Bureau could never positively link the Rays to the robbery.[46]

The House Select Committee on Assassinations conducted a more extensive investigation of whether the Rays robbed that bank. There is, as the Select Committee concluded, "substantial, albeit circumstantial" evidence that the Rays were the perpetrators of the unsolved crime.†[47]

The two thieves, described by witnesses as middle-aged white men similar in height and build to James and John Ray, left the bank and evidently a getaway car was waiting for them. Instead of taking a direct route out of town, the robbers actually headed deeper into Alton, indicating some familiarity with the town and confidence in their ability to elude the police while there. The shotgun and the clothing they used were found abandoned only several hundred yards from the home of Willie Maher. Their mother, as well as James, had previously had homes in the same neighborhood. Jerry Ray, in a critical admission to one committee witness (who asked for anonymity), privately confided that James and John had indeed robbed the Alton bank.[48] (Jerry, typically, later denied making the statement.)

The actions of James and John immediately after the Alton robbery indicate that both brothers had suddenly come into cash. The day after the robbery,

---

*   As Select Committee deputy chief counsel James Wolf concluded, "The participation of John Ray in all five bank robberies is supported by evidence, even though he was only convicted of the St. Louis, Mo., holdup." The committee had statements from other criminals who admitted being part of the holdups and who also provided information about John Ray's involvement.

†   The FBI had received a statement from Jack Gawron that James Earl Ray and another man had pulled the Alton robbery (MURKIN 4760, section 62, pp. 21–29). However, the other man named by Gawron turned out to be in jail at the time of the robbery, and there were other inconsistencies in his story. The author does not give it any credence in deciding whether the Rays robbed the Alton bank.

James spent $210 for a 1962 red Plymouth, and the following day he left for Canada.[49] Within a few weeks, John abruptly abandoned the Midwest for California and Mexico. When he returned to Missouri in late summer, he deposited $2,650 to two St. Louis bank accounts.[50] Although John claimed the money came from honest work in California, he could not substantiate a single job he had there.*[51]

Not surprisingly, all three brothers have publicly denied any role in the Alton bank robbery, although none had a verifiable alibi for the time of the heist.[52] Jerry Ray, seizing the drama in almost any situation, actually followed his Select Committee testimony with a trip to the Alton police station, where he offered to waive any statute of limitations and turn himself in. The police turned him away, saying he was not a suspect.

It is quite possible that the Rays, or at least John and James, were involved in the Alton robbery, and the success of the heist would again explain much of the money James used in the year leading up to the assassination. His departure for Canada was not unexpected, since he had been talking about leaving the States for some time, but it is suspicious that it happened right after the bank robbery, which would have netted his largest haul ever.

---

* John held very few straight jobs through the 1960s. In his testimony before the Select Committee in December 1978, John was asked what employment he had in April 1967, when James escaped from Jeff City. He said, "I can't—I can't—I believe I was a painter." He could not provide the name of the contractor who supposedly employed him (MURKIN 4760, section 62, p. 201). Just before his committee testimony, he had been arrested on suspicion of burglary. Many committee members suppressed laughter when Jim Lesar, his attorney, claimed that John had been arrested "when he wandered into a house by mistake."

20

Gray Rocks

On July 15, 1967, Ray spent the night in Indianapolis before traveling to Canada.[1] Two days later he registered under the name John L. Rayns at the Bourgard Motel in Dorion, about twenty-three miles outside Montreal. The following day he signed a six-month lease for a single room at the Har-K, a three-story collection of fifty-seven dingy apartments in a run-down industrial district of Montreal.[2] On the Har-K's ground floor was a raucous nightclub, the Acapulco, advertised by an enormous flashing yellow and red neon sign promising ACAPULCO SPECTACLES. Ray signed that lease using a new name, Eric S. Galt.

Galt became Ray's primary alias for the next nine months leading up to the assassination, and there has been much controversy over how Ray came by the name. There was a real Eric S. Galt who worked for Union Carbide and lived in Toronto.*[3] The real Galt's middle name was St. Vincent, and for a while he had

---

* Galt worked as a laboratory staffer, responsible for inspecting the company's manufacturing of proximity fuses used in such military weaponry as air-to-air missiles, artillery shells, and the like. Because of his position, he was required to have a security clearance, and the Royal Canadian Mounted Police had conducted the last one in 1961. Of course, the fact that Galt's employment had a military connection has prompted some conspiracists to speculate—without any supporting evidence—that there was a military or intelligence connection to Ray's aliases.

an unusual way of signing it—he abbreviated it to "St.V." and for the two periods drew small circles. It could look, at first glance, like StoVo. A few months
after Ray first used the alias, he applied for an Alabama driver's license, and
when asked what the *S* stood for, he said, "Starvo," raising the inference that
Ray (or someone) may have seen the real Galt's signature and misread it.[4]
Moreover, the real Galt lived in a Toronto neighborhood only a few miles away
from three other people whose identities Ray would appropriate when he was
on the run after the assassination. Ray and Galt also bore a passing resemblance to each other.*

Ray has said that he is positive he did not know there was a real Galt when
he first selected the alias. He seemed positive about very little else, however, and
has relished sowing confusion by presenting conflicting versions of when and
how he chose that name. In 1968 he told Huie he had come up with it "about
3 or 4 years before I escaped," but he testified to the House Select Committee on
Assassinations, "I didn't have no idea I'd use that name in Jeff City." He soon
suggested he found the name when he was working in Chicago, and then later
changed that to Birmingham. (Impossible, since Ray used Galt before he ever
visited Birmingham.[5]) As for how he found the name, he has, at various times,
said he took it from a phone book, a magazine, an advertisement, or a book.[6]
When asked how he found the distinctive middle name, Starvo, he shrugged. "I
couldn't say."[†7]

---

* Some claim that the real Galt bore a remarkable resemblance to Ray. That has raised
concern that Ray had selected, or been given, a look-alike identification that would later
mislead investigators in the hunt for King's assassin. Actually, Galt was fourteen years
older than Ray, and despite the overreaching efforts of writers such as Philip Melanson
to say that Galt "had a rugged, youthful appearance and looked to be in his forties," pictures of Galt from that time show he looked considerably older than Ray, who was
thirty-nine. Although only an inch taller, and ten pounds heavier, he had a different
hairline, a broader nose, and fatty bags under his eyes. No one could have visually confused the two men, but a verbal description—white, five-ten, 170 pounds—would have
been similar. Also, some buffs even claim that Ray and Galt had matching scars. In fact,
Ray's Jeff City prison records do not list any distinguishing scars, and when asked by the
Select Committee if he had any, Ray said, "None that I know of." One that he had on his
hand from a lawn mower accident years earlier had faded and was invisible (MURKIN
x–125, section 1, p. 11).

† Ray seems to enjoy the confusion he creates with his constantly changing answers.
He also readily admits that at times he lies: "Do you know you are a liar?" a *Playboy* interviewer asked him in 1977. "Yes, I know that." However, Ray has claimed he does so
only if he is not under oath. For instance, when the House Select Committee asked him
if he had been truthful in a long interview with CBS's Dan Rather, Ray said breezily, "I
don't recall. I wasn't under oath." As for his *Playboy* interview, Ray said he "intended"
it to be truthful but there may have been "certain inadvertent errors." As to his cooperation with the Select Committee, Ray noted that for his eight prison interviews, totaling

Several researchers and authors have found innovative solutions. George McMillan said Ray selected the Galt alias from books he read while imprisoned at Jeff City. Ayn Rand's *Atlas Shrugged* opens with the question "Who is John Galt?" and a villainous character named Ernst Stavro appears in the James Bond series.[8] However, Ray later said, "I'm sure I didn't get it out of there."[9] Author Clay Blair, Jr., thought it probable that Ray bought the name from "an underworld ring dealing in forged passports and papers."[10] However, in Ray's first weeks in Canada, he earnestly tried to obtain a passport through legal channels. If he had located an illegal ring, he would have merely purchased a usable passport. Moreover, he had no documentation such as a driver's license to go with the Galt name, false items that an underground ring would have provided along with the name. Finally, William Bradford Huie decided that when Ray drove into Canada he passed a road sign for the town of Galt—there is such a sign near Toronto—and later settled on the first name Eric when "seeking something different from the more common first names."[11] Ray also contested Huie's version—"that wasn't the, the way I got the name. I'm positive of that."[12]

The key question is whether Ray could have been given the name by a conspirator in the King assassination, even though the murder was nine months away. The mysterious person called Raoul, says Ray, directed almost all his actions in the year leading up to the assassination. Yet Ray arrived in Canada on July 15, and he used the Galt alias for the first time when he leased an apartment in Montreal three days later. In his own version, he did not meet Raoul for at least another week. Therefore, it was impossible for Raoul to have supplied the name Galt to Ray.*

1,700 pages of testimony, he had been assured by the committee's counsel that "nothing I said would be under oath," again implying there was a lower standard of truthfulness to the interviews that carried no perjury penalties. Once, when confronted with a direct contradiction between two versions of his 1967 escape from Jeff City, Ray asked the committee counsel, "Was I under oath when I told you the other part of it?" (HSCA vol. XI, p. 343).

* Ray's latest lawyer, Dr. William F. Pepper, published a book, *Orders to Kill*, in 1995. In it, Pepper presents one of the most convoluted and complex assassination theories that has ever been printed, outlining a mammoth conspiracy that involved the White House, the CIA, the FBI, Canadian and British intelligence, the Memphis police, military intelligence, Green Berets, the National Guard, and the mafia, among others. (See Chapter 32 for a detailed discussion of his theory.) According to Pepper, the real Eric S. Galt was a "highly placed Canadian operative of U.S. army intelligence." He even reproduces a photo of Galt that he claims was obtained covertly from a National Security Agency file about him. According to the NSA, there was never a preassassination file on Galt. Pepper says only that he obtained his information from an unidentified source, who allegedly told him "not to ask any questions." As with all his "revelations," the Galt

No books, no criminal ring, no road sign, no conspirator. The only realistic alternatives are either that Ray developed the Galt identification on his own, during a brief stopover in Toronto, or that one of his brothers had found it earlier and passed it to him when he left for Canada.

Did Ray have an opportunity to get the name himself? In the 20,000 Words he sent to Huie in 1968, he wrote that while traveling to Montreal, "I stayed one night in Toronto."[13] Once in Toronto, he either stayed at a fleabag motel that accepted cash as the only necessary identification or slept in his car, something that he sometimes admittedly did.[14] Although Galt was a quite traditional Canadian surname, there was only one Eric Galt in the Toronto telephone directory.[15] As Ray told the Select Committee, he might have randomly selected Galt from the phone book. Since he used it first on July 18, it is likely he picked it up on July 16 when he stayed in Toronto.* Is it not possible that he stumbled across the unusual way Galt signed his name? From credit card slips to auto registrations left in cars, thieves like Ray are adept at finding a different name when one is needed. "I have used a lot of aliases," Ray once admitted, "I can't remember how many—probably fifteen or twenty or maybe more."†[16]

There remains the possibility that John and Jerry Ray might have had the name ready for James before he left for Canada. Once he broke out of jail in late April, James did not leave the States for two months, giving them plenty of time to develop a usable name. Jerry told the author that he had been to Canada only once, in 1963, and it was to Toronto, where the real Galt lived.[17] James himself had fled to Canada after a robbery in 1959, so the brothers knew it was

---

information is not sourced, and is not supported by a single piece of corroborating evidence. Galt was dead, of course, by the time Pepper published his accusations, so there could be no action for libel.

* Why, though, if Ray had Galt's name on the sixteenth in Toronto, did he revert to his old alias of John L. Rayns when he checked in the next night at the Bourgard Motel in Dorion? Some charge that if he had already settled on Galt, he would have used it in Dorion. Yet since Ray did not have supporting documentation for Galt, he could not use it everywhere. "The only instances I would use Rayns," Ray said, "was when I'd go in the motel somewhere where you have to register with your license plate number." He had to do that at the Bourgard and therefore used Rayns. The next day, in Montreal, he was not required to produce any documentation when he signed the six-month apartment lease, so there he christened the Galt alias. He paid $150 for the first and last month's rent, and as Ray later said, "that was just the first step" in his efforts to establish a paper record for Eric S. Galt.

† The author also checked the Toronto newspapers—the *Star*, the *Telegraph*, and *The Globe and Mail*—for the time Ray was there to see whether Galt was mentioned in any article. Ray could have read such an article and appropriated the identity that way, but there was no mention of Galt in the local press.

a good place to "cool off." The Rays also had a habit of gathering identifications from various places just in case they ever needed them. "I know around the home there," James recalled, "we used to have 15 to 20 different social security cards."[18]

The night before Ray signed the six-month lease at the Har-K apartments as Galt, he said that he drove into one of Montreal's red-light districts. He paid $25 to a prostitute at a gambling club and went to an "apartment run by who ever she is working far." After he finished with her, he noted the address as he left.[19] The next night, after Ray had settled into his new one-room apartment, he drove back to the club and again picked up the same girl. He paid her another $25 at her apartment, had sex with her, and then "we were ready to leave and I put the gun on her and took her to the office."[20] Ray forced his way in and bound the pimp's hands and feet with the prostitute's stockings. "After a little persuasion" (presumably beating the pimp), Ray was told where they hid the money—in a cabinet—and found $1,700 there. He told the girl to get under the bed and then fled the scene.[21]

The reason he waited to get to Canada to pull his first solo crime, said Ray, was "that if I would have been caught (in the U.S.) I would have had to do time plus what I had left in Missouri. If I would have been caught in Canada they would have just sent me back to the U.S. Also, by robbing a brothel, I figured they mite not of called the police."[22]

An armed robbery entailed a fair amount of risk for a fugitive, and Ray would only have undertaken it if he desperately needed money. It is possible, however, that Ray invented the whorehouse heist to cover his involvement in the Alton bank robbery just five days before. He cannot recall the name of the Montreal club he supposedly robbed, has given conflicting amounts for what he stole, and has changed the dates, and indeed, no robbery that even remotely fit his description was ever reported.* What is significant, nevertheless, is that the day after he says he robbed the brothel, Ray went on a spending spree, most

---

* Huie first published the account of the whorehouse robbery in Look in 1968, and quoted Ray as saying he had gotten only $800 from the robbery. Huie said Ray gave the lower sum to his then lawyers, the Haneses. However, Ray's own letters to Huie state the amount was $1,700, and the $800 figure is likely a misunderstanding by Huie. Ray has varied the amount over the years, but only slightly—$1,600 to $1,700 to Dan Rather in 1977, and once $1,500 to the House Select Committee on Assassinations, and another time $1,700 to the committee. Also, Ray had changed his story and later told both Hanes and Huie that he had not really robbed a whorehouse but instead it was a supermarket. No supermarket in Montreal reported a robbery on those days. Before the Select Committee in 1977, Ray reverted to his whorehouse version, claiming he had deliberately

of it to create a new and sophisticated identity. On July 19, he spent about $200 for a dark brown suit, a pair of gray trousers, and some ties, T-shirts, underwear, pajamas, and swimming trunks at Tip Top Tailors. It was the first suit he ever owned. Later that day he got a haircut and had his nails manicured at the ornate Queen Elizabeth Hotel. Two days later, he ordered a tailor-made suit from the English and Scotch Woolen Company. He next bought a small television set and several books on hypnosis.[23]

A few days after his shopping spree, Ray sent a Canadian money order to Futura Books in Inglewood, California, for three sex manuals.[24] According to the advertisement that Ray answered, the books dealt with such issues as "sex impulse in men vs. women; masturbation in and out of marriage; precoital stimulation; problems of sexuality; frustrated wives with case histories; sex myths; aids to penetration; oral eroticism; enlarging the penis to a maximum; assistance in overcoming premature ejaculation, etc." The sex manuals were evidently part of Ray's "research" for the women he soon hoped to meet. He also purchased another Canadian money order and sent it to the Locksmithing Institute in Little Falls, New Jersey, as a $17.50 first payment on a mail-order course.[25] Although he later said there was "no particular reason" for taking the correspondence locksmithing course, he admitted that he "might do something illegal. . . . I didn't specifically have in mind learning to be a burglar at that age, but at the same time you could always use something like that when nothing else is available."[26] Locksmithing was, as he later put it, "a trade for which I'd always felt an affinity."[27]

But Ray was preoccupied with something else during his early stay in Montreal. When he had first arrived in Canada, he decided, "One thing was certain: I never in my life intended to return to the United States. What hope was there for me back there? The first thing I did in Montreal . . . was call a travel agency and ask what I.D. was necessary to get a passport. . . . I was never going to cross that border back into the United States."[28] Ray dreamed of moving to South America, Spain, Australia, or even an English-speaking country in Africa.[29] However, the travel agency gave him the wrong information, telling him that while he did not need any identification, he needed a guarantor to

---

lied to his own attorneys and to Huie because he was sick of "giving attorneys information that attorneys give to book writers and the book writers would give it to the FBI."

As for the issue of the robbery's timing, Ray started spending heavily on July 19. In the 20,000 Words, he indicated that between his one night required to case the place, and the second night to rob it, the heist did not happen until the evening of the nineteenth, after he had already started freely spending. That meant he already had money with him when he arrived in Canada, fitting into his role in the Alton heist. However, before the Select Committee, Ray retold the story and moved the robbery up by one day, thereby eliminating any problem over the timing.

swear that he or she had known him for two years.[30] "Later [after the assassi-nation] I found out this wasn't true," Ray recalled, "you can get a Canadian passport simply by swearing you are a Canadian citizen, and you don't need anybody else to swear with you. But right then I thought I needed somebody else, so I began looking."[31]

His haunt for his first eleven days became the waterfront—about thirty blocks from his apartment—where some six thousand ships a year docked, and hundreds of seamen arrived daily.[32] The Montreal waterfront, in addition to being one of North America's most active ports, had a well-deserved reputa-tion in the 1960s as a major thoroughfare for illegal contraband and was the entry point for the heroin pipeline run by the now-defunct "French Connec-tion" from Marseilles. It was there, in the waterfront's rough bars and the local merchant seaman's club, Mariners House, that Ray hoped to find a job on a ship (he had optimistically told his employers at the Indian Trail in Chicago that he had left to go to sea). He loitered around the wharves trying to educate himself about obtaining seaman's papers, and at times he shadowed sailors in the hope he might "possibly roll a drunk" for his papers.[33] He tailed two or three, but never found the right victim.[34]

One of Ray's hangouts was the Neptune Tavern at 121 West Commissioners Street. It was narrow and dark, filled with massive oak furniture, the only lights dangling from pilot's wheels suspended from the ceiling, and a giant pilot's wheel dominating the rear of the bar. A sign welcomed all seamen and promised a gen-erous exchange rate for English money, and a chalkboard listed the day's small menu. It was there, after three or four nights, that Ray says he "sort of let the word get around" that he had had a little trouble in the States, was looking for ID and money, and just might be available for activities that didn't involve too much risk.[35] As a result of those feelers, Ray says he met a man he calls Raoul, who over a series of meetings supposedly offered him the possibility of "travel documents" if Ray helped "take some packages across the border."[36] Ray assumed that Raoul, who he said had wavy hair and wore suits with open-necked shirts, was Spanish because he had a slight accent. He never learned Raoul's last name.*

---

* Ray, as he is wont to do, has added to the mystery about Raoul over the years by giv-ing different versions in his numerous recountings of the story to investigators, lawyers, journalists, authors, and conspiracy buffs. For somebody that he supposedly saw nu-merous times over a nine-month period, Ray is remarkably inconsistent in describing Raoul. According to Huie, Ray originally told his lawyers that Raoul was a thirty-five-year-old blond Latin, and then told Huie that he was instead "a reddish-haired French Canadian." Ray, typically, later denied saying Raoul was blond. At other times, he has described Raoul's hair as being "darkish red, real dark," "sandy-colored," or "auburn." As for Raoul's complexion, Ray has described it as everything from "ruddy, dark" to being lighter than his own pale coloration.

According to Ray, after several tentative meetings with Raoul at the Neptune, he decided not to accept his offer of travel documents in exchange for some border smuggling. Instead, Ray decided to try to find a woman who might vouch that she had known him for two years.[37] He called a local travel agency, which recommended that a single man might want to visit the Gray Rocks Inn, a stunning mountain resort widely known to vacationers for its beauty and sports, including golf, boating, swimming, and winter skiing.[38]

Ray's purchase of good clothes two weeks earlier, including his first suit, now seem part of his effort to find that "respectable Canadian woman" who would be willing to lie for him.[39] His trip to Gray Rocks was the next phase of his plan. If he had truly met a Raoul at the Neptune—someone who held out the easy promise of a passport for some help in smuggling—it is unlikely that Ray would have still pursued cultivating a woman to do his bidding. Considering that he had never had much previous success with women and his relationships with them were mostly limited to half-hour stints in run-down whorehouses, it was not a plan with which Ray could have felt very confident. The easier choice would clearly have been opting for Raoul's criminal deal. The fact that he set off for Gray Rocks means there was likely no such offer on the table.*

Ray paid the travel agency $153 for the minimum board for a week, and on Sunday, July 30, he drove in his red Plymouth the eighty miles along the Laurentian auto-route. His room had a spectacular view of the Laurentian Mountains, and while Ray knew his battered Plymouth "wasn't exactly gigolo material," he hoped that his new clothes might make him stand out to the resort's single women.[40] His first six days were uneventful, but on his last evening he met a very attractive brunette in her late thirties, Claire Keating.[†41] Keating

---

* In the 20,000 Words, Ray wrote that after the whorehouse robbery he had gone to Gray Rocks, and that he met Raoul *after* that trip. That, of course, would make more sense as to why he might have gone to Gray Rocks to try and meet a woman—if he had not yet met Raoul there would have been no offer for travel papers. However, the registration papers at Gray Rocks show that Ray did not check in until July 30, eleven days after the supposed robbery. In fact, he had spent that time hanging out around the waterfront. Before the House Select Committee in 1977, Ray admitted that his original version in the 20,000 Words was wrong and instead claimed to have met Raoul *before* he went to the mountain resort.

† Huie was the first person to find Keating. In his book, he does not name her, nor did most other writers of early books on the case. Later writers seemed unable to find out who she was, but her name is buried in Ray's 20,000 Words. The House Select Committee also published her name. When Huie went to Canada to interview her, because of Ray's awful reputation with women he had expected to find "a shapeless frump" but instead was "flabbergasted . . . [she was] most attractive. Not in the manner of a brainless sexpot, but in the manner of a cultivated, sensitive, efficient, tastefully dressed and coiffured mature woman. At almost any resort she could have her pick of the unattached men."

was a sophisticated career woman who had recently taken her first steps to get a divorce from a troubled marriage. She was spending a long weekend with a girlfriend at a nearby resort in St. Jovite. On Saturday, August 5, the two women attended an auto race at Mont Tremblant, and that evening went to Gray Rocks to "mingle with people."[42] There, in the Gray Rocks lounge, Keating recalled, "was this lone man sitting at a table. He was neat, well-dressed, and shy. I guess it was his shyness that attracted us. My friend said, 'Let's sit with this man,' and we introduced ourselves and sat down and ordered drinks and began to talk."[43] She found Eric was "a nice man" who "listened and didn't talk much." Keating liked that he "was not a take-charge guy. . . . He was so unaggressive. All around us were aggressive men, trying to paw you and take you to their cars or rooms. Eric wasn't that way. He wasn't loud or boastful. He spent his money generously, but not wastefully, and he made nothing of it."[44] At one point she cautioned him against spending too much, and "he sort of smiled and said, 'There's more where that came from.' "[45]

They drank and danced, Ray moving clumsily about the floor, and she tried to show him some steps. Instead of being bothered by his awkwardness, she found his "lost-and-lonely manner" endearing. As the night wore on, she noticed that "he seemed to become more confident" and quietly warned off other men who made plays for her. He told her he was from Chicago. "He said he worked with his brother in some sort of business," she recalled. "In fact, he was meeting his brother in Montreal the next day."[46]

They spent the night together in Ray's room at Gray Rocks, and she found him "perfectly normal, nothing unusual." She, of course, had no idea that it was the first time Ray had had sex with a woman other than the seediest of prostitutes in almost twenty years. It is hard to imagine the impact on Ray of his success with Keating. The man who had spent ten of the last twelve years in tough prisons, who had recently worked as a dishwasher earning less than $100 a week, was now cavorting at one of Canada's finest resorts with a woman who would have been the envy of many men. Ray was no longer passing himself off as a small-time ex-con from a poor white trash background, but instead as Eric Starvo Galt, a well-dressed businessman with access to ready money. He was living the life he had often read and thought about while in prison. If anything, the encounter with Keating at Gray Rocks must have been a strong impetus for Ray to maintain his new lifestyle at all costs, a vivid reminder that the last thing he wanted was to be arrested as a fugitive and sent back to Jeff City to serve the remainder of his twenty-year sentence.

Keating lived in Ottawa, but she and her girlfriend planned to visit Expo '67 in Montreal on their way home. On Sunday, August 6, Ray told them he had to rush back to Montreal for the meeting with his brother.[47] The next day, he called Keating and gave her his address at the Har-K apartments. Ray, Keating, and her girlfriend spent that evening at the Acapulco Club on the ground floor of the building. As she had at Gray Rocks, she tried to teach him some Latin dance steps, but on this night he did not seem so lighthearted. "He seemed much more serious," noted Keating, "perhaps worried. He told me he wanted to come to Ottawa and talk to me about a serious matter."[48] During dinner that night, they got around to talking about blacks. "I can't remember how the subject came up," Keating later told author William Bradford Huie. "But he said something like 'You got to live near niggers to know 'em.' He meant that he had no patience with the racial views of people like me who don't 'know niggers' and that all people who 'know niggers' hate them."[*][49]

That night Ray, Keating, and her friend slept across his bed in the small one-room apartment. "The place was not Gray Rocks," recalled Keating. "It was seedy and run-down, and Eric was embarrassed about it. When I left him next day, he said he would telephone, and he told me again that he was coming to Ottawa to talk about the serious matter. He was very serious."[50] Ray had obviously decided that Claire Keating was the right woman to ask about vouching for his Canadian passport application. But he was nervous, as he later wrote, about approaching her. "I didn't want to ask her too direct since she mite go to the police."[51]

But Ray did not drive to Ottawa for another eleven days. During this time he says he tried unsuccessfully to get some travel documents or work on a ship, and that he also again met with Raoul at the Neptune. This second set of meetings supposedly produced a tentative agreement whereby Ray would smuggle some unspecified contraband across the border in exchange for a "small amount of money and a passport."[52] Raoul even told him that if this operation were successful, there would be more work for Ray in the States and in Mexico.[53]

Ray, if he is to be believed, had made a relatively painless deal with his new-found friend—to take a few packages across the border in exchange for his coveted passport. However, again he left to see Claire Keating, determined this time to ask her to vouch for his passport. It would seem unlikely that Ray would pursue the passport through Keating if he had already reached an agreement with a Raoul-type character.

_____

* Claire Keating refused to be interviewed in 1977 by the House Select Committee on Assassinations, so the committee was able only to review the Royal Canadian Mounted Police interview with her done shortly after the murder. During her interview with the RCMP, Keating said Ray never mentioned any hatred of blacks and never mentioned Martin Luther King in her presence. However, Keating obviously did not want to be involved, and gave little information. Huie, on the other hand, had lunch with her, spoke to her extensively, and seemingly gained her confidence. As was Huie's custom with most sources he interviewed, he gave her $100 for the information. She provided Huie more details than she gave the RCMP (MURKIN 5451–5505, section 75, p. 205).

Instead, on August 18, he drove to Ottawa and checked into the Town and Country Motel. Ray tried to play on Keating's sympathy by saying he was without his car, so she took hers and drove him around the capital, showing him some sites. At first he seemed fine, bragging a little that he was now working for his brother. He said that while there was not much to do, he was paid well, and money was not a problem, since he could always get some.[54] But as they drove, she noticed he got quieter. "For a long period as we rode around," she recalled, "or while we were together at the motel, he said nothing. He just looked at me, like he was trying to get up the nerve to say something. I showed him where I work."[55]

When she did, Ray remembered, "she pointed to a big office building with the Canadian flag flying on a pole out front. It was a government agency. So much for my passport scam."[56]

Ray did not show it, but he was terribly disappointed to learn that Keating worked for the Department of Transport in the Canadian government.[57] He was somber the rest of the day and they did not spend that night together. The next day he left, and she never saw him again.

Returning to Montreal on August 20, the fickle Ray reversed the promise he had made to himself five weeks earlier—that he would never return to the United States—and instead decided to go home. He settled inexplicably on Birmingham, Alabama—possibly since, as his brother John had admitted, Ray was a fervent supporter of then governor George Wallace. At least, if he had to return to the States, Ray had selected a state that better fit his politics and racial views. He later wrote to the English and Scotch Woolen Company, where his tailored suit was still being made, and asked them to send it to Birmingham care of Eric S. Galt at the general post office delivery.[58]

The next day, August 21, Ray drove to Windsor, Ontario. "I stopped along the side of Highway 401 and buried the revolver."[59] He did not want to take any chance that it might be found on a search at customs.

Raoul was waiting at the rail station with an attaché case, according to Ray. Raoul removed three packages—which Ray assumed contained narcotics—from the briefcase and stuffed them behind the rear seat of the Plymouth.[60] "He said he would meet me on the other side," Ray claimed.[61] When Ray successfully crossed through the tunnel, Raoul was there, took him to a side street, and retrieved the bags from behind the seat.* Then he directed Ray back to

---

* One of the least plausible aspects of Ray's story is that if there was a real Raoul, it is extremely unlikely that a professional smuggler like Raoul would have trusted Ray, someone he had met only eight to ten times in a bar in Montreal, with a stash of narcotics. Since Ray would be left on his own with the dope, there was no guarantee that he would not just take off with the valuable load, leaving Raoul cooling his heels on the American side.

Canada, where he again met him, loaded a second batch of bags behind the seat, and told Ray to make the return trip to the States over the bridge.[62] As for the second run, Ray "noticed the customs officer was shaking down about every other car."[63] Remembering the portable television set he had previously bought in Montreal, he declared that, and although the agents searched his car, they did not find any contraband.[64] Ray used the name Rayns at customs since he had his driver's license in that name.[65] After thirty minutes, and paying a $4.50 duty for the television, he was waved through by the customs officer.* "Raoul was a little nervous and wanted to know where I had been," Ray wrote.[66] After Ray explained about the television, "he gave me $750.00 but told me he couldn't as yet get any travel Documents."[67] (Before the House Select Committee, Ray said Raoul paid him $1,500, and to CBS news anchor Dan Rather, he said it was $1,700 or $1,800.)[68]

Raoul then made Ray a new offer. "If I would go along with him he would not only get me traveling Documents but also 10 or 12 thousand dollars."[69] Raoul told Ray to "get rid of the car" and "go to Mobile, Alabama," and that he wanted Ray "to take weapons into Mexico or help in some way, [but] he assured me it would be relative safe."[70] There was every reason for Ray to say no. Since Raoul had just let Ray down on the all-important passport, there was certainly no guarantee that he would pay Ray any more money. Ray was a loner who preferred working by himself—he had complained bitterly that the only times he ended up in jail for long stretches were because he used accomplices. Ray says, though, that he instantly agreed to work for this virtual stranger. The only condition upon which he insisted was that since he suffered from allergies, the dampness on the Gulf Coast would bother him, and he preferred Birmingham to Mobile. Ray had been in Alabama when he briefly drove across it during his 1955 postal money order spree that landed him in Leavenworth.

Raoul agreed, and even promised to pay Ray's living expenses in Birmingham, as well as buy him a new car. All Ray had to do was wait to receive correspondence care of general delivery in Birmingham. Before he departed, Ray claimed that Raoul even gave him a telephone number in New Orleans, which he was to call if he did not hear from Raoul for a long time.[†71]

While there may be doubts about the key details of Ray's Raoul story, it is possible that Ray might actually have latched on to a small group of smugglers

---

* The FBI was unable to find evidence that Ray had in fact paid any customs duty when reentering the United States (MURKIN 5351–5396, section 73, p. 85).

† That supposed telephone number has been the source of considerable controversy, with Ray claiming he had written it backward and in code on two pieces of paper, one of which the police stole after his arrest. As for the other copy, James said he gave it to his brother Jerry, but "somebody knocked him in the head in St. Louis in 1971 and he lost

in Montreal—"I'd known guys like Raoul for years," Ray later wrote.[72] When Dan Rather interviewed Ray in 1977, he said that he had met "*some* people" (emphasis added) involved in dope smuggling. Later, when the Select Committee confronted him with that important admission, he tried to backpedal by claiming, "I am not really too precise on the language."[73] Ray had, in fact, smuggled goods in the Army, and later dealt drugs at Jeff City, so carrying a couple of packages of dope across the border would be worth the gamble if the price was right. An offer to make such a trip, combined with his failure to land a passport through Claire Keating, might have been enough to induce him to return to the States. Jerry Ray told author George McMillan that James had actually run into an ex–Jeff City inmate while he was in Montreal, and that inmate had supplied Ray with narcotics that he then ran between Montreal and Detroit. "The whorehouse robbery is bullshit," said Jerry. "What he did was run dope. He had decided kidnapping was too risky."[74]

What is not contested is that Ray stayed at a motel—under the name Rayns—outside Gary, Indiana, on August 21, his first night back in the States. One day after he supposedly received money from Raoul, Ray was, by his own admission, in Chicago visiting his brother Jerry.[75] Was Jerry the brother whom James told Claire Keating he was meeting the next day in Montreal? Was he the brother whom James told Keating he was in business with and through whom money was no longer any problem? James claimed he did not tell Jerry "where I was going or anything."[76] Knowing how close and trusting the relationship was between them, however, if there was a real Raoul, then James would almost certainly have told Jerry about his good fortune in plugging into a drug-smuggling ring that promised thousands of dollars for little work.[77]

---

the original." With only the first three digits recalled by Ray, conspiracy buffs have tried every combination of numbers looking in vain for a contact to the mysterious Raoul.

Although Ray claims Raoul was the person that set him up for the King assassination less than eight months later, the very description of Raoul using Ray for smuggling at the U.S.-Canadian border casts further doubt on the tale. Many researchers believe that Raoul was plotting the King murder from the time he met Ray, and was slowly bringing James into the plot. But David Lifton, the author of *Best Evidence*, a book setting forth an extensive conspiracy in the JFK assassination, spent several months researching the King case for an article he cowrote about Raoul in 1977. He says, "There is one major inconsistency [in Ray's Raoul story] which crops up again and again. Ray claims to be involved on three occasions in smuggling in both Canada, and at the Mexican border. This does not make sense. A plot to kill Dr. King would not involve the patsy in risky activities, anymore than a plot to kill Kennedy would tell Oswald to go out and take skydiving lessons. The entire plot could fall apart." Why go to all the trouble of setting up a false identity for the patsy, and make him available to be framed for the assassination, and then risk it all by involving him in smuggling for which he might be arrested and jailed?

Jerry has admitted that he and James met at a local hotel on North Avenue. James again asked Jerry to go into the porn business, to join him on the trip to Birmingham, but Jerry begged off, even though he was impressed at how much money James had—close to $10,000.[78] And most important, according to Jerry, his brother had not abandoned his idea that King should be killed. "Jimmy was going to Birmingham to take out citizenship papers in Alabama," Jerry said. "He believed that if he killed King in Alabama, or if he killed him anywhere in the South, it would help him if he showed he was a resident of Alabama. . . . Of course, if he killed King in Alabama, he believed Wallace would eventually pardon him, not at first, but after a few years when things had cooled off."[79]

Jerry noticed that his brother seemed to be "getting caught up in the Wallace campaign. He was talking as much that night in Chicago about getting Wallace in as he was about rubbing King out. He had it in his head that it would help Wallace if King wasn't around."*[80]

The following day, August 23, James gave his car to Jerry, telling him it was "hot" and that he should change the license plates. Jerry then drove him to the train station in Chicago, and Ray boarded a sleeper heading for Birmingham.[81] He was settling back into America, and ready to call the Deep South home.

---

* Jerry, expectedly, later denied making these statements to McMillan, then said he could not recall making them. However, the author has reviewed McMillan's contemporaneous notes for the interviews in question, and there is little reason to doubt that they reflect what Jerry told him.

As for James wanting to help the Wallace campaign, as an avid newspaper reader he would have followed the Alabama governor's political moves. While Wallace did not officially announce his presidential candidacy for another five months, during the summer of 1967 his movement was noisily under way. Wallace was actively campaigning in multistate appearances, exhorting his followers to "Stand Up for America," and putting his effort behind the creation of the American Independent Party, a third political party formed only in June.

21

Wallace Country

Alabama was the scene of many of Martin Luther King's greatest triumphs in the civil rights movement. It was also the home of some of his most venomous enemies. Because Ray chose Birmingham as the place to settle when he came back to the States, it is tempting to speculate that the decision to kill King had already been made, either by Ray or by someone who placed him there. Yet after moving there, almost nothing that he did during the next six weeks seemingly had any political nexus, much less made him look like a man obsessed with murdering King.

Ray arrived in Birmingham on Friday, August 25, and checked into the Granada Hotel, four blocks from the train station.[1] He used his old alias John L. Rayns in case the clerk asked for identification. "In the morning I picked up a newspaper in the lobby and started looking for rooms to let," recalled Ray.[2] He found one in familiar surroundings, a cheap rooming house in a poor southside neighborhood. Known as the Economy Grill and Rooms, it was a two-story stucco building with space for eighteen roomers.* The Spanish-style archway

---

* The rooming house was not far from the office of Dr. Edward Fields, one of the leaders in the militant and segregationist National States Rights Party (NSRP). After the assassination, the NSRP counsel, J. B. Stoner, became one of Ray's lawyers, and Jerry Ray worked for Stoner as a driver and bodyguard. Did Ray have contact with Fields or the

that marked the entrance through a small garden had a large sign proclaiming ECONOMY SLEEPING ROOMS. A poster announcing WE SERVE MAXWELL HOUSE COFFEE dominated the lobby desk. The residence's only public phone was in the long hallway. Ray registered with the manager, Peter Cherpes, whom he described as an "easy going middle-aged fellow of Greek extraction who didn't ask a lot of questions." (Cherpes was actually seventy-two years old.)[3] Ray signed in as Eric S. Galt and told Cherpes he was an ex-employee of Ingalls Shipbuilding Corporation in Pascagoula, Mississippi, and that he was in Birmingham for a long holiday that might extend up to four months.[4] When Cherpes jovially remarked that it was a "long vacation," Ray was serious, saying merely that he had been working hard and needed the break.

Cherpes assigned Ray to Room 14 and collected $22.50 cash in advance for a week's rent, which included breakfast and dinner.[5] "One reason I picked his place," Ray noted, "was that when he showed me the room, I noticed a side window opening onto a passage leading to the back of the building—a handy escape route if the occasion demanded."[6]

Ray was a model tenant. Cherpes later remembered him as a "good-looking" and "quiet fellow," who "dressed well, usually a suit with a tie . . . especially a plaid sports suit."[7] "You couldn't imagine a nicer guy to have around," said Cherpes about the roomer who paid his rent promptly every week and mostly talked about the weather.[8] Ray spent much of his time in the lounge watching television. He also ate most of his meals there, and Cherpes recalled, "He usually turned in early, didn't go out much. He never had telephone calls or visitors."*[9]

Ray did not mingle with the other roomers. Even at breakfast, when all the tenants gathered in the dining area, he arrived late, ate on his own, and then returned to his room, where he often spent much of the day.[10] This low-key approach paid off for a man who did not want to be distinctly recalled. While Cherpes may have had good memories of Ray, the other roomers did not recognize photographs of him, much less remember anything about him.[11] Even

---

NSRP—an organization that might well have wanted King dead—while he was in Birmingham? The FBI and the House Select Committee investigated whether there was any preassassination contact and found none. Dr. Fields, now living in Georgia, and the editor of the last segregationist newspaper in America, *The Truth At Last*, was adamant in telling the author that he had never heard of James Earl Ray before the assassination. He also, however, could not say whether any individual NSRP member had been in contact with Ray, as the organization had many members and he did not know all of them.

* The FBI not only checked all toll calls made from the pay phone at the rooming house, but also those on all public telephones in the neighborhood. It found no calls made to Ray's brothers, or to telephone numbers in Louisiana, where Ray claimed he had a contact number for Raoul.

Cherpes, when first shown two pictures of Ray, studied them carefully for several minutes, and the best he could say was that the photos "bear a very close resemblance to him, however, I can't be sure."[12] Ray's generic features and quiet demeanor were two of his greatest assets as a fugitive—he could pass as everyman, often leaving no clear impression on those who encountered him.

On August 28, two days after checking into the rooming house, Ray paid a seven-dollar annual fee to rent a safe deposit box at the Birmingham Trust National Bank as Eric S. Galt.[13] As a required reference, he gave a fictitious Karl Galt of 2515 Lafayette Street, St. Louis (his late brother Franklin had lived on Lafayette, but there was no number 2515).*

The next day Ray answered an advertisement he had seen in the classified section of *The Birmingham News* for a 1966 Mustang. The asking price was $1,995. Ray called the owner, William Paisley, a sales manager for a local lumber company, and arranged to meet him that evening.[14] Shortly after 7:00 P.M., he arrived at Paisley's house by taxi and inspected the car. Paisley offered to let him take it for a test spin, but Ray declined, saying he did not have a driver's license.[15] Ray liked the red leather interior but not the exterior color—a pale yellow that appeared to be white. "If you are going to do something illegal," Ray later said, "I'd rather not have a white car to do it in."[16]

But without much hesitation, he told Paisley, "I'll take it off your hands."[17] "He didn't try to cut the price at all," recalled a surprised Paisley, who was ready to drop his price by up to $300. But Ray said that he had been saving his money, and since he worked on a river barge, he had no place to spend it.[18] The fact that Ray, normally a penny-pincher, did not even try to negotiate a better deal is a good indication that he was flush with money. The most expensive car he had ever previously owned was worth $250.[†]

---

* The bank's records show that Ray accessed the safe deposit box only four times. When he rented it on August 28, it was not opened. He returned later that day, at 2:32 P.M., and had access to it for five minutes. That means he put something into it on his first use, since it was empty beforehand. He later told Huie that he put his Rayns identification there, because he did not want to run the risk of being stopped by police and found with two different names. On his subsequent visits—September 5 (four minutes), September 21 (four minutes), and September 28 (three minutes)—Ray certainly did not return just to look at his Rayns identification. He must have kept it for storing the bulk of his money while in Birmingham (MURKIN 2323–2324, section 21, p. 107).

† Conspiracist Harold Weisberg noted that the Mustang had an automatic transmission. He then quoted a newspaper article in which a gas station attendant, after the assassination, mistakenly said he had fixed a clutch problem on the car. Weisberg uses the erroneous secondary source to imply there were two Mustangs, one that Ray bought from Paisley, and a second one with a clutch that he drove. As is typical of the wilder

They talked a little after agreeing on the deal. Ray, an inveterate liar, spun a new story for Paisley. He said he worked on a barge line that ran between New Orleans, St. Louis, and Memphis but did not like the twenty-day stretches without a break.[19] Instead, he was now hoping to land a job with the Social Security Administration.[20] As for his private life, Ray said he was divorced from his wife, who lived in Rocky Ridge, an area south of Homewood, Alabama.[21] When Paisley said he was sorry to hear that Galt was divorced, Ray breezily said, "Yeah, that's the way it goes."[22]

Before leaving, Paisley and Ray agreed to exchange the money and car registration the next morning near Ray's bank. When they met around 10:15 A.M., Ray was neatly dressed in a sports jacket and open-necked shirt. He took a thick roll of cash from his shirt pocket.[23] Paisley was nervous as Ray calmly counted out $2,000, mostly in twenties, with some hundreds—"Man, let's be careful with this kind of money," warned Paisley.[24] When Ray finished, Paisley crossed the street to his own bank, the First National, got five dollars change for Ray, and then took him to an adjoining parking lot, where he gave him keys to the car.[25]

Cherpes, the rooming house manager, was pleased to help Ray transfer the car title and get his driver's license.[26] On September 6, Ray and Cherpes filed the driver's license application at the Jefferson County Courthouse in downtown Birmingham. This was the first time Ray was asked for the full middle name of his alias, and he provided "Starvo." On the application, he made himself a little younger (three years) and a little taller (two inches).[27] He listed the rooming house as his local address, said he was an unemployed merchant mariner, and that his last license had expired in 1962 in Louisiana. That was a good place to give as a reference, since at the time Louisiana was one of the few states that did not maintain previous records for driver's licenses. When Ray took his physical driving test, he passed with an 86 percent score and a notation that he "needs training as to posture and attention." The report listed his eyesight as a perfect 20/20.

Later in the month, Ray ordered camera equipment—a Kodak super-8 camera, model M8; a Kodak Dual projector, model M95Z; one HPI combination splicing machine, and a twenty-foot remote-control cable—for $337.24 from the Superior Bulk Film Company in Chicago.[28] On the back of the order coupon Ray requested that the equipment be sent special delivery to him—"I would like this order as soon as possible"—and that he also wanted any manuals about "sound stripers, descriptive circular on LSF automatic cine printer,

---

conspiracy charges, the issue is raised to imply some supposedly sinister connotation, yet Weisberg never explains why Ray would have wanted two Mustangs or what purpose it would serve in an assassination plot still over seven months away.

and the price of the Eumig Mark S Sound Projector."* He also sent a money order for $8.95 to the Modern Photo Bookstore in New York requesting the *Focal Encyclopedia of Photography*, described on the book jacket as "a one-volume photographic library." On the rear of the order coupon, which Ray had clipped from *Modern Photography* magazine, the FBI later discovered his left thumbprint.[29]

Ray has an explanation for almost everything he did in Birmingham, and, as might be expected, it revolves around Raoul, who Ray says directed his actions. Two days after he moved into the rooming house, Ray checked with the general delivery branch of the post office, and a letter from Raoul had arrived that very day. It directed him to meet Raoul that evening at a diner—the Starlite Café—across the street from the post office.[†] There they met. "We'll need a good set of wheels," Raoul supposedly told Ray. "But I don't want to spend more than a couple of thousand. Can you take care of that?"[30] The next day they again met at the Starlite, and Raoul gave Ray $2,000. After he bought the Mustang, Ray picked up Raoul from the Starlite and drove him to the rooming house. Even though they were at the Starlite on three occasions and at the rooming house most of that night, no one remembered anyone with Ray, nor did they recall anyone who could have been Raoul.

Raoul is then supposed to have told Ray that "there are some things I want you to buy."[31] He gave him $500 and the list of camera equipment to order, which Ray assumed Raoul just wanted to sell in Mexico, where it might fetch a higher price.[32] When Ray asked for some more money for living expenses, Raoul forked over another $500 without any questions.[‡][33] He also supposedly gave Ray a new contact telephone number, this time in Baton Rouge.[§] Finally,

---

*   The sound striper lays a magnetic coating for a sound track. The cine printer reproduces film. The Eumig projector was to record sound on film.

†   The letter was addressed to Eric S. Galt, for which Ray had no identification at that time. He said the postal clerk asked him for his middle initial and, when he said "S," then gave him the letter. As with Ray's other descriptions of how he met with Raoul, the letter routine at a general delivery post office requires a lot of luck to work correctly and seems a most unlikely form of communication. For instance, if Ray had not checked with the post office that day, or if the letter was delayed by even a day, Raoul and Ray would miss their evening rendezvous. Somehow, in his versions, Ray usually managed to check with the post office just after the arrival of Raoul's letters, usually directing Ray to do something later that very day.

‡   Later, in his book *Who Killed Martin Luther King?*, Ray changed the amount Raoul supposedly gave him, upping the expense money from $500 to $1,000.

§   Ray later said that when he left Birmingham, he drove through Baton Rouge. Curious about the number Raoul had given him, Ray said he went to a phone booth and checked all the telephone numbers in the Baton Rouge directory until he found it. The

Raoul asked for a set of keys to the Mustang. "I gave him a set of keys at his request," wrote Ray, "I think I got about 3 sets from the original owner."[34] (Paisley was adamant that he gave Ray only two sets of keys, and since Ray admitted to having two when he left Birmingham, there was no extra set for Raoul.[35])

Before leaving the rooming house, Raoul told Ray that "we would be taking something into Mexico in a couple of months and he would write me where to meet him."[36]

Again, Ray's version makes little sense from the perspective of a Raoul-type character. In a matter of days he had given Ray almost $4,000 and allowed him to buy and register a car under his new alias. He had no guarantee that Ray, a fugitive convict, would not abscond with the cash and car. A real Raoul could simply have used Galt's name to buy the car and camera equipment himself, thereby never risking the money. Meeting Ray in public places such as the café was an unnecessary risk that no seasoned criminal would take if he wanted to ensure that no one could later tie him to Ray. And, of course, Raoul was supposed to have stayed in Birmingham for a couple of nights while he met with Ray. But where? The FBI's postassassination investigation failed to find any hotel, motel, or flophouse with the right name or description.

However, from Ray's perspective, his movements and actions in Birmingham make perfect sense. Having given his battered car to Jerry, he needed a new one. Buying it from a private party was a smart idea, since Ray had cash and no driver's license, something that might have raised questions or suspicion from a car dealer. Nervous that the FBI might be close to tracing his John Rayns identification and social security number, it appears Ray came to Bir-

---

number was registered to a Herman A. Thompson. The House Select Committee on Assassinations extensively investigated Thompson. He had been an assistant chief criminal sheriff's deputy in East Baton Rouge for twenty-six years.

Under oath, Thompson stated he never knew anyone named or nicknamed Raoul. He adamantly denied ever knowing, meeting, or speaking with Ray or anyone using Ray's known aliases. The committee investigated whether Ray may have maliciously implicated Thompson as a means of settling a grudge or aiding a fellow inmate, but Thompson could not recall ever arresting, incarcerating, or transporting any person who had contact with the prisons where Ray had been an inmate.

Thompson said he was never a member of any white extremist organization and that he never had any complaints or disciplinary actions filed against him. His former employer confirmed his statements.

The committee concluded it "found no evidence to indicate that Herman Thompson was involved in the assassination or with an individual named Raoul." The committee concluded, further, that "Ray's allegation was merely an attempt to gain credence for his Raoul story and to raise an implication of official complicity in the assassination." Even Ray, at one point when pressed by the committee, suddenly said, "I thought that was a fraudulent number. . . . I concluded it was probably something just to put the heat on someone."

mingham in order simply to establish solid identification for Galt, and in this he succeeded. Although he still did not have a passport, birth certificate, or social security card, he now had a driver's license, car registration and title, and safe-deposit-box agreement, all showing him to be a resident of Alabama with a permanent address at 2608 Highland Avenue, the site of the rooming house.

Besides obtaining a car and getting documentation for his Galt ID, what about the camera equipment? Ray told Huie that he "didn't know what the stuff was," but that "after buying [it] and reading about films and cameras I got interested in pictures."[37] However, his detailed note to the mail order company exposes this as a lie and shows that Ray was already well informed when he ordered it.[38] Some researchers have speculated that he merely wanted to take numerous pictures of himself so that he could better decide how to disguise himself as a fugitive. Again, Ray told Huie that when he was in Birmingham, he expected that at any moment the FBI might put him on its ten most-wanted list.[39] But Ray did not just order a basic camera to take photos of himself; he asked instead for equipment that allowed him to film amateur movies, including the use of slow motion and settings for different lighting conditions. If he had merely wanted to take his own picture with a remote cable, he could have had the entire setup for less than $50, not the nearly $400 he spent. One filmmaker who reviewed Ray's order told author George McMillan that Ray had purchased "a completely self-sufficient movie-making unit of good quality."[40] Given its sophistication and the money he spent, a more likely explanation is that Ray was buying it for his own freelance venture into the porn business. Just a couple of months before ordering the camera equipment, Jerry said, the brothers had discussed that possibility at the Chicago summit meeting. A few weeks after that, James had ordered sex manuals from a California distributor. When he returned to the States in late August, he again asked Jerry to go into porn with him, but Jerry claimed that he had declined.

Moreover, James had already inquired about a sound unit, and in his order asked for the long remote cable. It meant not only that he contemplated commercial sales, but also that he might have thought about personally being in the films. A few weeks earlier, while in Montreal, Ray had sent a one-dollar money order to E. Z. Formula in Hollywood, California, the maker of a compound that promised to turn regular glass into a two-way mirror, something that would allow him to surreptitiously film women.[41] When asked about his interest in the chemical by the Select Committee, Ray dodged the question. "I really don't know what I ordered. . . . If there's something in there, I don't know all the technical terms of the stuff."[42] The only thing he lacked was the equipment to develop the films, but a host of independent printing companies existed in Los Angeles, a city to which he would soon move. To Ray, his initial order was likely a capital investment in what could prove to be a lucrative new business.

While in Birmingham, Ray continued paying for his weekly locksmithing correspondence lessons, but also added some new ventures: once-a-week dance lessons at the Continental Dance Club Studios, and membership in a lonely hearts club in Canada.[43] He says that he took the ten-dollar dance course because "I was thinking I mite half to go to a Latin American country and it helps socialy if you know a little something about the Latin Dances."[44] His instructor remembered him unkindly as a clumsy loner.[45] She tried to integrate him into the group of sixteen other students, but Ray was too timid. When she spoke to him, he would not look at her eyes but instead glance away or drop his head. He answered questions only with a simple yes or no.*[46]

As for the lonely hearts club, when Ray left Canada for Birmingham, he had taken some Canadian newspapers with him. In one of those, he saw an advertisement for "one of the international clubs. . . . These people who belong to these clubs are not criminals but they are not what the hippies refer to as squares. I still had not ruled out a Canadian passport and I thought I mite contack someone in Canada through one of these clubs."[47] He claimed that if he developed a relationship, he would eventually ask someone to sign his passport application.

It is unlikely that Ray really thought he should know Latin dance steps if he intended to make a successful flight as a fugitive to Latin America. Also, it is hard to imagine why he would still be interested in the difficult process of finding a Canadian to vouch that they had known him for two years so that he could get a passport, if supposedly his entire relationship with Raoul was predicated on the eventual payoff of a passport. It is more likely that Ray simply considered both the dance lessons and the lonely hearts club as ways of meeting women. He never got a bite from either.

Ray maintains that "about the 5th or 6th of October Raoul wrote me and ask me to come to Heuvo Larado [Nuevo Laredo] Mex" and that is why he left Birmingham.[48] At times he has described his upcoming venture as gunrunning and at other times as dope smuggling.[49] But actually, Ray had decided to leave before his alleged friend ever contacted him. In late September, Ray had telephoned the Chicago film company to tell them he would be leaving Birmingham no later than October 7, the last day through which his rent was paid at the rooming house.[50] He also wrote to the Modern Photo Bookstore in

---

*   The owners of the Birmingham dance studio had previously owned one in New Orleans. They mistakenly told the FBI that they remembered "Galt" had also taken a year-long course from them in the Big Easy in 1964. Of course, they were surprised to learn that Ray was incarcerated in Jeff City at that time.

New York on September 26 and said, "If you have not allready mailed the book (PLEASE DO NOT MAIL IT) I am moving and will shortly send you my correct address."[51] As for his safe deposit box, he made his final visit on September 28, taking three minutes to clear it out.* The notification to the camera company and the bookstore, and the last visit to his deposit box, mean that Ray had decided on his own to leave Birmingham nearly a week before he claimed to receive any direction from Raoul.[†]

Now that he was ready to leave, Ray decided it was time to replace the gun he had buried in Canada before he reentered the States. On October 1, he saw another classified ad in *The Birmingham News*. This was for a Japanese-made Liberty Chief snub-nosed .38-caliber revolver.[52] Ray called the seller, Walter Spain, drove to his house, and examined the gun that evening. Spain—who was also unable later to positively identify Ray from photographs—said he wanted $65 for it.[53] Ray pulled out a stack of bills and peeled off the money. He pocketed the pistol and left.[54]

There was a strategy in the length of Ray's stay in Birmingham, and he completed it when he finished building the paper trail for Galt. The last identification items for which he was waiting were the license plates for his Mustang,

---

*   Ray initially told Huie that he sent the safe deposit keys back to the bank from Baton Rouge while he was driving to Mexico. Bank records show the account, while inactive, was closed on December 13, nearly two months later. Some authors, such as Clay Blair, have contended that since Ray was in Los Angeles in mid-December, the timing of the account's closing raises the possibility of an accomplice. However, their conclusion appears to be based on a mistake by a bank clerk. When Ray returned the keys, he included a letter in which he wrote that he no longer needed the box since he was "moving to Louisiana." One of the bank clerks had noted when closing Ray's file that he had moved to Baton Rouge. When asked by the FBI why she listed Baton Rouge, she could not recall, but guessed that it may have been due to the envelope's postmark. There is no way to know, however, since by the time the FBI investigated, the bank had long ago destroyed the envelope that contained Ray's letter. It is more likely that the letter actually arrived in mid-October, and the clerk either wrote the wrong date into the bank's records or forgot to officially close the box until December. Such writers as Blair and Huie subsequently converted the likely clerical error into an incontrovertible fact in their versions.

†   By the time Ray wrote *Tennessee Waltz* in 1987, he realized that his story's timing meant he had made his decision to leave Birmingham instead of taking orders from Raoul. As a result, Ray altered the story in his book, saying that Raoul actually wrote him a letter "in late September" about the upcoming trip to Mexico. Before the House Select Committee, Ray said that he had called the contact number in New Orleans several times in late September, and an unidentified man, someone who kept track of Raoul and his whereabouts, coordinated Ray's departure for Nuevo Laredo. Yet in an interview with Dan Rather in 1977, Ray had said he did not know he was to meet Raoul in Nuevo Laredo when he left Birmingham.

James Earl Ray was born in the basement of this two-room house in the rough blue-collar town of Alton, Illinois.

Ray (left) at fourteen. By this age, he had already been picked up by the police for petty theft and had started visiting prostitutes and bars with his uncle Earl, a convicted felon.

LIFE

THE ACCUSED KILLER

RAY alias GALT
The Revealing Story of a Mean Kid

James Earl Ray, age 10, in third grade in Ewing, Mo. (under red arrow?)

MAY 3 · 1968 · 35¢

After the assassination, much of the press coverage focused on Ray's tough upbringing in a poor white family with a nearly one-hundred-year history of criminal behavior. *Life*'s cover story on young Ray (partially hidden on the right, second row) was one of the harshest portraits, describing him as a young bully who could not stay out of trouble.

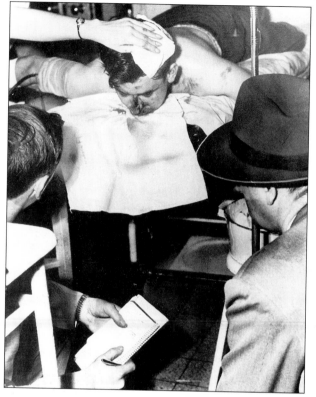

Ray botched a 1952 armed robbery of a taxicab in Chicago, and was shot in the arm by police before he surrendered after a wild chase through city streets. This was his third adult arrest, and he spent twenty-two months in state prison for the crime. (AP/WIDE WORLD PHOTOS)

Although he pulled dozens of successful robberies during the 1950s, Ray's luck again turned bad in 1959, when he was arrested for several supermarket robberies. Since it was his fourth major offense, the thirty-year-old Ray was sentenced to twenty years in prison. (AP/WIDE WORLD PHOTOS)

Ray as he looked in 1960 when he entered Missouri State Penitentiary, one of the toughest prisons in the United States. There he developed a reputation as a "merchant," dealing in drugs and other contraband. He was also known as a racist who abused drugs himself, primarily amphetamines. (FBI COPY OF MISSOURI STATE PENITENTIARY PHOTO)

Six years later, in 1966, Ray looked gaunt and haggard, perhaps from his drug abuse. That same year he made his second unsuccessful escape attempt. On April 23, 1967, Ray finally broke out. (PRISON PHOTO, MISSOURI CORRECTIONS)

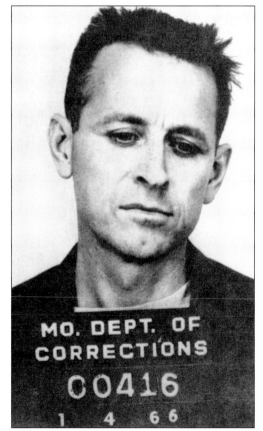

After escaping from prison in April 1967, Ray threw police off his trail by moving frequently across the United States and Canada, as well as Mexico, where he was when this picture was taken. It was during these travels that Ray later claimed to have met a mysterious man he called Raoul, who would later be at the center of his defense in the King assassination. (AP/WIDE WORLD PHOTOS)

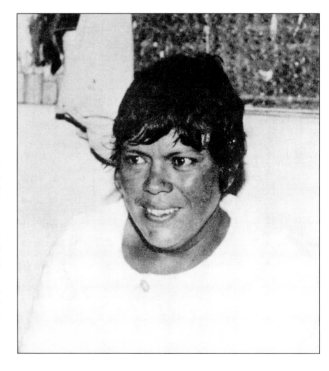

While in Mexico, Ray spent most of his time in Puerto Vallarta in the company of prostitutes. Among them, Manuela Aguirre Medrano, who used the professional name Irma La Douce, was with Ray the most. According to some who met him there, he also smuggled marijuana and took racy photos of some of the women. (HOUSE SELECT COMMITTEE ON ASSASSINATIONS)

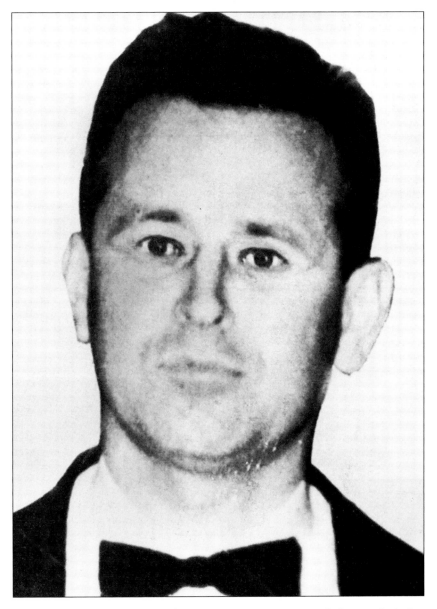

In his fugitive year leading up to the assassination, Ray spent nearly five months in Los Angeles. A habitué of local bars and flophouses, Ray also visited hypnotists and psychologists, took dance lessons, had plastic surgery, and attended bartending school. For his March 1967 graduation photo from the International School of Bartending—taken only a month before the assassination—Ray closed his eyes, with the hope that it might make him difficult to identify. An FBI sketch artist drew the eyes onto the photo. (FBI)

THE SANITATION STRIKE

Tensions were high in Memphis after 1,300 sanitation workers, most of them black, defied the mayor's order and went on strike in February 1968. A spontaneous February 28 demonstration for the strikers ended in violence when the police rioted, gassing and clubbing citizens. That provoked an outcry and led directly to Martin Luther King, Jr.'s decision to become involved in the Memphis strike. (MISSISSIPPI VALLEY COLLECTION, UNIVERSITY OF MEMPHIS)

Martin Luther King, Jr., and Ralph Abernathy (right) begin a march through Memphis on March 28, 1968. Young agitators in the crowd started breaking windows, and the protest soon turned violent, prompting the Tennessee governor to send in 4,000 National Guardsmen. King, sickened by the violence, vowed to return quickly to Memphis for another demonstration. (MISSISSIPPI VALLEY COLLECTION, UNIVERSITY OF MEMPHIS)

THE ASSASSINATION

At 6:01 P.M., on April 4, 1968, Martin Luther King was shot as he leaned over the railing of the balcony that ran in front of his motel room. Within minutes of the shooting, King's aides and friends, who had run to his assistance (King is lying on the floor), greeted police by pointing in the direction from which the shot had originated. (House Select Committee on Assassinations)

What most of the eyewitnesses immediately pointed to was the rear of two buildings, about eighty feet up a low slope across the street from the motel where King was staying. The buildings comprised separate wings of the flophouse where James Earl Ray, using an alias, had rented a room only three hours before the assassination. The window circled on the right is the bathroom from which the shot was fired. (Attorney General File)

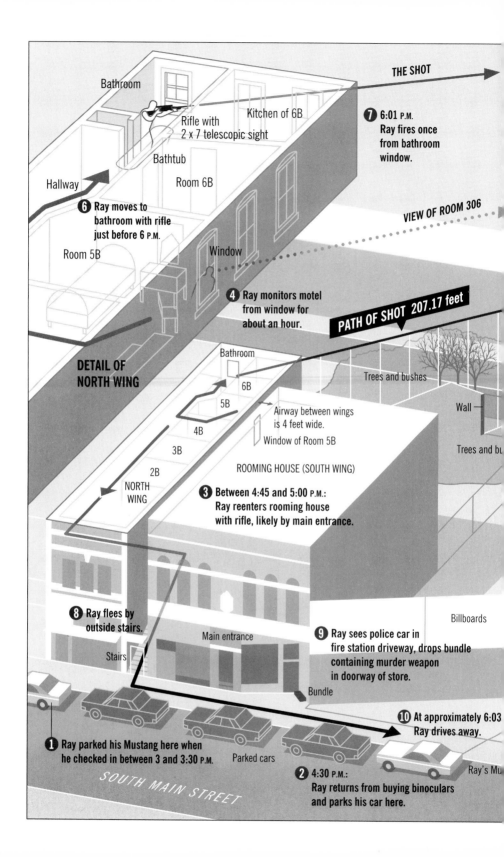

THE SHOT

7 6:01 P.M.
Ray fires once
from bathroom
window.

Bathroom

Rifle with
2 x 7 telescopic sight

Kitchen of 6B

Bathtub

Hallway

Room 6B

VIEW OF ROOM 306

6 Ray moves to
bathroom with rifle
just before 6 P.M.

Room 5B

Window

PATH OF SHOT 207.17 feet

4 Ray monitors motel
from window for
about an hour.

**DETAIL OF
NORTH WING**

Bathroom

6B

Trees and bushes

5B

Wall

4B

Airway between wings
is 4 feet wide.

3B

Window of Room 5B

Trees and bu

2B

ROOMING HOUSE (SOUTH WING)

NORTH
WING

3 Between 4:45 and 5:00 P.M.:
Ray reenters rooming house
with rifle, likely by main entrance.

8 Ray flees by
outside stairs.

Billboards

Main entrance

9 Ray sees police car in
fire station driveway, drops bundle
containing murder weapon
in doorway of store.

Stairs

Bundle

10 At approximately 6:03
Ray drives away.

1 Ray parked his Mustang here when
he checked in between 3 and 3:30 P.M.

Parked cars

Ray's Mu

SOUTH MAIN STREET

2 4:30 P.M.:
Ray returns from buying binoculars
and parks his car here.

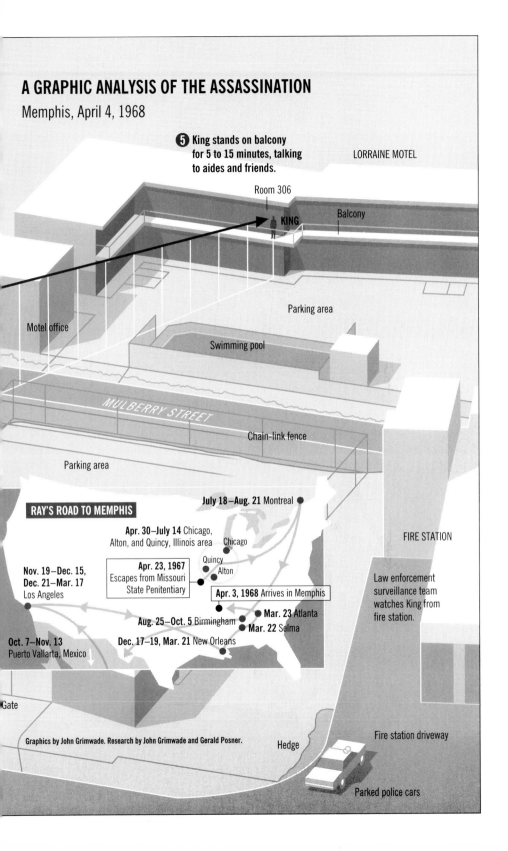

A GRAPHIC ANALYSIS OF THE ASSASSINATION
Memphis, April 4, 1968

5 King stands on balcony for 5 to 15 minutes, talking to aides and friends.

LORRAINE MOTEL

Room 306

KING

Balcony

Parking area

Motel office

Swimming pool

MULBERRY STREET

Chain-link fence

Parking area

RAY'S ROAD TO MEMPHIS

July 18–Aug. 21 Montreal

Apr. 30–July 14 Chicago, Alton, and Quincy, Illinois area

Chicago

Quincy

Alton

Apr. 23, 1967 Escapes from Missouri State Penitentiary

Nov. 19–Dec. 15, Dec. 21–Mar. 17 Los Angeles

Apr. 3, 1968 Arrives in Memphis

Mar. 23 Atlanta

Aug. 25–Oct. 5 Birmingham

Mar. 22 Selma

Oct. 7–Nov. 13 Puerto Vallarta, Mexico

Dec. 17–19, Mar. 21 New Orleans

FIRE STATION

Law enforcement surveillance team watches King from fire station.

Gate

Graphics by John Grimwade. Research by John Grimwade and Gerald Posner.

Hedge

Fire station driveway

Parked police cars

After Ray fled the scene of the assassination, police entered his room and discovered that the dresser and mirror had been moved away from the open window and replaced by a chair. Someone leaning slightly out the window could observe Dr. King's room at the nearby motel. (AP/WIDE WORLD PHOTOS)

Within a couple of minutes of the assassination, the police discovered a bundle in front of a store doorway underneath the rooming house. It included a rifle bought five days earlier by Ray. His fingerprints were on the gun and telescopic site, as well as other items in the bundle. (HOUSE SELECT COMMITTEE ON ASSASSINATIONS)

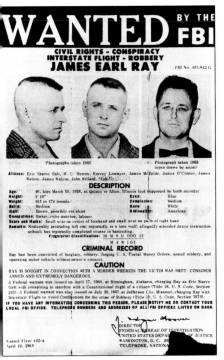

The FBI identified Ray from fingerprints and released a wanted poster for him fifteen days after the assassination. By then, he was hiding in Toronto, Canada. Ray applied for birth certificates of local Toronto residents Paul Bridgman and Ramon Sneyd. Living near those men was Eric Galt, whose name Ray had used during most of the year leading up to King's murder. Some conspiracists have claimed that the three Canadians bore a remarkable resemblance to Ray, implying that the names were supplied to him as part of a sophisticated plot. But, in fact, beyond being middle-aged white males, they do not look much like Ray. (FBI FILE COPY OF WANTED POSTER)

Paul Bridgman   Ramon Sneyd   Eric Galt

Ray obtained a Canadian passport in the name of Ramon George Sneyd. He then visited Portugal and England, trying in vain to join a mercenary group fighting in Africa. On June 8, 1968, sixty-five days after King's murder, an alert British policeman spotted the name Sneyd on a watch list at Heathrow Airport as Ray tried to board a plane for Brussels. He was arrested and extradited back to the States that summer. (HOUSE SELECT COMMITTEE ON ASSASSINATIONS)

STORY FOR SALE

Ray's first attorneys were Arthur Hanes, Sr., the former mayor of Birmingham, and his son, Arthur Jr. (above center). William Bradford Huie, a well-known writer (above right), signed a contract with the Haneses and Ray to obtain Ray's exclusive story and for all of them to split any profits. Barred from interviewing him in prison, Huie received Ray's story in handwritten notes and letters (right), which because of their cumulative size were called the 20,000 Words. Ray fired the Haneses just before his trial was to start in October 1968, and hired famed Texas trial lawyer Percy Foreman (above left). (Top: Mississippi Valley Collection, University of Memphis; sheet of Ray's writing: House Select Committee on Assassinations)

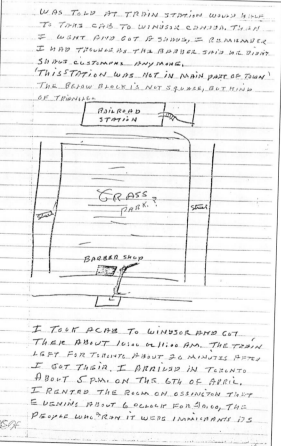

THE PROSECUTION

The prosecution team: District Attorney General Phil Canale (center), Executive Assistant Attorney General Robert K. Dwyer (left), and Assistant Attorney General James C. Beasley. Dwyer and Beasley were disappointed that they could not obtain a death penalty conviction. (MISSISSIPPI VALLEY COLLECTION, UNIVERSITY OF MEMPHIS)

Three days after his guilty plea, Ray wrote the trial judge, recanting the plea and asking for a new trial. It was the beginning of three decades of herculean legal efforts by Ray and a broad assortment of attorneys to win his freedom. (MISSISSIPPI VALLEY COLLECTION, UNIVERSITY OF MEMPHIS)

THE LEGAL GAME

J. B. Stoner (center), one of the country's most virulent racists, became Ray's attorney in 1969. Ray's brothers John (left) and Jerry (right) joined Stoner for an impromptu 1969 press conference in Memphis. The House Select Committee on Assassinations investigated whether either brother had any involvement in the assassination. (AP/WIDE WORLD PHOTOS)

In the late 1970s, when Ray appeared before the House Select Committee on Assassinations, he was represented by Mark Lane, a caustic conspiracy buff who had earlier written a book contending that Ray was a patsy. (AP/WIDE WORLD PHOTOS)

William Pepper (center), Ray's latest lawyer, as he was confronted in 1997 by two retired military officers, Colonel Lee Mize (left) and Major Rudi Gresham (right), over Pepper's charges that a military sniper team was in Memphis on the day King was killed. (COURTESY OF RUDI GRESHAM)

ATTEMPTS AT FREEDOM

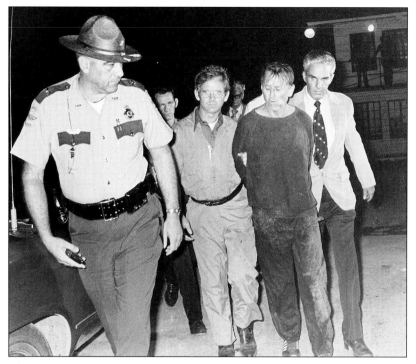

In 1977, Ray made a successful breakout from Brushy Mountain State Prison. It was his second attempt since pleading guilty to killing King. More than 125 prison guards, state troopers, and FBI agents, assisted by bloodhounds, combed through the thick wilderness in search of Ray, who was found only five miles from the prison, fifty-five hours after he escaped. (AP/WIDE WORLD PHOTOS)

In one of the bizarre turns in Ray's unusual life, during his 1977 trial for the escape, he met courtroom artist Anna Sandhu (right, appearing on *Today* with Jane Pauley in 1978). The two married, and she campaigned for his freedom— until she suddenly filed for divorce in 1990. She has said that the real reason she divorced Ray was that during a phone argument, she told him, "I've never believed you could have killed Martin Luther King," and Ray yelled, "Yeah, I did it. So what?" and then slammed down the receiver. (AP/WIDE WORLD PHOTOS)

On Thursday, March 27, 1997, Martin Luther King's son Dexter met with James Earl Ray in his Nashville prison. Ray's attorney, William Pepper, had urged Dexter King—who believes that a massive government conspiracy killed his father—to meet the confessed killer. During their meeting, Ray denied killing Dr. King. "I believe you, and my family believes you," said Dexter. (AP/WIDE WORLD PHOTOS)

which he had to purchase after October 1, when the old ones expired. On October 2, Ray bought the new tags: Alabama 1-38993.[55] While standing in line at the motor vehicles department, George Seibels, Jr., who ran successfully for mayor in the next month's election, came by politicking. "He shook hands with me and asked me to vote for him," Ray later boasted to Huie.

Now that he had his license plates, Ray made final preparations for his departure. Having endured Birmingham's sweltering summer, he was eager to leave. Although Ray later remarked that his time in Birmingham had been "uneventful," he had often been depressed during his six weeks there, and for a while his melancholy was so pronounced that he visited several local doctors.[56] His once again obsessive fretting about his health created some of the problem. He was sick for nearly two months, he later complained.[57] He had trouble sleeping. To one of the doctors he complained he had the "flu or something with a sore throat"—later he thought it was pneumonia.[58] For that, he received "some shots plus some pills [the antibiotics penicillin and tetracycline, and some sleeping pills]." Then later, "I was still feeling bad," so Ray saw a psychiatrist who prescribed antidepressant pills.*[59]

The shipment of the camera equipment from Superior Bulk Film finally arrived on October 4, but the company had substituted a Crestline super-8 camera for the Kodak.[60] Ray did not want the replacement, and the next day he wrote back saying that he "was well please with everything except the camera, which I am returning. The camera you sent me has only one film speed and I wanted the Kodak M8 which has 4." Impatient, Ray went out the same day he wrote that letter (October 5) and bought a Polaroid 220 Land camera. He soon wrote another letter to Superior Bulk Film, asking for a refund instead of a replacement.†

---

* Ray later wrote several lists for Huie titled "points that could be used against me." One was "mental history" and another was "received anti-depression pills from Dr. at Birmingham." The other two dealt with his two-month internment in the psychiatric ward while incarcerated at Jeff City and his use of hypnotists and psychiatrists when he was in Los Angeles after his Birmingham stay.

† The film company first tried mailing the Kodak camera to Galt in Birmingham, and then later a refund to him in Mexico. Both were returned. Ray did not receive the $140 refund for the camera until a week before King's assassination. He never cashed it before the murder and afterward had to destroy it because he "couldn't take the risk of cashing it." Even when he talked to Huie, months after the assassination, he was still bitter that he had lost that money.

As for his purchase of a Polaroid Land camera, Huie reported that Ray paid $245 for it, and McMillan repeated that, but it is almost certainly wrong. The author checked with Polaroid, and the 220 camera, an instant-developing still camera introduced that year, was the second-cheapest in the 200 series, with a manufacturer's suggested retail

Also on October 5, he sent a letter to the Continental Dance Club, apologizing that he could not attend the rest of the classes because he was leaving town, but that if he returned, he would resume his lessons.[61] Later that day, he told Peter Cherpes he was leaving for work on a boat in Mobile, Alabama.[62] He drove south, this time in his flashy Mustang, a Confederate sticker on the front bumper, breezily heading back toward Nuevo Laredo, Mexico.[63] "I knew it from my last visit to Mexico in 1959," recalled Ray. "On the outskirts there was an area known as 'Boystown,' a wide-open scene with about 35 bars that ran 24 hours except for a ten-minute break when the operators cleared the floor so someone could sweep up. I'd gotten to know Boystown pretty well on my last visit. I wondered if it was still the same wild place."[64]

---

price of $75. Even with accessories and film, it is unlikely that Ray could have spent $245 on the camera. Ray told the Select Committee that the Polaroid cost him $56, and he was probably right.

22

Mexican Holiday

R ay said he left Birmingham on the morning of October 6, 1967.[1] Before he reached Nuevo Laredo he drove partway to Dallas to visit a former inmate from Leavenworth. He claimed that since he thought he might be carrying drugs for Raoul, he wanted advice from the ex-con, who had himself been a drug smuggler. But he turned around halfway since it "might not be a good idea because he may be under surveillance himself."[2] He then stopped in Baton Rouge, checked into a hotel, and, he said, spent considerable time searching a phone book to find the number that Raoul had recently given him.[3]

The following afternoon, October 7, Ray was issued a tourist card in the name Eric S. Galt and crossed the Mexican border at Nuevo Laredo.*[4] It was there, he said, that he had his only Mexican contact with Raoul. They met at a hotel on the Mexican side of the border, and the two then crossed back into the

---

* If Ray drove partway to Dallas and then to Baton Rouge before arriving in Nuevo Laredo, it was an arduous feat, since he had some 1,400 miles to cover. He made the trip, by his account, in about thirty hours. The driving alone could easily take twenty-five hours, and then he needed time for his phone book investigation, food, and gas. He did not sleep for two days, providing the first evidence he may again have found a temporary source of amphetamines, the same drug that used to keep him up in multiday spurts at Jeff City.

United States.* From a second car parked near the border, they picked up a spare tire, and crossed again into Mexico.[5] Ray assumed the tire contained rare coins, jewelry, or even counterfeit money. "I don't believe you smuggle narcotics into Mexico," he said, "it would probably be something manufactured. Manufacturing products have a high resale value."[6]

They returned to the hotel in Nuevo Laredo where Ray had earlier checked in. "We talked a short while," Ray later wrote, "and he told me what he wanted me to do which was to haul the tyre and its contents through the customs check in the interior, I guess that would be about 50 klms. from the border (he also told me to keep the photographic equipment for the time being)."[7]

The next day, Ray and Raoul drove through the interior customs checkpoint in separate cars. In the car with Raoul was another man, whom Ray described as a Mexican with Indian features. When they were out of sight of the guards, they transferred the tire back to Raoul's car. Ray has claimed that Raoul then gave him $2,000 (though he told Huie it was $3,000) and that Raoul told him he "couldn't get the travel documents," but that he would have them the next time they met, and that he would also give Ray $10,000 to $12,000 for the next job, which "involved taking guns and accessories into Mexico."[8]

Although Ray said he was "mad as hell" that there was no passport, he agreed to let Raoul contact him again. He told Raoul he would probably stay in Mexico for a month and then head for Los Angeles. "Raoul said okay," recalled Ray, "but for me to let him know where I was by calling the New Orleans telephone number from time to time, and that he'd write me general delivery in Los Angeles."[9] (Before the Select Committee, Ray changed his story to say that Raoul had given him a new telephone number in New Orleans with which to stay in touch.)[10]

Ray may be partially telling the truth, at least about smuggling goods into Mexico. He had been to Mexico in 1959 when he was "cooling off" after pulling a $1,300 heist from a Madison, Illinois, gambling club. Then he had smuggled small appliances that had a high tariff in Mexico into the port town of Campeche.[11] He knew that fencing such items as jewelry and coins was profitable. It is hard to imagine that Ray, a habitual criminal, had suddenly turned straight since he had fled from Jeff City six months earlier; instead, he was likely still plying his trade. When the Select Committee asked Ray if he was smuggling goods while in Mexico, he gave a weak denial: "Uh, no, not particularly. I was thinking about it one time."[12]

---

* The FBI checked all the hotels and motels in Nuevo Laredo for the month of October under the names Raoul, John L. Rayns, and Eric S. Galt, and could not find that any of them were ever registered.

Ray's description of the smuggling sounds authentic. What does not sound truthful is what Raoul supposedly paid him—$2,000 to $3,000. In Canada, Ray claimed he was paid $750 for two runs across the border with a much higher-risk cargo, probably heroin. Yet in Mexico, where the *aduaneros*—Mexican customs officials—were notoriously lax about what came *into* their country, why would Ray be paid up to four times as much for only a single run, with a lower-risk cargo of jewelry or coins? If Ray made several thousand dollars, it is probably because he had stolen the goods himself while in Birmingham and then reaped all the profits when he fenced them in Mexico.

Additional evidence that Ray was involved in some type of border smuggling was uncovered when author William Bradford Huie visited the San Francisco hotel in Acapulco after the assassination. That is where Ray initially drove after crossing the border. It was the same hotel he had stayed in when he visited in 1959. The local police chief later accompanied Huie to the hotel, and they asked to examine the registration card of Eric S. Galt, which would indicate his arrival around October 10. However, when the hotel manager retrieved the registration book, he discovered that the space where Galt had signed his name had been carefully cut out. In compliance with police regulations, toward the bottom of the page was a handwritten explanation for the excision. According to the note, on October 14, only a week after Ray crossed the border at Nuevo Laredo, his registration had been examined and taken by a federal police officer from Mexico City named Ramon del Rio.[13] If Ray was under investigation in Mexico six months before King's assassination, it was almost certainly related to his border crossing.*

Ray did not like Acapulco the second time around. He stayed only four days. "The reason I left Acapulco was everything was money," he later wrote, "you couldn't even park or go to the beach without someone wanting pesos."[14] Several years earlier, while in Jeff City, Ray had read an article in *True* magazine about an up-and-coming resort, Puerto Vallarta.[15] He decided to go there. The three-hundred-mile drive north was difficult because of poor road conditions caused by the rainy season, so he stopped for three days in Gaudalajara, staying at the Pancho Villa motel.[16] While there, a local dentist treated him for an abscessed molar.[17]

---

* The Mexican government, pursuant to the author's repeated written requests for information about the original investigation, as well as access to Ray's file, finally said that they did not have any files or information about Ray. It is possible that what Huie interpreted as a federal police interest in Ray in 1967 was mistaken. Hotel proprietors are required by Mexican law to forward daily reports of foreign guests to the Federal Office of Tourism. After the assassination, a federal police officer may have come to the San Francisco hotel to excise the signature, and the October 14 reference on the bottom of the register refers merely to the date Ray checked out (he checked in on October 10).

Ray finally reached Puerto Vallarta on Thursday, October 19, and registered as Eric S. Galt at the Hotel Rio. On his registration form he listed Alabama
as his native state, Cherpes's rooming house as his permanent address, and as
his profession listed "Employed by Publisher."[18] He settled into a $4.80-a-day,
second-floor room that overlooked a small stream where fishermen stretched
their nets and locals fried fish along the banks at night. Although only a few
hundred miles from Acapulco, Puerto Vallarta was primitive and cheap in
comparison, largely undiscovered by the combination of jet-setters and package tours that would later convert it into another slick and pricey tourist
haven. It did not take Ray long to conclude "this was about the best town in
Mexico I had been in." After the assassination he told Huie, "When I get out of
jail again I'm going back there permanently."[19]

Ray spent the first three weeks at the Hotel Rio, and the last week at the
more expensive Tropicana, directly on the beach.* For Ray, his month in Puerto
Vallarta may have been the single season in his life when he felt as though he
was somebody. In a town where many of the streets were unpaved, donkeys
still transported goods, and jalopies were owned by only a small number of residents, Ray's Mustang conferred a special status. Since he now announced he
was a writer, and had a portable typewriter, notebook, and cameras to prove it,
he won even more attention, especially at the local whorehouses that became
his haunts.

While he was at the Hotel Rio, another visitor from Alabama heard about
the popular Southern American writer who had just come to town and knocked
on Ray's door. The tourist wanted to reminisce about their home state. Ray knew
he could easily be unmasked as a liar and simply listened, occasionally grunting
or nodding in agreement to whatever his visitor said. "I guess he thought I was
crazy as I didn't say mush as I didn't know mush about the state."[20]

"I spent most of my time on the beach," he recalled. "Their was one brothel
which I was in about 4 times plus two times during the day on business."[21] The

---

* While Ray was at the Hotel Rio for nineteen days, he did not make a single telephone
call from his room. William Bradford Huie inadvertently created one of the mysteries in
the case when he interviewed the manager of the Hotel Tropicana and reported in his
book that the day before he checked out Ray charged a single call to Corpus Christi,
Texas. However, according to Huie, the Mexican police had taken the charge record after
the assassination and never released it. Ray, meanwhile, denied making any calls while
in Puerto Vallarta. On this, Ray told the truth. Huie relied on the word of the manager
that the records did not exist, but in fact they did. Mexican authorities and the FBI reviewed the records, made available by the hotel's accountant, Carlos Manzo, and they
reveal that Ray made no calls from that room. In addition, 12,000 toll calls made
through the central exchange in Puerto Vallarta from October 15 to November 20,
1967, were checked, and none were placed in the name Galt (MURKIN 5101, section
69, pp. 150–51).

business he referred to was that a bartender wanted to trade a plot of land for Ray's Mustang.[22] Ray was tempted. He even thought about returning to the States to steal a Mustang and bring it back for the land swap, but eventually decided against it.[23]

While Casa Susana, the town's largest whorehouse, was his favorite hangout, he also visited other brothels. One that he boasted about to Huie was a place where a dozen horizontal cubicles, each a little larger than a telephone booth, were stacked on top of one another. The ends of the cordwood cubicles were open, and a blanket in each covered the floor. There, climbing wooden ladders to get inside, men paid twenty pesos ($1.60) to spend an hour with a local girl. Ray liked it because the cacophony of sex sounds that came from the adjacent cubicles heightened his excitement.[24]

In visiting the brothels, Ray struck up a relationship with at least two women. The first was Manuela Aguirre Medrano, a slightly plump prostitute at Casa Susana.[25] She went by the professional name Irma La Douce, after the popular musical of a decade earlier.[26] Although only twenty-three, she had the prematurely haggard appearance that was the trademark of many of the girls who eked out a harsh living for a few dollars a day.[27] There, in a run-down building, women from teenagers to grandmothers sat in metal chairs that ringed the ground-floor room, which also served as a primitive bar, a single jukebox blaring dated American show tunes. Local men used the whorehouse as a gathering spot, drinking at the bar and sometimes picking one of the women for a dance and a short visit to one of the grimy upstairs rooms. Children whose mothers were occasionally among those sitting along the walls ran in or through the room. It was there that Ray usually settled in after having a daily hamburger and Pepsi from the nearby Discotheque Café.[28] He spent the afternoons drinking beer, and switched to a wide assortment of liquor—gin, screwdrivers, Bacardi rum, and even tequila with Squirt soda—at night.[29] After a few drinks, he usually had enough courage to dance with the women.

Irma recalled him as someone who never laughed, and while he was not overly generous with her, he initially treated her kindly.[30] Ray always carried his English-Spanish phrase book, since Irma knew only a few English words. She tried to teach him some Mexican dance steps, something he wanted to learn but at which he was not very good. In return, he took her over the twelve-mile bumpy, gravel road to Mismaloya Beach, where *Night of the Iguana* was shot. Rodimir Biscara, a short, skinny bartender at the whorehouse who spoke a fair amount of English, sometimes accompanied them. An open-air cantina that served refreshments was at the beach and the owner remembered the three of them—the plumpish Irma, the fully dressed and solemn Ray, and Biscara, always flashing a big grin that showed a mouthful of rotting teeth—usually sitting under some remote palm tree.[31] Once, Biscara told the cantina owner that Ray was spending "a great deal of money" on Irma.[32] When Ray was still considering swapping his Mustang for some property, the three of them looked at land parcels together.[33] On those excursions, Ray sometimes took along his Polaroid, and on their way back to Puerto Vallarta he took pictures of Irma, one with her skirt lifted up to her waist, but he tore them up because he was dissatisfied with the way they came out.[34] Another time at the whorehouse, Irma prevailed over his objections and had a photographer snap a photo of them.[35]

One evening, when Ray was in Casa Susana having a drink with Irma, four black sailors from a private boat were at a nearby table. The group was quite drunk and rowdy, especially one short, heavyset man. Irma, in a statement she gave to the Mexican police a few months after the assassination, said she noticed that Ray seemed disturbed. She had trouble understanding him because of the language barrier, but believed he was insulting the black men, "goading" them. He even walked to their table and angrily said something before stepping outside. In a moment he came back, again strode to their table, and said something else in an agitated state. When he returned to Irma, he asked her to feel his pocket, and she reached over and ran her hand over what appeared to be a pistol. When one of the four blacks walked up to Ray in a conciliatory manner, Ray rebuffed him. Then one of the black men took the shorter one by the arm, and they left the whorehouse. Although Ray wanted to pursue them, she warned him that the police would soon be coming around for their nightly rounds, and he abandoned the idea.[36]

Almost ten years after she told her story to the police, the House Select Committee on Assassinations interviewed Irma. In her later version, she downplayed the confrontation's racial overtones. She told the committee she remembered only two blacks, and that one of them was so drunk that he grabbed her to steady himself as he walked past their table. He then apologized. But Ray got angry and "stood up, he had something, I imagine a weapon, to take care of him."[37] Ray began calling him names: "Son-of-a-bitch, chicken, and many such things."[38] The other black sailor took his friend by the arm and they left the whorehouse. However, Irma said she believed that Ray became so agitated "because he [the sailor] touched her," not because he was black. She said that because of the language difficulties between them, she did not remember him ever talking badly about blacks.

Irma, who was seldom treated with anything but contempt by locals, interpreted Ray's trips to the beach and the money he spent on her as true affection. On three or four occasions, he got so drunk that he even asked her to marry him.[39] She said no because he still slept with other women, and the final time she said no, he pulled a pistol on her. "He scared me," Irma recalled about the incident that prompted her to stop seeing him.[40] Although Irma might like to have thought that Ray was being chivalrous in his argument at Casa Susana, given his demeaning view of blacks it is instead likely that the sailor's race incited him, more so than someone accidentally touching his eight-dollar-a-day prostitute. His regard for Irma was actually so low that when he was angry with her about other matters, he simply used one of the other whores—one named Arcelia Gonzalez and another Margarita Montes Meza, who used the professional name "La Chilindrina" (the Little Trifle)—while Irma stood by helplessly.[41] He asked both of the new girls to go to a nearby recreation area at the coast, possibly so he could take photos of them, but both declined.[42]

When Irma finally shied away from him, Ray found another woman, nineteen-year-old Elisa Arellano Torres, a cigarette girl and photographer's assistant at the town's most expensive hotel, the Posada Vallarta.[43] She was younger and prettier than Irma, and Ray took her for a week to a cheap motel at Playa del Gloria, located on the road from Puerto Vallarta to the airport.[44] The owners remembered that the couple, who checked into a corner room, was "strange." Ray sometimes left at dawn, returned later, and then locked the door to his room, where he spent the rest of the day with Elisa.[45] Author George McMillan believes that it was with Elisa that Ray took his first sexual pictures.*[46]

Elisa found Ray an introvert who did not like noisy crowds or loud sounds. He often complained that he was tired, and she later said that while she wondered if he was "maybe a mental case," he was generous to her so she stayed.[47]

"About this time," Ray wrote, "I thought of having plastic sugery."[48] He said that the idea first came to him when he was discharged from Leavenworth in 1958. The discharge officer did not think Ray's prison photo looked like him, so he was forced to wait until they matched his fingerprints. While most said Ray was nondescript, he nevertheless fretted that he had "pronounced features"— a pointy nose and jutting right ear—and it might be easy to identify him, and he thought surgery could "change my facial features so it would be harder to identify me throught pictures circulated by law officials."[49] That photos taken of him at the Mexican beaches made him look considerably younger also encouraged him to consider plastic surgery.†[50]

---

* There were rumors that he had actually made nude photos of both Elisa and Irma, and maybe even a short blue film with Elisa, but they have never been substantiated. None of the pictures Ray took of the women have been found, although copies of a simple photo of Ray and Irma, taken by another photographer at Casa Susana, was turned over to the FBI. That photo was released in mid-1968 when the hunt for Ray was in high gear.

† Typically, Ray changed his testimony several times before the Select Committee about whether he had taken pictures of himself in Mexico. He once denied taking any photos, then admitted to one, and then admitted to a couple, at other times saying perhaps he took some more.

But evidently not even the relaxation afforded by his indolent lifestyle in Puerto Vallarta could keep Ray away from the rackets that were second nature to him. In one of his letters to Huie, Ray said, "Their is another bartender who works at one of the hotel's [Luis Garcia at the Hotel Oceano] who mite give you some information on my somewhat illegal activities, but I think you should talk to him first, then I will verify what he says."[51] Luis Garcia was the only visitor Ray ever had while he was at the Hotel Rio for three weeks. One day, when Ray was not there, Garcia had arrived and seemed agitated about something he had left in Ray's car.[52] William Bradford Huie interviewed Garcia and concluded he was Ray's source for the marijuana he sold. Garcia denied it.[53]

Soon after the assassination, the FBI picked up information that Ray might have sold marijuana while in Mexico. But Ray had a ready, albeit unlikely, explanation. "I think that one reason for this charge was that on the way to the beach I picked up a hippie who was hitchhiking, he probably remembered my car from newspaper reports. Anyway several of them was living on the beach and I was talking to one of the girls about the effect the drug [marijuana] had on you, and I think out of this conversation and by them knowing me on sight they mite have informed on me to the FBI. Also, I would think that the hippies would be sympthic to people like King. And if they thought I was involved they would inform."[54] His version is more telling than he intended. Ray detested informers, yet he used that word to describe what the hippies did to him. If they had concocted a story about him, he would have said that they made one up to hurt him, but rather his use of "they would inform" implies that they told the authorities about whatever he was doing with marijuana.

Others who knew Ray in Puerto Vallarta reported that when he was offered a cigarette, his answer invariably was "I don't smoke anything but marijuana."[55] Ray took several American hippie girls to the same isolated stretch of beach that he visited with Irma.[56] Elisa, his last girlfriend, said Ray bragged to her that he had made several trips to Yelapa (nearby at the coast) to buy marijuana.[57] He was obviously familiar with Yelapa, as he had told Irma that he had been there for business, and had asked another prostitute, Arcelia Gonzalez, to accompany him there.[58] Also, early in his stay in Mexico, when Ray had to replace a damaged tire, he bought a slightly larger tire than the car needed and fitted it with an inner tube.[59] An inner tube is a handy means of hiding several pounds of contraband pressed against the wall of an oversize tire.

During his "working" vacation in Puerto Vallarta, Ray also did some further research on finding a country to which he might want to permanently move. While reading a copy of *U.S. News & World Report*, he saw an advertisement for immigrants wanted in Rhodesia. The ad listed an address to write to for more information, and Ray sent a letter saying that he was interested in immigrating to an English-speaking country. He did not get an answer before he left Mexico.*[60]

By mid-November, Ray was ready to move on, later claiming, "It became clear that I couldn't accomplish anything further in Mexico in the way of securing permanent residency."[61] Mexico was not a country to which he seriously considered relocating. He later gave several reasons. "I don't believe you can live in Mexico. There's a language problem. . . . They don't have no middle class, see, you are either on top or on the bottom and I think It would be difficult to accustom yourself living on the bottom because there is all types of ailments and things. . . . [p]eople that lives down there for years and years they immune to that, whereas probably if somebody like me that hadn't been use to that water, they'd probably wind up poisoned or something."[62]

Ray failed to mention another key reason: Elisa jilted him. He had grown fond of her, and had given her the most money he had ever given a woman, 600 pesos [$48], with a promise that he would soon have more. He told her to take the money and rent an apartment where they could stay together. But she took the cash and skipped town with her two children. When Ray showed up at the lush bar at the Posada Vallarta looking for Elisa, the bartender gave him a "Dear John" note from her.[63] Elisa later claimed that the real reason she left him was his insistence that she buy marijuana for him.[64]

He visited Irma La Douce one last time, said he was leaving, and promised to return when he finished some unspecified business.[65] His new destination was Los Angeles, and on November 13 he checked out of the Tropicana and headed for the West Coast, stopping in the border town of Tijuana. There he checked into a motel and thoroughly searched his car to ensure there was nothing that might alert a customs check to his fugitive status.[†] Almost ten years after the assassination, Ray told a story publicly for the first time to the

---

* Of course, Ray's interest in Rhodesia has raised much speculation about his racism and the eventual role it might have played in the assassination. He read too many newsmagazines and newspapers not to know that Rhodesia was one of the last bastions of a segregated, white-dominated society and government. It was also a staging ground for white mercenaries who fought in some of the local civil wars that ravaged its black neighbors. Certainly the assassin of Martin Luther King, Jr., might well have been considered a hero, or at least a respected character of high notoriety, in a place like Rhodesia.

[†] Ray's careful cleaning of the car prior to passing customs is another good indicator that he was involved in some type of contraband dealing while in Mexico. Although he contends he was worried about revealing anything that would unmask his fugitive status, he knew there was nothing like that over which to fret. However, some remnant of stolen property or marijuana would have concerned him.

Canadian Broadcasting Corporation: that his search of the car produced a business card, slipped into a pack of cigarettes, lodged between the right front bucket seat and the gearshift. That card, according to Ray, contained some unusual information—information that has produced one of the case's enduring controversies. On the front of the card, Ray said, several things were written or printed, including a name that had been inked out, a city (a "two-part name, like New Orleans"), and the initials LEAA. On the rear of the card was a handwritten name—"Randy Rosen-something"—and an address, "1180 Northwest River Drive, Miami, Fla."[66] Ray was unsure of the significance, if any, of this information. "I could only speculate whether the cigarette pack had been accidentally dropped or intentionally planted," he wrote.[67] Nevertheless, he copied the information to a separate sheet of paper (listing all the numbers backward), and then threw that paper out when he was later on the run after the King assassination (he has changed his story about when he threw it out, but is adamant that he no longer has a copy).[68]

In his 1977 interview with Canadian Broadcasting, Ray intimated that the person listed on the card—whom Jerry Ray supposedly tracked down—was Randolph Erwin Rosenson, and that Rosenson might have information about Raoul. Ray speculated that this was possible since Raoul had supposedly been in the car five weeks earlier and may have dropped the cigarettes and card there (of course, if the card story is true, it could also have been dropped there by any of the local Mexicans or American hippies that Ray gave rides to during his stay in Puerto Vallarta, or even the previous owners of the Mustang in Birmingham).

The House Select Committee on Assassinations conducted an exhaustive investigation into Rosenson's background, associates, and movements in the 1960s. It uncovered evidence that Rosenson and Ray had had several opportunities to meet prior to the King assassination. For instance, Rosenson, who had a drug-related felony conviction, used a carnival operation as the cover for his smuggling. Rosenson traveled extensively in his work, and had been in Mexico in late 1965 and early 1966.[69] The committee could not show that he was there in 1967 when Ray visited. However, he was frequently in New Orleans, a city Ray visited briefly in December 1967. Rosenson traveled in many of the same New Orleans circles as the person with whom Ray visited New Orleans, Charles Stein. Both Rosenson and Stein were known to the New Orleans Police Department for similar crimes, had mutual acquaintances, frequented the same bars, and had even retained the same lawyer.[70] Moreover, Rosenson was also in Los Angeles and Birmingham at the same time as Ray during 1967 and early 1968, and in Birmingham during March 1968 when Ray purchased the murder weapon.[71] Ray and Rosenson even used the same Birmingham bank.[72]

The Select Committee interviewed Rosenson on six occasions, and once he appeared in executive session. He adamantly denied knowing Ray or any Ray family members or known associates, including a Raoul or Charles Stein. Further, he emphatically denied any role in the King assassination and could not offer any reason as to why Ray implicated him.[73]

The Select Committee concluded, "Despite the opportunities for Ray and Rosenson to have met, an extensive field investigation, including interviews of Rosenson's relatives, friends, business associates, criminal contacts, and numerous law enforcement officials, failed to establish a definite link between Ray and Rosenson. The committee concluded that Rosenson was not involved with Ray in a conspiracy to assassinate Dr. King."*[74]

Rosenson's lawyer before the Select Committee, Gene Stanley, told the author, "Originally Rosenson lied to the committee investigators about Ray and he gave them all this bull, he was trying to bait them by lying through his teeth. I spoke to them and to him. He finally leveled with them and really did not know anything about Ray. But as he said, 'I met a lot of people I've never known, and if I was on drugs, I might have met him and not known it.' "[75] According to Stanley, the HSCA investigators thought "there might be a person who was involved in drug smuggling who may have had contact with Ray and Rosenson. That person wasn't Raoul, but it may have been somebody who was operating in Mexico. The problem was with Rosenson's mind, since it was so fried on drugs he could not even remember what he did a couple of years ago."[76]

It is possible that Ray and Rosenson met and somehow formed a smuggling link, and that Rosenson was truthful when he said he had nothing to do with the King assassination. Also, it is possible that Ray, after he was in jail for the

---

* One of the issues that conspiracy buffs use to keep the Rosenson issue alive are the initials—LEAA—that Ray said were on the front of the card. "The L.E.A.A. stood for the Law Enforcement Administration," alleges William Pepper, Ray's latest lawyer, "which at the time was sponsoring a number of pilot projects in selected cities." However, the problem is that the LEAA was not created until August 1968, almost a year after Ray crossed into Mexico. Ray has since tried to cover the mistake by claiming there were two early LEAA pilot projects in New Orleans, and Newark, New Jersey. However, the author checked and the name—Office of Law Enforcement Assistance—was never even mentioned before the August 1968 Omnibus Crime Control and Safe Streets Act was passed. As for the pilot projects, there was nothing remotely related to the agency's eventual name, or the use of initials such as LEAA. Moreover, as opposed to the implication of some conspiracists, the Office of Law Enforcement Assistance was not a law enforcement operation. It was instead a block-grant program, coordinated as a research and statistics agency. By coincidence, the LEAA was actually formed by Lyndon Johnson because, in the wake of the riots that ravaged some cities after the King assassination, he wanted to provide additional funding to those particularly hard hit.

King murder, read about Rosenson in the papers, and then placed him into the story just in time for the Select Committee to waste precious time and resources tracking down a tale that proved to be a dead end. Was it one of Ray's ploys to prevent the committee from investigating other leads that might have brought it closer to the truth about his role, and the scope of any real conspiracy in the King assassination?

23

Dancing in Los Angeles

Ray passed through customs at Tijuana without incident. He drove leisurely, arriving in Los Angeles on Sunday, November 19, in the middle of a torrential rainstorm. That afternoon, he spotted a vacancy sign for AIR-CONDITIONED APARTMENTS at a two-story, deco-style building at 1535 North Serrano Avenue. The manager, Margarita Powers, showed him a bachelor apartment—number 6 on the first floor—and he took it immediately, paying her $127.50 in cash, which covered a month's rent, a cleaning fee, and a key deposit.[1] Southern California would be his home for the next four months, until March 17, eighteen days before Dr. King was murdered in Memphis.

Ray's initial time in Los Angeles was merely a continuation of the lazy, drifting lifestyle he had enjoyed in Mexico. His new apartment was a few doors south of Hollywood Boulevard, a sleazy area claimed in late 1967 by hippies and transients as their own, marked by flophouses, all-day bars, and inexpensive shops. Western Avenue, just around the corner, was a haven for streetwalkers, including the city's largest transvestite contingent.

The day after he arrived, Ray wrote to the Chicago film company, from which he was still waiting for his refund. "I will be at the below address for five months," he told them.[*2] "I had a phone installed as I wanded one to inquir

---

* Ray actually would leave his North Serrano apartment in January, but he would move only three blocks. The fact that on his second day in Los Angeles he predicted how

about jobs," Ray later wrote. He had surprisingly decided to look for a straight job. Although he appeared to have money left over from Mexico—he bought a $90 console television soon after arriving in Los Angeles—it seems that he expected to stay in Southern California long enough that he wanted to replenish his cash without resorting to crime.[3] Though smuggling might be worthwhile in a country such as Mexico where law enforcement was lackadaisical, it was a much greater risk in the States, where being arrested meant being sent back to finish his twenty-year sentence at Jeff City.

At first the phone company told him there would be a delay, since the main office was swamped with new orders. But he managed to get a fast installation by claiming that he worked in Governor George Wallace's campaign to get his party—the American Independent Party—placed on the California ballot for the following year's presidential election. Ray had actually called the local Wallace headquarters to ask how long they would be operating in California, because he thought that since Galt was an Alabama identification, it "would be a good cover."[4] It is a reminder that Ray had stayed abreast of the news while in Mexico and that he was at least following the developments in the Wallace campaign. California was a major testing ground for the incipient Wallace effort, and his supporters had to present the California secretary of state with 66,059 signatures by January 1 to qualify for ballot status. If Wallace and his new party failed there, it would sap the momentum needed to qualify in other states.

Shortly after Ray arrived in Los Angeles, Wallace visited the state and campaigned in large, boisterous rallies from San Francisco to San Diego. The *Los Angeles Times,* which Ray read, extensively covered the third-party effort. At the same time that Wallace dominated the California political news, there was also steady coverage of King. He had finished serving the five-day jail sentence for his 1963 Birmingham contempt conviction, and the press increasingly focused on his October call for "escalating nonviolence to the level of civil disobedience."[5] King had ratcheted up his rhetoric by blaming the 1967 summer riots on "the greater crimes of white society."[6] A few weeks after Ray moved to Los Angeles, King held a press conference in which he predicted that "waves of

---

long he would be there has prompted speculation that his moves were preplanned, possibly coordinated by someone else, leading ultimately to the King assassination. But that overlooks the importance that Ray attached to staying on the move as a fugitive. He had convinced himself that law enforcement would trace him if he stayed too long in any single city. In Birmingham, he originally told the rooming house manager that he would be there only four months (he left in six weeks) and in Mexico claimed he would be there a few months (again, less than two). The only difference in Los Angeles is that his estimate was closer to being right, only a month off.

the nation's poor and disinherited" would swarm to Washington, D.C., the following April. Announcing that it was time to "confront the power structure massively," King acknowledged that his march on Washington was intended to "develop massive dislocation."[7] None of this would have gone unnoticed by the man in Apartment 6 on Serrano Avenue—who was viewed by his neighbors as a quiet loner who shied away from even the casual chitchat that passed as conversation between apartment dwellers in a large city.

Ray's phone was finally installed on November 27. But instead of calling around to look for work, his first call was to a Dr. Mark O. Freeman, a Beverly Hills clinical psychologist who specialized in self-hypnosis.[8] Ray made an appointment that same day for 5:00 P.M.

"I had read quite a bit about hypnosis in the penitentiary," Ray later recalled.[9] While in Canada four months earlier, he had bought several books on hypnosis, including *Psycho-Cybernetics* by Dr. Maxwell Maltz, a plastic surgeon who had developed a commercially popular theory of "self-image" from his experiences in cosmetic surgery. The book's dust jacket made a pitch that might well have appealed to Ray: "A New Way to Get More Living out of Life." Personality, according to Maltz, had a "face." If it "remained scarred, distorted, 'ugly,' or inferior, the person himself acted out this role in his behavior." Maltz talked of changing the type of person whose "image of the world in which he lives is a hostile place. . . . Frustration, aggression, and loneliness are the price he pays."[10]

Ray, neatly dressed, his short dark hair slicked back, arrived promptly for his appointment with Freeman. He told Freeman that he wanted to "overcome his shyness, gain social confidence, and learn self-hypnosis so that he could relax, sleep better, and remember things better."[11] Of course, it is also possible that Ray thought self-hypnosis might help him in planning alibis for crimes, not being anxious about getting captured, or being better able to maintain a cover story as a fugitive when interrogated. If he read Maltz's book, he may even have thought self-hypnosis would make it possible to adopt a new identity and suppress his old one.

When Freeman asked some introductory questions, Ray astonishingly gave truthful answers, including his real name, and that he came from East St. Louis and was born March 10, 1928.[12] "I gave him my right nane since I thought he mite get me under hypnosis and find out my right name," Ray later wrote.[13]

"You've got to keep in mind that I get a lot of angry people around here," Freeman said later. "I get a lot of rough stuff around here. I mean psychotic, that stuff. But I couldn't pick up on any of that with Ray. He made a favorable impression on me. He was a good pupil. I'd show him how to go under, and pretty soon he'd be lying on the couch on his back and start talking. I taught him eye fixation, bodily relaxation, how to open himself to suggestion. I gave him lots of positive feelings of competence."[14]

Ray saw Freeman six times—$25 for each hourlong session—with several days between visits. During the course of the treatment, Ray assured him that he had no "deep dark secrets."[15] While Freeman did not hear anything startling from Ray, he found him an excellent hypnotic subject, and did discover Ray's tremendous shyness as well as his dislike for blacks.[16] He also found Ray "young and immature for his age," and that his expectation about hypnosis was unrealistic: "He had the old power idea of hypnotism. That is, that you can go around looking people in the eye and can hypnotize them and make them do what you want them to do" (something that might have appealed to Ray if he wanted to convince women to be in porn films).[17]

While Ray was seeing Freeman, he finally began looking for work. He answered several classified advertisements in the *Times*. Among the jobs he applied for were temporary work at the IRS helping taxpayers fill in tax forms, a job as a vacuum cleaner salesman, and even a position as a maintenance man at the Big Bear ski resort. He was frustrated, however, because the positions required a social security card, something he had not yet obtained for Galt.[18] "I didn't want to give the Rayns name," Ray recalled, fearful that the FBI might have finally traced it from when he had used it during the spring at the Indian Trail restaurant near Chicago.[19]

Ray then placed two advertisements in the *Times*, one for restaurant work and the other for general labor, hoping he might "get a job that didn't require a social security card."[20] He had no luck—all the offers wanted local references. Briefly, Ray's interest was reignited by a seafaring job. He called the Coast Guard in vain to ask about any shortcuts for getting a job on a ship, and also made a few futile inquiries about seaman's papers. "It's not quite as easy in the United States as it is in Canada," Ray later recounted. "See, Canada don't require fingerprints or anything, and the United States, in order to get the Seaman's papers, I found out you have to, they have to take one print. So I was trying to scheme around and find out how I could get someone else's prints on there rather than mine. But I never did carry it through that far."[21]

On December 5, Ray made one of his patently quirky moves—he put down a $100 cash deposit on a $499 dance course at the National Dance Studio in Long Beach. It was a premier school, with twenty-five private hourlong sessions and twenty-five group lessons focusing on recreational dances such as the fox-trot, swing, rumba, and others.[22] On his membership application, the dance instructor listed that Ray had previously taken cha-cha and fox-trot lessons while in Birmingham, had owned a restaurant in Mexico, and would be leaving "in a couple of months to work on a ship—wants to travel."[23] The National Dance Studio commanded an extravagant price and was certainly a considerable step up from the lessons he received from Claire Keating in Canada, Irma in Mexico, or the ten-dollar classes in Birmingham. Ray later complained about the price: "The ad in the paper said it would cost $32.00, but they coned the country boy." Still, he insisted that he wanted to take the course because "I thought I mite stay in Mexico . . . also, about this time I found out you could go to Columbia S.A. without a passport."*[24]

Ray had begun visiting the neighborhood bars when he first moved in, and settled on two as his new haunts. The Sultan Room had erotic décor, sixty-cent drinks, and a pool table in the rear. It was on the ground floor of the five-story, yellow brick St. Francis Hotel-Apartments, only three blocks from his apartment. His other favorite was the Rabbit's Foot Club, a dark, musty bar around the corner on Hollywood Boulevard. The few who remember him at the bars recall that he claimed to be an Alabama businessman who had just returned from Mexico after several years of operating a bar, which he had sold to his Mexican partner.[25] He was looking to open a new tavern. Occasionally he used a couple of Spanish phrases as if to authenticate his story.

Although he made no close friends, it was at the Sultan Room that he met a cocktail waitress, Marie Tomaso—she had used several names over the years, but finally adopted the professional name Marie Martin when she worked as an exotic dancer.[26] Thirty-five, with a plump face and sporting a long, jet black wig, she first saw Ray sitting by himself, nursing a steady supply of straight vodkas.[27] She noticed him because the bar, which was usually crowded with elderly retirees, who occupied most of the upstairs hotel, did not get many strangers. Always dressed neatly in a dark suit and light shirt, he seemed very pale, she thought, as though he did not get outside often.[28] The thrice-divorced Martin walked near Ray one evening, and suddenly he asked if he could buy her a drink. He spoke so softly that at first she was not sure he was talking to her. She agreed, and it was the start of their friendship.[29] "She started telling me something about her family," Ray recalled. "She said she had a boyfriend doing five years in San Quentin for possession of marijuana."[30] Later that evening, she asked him for a ride home, and on the way she told him that she was originally from New Orleans.[31] He talked mainly about the bar he claimed to have owned in Mexico. She reminded him, he told her, of a girl he knew in Guadalajara, where he had lived for six years.[32]

---

* The unusual part of Ray's actions, especially if he is to be believed about desperately wanting a passport, is that he spent his money on nonessential items instead of obtaining his travel papers. For instance, he admitted before the Select Committee that as an ex-convict he knew it was possible to buy a forged passport for about $1,000. Yet, while he never did that, he spent nearly $800 in Los Angeles alone on the dance lessons, his psychological sessions, and later a bartending course.

On Thursday, December 14, Martin's cousin, Rita Stein, a go-go dancer, dropped by the Sultan Room.[33] Dark-eyed and full-figured, the women resembled each other. Martin introduced Ray, and the two women sat with him. Rita noticed that Ray never looked at their eyes, even when he spoke to them.[34] Soon, Marie turned to him.

"Rita's got a problem," she said. "Her two girls are living with her mother in New Orleans and they're going to put the kids into a children's home unless she brings them back here. We've been looking for a ride to New Orleans . . ."

She stopped and stared at Ray. She knew he was ill at ease when he began pulling on his right ear and smiling crookedly as though he was the only one in on a private joke.

"You wouldn't want to drive me down to pick them up, would you?" She was half joking.[35]

Ray considered it seriously. "Well, maybe I would. I'm on vacation and not working."

"You would?!" Martin and Stein were delighted. Stein acted as though Ray had given a firm commitment. "You've got to meet my brother, Charlie. He'd go with you and help you drive."*[36]

Ray did not object, but he clearly had expected the women were planning to accompany him.

Stein ran the few blocks to her apartment on Franklin Avenue. There, her thirty-eight-year-old brother, Charlie, was baby-sitting her two youngest children. He was a hulking figure, six-two, 240 pounds, bald except for some long, straggling locks of hair that went past his shoulders, and with a thick black beard. Neighbors thought of him as merely a hippie, regularly dressed in his torn jeans, beads, and sandals, often lying on the grass at night searching the sky intently for flying saucers. His own mother thought he was "crazy but harmless."[37] A believer in "Cosmic Philosophy," he often talked to plants, trees, and animals, convinced that he had the ability to communicate with other lifeforms.[38] Charlie Stein said he was a songwriter and budding psychic healer— he claimed to have recently cured Marie of arthritis by laying his hands on her and having her bury her panties in a hole he dug in the backyard. But at different times, the sixth-grade dropout had operated a garage, boxed, played competitive chess, worked as both a barker and bouncer at New Orleans strip shows, and even managed a bar for a while in the Big Easy. Stein, who was di-

---

* In Ray's version, he first mentioned to the women that he was going to New Orleans for business, and then they asked if he would pick up the children. However, both Martin and Stein gave contemporaneous statements to the FBI that indicated they initiated the idea of the New Orleans trip. Ray obviously realized later that if it was their suggestion, he could not very well claim that he had planned the trip in conjunction with Raoul as part of a plot that led to King's death.

vorced four times, also had two things in common with Ray, although they did not know it—he had become a union member as a merchant marine, and he had a criminal record.*[39]

Rita excitedly told him that she had met "a guy in the Sultan Room who's willing to drive down."[40] A half hour later, Stein made his way to the Sultan. Ray was leery of the "big, swarthy, balding" stranger.[41] Charlie said that Ray gave him a limp handshake (the same weak handshake that is a trait of the three Ray brothers), and he felt strong "antivibrations" from him.[42] But Charlie was also eager to visit New Orleans to see his mother, as well as a young son from a previous marriage. Could Ray leave tomorrow, Friday, giving them the weekend to drive there? After having said yes so quickly when Marie asked for the ride, it was difficult for Ray suddenly to change his mind. "Since police loved to stop hippies for no cause in those days, Charles was not exactly the type of character an escaped convict would choose to travel with," said Ray. But he did not want to "welch on my commitment to Marie."[43] So, instead, he made the trip appear to be no big deal by saying he had some business of his own there, and that he would pick up Charlie at 10:00 the next morning.

When Stein left, Ray turned to Marie. His face was clenched and drained of the little color it normally had. "If this is a setup, I'll kill him." He almost seemed to hiss the words, his teeth clenched in anger. "I have a gun. If he tried to pull anything on me on the trip—"[44]

"Oh, Eric, it's not a setup," Marie interrupted. "If Rita doesn't get her girls back, they go into a children's home."[45]

Ray, typically, claims that his decision to make a December trip to New Orleans was at Raoul's direction. He gave two different versions to Huie about how he was called to New Orleans. In the first, Ray said that shortly after he arrived in Los Angeles in November, "I then called Raoul in New Orleans, someone else ansered and ask me if I could come down around xmas, I agreed."[46] In another account, there was no telephone call but "Raoul had written me and

---

* Beyond running illicit prostitution and gambling, Stein had a 1961 arrest in New Orleans for possession of narcotics, but no conviction on that. Several police officers in New Orleans told the House Select Committee that they believed, however, that Stein dealt in narcotics while there. After his meeting with Ray, Stein did have a 1969 conviction for growing marijuana in California, and a 1974 conviction for dealing in heroin. Stein's brother-in-law had had a narcotics record and died of a morphine overdose in 1966. This background, coupled with Ray's connection at different times to illegal drugs, raised the possibility that the meeting was not as coincidental as they have recounted it. The FBI seriously considered the possibility that Stein and Ray made the New Orleans trip to score narcotics, but could not prove it. The House Select Committee conducted an extensive investigation of Stein, his background, associates, and activities, concluding finally that he and Ray met "fortuitously . . . had separate and independent reasons for making the trip" and that "no evil purpose" existed between them.

told me to meet him at a certain bar in New Orleans at a certain time on December 15" (note, however, that while Ray claims he was supposed to meet Raoul on December 15, he did not even leave Los Angeles until that date).[47] Before the Select Committee, he reverted to the phone-call scenario.[48]

In both of Ray's stories, the trip had been planned for several weeks. However, his activities in Los Angeles reveal otherwise. Ray had a session with Dr. Freeman on Thursday, December 14, from 10:00 to 11:00 A.M. When he left, he made an appointment to see Freeman the following Monday at 3:00 P.M. However, later on Thursday he met Rita Stein and agreed impetuously to travel to New Orleans. So on Friday morning, Ray called Dr. Freeman to say he was unexpectedly leaving town as his brother had found a job for him in the merchant marine in New Orleans.[49] Also on Friday, he telephoned the National Dance Studio and canceled his Monday lesson, saying he would be out of town on a short trip. If he had already had a trip planned to New Orleans for a couple of weeks, he would not have made appointments at Freeman and the dance studio for the time he would be away, and then have had to cancel them hurriedly on the morning of his departure.

Ray, wearing a dark brown suit with a white shirt, picked up Marie Martin at the St. Francis on Friday, December 15, near noon.[50] He then drove her to the Steins', where she explained to Rita and Charlie that Ray had a last-minute condition: that before he would make the trip to New Orleans, he wanted them all to sign petitions to place George Wallace on the California ballot. He even offered to pay all the trip's expenses if the three agreed.[51] "I just want you to register so Wallace will have enough signatures to get his name on the California ticket," Ray told them.[52] The California primary, he explained, was scheduled for next June.[53] Ray later denied that it was his idea to have them sign the Wallace petition—he said "they requested it," although that was unlikely since none of them were registered voters, much less politically active.[54] After his arrest, when he learned that the three had no political interest, he came up with an equally dubious reason for their supposed desire to register for Wallace: Marie Martin had a boyfriend in jail and she thought she might help him by making some political connections.[55]

After Ray had set forth his condition for the New Orleans trip, the three agreed, and Ray drove them to Wallace's North Hollywood office, where he watched as they signed the petition. Ray walked around the office looking at the campaign literature, and Charlie Stein thought that he seemed to know his way around the headquarters.[56] Later, Ray denied having been inside, and Wallace workers claimed they did not recall ever seeing him there.[57]

After dropping the women off at their apartments, Stein and Ray set off for New Orleans that afternoon. They were a strange pair, with almost nothing in common, and said little to each other. "The trip was uneventful," recalled Ray, "except that once in a while as he was driving and I was sleeping Charlie would nudge me awake and exclaim that a flying saucer had just passed the car."[58]

They drove overnight, sharing the driving. Early Saturday, during a snowstorm, Ray was at the wheel when the car skidded several hundred yards off the freeway, coming to rest against a wire fence. That prompted him to stop in El Paso, where he bought a used tire for four dollars to replace a threadbare one.[59] At rest stops, Ray ordered hamburgers with everything on them, together with a beer, which he usually drank in the car, one hand on the steering wheel and the other holding the bottle.[60]

Stein remembered that he once thanked Ray for making the trip, but Ray said, "I'm not doing any favor—I've got business in New Orleans."[61] Ray mentioned a name—something that sounded Italian—but Stein could not remember it. A couple of times, Ray stopped at gas stations to make telephone calls, which each lasted five or ten minutes.[62] Ray, in fact, later admitted to making two calls when traveling to New Orleans, both to his brother Jerry.[63] "I just called him," recalled Ray, "I just wanted to tell him I was all right and, of course, I didn't want to call him from California." (He feared that if the FBI was watching Jerry they might trace the call to his current hideout.) Ray said, "There was no significance in the calls. They weren't of no importance."*[64]

Although there was little conversation during the ride to New Orleans, at one point Ray told Stein that he had done a lot of traveling in the Mustang, and that he had had trouble in black areas because of his Alabama plates. He had also told Marie Martin about his problems with blacks.[65] If blacks wanted to be free, Ray said, they should live in the North or West, but if blacks wanted to remain as slaves, then they should stay in the South.[66]

At one point, Stein, having forgotten Ray's last name, asked him what it was. "It's Galt—Eric Starvo Galt. Galt!" Ray shot back. It was as though Ray wanted him to remember the name.[67] Stein did not think Ray looked like an Eric: With his greased-backed hair and affinity for cowboy tunes, he seemed

---

* After the assassination, journalist Louis Lomax rented a white Mustang and with Charlie Stein tried to re-create the drive from Los Angeles to New Orleans, especially to find one particular pay phone along the route that Ray used. Stein wanted $4,000 to make the trip but settled for agreeing to split the assassination's $100,000 reward with Lomax. They never collected it. Their collaboration resulted in a syndicated series of articles with wildly imaginative assertions, including, among others, that Ray had really called an industrialist in New Orleans who financed the King murder; that he secretly made another trip to New Orleans around Valentine's Day; that there was a girl, Jeri, in the plot, who worked at the Sultan Room (there was no such person); that after the murder, instead of fleeing to Toronto, Ray really hid in Milwaukee with the phantom Jeri; and that the FBI helped Ray. Even Ray felt compelled to comment on Lomax's articles in his prison letters to Huie. He found them "silly" and assumed they were "just something he [Lomax] made up."

more like a country boy. From their brief conversations, Stein had the impression that Ray, who was knowledgeable about the details of Wallace's presidential campaign, was somehow involved with it.[68]

The two drove nonstop, and while Stein said Ray was not a user of hard drugs, it was possible he was a "pillhead" and took some during their trip.[69] The unlikely duo arrived in New Orleans on Sunday, December 17. Ray decided at the last moment not to stay at Stein's mother's house, and instead checked into a motel on Stein's recommendation, the Provincial, in the heart of the French Quarter.[70] He signed in as Eric S. Galt, gave the Birmingham rooming house as his permanent address, and was assigned a small, twelve-dollar-a-night room.[71] After registering, Ray dropped Stein off at his family's home.* The next evening, Ray was anxious to return to Los Angeles. He drove to the home of Stein's married sister, Marie Lee. When Ray arrived, he parked the car and walked up a path to the front porch, where Stein and his sister were sitting. "Eric, say hi to Marie," said Stein. "Glad to know you," said Marie. Ray did not acknowledge the introduction. Instead, he leaned against a porch post and stared at the ground.[72] After a few uncomfortable moments, Marie went inside the house. "You ready to go back?" asked Ray. Stein, who had expected that they would be there at least a few days, pleaded to stay another day. Ray finally agreed.

Ray's thirty-six hours in New Orleans have sparked tremendous speculation about what he did, whom he met, and whether the groundwork for killing King was laid there some fourteen weeks prior to the assassination. By the time the FBI had traced him to the Provincial Motel after the assassination, it was possible to determine from the motel's records that he had not made any long-distance phone calls while there, but the records that would have shown if he made local calls, and to whom, had already been destroyed.[73] New Orleans was, of course, where Lee Oswald had spent his summer only four years earlier, just before he killed Kennedy. With its anti-Castro Cubans, right-wing paramil-

---

* Anthony Charles DeCarvelho, a cab driver in New Orleans and a friend of Stein's, told the Select Committee that he had met Ray at Stein's mother's house on the night they arrived. Ray then requested a cab ride to the Provincial Motel because he had to meet someone. DeCarvelho made the trip and waited for Ray, who took about ten minutes and then returned to the car satisfied that his meeting had gone well. However, when DeCarvelho was interviewed in 1968 by the FBI, only three weeks after the assassination, he told no such story. He said then he had only met Ray when he and Stein were leaving New Orleans, and did not speak to him. Moreover, his story was at variance with the descriptions supplied by both Stein and Ray, and it made no sense for Ray not to use his own car if he had such a rendezvous, rather than create a witness to a clandestine meeting. The Select Committee concluded that DeCarvelho's information about Ray was "unreliable."

itary groups, a dominant mafia family headed by Carlos Marcello, and a corrupt police and judiciary, it is easy to believe in conspiracies brewing in the Big Easy. When Ray was there, conspiracy and assassinations were topic one, as District Attorney Jim Garrison had forced through an indictment against prominent businessman Clay Shaw just that March. The trial had not yet begun, but the international press had swarmed into the city to discover whether Garrison had uncovered a plot behind the president's murder.*

It was in New Orleans that Ray claims to have had his first meeting with Raoul since the supposed rendezvous at the Mexican border.[†] Again, Ray has given many different versions. In the original, he met Raoul at Le Bunny Lounge, a bar at 611 Canal Street, and said, "Raoul was interested in a job he wanted us to do in about two or three months."[74] In a subsequent rendition, instead of giving the general time span of two to three months, Raoul was precise, promising he would contact Ray in April, the very month in which King was killed.[75] Before the Select Committee, nine years later, Ray reverted to claiming that "there was no date set at that time."[76]

Raoul still had no travel documents for Ray, but promised them the next time, together with the long-awaited $12,000 payoff. Another time, instead of travel documents, Ray asserted that Raoul promised to relocate him to Cuba, and that from there he could go anywhere in the world.[77] When Ray asked what the next job entailed, Raoul "said not to worry about it and not to ask questions."[78] In a second version to Huie, instead of telling Ray not to ask questions, Raoul told him it involved gunrunning. Before the Select Committee, nine years later, it had changed to "some type of military equipment."[79]

Originally, Ray said Raoul gave him $500 in twenties to prevent him from asking questions. Ray's next story had him receiving the money merely be-

---

* Stein, Ray's travel mate, was coincidentally a close friend of Garrison's, and both belonged to and played chess at the New Orleans chess club. When Stein was arrested in 1962 on a vice charge, Garrison commented, "He is a good boy but keeps bad company." Garrison eventually dismissed the charge (MURKIN 2635–2673, section 27, p. 83).

† Charles Stein surprised the Select Committee in one of his interviews with its investigators when he announced that Ray had mentioned the name Raoul on their drive to New Orleans. If true, it would be the only independent, contemporaneous corroboration that Raoul existed. However, when asked by the FBI in February 1969 if Ray had ever mentioned Raoul, Stein said he had never heard the name. Finally, when placed under oath by the committee, Stein backed off his new story. "I don't know," he said when asked if Ray mentioned Raoul. Moreover, Stein was working with some people on a film about the King assassination at the time of his changed testimony, and the film was offered to the committee for a substantial amount of money. The Select Committee concluded that Stein's change of testimony about Raoul was prompted "not by a specific factual occurrence, but rather by the passing chance of financial gain."

cause he was short of cash, and it had nothing to do with silencing him. Then, suddenly, Ray claimed that instead of a mere $500, Raoul had actually given him $2,500.[80] Before the Select Committee, he dropped it back to $500.[81]

While there may have been no Raoul, it is possible that Ray met with someone in New Orleans connected to his Mexican smuggling or even an old jail mate. However, if he met with anyone, it was more likely one of his brothers. When James had canceled his appointment with Dr. Freeman in Los Angeles, on the day he left for New Orleans, he said his brother had found a job for him in New Orleans. On his way to the Big Easy, Ray admitted, the only person he called was Jerry. James later told his Los Angeles dance instructor, Sharon Rhodes, that when he visited Louisiana in December, it was to see his brother.[82] And most important, in a private conversation with a Select Committee witness (who asked for anonymity), Jerry admitted that he was in New Orleans with James in December 1967.[83]

Jerry publicly denies being there, saying instead that he was visiting St. Louis for the Christmas holidays. But St. Louis is only 675 miles from New Orleans, making it possible for Jerry to have quickly made the trip there after James called him from the road.[84] Of course, the visitor in New Orleans could also have been John Ray, who had recently begun preparing for the opening of his own tavern in St. Louis and had no time clock or work schedule that could curtail his movements.

The timing of a December meeting between the brothers is important because that is the time when John and Jerry may have independently learned about the standing $50,000 bounty that the St. Louis lawyer and segregationist John Sutherland was offering for King's murder. That was the same offer Ray himself might have found out about before he escaped from Jeff City.

Ten weeks before Ray left for New Orleans, on October 1, 1967, Carol Ray (then using her married name, Pepper) took out a lease on commercial space on Arsenal Street in St. Louis. She had decided to go into a joint venture for a bar—the Grapevine Tavern—with her brother John, but because of his criminal record she did not want to jeopardize the liquor license by putting his name on the lease.[85] For the next two months, John Ray was a regular in that St. Louis neighborhood, preparing the bar for its grand opening. A couple of weeks before James's visit to New Orleans, the Grapevine finally had its gas and electricity turned on, and although it did not technically receive its liquor license until January, it was unofficially open for business for neighborhood locals.[86] John had made friends in the area during the bar's construction, and it was immediately popular, according to him, with a "rough blue collar" crowd.[87] It was also, according to St. Louis police intelligence files, a place where ex-convicts gathered, often to plan burglaries and robberies, and it had a reputation among criminals as a place where "jobs" could be found.[88]

Later the Grapevine became a center of pro–George Wallace activity.[89] John Ray's sudden engrossment in politics was out of character, as he had never shown any interest before 1968, and as an ex-felon he was barred from voting. However, that year he converted the Grapevine into a distribution center for Wallace literature, and actually drove prospective voters to the Wallace registration office.*[90] Sutherland and John Kauffmann, the man he had used as a go-between to pass along his offer of money for King's death, were major Wallace supporters. Sutherland even paid the salary of the American Independent Party's Missouri state chairman.[91] Many of the party's rallying meetings were held near the bar, even when it was under construction in late 1967. One of the party's most active organizers lived only a hundred yards from the Grapevine.[92]

The Grapevine was a place where a bounty on King could have been comfortably discussed.[93] "I ran a tavern in a racist neighborhood," John later said.[94] When pushed by the Select Committee on how King was discussed at the Grapevine, John acknowledged that King was "a controversy figure," to whom John was personally "opposed," but that he could not remember any "*serious* discussion to do bodily injuries or conspiracies" about King (emphasis added).[95]

Moreover, starting in January, John Ray employed Naomi Regazzi as a bartender. Her husband was friendly with at least one person who knew of the bounty (Russell Byers) and a convict at Jeff City (John Paul Spica) who might have been aware of it.[96]

If John learned of the bounty, he and Jerry would almost certainly have talked about it—$50,000 was too tempting to summarily dismiss. But, as the Ray brothers always operated, a decision that big, especially one that involved a step up to murder, could not be made without the untitled leader of the clan, James.[97]

Not surprisingly, the Rays and Naomi Regazzi all disavow any complicity in the plot. John denied ever learning of Sutherland's offer through his Wallace work or passing it to James, much less visiting New Orleans in December 1967. Jerry Ray made the same denials. Regazzi said she was separated from her husband, did not meet John Ray until late December, and anyway claimed she never knew of any offer to kill King.[98]

---

* John later told a reporter for the *St. Louis Post-Dispatch* that he and James were "both strong supporters of George C. Wallace," and that when John visited James at Jeff City in 1967, "maybe we talked about him a little."

Whatever Ray was up to in New Orleans, he certainly gave no indication to
Charlie Stein. They left New Orleans on Tuesday. Stein and Ray shared the driving, and Rita Stein's twin eight-year-old girls sat in the Mustang's backseat.
They drove the 1,850 miles almost nonstop, stopping once for a snowball fight
in Texas and then after that only for food and gasoline.[99] The girls recalled that
Ray never spoke much, but that he used to hum loudly, accompanying radio
music that to them sounded like a train whistle.[100] They arrived in Los Angeles
on Thursday, December 21, two days after leaving New Orleans. Ray visited the
National Dance Studio that same day, and even though he had an agreement
to pay the balance of his enrollment fee in installments, he paid $364 cash.[101]
Such a large expenditure, hours after his return from New Orleans, again
raised the specter that somehow he had come into money while there.

Four days later, Ray had his first Christmas outside prison in eight years.
Rita Stein invited him over for dinner with some of her friends and family, but
Ray declined.[102] Huie later assumed that it must have been a "memorable" day
for Ray, and asked what he did that Christmas. "I don't remember anything
about that Christmas," Ray said. "You ought to know that Christmas is for family people. It don't mean anything to a loner like me. It's just another day and
another night to go to a bar or sit in your room and look at the paper and drink
a beer or two and maybe switch on the TV. No, I don't remember anything
about Christmas."[103]

24

The Swingers Club

A few days before the close of 1967, Ray wrote a telling letter to the American–Southern African Council in Washington, D.C.

> Dear Sir: I recently read an article in the Los Angeles Times on your council. The John Birch Society provided me with your address. My reason for writing is that I am considering immigrating to Rhodesia, however, there are a couple legal questions involved:
>
> One: The U.S. government will not issue a passport for travel to Rhodesia.
>
> Two: Would their be any way to enter Rhodesia legally (from the Rhodesian point of view)?
>
> I would appreciate any information you could give me on the above subject or any other information on Rhodesia.[1]

The American–Southern African Council, a group established to improve relations with Rhodesia and South Africa, responded to Ray with a form letter, enclosing literature about the country.[2] It was not, of course, the first time Ray had shown interest in going to one of Africa's two countries whose governments preached and practiced political and social race segregation. Ray's initial curiosity about Rhodesia arose while he was at Jeff City, when he told other prisoners that he considered it one of the places to which he might one day move. Once, when his brother John visited him at Jeff City, James mentioned that he thought Ian Smith was doing a good job as Rhodesian prime minister. Ray's comment came the month after the Smith government had condemned three black men to death for murder. Queen Elizabeth commuted their sentences, but Smith defied the crown and hanged them anyway.[3] And from Mexico, Ray had answered a magazine advertisement and sent off for information about immigrating there.

In addition to his growing interest in Rhodesia, the December 28 letter also disclosed that Ray, often incorrectly thought of as apolitical, had been in touch with the John Birch Society. A check of the Birch Society's records in Los Angeles revealed that while he had called them, he was not a member.[4] But Ray, after the assassination, realized that even such a brief contact might be significant, and in his letters to Huie listed the call and some to "other organizations" as one of five points that could be used against him by the prosecution.[5] The "other organizations" that Ray thought could be problematic were never identified.

A few days after his inquiry about Rhodesia, Ray drove to Las Vegas to celebrate his first New Year's Eve out of prison since 1959. He went alone and slept in his car, and while he did not gamble, he watched others at the clubs along the Strip.[6]

Since his return from New Orleans in late December, Ray had not made a new appointment with Dr. Mark Freeman, the clinical psychologist he had visited five times. "He didn't know nothing about hypnosis," Ray later complained.[7] Instead, on Thursday, January 4, Ray turned up at the office of the Reverend Xavier von Koss, head of the International Society of Hypnosis. The middle-aged Koss, who advertised himself as "an internationally recognized authority on hypnosis and self-hypnosis in the field of self-improvement," was well known for seminars to help businessmen develop more self-confidence.

"I remember him clearly," said Koss. "He seemed very much interested in self-improvement. He wanted to find a way to improve himself and his life. He had read several books on the subject and was impressed with the degree of mind concentration which one can obtain by the use of hypnosis. . . . He also seemed to be aware of self-image and its importance to a person."[8]

When Koss questioned Ray about his goals in life, "he told me he was considering taking a course in bartending. . . . But when I emphasized that he must complete his course in bartending, that he must work hard, that he must go to night school, that he must construct a settled-down life, I could feel a wall rising between us. I lost him. His mind moved far away from what I was saying to him."

Koss classified Ray as a "recognition type—he desires recognition from his group, from himself. He yearns to feel that he is somebody. The desire for recognition for him is superior to sex, superior to money, superior to self-preservation."[9]

When he tested Ray for hypnosis, he encountered a "strong subconscious resistance, he could not cooperate," but Koss was not surprised, as that was typical of people who hid something they were fearful of revealing. Feeling sorry for Ray but unable to help him, he merely recommended some books. In addition to the Maltz book, *Psycho-Cybernetics*, which Ray already had, Koss suggested *How to Cash In on Your Hidden Memory Power* by William Hersey and *Self-Hypnotism: The Technique and Its Use in Daily Living* by Leslie LeCron. When Ray was eventually captured two months after the King assassination, he was carrying well-worn copies of each of those books.

Besides his visit to Koss, January was a whirlwind of activity for Ray. He was still sending money orders for his weekly locksmithing correspondence classes. And every two to three days he attended hourlong sessions at the National Dance Studio. There, where he saw the same instructors and students for seven weeks, he failed to make a single friend and was considered by others to be either "unsociable," "bashful," or a "true introvert."[10] Showing up for classes invariably in a dark suit, shirt, and tie with a tie clip and cufflinks, wearing imitation-alligator loafers, he often stood awkwardly on the side, staring at his feet while pulling on one of his earlobes, waiting for his next partner to take him onto the dance floor.[11] Once he attended a party for twenty students, but he spent the night mostly by himself, and even after some drinks could manage only a stiff conversation confined to dancing.[12] His dancing, at least, had improved. In Birmingham his instructors remembered him as clumsy, while in Los Angeles most judged him fair to good. Although his instructors recalled that he was "crazy" about dancing, his personal stiffness held him back.[13]

In the middle of his dance lessons, on January 19, Ray enrolled in a six-week, $220 course at the International School of Bartending on Sunset Boulevard.[14] On the application, he listed Marie Martin and Rita and Charlie Stein as references, and concocted a recent employment with a fictitious Mr. Willer.[15] He attended classes six hours daily, five days a week, saying later that since bartending was a universal job, it might make it easier for him to get work when he eventually settled into a new country.[16] He told other students that he had been a chef in the merchant marine, but that the work was so hard he had abandoned it.[17] It might be a coincidence, but Ray's brother John had officially opened the Grapevine Tavern a few weeks earlier, and Ray may have thought he would one day settle into one of the family's few straight enterprises.

Two days after enrolling in the bartending school, Ray moved several blocks from Serrano Avenue to the St. Francis Hotel-Apartments on Hollywood Boulevard.[18] An FBI report later described his new building as a "den of iniquity" teeming with prostitution and drug trafficking.[19] Ray wrote his former landlord a short note and enclosed his apartment key, but gave no reason for the move.[20] Later, Ray said that he relocated because he had given Dr. Freeman "my right name, I had also given him my phone no. and . . . I moved from Serrano St. address as I thought I mite be put on the top 10 and he would find out."[21] While most of his neighbors at the St. Francis were retirees, Ray liked that the Sultan Room was on the ground floor. His $85-a-month room had no telephone and was adjacent to the building's two-story orange neon sign, which bathed his small apartment in a steady, eerie glow.* The only time other residents saw him was occasionally on Thursday nights, when Ray visited the television room, off the main lobby, to watch the evening's prizefights. At those times, he sat by himself and did not talk to anyone.[22]

Not long after he moved to the St. Francis, Rhodesia was again on Ray's mind. This time he wrote to the Orange County, California, chapter of the Friends of Rhodesia, another organization that attempted to foster better relations with the United States. Ray thanked the group's president, Ronald Hewitson, for his previous help in "clarifying most of my questions regarding immigration" (Hewitson later claimed he could not find a copy of the first letter to which Ray referred).[23] In his second communication, Ray said he did not intend to leave for Rhodesia until November 1968, but that in the meantime he wanted to subscribe to *Rhodesian Commentary,* a publication that extolled the white-run country. If Ray had decided to kill King by this time, it appears his plan did not yet include a timetable.

But Rhodesia was again only briefly on his mind. On January 29, he sent a $4.25 money order to the Los Angeles *Free Press,* an underground newspaper filled with personal classifieds. Ray's ad ran in the February 2 issue: "Single male Cauc. 36 yrs, 5-11, 170 lbs, Digs Fr. Cult. [oral sex], desire's discreet meeting with passionate married female for mutual enjoyment, and/or female for swing session apt. furn. will ex. photo. Write Eric S. 406 So. 2nd St., Al-

---

* The FBI checked all calls placed from the St. Francis's two pay telephones and none could be connected to Ray. The hotel's manager, Allan O. Thompson, initially told the FBI that Ray had never received a single call. However, later he changed his mind and said that he had had a conversation with a man he refused to identify, who "prompted his recollection" that Ray had actually received four calls from a "James C. Hardin," originating from Atlanta and New Orleans. Since Ray was not there to receive the calls, Thompson supposedly passed the information to him. Thompson also claimed that in mid-March, Hardin—described as a middle-aged white male, with a dark complexion and dark hair and a Southern accent—showed up at the hotel looking for Ray. Again, Ray was not there. The FBI, despite a nationwide search, could never find anyone by that name or alias who fit the story. The Bureau concluded Thompson's revised story was wrong and might have been motivated by his desire to cash in on the case's $100,000 reward (MURKIN 4061–4142, section 51).

hambra, 91802."*[24] The day before Ray's advertisement ran in the *Free Press*, he also paid one dollar to a local correspondence club—the Local Swinger—for the names and addresses of five swingers.[25] Ray took at least a dozen Polaroid photos of himself and sent them to women whose advertisements he answered in the *Free Press*, as well as to the women whose names he received from the Local Swinger.[26] Typical was his February 17 letter to one of the women:

Dear Miss:

I am answering you listing in the Local Swinger since I think I share most of your interests, with emphasis on French cult. and swing sessions. I have just returned from Mexico after five yrs. and the few females I have met don't go for the swing parties and it takes two to swing. The same routine gets boring, don't you think. Will close until I here from you.

Sincerely,
Eric S. Galt
5533 Hollywood Blvd.
Hollywood, Calif.
90028
Ph. 464-1131[27]

Later in the month, Ray bought more sex manuals from Futura Books for $6.44, and also ordered a set of Japanese chrome handcuffs for $9.98.†[28]

What was Ray's motive in soliciting swingers and sending out his own photos? It initially seems another effort to get women for his still-stagnant porn venture. Stuck with $400 in camera equipment and not having used it yet except for some poor-quality photos in Mexico, he must have been frustrated. He did not, by the accounts of those who still saw him alone at the St.

---

*   The Alhambra address was a mail-forwarding service Ray used for February for the *Free Press* ads. Ray later fretted that the prosecutors might use his placement of those classifieds against him since the *Free Press* was "a very liberal publication."

†   Tiffany Enterprises ran the advertisement for the handcuffs, but the International Police Equipment Company of Los Angeles filled the order. When Ray's order was received, the company was temporarily out of stock, and it shipped the handcuffs late. They arrived at Ray's forwarding address in Atlanta. Also, in late May, solicitations to purchase lewd films, addressed to Eric S. Galt, arrived at his former Los Angeles address. Somebody had purchased the Galt name from a mailing list and thought he would be a potential customer for video pornography, unaware that he was then the subject of an international manhunt for the King murder.

Francis apartments, meet anyone through the *Free Press* or the Local Swinger. Yet Ray has offered a different reason for placing the personal classifieds and then distributing his photos, and it ties to something surprising he did in mid-February: He had plastic surgery. "I didn't get plastic surgery to change my personally or future as you mite have construed by reading the Maltz book," Ray wrote. "I got the surgery to change my facial features so it would be harder to identify me throught pictures circulated my law officials. . . . What I did was circulate a lot of pictures around through this club [the Local Swinger] then I had plastic surgery. The reason I did this was that I knew sooner or later the F.B.I. would get me on the Top 10, and I assumed someone that I had mailed a picture to would sent it to the F.B.I., meanwhile I would have had my features altered plus the fact that the pictures have made me look considerable younger."[29]

Ray visited Dr. Russell Hadley on Hollywood Boulevard on February 19. He had an initial consultation regarding rhinoplasty, filling out an application in which he lied as usual about his age (three years younger) and listed his nearest relative as the fictitious Karl L. Galt. He told Hadley that he wanted the surgery because he was getting work in a television commercial and needed the improvement.*[30]

Ray paid $200 cash for the surgery, which was done on March 5. The doctor's records show a "nasal tip reconstruction for pointed tip. Under local anesthesia in office." Two days later, Ray returned to have the nasal packing, a

---

* By mid-February, when he had his consultation with Hadley, Ray was evidently also making preparations to leave Los Angeles soon. He swapped his more expensive console television for Marie Martin's small portable set, telling her that he was going to do some traveling and wanted a set that he could carry in his car. Louis Lomax thought Ray actually made a secret trip to New Orleans in February, in order to get his final orders on the assassination. Others have speculated that Ray visited Chicago for several days, where his two brothers were admittedly at the Atlantic Hotel for a brief reunion. However, the Mustang's odometer shows neither of those trips was possible. On February 13, Ray had the car serviced at a local gas station and the odometer showed 34,185 miles. When the car was found by the FBI after the assassination it had an additional 5,000 miles, almost all of which can be explained by Ray's known destinations through his abandoning of the car after the assassination. An extra trip to Chicago or New Orleans would have required several thousand more miles.

Also, toward the end of the month, Ray fired off one of his unusual letters, for which there is no apparent explanation—he wrote the Social Security Administration in Baltimore asking "what effect the amendments to the Social Security Act 1956, 1960, 1961, 1965 had in regards two who was covered, such as the number of employes a firm could hire without paying social security." They answered him after the assassination.

standard procedure in rhinoplasty, removed. On March 11, the day after his fortieth birthday, the stitches were taken out.*[31]

Rhinoplasty is a major cosmetic procedure, yet following the surgery Ray "got to the hotel, [and] I moved the bandage to the right to change my appearance more." Trying to further alter the shape of his nose within hours of surgery must have been excruciatingly painful, and it is further evidence of how badly Ray wanted to change his appearance. No sooner did he have the rhinoplasty than "I intend to go to another dr. and have my ear changed (these things are not noticeable on person to person contack but they show up in pictures) I didn't have time for the ear."[32] Again, Ray emphasized his fixation on his imaginary importance to the FBI: "The reason was that I expected to be put on the top 10 any day since I excaped over the wall."[33]

Ray's mistaken belief that he was about to be placed on the FBI's ten most-wanted list is not just a simple error in judgment, but calls into serious question how far he was removed from reality. It would not take a very clever man to discern that Ray, a petty thief who had managed to escape from a state prison, and had in the meantime failed to be fingered for any subsequent crime, would be of little or no interest to the Bureau. That he thought of himself as daring enough to be in the FBI's criminal elite, indicates that while few thought of him as confident, he obviously considered himself as somebody to be reckoned with. If he had learned of the bounty on King in New Orleans, instead of being intimidated by the assignment, Ray would likely have embraced it as a confirmation of how clever he thought he was. It was as though Ray's nearly ten months of freedom had somehow emboldened him. Not only had he pulled off a successful escape from a maximum-security prison, but he had managed to stay free while traveling through three countries, visiting his family, and smuggling narcotics, and he had more money than at any other time in his life.

Not surprisingly, he denies that he was thinking of murdering King when he had plastic surgery and sent out the presurgery photos. He contended, "I certainly wouldn't have circulated my picture around if I thought I was going to be the object of a world wide manhunt the next month, plastic surgery or not."[34] That initially sounds reasonable. But Ray contradicts himself by saying that on the one hand he wanted to distribute photos to create confusion in a manhunt since he expected to be momentarily placed on the most-wanted list, and on the other hand

---

* A typical part of all plastic surgery is the taking of before and after photos, so that the patient can best determine the results. In Ray's case, on the day the first photos were taken, something was wrong with Dr. Hadley's camera, and the pictures did not turn out. By the time the "after" photos were due to be taken—six to eight weeks later—Ray had left Los Angeles.

he would not have sent his pictures around if he knew law enforcement would be hunting him for the King murder. Placement on the Top Ten, for any reason, would mean the start of an international game of hide and seek once his picture was broadcast as part of a wildly successful weekly television program, *The F.B.I.* One of the reasons Ray might have concluded that "sooner or later the F.B.I. would get me on the Top 10" was that he was then planning the assassination.

When Ray eventually realized that his strong interest in altering his appearance so near the King assassination might signal foreknowledge of the murder, he changed his reason for sending out his photos and having the surgery. No longer did he tie it to a plan to mislead law enforcement in case of a large manhunt, but claimed it was merely because "I wanted to collect some extra names and addresses in case I needed a new identity. And in the process of meeting marks, I might even recruit an ally."[35] But that rationale, written almost twenty-five years after his contemporaneous explanations to Huie, rings hollow.

It is also notable that in his first account Ray asserted, "I didn't have time for the ear [surgery]." While he lived in Los Angeles, however, he was enjoying an eclectic lifestyle that was not constrained by any deadlines. That he did not "have time" for the ear surgery, and had to suddenly leave Los Angeles only eighteen days before King's murder, is another indicator that he may already have settled on making an attempt on King. It is probable that notwithstanding his denials, the plastic surgery and the circulation of presurgery photos were part of groundwork for the assassination. Something certainly provoked this rather significant effort at subterfuge, for if all Ray wanted was his long-claimed passport and move to Africa, the surgery and photos would have been unnecessary.

Furthermore on March 2, three days before he had the rhinoplasty, Ray had graduated from bartending school. As part of the graduation, he had a picture taken, holding his completion certificate, with the school's manager, Tomas Lau. Ray fretted about that picture. While he could not arouse suspicion by being the only student to refuse to have a graduation photo taken, he did his best to make it useless for further identification. In it, dressed in a barman's jacket and bow tie—the first time he had ever worn a bow tie—Ray appears to be in a tuxedo. At the moment the picture was snapped, he closed his eyes, later saying he hoped not to be identified.*

---

* Ray's closing of his eyes worked. An FBI sketch artist later drew the eyes in, and the photo did not look like Ray, even to his own family. Yet it ended up as one of three photos on the international wanted posters for the King murderer. The other two were eight-year-old mug shots of Ray sporting a crew cut. Those pictures also looked markedly different from the 1968 Ray. All the wanted-poster photos aided Ray in staying free, and also confused many of the initial witnesses approached by the FBI.

Near this time, Ray was involved in an incident at one of his favorite bars, the Rabbit's Foot, that has aroused much controversy concerning his racial attitudes near the assassination. "On this particular nite," Ray wrote to Huie, "they was someone sitting next to me who talked about 30 minutes without stopping about the state of the world. Their was also a young girl sitting on the other side of me. I mite of told the guy who was talking to me where I was from as I think he ask me, or she mite have seen my car with the Alabama license on it. Anyhow, when the conversationalist left she started by asking me how come they deny colors their rights in Alabama. I think I ask her if she had ever been there or something like that and walked out. Their was two guys next to her and when I went out they must of followed me. . . . Anyhow, the big one grab me from behind and pulled my coat over my arms (I had a suit on) the shorter one started hitting and asking for my money."[36] Since Ray did not have his ".38 equalizer" with him, the men were able to steal his watch and jacket. When he got to the Mustang, he realized that his car keys were in the jacket, so he waited until the following morning to make sure the police had not been called, and then had a local locksmith make a new pair for him.*[37]

However, witnesses to the confrontation told the FBI a quite different version. Bo Del Monte, a Rabbit's Foot bartender, was interviewed only a few weeks after the assassination. He knew Ray as Doug Collins, a name he said Ray used at the racially integrated bar. Del Monte recalled that Ray and the female patron, Pat Goodsell, got into such a donnybrook that Ray dragged her toward the door and screamed, "I'll drop you off in Watts [Los Angeles's largest black ghetto] and we'll see if you like it there."[38]

James Morrison, another bartender, recalled that when he once discussed Robert Kennedy and politics with Ray, Ray became incensed and enthusiastically praised Wallace.[39] He confirmed Del Monte's recollection that on the night of the fight over blacks and the civil rights movement, Ray dragged Goodsell toward the door while shouting. Another customer, who knew Goodsell, broke up the argument.

---

* William Paisley, who sold Ray the Mustang, said he had given Ray two sets of keys. Ray claimed he gave one set to Raoul in Birmingham. If he lost a set in Los Angeles, the fact that he had to have an extra set made is often used by Ray and his supporters to credit the existence of Raoul. However, the FBI was unable ever to locate a locksmith that made a new lock for any Mustang near the time of the incident, calling into question whether Ray lied about losing his keys. Moreover, even if he only had one set while in Los Angeles, there are several possibilities as to what happened to the second set, from Ray having lost it during his cross-country and international travel to his having sent it to one of his brothers.

When the Select Committee reinvestigated the issue in 1978, it discovered that the woman, Goodsell, had died, and it located only one of the bartenders, Del Monte. Ten years after his original interview, he downplayed the altercation and Ray's right-wing politics. In his second version, Del Monte said that Ray did not discuss Wallace, and that on the night of the incident, there was no fight—"there were a lot of people sitting at the bar taking part in a philosophical discussion concerning someone in the group saying blacks could come into a white area and be safe and whites could not go into a black area and be safe."[40] Before the Select Committee investigators, Del Monte added that he suspected that Ray, who had been a regular at the bar for three months, was on heroin, because he had the sullen and drawn look of an addict, and often nodded into a stupor at the bar.*[41] However, the Select Committee also located Dennis LeMaster, the FBI special agent who had spoken with Del Monte in 1968. He was adamant that his original reports of interviews with both Rabbit's Foot bartenders were accurate and that he had had no reason to exaggerate or falsify anything in them.[42]

While the actual argument in the bar adds little to understanding the fervor of Ray's racism shortly before King's assassination, the subsequent mugging in the parking lot raises a perplexing issue. It happened sometime in late February, but no one can pinpoint the exact day. What is known is that on Wednesday, February 28, somebody telephoned the Highway Bureau in Montgomery, Alabama, and requested a duplicate license for Eric S. Galt. The Highway Bureau mailed the duplicate and a bill for twenty-five cents that same day to Galt's permanent Alabama address, the rooming house Ray had occupied during the 1967 summer.[43] (The rooming house had a hallway table where mail was placed for tenants.) Four days later, the twenty-five-cent fee was sent to Montgomery by mail. Who picked it up if Ray was in Los Angeles? Moreover, Ray is adamant that he did not lose his license in the parking-lot mugging.

Memphis prosecutor James Beasley said "any friend" could have received the license for Ray, but had no guess as to who that could be.[44] William Bradford Huie's investigation concluded that Ray had lied and that in fact he had lost his license when his wallet was stolen in the parking-lot dispute. Ray telephoned the Alabama Highway Bureau for a replacement, according to Huie, and then instructed the Birmingham post office to send any mail to him care of general delivery in Los Angeles. He also sent the Highway Bureau the twenty-five-cent fee.[45]

---

* One indication that Ray may have again been using drugs is that he admitted in the 20,000 Words that he had visited a "pill doctor" in Los Angeles, but could not remember the man's name. The FBI could not find that doctor.

When pressed on the issue by the Select Committee, Ray was vague, giving the impression that it was another matter in which he was being less than honest. Asked whether he remembered ordering a duplicate license, he said, "I don't recall. I got these vague ideas that I may have ordered two of them or something, but that wouldn't make much sense, but if I'd lost the driver's license I'd have most likely lost the registration, but I just can't recollect losing it at that time."[46] It is even possible that Ray did not lose his license when mugged, but that the incident scared him enough so that he wanted a backup. In either case, it appears probable that Ray ordered the duplicate license for Galt and there was no confederate retrieving a copy in Birmingham.*

In early March, Ray made final preparations to leave Los Angeles. He had stopped taking dance lessons weeks earlier, forfeiting some of his money and telling the instructors that he was accepting a bartender's job. But in fact, when the manager at the bartending school, Tomas Lau, called Ray a week after his March 2 graduation and offered him work, Ray declined, saying that he was leaving town in two weeks to visit his brother.[†47]

Shortly before his departure from Los Angeles, Ray ran into Marie Martin and told her he was heading south. Once again, she asked him if he would mind stopping in New Orleans, to drop off a package with her family, and he agreed.[48] Ray appeared in need of money, she thought, which she considered unusual for him, as he always seemed to have a ready supply of twenty-dollar bills. When she mentioned it, he told her he was waiting for money from his brother.[49]

On March 16 and 17, 1968, Martin Luther King visited Los Angeles. Newspapers and local television and radio extensively covered the visit. On his first night, King addressed the California Democratic Council and called for President Johnson's defeat. The following night, he spoke at the Second Baptist Church about the "meaning of hope." There is no evidence that Ray stalked King or tried to get near him on either of those days. If he had decided to move against King, his brother Jerry is almost certainly right when he said that Ray

----

* Although the issue is one of the favorites of conspiracy buffs, no one has ever offered a reason as to why anyone would want a second Galt license for a plot to kill King. No issue later developed in the case in which a second person passed as Galt, or another Galt identification was presented anywhere. As with many similar issues, the replacement license sometimes consumes pages in conspiracy books, but what possible sinister implication it might have had, even if true, is never explained.

† At the graduation ceremony, a fellow student, Richard Gonzalez, had also overheard Ray say that he was soon leaving for Birmingham to visit his brother.

believed killing King could be done only in the South, where people might be
willing to view the crime sympathetically.

On March 17, St. Patrick's Day, Ray executed a change-of-address card ad-
vising that his old address at the St. Francis apartments had been changed to
general delivery at the main post office in Atlanta. He noted on the card that
the new address would be good only until April 25, 1968.[50] If killing King was
on his mind, he had given himself a small window.*

---

* In the 20,000 Words, Ray said Raoul told him in a letter that he would meet Ray at
a bar in New Orleans and then "we would go from New Orleans to Atlanta, Ga." To Dan
Rather, nine years later, Ray changed his story—"I never knew I was going to Atlanta
until I arrived in Birmingham, and there was no forwarding address—of course, that
would be very damaging against me." When questioned by the House Select Committee,
he was asked if he had filed a change-of-address card while in Los Angeles. "No, I
didn't," said Ray. "I'm positive I didn't." The committee then produced his change-of-
address card, submitted while still in Los Angeles, and confronted Ray. He then backed
down and admitted that when he left Los Angeles he had known that he was heading to
Atlanta (HSCA vol. II, p. 51).

25

Memphis Bound

U nlike his rushed trip to New Orleans over the Christmas holidays, Ray's drive east from Los Angeles was a leisurely one. Using his Galt alias, he stayed at cheap motels along the way.[1] On the night of March 20, he reached New Orleans.[2] He dropped off a box of clothes with Marie Martin's family the following day.[3] While there, the local newspapers and radio reported that Dr. King would be in Selma, Alabama, on March 22, recruiting for his Poor People's Campaign.* Selma had been made famous by King's groundbreaking work there, and would have been one of the most dramatic places to assassinate him. Ray drove there on March 22 and spent the night at the Flamingo Motel. His appearance in Selma raises the suspicion that Ray was finally stalking his target.†

---

* Although King had been scheduled to stop in Selma, he changed his plans at the last moment and instead stopped in Camden, Alabama, about thirty miles away.

† In the November 11, 1968, edition of *Look*, Huie wrote that Ray had been stalking King in Selma. Ray had read the galleys before publication, as had his brother Jerry, and both had discussed and approved them. Later, Ray denied stalking King, claiming he did not know King was scheduled to be in Selma, and was only in Selma himself because he got lost while driving to Birmingham. It is not easy to get lost traveling on the straight route from New Orleans to Birmingham, especially ending up in Selma, which requires a turn off the main freeway and then another sixty miles to the city. Moreover, Ray was

The next day, when King left the area, Ray also left. He drove to Atlanta, King's hometown, passing through Birmingham on the way.* On Saturday, March 23, Ray, using his Galt alias, rented a $10.50-a-week room in a decaying rooming house in the heart of Atlanta's small hippie community. The faded green, two-story house at 113 Fourteenth Street catered to transients, handling up to 500 boarders a year. A small yard overgrown with weeds marked the front, and a gravel lot in the rear served as a parking lot. Ray's eight-by-ten-foot room had a worn black and gray tile floor, a single bed, a dresser, and a washbasin. His window faced another similar rooming house next door.

James Garner, the rooming house manager, was drunk much of the time Ray was there.[†4] Still, he remembered Ray—who claimed he was a "jack of all trades"—as being neatly dressed in a dark suit, nice, and well mannered.[5] He saw Ray—always alone—a few times over ten days. After the assassination, when the FBI searched Ray's room, they found, among many other items, a map of Atlanta, with four penciled circles on it. One circle was near King's former home, one near the SCLC headquarters and Ebenezer Baptist Church, where King's father was the pastor, and one at the Capitol Homes housing project, where the Mustang was found abandoned after the assassination. Ray's thumbprint was on the map.[6] Over a dozen other maps were found in Ray's possession, but none bore pencil marks such as those on the Atlanta one.[‡]

---

an experienced driver who had driven without problems through Canada, the United States, and Mexico. He regularly used maps, over a dozen of which were found in his belongings after the assassination. It would be an unlikely coincidence that the only time Ray got lost while driving around the country was on a day that put him in a city where Dr. King was scheduled to be. It seems more plausible that Ray was indeed stalking King and getting a feel for the security around him.

* He arrived in Birmingham around noon, and claims he met Raoul at the Starlite Café and then drove with him to Atlanta. No one at the café later remembered Ray or a person who fit Raoul's description.

† Ray says that when he rented the room on the twenty-third, the manager was drunk. When Ray returned the following day he convinced Garner he had already paid the rent, when in fact he had not. Ray also claimed that Raoul accompanied him to the rooming house on the twenty-third, but Garner does not remember seeing anybody with Ray.

‡ Ray supporters often ignore or distort the evidence about the Atlanta map. Harold Weisberg, for instance, flatly but incorrectly writes, "*No* Ray print on the *marked* map of Atlanta!" (emphasis in original). The author obtained an order of the court in Memphis to examine personally the physical evidence in the case, and part of that review involved inspecting Ray's maps. Ray has claimed that he often marked maps to get his bearings. Although all the maps reviewed by the author are in poor condition due to the FBI's application of a solvent for finding fingerprints, the pencil markings on the At-

While Ray had moved to Atlanta, King had not returned there from Selma. Instead, he traveled to New York, where he stayed through March 27, and then went on to Memphis on the twenty-eighth for the sanitation strike.

Ray was not certain how long he might remain in Atlanta. He paid the $10.50 weekly rent on March 24, and again on March 31. On an envelope found in his room after the assassination, he had made notes indicating he also intended to pay the rent for the week starting April 7—which, of course, turned out to be after the assassination, indicating that by late March, Ray had not yet selected a time or place to try to kill King. There is also evidence that if Ray had been hired to kill King, he had not yet received any money, since, short of cash, he exchanged up to $700 of the Canadian money he still had.*[7]

Ray said everything he did in Atlanta revolved around Raoul. His evolving versions of events there provide a good example of how he has adapted his Raoul story over time. For instance, in his original account of his stay in Atlanta—the one he told to Arthur Hanes, Sr.—Ray did not mention having any meal at a restaurant with Raoul.[8] Then, in September 1968, Hanes found a restaurant receipt—from an Atlanta restaurant on Peachtree Street called Mammy's Shanty about five blocks from Ray's rooming house—in Ray's belongings collected by the FBI. The undated receipt showed that food (London broil for $1.85) was served to two people. Hanes asked questions concerning the receipt and Ray said he knew nothing about it.[9] When Ray was asked if he had ever ordered London broil, he did not even know what it was.[10] However, Ray is excellent at incorporating bits of information he learns from one source and developing them into a cohesive story he spins to somebody else. After learning of the receipt, he wrote to Huie that on the night he had arrived in Atlanta, he and Raoul "went to a restaurant on Peachtree Street as I hadn't eaten since breakfast."[11] After Ray fired Hanes, he suddenly told Foreman that he had gone to a "restaurant on Peachtree street" with Raoul. Huie subsequently visited the restaurant and could not find anyone who remembered Ray.

Ray also contended that he wanted Raoul to have easy access to his Atlanta room, so he had an extra key made for him.[12] Before the Select Committee, he at

---

lanta map are still visible, and no other map has similar ones. Ray himself realized that the markings were highly incriminating. "I could never explain that away to the jury," he admitted to the Select Committee. Instead, he said the markings related to restaurants and banks he visited. "I gave it a lot of thought," Ray said, "and that's the best I could come up with" (HSCA vol. IX, p. 224).

* The fact that Ray was worried about running low on cash and had to use his Canadian funds indicates that if he had been hired to kill King, he had not been paid anything by late March, only a week before the murder.

first did not mention the key, saying only that Raoul had trouble getting in and out of the rooming house without the manager, James Garner, noticing him.[13] Another time he told the committee that he left the door unlocked for Raoul but Garner's sister kept relocking it.[14] In yet another committee interview, he reverted to the key story and even claimed that he personally tried to make a copy from a blank key and some tools but gave up after a couple of days because it was too difficult.[15] Still, no one at the rooming house ever saw Ray with anyone.

Thus, Ray's stories of his association with Raoul are not independently corroborated. There were, however, plenty of witnesses to what Ray did by himself during that time. On March 27, he drove 122 miles to Birmingham, Alabama, to visit the Gun Rack.[16] That was the store where the clerks remembered him from at least one earlier visit and his constant barrage of questions.[17]

The following day, back in Atlanta, he purchased a postal money order for $7.50 and sent it to his locksmithing school in New Jersey, notifying the school that he had relocated to Atlanta.[18] This indicates that Ray expected to be in Atlanta for at least a few more weeks (his change-of-address card submitted in Los Angeles showed that he expected to be in Atlanta until April 25).[19]

On Friday, March 29, Ray walked into the Long-Lewis hardware store in Bessemer, Alabama, about ten miles outside Birmingham, where he again asked asked about high-powered rifles and ballistics.*[20] A little later, at Aeromarine Supply Company, across the road from Birmingham's municipal airport, Ray—using the name Harvey Lowmyer—finally paid cash for a .243-caliber rifle with a 2×7 Redfield scope and twenty rounds of ammunition.†[21] He paid the $248.59 bill in cash.[22] (The next day, Ray also bought some additional ammunition, a cheaper box of older Army ammo, from an unidentified store.)[23]

---

* Questions by Ray such as how much bullets might drop at anywhere from 100 to 600 yards, indicates that he was evidently not considering an assassination at close range, which would immediately lead to his capture. Instead, his interest was in a long-range shot, sufficiently removed from the actual kill so that he would have a fair opportunity to get away. The only other assassin in Ray's memory who had at least managed to escape from the crime scene was Lee Oswald, who also had shot from a long distance with a high-powered rifle.

† Ray told William Bradford Huie that he did not buy the gun in the Atlanta area because his only valid identification was the Alabama license for Eric S. Galt. So he made the two-hour trip to Birmingham, a city with which he was familiar from his 1967 stay there. His intent was to buy the gun under a new alias, making it more difficult to trace him. If the Alabama stores required a proper ID, he had decided he would reluctantly resort to his Galt driver's license. As for the name Ray did use, a Harvey Edward Lohmeyer had worked in a prison kitchen with John Ray, James's brother, in Illinois during the late 1950s. On the receipt, the name is printed as "Lowmeyer" but it appears the scribbled signature is "Lowmyer." Some authors, such as Gerold Frank in An American Death, use Lowmyer as the name.

That same day, Ray called Aeromarine and said that he needed to exchange the .243 for a more powerful .30-06, because his brother had told him he had bought the wrong gun.*[24] The clerk told him he would have to come back the next morning, so Ray spent the night at a local Travelodge Motel. On March 30, Ray returned the .243 rifle to Aeromarine when it opened at 9:00 A.M. Around 3:00 P.M. he picked up the Remington Gamemaster Model 760 .30-06-caliber rifle—the one that would be left, five days later, in front of the Memphis rooming house from which an assassin killed King.

Raoul is central to Ray's explanation as to how and why he bought the rifle. In Ray's version, Raoul gave him $700 to buy a "large-bore deer rifle fitted with scope, plus ammo," as a sample to be shown to Mexican buyers in a gunrunning scheme.[25] If the Mexicans liked the rifle, they would buy another ten. Ray has never explained why foreign gun smugglers would have to buy guns from Raoul and Ray when they could buy them over the counter in most American gun stores—in cash and with no identification—just as Ray had bought the rifle at Aeromarine.† Nor does he have an explanation of why he spent hours at three shops asking technical ballistics questions if Raoul had only instructed him to buy a rifle for resale.

As before, Ray has constantly changed the details. Sometimes he has said that Raoul accompanied him on the first trip to Aeromarine Supply and simply sat in the car; other times Raoul went with him to Aeromarine only on the second day; and on still other occasions Ray says Raoul was not with him on either visit.[26]

When he returned to the Travelodge with the first gun, the .243 caliber, Ray says, Raoul looked at it and without any explanation declared "it was the wrong kind."[27] In an interview with the Select Committee, Ray said Raoul stayed in Birmingham overnight so he could approve the selection of the .30-06 before leaving. But in another version, Raoul left Birmingham that same evening, before Ray returned the next day to get the .30-06.[28]

---

* Jerry Ray boasted to author George McMillan (in a February 23, 1975, interview maintained with the McMillan papers at the Southern Historical Collection) that he was in Birmingham with James on the day the rifle was purchased. However, he asked McMillan to understand why he could not answer more questions about where and when they test-fired the rifle. According to McMillan's notes, "Jerry let it slip to me, 'the rifle had to be one that would do it in one shot.' " Jerry has since denied telling McMillan that, and now claims he was at work consistently through this period, with only Tuesdays off. The rifle transactions at Aeromarine Supply took place on Friday and Saturday. Some coworkers supported Jerry Ray's claim, although his work records no longer exist so the issue cannot be definitively settled.

† As a result of King's murder, a federal law was passed that required gun sellers to obtain the purchaser's name, age, address, place of birth, and home telephone number, and to produce a valid identification such as a driver's license.

In most renditions, including his Select Committee testimony, Ray contended Raoul directed him to take the weapon to Memphis a few days later. However, in 1977 he told the Canadian Broadcasting Corporation that he gave the rifle to Raoul in Birmingham and never saw it again.[29] In almost every account, Ray said Raoul handled the rifle after Ray touched it for the last time. Yet he cannot explain why only his prints were on it. If the gun had been wiped clean of prints, Ray's would have been removed with anyone else's. He once suggested Raoul may have worn Band-Aids or wax over his fingertips to prevent prints being left behind, but admitted he never noticed Raoul wearing either.*[30]

There is strong evidence that after Ray picked up the .30-06 from Aeromarine Supply, he returned to Atlanta by the early evening of March 30. Garner remembered collecting the second week's rent the next day. On April 1, Ray dropped some of his clothes at Atlanta's Piedmont Laundry. That is where Estelle Peters, the manager, signed him in on her ledger as Eric Galt.[31]

Yet Ray told Huie that after he got the .30-06 rifle in Birmingham on March 30, he did not return to Atlanta but instead began a leisurely drive toward Memphis.[32] Ray asserted he had dropped off the laundry in Atlanta and paid his second week of rent before he left for Birmingham and the gun stores.[33] Although Memphis was only 312 miles away from Birmingham—some five hours drive—in Ray's version to Huie it took him five days to get there. The reason the early departure for Memphis is a critical issue is that Ray is claiming he left for the city two days before the Southern Christian Leadership Conference publicly announced that Dr. King would return there for another march. The SCLC made that decision only on March 30. So if Ray was directed to Memphis as early as March 30, it would be potent evidence of a sophisticated conspiracy.[34] However, if Ray did not leave Atlanta until April 1, or later, after reading about it in the newspapers, that would be strong proof that he was indeed stalking King.

Problems with Ray's story of an early departure directly for Memphis were evident to Hanes and Huie as early as mid-1968. Ray had told Hanes that on the journey to Memphis he met Raoul at an unidentified motel in Mississippi on the night of April 2. There, he not only gave Raoul the Remington rifle, but Raoul also told him to rent a room at the South Main Street rooming house in Memphis around 3:00 P.M. on April 4 under the alias John Willard.[35] When Hanes heard that story, and then told Huie, both realized that the unidentified Mississippi motel was critical to Ray's defense. "A witness might be found,"

---

* Ray never fails to contradict himself if asked the same question enough times. He once told the Select Committee that he never saw Raoul handle the rifle (HSCA vol. II, p. 15).

wrote Huie, "who could identify Raoul or who saw a man leaving Ray's room with a box large enough to hold a rifle."[36] As a result, Hanes, Huie, and a private detective searched extensively for the motel. Ray, who had provided Hanes and Huie remarkably accurate diagrams and maps for locations and motels he visited in Canada, Mexico, and other parts of the United States, could not draw anything reliable about the motel at which he supposedly met Raoul, but he claimed that it was no more than five miles south of the Tennessee-Mississippi state line.

"We went to every motel in Mississippi within twenty miles of Memphis," recalled Huie, "and we could find no evidence that Ray under any of his aliases, or anyone driving a white Mustang with an Alabama license, had registered at any of them between March 30 and April 3. Similarly, with the motels near Corinth and Florence."[37] When Huie and Hanes learned that James Garner, the manager at the Atlanta rooming house, recalled Ray was actually in Atlanta through the night of April 2, they confronted Ray. In a letter to Huie, Ray suddenly changed the night that he transferred the gun to Raoul to the following evening, April 3, at the New Rebel Motel in Memphis. That was a place where the FBI had confirmed that Ray had spent the night as Eric Galt.[38] But still, his changing story about the April 2 meeting, and the fact that he could name none of the motels he supposedly stayed at during his five-day trip to Memphis, left Hanes and Huie uneasy about his entire story.

Before the House Select Committee on Assassinations in 1978, Ray continued to insist that he had left for Memphis directly from Birmingham, even that he set out a day earlier than he told Hanes and Huie. "After this conversation [with Raoul] I stated a slow trip toward Memphis on the 29th."[39] That was before the SCLC had even decided that King would return for another march, so no one could have had the knowledge to direct Ray there. It was also the day before Ray picked up the .30-06 rifle from Aeromarine Supply in Birmingham, so it was physically impossible for him to have left that early.

That did not stop Ray from embellishing even this story. He told the committee that he spent one night in Decatur, Alabama, one in Florence, Alabama, another in Clinton, Mississippi, and two nights outside Memphis near Corinth, Mississippi, at the DeSoto Motel.*[40] The committee's chairman, Ohio congress-

---

* Ray actually picked up the name DeSoto from one of the guards assigned to Cell Block A during 1968 and 1969. The guard, listening to Ray's story, suggested that he might have stayed at the DeSoto Motel. Harold Weisberg, who served as an investigator for Ray in the 1970s, says that in 1974 he confirmed that Ray had stayed at the DeSoto on April 2. Weisberg's "confirmation" was talking to the manager and maids who suddenly, six years after the event, claimed to remember Ray staying there one night on April 2. Of course, they could provide no records to substantiate the visit, claiming the FBI took their records shortly after the assassination, something there is no indication of in FBI files.

man Louis Stokes, questioned Ray to ensure there was no misunderstanding about his story and the importance of it.

"Now, you said in your statement to us here that after purchasing the rifle you didn't return to Atlanta, isn't that true?"

"That is correct, yes," said Ray.

"Do you want to change anything at all about that statement?"

"No," Ray replied with unusual vigor and confidence. "I don't want to change that one regardless of how many documents you have up there. I know I didn't return to Atlanta. *If I did, I will just take the responsibility for the King case here on TV*" (emphasis added).[41]

What followed in the televised assassination hearings seemed as though it had been scripted for a Perry Mason climax. Stokes presented Ray with copies of receipts from Atlanta's Piedmont Laundry showing Eric Galt dropped off clothing on Monday, April 1, a day Ray claimed he was in Corinth, Mississippi.[42] There were two receipts, neatly handwritten by the laundry's manager, Estelle Peters, one showing the clothes Galt left for dry cleaning, and the other listing clothes for washing. Clearly on the top of each receipt was the name Eric Galt.

Ray and his lawyer, conspiracy buff Mark Lane, were visibly stunned. Lane tried to divert the discussion to the issue of whether the rooming house manager, James Garner, had really spotted Ray in Atlanta during those days. But Stokes would have none of it, directing Ray back to the receipts, and also providing him with a statement from Estelle Peters confirming the accuracy and authenticity of the receipts.[43] Ray asked for time to read the document since "this is an important area."[44] Picking up the cue from his client, Lane requested a recess. Two hours later, they reappeared. Lane began with a vitriolic attack, calling Peters's statement a "doctored document" and charging that the entire congressional inquiry was "McCarthy-like," "indecent" and "very unfair."[45] Some of those on the committee familiar with Lane's pugnacious tactics smiled. His histrionics meant the committee had hit home on a key issue. But Stokes, a prosecutor before he was elected to Congress, ignored Lane and instead started questioning a visibly nervous Ray. "I can't recall," protested Ray, "unless this lady made an error on this, or this is some kind of forged document because I know I did not take the laundry in April 1."[46]

Once Ray mentioned the possibility of a "forged document" Stokes produced another exhibit, a chronological, handwritten "counterbook," a ledger listing each order dropped off at the Piedmont, including the date it was left and the date it was picked up. The laundry's practice was to have the clerk write the order information into the counterbook within a few minutes of the customer's drop-off.[47] Galt's two orders were listed on lines 30 and 31 of one of two pages for laundry brought in on April 1, 1968, and the book also showed the laundry was retrieved the day after the assassination, April 5.[48]

The committee exhibit presented to Ray was 198 pages long, covering nearly 10,000 laundry orders. There were no blank or missing lines on the pages, and Ray's entry was almost squarely in the middle of one. Because of the way it was created, with various handwritten entries for each of thousands of laundry jobs at Piedmont, it was virtually tamper-proof. It showed that Ray's protestation of forgery was meritless. But, of course, that did not stop Ray and Lane from offering it as the only possible defense. Just hours earlier Ray had painted himself into a corner by challenging Congressman Stokes, saying that if the committee could prove he returned to Atlanta after buying the rifle in Birmingham, he would "just take the responsibility for the King case here on TV."

Lane asserted, "If this in fact is a forged or deceptive document, we have the right to know it. It should not be shown to him to trick this witness. . . . It looks as if there has been something added or subtracted to this document, from this document. Something may have been superimposed upon it." Although Ray finally admitted, "I picked up the laundry on April 5," he would not budge about not putting it there on April 1.[49]

"That was the end of it for almost everyone on the committee," one investigator told the author. "It was such a clear lie about a major part of his story. Ray was simply caught red-handed, yet he continued dissembling without taking a second breath. It showed us what we were dealing with, a pathological liar who did not change his story even when documents proved him wrong. It was the final proof that we certainly weren't going to get the truth about anything from Ray."

26

The Alibi

Ray learned of King's trip to Memphis the way everyone else did, through the public announcement on April 1 by the Southern Christian Leadership Conference. King was scheduled to lead a new march on Friday, April 5.

Ray left for Memphis on the same day that King flew into the city, April 3. It was a seven-hour drive, and along the way, at a Rexall drugstore in Whitehaven, Tennessee, he purchased a Gillette shaving kit.[1] Later, he stopped for a haircut.[2] Around 7:15 P.M., with a thunderstorm raging, he pulled into the New Rebel Motel at 3466 Lamar Avenue, just within the Memphis city limits. When Ivan Webb, the night clerk, patrolled the motel's grounds at 4:00 A.M., Ray's room was still brightly lit.[3]

Although he has varied his story over time, Ray's most persistent claim is the following: He met Raoul at the New Rebel Motel on April 3, and was told that the next day they would complete the first stage of a gunrunning operation. Raoul directed Ray to change motels to the South Main Street rooming house.[4] While Raoul thought Ray should use his own name (he was known to Raoul as Galt), Ray said he would prefer to use a different alias, John Willard.*

---

* Ray told the Select Committee that he could not recall how he came up with the Willard name, although he claimed to have used it "indirectly once before." However,

The final part of the plan was for Ray to meet Raoul at Jim's Grill, on the ground floor of the rooming house, at about 3:00 P.M.*

When the Select Committee asked Ray why he could not have done the gun deal at the New Rebel, he said "Well, I don't know, I, uh, I couldn't ask that. I was always moving, seems like I was always going from one place to the other. I assumed that the place [rooming house] was, uh, a place like that would be more conducive probably to something illegal. . . . Nothing would be suspicious down there, or anything, any type of transaction would be normal."[5]

Ray also told the Select Committee that he gave Raoul the Remington rifle at the New Rebel on April 3. "That was the last I saw of the weapon," he said.[6] Of course, if that gun was used to kill King the next day, then Ray was being set up as a patsy—the reason the conspirators had him buy the gun was so it would be traced to him. The same would be true of the rental of a room at the rooming house. But it would also be logical that a key element was to have Ray bring the rifle into the sniper's nest, in the hope that some witness might be able to identify him entering with the murder weapon. Raoul, as recounted by Ray, had assiduously tried to dissociate himself from the rifle. He would be the last person who would run the risk of personally taking the rifle into the rooming house, or carrying it on the public transportation that Ray believed Raoul used in Memphis.[7] When the Select Committee asked Ray why Raoul would not have wanted him to keep the rifle, all he could say was "I really don't know why."[8]

On the morning of April 4, Ray checked out of the New Rebel, bought a local newspaper, had breakfast, and then spent the rest of the morning and early afternoon in an unidentified "beer house."[†9] Ray said he drank part of "three or four beers."[10] Rare as it was for him to drink beer, it may have been necessary to give him the extra nerve for the afternoon's assignment.[‡]

---

there was a real John Willard living in the same Toronto suburb as three other men whose names Ray used.

*   There was a Jim's Grill near the rooming house, and also a Jim's Grill directly underneath the rooming house. Ray told Dan Rather that he initially went to the wrong one, before finding the right one at the rooming house.

†   In one of his interviews with the Select Committee, Ray said he had stayed at the New Rebel until 2:00 P.M. and then left directly to meet Raoul at the rooming house (HSCA vol. IX, pp. 14–15).

‡   Author George McMillan wrote that Jerry Ray, while on a break on his job at the country club, received a telephone call from James on the morning of April 4. McMillan says it lasted less than three minutes, and that James said, "Jerry, tomorrow it will be all over. I might not see you and Jack for a while. But don't worry about me. I'll be all right! Big Nigger has had it!" Jerry Ray has emphatically denied giving that story to McMillan.

One of the most suspicious things Ray later did was to try and downplay his knowledge in general of Martin Luther King, Jr., and especially that King was in Memphis that day. Ray admitted buying a copy of April 4, *The Commercial Appeal*, in which King was the subject of a front-page story, with his photo prominently displayed. Yet before the Select Committee, when asked, "Did you know who Dr. King was?" Ray incredibly said, "I probably had a vague idea, but I don't have any strong idea." When pressed, "Did you know there was such a person as Dr. Martin Luther King, and that he was purported to be a civil rights leader?" he responded, "At that time, at the particular time I was in Memphis I had no idea, but I probably, I may have had a vague idea that there was such an individual."[11] He said he had never heard that King was in Memphis.

Ray drove to the South Main Street area and parked his Mustang near the rooming house.* He met Raoul, he said, at Jim's Grill downstairs (in other versions, he claimed he first saw Raoul upstairs in Room 5B, and in another story said he rendezvoused with him first in the Mustang).[12] After being directed by Raoul to rent a room, Ray went upstairs and rented Room 5B from Bessie Brewer, giving his name as John Willard. Raoul then settled into that room and asked Ray to find a pair of "infrared" binoculars.[13] That prompted Ray's visit to the nearby York Arms Company, where he bought a $39.95 pair of binoculars.†

The author, however, reviewed notes taken by George McMillan of his interviews with Jerry Ray, and his contemporaneous notes reflect precisely such an interview (McMillan/Southern Historical Collection). Also, McMillan gave a sworn statement to the House Select Committee that the quote was accurate, and had been given to him by Jerry. William Bradford Huie confirmed to researcher David Lifton, as well as to the Select Committee, that Jerry had told him about the same phone call in November 1968. However, Huie did not print the information since he did not believe Jerry's story. The committee investigated the issue and concluded that Jerry had indeed told both authors about such a call, but since his "credibility was highly suspect" it assumed that he concocted the story "motivated by a simple desire for financial gain."

*   As with almost every issue of the day on the assassination, Ray has given multiple versions, even on apparently simple matters such as where he parked his car. It appears Ray parked it directly in front of the rooming house, near Jim's Grill. However, Ray once told the Select Committee that it was six blocks away, and another time told the committee it was eight or nine blocks; to one of his attorneys, Robert Hill, he said it was a mile; to the Canadian Broadcasting Corporation and in his habeas corpus proceeding he said it was two or three miles.

†   In the 20,000 Words, Ray said he made one trip to the store. To the Select Committee, he said he got lost the first time, returned to the rooming house to get more information from Raoul, and then found it on his second trip. The salesman, Ralph Carpenter, said Ray never inquired about any infrared binoculars, the type that Raoul supposedly sent him to find.

After Ray had dropped the binoculars back at the rooming house, Raoul told him to disappear for a while. Originally, Ray told Hanes and Huie that he simply went downstairs and waited in Jim's Grill.[14] However, they noticed an immediate problem. "With his remarkable memory for detail," wrote Huie, "Ray accurately described the interiors of taverns in Montreal, Chicago, Puerto Vallarta and Los Angeles. So we asked him to describe the interior of Jim's Grill. He described it—and missed it by a mile. Then Mr. Hanes drilled him in the correct description of Jim's Grill."[15] After Hanes was fired, Foreman came aboard and asked Ray where he was just before King's killing. Ray told him he had been in Jim's Grill. "Word for word," recalled Huie, "his description was what Mr. Hanes had given Ray, not the inaccurate description Ray originally gave Mr. Hanes."[16]

As might be expected, over time Ray has added to his story of where he was in the critical hour leading up to the murder. He is vague about times and the places he supposedly visited, often mentioning a number of possibilities, so that if one fails another might be used as an alibi. Among other stories, he went to a movie theater;[17] was in a drugstore;[18] stopped in one of several restaurants (one of which may have been an ice cream parlor), the names of which he was not certain;[19] and took forty-five minutes retrieving his car, parked in a lot he could not pinpoint, and then sat in the car for another fifteen minutes.[20]

As for the moment of the murder itself, he first told Huie that he was outside sitting in his Mustang and heard the shot. The next thing he knew, Raoul came running out of the rooming house, jumped into the backseat, and covered himself with a white sheet. Ray immediately drove away. After eight blocks, Raoul told him to stop, then leaped from the car. Ray continued driving to Atlanta and never saw Raoul again.[21]

Once Ray learned there were witnesses at the record store, Canipe's, who saw only one man run into the empty Mustang and only one man drive away, he claimed the Raoul story "was more or less a joke."[22]

He got a new idea from an article that appeared shortly after the assassination in *The Memphis Press-Scimitar.* Willie Green, a gas station attendant, was quoted as saying he noticed a "nervous fellow" pacing near the station's phone booth around the time of the assassination. The station was about six blocks from the rooming house. Green identified Ray as the man he had seen. He also recalled a white Mustang.

After reading this information, Ray completely abandoned the white-sheet story he had given Hanes, and he presented a new alibi to Foreman when he came aboard in November 1968.[23] Ray claimed he was probably at one of several gas stations when the assassination happened, trying to fix a spare tire that had gone flat the previous day.[24]

"I went to, I think," he told CBS's Dan Rather in 1977, "a service station down about, I would say it was about five blocks from Main Street."[25]

The Select Committee, the next year, questioned Ray about his latest alibi. "I will go back to my question," said Congressman Stokes. "I want to know, where were you when Dr. King was killed?"

"I believe I was in the service station, but I'm not positive," Ray said tentatively.

"You see," said Stokes, quite exasperated by Ray's evasive answers, "it is pretty difficult for us to understand when you say, 'I believe I was but I'm not positive.'"

"Well, it is difficult to pinpoint where you was at a certain time. At six o'clock I could have been at the service station or I could have been driving down the street preparing to come back into the rooming house area. . . . My best recollection, I would be in the service station or just leaving it."[26]

Ray said he could not recall the name of the station. "Anyway, there's two or three of them in that area."*[27]

The committee members were perplexed as to why Ray had failed to tell Hanes about this alibi. "Well, when you were picked up," asked Stokes, "and brought back from London knowing you were charged with this crime, wasn't it important to tell your attorneys what gas station you were in?" Ray said that he did not tell Hanes because he feared that Hanes and Huie were passing along the information he gave them to the FBI. "I was a little hesitant," he said, "in giving Mr. Hanes certain information."

"All I want to know," persisted Stokes, "is why you didn't tell this man who is representing you in a capital case the truth."

"I just didn't tell him that," said Ray. "I intended to tell the jury that."[28]

Mark Lane, Ray's attorney before the Select Committee, worked hard to bolster his client's alibi. In addition to providing the names of witnesses who might have seen Ray at the gas station, Lane also made a major issue of his discovery of a witness in the rooming house who could supposedly identify a different man than Ray fleeing the scene of the crime.

The rooming house witness was Grace Walden, Charlie Stephens's common-law wife. They had lived next door to the room Ray had rented, and Stephens was one of two witnesses who could possibly identify Ray as fleeing

---

*   While Ray had told Dan Rather that the station was "about five blocks from Main Street," in his first interview with the Select Committee staff, Ray said the station was "three blocks north and three or four blocks east from the rooming house." In a May 1978 interview with the staff, Ray was certain the station was "three or four blocks down north and then turn right and go four or five blocks more, somewhere along in that area."

the scene after the shot. Lane claimed, in an article he wrote for the November 1978 *Hustler* magazine, that Walden also saw a man flee, but that it was not Ray. Not only that, but she was also offered a $100,000 reward to lie and pinpoint Ray as the man she saw, and when she refused, the government silenced her by forcibly committing her to a mental hospital.[29] Lane called Walden one of the case's "most important" witnesses.

Walden told Lane that after she heard gunfire, she looked out of the doorway of her room, 6B, and "then I saw him. He was moving fast. Not running, but walking very fast right past our doorway." She later said she told the police that the man was five-five, very thin, about sixty years old, and wearing "a hunting jacket and . . . a loud colored checkered shirt." Lane contended that Walden was told she would be in "grave danger" if she testified on Ray's behalf at trial.[30]

Once he established Walden as a supporting witness to his contention that Ray was not at the rooming house, Lane then produced the names of witnesses who supported the story that Ray was at a gas station when King was shot. One was Willie Green, the gas station attendant originally quoted in *The Memphis Press-Scimitar* in 1968. Although Lane had not personally spoken to Green, he chastised the committee that "nobody from the government" had interviewed Green. He also listed two additional people, Dean Cowden and Thomas Wilson. The defense team investigator, Renfro Hays, had found both. That immediately raised the suspicions of some committee members, since Hays had developed many bogus leads with questionable methods, including paying money for stories. Adding to the uneasiness over the new witnesses was that their story had broken in the *National Enquirer* under the banner headline *"Enquirer* Uncovers New Evidence . . . James Earl Ray Did Not Kill Martin Luther King."[31] Lane assured the committee, however, that he had personally interviewed both Cowden and Wilson, and he vouched for their credibility.*[32]

Cowden was a commodities broker with a local Memphis trading firm in 1968, and he told the *Enquirer* that on the day of the assassination, "I bought gas at a Texaco station on the southeast corner of Linden Ave. and 2nd St. in Memphis [about 6½ blocks from the rooming house]." He said he saw Ray, sitting in a white Mustang, as late as 5:50 P.M. About five minutes after the assassination, Cowden said he saw Ray again near the gas station, "walking in a leisurely, casual manner with no haste."[33] As for Thomas Wilson, a retired car

---

* Harold Weisberg, in his quest to free Ray, personally interviewed dozens of people in the 1970s in the vicinity of the rooming house, looking in vain to find support for Ray's gas station alibi. He found two "new" witnesses who claimed to remember seeing Ray and his Mustang in front of the rooming house at the time of the shooting, something contradicted by contemporaneous witnesses interviewed by the police.

salesman, he saw a man in a white Mustang at the same service station around 5:45 P.M. "I feel absolutely sure beyond any doubt that the man I saw was Ray."[34]

There are, however, problems with the credibility of each of these witnesses. Grace Walden was indeed committed to several mental institutions for nearly ten years after the assassination—but not, as Lane contended, in an effort to silence her. Walden was in fact an alcoholic who had previously tried to kill herself.[35] Her husband, Charlie Stephens, took her to a local Memphis hospital on July 8, 1968, because she had hurt her foot. Walden was in such an anxious state that a staff psychiatrist, Mary Slechta, was called to examine her. Slechta concluded that Walden was suffering from a psychotic depression and was suicidal.[36] Three weeks after being committed to the psychiatric ward, Walden tried to hang herself. She began hearing voices. The hospital filed a "lunacy warrant" on her and on July 31 she was committed by the Shelby County Probate Court to the Western State Mental Hospital in Bolivar, Tennessee.[37] There she was diagnosed with schizophrenia, chronic brain syndrome induced by alcoholism, and delusional behavior.[38] She suffered from "confabulations," a tendency to concoct stories to fill in considerable gaps in her memory.[39]

Mark Lane eventually fought to get Walden released, did so in May 1978, and was appointed her coguardian. In the meantime, she had given different stories about the person she claimed to have seen fleeing the rooming house. One time she even said, "I think he was a nigger."[40]

Walden's "revelation" was made on November 5, 1968—when she was already committed to the Western State Mental Hospital—to the indefatigable Renfro Hays. On that occasion, she told Hays that the man she saw fleeing the rooming house was about five-two.*[41] But her statement to Hays was not her first about the case. On the day of the assassination, Walden had told the Memphis police that she heard "about five" firecrackers explode, but was bedridden in Room 6B and did not get up to see anything.[42] The day after the assassination, and also in subsequent interviews over several weeks, she told the FBI that she had heard footsteps walking rapidly in front of her apartment door, but since she was bedridden, she saw nothing.[43] She told several newspaper reporters, who subsequently submitted affidavits to the Select Committee, that she did not get out of bed or see a thing.[44] Moreover, she was unable to see into the hallway from where she was lying.[45] A reward of $100,000 was never even

---

* In his 1978 *Hustler* article, Lane quoted Walden, who was five-three, as saying the man she saw was "maybe two inches taller than me." But in his 1977 book, *Code Name "Zorro,"* Lane quoted the original Walden statement, "this man was not quite as tall as I am." Still, in the next paragraph, Lane somehow summarized Walden's testimony incorrectly as describing a man "approximately five feet, five inches tall."

mentioned to her by the FBI or Memphis police since she was not considered a witness who had seen anything probative.[46]

As for Dean Cowden and Thomas Wilson, who saw Ray at the gas station around the time of the shooting, Lane promoted them as heavily as he did Grace Walden. In his book *Code Name "Zorro,"* published just before the Select Committee started its work, Lane wrote, "Cowden told me that during the past nine years he had never been questioned by the Memphis police or the FBI. With all the personnel available to them, they had not located the decisive alibi witness in the case. But Renfro Hays had."[47]

When the Select Committee quizzed Dean Cowden, he told a story different from the one related by Lane. The forty-three-year-old Cowden admitted that he was not even in Memphis on the day King was assassinated, but was at work as the store manager of Fair Incorporated in Beaumont, Texas, over five hundred miles away.[48] The Select Committee showed Cowden the story in the *National Enquirer* in which he was extensively quoted.

"Is this story true?"

"This story is completely false," Cowden told a stunned hearing room. He also admitted that the story he had given Lane was false. "It was a rehearsed story."

"With whom did you rehearse the story?"

"Renfro Hays."[49]

It turned out that during a period in 1973 when Cowden was drying out from a long bout with alcoholism in the psychiatric ward of the Memphis Veterans Administration Hospital, he met Renfro Hays, who was then a patient in the same ward.* Hays later helped support him for about four months. Around December 1975, Hays came up with the story about Ray's gas station alibi. Hays, who was trying to sell film or book rights to the King murder and his investigation of it, convinced Cowden to tell the lie and said, "If I make a million out of this, you know, I will always take care of you."[50] Hays also told Cowden that he would have someone else ready to confirm the story; as Cowden recalled, "It wouldn't be salable unless he had collaboration."[51] Lane was not in on the fraud, Cowden told the committee, but "I really think if I had been the lawyer and Mr. Lane had been the witness, I believe I would have asked a little harder questions."

As for Wilson, the man who had corroborated Cowden's story, he had died on April 5, 1978, just before the Select Committee was prepared to take his statement. However, the committee had already learned that at the time of the assassination, Wilson was a mile away from the gas station where he suppos-

---

* At the time of Cowden's testimony, Renfro Hays was back in the psychiatric ward of the same hospital.

edly saw Ray.[52] Wilson was with a friend at a local shoe repair shop, and had been there since 5:30 that evening, half an hour before the assassination. They did not leave the shop until after King was killed.

Larce McFall, the owner of the Texaco station at which the two witnesses claimed to have seen Ray, and his son, Phillip, were both working at the time of the assassination. At 6:01, when King was shot, they were washing a truck for a customer. There was no sign of anyone who looked like Ray. There was no request by anyone to repair a flat tire that day, and no white Mustang appeared at any time at the station. Both McFalls had provided that information to the Memphis police and the FBI shortly after the assassination, when everybody within several blocks of the rooming house had been questioned about what they had seen on the day of the murder.[53]

What about the final witness cited by Lane as support for Ray's alibi, Willie Green, the Esso gas station attendant quoted in *The Memphis Press-Scimitar* in 1968? There was actually a warning sign in Green's early statement to the newspaper, when he claimed that the FBI had shown him a photo of Ray before the Bureau even knew that Eric S. Galt was James Earl Ray. But he stuck to his story, which he told again to the *Press-Scimitar* in 1977: Ray had arrived shortly before King was killed, he said, and was "the most nervous fellow I ever saw. . . . so nervous he could hardly make a phone call."[54]

But the author discovered internal working files of the *Press-Scimitar* reporters that covered the case, which were donated to the University of Memphis's collection on the sanitation strike. Among the many documents are several pages of typed notes, listing the names of people who were either already interviewed or still needed to be interviewed by staff reporters. On the "ray 7" page is the following listing: "Willie Green, an attendant at a service station at 189 Linden, said the Galt picture resembled a nervous man who used a phone booth near the station right *after* King was slain and paced up and down there until he [Green] closed for the curfew" (emphasis added).[55] In his original notes, the reporter took Green's statement as placing a Ray look-alike at the station not at the time of the assassination, but afterward, and then keeping him there for a few hours until the police closed down the city. Ray had actually left the area in his Mustang a few minutes after 6:00 P.M.[56]

There are no witnesses to support Ray's ever-changing story of being at a service station at the time of the assassination. Rather, after Ray returned to the South Main Street rooming house after buying the binoculars, there is no evidence he left before King was murdered.

27

On the Run

Within two minutes of the shooting, Ray had left the scene of the assassination and was on his way toward the Mississippi state line.[1]

Ray's story was that he was on his way back to the rooming house from the gas station when he "ran into a police roadblock."[2] Since he was a fugitive, Ray immediately turned around and drove away. "When police are around," he said, "I try to avoid the area." Before the Select Committee, Congressman Louis Stokes asked Ray why he did not just drive to another part of town. "It was my intention," he said, "to drive out into Mississippi on the highway and stop at a service station and make a telephone call and attempt to find out if anything had taken place illegally."[3] He was "apprehensive" that something had gone awry with the gun deal at the rooming house.[4] That was despite the fact that Raoul had supposedly assured him there would be no gun deal until Ray returned to the rooming house later that night.[5] "I was playing it safe on assumptions of what might have been," recalled Ray.[6]

He was already in Mississippi, he recalled, when he heard a radio news bulletin that Dr. King had been shot in Memphis.[7] A little while after the first news flash, Ray heard another report that the police were looking for a white Mustang.[8] From the time of the first broadcast, Ray said, he was "really" in a hurry and he drove the 350 miles straight to Atlanta without stopping.[9] Fearful that his car would be spotted, he stayed largely on dark side roads, and the journey took him nearly eleven hours.[10] As he drove along, he threw out "everything I could get ahold of," including "the camera equipment . . . I didn't know what else I threw out . . . anything I could get my hands on I threw out the back seat of the car. . . . I just wanted to get rid of everything that would connect me with the Mustang. Or that would connect me with anything."*[11]

When he reached Atlanta, it was shortly after dawn on April 5. He parked the Mustang in the rear of the Capitol Homes housing project, figuring that "if it's in a parking lot it might sit there a few days" before the police found it, and he "wiped the fingerprints off the car."[12] He had already stopped twice, once at a gas station, and wiped down the interior.[13] "I know I wiped everything off the Mustang after they started looking for me."†[14]

Ray's hurried departure from Memphis has the earmark of guilt. Ray later said he only "vaguely" knew who Dr. King was, and did not know he was in Memphis—much less that he was staying at a motel only two hundred feet away from the rooming house where Ray had his room. However, the initial bulletins did not say where King was shot, so if Ray had been telling the truth about his ignorance of King and his whereabouts, the news of the shooting would have caused no panic in him. But his reaction was to drive eleven hours to Atlanta, throw hundreds of dollars' worth of goods from his car window, and wipe his fingerprints off the vehicle. When asked by the Select Committee why he threw out his camera equipment, he admitted, "I don't have any rational explanation."[15] Why did he wipe the fingerprints off the car? "Naturally, I would have any fingerprints off of everything if I was going to commit a crime," he said.

Once he reached Atlanta, "I went back to the rooming house that I had rented."[16] He had to retrieve the pistol he had left there before making the trip to Memphis.[17] "I had it in my mind," recalled Ray, "that if I was short of money I may have to do some holdups to get out of the country, whichever country I was in, Canada or something like that."‡[18] He also quickly had to decide what

---

* Ray had recently received his long-overdue $140 refund check from Superior Film Company for the camera he had returned the previous October. He told the Select Committee that, afraid of cashing it, he also threw that check out the car window while returning to Atlanta. Later, he told the committee he held on to the check and actually got rid of it in Canada.

† Harold Weisberg uses the absence of Ray's prints on the car to raise conspiracy speculation: "Who drove it from Memphis to Atlanta if Ray's fingerprints were not there to identify him as the driver?" Weisberg never mentions that Ray himself wiped them off the car.

‡ The Select Committee grilled Ray on why he had not taken his pistol with him to Memphis if he thought he was really going to be part of a gun deal with Mexican smugglers he had never met. He never had a satisfactory answer, finally saying, "I'm not able to articulate it."

to take with him. Anything bulky, such as his typewriter, was abandoned. Ray also deliberately left some other items—a Los Angeles *Free Press*, a John Birch Society pamphlet, and two pairs of pants in sizes too small for him—"you know, to try to throw the police off."*[19] Despite leaving behind the Atlanta map with his fingerprint and the pencil markings showing that he had stalked King—an obvious mistake—he did his best to make the room useless to investigators when they found it. "I wanted to get the fingerprints off there. . . . I think I did wipe my prints off various things in the rooming house. . . . I think I cleaned the place up the best I could and got rid of all the junk."[20]

By 9:00 A.M., Ray was at the Piedmont Laundry around the corner from his rooming house.[21] Estelle Peters, the same manager who was there when he dropped his clothing off on April 1, was on duty. While Peters retrieved the dry cleaning and small bundle of laundry, she noticed that Ray "kinda paced in the front. And he just acted a little bit nervous."†[22]

After picking up his clothes, Ray took a cab to the bus station and put his luggage in a locker. He had worked out a route to Canada, where he had fled twice before as a fugitive. He went to a local bar until it was time to catch his first connection, a bus to Cincinnati.[23] Ray became nervous because the 11:30 A.M. departure was delayed for two hours, but finally the bus left. He reached Cincinnati about 1:30 on the morning of April 6, and had a half-hour layover before getting the next bus to Detroit, where he arrived about 8:00 A.M.[24] There he took a taxi for the short ride to Windsor, Canada. Less than forty hours after the murder, he had safely made it to another country.[25] With some time to spare before he left for Toronto, Ray visited a local barber and had a shave.[26] His train departed in the early afternoon, and Ray was in Toronto by 5:00 P.M. on April 6.[27]

He rented a room in a second-rate rooming house at 106 Ossington Avenue, an area where many immigrants lived.[28] The manager was Polish-born Feliksa Szpakowska, who also lived there with her husband, Adam, and nine-year-old daughter.‡[29] "The woman couldn't hardly speak any English," recalled

---

* Ray later said, "I think they [the smaller clothes] belonged to this guy they call himself Raoul."

† When asked why he risked taking the time to get his laundry, Ray told the Select Committee, "Well, I guess to have clean clothing, that's all."

‡ Szpakowska said Ray checked in April 8, not the sixth. But she did not maintain good records, and April 8 was based on what she recalled a couple of months later. It appears likely that Ray did check in on the sixth, and that Szpakowska did not mark his arrival until the eighth. Although less likely, if Szpakowska is right, Ray deliberately covered up a missing two days immediately after the assassination. That would almost certainly be the time in which he could have rendezvoused with his brothers. Jerry Ray claims he was at work then, but the work records are destroyed, and his credibility is highly suspect. John Ray had no alibi for those days.

Ray, "and the man not much better."[30] Ray, who had seen a vacancy sign in the front window, took a room with a bay window that overlooked the street.[31] His $10-a-week room had a console television in the corner, a small painting of Jesus on the wall, and an embroidered doily that read HOME SWEET HOME. He had planned to give Szpakowska a new alias, figuring that it was time to abandon Galt, but she did not ask for his name. She later told the authorities that she never got American names right anyway.[32] Szpakowska recalled that her tenant was quiet and ventured out during the days.[33] He kept to himself, ate alone in his room, and put his head down when he would walk past her. Every evening she heard his television, and in the morning when she cleaned his room, she would find a stack of newspapers by his bed.

While he followed the news carefully, he was initially preoccupied with obtaining new identification, particularly a passport. He intended to head for Europe, and then for Rhodesia or South Africa. Seeking a suitable alias, Ray first visited a graveyard to search tombstones for names of men who had birth dates near his, but found that too difficult. The office of a Toronto newspaper proved more helpful. There he viewed microfilm of past issues, searching for birth announcements that might be suitable to appropriate as his own.*[34]

Ray needed to find someone who not only fit his age, but who also did not have a current passport. He feared that anyone who had a passport picture on file might not look like him, therefore his application would be immediately revealed as fraudulent.[35] Moreover, Ray was still under the mistaken impression from his 1967 trip that he needed a guarantor to vouch for his passport. He had devised a plan to develop two false identifications and use one for the actual passport application and the other as the guarantor.†[36]

On Wednesday, April 10, Ray sent $2 and a handwritten letter to the Bureau of Vital Statistics requesting a copy of a birth certificate for Paul Edward Bridgman, listing both his father's name and mother's maiden name, and the

---

* Since Ray thought he looked younger than he was, he looked at birth announcements for 1932, four years after his own birth date. He has given different versions of how many names he pulled during his search. In the 20,000 Words he said he found ten, but to the Select Committee he once said four or five, and another time three. In addition to the newspaper office, the name of which Ray has never remembered, at other times Ray contended he did the work at a library. Both afforded that type of research.

† Ray's plan was a risky one, but the only one he thought available. He intended to apply for the passport under one name, with his thick horn-rimmed glasses, and then return the next day and, without his glasses and with the second identification, go to another clerk and vouch for his "friend's" passport application that had just been filed. He had even gone far enough in his planning that he "went to Brown's Theatrical Supplies on Yonge Street and bought a makeup kit."

Ossington Avenue address.[37] Ray then gave Szpakowska a piece of paper with the name Bridgman on it, telling her it was his, and that if any mail arrived for that name, to please give it to him.[38] The next day, April 11, Ray had passport photos taken at the Arcade Photo Studio, giving his name as Paul Bridgman.[39] The manager, Mabel Agnew, remembered Ray because he would not smile, but instead just stared glumly into the camera.[40]

The next day, the real Bridgman—a thirty-five-year-old coordinator of language studies for the Toronto Board of Education—received a telephone call from Ray, who identified himself as an official in the Canadian Immigration Department.[41] Ray asked questions about Bridgman's passport, and learned that Bridgman had one. That meant Ray could not use the Bridgman name to obtain a new passport, but he thought he might still be useful as a guarantor.[42] That same day, April 12, newspapers reported the FBI was looking for a thirty-six-year-old white Alabama resident, Eric S. Galt, for questioning in connection with the King assassination.[43]

A few days after calling Bridgman, and evidently after several failed attempts to reach other men whose names he had gathered from the newspaper archives, Ray talked to Ramon George Sneyd, a thirty-five-year-old policeman (Ray did not know his profession).[44] Again pretending to be a passport official, Ray asked a question about Sneyd's passport, only to discover he did not have one. He had found the name under which to apply.*[45]

On April 14, the Bridgman birth certificate arrived at Ray's Ossington Avenue rooming house. That was surprising, because unbeknownst to Ray, Mrs. Szpakowska had not understood him when he said his name was Bridgman, and she said she had twice told callers from the Registrar's Office that Bridg-

---

* One of the mysteries of the case is that all four Canadians whose names Ray used before and after the assassination—Eric Galt, John Willard, Paul Bridgman, and Ramon George Sneyd—lived in Scarborough, a suburb of Toronto. Although newspaper accounts after the assassination said all four men lived within blocks of one another, they actually lived up to four miles apart. The men did not know one another. The four men never reported losing their identification or having any other problem with their names being appropriated. Three of the four, Galt, Bridgman, and Sneyd, bore a passing resemblance to Ray, which has raised the legitimate suspicion that the aliases were provided to Ray as part of an elaborate conspiracy. There is evidence, however, that despite his denials, Ray visually checked on the three who resembled him. A Toronto map was later found in Ray's belongings, and while it was destroyed years later by the Royal Canadian Mounted Police as part of their regular procedure for the destruction of files, reports about the map indicate it had marks near the homes of those three men, as well as marks along the public transportation route from Ray's rooming house to Scarborough. Sophisticated plotters would have either been ready to dispose of Ray after King's murder or to have had ready identification and travel papers for him.

man did not live there.[46] When the letter arrived for Bridgman, she gave it back to the postman, saying that she did not know the name.*

Around this time, Ray had a freak run-in with the police, one that could easily have led to his arrest if the officer had been more alert. A few blocks from his rooming house, Ray was stopped by a policeman who cited him for jaywalking.[47] As he wrote the summons, he asked Ray for his name. Ray was afraid to give Bridgman or Sneyd in case he was asked for identification, and Galt had already been named as the man wanted for questioning in the King murder. However, Ray "gave him the Galt name because that's what I had the driver's license and everything."[48] When asked for an address, Ray gave one he had picked up during his correspondence with women through the lonely hearts club magazine a few months earlier.[49] "I got a bunch of these addresses out of the Lonely Hearts Magazine," he recalled. "I was using these addresses if the police stopped me and they wanted to know where I was."[50]

When he returned to the rooming house after that incident, he destroyed all his Galt identification.[51] He also disposed of all other documents he thought were incriminating, including the business card he claimed to have found in his Mustang in 1967 with the name Randy Rosenson on it, and also the scrap of paper on which purportedly he had kept Raoul's New Orleans and Baton Rouge telephone numbers.[52]

Tuesday, April 16, was a busy day for Ray. First, he rented a new room at another run-down rooming house, at 962 Dundas Street, on the edge of Toronto's red-light district. He noticed a FOR RENT sign in the window, paid nine dollars for a week's rent, and agreed to move in on the nineteenth.[†53] The landlady was thirty-two-year-old Sun Fung Loo, who knew even less English than Mrs. Szpakowska.

Ray needed a new address because he had another letter ready to send to the Bureau of Vital Statistics, this time requesting a copy of Ramon George Sneyd's birth certificate.[54] Ray was fearful of listing the Ossington Avenue ad-

---

* Szpakowska initially told the authorities that she had known Ray as Bridgman and had told him his letter was on the hallway table but he never picked it up, so she returned it to the postman. However, she later admitted to Huie that she did not know Ray's name at all. Ray never knew what happened to the Bridgman birth certificate until Huie informed him after the assassination.

† The fact that Ray asked to move in on the nineteenth is further evidence of the fact that he had probably moved into the Ossington Avenue rooming house on April 6, as he said, and not April 8 as Szpakowska remembered. The nineteenth would be the end of two weeks of rent at Ossington Avenue, and Ray was careful to watch his money in this period. Ray told Huie that he had less than $1,000 when he started his postassassination run and expected most of it to be spent on air travel.

dress for Sneyd as he had for Bridgman, on the chance that if the same clerk handled both requests, it might seem unusual. Now, armed with the Dundas Street address, Ray sent off his request for Sneyd. Later that day, he appeared at the office of the Kennedy Travel Bureau, one of Toronto's most respected travel agencies. He explained to Lillian Spencer, the manager, that he wanted to buy a ticket but that he did not have a passport, nor did he have his birth certificate with him.[55] He had lived in Toronto years ago, but did not think he could locate anyone who could vouch for him.[56] At first he asked about a round-trip ticket to South Africa, but that cost $820, so instead he settled on a twenty-one-day excursion round-trip ticket to London, for $345. That he could not afford to buy the ticket he wanted to South Africa is solid evidence that if Ray had killed King in the hope of collecting a bounty, he had not yet received it while in Toronto.*

It was at that travel agency that Ray learned the good news that he was mistaken about needing a guarantor to obtain a Canadian passport. Spencer informed him that Canada actually had an extremely simple process for obtaining a passport (the law was later tightened due to the ease with which Ray obtained one).[57] Ray only had to complete a passport application together with a Statutory Declaration in Lieu of Guarantor. The form required that he swear he had been born in Canada, and it further stated: "There is no one in Canada, eligible under the Canadian passport regulations to vouch for passport applications, who knows me well enough to vouch for my application. The reason for this is:" Ray then wrote, "I have been in Toronto only three weeks."

He said he was single and had never before applied for a passport, listed his new rooming house on Dundas Street as his permanent address, and said that he was five-eight, 168 pounds, with black hair and blue eyes, and that he was a car salesman with a scar over his nose. To the question "Person to Notify in Canada in Case of Emergency," he wrote, "Mr. Paul Bridgman, 102 Ossington Avenue, Toronto, a Friend." Ray signed all the forms as Ramon George Sneyd.[58]

Henry Moos, the travel agency's owner, notarized both forms, and sent them out the next day, with Ray's pictures and a five-dollar money order he had provided, to the passport office in Ottawa.[59]

Before he left the agency, Miss Spencer helped him pick his travel dates. His passport might take ten days to two weeks, she told him. Ray selected Monday,

---

* Ray asked for a round-trip ticket although he had no intention of returning to Canada once he arrived in England. However, he thought a round-trip would arouse less suspicion than a one-way ticket. The twenty-one-day excursion ticket bought by Ray was the cheapest available. Although $345 Canadian, it was only $275 U.S.

May 6, the first day he could leave under the rules of his excursion ticket, for his departure. She booked him on BOAC (British Overseas Airways Corporation) flight 600 to London. Before he left, Spencer told him that when he returned to pick up the passport, he would need to pay for his tickets, and also have proof that he had had a vaccination.*

The next day, April 17, the FBI issued a fugitive warrant for Eric Starvo Galt, wanted for conspiracy in the death of Dr. King.[60] Fortunately for Ray, while the news was international, the hunt was still focused in the United States. Moreover, the first photo available was the bartending graduation photo of Ray, with his eyes closed. It did not look very much like him. Accompanying that on most stories was the same picture with the eyes drawn in by an FBI sketch artist. That looked even less like Ray. Among many who had seen Ray—including Peter Cherpes, the Birmingham rooming house manager; Bessie Brewer, the manager at the Memphis rooming house; and William Paisley, who sold Ray his Mustang—few thought that the man with the bow tie looked like the man with whom they had dealt.

The news of the warrant hit the Canadian newspapers on April 18. The *Toronto Star* carried it on the front page. One of the few people who thought the photo looked like someone she knew was Mrs. Szpakowska, the landlady at the Ossington Avenue rooming house. "Bridgman is the man who killed Martin Luther King," she announced to her husband. Fortunately for Ray, Szpakowska's husband thought she was crazy and refused to allow her to call the police.[61] By the next day, Ray had moved out. When Szpakowska went to his room to clean it, she noticed he had left the newspaper on the bed, open to the same photograph.[62]

The day that Ray moved into the Dundas Street rooming house, Friday, April 19, the FBI announced that Eric S. Galt was really James Earl Ray. It was bad news for Ray. But fortunately for him, he was now in a house with a Chinese landlady, her husband, and three small children whose English was not only poor but who also seemed to pay no attention to English-language news reports. Loo said that Ray basically stayed in his room. However, on Sunday evening, April 21, he did leave. He knew it was the night that the widely popular television program *The F.B.I.* was on, and since his Dundas Street room did not have a television, he wanted to find a bar that had the

---

* Spencer said that Ray had one of those anonymous faces that faded quickly from memory. She told Huie, "Ray is not the sort of man one notices or remembers. A few minutes after he left the office his features had faded into the wallpaper for me." This was, of course, one of Ray's greatest attributes in blending into his surroundings and not standing out as a fugitive, even after his photos were published.

show. He expected finally to be on the FBI's ten most-wanted list. The first three bars he visited had their televisions tuned to *The Ed Sullivan Show*, but the fourth had it tuned to *The F.B.I.* Ray sat at the end of the bar and ordered a vodka and orange juice.

"Good evening. The FBI is engaged in a nationwide search to locate James Earl Ray, also known as Eric Starvo Galt, in connection with the fatal shooting of Dr. Martin Luther King, Jr. Ray, an escapee from the Missouri State Penitentiary, is forty years old, five feet ten inches tall, 174 pounds, has brown hair, blue eyes, and a medium build. Consider him armed and extremely dangerous. If you have seen Ray, notify the FBI immediately."

None of the other customers recognized the plain-looking man just feet away from them.[63]

Although Ray had expected it, the announcement was still sobering. The size of the reward by the city of Memphis and the Scripps-Howard newspapers—$100,000—startled him. He had not foreseen that Memphis, where he thought King had caused so much trouble, would put up such a large amount of money to bring in his killer.[64]

The next day, Monday, April 22, Ray left by bus for Montreal, where he thought he might find a ship that would take him abroad without insisting on a passport.[65] He took a room on the opposite side of town from where he had lived in 1967. "I was going to rent passage on a ship that sailed around the coast of South Africa and try to slip in at one of the stops or get overboard and swim to shore."[66] A Scandinavian liner offered a $600 ticket to Mozambique, but required a passport, so he had to pass. While in Montreal, Ray heard that Canadian authorities had detained some men who resembled him. That scared him. As a result, "I never left the room except for meals." He gave the landlord the name Walters and used a phony name and address at the shipping office.[67] On April 26, he returned to Toronto, and paid nine dollars to Mrs. Loo for another week's rent.*[68]

On April 29, he visited a doctor to get the required vaccinations.[69] On Thursday, May 2, he telephoned the Kennedy Travel Bureau and learned that his passport was ready. He went there that afternoon, paid $345 Canadian cash

---

* Ray told the Select Committee that he stayed in Montreal until May 1, but not only did Mrs. Loo record the receipt of the rent on April 26; Ray also did other things in Toronto before May 1, all of which have been corroborated. Further, when Ray left for Montreal, he wrote to the Kennedy Travel Bureau, saying he was going to the town of Capreol, so that if they tried to contact him, they would realize he was out of town. Capreol is a small railroad town with some fishing lodges, but the Royal Canadian Mounted Police investigated the area and determined Ray had not stopped there, but only in Montreal.

for the ticket, and picked up his travel documents.*[70] When he saw the passport, he was disappointed because the name had been misspelled as Ramon George Sneya.[71] (On Ray's application, his *D* for Sneyd could easily be mistaken as an *A*.) Now his passport did not match his birth certificate. Moreover, the name under his photo on the passport said Sneyd, but the title page had the misspelling. Lillian Spencer, the agency's manager, checked with Ottawa and told him she could have it corrected in three days. But when he returned on May 4, she had forgotten to send it off.[72] Ray had no option but to travel with the misspelled passport, hoping that he might be able to fix it abroad.

On Monday, May 6, Mrs. Loo discovered that Ray had moved out. In his room, he had left behind a blue overnight bag. It contained a small metal strongbox; six rolls of unopened movie film; some Band-Aids; cold cream; maps of Toronto, Montreal, and Canada; and three sex magazines bought at a reduced price from a local back-issue store. She put the bag aside in case he returned, and after his capture she turned it over to the police.[73]

Meanwhile, Ray caught BOAC flight 600 to London at 6:00 P.M. He landed at 6:40 A.M. on Tuesday, May 7.

"When I arrived in London I called the Portugerse Embassy about a visa to Angola," wrote Ray. "I was told it would take one day to process. I then took a plane to Lisbon, and spent most of the time there trying to get a ship to Angola. (I was going from Angola into one of the English speaking countries if I could not get a job their)."[74]

Ray's flight to Lisbon had left at 10:55 the same night he had arrived at Heathrow. He had exchanged the return portion of his excursion trip from Toronto, and even received a fourteen-dollar refund in addition to the ticket to Portugal. During the two-and-a-half hour flight he sat by himself. He arrived in

---

*   Earlier that day, when Ray was in his room, a heavyset, middle-aged Caucasian appeared at the rear door and asked Mrs. Loo for "Mr. Sneyd." She went upstairs and told Ray, who came down and greeted the visitor. Loo watched as they briefly spoke, and then the heavyset man passed an envelope to Ray. When the Toronto papers later learned of the visit, they dubbed the stranger the "Fat Man" and began a frenetic search for him. Most speculated that the envelope contained a payoff, especially since later that day Ray paid cash for his airline tickets. However, the "Fat Man" turned out to be Robert McDouldton (identified as the "Fat Man" for the first time here), a paint company salesman who worked in the Dundas Street area. He had used a public telephone booth and found an envelope addressed to Sneyd with no return address. Huie reports that Ray said the envelope contained the Sneyd birth certificate, which had finally arrived. Ray had carried the envelope in his jacket pocket, and when he called the travel agency from a phone booth, he had written the departure time on the back of the envelope. Then he walked away from the booth, leaving it there. Mrs. Loo later identified McDouldton as her visitor, and the Toronto police investigated and cleared him of any sinister association to Ray or the case (MURKIN 4351–4440, section 55, p. 146).

Lisbon at 1:15 A.M. on May 8.[75] At customs, the clerk, Antonio Rocha Fama, warned him to correct the misspelling in his passport, which he promised to do.[76] Ray found his way to the third-class Hotel Portugal. There he rented a $1.80-a-day room.[77]

Lisbon was a sensible stopover, considering Ray's desire to get to white Africa. The Portuguese capital had become a major European recruiting center for white mercenaries who wanted to fight in the war in Angola. But finding a ship or a mercenary unit was easier said than done.

Gentil Soares, the clerk at the Hotel Portugal, remembered Ray as someone who was unfriendly, never used room service, and never tipped. He walked through with his head usually cast down, never made or received any telephone calls, and was never with any other men. He did, however, try to bring prostitutes back to the hotel, but when told he could not have women in his room, he left with them.[78] One, Gloria Sausa Riseiro, spent a night with him, and she remembered that he was obsessed with buying British and American newspapers. She did not know what he read in the papers. Since he spoke no Portuguese and she spoke no English, she told the authorities they spoke "only the international language of love."[79]

Ray frequented numerous bars near his hotel: the Texas, Bolero, Niagara, Galo, Bar Bohemia, and Fontoria Nightclub.[80] Most were hangouts for sailors. On his eighth day in Lisbon, "I finally found a ship, a one way ticket cost 3,777 Escudos [$131], I then went to get a visa but was told it would take 7 days to process the visa, the ship was leaving in two days, so I missed the ship."[81]

He then checked with South African Airways (SAA) and picked up a timetable. After his arrest, Ray still had the SAA timetable, with a checkmark next to the schedule for Salisbury, Rhodesia.[82] He also visited the South African Embassy. There he identified himself as a Canadian and said he wanted to go to South Africa to search for his brother, who was fighting somewhere in Africa as a mercenary. Was there an organization in South Africa that recruited mercenaries, and therefore might be able to help him? The embassy officials informed him that the mercenary recruiting office had closed in Johannesburg and they did not know where it had relocated.[83]

Ray also visited the Rhodesian mission, spun the same story, and asked for an address of an organization in Salisbury that recruited mercenaries, but he received no assistance.[84] He then went to the unofficial legation for Biafra, which had broken away from Nigeria and was headquartered in Lisbon. He again asked about joining a white mercenary group in Africa, but the legation could not help him.*[85]

---

* There were some later reports that Ray had actually met two soldiers while at the legation and that one was black, which made him leave. He adamantly denied that.

As his funds dwindled, Ray decided to return to London because he found it easier to operate in an English-speaking country.[86] Before leaving, he visited the Canadian Embassy on Wednesday, May 15, and tried to cancel his incorrect passport and have a new one issued. Manuela Lopes, the consular clerk, remembered Ray said he "did not want to spend all of his time waiting around the Embassy."[87] She helped him fill in the forms. He needed so much help that she concluded he was not well educated. Aubrey Morantz, the embassy's second secretary, checked and approved Sneyd's documents, including his birth certificate.[88] Earlier, he had had passport photos taken at the nearby Foto Lusitania.[89] Ray picked up the new passport on Thursday, May 16, and left the next day for London.[90] He would still have to show his canceled passport together with his new one when passing through customs.[91]

Back in London, he settled into a cheap hotel named Heathfield House, in the Earl's Court neighborhood, an area filled with Australians and Americans.[92]

On Tuesday afternoon, June 4, Ian Colvin, a journalist in the Foreign Room of London's *Daily Telegraph,* found a note at his typewriter. "A Mr. Sneyd called, will call later."[93] At 5:00 P.M., the phone rang. "This is Ramon Sneyd. I want to join my brother who has been in Angola."[94] Ray said he was a Canadian who had read Colvin's articles about mercenaries in Africa. He sounded nervous and wanted the telephone number of Major Alistair Wicks, former second in command of the Five Commando unit in the Congo, who was mentioned in one of Colvin's articles.[95] Ray claimed that his brother was missing and he hoped that Wicks might put him in touch with a group who could help locate him.[96]

Colvin was wary of giving out any information about Wicks, and instead offered to pass along Sneyd's number. By then, Ray had moved to the New Earl's Court Hotel, and he gave that number. He had stayed at the Heathfield for ten days, moving on May 28. While there, he had received no mail, telephone calls, or visitors.

Two days after the first call to Colvin, Ray called again. He had not heard from Wicks, he complained, and wanted Colvin to know that he had again moved, this time to the Hotel Pax. Colvin had indeed passed along Ray's message to Wicks, but Wicks did not recognize the name and had decided not to return the call.[97] This time Colvin questioned his caller and Sneyd admitted that his brother was not really missing, but that he had not heard from him in four months. Then Sneyd admitted that it was not so much that he wanted to search for his brother, but he actually wanted to become a mercenary himself.[98] Their conversation was interrupted several times because Sneyd was calling from a pay phone and often got disconnected when his money ran out, forcing him to redial. It was a bad time to join the mercenaries, Colvin explained, as both the British and African governments frowned on them. Anyway, he told Sneyd, the place to get information was not London but Brussels. While he did not have the information at hand, he would be happy to send Sneyd the address of Jean Gerard-Liebro, someone in touch with affairs in the Congo.

Almost the moment he hung up, Colvin felt uneasy about his caller. Sneyd seemed "overwrought and somewhat incoherent," and instead of sending the information about Gerard-Liebro, he instead forwarded a simple postcard suggesting that Sneyd contact the Belgian Embassy.[99]

At the New Earl's Court Hotel, the receptionist, Janet Nassau, remembered that Ray was trying to trace a Major Wicks about whom he had read. She liked her new guest and sometimes tried to talk to him, but found him incredibly shy.[100] She and some others tried to assist him on Wicks, but "he was so incoherent nobody seemed able to help him." On June 4, after Ray called Colvin from a pay phone a few feet from the lobby's main desk, he asked Nassau about his bill for the first week. He was worried because he was running low on money. "I'll have to go to my bank and make a withdrawal," he told her.[101]

That afternoon, one of the tellers in the Fulham branch of the Trustee Savings Bank looked up to see a white man with large sunglasses, wearing a blue suit, standing in front of her window. He pushed a small, pink paper bag toward her with a handwritten notation, "Place all £5–10 pound notes in this bag."[102] The teller could see the tip of a pistol between the fingers of one of his hands. She grabbed £105 (then equivalent to $240) and pushed the bills over the counter. He pocketed them and slowly walked out, leaving the bag behind. Later, it was discovered that the bag had James Earl Ray's right thumbprint on it.*[103] That Ray risked a robbery in England is further evidence that he had not yet received any money for having killed King. When he was arrested only four days later, he had just over £51 (about $117). He told Huie that his major error while on the run was not to have committed a crime when he was hiding in Canada between April 22 and May 6. "That's where I made my mistake," he insisted. "I should have pulled a holdup. But I didn't. And I let myself get on that plane to London without enough money to get where I intended to go."[104]

---

* Ray has adamantly denied robbing the bank, but his fingerprint is irrefutable evidence that he did. The House Select Committee concluded that Ray, on May 27, had also tried unsuccessfully to rob a Paddington area jewelry store at about 5:30 P.M. Maurice and Billie Isaacs, the owners, later identified photos of Ray as the person who attempted to rob them at gunpoint (see MLK Exhibits F-238 and F-239). However, contemporaneous FBI documents indicate that Scotland Yard did not pursue its investigation of those robberies because they were "extremely fearful that if information re: the jewelry shop job and information implicating Ray in any other jobs leaks to the press, that Ray's solicitor will insist Ray be charged in order to clear him of any or all jobs he allegedly committed." That would have substantially delayed his extradition to the States for the King assassination. (MURKIN 4901–4982, section 66, p. 46.)

After robbing the bank, Ray checked out of the New Earl's Court Hotel, telling Nassau that he was leaving for the airport. Actually, he went looking, in the midst of a violent rainstorm, for another room. The YMCA was full, and he was directed to the nearby Pax Hotel in Pimlico. The Pax was a private house, but its owner, Swedish-born Anna Thomas, let out several rooms. At 5:00 P.M. on Wednesday, June 5, she opened her door. Ray was standing there dripping wet in a beige raincoat, a suitcase in one hand and books and newspapers under his other arm. Introducing himself as Sneyd, he took a room for $3.60 a day, including breakfast. Before he settled in, he complained of a bitter headache, and she gave him some aspirin.[105]

When Thomas brought his breakfast the next morning at 7:45 and knocked on his door, there was no answer, so she left the tray. When she began walking away, she saw him open the door.[106] He was fully dressed and took the tray without saying a word.[107] He followed the same routine for the next two mornings, and stayed in his room except for briefly going out each day to buy some newspapers. On the second day she asked him to sign the hotel register, but he did not, only telling her again that his name was Sneyd, and this time adding that he planned to go to Germany.[108] While he was there, he received four telephone calls. Two were from a British European Airways representative about changes in his flight schedule, and the other two did not leave any message.*[109] Thomas took the messages and slipped them under his door. One day when he left to buy headache pills, she went into his room to tidy up. She noticed that he had washed his own shirts, and on the bed were newspapers open to the extensive news about the assassination of Senator Robert Kennedy.[110]

At 9:30 A.M. on Saturday, June 8, Ray seemed particularly harried when he paid his bill, and he left the rooming house in a rush with all his belongings.[111] About two hours later, at Heathrow Airport, Detective Sergeant Philip Birch would be waiting with the Watch List at the immigration desk in Terminal Two. Sixty-five days after he had fled the scene of the assassination, Ray's luck had finally run out.

---

* Thomas thought they could have been from the *Daily Telegraph*. Although Colvin said he never called Ray, it is possible that Major Wicks or somebody else connected with the mercenaries may have finally returned a call, but after Ray's arrest were embarrassed to admit it. Thomas thought one of the callers, a woman, sounded American. It is also possible that it was Carol Ray, James's sister, checking on him—Carol and the rest of the family, of course, have consistently denied knowing his whereabouts when he was on the run, but considering the special bond among the Rays, it would not be surprising to discover that it was her or another family member.

PART III

The Search for Truth

28

"The Legal Truth"

A conspiracy in the King assassination has seemed likely to many since the day of the murder. King had numerous enemies, any of whom might have sponsored a triggerman. Ray's capture only fueled the speculation. Questions of how a career thief was suddenly transformed into a competent assassin were not answered by the Memphis plea agreement. And Ray's sixty-five-day odyssey after the killing, involving travel to three countries and the use of foreign passports, seemed far beyond the capability of the poor, uneducated hillbilly charged with the crime. William Bradford Huie's articles about Raoul nurtured the conspiracy talk. A public opinion poll soon after the plea revealed two-thirds of those questioned believed there was a conspiracy.[1]

But Huie made a U-turn in his third *Look* installment, published in April 1969. He admitted he had made "a serious mistake" and now believed Ray alone had killed King. He concluded that Raoul was merely a composite of criminals Ray had likely encountered in his fugitive year leading up to the King assassination.[2] That conclusion was shared by Clay Blair, Jr., in his paperback *The Strange Case of James Earl Ray*, rushed out in March 1969 at the time of Ray's plea. Huie followed Blair with a longer version of his lone-assassin thesis in book form, *He Slew the Dreamer*, the following year.*

---

* Delacorte Press originally signed the Huie book as "They Slew the Dreamer," but the title was modified after Huie changed his mind about what happened in the murder.

But for every former conspiracy believer like Huie who was now convinced that Ray had indeed killed King alone, there was an ever growing number of skeptics about the case. *The Greatest Police Fraud Ever: The James Earl Ray Hoax,* by German leftist Joachim Joesten, declared that Ray was "the ideal fall guy," that there was a Ray double, and that "Dr. King was *not* shot from Mrs. Bessie Brewer's flophouse window; instead, the fatal shot came from a Memphis replica of the famous grassy knoll in Dallas" (emphasis in original). According to Joesten, "the real assassin has been quietly spirited away to a foreign haven where he is to await his next assignment under the protection of the CIA."*[3] Harold Weisberg, a former chicken farmer who eventually self-published half a dozen convoluted books on the JFK case, also brought out one on the King case, *Frame-Up,* in 1969.[4] Included in Weisberg's speculation was the two-Rays theory—"there were at least two men, only one of whom was arrested and charged." Although both the Joesten and Weisberg books were riddled with errors, they nevertheless added to the early conspiracy fever.

And Ray himself, through a succession of lawyers, did his best to create confusion in the hope that enough controversy might force the state to grant him a trial. When J. B. Stoner—the National States Rights Party (NSRP) counsel, the founder of the Stoner Anti-Jewish Party, and a cofounder of the Christian Anti-Jewish Party—took over from the dismissed Percy Foreman, the conspiracy speculation accelerated.[5]

The forty-one-year-old Stoner, who thought Hitler was "too moderate," had the distinction of being one of the country's most vicious racists. His newsletter, *The Thunderbolt,* said King's killer was "actually upholding the law of the land [and] he should be given the Congressional medal and a large annual pension for life, plus a Presidential pardon."[†] In 1969, Stoner had a new

---

* German leftists were particularly attracted to the King case, in part because they simplistically saw the murder as the right-wing plot of a secret government to end the civil rights movement. One of the most talked-about plays in 1970 in Germany was Rolf Hochhuth's *Guerrillas,* in which the CIA organized the King murder.

† When Stoner was asked about King the night of the assassination, he said, "He has been a good nigger now since six or seven o'clock tonight." Stoner had joined the Chattanooga Klan at eighteen. In 1944, he petitioned Congress to pass a law establishing that "Jews are the children of the Devil." The following year he organized the Stoner Anti-Jewish Party and worked toward passing laws to make Judaism a crime punishable by death, including the use of gas chambers, electric chairs, and firing squads. In 1950, the Chattanooga Klan expelled him because he was so extreme. In 1964, Stoner ran for vice president on the NSRP ticket, and he later ran unsuccessfully for governor and senator from Georgia. In 1980, he was convicted of conspiracy to bomb a black church in Birmingham nineteen years earlier. In the 1990s, Stoner founded a new organization, Crusade Against Corruption. He frequently lectures about how AIDS—since it affects many gays and minorities—is "God's gift because he loves us white people." Some of

roommate: Jerry Ray. Jerry worked for Stoner for more than ten years as an un-official bodyguard, driver, and general gofer and aide.[6] Jerry became a mini-celebrity among white supremacists—the NSRP even feted him at a dinner at which he was introduced as "the Honorable Jerry Ray, brother of James Earl Ray."[7] In 1970, when Stoner ran for governor of Georgia (he got less than 3 percent of the vote), Jerry Ray was his campaign manager. That same year, Jerry was arrested for shooting a seventeen-year-old member of the American Nazi Party who broke into the NSRP headquarters to steal party files. Stoner defended him that November, and he was acquitted.*

Jerry Ray and J. B. Stoner formed a quick bond because they shared a simi-lar disparaging view of blacks and Jews, the same bigotry all the Ray boys had grown up with. "It might take another 50 or 75 years but the Jews are like the Nigger beast," Jerry wrote, "give them a rope and they will hang themselves. I am sure when History is written my Brother James Earl Ray, and the Hon. Gov. George Wallace will be Heroes alongside of JB Stoner." He called Sirhan Sirhan a "hero" and said that when Robert Kennedy was assassinated, he "celebrated."[8]

Stoner and Ray also shared a similar tendency to embrace wild conspiracy theories, usually with the federal government cast as the villain. A few months after James's guilty plea, Stoner became the first of Ray's attorneys to charge publicly that "agents of the federal government" had killed King, "but so far I have been unable to find out what their motive was."[9] Stoner said he had evi-dence that King's murder and Ray's conviction were part of the same plot—"Mr. Ray was just a fall guy so they [the federal government] could consider the case closed."

A few weeks after Stoner's announcement, Jerry Ray released to a St. Louis radio station a statement, supposedly from James, that confirmed Stoner's

---

James Earl Ray's supporters are clearly ashamed of his Stoner connection. Ray's current attorney William Pepper, in his 1995 book, *Orders to Kill*, writes about every possible aspect to a conspiracy in the case, but does not even mention Stoner or the NSRP.

* If Jerry Ray, or any of the Rays, knew Stoner *before* the King assassination, that would be critical. Stoner and many in his NSRP celebrated King's death, and could be prime suspects if there was an early Ray-Stoner connection. Jerry testified before the House Select Committee that he had never heard of Stoner until after the assassina-tion. Harry Avery, the commissioner of the Tennessee prison system, said that Jerry had admitted to him that Stoner had "been our lawyer for at least two years before Martin Luther King was killed." Jerry Ray said Avery was "lying" and called his testi-mony "a joke, a sick joke." Whatever the relationship, when James Earl Ray gave waivers of his attorney-client privilege to the House Select Committee so they could in-terview his former lawyers, he refused to give one only for Stoner, leading many to be-lieve that even if Stoner was not involved in King's murder, the Rays had confided the truth to him.

charge. "In the spring of 1968," James said, "I was working with agents of the
Federal Government, including Raol. They told me that I was helping them to
supply arms and guns to Cuban refugees to overthrow Castro and the Communists in Cuba. The reason I made trips to Mexico was in regard to helping the
agents of the Federal Government to supply arms to Cuban refugees there to
overthrow Castro. The federal agents led me to believe that I was in Memphis in
April for the same purpose. . . . I now realize that they had no interest in over-
throwing Castro, and their whole purpose was to use me to cover up their own
crime. Two federal agencies are guilty, and I am fully innocent."[10]

Actually, Jerry Ray had written the statement without consulting James,
and Stoner allowed him to release it. James was initially so angry that he temporarily barred Jerry from visiting him.[11] It was nine years before the House Select Committee unmasked Jerry's fraud.[12]

In addition to the false statement, Jerry began telling the media that the FBI
was so eager to stop James from seeking a new trial that it had "tried to frame
me with false charges" and "planted evidence in the automobile of our brother,
John Ray, of St. Louis, and succeeded in sending him to prison even though he
was innocent."[13] (John had received a twenty-year sentence for driving the getaway car in yet another bank robbery.) Jerry charged that the Bureau of Prisons had tried to kill John by placing him in the "black jungle," where black
inmates were crammed into cells. (John Ray actually refused to be placed into
any prison cell with blacks.*)

While Jerry Ray and Stoner battled to win over public opinion, Stoner and
Memphis attorney Richard Ryan and Chattanooga counsel Robert Hill initiated appeals in the Tennessee courts to try and get a new trial for Ray.[14] They
also filed a lawsuit—*Ray* v. *Foreman*—against Foreman, Hanes, and Huie in the
U.S. District Court in Nashville. It charged them with violating Ray's constitutional rights and tried unsuccessfully to enjoin the publication of Huie's book.

In the early summer of 1969, only a month after the request for a
new trial was made, criminal court judge Arthur Faquin ruled that Ray had
given up his right of appeal when he pleaded guilty.[15] The Tennessee Court of
Criminal Appeals, and subsequently the Tennessee Supreme Court, upheld
Faquin's ruling.[16] Ray's attorneys then resubmitted a motion for a trial, based

---

* Jerry also complained that the Bureau of Prisons almost had John killed by putting
him in a shoe shop with a "half Jew and half Indian who is completely crazy." He also
wrote, "They [prison officials] only put the Whites in solitary and never the blacks. To
show how biased against Whites they can be, the federal officials have ordered that Martin Luther King's birthday always be celebrated as a holiday in all federal prisons. It is
time to end the jungle conditions in the prisons and to return them to the control of the
decent White people."

on a new contention that Foreman had induced Ray to plead guilty on the false promise that he would be paroled in two years.[17] Criminal court judge William Williams rejected that argument and was affirmed twice on appeal.

Ray had no better luck in his civil lawsuit against Foreman, Hanes, and Huie. It came to trial in the District Court in December 1969 and was dismissed by Judge Robert McRae as legally insufficient.[18] The Sixth Circuit Court of Appeals affirmed the dismissal.[19]

In 1971, after the State Court of Appeals had rejected his second application for a new trial, Ray decided to try an alternate route to freedom. This time he would attempt to escape from Brushy Mountain State Penitentiary. As with his earlier escape attempts from Missouri State Penitentiary in the 1960s, Ray's effort was ambitious and had taken weeks of planning. He used a welding rod provided by another inmate to remove part of two concrete blocks in his cell, working at the job for several days and carefully replacing the mortar he removed with a temporary paste so the guards would not notice anything unusual when they inspected his cell.[20] And for several days he worked with a hacksaw on some bars that blocked an air vent through which he needed to crawl. Every night when he worked on cutting the bars, he put a dummy into his bed so as not to arouse the guards' suspicions. Finally, on May 2, Ray squeezed into the vent. He again left the dummy in his bed. Working his way through the long vent, he eventually reached the prison yard behind his cell block. Then, using a crowbar, he removed a manhole cover on a steam tunnel. His plan was to crawl through the tunnel to go under the prison wall, emerging outside the prison. But the steam tunnel, which was several hundred degrees Fahrenheit, proved too hot for Ray, so he retreated to the prison yard and hid.[21] Around 3:15 A.M., guards finally found him hiding in the shadows of one of the large prison buildings.

Nine months later, Ray made another unsuccessful escape attempt, this time trying to cut through the roof in the prison gymnasium.

After two failed escapes, Ray was at least temporarily resigned to put more energy into his legal efforts. He had new lawyers: Bernard Fensterwald, Jr., the founder of the Washington, D.C.–based Committee to Investigate Assassinations, and his assistant James Lesar, as well as Memphis-based Robert Livingston. As with many attracted to the cause, Fensterwald was a conspiracy believer who was not only willing to credit Ray's tales, but also brought along many of his own theories about political murders, particularly from his work on the JFK assassination. His Committee to Investigate Assassinations, for instance, had a board of directors that included his friend Jim Garrison, the district attorney of New Orleans, and former FBI agent William Turner, both of whom thought a wide-ranging government plot killed JFK. Later, key members of Fensterwald's group included Penn Jones, who invented the bogus issue of mysterious deaths in the Kennedy case; Richard Popkin, the originator of the two-Oswalds theory; and Fletcher Prouty, the former military officer who spun a wild tale of CIA involvement in JFK's murder. A friend of Fensterwald's, conspiracy buff Harold Weisberg, became an investigator for Ray, searching for new witnesses who might bolster or even go beyond Ray's version of what happened.

Having exhausted his right of appeal in the Tennessee courts, Ray and his lawyers decided to file a special writ of habeas corpus in federal court.[22] Ray had been ineffectively represented, they argued, and Foreman and Huie had maneuvered and coerced him into a guilty plea in order to enhance the success of their articles, books, and movies about the case.[23] The legal maneuvering that followed was Herculean. In March 1973, a federal district court rejected Ray's argument that his constitutional rights had been violated.[24] Ray appealed, and in a 2 to 1 decision the Sixth Circuit Court of Appeals sided with him, ruling in January 1974 that he was at least entitled to an evidentiary hearing.[25] The state of Tennessee appealed that decision to the Supreme Court, but that June the high court declined to hear the case.*[26]

After the habeas corpus proceeding was returned to district court, an evidentiary hearing that extended over eight days was held in October 1974. When Foreman took the stand, he was surprisingly hesitant, and at times seemed, unwittingly, to bolster Ray's case that he had done little to prepare Ray for trial. His weak performance prompted press speculation that Ray might well get the trial he had forgone six years earlier.[27] But in February 1975, U.S. District Judge Robert M. McRae, Jr., ruled Ray had had adequate counsel after his arrest and that his guilty plea was voluntary.[28] Over a year later—in May 1976—the U.S. Sixth Circuit Court of Appeals affirmed McRae's ruling.[29] That

---

*   While Ray's legal machinations were under way to win a new trial, he made sure that his lawyers also stayed busy on several civil fronts. After the publication of Gerold Frank's An American Death in 1972, Ray sued former Memphis prosecutors Phil Canale and Robert Dwyer, charging that they were in collusion with Frank and his publisher, Doubleday, to keep him in prison. He unsuccessfully sought $300,000 in damages. In 1976, he brought a $3 million suit against, among others, Time magazine and authors George McMillan, William Bradford Huie, and Gerold Frank, for libel and civil rights violations. Judge Harry Wellford ruled that because of his past criminal convictions Ray was "libel proof," and he dismissed the suit. That did not stop Ray from filing another suit against George McMillan, the publishers Little, Brown, William Bradford Huie, and others. U.S. District Judge Bailey Brown rejected that action. And while Ray was active, his brother Jerry also was litigious, filing a $2.25 million suit against McMillan, Time, and a former assistant attorney general. It was also unsuccessful.

December, the case was back before the Supreme Court, which again declined to review it. As a result, Ray decided that he did not like his current batch of attorneys, and he dismissed Fensterwald, Lesar, and Livingston.

While the habeas corpus proceeding was pending on appeal, William Sullivan, the former assistant director of the FBI's Domestic Intelligence Division, testified before a Senate committee in November 1975 that Dr. King had been a target of an extensive FBI campaign designed to neutralize him.[30] The FBI's counterintelligence program against the Communist Party (COINTELPRO) had also included a secret war against King from late 1963 until his death. According to Sullivan, during the operation—which included extensive physical and electronic surveillance—"no holds were barred."[31] Those widely publicized disclosures of the FBI's gross abuses revived the question of whether the Bureau might have either plotted to kill King or covered up for the real killers during its investigation. To examine that question, on November 24, 1975, the Justice Department began reviewing the FBI's investigation. Its report was released fourteen months later. It strongly condemned the FBI's campaign against King, but found the Bureau's murder investigation into his death to have been generally thorough. The report further tarnished the FBI and Hoover vis-à-vis their personal and sometimes illegal crusade against King, but it did nothing to help Ray. "We found no evidence," the Justice Department concluded, "of any complicity on the part of the Memphis Police Department or of the FBI. . . . We saw no credible evidence probative of the possibility that Ray and any co-conspirator were together at the scene of the assassination. Ray's assertions that someone else pulled the trigger are so patently self-serving and so varied as to be wholly unbelievable."[32]

Meanwhile, Congress had begun considering its own investigation into the King case. Texas representative Henry Gonzalez introduced a resolution in the 94th Congress (1975) calling for a new investigation of not only King's murder but also the shootings of John and Robert Kennedy and George Wallace. In April 1975, Virginia congressman Thomas Downing introduced a resolution for a reexamination of only the John Kennedy assassination. A tied vote in committee killed any new investigation that year.

But in 1976, the momentum for a new investigation revived when Coretta Scott King met with the Congressional Black Caucus and urged them to seek the truth in a case she remained personally convinced involved a major conspiracy. The caucus then spearheaded an effort to meld the Downing and Gonzalez drafts to empower a select committee to investigate both the King and JFK deaths. Their efforts resulted in House Resolution 1540, introduced on September 14, 1976, and passed by a vote of 280 to 65 on September 30. The Black Caucus wanted Mark Lane as general counsel, but eventually Richard

Sprague, a prominent Philadelphia prosecutor, was selected. Sprague did not last long, however. He submitted a $6.5 million budget for 1977, considered excessive by some in Congress, and announced he would use polygraphs and stress analyzers on witnesses. Thomas Downing had briefly been the committee chairman, but when Henry Gonzalez replaced him, Gonzalez tried to dismiss Sprague. But Sprague refused to leave unless the entire committee voted him out. In the ensuing standoff, Gonzalez resigned, and it appeared that any congressional investigation was dead.

In March 1977, House Speaker Tip O'Neill appointed Ohio congressman Louis Stokes as the new chairman. Stokes persuaded Sprague to resign, eventually got two years of funding, and hired G. Robert Blakey, a respected attorney and academician, as general counsel.

Starting in the spring, the committee began a series of interviews with Ray. It had completed five when, on June 11, 1977, the forty-nine-year-old Ray finally made a successful escape from Brushy Mountain State Penitentiary. Ray and five other prisoners used a ladder made of lightning-conductor wire and pipes to scale a fifteen-foot wall. A seventh prisoner, the last up the ladder, was shot and captured before he could get outside.*

More than 125 prison guards, state troopers, FBI agents, and Tennessee Bureau of Criminal Identification agents, assisted by bloodhounds, combed through the thick wilderness that surrounded the maximum-security prison. Fifty-five hours after he escaped, the bloodhounds found Ray, exhausted and cold, hiding under a pile of leaves in the dense woods. He was only five miles from the prison.[†]

---

* William Pepper, who became Ray's attorney in the 1980s, writes in *Orders to Kill* that Ray "was no sooner over the wall . . . when a large SWAT team (upwards of 30 FBI snipers) took up position in the area. The function of snipers is not to apprehend. It is to kill." Pepper claims the reason the FBI snipers had been assigned to kill Ray was that "some people feared what James might have testified to before the HSCA." He fails to mention that the Select Committee had already interviewed Ray five times by the time he escaped. He also does not explain how thirty FBI snipers somehow missed Ray. While that allegation is typical of the fantastic charges that fill Pepper's book, he also contends that a New Orleans mobster wanted Ray killed immediately after the assassination, but "the killing had been botched up." Again, he does not explain why, if professional hit men were supposed to kill Ray in 1968, they had never finished the job in the intervening decades. Although prison is one of the easiest places to have someone killed, Ray was safe there. "The fact that Ray is still alive is one of the best arguments against the existence of any sophisticated conspiracy," former Select Committee counsel Robert Blakey told the author. "If the mob, government, or anything like that had been involved, Ray would not have lived for very long after King was murdered."

† In one of the bizarre turns in Ray's unusual life, during his 1977 trial for the escape he met an attractive, blond courtroom artist, Anna Sandhu. The thirty-two-year-old

After he was returned to prison, Ray completed another three interviews with the Select Committee. The committee's investigators were tough in their questioning. They would not let him modify or change his story without offering a solid explanation. That unsettled Ray, who was accustomed to softer treatment from his own lawyers and investigators. "I could see the handwriting on the prison wall," wrote Ray. "The fix was in at the Select Committee, and an interview with *Playboy* to which I'd agreed was turning out to be more aggravation than it seemed to be worth."[33]

The *Playboy* interview was published in September 1977, while the Select Committee interviews were still under way. It, too, was the result of hours of interviews. Even Jerry Ray talked to the magazine. Most significant, however, was that James, on the advice of his new Nashville attorney, Jack Kershaw, agreed for the first time to undergo a polygraph examination. *Playboy* hired Douglas Wicklander, a well-known polygraph expert at the firm of John E. Reid & Associates, to administer the test.*

To the key questions—"Did you kill Martin Luther King, Jr.?" and "Did you fire the shot that killed Martin Luther King, Jr.?" and "Do you know for sure who killed Martin Luther King, Jr.?"—Ray answered no.

Wicklander reviewed the polygraph tape with John Reid, the company's owner (also the inventor of the portion of the polygraph machine that mea-

---

Sandhu and Ray enjoyed their brief courtroom conversations, and when Ray testified before Congress in 1978, she was in the public gallery. Convinced that Ray was innocent, and that he might win release easier if he was married, Sandhu proposed to him. The two were married in a surreal thirty-five-minute ceremony on October 13, 1978. The Reverend James Lawson, a former friend of Dr. King's, who had come to believe in Ray's innocence, performed the service. Mark Lane was best man. Sandhu then went on a national press tour to proclaim her husband's innocence and ask for a new trial or a pardon. She visited Ray in prison at least twice a week for several years, and Ray tried to polish his image by taking a Bible study course with Sandhu, saying he had returned to Christianity. Sandhu, though, filed for divorce in November 1990, citing "inappropriate marital behavior." The divorce was finalized in 1993. Sandhu went on another national press tour, including appearances on *Geraldo!* and *The Phil Donahue Show* in which she now claimed that Ray was an expert manipulator and she no longer believed him innocent. In 1997, she told the *National Enquirer* that the real reason she divorced Ray was that during a phone argument she told him, "I've never believed you could have killed Martin Luther King," and Ray yelled, "Yeah, I did it. So what?" Then he slammed down the receiver. Ray's answer to that is that he would never have made that admission on a prison phone because he always assumes that officials are listening.

* Wicklander had personally administered over 2,500 polygraph exams, had written a text used by trainees in the field, and had designed the "control question" technique that had become standard in the profession.

sures changes in blood-pressure levels), and Joseph Buckley, the company's director. All concluded that Ray was lying on each key answer.[34]

To explore the possibility of a conspiracy, Wicklander then conducted a second test. "Did anyone ask you to kill Martin Luther King, Jr.?" he asked Ray. "Did you arrange with anyone to kill Martin Luther King, Jr.?" "Did anyone give you any money to kill Martin Luther King, Jr.?" Ray again answered each question no. This time the examiners decided he had told the truth on those questions. *Playboy* asked the polygraph examiners if they had any doubts about their conclusions. Their answer was "None." As *Playboy* wrote, the "polygraph tests indicate that Ray did, in fact, kill Martin Luther King, Jr., and that he did so alone."

At the close of the interview with Ray, *Playboy* informed him that he had failed the tests. He seemed unfazed, calling the equipment a "medieval contraption," and said, "I had a headache all day. I took a bunch of aspirin. I don't know if that would affect the test or not."[35] (It would not.) Years later, in his book *Who Killed Martin Luther King?*, Ray called the *Playboy* interview "a prosecutor's brief" and suggested that the article was the result of a conspiracy: Hugh Hefner, *Playboy*'s owner, had slanted the interview in order to curry favor with federal authorities because of the drug conviction of a Hefner aide.[36] Because of the *Playboy* results, Ray fired his attorney, Jack Kershaw.

Now, as Ray continued to appear before the Select Committee, he had a new attorney: longtime conspiracy buff Mark Lane. Lane had attracted Ray's attention with his book *Code Name "Zorro,"* cowritten with comedian and political activist Dick Gregory.[37] In that 1977 book, Lane argued that the FBI had killed King and that Ray was a dupe.

"Lane and I could see my inquisitors were trying to maneuver me into making misstatements," wrote Ray. "After my December 2, 1977 session with them, I stopped altogether."[38] But Ray was still scheduled to testify under oath the following year, at public hearings. To counteract the negative publicity of the *Playboy* publication, Lane arranged in December 1977 for Ray to submit to another polygraph. The results would be aired on columnist Jack Anderson's syndicated television program.

This time the test would be administered by fifty-six-year-old Chris Gugas, perhaps the most experienced polygraph expert worldwide. Gugas had conducted over 30,000 tests personally and supervised several thousand more. A widely respected lecturer and expert witness, Gugas was past president of both the National Board of Polygraph Examiners and the American Polygraph Association, and had worked for many private companies as well as having directed the CIA's polygraph program.[39]

Before starting the exam, Gugas had a long talk with Ray. During that conversation, Ray told him that he had "read up on the polygraph after that last fellow from Reid's gave me my test. He called me a liar, and I wanted to make sure I knew something about the polygraph before I took your test."[40] When they got to talking about Mark Lane, Ray told Gugas, "He's been a true friend and an honest attorney." Lane had taught Ray that "there is the truth, and there is the legal truth." "And he's right," Ray told Gugas. "The evidence they have against me won't stand up in any objective court."[41]

When the exam finally started, Gugas ran several simultaneous polygraph tapes, a procedure he had devised to ensure greater accuracy on reading the results. The questions were much the same: "Did you shoot Dr. Martin Luther King, Jr.?" "Were you involved with any other person or persons in a conspiracy to shoot Dr. Martin Luther King, Jr.?" "Did you know Dr. Martin Luther King, Jr., was going to be shot?" and "Did you point any weapon toward Dr. Martin Luther King, Jr., on April 4, 1968?" Ray answered "No" to each. During the exam, Gugas noticed that Ray "kept applying pressure to his left arm, the one that held the blood-pressure cuff . . . only at certain questions. . . . I thought he was attempting to beat the polygraph."

Immediately after the tests, Lane eagerly asked Gugas for the results. But since Ray had "tried to manipulate the process," Gugas told Lane he needed several hours to examine the charts carefully. When Ray later appeared on Jack Anderson's television program, he not only denied killing King but also said he knew nothing about the assassination. Then Gugas came on and Anderson asked him for the results. Gugas said the results showed "Ray had lied about not shooting Dr. King, but had told the truth when he said there was no conspiracy." It meant, said Gugas, that "Ray had acted on his own."*[42]

---

* The House Select Committee appointed three experts to review the polygraph examinations administered to Ray. As for the two-part *Playboy* test, the panel unanimously concluded that Ray had lied when he denied participating in King's murder. Yet when Ray said no one had told him to shoot King, as opposed to Wicklander's definite conclusion that Ray had also lied there, the panel interpreted the results as inconclusive. As for the Gugas exam, the panel thought that "the apparent attempt by Ray to create artificial reactions to control questions" had affected the results. Nevertheless, it agreed that Ray lied both when he said he did not know who shot Martin Luther King and that he did not shoot King. The answers relating to the possibility of a conspiracy, however, were inconclusive (HSCA vol. XIII, pp. 143–51).

Jerry Ray repeatedly bragged to the author about passing two polygraph examinations. He says they indicated that he was telling the truth when he denied having any part in the Alton bank robbery or the King assassination.

Lane's attempt to counter the effects of the *Playboy* polygraph had back-fired, but Ray did not dismiss him. When the Select Committee began its public hearings in August, Lane was still at Ray's side.

Lane aggressively represented Ray before the committee. He often attacked the process as unfair and prosecutorial. The committee, in turn, officially chastised Lane in its final report, issued in July 1979, for bogus information he had tried to pass as credible. "The facts were often at variance with Lane's assertions. . . . In many instances, the committee found that Lane was willing to advocate conspiracy theories without having checked the factual basis for them. In other instances, Lane proclaimed conspiracy based on little more than inference and innuendo. Lane's conduct resulted in public misperception about the assassination of Dr. King and must be condemned."[43]

As for King's murder, the committee concluded that while "no Federal, State or local government agency was involved in the assassination of Dr. King . . . on the basis of the circumstantial evidence available to it . . . there is a likelihood . . . of a conspiracy."[44] St. Louis attorney and segregationist John Sutherland, who the committee discovered had a standing bounty of $50,000 on King during 1967 and 1968, was the plot's likely money man.

But for Ray personally, there was little comforting news. The committee concluded not only that Ray "knowingly, intelligently, and voluntarily pleaded guilty," but also that he alone "fired one shot at Dr. Martin Luther King, Jr. The shot killed Dr. King."[45]

Ray dismissed the Select Committee as a "Five million dollar hoax orchestrated by professional hoaxers."[46] Yet, while he seemed unconcerned, he must have realized that its conclusions were yet another obstacle—and a major one—in the way of obtaining a new trial. Ray still used Mark Lane as his attorney. No one else was volunteering for the job.

Lane made another application for a new trial the same month the Select Committee issued its report. It was quickly rejected.[47] Ray then went on a litigation binge. He sued Congressman Stokes and the committee, seeking $75,000 in damages to his reputation. The suit was dismissed.[48] He also filed separate actions against one of the committee's members, Representative Harold Ford, who had said Ray had killed King alone, and also against the U.S. Department of Justice and an Illinois sheriff, both for providing evidence to the committee that Ray and his brothers might have robbed the Alton, Missouri, bank in 1967. Those suits were also dismissed.[49] The same fate befell a new legal action against Percy Foreman, this time for malpractice.[50]

In November 1980, over a year after the Select Committee had issued its final report, Ray submitted a clemency appeal to the Tennessee Board of Parole. By March 1981, he had completed his answers to the Board of Parole, the first step in the process. Two months later, while the clemency appeal was pending, several black inmates attacked Ray at Brushy Mountain. The assault took place in the law library in the early morning. Ray was stabbed twenty-two times with a twelve-inch homemade knife made from a metal window brace. There were wounds on his cheek, the side of his neck, his left hand, and his chest. He needed seventy-seven stitches to close the punctures, but none of the wounds was deep or serious.

However, there were immediately questions about the nature of the attack: The attackers were alone with Ray for several minutes and were not stopped by guards until they had finished and were on their way out of the library.

Lane flew to the hospital where Ray had been taken and refused to allow a state photographer to photograph the wounds. That kicked off speculation that Ray might have staged the attack in order to win sympathy for his clemency appeal. The prison authorities eventually charged three inmates: Dock Walker, Jr., John Partee, and Jerome Ransom, all members of Alkebu-lan, a black nationalist prison organization.[51] Another inmate, William Wynn, came forward and testified that he had overheard Ray offering $50 for someone to stab him. Wynn passed a lie-detector test. Tennessee Bureau of Investigation and Corrections Department officials concluded that the stabbings were not intended to kill Ray, but were done by the three inmates to attract attention to their organization.*[52] Mark Lane contended that the knifing was part of a conspiracy to silence Ray.[53]

Following his recuperation from the stabbing, Ray continued his litigation spree. He sued *Playboy* over his 1977 interview and polygraph exam, contending the test was "rigged" and hurt his chances for any successful appeal. Ray also named Jack Kershaw, his former lawyer, as a defendant, asserting that he had profited from the article, to the detriment of Ray's legal case.[54] Two months after he initiated the *Playboy* lawsuit, Ray brought an action against several Tennessee officials, a television reporter, and a local congressman. "I believe they conspired to have me stabbed," he told a newspaper. "I think they wanted to keep me from talking."[55] The courts quickly rejected all of Ray's new litigation. Predictably, at the same time, the Parole Board voted four to one against even granting Ray a hearing.[56]

For the first time since the assassination, the case and Ray temporarily became quiet. In the mid-1980s, Ray and his lawyers seemed to have run out of legal options and enthusiasm. But just at the point when many had begun to

---

* When the three were tried two years later, Ray was placed on the witness stand, but said he could not identify any of them. All three were convicted of first-degree assault with intent to commit murder, and their jail sentences were extended.

forget about the confessed killer and the chances for further dramatic developments, yet another lawyer entered the case, one who would put Ray and the
controversies surrounding King's assassination in the spotlight as never before. British-based Dr. William Pepper, who had been at the periphery of the
proceedings a decade earlier, was about to become Ray's new lawyer.*

---

*   It was Pepper's January 1967 article in *Ramparts* about the horrors the U.S. military
had inflicted on the children of Vietnam that had originally caught Dr. King's attention
and eventually led to his strong moral stance against the war. Pepper had moved to England in 1980, claiming in *Orders to Kill* that he was forced to move because the mafia
in New England had made him "a marked man" after he led a successful effort at re-
organizing a school system "rife with corruption." Actually, a company of which Pepper was the president had received more than $200,000 from the state of Rhode Island
to run a foster-care program for troubled youths. On July 6, 1978, Pepper was charged
with four felony counts of transporting two teenage boys "to engage in lewd and indecent activities." The local police also learned that in 1969 a U.S. Senate subcommittee
heard statements from two young boys who said Pepper had sexual contact with them
when they were eight. No charges were filed against him then. Shortly after his arrest, a
state audit charged that more than half of the money given to Pepper's firm could not
be accounted for. His legal problems worsened when a real estate company sued him
civilly, claiming he had reneged on a deal to sell his $350,000 Westchester, New York,
home. Eventually, the felony morals charges were dropped to misdemeanor charges. He
left for England, and finally in 1990 the morals charges were dismissed for lack of prosecution. Pepper denied the charges and claimed that his legal problems were part of a
conspiracy to punish him for his anti-Vietnam stance in the late 1960s and his friendship with Dr. King.

29

The Mock Trial

O ne of the first persons Pepper talked to about the case was Renfro Hays, the discredited private investigator who had concocted the false stories concerning Ray's alibi. "Hays single-handedly did more damage to the case and the pursuit of truth than anybody else," says Wayne Chastain, a former journalist turned lawyer who later became one of Ray's attorneys.

But Pepper listened attentively to Hays and his startling tales, among them that a CIA mercenary had been in Memphis the day before the killing and had cut down a tree branch that blocked a clear shot from the rooming house; that a state trooper in Louisiana was really the shooter Grace Walden saw fleeing the rooming house; that a twelve-year-old black youngster had seen the shooter, and after he told the authorities what he saw, "the police came and took the boy away; he wasn't heard from again"; and that a local safecracker had opened the door to Ray's room at the boardinghouse on the day of the assassination and had seen three to four men inside, none of whom looked like Ray.[1]

"I was intrigued," said Pepper, who has a reputation even among friends as someone very receptive to broad conspiracy theories. "Hays seemed to be both sincere and fearful."[2]

After meeting Hays, Pepper decided to represent Ray on his appeal before the Sixth Circuit regarding the denial of yet another evidentiary hearing. "On my next visit to Memphis," recalled Pepper, "Renfro Hays introduced me to Ken Herman, another local investigator, whose services I engaged."[3]

Kenny Herman, then a fifty-two-year-old self-styled private investigator, was certainly every bit as colorful as Hays. Overweight, darkly tan, and with orange-tinted hair worn in a 1950s pompadour, he presented an offbeat image. Herman liked to boast that his one-story, bright pink home was "built by Elvis."* His first successful business was the Elvis Presley Information Center. "I sold Elvis before anyone else thought of it," recalls Herman. When Elvis died, Herman stocked up on a thousand newspapers, which he keeps in his attic, planning to hold them until the twenty-fifth anniversary in 2002. "Then I'll cash in," he says determinedly.[4]

Herman has dabbled in a dozen other ventures besides the Elvis souvenir business, but his true love is country music. "I was playing in a local club here in town on the night King was killed," he recounts. "They closed the whole city down that night with the curfew and all, and I was the only guy with a car. I had to give all the black musicians rides home, and there were riots all around. It was wild." Always thinking of a way to make a quick buck, Herman even profited by the assassination. "I rented my German shepherd to a furniture store because of the looting and all that followed. I rented out about twenty-five to thirty dogs, anything that could bark."

But his old acquaintances, including Elvis Presley and Johnny Cash, had gone on to star-studded music careers, leaving Herman behind. According to some friends, he was bitter. Although Herman was never able to get a private investigator's license—a criminal record bars him from having one—it did not stop him from doing civil and criminal investigations for local lawyers. He enjoyed that work, and running into Bill Pepper and the Ray case promised to put him in the limelight, something he relished. Herman quickly became Pepper's chief investigator.

On the legal front, Pepper initially had as little success as his predecessors did. The Sixth Circuit Court of Appeals rejected the petition to grant Ray an evidentiary hearing. The United States Supreme Court refused to hear the case in October 1989.

But Pepper, as had Mark Lane before him, realized there were other ways to press Ray's case. Although there were ever fewer legal options available

---

* His house is a museum of kitsch, from iridescent Jesus night-lights to small plaster replicas of the Parthenon and the *Pietà*, to his own executions of paint-by-number nudes. The chain-smoking Herman, comfortably ensconced in his perpetually dark living room, will gladly play one of his guitars and sing Merle Haggard songs for visitors. He also enjoys providing tours of the house, "a bit of Florida in Memphis," ranging from the safe that he boasts holds two kilos of gold to the rickety kitchen table that he says was the site of many of his breakthroughs in the Ray case.

through the courts, public opinion had yet to be extensively exploited. Even after twenty years, the King murder had attracted only a small portion of the media attention given to the JFK assassination. There were only a handful of books and no major documentaries or films. Pepper, with Herman doing the fieldwork, set out to change that.

"In early summer 1989," recalled Pepper, "I became involved in assisting the production of a BBC documentary on the assassination, *Inside Story: Who Killed Martin Luther King?*"[5] That show made a case for a widespread CIA-led conspiracy, with Ray as a patsy.

Much of that show was a rehash of interviews with longtime conspiracy buffs. "No question a secret [intelligence] unit carried out the Kennedy and King assassinations," said Fletcher Prouty, the former military officer who had developed some of the wildest and least sustainable theories in the JFK murder.* Harold Weisberg appeared to say, "There is no evidence that Ray ever shot a rifle in his life." He seemed not to know about Ray's marksmanship in the Army or the practice session he had with the .30-06 he bought only days before King's murder. Ed Redditt, the black Memphis policeman who had been assigned to watch King and was removed from duty the day of the assassination following a bogus death threat, reappeared to imply his removal was part of a conspiracy. It was the same charge for which the House Select Committee had chastised him nearly a decade earlier.

The show also had new material that Pepper and Herman had helped develop. Earl Caldwell, a former *New York Times* reporter who was at the Lorraine on the day of the assassination, said he saw a white man emerge from the bushes across from the motel just after the shooting. Caldwell complained that no one had ever interviewed him about what he saw that day.[†] But the highlight of the show was an interview with Jules Ricco Kimble, then serving a double life sentence in Oklahoma for murder. He claimed he was a CIA hit man who had handled Ray in Canada in 1967, took care of all his false identifica-

---

* Prouty would later become an adviser to Oliver Stone, and the mysterious "Mr. X" in the film *JFK* was based on him.

† Since telling that story in 1989, Caldwell has repeated it in several television interviews. Pepper and Herman apparently did not know that while Caldwell might not have been interviewed by law enforcement, he was extensively interviewed by author Gerold Frank only a year after the assassination. According to Frank, Caldwell was in his first-floor motel room, at the Lorraine when the shot was fired, and initially thought it was a bomb, and then a firecracker. He went outside only after he heard considerable screaming and commotion, and then saw King's legs dangling over the edge of the upstairs balcony. He then ran back inside his room to get a pencil, and by the time he again came outside, a crowd of uniformed men was racing toward him, as though they had been hiding in the bushes. Frank reported that Caldwell's first thought was that the police

tion, and flown him to freedom after the assassination. Kimble even maintained that he was Raoul.

Kimble also insisted he flew two snipers to Memphis the week before the assassination, and that Ray was merely a pawn. Ray then appeared on the show to say that Kimble looked very much like someone he had seen on the day of the assassination in Jim's Grill, beneath the rooming house. Support for Kimble's veracity came from a bizarre source, New Orleans district attorney Jim Garrison. Years earlier, Garrison had linked the self-promoting Kimble to the JFK murder, and he now said that "every single statement Kimble gave us turned out to be true without exception—the only information that is not true is what had been planted at that time in his mind at the end of his service by the CIA." According to Garrison, the CIA had somehow inserted the thought into Kimble that he really worked for the Ku Klux Klan, which, according to Garrison, "is really pretty standard operating procedure for intelligence agencies before they dismiss someone."

The producers evidently were not troubled by the fact that the House Select Committee had extensively investigated and dismissed Kimble's ever changing claims ten years earlier. He was not even in Canada at the time Ray had been there. Moreover, under intense questioning from the committee, Kimble had actually admitted that he had never met Ray.[6]

Pepper, however, felt comfortable enough with the show to be interviewed and endorse its theory. Although he had only recently begun his research, the program demonstrated that he already embraced some of the weakest conspiracy issues. He announced not only that the bundle containing the murder weapon had been dropped there by somebody who "had a specific role," but also that the fatal shot came from the bushy area behind the rooming house, not from the bathroom of the house itself. "It is not enough to say that the FBI did it," concluded Pepper. "It is much more complicated than that."

Following the BBC show, Pepper said, "I began to flesh out the bones of the idea of a television trial. . . . I spent two years getting nowhere. Finally, Thames Television in London expressed interest in producing the program. . . . In early 1992 I signed a contract with Thames. It was agreed that both counsel and the judge would be paid reasonable professional fees. I insisted the Ray family also be paid a fee."[7]

---

had been shooting at King, although at the time he did not realize a large contingent of police had been nearby in a fire station (Frank, *An American Death*, p. 82). Somehow, in the nearly twenty years that had intervened between his contemporaneous interview with Frank and his 1989 television interview, Caldwell's memory had changed to a sighting of a possible assassin in the bushes, something that he was physically too late to see in any case.

Jack Saltman, a veteran British television producer, was assigned to the program, and Home Box Office became the American partner. Hickman Ewing, Jr., the former U.S. Attorney for the Western District of Tennessee, agreed to play the prosecutor, and Marvin Frankel, a respected ex–New York District Court judge, was chosen as the jurist. The jury would be composed of people from four states who had completed written questionnaires and submitted to videotape interviews.

Once the mock trial had Thames and HBO financing, one of the first things Pepper did was introduce Saltman to Kenny Herman. By this time, Herman had found a sidekick, six-four John Billings, a forty-three-year-old self-described "mercenary" who had left a rough narcotics-running gang operating out of Arizona and Mexico to become a private investigator.[8] The producers gave Pepper $140,000 to investigate the case, and he used Herman and Billings. But once the word spread among conspiracy buffs that a major television production about the King case was under way, and that Ray's defense lawyer had money to spend, Pepper was besieged. Soon he was paying for leads so wild that even Herman and Saltman were angry.[9] "He spread the money way too thin," complains Herman. "Pepper believes anyone with a story. He's really, really naive. He paid $14,000, sight unseen, for a photo that was supposed to show some military guy shooting King. Of course, there was no picture. He paid $25,000 for stuff about the Army that I knew was junk."*[10]

But despite the discord on the defense team, the money allowed them to prepare effectively for the televised mock trial, often freshly packaging old issues with new witnesses. From the start, Pepper was willing to use a tactic that Jim Garrison had employed with disastrous results: "We wanted several witnesses to be hypnotized to determine whether they could remember anything further," he recalled.[11] The possibility of planting new memories instead of recalling old ones was a risk he evidently thought worthwhile. Most of the matters upon which Pepper and his investigators focused had been settled conclusively fifteen years earlier by the House Select Committee, yet that did not stop them from resurrecting old canards as evidence of a conspiracy: King had never before stayed at the Lorraine and his room was changed at the last moment in order to give an assassin a better shot; two white Mustangs were parked in front of the rooming house on the day of the assassination; and the bullet taken from King's body was mysteriously broken into three pieces as part of a ballistics cover-up.† Pepper relied on the early statements of Solomon

---

* For a detailed discussion of Pepper's theory about the Army and the King assassination, see Chapter 32.

† The confusion over the bullet developed because a Memphis police lieutenant, J. D. Hamby, had signed an affidavit that he had received "one battered lead slug" from the

Jones, the driver assigned to King by the local funeral parlor, about an unidentified man in the bushes across from the Lorraine. Caldwell once again "confirmed" that sighting. James Orange, one of King's aides, now came forward with a new story: that after he heard a shot he saw smoke coming from the same bushes.*

Orange's memory went beyond the smoke he claimed he remembered: He also said that the bushes from which he had seen the smoke emanating were cut down the day after the assassination. That was one of Pepper's favorite issues at the trial—whether the shrubbery across the street from the Lorraine had been mysteriously chopped down the day after the murder, leading to the suspicion that not only had evidence been destroyed, but that it would have shown that a shot from the rooming house bathroom was blocked by the thick foliage. Actually, a Memphis newspaper reporter, Kay Pittman Black, had first raised the question about the shrubbery shortly after the murder. It had become one of the case's enduring areas of speculation, with some conspiracy buffs earnestly comparing numerous photographs to see if the foliage seemed denser the day before the assassination. The House Select Committee tackled the question and could find no records of the City Public Works Department that showed such a cleanup took place, but could not rule it out. In his preparation for the trial, Ken Herman found a public works employee, Willie Crawford, who said that he and another worker had been ordered to the vicinity of

---

Memphis coroner, Dr. Jerry Francisco. By the time the FBI finished its ballistics work with the bullet, it was in three pieces. Pepper added to the mystery by getting former Memphis homicide chief N. E. Zachary to say that when he passed the bullet to the FBI, it was already in three pieces. Was either Zachary or Hamby lying about the condition of the bullet? Had someone intentionally broken it because of fear it might not ballistically match Ray's rifle, dropped at the scene? Actually, the death slug removed from King was in one piece and Zachary's twenty-five-year-old recall was mistaken. Dr. Francisco, who performed the autopsy, is still the Memphis coroner. When the author met him in April 1997, Dr. Francisco produced a color slide of the bullet removed from King, and although battered, it was a single piece. The author then interviewed the FBI's Robert Frazier, now retired, who confirmed the bullet was intact when he received it from the Memphis police. "I am the one responsible for it being in three fragments," he says. "The nose was folded back over the bullet, so in order to examine the microscopic marks and the rifling characteristics, I had to peel the nose of the bullet back. The pieces broke off because the brass gets overstressed. That is typical in any firearm examination where the bullet has mushroomed and you have to get it peeled. I've done thousands of such exams, and very frequently a bullet would fragment like that."

* The problem with Orange's revelation, revealed almost twenty-five years after the event, is that modern firearms and ammunition, such as the Remington Gamemaster rifle and .30-06 bullets, are smokeless. For a fuller discussion on Solomon Jones, see Chapter 6.

the Lorraine the day after the murder in order to cut and clean up the backyard of the rooming house.

But evidently no one checked the local Memphis newspaper archives, where the answer to the mystery is resolved. Trees were indeed cut down and foliage thinned, according to *The Memphis Press-Scimitar*, which reported on the event contemporaneously. However, the work was not done until early August, four months after the assassination.[12]

While Pepper's revelations were generally not new, and there was evidence available to rebut them, the prosecution, led by Hickman Ewing, was not well prepared. Pepper successfully flooded the trial with issues that Ewing had trouble refuting. When James Earl Ray finally testified, from a room in his jail, he performed much better than when he had been grilled by the House Select Committee fifteen years earlier. Unknown to the jury and the viewing public, Ray was being coached by Kenny Herman's sidekick, John Billings. He sat with Ray but was off camera, and passed notes to help Ray with his answers.[13]

The essence of the defense position was summarized by Pepper when he told the jury, "James Earl Ray was manipulated—by forces he does not understand and that he cannot identify. He was a patsy." The scattergun approach worked with the jury, which returned a not-guilty verdict on April 4, 1993, the twenty-fifth anniversary of the murder. Pepper used the verdict to ask the Tennessee governor, Ned McWerter, to free Ray, and for Amnesty International to come to his aid since he was "a true prisoner of conscience." Both rejected Pepper's requests.

Despite the rebuffs, Pepper considered the trial a success. "Its preparation had provided a foundation for the opening up of the case as had never before been possible," he said.[14]

But not everyone who worked with him shared the good feelings. "Pepper turned out to be an idiot," says British producer Jack Saltman. "He was just the easiest touch in the world. Pepper made me commit a lot of money to Jerry Ray, since he couldn't pay James directly. This was a way to pay Jerry. I said it was O.K. if he really worked as a researcher for Pepper. I doubt that Pepper got his money's worth from Jerry. That is part of Pepper's ineptitude. I gave him a lot of money for the show and he did not pay a lot of other people."[15]

Kenny Herman says that he and Billings spent about $40,000 of the production money chasing their own leads, and he personally ended up $17,000 short from Pepper by the time the show aired. Billings was $5,000 in the hole.[16] After the mock trial aired, the two investigators stopped working for Pepper. "But that was all right," says Herman, "because we got a lot of research done for that show, and Jack [Saltman] wanted to produce more shows about the case. Jack and I became partners, and we just agreed to split any money that came in. I'd take care of Billings from my share. And the HBO movie did the trick because people started coming out of the woodwork, and that gave us plenty of things to follow up on."[17] These people coming out of the woodwork were about to change the nature of the case.

30

The Confession

O n December 16, 1993, sixty-seven-year-old Loyd Jowers, the owner of Jim's Grill, which had been beneath the South Main Street rooming house in Memphis, appeared on ABC's *Prime Time Live*. He told cohost Sam Donaldson that he had been paid money to kill King and had hired a gunman to do it. Jowers named Frank Liberto, a deceased Memphis produce dealer who was long rumored to have had mob connections, as the moneyman.[1] Hidden in shadows during the program, Jowers was a powerful witness, who despite the pleading of the ABC producers refused to say more. His attorney, Lewis Garrison, a personal injury and workers' compensation lawyer with an affinity for loud checked suits, closed off further discussion—his client wanted immunity from prosecution before he said anything else.[2]

The Jowers "confession" had the apparent earmarks of authenticity. Many researchers of the case had long suspected that Liberto had some involvement in the assassination. John McFerren, a local civil rights worker, said he had heard Liberto, only an hour before the assassination, tell someone on the telephone, "Kill the son of a bitch on the balcony. Get the job done! You'll get your five thousand." Now Jowers had provided firsthand evidence tying Liberto to the King murder.

Moreover, Kenny Herman, William Pepper, John Billings, and Jack Saltman had worked hard to encourage Jowers to reveal information they thought he was withholding from their HBO mock trial. Pepper had already brought the Jowers information to the attention of the then district attorney general, John Pierotti. Billings was convinced that the investigative work he had done with Kenny Herman was a major breakthrough. "This isn't just a theory," he told a local newspaper. "We know beyond a doubt that James Earl Ray had nothing at all to do with the assassination."[3] Herman, meanwhile, had been looking for witnesses to corroborate Jowers's story.

"Somebody had told me there were waitresses who had worked at Jim's Grill and that I should try to talk to them," Herman told the author. "When I interviewed Jowers before he went on television, he didn't admit anything to me, but told me the names of the girls were Betty and Bobbie. I found Betty Spates. She was actually working across the street from Jim's Grill, at a paper company. She was only sixteen then [1968], and had been Jowers's lover. She told me that on the afternoon of the assassination, she had gone over to the restaurant to visit Jowers, and when she went into the kitchen he was on his knees and had a big gun, a long rifle with a flashlight on top of it, and he disassembled it in front of her. Then he said to her, 'You won't hurt me, will you?' "[4]

Spates told Herman that a week before the murder, she found something else in the kitchen. There were two stoves there, one used for cooking and one that was not used at all. Inside the second one was a box, two feet square and at least seven inches high. It was stuffed with money. "And she remembered there were no ones or fives," says Herman.[5]

When Herman interviewed Bobbie, Betty's sister, she remembered that the morning after the assassination, Jowers picked her up to drive her to work. She was a part-time waitress at his restaurant. " 'You missed everything,' he told her," says Herman. "Then he said he had found the gun used to kill King. But he never showed it to her."[6]

The third witness Herman uncovered was a former taxi driver, James McCraw. "On his third or fourth interview," recalls Herman, "McCraw said that after the assassination, Jowers had shown him a box that contained a gun. 'That's the gun that killed Martin Luther King,' Jowers bragged."[7]

Armed with this new revelation, Herman had driven to Martin, Tennessee, and confronted Jowers with the evidence he had gathered. Jowers denied any complicity and called McCraw and the others liars. It was not until the *Prime Time Live* interview that Jowers abandoned his denials and "confessed" he was part of the conspiracy.

Since that 1993 television appearance, Pepper and other new Ray lawyers, such as Memphians Jack McNeil and journalist turned attorney Wayne Chastain, have tried earnestly either to get the district attorney general to grant

Jowers immunity from prosecution, or to get the grand jury to indict him. Both efforts have consistently failed.*

While the lawyers pushed the legal fronts, Herman and Saltman tried to sell Spates's story of what she knew about Jowers. "For a while it looked like Fox was going for it," says Herman. "We were all going to make a bundle, but after she talked to them it didn't go anywhere."[8] In 1997, a few months after Dexter King, Martin's son, had met with James Earl Ray and endorsed Ray's innocence, Dexter also held a secret meeting with Jowers. The King family, relying largely on Pepper's advice, came to believe that Jowers is one of the keys to unlocking the truth of what really happened on April 4, 1968.

The Jowers confession, however, is not nearly as straightforward as the story presented by Herman and Pepper. Jowers had first been interviewed at length by the Memphis police and the FBI starting on the afternoon of the assassination. The stories he told them are quite different from what he said to *Prime Time Live.* He originally said that on the day of the murder he arrived at Jim's Grill around 3:50 P.M. A white Mustang with out-of-state license plates was parked in his usual parking space directly in front of the restaurant.[9] (That was Ray's car, shortly before he drove it away to buy binoculars.) After parking next to the Mustang, the forty-one-year-old Jowers went into the restaurant. There were a dozen men inside that he recognized, and one stranger, a white man, who was eating eggs and sausages. It was unusual to have a stranger in his out-of-the-way grill—most of the customers were local workers or residents.[†10]

Jowers was standing at the cash register at 6:00 P.M. when he heard a loud noise. He said it sounded like it came from the rear of the building, possibly the kitchen.[11] Thinking that one of his skillets had fallen to the floor, he began walking toward the rear to see what had caused the noise.[12] When he reached

---

* The latest failure was in December 1997. Jack McNeil, together with Herman and Billings, relied on a seldom used statute (4012-104 of the Tennessee Code Annotated) to bypass the district attorney general's office and brought the Jowers information before a three-member panel of the grand jury. That panel had to then decide whether enough evidence existed to recommend that the entire thirteen-member grand jury hear the evidence and consider issuing an indictment. The panel voted unanimously against forwarding the matter to the entire grand jury.

† Ray, not knowing that Jim's Grill seldom saw strangers, told Hanes and Huie that he had met Raoul there. Later that same afternoon, after Raoul supposedly told Ray to leave the rooming house for a few hours, Ray said he again stopped in the grill. However, no one remembered seeing anyone who looked like Ray or his description of Raoul in the restaurant on the day King was killed.

the last booth in the small restaurant, he stopped and asked a regular patron, Harold Parker, if he had heard a noise. Then Jowers looked inside the kitchen door, saw nothing suspicious, and started back to the front of the restaurant. As he was walking toward the cash register, the stranger stopped him and asked for a beer. Jowers served him, and then continued toward the cash register. Then he looked outside and noticed the Mustang was gone. A moment later, a policeman, with his gun drawn, rushed inside Jim's and ordered Jowers to lock the door and not to let anyone out until the police had arrived to take the names and addresses of everyone there.[13] Jowers estimated that the policeman had appeared at the door only several minutes after he and the dozen customers had heard the loud noise.[14]

The next morning the same stranger reappeared and again asked for eggs and sausage. Jowers noticed he was well dressed and considered him "out of place" for the neighborhood.[15] Therefore, he reported him to the police as a suspicious person, and the police arrested the stranger just as he left the restaurant.[16]

Jowers's subsequent descriptions of that stranger should have been the first warning sign that there might be questions about his reliability as a witness. Ten months after the assassination, he told investigators for the district attorney general that the stranger had since become a "regular customer" and his name was Jim Sanders.[17] Then he told Renfro Hays that he had not seen the stranger since the murder, and after looking at a photo lineup said it was actually Walter "Jack" Youngblood, a self-proclaimed adventurer who boasted of ties to the CIA.*[18] Then, years later, Jowers told another researcher that he no longer thought the stranger was Youngblood.[19] But when Pepper showed him photographs of Youngblood, Jowers again flip-flopped. "Yep, that's him all right."[20]

Actually, the stranger's arrest record is in the district attorney general's files, and he was Gene Crawford, a drifter who turned out to have no connection to the case.[21] He was released soon after his arrest. He did not even bear a resemblance to Jack Youngblood.

But even before the Youngblood identification became an issue with Jowers, the district attorney general's office had learned, in early 1969, of a witness

---

*   A local attorney, Russell Thompson, and two Memphis ministers, James Latimer and John Baltensperger, gave variations of a story in which they were visited by a stranger within days of the assassination. The stranger, depending on the version, claimed either his roommate or himself had killed King. The stranger also talked about the Kennedy assassination, which was supposedly a mafia contract. It is not clear why the stranger would have "confessed" his involvement to any of those three strangers, but Pepper at least accepts their accounts as true, and speculates in Orders to Kill that the stranger might have been Youngblood.

who not only insisted that Jowers was involved in the assassination, but also claimed to have seen Ray outside the rooming house at a time so close to the assassination that he could not possibly have gotten back inside in time to shoot King. A month before Ray pleaded guilty, the prosecutors sent investigators to interview the witness, who turned out to be none other than Betty Spates, then seventeen, the same person who popped up twenty-four years later with a different version of the Jowers story for Kenny Herman. At the time, prosecutors did not know that Spates was having an affair with Jowers. When they interviewed her on February 12, 1969, Spates admitted her claims about Jowers were a hoax, and claimed that she had been offered $5,000 by supporters of Dr. King to concoct the story because they did not believe Ray had shot King and wanted to force the prosecutors to expand the investigation.[22] That temporarily closed the Jowers file for the district attorney general.*

Spates's accusation, and her subsequent retraction, was never made public, and as a result, Jowers stayed out of the limelight in the assassination investigation. Early buffs such as Harold Weisberg and Mark Lane, who often made tenuous assertions about people only remotely connected to the case, barely mentioned Jowers in their books.[†23] The only other time he appeared in the case, prior to his sensational confession, was in October 1974, when he testified for Ray in the habeas corpus proceeding, saying that he personally knew Charlie Stephens was "pretty drunk" the day of the assassination and therefore might not be reliable.[24]

However, when Pepper sent the new Jowers evidence to the district attorney general, John Pierotti, in late 1993, Pierotti decided it required a serious investigation.[‡] He appointed a small group within the office to investigate the claim,

---

* The prosecutors had learned of the Betty Spates allegation after she had told a local bail bondsman, James Alexander Wright, that James Earl Ray had not killed King, but that her boss had. The bail bondsman, in turn, had told the Memphis police, who informed the prosecutors. The two investigators for the district attorney general who took Spates's recantation, John Carlisle and Clyde Venson, did not remember obtaining it when asked by Jack Saltman in the mid-1990s. Betty Spates has denied telling a bail bondsman any story, and also denied ever talking to state investigators in 1969. Realizing that such an early involvement in a similar, but fraudulent, story is deadly to Spates's credibility, Saltman and other buffs have tried to raise the inference that the investigator's report in the district attorney general's office is a forgery.

† He was evidently so unimportant to them that both misspelled his name as Lloyd, instead of Loyd. Weisberg mentions him only twice and Lane only once, both in connection with his owning Jim's Grill.

‡ Pepper is naturally suspicious. When he travels, he usually uses a pseudonym, and journalists who have interviewed him when he appears at court say he often wears a bulletproof vest.

as well as other new evidence that Pepper and Herman had uncovered relating
to the long-standing mystery of Raoul (see Chapter 31). Leading the special
task force was John Campbell, a thirty-six-year-old assistant district attorney
general. Campbell, a native Memphian who resembles a young James Caan, is
a devout Catholic and family man, considered by his peers to be one of Memphis's smartest prosecutors. With a rapid machine-gun style of talking, and
dressed stylishly in double-breasted suits and an endless assortment of new
shirts and ties, he reinvigorated the prosecution's dormant investigation of the
case. The best evidence that Campbell was serious in pursuing leads in the King
murder was his request that Mark Glankler be assigned as his investigator.
Glankler, whose father is one of the city's premier attorneys, is a former member of Airborne Special Operations, and before joining the district attorney
general's office was a crime-scene detective for the nearby Germantown police.
The then thirty-nine-year-old Glankler showed a natural affinity for investigative work, winning more merit citations in less time than anyone in department history.

"I didn't know if there was a conspiracy or not in the King assassination,"
says Glankler. "But I knew that once I was on board, I would do my damnedest
to find out if there was anybody or anything out there that had not been found
in the original investigation. My only charge from the general was to find the
truth, whatever that happened to be."[25]

Glankler, together with another investigator, Johnny Simmons, from the
Tennessee Bureau of Investigation, began collecting background information. One of the first things they learned was something that Jowers did not
tell Sam Donaldson on the ABC program: that he had actually provided Pepper and Herman the name of the assassin he hired—Frank Holt, a black man
who had been a local laborer in Memphis in 1968.[26] Holt was supposed to
have shot King from the thick foliage behind Jim's Grill, and Jowers said he
later disposed of the rifle. It turned out that Holt had been walking to Jim's
Grill when the assassination had occurred, and a policeman made him go inside and stay there after the murder. He was one of the dozen patrons from
whom police later took names and addresses that same afternoon.[27] Now
Jowers claimed Holt had been there because he had hired him to kill King.
Jowers then said he had Willie Akins, a man who did some odd jobs for him,
kill Holt.*[28]

---

*   Akins is currently serving a sixty-year sentence in Huntsville, Texas, on a narcotics-
related conviction. The author interviewed Marvin Ballin, Akins's former attorney
in Memphis. "I wouldn't believe Willie if he swore on a stack of ten Bibles. He would
tell a story for money in a New York minute. I always had that feeling when I spoke to
him."

If Holt was dead, it was a safe name for Jowers to give, since no one would be able to test the reliability of his accusation. Holt, however, was alive. Glankler had picked up word that he was living in Florida. He went there searching for him, as did Kenny Herman, who had heard the same thing. The rumor was quickly spread among reporters that the man Jowers had identified as the assassin might still be living, and soon they, too, were hunting for him.

Reporters for *The Tennessean* beat everyone else to the sixty-two-year-old Holt. He was stunned when he heard the accusations against him, and adamantly denied having anything to do with King's killing. To clear his name, he asked for a polygraph, which he took and passed.[29]

Once Holt was found, Jowers and his boosters quickly changed their stories. Pepper claimed that Jowers had merely named Holt in order to "distance himself" from the assassination.[30] Akins, who was supposed to have killed Holt on Jowers's orders, now said Holt had disappeared before he could dispose of him.[31] Jowers privately told his attorney, Lewis Garrison, that Holt might still be involved, but that he was not the shooter.[32]

Pepper, Herman, and Saltman were not dissuaded by the exposure of Jowers's purported hired assassin. Instead, they went their separate ways to exploit the story. Pepper filed an unsuccessful habeas corpus proceeding to free Ray based on Jowers's confession, and Herman and Saltman approached various media outlets hoping to package and sell the story. Disagreement on how best to publicize the story led to the final break between the Pepper camp and what had become the Saltman, Herman, and Billings team.[33]

Pepper set out to obtain sworn statements from the witnesses who had earlier been interviewed by Herman. He intended to use them in a legal action to free Ray. Betty Spates signed an affidavit on March 8, 1994, in which she greatly expanded on her earlier statement to Herman. In her new version, she not only repeated that she had seen Jowers disassembling a rifle at about 4:00 P.M. on the day of the assassination, but now claimed that she also saw him with a rifle when she visited before noon, and again when she returned to the grill around 6:00 P.M. During this last visit, as she walked into the kitchen she heard "a sound like a firecracker" and then "within seconds Loyd [Jowers] came running through the back door carrying another, different rifle. He was white as a ghost and very excited. . . . He looked like a wild man. His hair was all messed up and he had obviously been on his knees on the damp ground because the knees of his trousers were wet and muddy."[34]

Even Pepper, who had spent thirteen hours with Spates in preparation for her affidavit, said, in an understatement, "It was somewhat worrying that this was the first time she had mentioned a second gun."[35] Worse yet for her credibility, but never revealed by Pepper, was that Spates had independently told another of Ray's attorneys, Wayne Chastain, that she had also seen Jowers in the foliage behind his restaurant around noon, testing the gun sight by aiming the rifle toward the Lorraine Motel.[36]

Although the scene Spates described with Jowers was supposed to be one of great panic and excitement, the seventeen-year-old, who admittedly knew nothing about guns, swore that she could tell the gun was different from the one she had seen earlier, since the barrel was shorter and the handle was darker. She watched Jowers hide the rifle on a shelf under the counter. Somehow, no one else in the restaurant saw or heard any of the commotion.

In her affidavit, Spates said that Jowers only twice referred to the incident in subsequent years, but she knew she should not talk about it since Willie Akins, Jowers's part-time worker, had supposedly shown up in 1983 and 1984 and tried to kill her and her two sons, once firing "three shots into a sofa where I was sitting. . . . He told me that Loyd had paid him $50,000 to kill me." Akins also told Spates that "he had followed my sister Bobbi off and on over five years, trying to get her to go out with him so that he could kill her."[37] Spates said she never called the police to tell them about the threats or the attempted murders.

Beyond the credibility problem of a story about a hired killer who shoots a sofa instead of his intended target, there were serious questions with tangential parts of the story she continued to spin to investigators: She said that Jowers had bought her and her sisters a home in Memphis (he had not, and in fact they had borrowed money to get it themselves); she claimed to be working at Jim's Grill that day (she was never officially employed there); she asserted that in 1968, and again in 1973, several unidentified men offered her placement in the witness protection program if she would tell what she knew about Jowers and others (there is no evidence that any such government offer was even considered for Spates); and she said that Jowers had given her the rifle to dispose of, and she had given it to her brother, Essie (she later recanted that).[38] Although she insisted she was in the restaurant at the time of the assassination, the police did not list her as being there. Betty claimed that was because she was black and all the blacks in the restaurant were told to go into the kitchen, where they were ignored while the police took information only from the white customers. In 1968 in Memphis, that sounds plausible. However, Memphis police records show that of the twelve people whose names and addresses were taken down, three were black.[39]

But the key development regarding Spates's story came on January 25, 1994, when Mark Glankler of the district attorney general's office, together with his partner, Johnny Simmons, interviewed her.[40] Spates started by changing her story that she had been at Jim's Grill at 6:00 P.M. She said she had been there "before noon."[41] She admitted that she could not have been at the restaurant at 6:00 P.M. because she distinctly recalled being at the Seabrook Wallpaper Company across the street (where she was a shipping clerk), and "I remember these girls were crying, saying that Dr. King just got killed. . . . And I [then] ran across the street."[42] One of Betty's sisters, Bobbie, did work at Jim's Grill as a waitress, and Betty initially feared something had happened to her. That was why, she said, she ran from her own office to the restaurant after hearing about a shooting. Although she insisted she had seen a gun around noon, she was adamant now that she saw no gun near or after the assassination. As for the box of money, she at first said she had not seen that, but had been told about it by another of her sisters, Alta. (Alta told *The Tennessean* that Betty was simply not trustworthy.) Later, Betty changed her story back again— she had personally seen the money.[43] Spates informed the state investigators that Herman had paid her $500 "as a Christmas present" for her statement. (Herman told the author that Betty was about to be cut off by the local utility company, so he had merely helped her out.)

Finally, after some prodding from Glankler and Simmons, Betty Spates began to confess. She claimed that the story of Jowers having a gun at the time of the assassination had been planted by Herman and Saltman, together with the help of Jowers's attorney, Lewis Garrison. Herman and Saltman, she said, "wanted me to put on a recorder that Loyd was standing in the back door and a black man passed the rifle to him and ran and jumped off the banister, came around the front of the building and the police pushed this same guy that was supposed to have shot King in the door of the restaurant. . . . It was supposed to be that homeless man, Frank Holt."[44] Spates contended that Lewis Garrison, whom she described as "a very mean man," had actually given her the name Holt.[45] (Herman, Saltman, and Garrison adamantly deny all of Spates's charges.)

One night, Spates told the investigators, Jowers, Garrison, and Willie Akins telephoned her on a conference call. To ensure she had a witness to the conversation, she had her son and daughter pick up extension lines and listen to the conversation. The men, she said, told her "that if I had only said that I seen him accept this gun from this black man at six o'clock that we could of split $300,000. So see, I wouldn't have to work anymore." Three hundred thousand dollars was evidently the amount that Jowers and others thought the story was worth for sale. Jowers knew that Spates was behind in her house payments and also owed two years of back taxes. When the investigators asked her if Jowers's motivation in confessing to the crime was to profit from a book or movie, Spates replied, "Yeah, it sure is. . . . [B]ecause its so many people that has said, they say they're from London, they have said how much money that could get for the book that's going to be written and the movie that will be made."[46] Asked if she believed Jowers's story was truthful, she did not hesitate: "No."

Spates's recantation contradicted the sworn statement she provided Pepper a few months later in March 1994. When he learned that she had told two

completely different stories, Pepper said, "We found [it] distressing."[47] He finally obtained a copy of the signed transcript of Spates's interview with the
state investigators and confronted her about the discrepancies. "She said she
didn't read it because her glasses were broken," Pepper asserted.[48] He also put
part of the blame for her changing story on "a brain tumor that affected her
memory from time to time, but until then I had not taken it seriously."

However, unknown to Pepper, Herman, and Saltman, the district attorney
general's investigation had uncovered more evidence that Jowers's story was
not true and perhaps contrived to make money. Lewis Garrison, who represented Jowers, had also represented Willie Akins, the man who supposedly had
tried to kill Frank Holt for Jowers, as well as James McCraw, the taxi driver who
provided corroboration for Jowers's tale. Glankler and Simmons had separately
interviewed Bobbie, Betty's sister. They learned that Herman and Pepper had
visited her initially in December 1992, and she told them that while Jowers
used to keep extra money, a couple of thousand dollars, in the second stove in
the kitchen, there was none there around the time of the assassination. She
had not seen a suitcase filled with cash, and certainly had not told Betty anything of the sort.[49] Bobbie never saw Jowers with a gun, nor had Betty ever told
her about seeing him with a rifle.

Herman and Pepper claimed that, on the day after the assassination, Jowers
told Bobbie that he had the gun that killed King. She also denied that to the
state investigators. Jowers merely said, Bobbie contended, that the murder
weapon had been found by the police right near the restaurant, and that
she had missed all the excitement because she had left work by the time of the
murder.[50]

Bobbie also warned the state investigators that her sister Betty was not honest. "You know you can't believe half of the things Betty says, and that's true."
Betty would, according to Bobbie, lie about "anything . . . Betty would tell a lie
about and then if you don't believe her then she'll sit and cry, make sure so you
will believe what she says. Betty is a big liar."[51] When asked what motivated
Betty to make up the story, Bobbie simply replied, "Money . . . Just to make
money."

With Bobbie's permission, Glankler tape-recorded a telephone conversation between her and Betty on January 21, 1994. Betty, of course, did not
know that her sister was talking to her on behalf of the prosecutors. In that
conversation, Betty admitted that her story about passing a gun from Jowers to
her brother, Essie, was false. "All them lies they got in the paper," she said. "And
then there is Essie, walking around lying. I can't get over that."[52] Essie did not
even live in Memphis at the time of the assassination, Betty said, and anyway,
she had no gun to give him. Again, she said she had only been to the restaurant
around noon, and admitted, "When Martin Luther King got killed I wasn't

there [at Jim's Grill]." It was Jowers, she told her sister, who told her to modify the time in her story. She claimed that on that early visit, Jowers did have a gun, but it "wasn't no bigger than a pistol," not the rifle with a scope she had described to Herman and Pepper.[53] She also admitted she had never seen any money in the stove.[54]

Bobbie then asked her, "Well, why'd Loyd tell you to tell them that you see'd him coming in the back door at six o'clock?"

"Because he can, they can make it into a movie, he'll get paid. . . . That's why Loyd doing this here. He'll get paid $300,000 if he had somebody back this statement up. . . . I was trying to get some money for my, to pay my income tax . . ."[55]

Betty finally admitted to her sister, "I ain't seen no gun."[56]

If Spates's story was concocted, what of the other witnesses who helped corroborate part of Jowers's story? One, John McFerren, supported the proposition that Memphis produce dealer Frank Liberto—who supposedly paid Jowers to arrange the assassination—was indeed connected to the assassination. Pepper and others believe that if Liberto's involvement in the murder is firmly established, that adds credibility to Jowers. Even independent of Jowers's confession, McFerren's story has long been considered one of the most powerful in the case—that of a man without any apparent reason to lie, who may have fortuitously stumbled upon evidence of a conspiracy.

What exactly had McFerren, a civil rights activist who lived in nearby Somerville, said? On April 4, 1968, he went to the Liberto, Liberto and Latch produce market in Memphis. About an hour before the assassination, he overheard a heavyset man, whom he later identified as Liberto, shout into a phone, "Kill the son of a bitch on the balcony. Get the job done! You'll get your five thousand." A little later, he heard Liberto again on the phone, this time saying, "Don't come out here. Go to New Orleans. You know my brother. Get the money from him."[57] The House Select Committee concluded that "an indirect link between Liberto's brother, Salvatore, and an associate of New Orleans organized crime figure Carlos Marcello was established."*[58]

Three days after the assassination, McFerren, afraid of contacting the police, instead called Baxton Bryant, the executive director of the Tennessee Council on Human Relations, a local civil rights organization.[59] In turn, Bryant brought in David Caywood, a prominent attorney who was chairman of the

* Based on McFerren's story, a writer, William Sartor, hypothesized that organized crime was responsible for the King assassination. In his investigation, Sartor attempted to connect Frank Liberto with organized crime figures in Memphis and New Orleans. In an unpublished manuscript, often referred to by conspiracy buffs, Sartor offered one of the wildest mob-related theories about the case; the only thing missing was evidence.

Memphis branch of the American Civil Liberties Union. Bryant and Caywood drove to Somerville, picked up McFerren, and took him to Memphis. After midnight, in a suite at the grand Peabody Hotel, FBI agents and Memphis police officers interviewed McFerren. The authorities then interviewed Liberto and his family members in New Orleans, as well as James Latch, vice president of the produce company.[60] All those interviewed denied any involvement in, or knowledge of, King's murder, but both Frank Liberto and his partner, Latch, admitted making disparaging remarks about King in the presence of their customers.[61] The authorities finally closed the file, concluding that while they could not be sure of the significance of what McFerren claimed to have heard, they were convinced that Liberto was not involved in any plot to kill King.[62]

The House Select Committee on Assassinations reinvestigated the McFerren story, saying, "Because Liberto lived in the Memphis area and because of reports that he had displayed pronounced racial bias, the committee determined that McFerren's story warranted additional investigation."[63]

The committee conducted extensive interviews of Liberto, family members, neighbors, and business associates. It also investigated the backgrounds of Liberto and his brother through the FBI and municipal police departments. Liberto and members of his family, under oath, provided the committee essentially the same information they had given the FBI in 1968. The committee could find no link between Liberto, his family, or his associates and the King assassination.

Moreover, there are serious problems with McFerren's full story. In 1968 he had told the FBI, as well as the Select Committee, that James Earl Ray had worked at the Liberto produce company before the assassination, either in the fall or early winter of 1967.[64] Once, according to McFerren, Ray had even loaded groceries into his car.[65] McFerren also said that Ray was so dark that he initially thought he was Cuban, Mexican, or Indian.[66] He described Ray as about twenty-five years old, with jaundiced skin, coarse black hair, and a fungus on his cheek and neck—"jungle rot" he called it—that left scars and pock marks.[67] Of course, Ray was not even in Memphis at the time McFerren says he worked at Liberto's company.

McFerren also claimed he had positively picked out a photo of Ray for the FBI.[68] However, an FBI memorandum states that when McFerren was shown six photographs of possible suspects, he immediately eliminated three, including one of Ray.[69] On three different occasions, he quickly eliminated Ray's picture. As for the three photos he narrowed it to, one was of a man who had been in prison when King was killed, and two others were not in Memphis on the day of the assassination.[70] The person he finally picked from the photos was a five-five, 152-pound, twenty-five-year-old white man who looked nothing like Ray.

When the FBI agents finally told him which photo was Ray, McFerren suddenly said that he resembled the man who had worked at the market, especially since "the hair is combed the same way."[71]

He also said, regarding the second telephone conversation at the produce market, that he overheard another worker answer the phone and, in passing the receiver to Liberto, say, "Ray wants to speak to you."[72] Among his new disclosures to committee investigators was that Governor George Wallace was supposedly behind the King assassination, and that from his own investigation he had discovered that the same man who killed JFK had also murdered King.[73]

And there are other inconsistencies. The author interviewed David Caywood, who was the ACLU attorney who picked up McFerren in Somerville and took him to the Peabody Hotel, where the police and FBI interviewed him. When asked if he recalled what McFerren told him, he recounted basically the same story that has been given over the years, but said McFerren left out the part of the story that claims Liberto said, "Kill the son of a bitch on the balcony." Even with the passage of years, Caywood was certain that McFerren had never included the phrase "on the balcony." "That would have jumped right out at me," he says. "It would have set off all kinds of bells because the day before King was shot, I was on that very balcony at the Lorraine with him. McFerren did say something about 'shoot the son of a bitch,' but there was nothing about the balcony in anything he told me."[74] By the time the police and FBI interviewed McFerren a few hours later, he had added the balcony to Liberto's purported conversation. That is a critical addition, of course, because it ties the statement directly to the King assassination.

McFerren, over the years, has complained that people followed, threatened, and hurt him because of the information he had.[75] For instance, in 1976, after an initial conversation with House Select Committee investigators, he claimed that he had been shot (the Justice Department did not confirm it) and that "they" were out to get him, but he could not say who "they" were since the police were also after him and his phone was bugged.*[76]

The Select Committee said, "On the basis of witness denials, lack of corroborating evidence and McFerren's questionable credibility, the committee con-

---

* When the author tried to interview him in 1997, McFerren said, "I don't know you are who you say you are. You could be anyone. Send me some proof of who you are." He was subsequently sent a letter of introduction and several previous books. On another trip to the Somerville area, the author again called and asked for an interview. McFerren still refused. "You could have just bought those books and made up some letterhead. I don't know you are the person who wrote those books. Lots of people are trying to get to me. I won't be around here if you come near."

cluded that his allegation was without foundation and that there was no connection between his story and the assassination of Dr. King."*[77]

The McFerren-Liberto story, instead of bolstering Jowers's tale, casts even
further doubt on its authenticity.

The last major witness cited by Pepper and Herman to support Jowers is
James McCraw, the cabdriver. Ten months after the assassination, McCraw gave
a statement to the untiring investigator Renfro Hays. McCraw said that on the
day of the assassination, he had been dispatched around 6:00 P.M. to pick up
Charles Stephens, the boarder who was one of the prosecution's chief witnesses, but discovered he was too drunk to get out of bed.[78] With coaxing from
Hays, McCraw later added that he noticed that the bathroom, which was at the
end of the hallway near Stephens's room, was empty. He never mentioned anything about Jowers or a murder weapon until Pepper and Herman reached
him. The cabdriver, twenty-four years after the event, suddenly remembered
that the day after the assassination, Jowers had shown him the murder
weapon.[79]

The district attorney general's file on the assassination includes taxi company records subpoenaed in 1968, including the master sheet containing
names of employees, times they went on duty, mileage driven and gas used
while on their shift, and the like. On the day of the assassination, McCraw went
to work at 3:15 P.M. and had no call or pickup at the rooming house, where he
claims he saw Stephens and the empty bathroom.[80] "We had no reason to believe that he was even there," says Jim Beasley, the former assistant district attorney assigned to the prosecution.[81] There is also no reason to think that
McCraw's confirmation about Jowers showing him the murder weapon the
next day is any more credible than his statement about visiting the rooming

---

*   A possible motivation for McFerren's story was revealed in an April 18, 1968, interview with the FBI. A week before the assassination, McFerren said, he had been to Liberto's produce market, and one of the workers asked him, "What do you think about
your buddy?" When McFerren asked, "Who are you talking about?" the worker replied,
"Martin Luther King." "I tend to my own business," McFerren said. At that point,
Liberto, who was sitting nearby, said, "Somebody ought to shoot the son-of-a-bitch."
Liberto, after the assassination, admitted that he and some coworkers had made derogatory remarks about King, and might even have said something like McFerren
recounted in that conversation. McFerren, meanwhile, was a civil rights activist and
president of Somerville's Civic and Welfare League, and might have actually thought
after King's murder that the remark he heard the previous week did indicate some level
of foreknowledge on the part of Liberto. In order to boost the impact of his statement,
he may have moved it up to an hour before the assassination and added in some details
he knew about how King was killed. The story might also have been as simply motivated
as punishing Liberto for having made the crude remark the previous week (MURKIN
ME Sub. D, section 3, p. 50).

house at the time of the assassination. Not only did attorney Lewis Garrison represent both Jowers and McCraw, but Garrison admitted to the author that McCraw and Jowers had known each other for many years, and that Jowers even employed McCraw after the assassination. It is possible that McCraw's corroboration was an instance of trying to help his friend Jowers make the big score that he hoped the King confession would bring.*

The state investigators, Glankler and Simmons, have also spoken to Jowers's relatives, including a sister in Memphis. "She knows that he is not telling the truth, but she won't say much more to get him in trouble," Glankler says. "They are really afraid that he has already said so much that he might actually go ahead and get himself indicted."[82] Glankler also located a friend of Jowers's, Robert Ferguson. "Jowers told me before he ever went on TV that he was going to have a movie made about the King assassination," recalls Ferguson, who counts himself as one of Jowers's closest friends for nearly a decade. "And he told me he was going to be in the movie. I did not believe it then, and do not believe it now. I think it was one Budweiser too many in his mouth."[83]

Ferguson brought up something that Pepper, Herman, and Saltman have failed to disclose: Jowers has been an alcoholic since the late 1970s. "He's drunk seventy-five percent of the time," his lawyer, Lewis Garrison, told the author.[84]

Moreover, Jowers's own story has changed dramatically during the past few years, growing in scope and ambition, casting further doubts on his reliability. Jowers refused to meet with the author, but Lewis Garrison did pass along Jowers's latest version. When the author met Garrison in his Memphis office in April 1997, he had spoken with his client only two days earlier.

Jowers now claims that Liberto approached him in early March 1968, "when they knew Dr. King was coming here."[85] (The SCLC had not decided that

---

* Another witness sometimes cited to boost Jowers is Nathan Whitlock, a thirty-eight-year-old cabdriver whose mother owned a Memphis pizza parlor that Liberto frequented in the 1970s. Whitlock claimed that when he was only eighteen he had heard the rumors about Liberto and the King assassination and confronted him. Liberto supposedly told him, "Well, I didn't kill [King], but I had it done." When Whitlock asked about Ray, Liberto said he was "nothing but a troublemaker from Missouri" and a mere "set-up man." Whitlock swore to this in a November 3, 1994, deposition in a civil suit Pepper filed on behalf of Ray against Jowers. ABC News, and Sam Donaldson, used Whitlock to substantiate the story they aired about Jowers. But it stretches credulity that Liberto, who supposedly masterminded the King assassination and kept it a secret from everyone, somehow admitted it to a teenager who suddenly confronted him. Even Kenny Herman, who liberally accepts most new testimony, is skeptical about Whitlock. "Oh, watch out, he's definitely capable of making up stories, and he's very interested in what money he might make out of this," Herman told the author. "He's always asking when the big payoff is coming."

King would return to Memphis until March 30, 1968.) Further, there was no
$100,000 payment for the murder. Some money was involved, but primarily
Jowers did it in order to cancel gambling debts he owed Liberto. Jowers says
there were at least two meetings to plan the assassination, both held at Jim's
Grill. Each one was attended by Marrell McCollough, the Memphis police department undercover officer; Sam Evans, head of the police tactical units; Inspector N. E. Zachary, chief of homicide; and two or three others that Jowers
did not recognize.* As for Ray, Jowers now claims to have seen him at least
three times on the day of the assassination, always at the grill, and says that
while Ray was part of the plot, he was not the shooter.

According to Garrison, another man who appeared at the restaurant gave
Jowers money in a box. "Jowers is hard of hearing," says Garrison, "and
thought the man said his name was Royal, but he now knows it was Raoul."[86]
Garrison says Raoul was the one who killed King. "Raoul came in around five-
thirty and took the gun and went out back. Later he gave the gun to Jowers
after the shooting, and Jowers wrapped it in a tablecloth. The next day he came
and retrieved it."[†]

In fact, all the fanfare about Jowers and his confession might never had gotten
off the ground if researchers had merely compared Jowers's original statements to the FBI and the Memphis police to the statements of other customers
in Jim's Grill. Jowers had initially said that after hearing the loud noise, he

---

* Most people named by Jowers are deceased. Lewis Garrison told the author that
"Zachary is also dead, so we can't follow up with him." Actually, the author found
Zachary; he is still living in Memphis, and was infuriated at the allegation. "I will be very
happy to take them into court for that slander," he said. "I could use a little extra money
in my retirement." McCollough is alive, works for the CIA, and has steadfastly refused to
comment on the case or his surveillance on King.

In October 1997, when Jowers met with William Pepper and Dexter King, he again
changed his story and included two more Memphis policemen, John Barger and Earl
Clark, in the plot. Both were also deceased.

† Although Garrison was still saying, as late as August 1997, that the real murder
weapon had disappeared after the assassination and that the gun found with Ray's
prints was a planted weapon, he was evidently unaware that his client had flip-flopped
on that very issue. When a Criminal Court judge, Joe Brown, ordered in March 1997
that Ray's rifle be tested once again to see whether new technology might be able to ex-
clude or include the death bullet as having come from that gun, Jowers evidently feared
the tests might match the bullet to Ray's gun. That, of course, would gut his story. So he
called Mark Glankler, the state investigator, and told him, "Ray's gun *is* the real gun.
That was the one that shot King." It is not clear how that could fit into any previous version he has told.

walked toward the kitchen but paused by the last booth and asked a regular patron, Harold Parker, if he had heard a noise.[87] When Parker was interviewed by the FBI on April 15, 1968, he was unaware of what Jowers had told the authorities, yet he confirmed that Jowers had stopped by his table and asked if he had just heard the noise. A few minutes later a deputy sheriff entered the restaurant and told everyone to remain there.[88] That corroboration of what Jowers really did is the most effective refutation of the claim that he was running back inside the restaurant with the rifle that killed Martin Luther King.

Some people, convinced of a widespread conspiracy, are not dissuaded by the facts. "If you grant Jowers immunity," said Martin's son Dexter King, "he will tell everything he knows. There's a cover-up going on. They don't want him to talk. They're contributing to suppressing the truth."[89]

"We will not give him immunity," says John Campbell, the assistant district attorney general who has led the investigation into the Jowers story. "From investigating it, it looks real bogus. But if we get pressured into giving him immunity, that would be a disaster. Overnight, the value of Jowers's story would skyrocket. With immunity, he could say anything he wants to. Hell, he could hold a press conference and say he killed King and there would be nothing anybody could do about it. Also, just by the fact that he had immunity from the state, it would imply we thought there was some validity to his story, and that would also increase the value of what he could sell it for. We are not going to help someone, or a group of people, make a financial killing with a false story."[90]

31

Exit Raoul

It is significant that in Loyd Jowers's recent versions of his confession, he has included Raoul at his restaurant on the day King was murdered. Raoul is still an integral part of Ray's defense, and Pepper, Saltman, Herman, and Billings claim a breakthrough regarding Raoul that is as startling as their work with Jowers. Some who have seen the results of their Raoul investigation believe the longstanding mystery has been resolved. "Raoul has been found," announced Dexter King in April 1997 after meeting with Pepper.[1]

The break in the Raoul investigation came much the same way as that with Jowers—in the wake of the 1993 HBO mock trial of James Earl Ray, somebody came forward claiming to have new information. In mid-1994, Glenda Grabow, a forty-nine-year-old attractive blonde from Booneville, Tennessee, came to the attention of Lewis Garrison. Her husband, Roy, first called Garrison. "He told me that his wife had some information that I'd probably be interested in," recalls Garrison. " 'I've been trying to get her to come forward for twenty-five years. But she's real scared.' They came in a couple of days later. Turns out she had known Raoul down in Texas. She had some picture of his cousin."[2]

Glenda and Roy had read about Garrison and his representation of Jowers. They had decided that if Garrison was good enough for Jowers, then he was the one to whom they should speak.

"Garrison called me right away," recalls Kenny Herman. "He knew all I was doing on the case, and I knew him anyway."[3] Herman met Glenda and Roy and heard an astonishing story, which William Pepper set forth in his 1995 book, *Orders to Kill.* Glenda had grown up in Houston, where she met a Spanish man in his early thirties. Although she called him Dago, she said his real first name was Raul.* She met him in 1962 when she was only fourteen. At the time, Glenda said, she was being physically abused by an older relative, and she became friendly with Raul, who was protective of her. In 1966, Raul moved away. Around this time, she and Roy made the acquaintance of another Spaniard, named Amaro, who had the same surname as Raul—which in this book is given as Mirabal.[†] She did not know it, she said, but Amaro was Raul's cousin. Through Amaro, Glenda became involved with a group that made false passports and dealt in arms smuggling. In 1970, Raul moved back to Houston. By that time, Amaro had confided to her that Raul had killed Martin Luther King.

Reunited with Raul, Glenda helped him in the arms and passport business, frequently driving him to a local movie theater, where he met with associates of Carlos Marcello. One day in the mid-1970s, she visited a house where Amaro and Raul were meeting with several other men. She happened to be carrying a souvenir-type key ring that had small pictures of John Kennedy, Robert Kennedy, and Martin Luther King. When Raul saw it, she said, he exploded in anger.

"I killed that black SOB once and it looks like I'll have to do it again." He then stomped the plastic key ring to bits and dragged her into another room, where he raped her.[4] Glenda never reported the rape to authorities, and made an effort to keep her distance from Raul.

In 1978, when one of Roy's brothers was arrested for murder, she says they mortgaged their house for $5,000 and hired trial lawyer Percy Foreman. Foreman, besotted by her glamorous looks, had an affair with her and always wanted her around the office. When he learned, however, what she knew of Raul and the King murder, he changed. Foreman also knew Raul, Glenda asserted, and in 1979 Foreman said her life was in danger. Not long after, she lost control of her car on the freeway when a tire, which had been sabotaged, came

---

* This man spelled his name differently (*Raul*) not the way Ray and his previous lawyers spelled it (*Raoul*). Ray and Pepper have now changed their spelling of the name to *Raul* so it matches that of the person described by Grabow. In this chapter, whenever referring to the person described by Grabow, the author also uses the *Raul* spelling.

† Court documents that identify the person fingered as Raoul are sealed, because in absence of proof that he is involved in the case, disclosure of his name would certainly injure his reputation. Press reports about him, even in those instances in which journalists have known his name, have not included it.

off. That made her and her husband leave Houston.[5] Until she told all this to Garrison, she had kept it a secret out of fear for her life.

Garrison and Herman listened intently to her story. "Glenda and Roy are real simple country folk," says Herman. "Too simple to make it up." Herman told Saltman about what he heard. Both men were intrigued.[6] When Saltman met Glenda, he thought she was "near a fruitcake, undoubtedly unusual, as flaky and as totally screwed up as they come, but her story was either the work of a genius in terms of creativity or it is true."[7]

Glenda and Roy said they were willing to go to Houston to see if any of the people they knew were still around, so Herman gave them $300 for expenses. Roy ended up giving $100 back, which convinced Herman and Saltman that the couple was not after money, and therefore enhanced their credibility.[8]

When the couple returned and told Herman that some of the people they had known were still in Houston, Herman and Saltman decided to make their own research trip.[9] Glenda had told them that Amaro was a seaman, so the two men visited the Seafarer's International Union in Houston and discovered there was indeed a listing for Amaro. "Jack used his English background to charm everyone," Herman recalls, chuckling at the memories. "He used to always talk about how he knew Prince Charles, and after that they'd want to do anything to help him."[10] At the union, Saltman managed to convince a clerk to "leave Amaro's file on the desk when he went to the bathroom, and I looked at it. It told us that he had gone to Brazil in 1990."[11] Amaro would have been in his nineties if alive, but when the two men checked further they determined that he was dead. When they discovered how old Amaro was, they decided Glenda was wrong in concluding that Amaro and Raul were cousins, and it was more likely that Amaro was his uncle.

They spent another four days in Houston, talking to people who remembered Amaro. "Quite a few people remembered him and Glenda," says Herman. "We couldn't find anybody then who knew Raul, but that was because he would only show up for a week or so at a time and then disappear again."[12]

Herman then made what he considered a breakthrough. He used a $39 CD-ROM with U.S. telephone numbers and searched for a Raul Mirabal. He found two. "One was too old," he says. "The other one lived in New York, and was the right age."[13]

It did not seem to bother Herman that for him to have located the right person, he had to assume that a criminal who was involved in smuggling narcotics and guns with Ray, and then was the mastermind of the King assassination, used his real first name with Ray and then, after all the crimes, not only failed to change it, but actually listed himself in the phone book. "I don't know," says Herman, who shrugged his shoulders when questioned about how unlikely that was. "I've seen people do some strange things. It's possible," he said, as though he was trying hard to convince himself it was a reasonable assumption.*

"Well, in any case, I've got a law enforcement contact," he boasts, "who can get into CIA records, and he got me one page of Raul's last name, his address, the Portugal arms factory he worked at before he came to the U.S. It was his immigration file. I went back to my contact the next week to get more info from the CIA file but my source told me it had all been removed by then."[14]

"Kenny called me up," recalls Saltman, "and said, 'I found Raul!' He gave me his number so I called him. Now, I have a tape unit on my phone where I can record conversations, but I didn't start it. It turned out to be the day of his daughter's wedding. 'I am a friend of your uncle's,' I told him, 'and I met him when I was in Liverpool. Your uncle used to be in the merchant marine and he lived in Houston and you used to live there with him?' 'Yes,' he said. 'But it is my daughter's wedding. Please call back later.' Then I never got him again."[15]

Starting in October 1994, Saltman and Herman placed the New York Raul under a full investigation. John Billings wanted to use hard tactics. "I wanted to just get the truth out of him," says Billings. "I would have done it the way I'm used to, put him in the trunk of a car with a bag over his head. A bag really scares them into talking. If you don't use a bag, and just try to knock it out of them, it takes two or three days to break someone."[16] Saltman and Herman overruled him. Instead, using a 500mm telephoto lens, Herman stalked Raul's suburban house, snapping photos of him and his wife, daughter, grandchildren, and neighbors.[17] Herman began checking real estate records, credit unions, tax records, and local employment rolls. Although Raul was retired, Herman could not initially determine where he had worked. With a New Jersey–based freelance television producer, Mike Chrisman, he decided to get Raul's fingerprints to see whether they might match any of the unidentified prints left over from the King assassination. In November 1994, state elections were held in New York. Using election poll canvassing as a cover story, Chrisman knocked on Raul's door. "He had written down ten or twelve questions about which political party was best, and things like that," recalls Saltman. "The questionnaire was inserted into a plastic folder and when Raul took the folder he left his prints on it."[18] John Billings, who learned how "to lift prints in the Boy Scouts," found eight prints on the plastic folder, three of which were good for identification.[19] Raul and his family had no idea they were under suspicion.

From his secret source, Herman obtained a faxed copy of a photo that purported to be Raul's November 1961 snapshot from his Immigration and Natu-

---

* Jerry Ray testified before the House Select Committee that "the guy just calls him[self] Raoul. . . . That wasn't his real name."

ralization file. Herman then decided to put together a photo lineup to show to Glenda and others who might have been able to identify Raul from the 1960s. "It wasn't professional, but it was pretty good." (Herman showed the author how he used a handheld video camera to shoot the photos and a video-capture software program to transfer them to his computer. Then he adjusted them to appear similar in density and contrast). He could not remember all five of the other people whose pictures he used, but he took them from books in his study. "One was Carlos Marcello [the New Orleans godfather]," he says, "another was Frank Ragano [Marcello's lawyer], and Allen Dorfman [one of Jimmy Hoffa's closest associates]. I'm not sure of the other two."[20]

When Herman showed the six-person photo lineup to Glenda Grabow, "she pointed Raul out with no hesitation. She was sitting at the kitchen table in my house and zeroed right in on the guy."[21] Saltman was there that day, and he suggested that the group visit Grabow's younger brother, who lived nearby and had said he remembered seeing Raul. He also picked him from the lineup.[22] The next day, he repeated the identification in front of John Billings, who notarized his statement.

Over the next few months, Herman and Saltman found others they say picked the right picture. One of them was April Ferguson, a federal public defender based in Memphis who had been lover and cocounsel to Mark Lane when he was Ray's attorney before the House Select Committee in the late 1970s. Once more, the setting was Herman's kitchen table, and again Saltman was there. "I put the spread on the table," recalls Herman. "She picked out the photo right away, real fast. 'That photo used to be passed all around back around the time of the congressional hearings,' she told us. 'I remember seeing it back then. Investigators for the committee had it . . . we had no money to follow up on it then.' "[23]

The next confirmation was from Gene Stanley, the attorney who had represented Randy Rosenson before the Select Committee in 1978. It was Rosenson's business card Ray claimed to have found under his car seat when he reentered the United States from Mexico in October 1967. "It turned out we had actually interviewed Stanley for the HBO trial but he never ended up appearing, since his testimony would have been double hearsay," says Saltman. "He also said that in 1978 they [Select Committee investigators] had shown him that photo and told him it was Raul."[24]

Both April Ferguson and Gene Stanley convinced Saltman and Herman that the Select Committee had focused on the same Raul they had uncovered, but then somehow the investigation stalled.

But the most important person identifying Raul in the photo lineup was James Earl Ray himself. In over twenty-five years, Ray had failed or refused to identify anyone positively as Raoul—he told the Select Committee that he would not do so, even if shown a photo. However, Ray had intimated at times that one or another person looked like, and might even be, Raoul. For a while, the candidate was one of the three tramps whose picture was snapped at Dealey Plaza after the Kennedy assassination.[25] Then the candidate was Randy Rosenson, whose card Ray found in his Mustang. Another time it was possibly Raul Esquivel, a Louisiana state trooper who had been traced through a telephone number that Charlie Stein, Ray's travel mate to New Orleans in 1967, suddenly "remembered."[26] Then, when Esquivel seemed unlikely as a possible Raoul, it was Jules Ricco Kimble, the racist who claimed the assassination was part of a convoluted CIA plot.[27] Yet another time, Ray, as well as his brother Jerry, implied it could be a man named Reynard Rochon, but when he turned out to be a successful black accountant in New Orleans, the suspicion did not go very far.[28]

By failing to positively identify any single person, Ray had thus far avoided putting himself on a ledge from which his long-standing alibi might crumble. Therefore, when Saltman and Herman decided to approach Ray, they were not hopeful he would make a concrete identification. Kenny Herman and John Billings visited Ray in prison. "He looked at the pictures very carefully," recalls Herman. "He was really examining them. Then he picked out the shot of Raul."[29] The following week, John Billings and Jack Saltman again visited Ray. They once more laid the photo spread in front of him. "James not only picked it out instantly, but also said he had seen the same photo in 1978," recalls Saltman.[30] Ray also identified the photo before his lawyer, William Pepper, as well as in a deposition in 1995 taken by attorney Lewis Garrison.[31] His positive identification of Raul was a critical turning point in the case.

When William Pepper had picked up word about the breakthrough, he and his Memphis cocounsel, Wayne Chastain, wanted to be let in on the investigation. "Pepper thought he [Raul] lived in Philadelphia, and that his family was in Brazil," says Saltman. "Finally, we told Pepper everything and gave him all the details about Raul."[32] By the spring of 1995, Pepper began devising ways to make Raul part of a legal proceeding in Memphis, one that might force him to be publicly exposed. "We want to depose this guy," said Pepper. "We think that's the case right there."[33] Pepper also added a witness of his own, who had selected the right photo from the picture lineup: Sid Carthew, a merchant seaman who claimed he had met a Raul in the Neptune Tavern in 1967, and that Raul had been interested in selling guns.[34]

At that point, Memphis district attorney general John Pierotti says, Saltman called and told him that Raoul had been found, that they had some fingerprints, and that they would provide the information to Pierotti's office so long as they had the exclusive right to broadcast the final results of the investigation. Pierotti said no.[35]

Unknown to Saltman, Herman, and Billings, the district attorney general had found out about the New York Raul shortly after Glenda had first contacted Lewis Garrison. One day early in the investigation, at the prosecutor's office, another of Ray's Memphis lawyers, Mac Dickinson, had let slip the name of the New York Raul.[36] Pierotti had turned the Raoul issue, together with the Jowers matter, over to the special squad he had formed inside the prosecutor's office.*

Mark Glankler and his partner, Tennessee Bureau of Investigation agent Johnny Simmons, began collecting background information on the New York Raul. First, they got his Immigration and Naturalization file. Then they checked all records through local, state, and federal law enforcement. Once they discovered that he had been employed by one of the "Big Three" auto-makers, they started compiling his work records, pension contributions, and a list of fellow employees to interview.[37]

In November 1994, not long after Herman and Saltman had been there, Glankler, Simmons, and two New York State police officers went to Raul Mirabal's house. No one was home, so they left a business card with a local telephone number. When he returned later that day, Raul called the number on the card. Glankler told him that he needed to talk to him about an ongoing investigation. The heavily accented Raul let them come to his home.[38] When the police and investigators arrived, just Raul and his wife were there—their daughter and son-in-law, who lived with them, were still at work. Glankler began asking Raul questions about his background, work, family, and travels. Finally, perplexed, Raul wanted to know what all the questioning was about. At that point, Glankler took out a file several inches thick and explained to the shocked retiree that James Earl Ray's investigators thought he was the master-mind of the King assassination. "At first I laughed," Raul told the author in his only on-the-record interview. "I thought it's crazy. I didn't take it very seriously because it made no sense to me. I was not the person, so it was a mistake, and would all be over with. That's what I thought, at least."[39]

"I tried to explain the implications to him," says Glankler. "I had to search his house, to look for anything incriminating. Eventually, I was very comfortable with what he had to say."[40]

Glankler asked for, and received, permission to take Raul's fingerprints. Then he warned the Mirabals not to speak to anyone and to be wary of

---

* The special team, led by Assistant District Attorney General John Campbell, not only had the Jowers and Raul stories to track down. Other "leads" continued to pour in after the HBO trial. Among them, one involved a Raoul who supposedly lived in Mississippi, another was about a Raoul in Pennsylvania, and there was even an intricate tale of a man who claimed to be oilman Bunker Hunt's accountant. He said he could prove Hunt had paid for the King assassination. None of the new leads panned out when investigated.

strangers near the house. Mrs. Mirabal became anxious. Is it possible, she asked, that if people learn of this, someone might believe it and attack us or our children or grandchildren? Glankler said it was unlikely, but he was concerned about what could happen to the Mirabals if the Ray team publicly fingered them. "They were a little scared by the end," he recalled.[41]

What had Glankler and Simmons learned from their own investigation that convinced them that Ray's team had almost certainly fingered the wrong man?[42] Raul was sixty years old, having immigrated to the United States in December 1961. In Portugal, he had worked for six years as a secretary in a munitions factory, after having served his mandatory four years in the army.* He was the first member of his family to come to the States, and had no family member called Amaro. The only reason his last name was even Mirabal was that as the youngest of three brothers, he followed a Portuguese tradition and carried his father's middle name as his surname.[43] Otherwise, he would not even have come up in a search by Ken Herman. More important, he had worked from January 1962 to 1992 for the same automaker. His employment records revealed that he took normal vacations, but had never taken an extended leave of absence, or the time necessary to have been with Glenda Grabow for months at a time.[44] He was at work on the day of the King assassination. Moreover, until 1980, he had never been anywhere else in the United States except for Portland, Oregon, where he once went for his work. On the way back to the East Coast, his plane stopped in Chicago, but he did not leave the airport. He has never been to Texas or Tennessee.

When Glankler and Simmons left Raul, they still had one thing left to do before they were completely convinced that Ray's team had picked an innocent man—run his fingerprints against all unmatched prints in the King file. The report from the FBI came back with no matches. That essentially closed the file for the district attorney general, but unfortunately for Raul, Ray's defense team was increasing its efforts to prove his guilt.

When Saltman learned that Raul had held a job for thirty years and could not have been where Grabow claimed he was, he developed a ready answer: "We were told by a very big firm of investigators that two FBI agents were told

---

* Of course, conspiracy buffs such as Pepper try to tie the fact that the New York Raul once worked in a munitions factory with the fact that Ray claimed his Raoul had asked him to buy a rifle for a gun-smuggling operation in Memphis. Also, when Raul applied for his work at the American automaker, he listed his former munitions job as "mechanic's assistant." He told the author he did so because he thought having a mechanics background would be helpful at the assembly line factory to which he had applied. However, to Saltman, it means that Raul "was shipping arms illegally from the arms factory he worked in—he was in a department shipping weapons, and was known to be shipping privately guns out."

to create a false legend for this man."[45] "They can make up paperwork to say whatever you want it to say," says Billings. "Hell, think about it. They can kill people by inducing heart attacks and putting cancer cells into bone marrow to get cancer growing in you [which is medically impossible]. If they can do that, they can certainly come up with some paperwork to cover something up."*[46]

Meanwhile, Glenda Grabow began calling Raul's home almost nightly, saying, "Don't you remember me, please, don't you?"[47] Herman took Grabow to Raul's neighborhood and they camped out, waiting for him to leave the house. Warned by Glankler, who had picked up word of the trip, Raul and his family remained inside for several days. Meanwhile, Raul, who had started a small import business in his retirement, discovered that Herman and Billings were questioning his colleagues, raising insinuations about him that were causing concerns even among longtime friends.†[48] One day, Saltman and Herman showed up at Raul's house, wanting to talk to him. His wife answered the door. When she realized who they were, she ran to the rear of the house, screaming in anger. His daughter sprinted to the front and sent them away.

"It was starting to wear on us after several months," recalls his daughter. "We all live in the same house, and my mother is a very nervous person anyway. Well, this really put a terrible strain on us. We had to tape our calls to give over to the state police so they could monitor what was happening."[49]

"It was a turmoil," recalls Raul. "We were always worried that if this crazy charge comes out, it would endanger us."[50]

Early in the spring of 1995, William Pepper called and talked to Raul's daughter. He wanted to meet her father. The family said no. Pepper's response was to serve Raul with a summons on July 5. It was actually an existing civil suit that Pepper had brought for false imprisonment, on behalf of Ray, against

---

* Billings is an avid conspiracy buff who says that in his business as a private investigator "there is no such thing as coincidence." He talked to the author about far-fetched plots. Among them, he thinks the prison recently tried to give Ray a diet that would kill him. Billings was even suspicious of my wife and me, reluctant to talk to us because of my 1993 book, *Case Closed*, in which I concluded Oswald acted alone in killing JFK. As for Billings, the day we met at his home, he had just received a telephone call informing him that he could not visit Ray the next day since Billings had a charge pending against him for sneaking contraband (a knife) to a prisoner. "I find it really suspicious," Billings told us, "that you walk through my door at the very moment I get a call that says I cannot see James tomorrow. Something is not right about that. It just can't be a coincidence."

† Saltman and Herman both told the author that they had questioned distributors in Raul's new business and that no one knew him, something they found suspicious. In fact, the other importers did know Raul. When they were contacted by the investigators and asked a series of detailed questions, they proclaimed ignorance, and then called Raul directly to tell him about the unusual inquiries.

Loyd Jowers and the unidentified Raoul. Now that Pepper had a name, he added the New York Raul to the suit.

"What is this?" Raul asked his daughter. "What do we do now?"[51]

"I knew we could not use a small-town lawyer to stop this," she says. The next day at work, at a financial institution, she talked to her boss. He referred her to the company's attorneys, a prestigious Manhattan firm, Reboul, Mac-Murray, Hewitt, Maynard & Kristol. A meeting was set up, but when Raul's daughter explained their problem, the company lawyer mistakenly assumed it was a criminal matter and called in Ed McDonald, a partner and the former U.S. attorney for the Eastern District of New York. McDonald immediately realized it was a civil suit and brought in Janet Mattick, a partner specializing in civil litigation.

"I really felt sorry for these people," recalls Mattick, "so I suggested to Ed that we should take it on pro bono. They clearly did not have the money to pay us, and since it was a Tennessee matter, they were already going to have to hire local counsel there and that would certainly cost them. Ed agreed."[52] "I'll eat my shoes in front of everyone if this guy had anything to do with the King assassination," McDonald announced to the firm's partners.*[53]

In Memphis, John Pierotti had resigned as the district attorney general, and he persuaded a colleague in private practice, David Wade, to take the case on a reduced fee. Still, as the legal wrangling intensified, the costs mounted.

"It's the part that made my father so very upset," recalls Raul's daughter. "These were his life savings that he had put aside after thirty years of work, and now he was spending it on lawyers over something that he knew was completely false. It really hurt."[54]

In Memphis, the court records were temporarily sealed to ensure that Raul's name did not become public. Soon, however, Pepper sent a notice of deposition for Raul's wife and extensive interrogatories for both of them. Janet Mattick, who had already made a motion to dismiss, asked the court to postpone the deposition, and she advised her client not to appear. That left Pepper cooling his heels at the appointed time and place.[55] The motion to dismiss was finally granted in February 1996, and the court permanently sealed the record.

But even the dismissal of the suit did not end Raul's problems. Ray's team then turned to selected press contacts, and the next thing the supposedly anonymous Raul knew, a Memphis reporter showed up at his door, a New York *Daily News* reporter camped outside his house, and local television cameras

---

* There has been much suspicion over the fact that such a prominent firm represents Raul, who evidently could not afford their services. However, few know about the firm's pro bono decision.

chased him from his backyard.[56] Although none used his last name or precise location in their reports, it did not help his mood. "Even when the suit was dismissed, it did not make me feel better," he recalls. "My whole life was in chaos. I couldn't go into my own backyard, or walk around in the town. We actually thought of moving back to Portugal, but my wife and I did not want to leave our grandchildren."[57]

Behind the scenes, unknown to Raul and his family, things were getting worse. Saltman was now trying to sell the story to an American television network, with himself as producer and Herman and Billings as consultants. ABC News, which had broken the Jowers story, was interested. "Yeah, I talked to the producer all the time," recalls Herman. "They actually got copies of seven of the thirty-seven unidentified prints in the King case, and they wanted to match the three prints we had lifted from Raul. They came to my house. But eventually there was no match between the prints, so they sort of lost interest."[58] Then Saltman got the attention of *60 Minutes*. The leading CBS news program spent nearly a month looking into the story. "*60 Minutes* was really interested," says Saltman. "They paid plenty for three weeks of our research. But they wanted more and told us they would run it when we had a smoking gun. At that point I wouldn't need them—I could do the show myself."*[59]

In March 1997, Saltman and Herman went to the district attorney general and met with John Campbell and Mark Glankler. Not knowing that the prosecutor's office had been aggressively investigating the case for more than two years, Saltman and Herman hoped to convince the office to undertake an inquiry into the man they had pinpointed as Raul.

"We had three good prints from Raul," says Saltman. "We gave them to Glankler and said, 'Please match this against the prints unidentified in the case.' He never got back to me. I don't know if they have done anything with it."[60]

"I don't know what Saltman is talking about," says Campbell. "We gave them all the info about the prints about a month later. They know there is no match there. Maybe they just don't want to hear that."[61]

"The shame in all of this fiasco," former district attorney general John Pierotti told the author, "is that I think this is a cruel hoax against this innocent man in New York. I do not have the proof, but I bet the Ray people know it's wrong."[62]

---

* *60 Minutes* was still interested in the Raul story as late as January 1998. Mike Chrisman, who worked with the CBS team at the time of their original interest, said that producer Phil Sheffler still called on a "regular basis" to check on the status of the research. "If we can put a couple of more things together," says Chrisman, "they are ready to run a program."

The author uncovered information that supports Pierotti's view that the Ray team has at least not told the truth about everything it discovered. This conclusion centers on Glenda Grabow, the woman who instigated the entire Raul hunt. The author obtained a two-hour video of Grabow being questioned by Jack Saltman. It raises extremely disturbing questions about the accuracy of her story as well as her own stability. In it, Grabow refers to Raul as Dago. Pepper has said that Dago was only a "nickname."[63] However, at the beginning of the tape, when she first refers to him as Dago, Saltman interrupts her and says, "Let's call him Raul for this interview." (In September 1997, Grabow told the district attorney general's office that she never knew his name was Raul until she learned it in a session when the defense team placed her under hypnosis.[64]) During the often rambling tape, Saltman sometimes asks leading questions and puts words in Grabow's mouth. At one point, when she stumbles with an answer, he says, "It doesn't matter if you get it wrong, we can go back." At several points, the tape is stopped and then restarted. Grabow appears to be medicated, often having trouble understanding straightforward questions, laughing at inappropriate times, and occasionally wandering away from the conversation.

She tells a remarkably different story to Saltman from the one presented to the public in William Pepper's *Orders to Kill*. On the tape, Grabow's most explosive disclosures are not about the King assassination, but rather about Raul and the Kennedy assassination. According to Grabow, she had seen Jack Ruby in Houston four or five times during 1962 and 1963 (even though there is no evidence that Ruby was ever in Houston), and he used to meet there with Raul. Two to three weeks before JFK arrived in Texas, Ruby again visited Raul in Houston. "They talked, 'He's coming to town,' " Grabow says. "He [Ruby] brought some uniforms, a light blue, and a tan, and a dark uniform, and hat all in paper bag, and they were talking about stuff like Mr. Lee and stuff. I wasn't paying too much attention."

On November 21, Grabow says she went to Houston's airport to see President Kennedy arrive. As she pulled up along the road with her husband, Roy, she saw other cars parked there. One was in a ditch, and she saw a man standing on its hood with what appeared to be a rifle. Then she nudged Roy to look at him. "He [Roy] said it was probably Secret Service," said Grabow. "And I went to the car and got my glasses and put them on. He knew I was watching him. No doubt, it was Raul, and it was a gun in his hand. A big rifle with a telescopic site. When Raul saw me and Roy he acted real mad and he jumped down off the hood of the car and threw the gun in the backseat and started racing up and down the road because he really didn't know which direction the president was going to go."

The next day, when she heard that JFK had been killed in Dallas, "I just knew it was Raul," says Grabow. "Raul told me he was in Dallas on that day when JFK was killed. He told me later. He said he was there with Mr. Lee. He was upstairs with Oswald. He was shooting the gun, not Oswald."

Of course, the real Raul was working in his car factory during all of 1962 and 1963, and not on vacation at the times Grabow said she saw him in Texas.

At other points in her astonishing story, she claims that Ruby molested her once in a car, and that he was involved in "Lolita" films and books with Raul and Jack Valenti, the current head of the Motion Picture Association of America. "He [Raul] said he wanted to make a million dollars with Jack Valenti," she said. Jack Ruby actually produced the books, according to her, and she was even photographed, nude, when she was only fourteen. Also, "in the late 1960s and early 1970s, I used to take Raul and drop him off at the Alabama Theater." There, before the theater opened to the public, Raul would meet with associates of Carlos Marcello and Jack Valenti.

As for the King assassination, she gives different versions throughout the tape. She repeats the story that Pepper relates in his book—that Raul stomped on a keychain with King's picture—but adds the words "I killed this black so and so, do I have to kill him again" only on her third rendition. Also, Grabow says that Raul admitted to her that he was at the scene of the King murder and "he tripped over some mimosa tree, and somehow leaned on it or tripped over it, and he said no one could have missed all the stuff he knocked off that tree." There was no mimosa tree in the area of the Lorraine Motel where King was killed.[65] When she repeated the story of the tree for the third time, Saltman asked her, "He told you he tripped over the tree after he shot Dr. King?" She had never mentioned Raul shooting King. But after Saltman feeds her the question, she softly replies, "I guess that is how it was."

Sometimes, Grabow says she saw Raul the week after the King assassination. At other times, she says she did not see him for several years. She describes in detail her supposed affair with lawyer Percy Foreman, and the fact that he knew Raul and told her to leave Houston because her life was in danger.* As to the possibility that someone tried to kill Grabow by sabotaging her tire, even Saltman told the author, "That is the one area I am a little skeptical about."[66] Pepper, in his published account, says she and Roy moved from Houston because they were fearful of being killed for what they knew about the assassination. What he does not disclose is that Grabow admits on the tape that after a few years they moved back to Houston.

---

*   It appears that Grabow did at least know Foreman. She still has an autographed sketch of him. As to whether they had a sexual affair as she claims, there is no way to confirm or dispose of the allegation.

Armed with this information about Grabow, the author interviewed investigators Herman and Billings. They showed no surprise and readily admitted that that was her story and they believed it. "There's even more," says Herman. "When we put her under hypnosis she gave a new thing out, that Amaro and Raul had a fifty-five-gallon drum in the room, and she heard a noise of someone inside the drum. Then they both shot it full of bullets. Then the noise stopped, and the two dumped the drum into the river port."[67] Also, according to both investigators, Grabow swears that her oldest daughter is Jack Ruby's child.[68]

"We have thought of secretly clipping the hair from some of Ruby's relatives," admits Billings. "Then we could prove that her child is Ruby's and that would tie everything together."[69] "We found a firm, Valenti and Mirabal, in Orange County, California," whispers Herman, as though he is imparting highly classified information. "It was an import-export business, and after John [Billings] started to make inquiries, they changed their name. Some coincidence, huh? Jack Valenti is key here. Kiddie porn. What do you think now of the fellow who tells Americans what they should see in movies?"*[70]

"We are almost sure that the person taken in a picture with Oswald in New Orleans is really Raul," says Billings. The photo is actually of a man that Oswald picked from an unemployment office to help him distribute leaflets on a street corner in 1963.†

By October 1997, Billings had taken Grabow to meet a number of Kennedy assassination buffs in Dallas. Once they heard her story, some of them became convinced that they had seen Raul at Jack Ruby's club in Dallas. Billings and Herman had latched on to a new theory that Jack Ruby might even be alive, part of the witness protection program.[71]

When I asked Ray's investigators why all the information about the Kennedy assassination and Raul had not been published, Billings had a quick answer. "I was the one who called Pepper when we heard what Glenda said. I

---

*   When the author spoke to Jack Valenti, he was flabbergasted to hear about the accusations. "I don't even know what to say," he replied. "How can you answer something that is just so crazy? How do these people invent these things? It's just pure fantasy, completely and utterly false. It's either malicious or the product of someone who is disturbed." It was impossible for Grabow to have seen Valenti in Houston during most of the time she claimed, since he was living and working in Washington, D.C., in a high-profile job in the Johnson administration.

†   Billings, who seems the more rabid conspiracy devotee of the two investigators, told the author that he feared he was so close to the truth in the King assassination that the government might kill him. "That's why I have just rewritten my will, so that if I am killed, my vital organs go to James Earl Ray. That way, Ray could get the new liver he needs [because of his terminal cirrhosis]. It is also my life insurance policy to make sure the FBI doesn't do away with me."

told him, 'I have good news and bad news for you. We have found Raoul. That's
the good news.'

" 'What's the bad news?' asked Pepper.

" 'We can tie him into the Kennedy assassination a lot better than the Martin Luther King assassination.'

" 'Oh, no!' Pepper yelled. 'We can't say that! That would ruin everything.' "[72]

In *Orders to Kill*, Pepper omitted all of Grabow's claims about Raul killing
JFK, Jack Valenti being in the kiddie porn business, and Ruby having had an affair with her.

But what about the other witnesses who identified the early 1960s photo of
Raul in a picture lineup? Her brother, it turns out, was only six when he remembers seeing Raul. Saltman was not troubled by that. "Granted he was only
six," Saltman says, "but his memory still seems good. I do not believe it was a
setup with his sister."[73] April Ferguson, who supposedly picked out the photo
on Kenny Herman's kitchen table and remembered that Select Committee investigators had shown it to her, backed off when contacted by the author. "I
have no idea, I can't tell you anything one way or the other," she says. "I personally don't even remember ever talking to anyone for the Select Committee.
Why would they want to talk to me? It was so long ago. I think I saw the picture
before, but I cannot recall the circumstances."[74] Gene Stanley, Randy Rosenson's attorney, does not support Saltman's claim either. "I could not identify
any photograph at the trial. No way. If I saw any photograph from the Select
Committee investigators, I couldn't identify it today or identify it in 1993. Hell,
it's fifteen years later."[75]

Sid Carthew, reached in England, had a most unusual response to the author's inquiries about his identification of Raul from a photo lineup. "I'm sorry,
but I won't talk to you unless William Pepper gives me permission. And I want
you to know that I am not a Nazi [something the author had never heard before Carthew raised it], I do not know Nazis in the United States, and I do not
know James Earl Ray. It's just a shame that an innocent man is being held for
killing that King." He then hung up.[76] It turns out that Carthew was actually
the Yorkshire regional organizer for the fascist British National Party for years,
and had been a self-proclaimed "nationalist" since the 1960s.[77] Carthew's extreme political affiliation raises the question of whether he might try supporting Martin Luther King's killer by concocting a story to help set him free.[78]

But, of course, the most important identification is that made by Ray. Finally, after almost three decades, he decisively picked out a photograph of Raul.
Now that Raul turns out to be an innocent man completely unconnected to the
case, Ray's long-standing alibi falls apart.

On a brilliantly sunny autumn day in Manhattan, the author met with Raul in his midtown Manhattan lawyer's office. It had taken months of talking to his counsel, Janet Mattick, to convince her to produce her client. Raul was impeccably dressed in a gray pinstriped suit, set off by a crisp white shirt, dark blue tie, and a cotton pocket handkerchief. His thick hair was neatly cut and combed. He was of average height and trim. His daughter and son-in-law accompanied him. He was clearly uncomfortable at having to discuss the assassination of Martin Luther King. "I am still not sure why I am here, why I am answering all of this," he said somberly. "They have turned my life upside down. This is the time of my life, my retirement, when I should be enjoying what I have worked thirty years for. And now I cannot go outside my own house without worrying that someone is there with a long-range camera to take my picture. They talk to my friends, people wonder what is happening. And my life savings, a lot went to lawyers to fight this. I didn't think this could happen in America. When Dexter King said that I had been found, my wife and I were shocked. This will never end for me, I fear. There will always be someone crazy out there who will believe it. Doesn't the truth matter anymore in this country? Who will give me back my life?"

But to the Ray defense team, there are more important things at stake than Raul's reputation. "The Oliver Stone film will be the last big thing done on this case," says Kenny Herman, leaning forward while he lights another cigarette. "And you know how they are in Hollywood. Hell, they aren't interested in the facts, they just are looking for the best story. I actually don't know whether Ray did it or not. But I know the whole case has changed as a result of what we have uncovered. We have one hell of a story for 'em out in Hollywood."[79]

32

Military Hoax

Jowers and Raul were the two major breakthroughs trumpeted by the Ray defense team. However, quite separate from those matters, William Pepper, in *Orders to Kill*, developed another startling theory, and it was this one that originally captured the attention of the King family. It solved the King assassination without any necessity for Raul or Loyd Jowers. It was instead a convoluted hypothesis that centered on a covert team of Green Beret snipers from the 20th Special Forces Group that was supposedly in Memphis on the day King was killed. Two snipers, according to Pepper, had both King and his top aide, Andrew Young, in their gun sights at the very moment someone else, probably an unidentified military sniper, carried out the assassination.[1]

Pepper's interest in the military and the assassination began in 1993 when Steve Tompkins, a reporter for *The Commercial Appeal*, wrote a controversial 6,000-word article charging that the Army had conducted extensive surveillance on three generations of the King family. The result of a sixteen-month investigation, the article mixed solidly sourced reporting with innuendo and speculation. By March 1968, Tompkins said, the "Army's intelligence system was keenly focused on King and desperately searching for a way to stop him." The most sensational charges were unattributed and buried at the end of the story. In Memphis, Tompkins wrote, the Atlanta-based 111th Military Intelligence Group "shadowed" King, using "a sedan crammed with electronic equipment." Tompkins also used two anonymous sources to charge that "eight

Green Beret soldiers from an 'Operational Detachment Alpha 184 Team' were also in Memphis carrying out an unknown mission" on the day of the assassination. The 20th Special Forces Group, according to more unnamed sources, used "Klan guys who hated niggers" as its intelligence-gathering network.*[2]

When Pepper became Ray's lead counsel, and then received $140,000 payment for the Thames-HBO mock trial, he hired Tompkins as a consultant. Tompkins told Pepper he would not reveal his two secret sources, but he did disclose that they were living in Latin America. He offered to be the go-between. Pepper agreed, and never actually spoke to the two men, whom he code-named Warren and Murphy in his book.†[3] While Tompkins's *Commercial Appeal* article was the starting point, Pepper eventually went much further, reprinting supposed White House orders to the Alpha 184 team and giving precise details about how a secret squad shadowed King with snipers.

When Pepper's book was published, a friend of General William Yarborough, the father of the Green Berets, brought it to the attention of Yarborough's former chief aide, retired major Rudi Gresham. "I thought it was just crazy," recalls the fifty-two-year-old Gresham. "There were things in there that were impossible, that told me that Pepper did not understand how the military worked. I knew right away that he was either really careless with the facts, or someone had sold him a bill of goods."[4]

---

*   Actually, Tompkins's article was rooted in fact. Senate hearings in 1971 had examined abuses in an Army surveillance program established under President Johnson after riots in 1965 and 1967. The program, designed to provide the Pentagon with "early warning" of civil disturbances that might require federal troops, involved sending Army observers to antiwar demonstrations, civil rights rallies, and other political gatherings. Senate investigators found the Army sometimes exceeded its authority, crossing into improper political surveillance that included keeping dossiers on civilians. General William Yarborough, who helped direct the intelligence program, told the author, "I can't give the Army a clean bill of health from that time. But we were not enthusiastic about being soldiers assigned to correct a civilian problem. We did not want it."

In Memphis the local 111th Military Intelligence Group closely monitored the 1968 sanitation strike. Five agents watched public gatherings and used civilian, police, and FBI sources to report on King and others. However, some reporters criticized Tompkins's article for going too far afield in its conclusions, and it prompted a scathing reply from General Yarborough. Shortly after that article, Tompkins, who had resigned in 1984 from *The Wichita Eagle-Beacon* after an internal investigation into a discrepancy about a critical date in a story he wrote, also resigned from *The Commercial Appeal*. He says his departure from the Memphis paper was not connected to his military story, but rather because he "wanted to pursue other goals."

†   Pepper later added yet a third source to his story, a man he code-named Gardner, who he claimed had been legally dead for years, then appeared and confirmed details of Warren and Murphy's story, before again disappearing.

Gresham was a former Special Forces officer who had served as Yarborough's aide through the 1960s, before becoming the assistant to the Army's chief of intelligence. In Pepper's book, Yarborough was named as the officer in charge of military intelligence at the time the conspiracy against King supposedly gained momentum. Gresham was outraged at the accusations against the military, but particularly against Yarborough. When he spoke to Yarborough, the retired general wanted to sue Pepper. Gresham, however, concluded that Pepper had written the sections about Yarborough "right on the borderline, just as a good lawyer would," and he advised Yarborough not to sue. "Let me handle this," he told his former superior officer.[5]

Gresham was a member of the Special Forces Association, a group of retired and active Green Beret soldiers that Yarborough had founded. The association also asked the energetic Gresham to conduct a preliminary investigation of Pepper's charges against the military.

Pepper had alleged that military snipers assigned to Memphis were part of the 20th Special Forces Group (SFG), a National Guard unit. "That seemed very odd," says Gresham, "that you would have an operation of this sensitivity and assign weekend soldiers to it. Anyway, in the 1960s, the only way the federal government could take troops from the States was to federalize them [through a presidential directive]."[6]

Pepper charged that during 1967, Warren and Murphy were deployed with the 20th SFG in Los Angeles, Tampa, Detroit, Washington, and Chicago, always on "sensitive" surveillance missions.[7] Gresham knew that all National Guard units have a seasoned combat veteran as an adviser. When he looked up the name of the adviser for the Birmingham-based 20th SFG, "it turned out to be an old friend, Colonel Lee Mize."[8] Mize, an Alabama native, was a decorated Vietnam veteran who had completed four tours of duty. He was the senior Army adviser for the 20th from 1967 through 1969.[9] Gresham called him.

"Hey, Lee, was your unit ever activated and sent out of state?"

"No."

"Was the 20th ever activated at all?"

"No. If they were federalized, I would have been the first to know of it."[*10]

---

* Although Gresham shared with the author the results of his investigation, the author obtained documents that independently corroborated anything cited to Gresham in this chapter. For instance, the author checked the records for the 20th unit and confirmed that the unit was not federalized at any time during 1967 and 1968. While the 20th was never activated, the unit did go out of state for training sessions to Atlanta, as well as remote areas in Florida and Idaho. Additionally, it did some unconventional warfare training at Fort McClellan, Alabama. The records for the 20th show it was never in the places Pepper put it in 1967, namely Los Angeles, Tampa, Detroit, Washington, Chicago, and Camp Shelby, Mississippi.

Gresham sent Mize a copy of the book in late 1995. "It's the biggest horse-shit I've ever seen" were his first words when he called Gresham after reading it. In the book, Pepper named Captain Billy R. Eidson as the leader of the eight-person Alpha 184 covert team that went to Memphis on April 4, 1968. Pepper claimed that, once in Memphis, Eidson introduced the two snipers, Warren and Murphy, to Lieutenant Eli Arkin of the police intelligence unit.[11] And Eidson was the one that gave the snipers their targets—King and Andrew Young—telling them "they were enemies of the United States who were determined to bring down the government."[12] Eidson could not be questioned, however, said Pepper, since he was dead. Pepper quoted Warren as saying that after the assassination the "clean-up process had begun"; Warren and Murphy fled the country, but Eidson likely ended up with a bullet in the back of his head.[13]

"Hell, that's just crazy," Mize told Gresham. "Billy Eidson ain't dead. Eidson has a daughter in Birmingham and he visits me about every six months."

Gresham next called Ian Sutherland, the colonel who had been in charge of the gunnery training at Fort Bragg. Pepper had alleged that Warren and Murphy had undergone sniper training. Sutherland laughed when he heard the charge. "I would have known about any sniper training," he told Gresham. "That's ridiculous. I was the gunnery officer and even if TDY ["temporary duty," being sent elsewhere for training], I would have known about it."[14]

Pepper claimed that Warren and Murphy had been transferred from the 5th Special Forces Group in Vietnam to the 20th SFG in Mississippi.[15] A friend in the Army ran a computer check for Gresham to determine whether there had been any such transfers. There were none until 1971.[16]

Around this time, Gresham had also started checking on the military order to "recon riot site Memphis prior to King, Martin L. arrival," that Pepper reproduced prominently in his book. It purported to be a "secret/crypto" order from Special Operations to the 20th SFG, Alpha 184 team.[17] If authentic, the order would prove the existence of the military units about which Pepper was writing, and that they were involved in a covert operation against King. At a party, Gresham ran into an old acquaintance, Daniel Ellsberg, the man responsible for releasing the Pentagon Papers to *The New York Times* in the 1970s. When Ellsberg had worked as the special assistant to the assistant secretary of defense, "one of my jobs was to winnow through cables and see which ones he should see. I saw everything from Vietnam. There were usually two piles, almost six feet tall, and this was a daily intake. It is hard to overestimate how many cables I have read."[18]

Ellsberg had previously seen the order and told Gresham that "at first glance, it looks real," but after inspecting it closer he had noticed problems that indicated it was "a deliberately constructed fraud."[19] The most disturbing error was that the date was wrong, indicating that the cable was sent on April 30, twenty-six days *after* King had been killed. "It might have been a typo," says Ellsberg, "but it would have been very unusual. It is so critical to get the date and time group right in the military. It is a very serious question about the document. In the tens of thousands I have seen, I have seen typos, but never a date-time group error, since the cables are filed by that. If that were a typo, there would certainly be a follow-up correcting it. On its own, it indicates the cable is almost surely a fake."[20]

Other problems included a zero at the front of the date line. "I have never seen anything like that," remarks Ellsberg. The name of the originating unit for the cable is listed as "Lantcomn." "That is actually Atlantic Command," says Ellsberg, "and would have no second *n* in it." Also, the cable showed that it came from "Cincspecops" (Central Command for Special Operations) but Special Operations was not even in existence in 1968.[*][21]

In February 1997, Pepper appeared on *Montel Williams* and repeated the charges about a covert military team at the center of the King assassination. Again, Yarborough wanted to sue, but Gresham counseled patience. He had dealt with the media when he worked as Yarborough's aide. "What do we do?" Yarborough asked him. "Nothing," replied Gresham. "The *Montel* show is a secondary media market. We just ignore it."[22]

Pepper next appeared on Court TV with celebrity lawyer Johnnie Cochran and Dexter King. Then he reappeared on *Montel Williams* in March. "Pepper went the whole nine yards," recalls Gresham. "He had gotten the King family involved, and Dexter was there saying what a great book it was, and how powerful the facts were. This made me feel very uncomfortable. Everybody wanted to do something, and I had to restrain them."[23]

But instead of merely fading away, as Gresham had hoped, Pepper began to get more publicity because he now had Dexter King in tow. On CNN's *Larry King Live*, Dexter again endorsed the book, saying it was the source for the new information that had been uncovered. "When it went on *Larry King*, I knew it

---

* Pepper had actually sent the order to Ellsberg, through an intermediary. Ellsberg conveyed his doubts to Pepper, who replied that he had checked with his source, "Warren," and now thought it possible that the date might actually be a subsequent rerouting for filing or some other purpose. Ellsberg, however, says, "This explanation doesn't make sense to me." If it were a rerouting then the original date would show in the cable's heading. "Why, also," asks Ellsberg, "would anyone send a highly secret order around for filing, twenty-six days after King was assassinated?" If real, this cable would never have seen the light of day after King's death. Pepper reproduced the order in his book without any caveats. Both Ellsberg and Gresham agreed that Pepper's silence was "disingenuous at best."

was a different ball game," recalls Gresham. Returning to his Florida home, he had a message from Yarborough that a producer from ABC, Courtney Bullock, had telephoned. When Gresham returned the call, Bullock said she was a producer with the newsmagazine *Turning Point* and they had completed 70 percent of a show on the King assassination and Pepper's new charges. "We can help you with lots of information," Gresham assured her. But he was afraid that he did not know enough about the 20th Special Forces Group to go on television and defend them—he needed extra time for more research. "We won't do the interviews yet," he told Bullock, "but we'll work with you and then see where we are at in a few weeks." She agreed.

For the next three weeks, from 6:00 A.M. to midnight, Gresham, spending thousands of dollars of his own money, worked to find the holes in Pepper's contentions.

First he called Lee Mize: "It's not enough to know that Billy Eidson is alive. We need to find him."

Then he located General Henry Cobb, who had been the commanding officer (then a colonel) of the 20th for thirteen years, including 1967 and 1968. "I had never heard of any of those charges before Gresham called me," recalls Cobb. "At first I was shocked. We never went to Memphis. Never went to L.A., or Fort Shelby, or Bobby Kennedy's house, or any of those places Pepper mentioned. We were federalized once by JFK in 1963, and never again. You couldn't get into my unit unless I knew about it, and those guys [Warren and Murphy] just didn't exist."[24]

Cobb also knew Eidson and that he was alive, but "I had never heard of either one of those other names," he says.[25] "General, your word is fine," Gresham told him, "but I need proof for ABC, I need rosters. I need backup for everything, General."[26]

At Cobb's suggestion, Gresham called Major General Clyde Hennies, the adjutant general of Alabama, and immediately obtained the rosters for the 20th Special Forces Group. They proved the unit was never in Mississippi, Los Angeles, Memphis, or anywhere else Pepper had placed it.*[27] Gresham asked for the personnel lists for 1967 and 1968. He was interested in another contention by Pepper: Besides naming Billy Eidson as the commanding officer of the sniper unit, Pepper had also named a Lieutenant Robert Worley and a buck sergeant, J. D. Hill, as other members. Both Worley and Hill were dead, contended Pepper. Hill had been shot by his wife, although Pepper implied there might have been something more sinister behind that murder.[28]

---

* The author has reviewed the rosters for the 20th SFG for 1967 and 1968 and they show that the unit, as Gresham said, was never in any of the cities cited by Pepper.

"And guess what," says Gresham. "When I got the personnel lists for April 1968, there was Colonel Henry Cobb and Major Billy Eidson, but no Robert Worley or J. D. Hill."[29]

Cobb and Mize had raised another puzzling issue. Neither had even heard of a unit called the Alpha 184, the supposed moniker for the eight-man covert team that was in Memphis on April 4, 1968. Did Tompkins make it up and Pepper just repeat the mistake? Gresham pored through the history of the 20th, from its inception as a rangers unit in 1959, until he discovered that a group 184 had indeed existed, for only one year in 1960.[30] It was disbanded eight years before King was killed.

Meanwhile, the effort to find Billy Eidson continued. Somebody remembered that he had worked at the Birmingham fire department. Gresham called and wanted to know where they sent Eidson's pension check, but the young clerk initially would not give out any information. After a half-hour lecture about the Martin Luther King assassination, she relented and gave the telephone number of Eidson's daughter in Birmingham. Gresham called the next day and told her about Pepper's charges. "She almost had a heart attack," he recalls. Her father was living in Costa Rica, having married a young woman there.* She gave Gresham the telephone number. On his first call, he reached Eidson, who said he had never heard of Tompkins or Pepper or an Alpha 184 unit. Then Gresham, without explaining the reason, started asking him questions.

"Was your unit ever deployed in Memphis?"

"No."

"Ever in California?"

"No way." He laughed.

"Did you ever have a second in command named Robert Worley?"

"No."

"What about a J. D. Hill?"

"Nope."

"Did you ever have two Vietnam vets from SOG in your unit?"

"Hell, no. If I had two like that I would have been tickled pink. But why would two SOG fellows ever come over to the National Guard?"[31]

After finishing those questions, Gresham told Eidson, "Look, I'm about to tell you a story you won't believe." When he finished, Eidson laughed. "Well, that's the most ridiculous thing in the world," he said. "People don't believe that, do they?"[32]

---

* Eidson had left the country shortly after having trouble with the law in Birmingham. He killed a man in a bar brawl, and a jury held him responsible for criminally negligent homicide. He received twelve months probation instead of a jail sentence.

"They do," Gresham said. "Martin Luther King's own son believes it."[33]

"Well, it's crazy, I was on duty at the fire department in Birmingham. Anyone can check it. Hell, I've never been in Memphis."*

The next morning Gresham called Eidson again. By this time, the enormity of the charges against him had sunk in. He was angry with Pepper. "He's crazy," he shouted. "What did I ever do to him? I can't believe that King's son thinks I killed his daddy." Eidson was also a little worried. "What if some fool reads that book and goes after me or my family?"[34] Gresham had no answer.

Meanwhile, Gresham continued faxing updates and talking daily with ABC producer Bullock. Once she learned that Eidson was alive, she immediately wanted to fly to Costa Rica to film him. Gresham, who was now the only person with Eidson's trust, said no.

Forrest Sawyer, one of *Turning Point*'s hosts, called Pepper. They had already interviewed him for the program, but now asked for another. Pepper was wary, but agreed. Meanwhile, Gresham kept digging. By this time, he had buttressed Daniel Ellsberg's opinion about the military order Pepper reproduced in his book: General Ray Davis, a four-star Medal of Honor recipient; Admiral Elmo Zumwalt, former chief of Naval Operations; and Colonel Harry Summers, a syndicated columnist and a military college instructor, had all chimed in with opinions that it was a fake.[35]

In early June, Gresham decided it was time to officially become part of the ABC program, which was scheduled to air on June 19. He agreed to visit New York with Billy Eidson, Lee Mize, Henry Cobb, and Jimmy Dean, the administrator of the Special Forces Association.[36] Just before they all left for New York, Courtney Bullock telephoned. She had tracked down J. D. Hill, the soldier Pepper claimed had been part of the sniper's team. He had been in the 20th Special Forces Group but had left the unit on May 7, 1966, and did not return to duty until May 7, 1968. He had not even been in the service at the time of the King assassination.[†]

---

*   After much wrangling with the personnel office in the Birmingham fire department, Gresham finally obtained copies of rosters that showed Eidson was on active call on April 4, and that he worked the following day. He was not back with the National Guard until July 10. Eidson, who worked part-time with a house-painting crew, was on a job in Birmingham, with other workers, on April 4.

†   The author has reviewed the personnel records that show Hill's departure from and return to the 20th. Hill was buried in Mississippi in 1976. "We finally got a copy of the police report on his death," says Gresham, "and he was a real son of a bitch who kept beating his wife until she finally killed him one day. She did not get charged with any crime." It would not be until after his visit to New York that Gresham found a Worley who had served in the National Guard, but he also was not on duty in 1968. He was actually a full-time pharmacist in Louisiana, and died in a car accident.

The group of former soldiers arrived in New York on Thursday, June 5, 1997. The following day their interviews were taped. They were then taken to a room adjoining a studio where Forrest Sawyer was taping an interview with Pepper, who had also flown into New York. They listened on headphones as Pepper admitted that prior to printing his charge about the 20th Special Forces Group being involved in the King assassination, he had never spoken to anyone at the 20th, or tried to get a comment from the unit. "If I had done that," Pepper offered weakly in his defense, "all types of doors would have closed to me."[37]

Reporter Steve Tompkins, whose original article in *The Commercial Appeal* had kicked off Pepper's interest in the military and King's murder, was also interviewed for the program. Sensing that things were turning against Pepper, he had started backing away from the story that he helped create. Sawyer played for Pepper a tape on which Tompkins now said that he did not believe the military was involved in any assassination plot. "I find that very interesting," said Pepper, looking quite uncomfortable. "I find that very interesting because he was the one who carried information back to me with respect to the assassination."*

Finally, Sawyer got around to Billy Eidson. "I believe Eidson, one was killed in New Orleans," said Pepper.

Sawyer then played a videotape of Eidson and informed Pepper that he was still alive. Pepper was visibly shaken and his lower lip twitched. "That's what you say, and that's what he says," Pepper contended. Sawyer did not hesitate. "Would you like to meet him?" "Would it serve any purpose?" Pepper asked, now squirming in his chair. "O.K., fine, I'll be glad to talk to them."

Sawyer gave a signal and Eidson and the other men walked onto the set as the cameras rolled. Pepper stood up and went to shake Eidson's hand. "I don't want to shake your hand," Eidson said to him. "I just want to look at you."

Sawyer told Pepper, "I think you may owe the American people an apology." Pepper kept saying he needed time to gather documents and proof that would change ABC's mind before the scheduled air date of June 19. Claiming that his publisher had checked his facts, and that Tompkins could provide written statements from Warren and Murphy, he dodged the questions from the five veterans for nearly two hours. Meanwhile, he kept telling Eidson, "I would never have written about you if I had any idea you were alive."[38] When told the

---

* Tompkins actually signed a September 11, 1995, affidavit drafted by Pepper, in which he endorsed the accuracy of the draft manuscript Pepper had shown him about the military and the two snipers, Warren and Murphy. When asked about that affidavit, Tompkins claimed that he had not read it carefully, and in any case had seen only one chapter from the entire book. He later said, "Pepper took my series and embellished the hell out of it."

military order he reproduced was a fake, he said he was not surprised—"What do you expect them to do, acknowledge it?" But Gresham did not let him off the hook so easily. "Who authenticated the order for you?"

"Oliver Stone had some military person check it, and it was fine," Pepper told the slack-jawed group.[39]

"I was starting to get real mad around this time," recalls Gresham, "and I told him that he had it all mixed up. It wasn't possible for Warren and Murphy to have come from the 5th in Vietnam and ended up in the National Guard. Pepper admitted that they had never served in Vietnam."*[40]

Pepper finally mentioned some names, saying that a Joe Stone, a former military officer who was now living somewhere in Latin America, was one of his sources. He also claimed to meet regularly with John W. Downie, of the 902nd Military Intelligence Group, and said he would produce him. Sawyer reminded Pepper that the show was scheduled to air on June 19, and that he had until then—two weeks—to develop new information.

Gresham also used that time to clear up loose ends. The Pentagon finally provided written confirmation that Pepper's military order was a hoax. "We continued checking on other things that Pepper had thrown out in that meeting," recalls Gresham. Mainly, he looked for Joe Stone and John Downie, the two sources Pepper had mentioned.†

Downie turned out to be a colonel who had been subpoenaed in 1973 before Congress and testified that the Army had surveillance on King. He had died in June 1987 and was buried in Arlington.

When Gresham informed ABC, and they in turn told Pepper, he did not miss a beat. "He's assumed another identity," contended Pepper.[41] (Pepper now denies giving the name Downie, but at least five people in the ABC room at the time have told the author they heard it.) Gresham, not one to be dissuaded by a mere contention, kept digging and found Downie's daughter. "She was flabbergasted," he recalls. "Yes, she confirmed, he was definitely dead."

---

* If Warren and Murphy are fictitious characters, there may be an indication of where Tompkins and Pepper obtained the names. *The Phoenix Program*, a 1990 book by Douglas Valentine, is about a government campaign against the antiwar movement. Valentine wrote, without citing any sources, that as part of the campaign, the 111th Military Intelligence Group in Memphis kept Martin Luther King under twenty-four-hour-a-day surveillance and took photos at the moment he was assassinated. In the book, two military men with the names Warren and Murphy appear. Excerpts from *The Phoenix Program* were found in Tompkins papers at *The Commercial Appeal* after he left.

† Peter Bull, another producer at ABC, talked to Tompkins, who denied that Joe Stone was one of his deep sources, but did admit to having spoken with Downie. Tompkins told the author that "Joe Stone" was simply a pseudonym he happened to have given one of his deep sources.

Joe Stone turned out to be an active warrant officer in the Alabama National Guard. "I know nothing about it," Stone told Gresham when the two finally spoke. "I don't know Pepper, don't know Tompkins, know nothing about them. I don't know why the hell they would have named me, but I can assure you that you have the wrong guy."[42]

By this time, only days before the show was due to air, Tompkins had even backed off further, saying that while he had provided the military order to Pepper, he had told him not to use it as he had questions about its authenticity. "We [*The Commercial Appeal*] didn't print it because we didn't believe it," he said.[43] Oliver Stone, when contacted, told ABC he had not verified the military order for Pepper.

"After realizing what a liar Pepper was," says Gresham, "I wanted to warn the Kings." So he talked to an old Army buddy, Major Harold Sims, a former executive director of the Urban League, who had served on the board of directors at the King Center in Atlanta for twenty-five years. Sims sent a fax to Dexter urging him to talk to Gresham. "He never called me," says a clearly disappointed Gresham.

The *Turning Point* program aired on June 19, 1997. Dexter and other members of the King family were on the show.

"Who do the Kings hold responsible for his assassination?" asked Forrest Sawyer.

"Army intelligence, CIA, FBI," Dexter answered immediately.

"Do you believe that Lyndon Johnson was part of the plot to kill your father?"

"I do."

With Dexter were his mother, Coretta; his brother, Martin III; and his sisters, Yolanda and Bernice. When Sawyer asked, "Is everybody united in the belief that James Earl Ray not only did not pull the trigger, he didn't know there was going to be a murder that day?" the group all nodded their agreement. Sawyer wanted to make sure there was no dissent. "Everybody?" "Absolutely," declared Martin III.

Turning Point only aired a fraction of what their producers and Gresham uncovered, primarily focusing on the error over the living Billy Eidson. However, following the show, the Kings held an emergency meeting the next night. They decided to adopt a lower public profile in the coming months, but the general consensus, incredibly, was that Pepper was still on the right track, and the fact that a major television network aired a program discrediting him confirmed to the Kings that the cover-up was alive and well.

Six days after the program, Billy Eidson filed a libel suit against Pepper and his publishers, Carroll & Graf, for $15 million. Meanwhile, Pepper, in conversations with journalists, began raising the possibility that the man ABC presented as Billy Eidson was a phony, intended only to discredit him, and that the real Eidson was dead. Gresham worked for the CIA, he charged, and was out to destroy him.[44] He complained that his sources had "gone underground" since the program, hindering his investigation.[45] But Pepper's protestations of an ever widening conspiracy, now directed at him, sounded increasingly hollow. By his high-profile hijinks, he somehow had converted the assassination more into a battle over his theories and credibility than a battle to free his increasingly forgotten client, James Earl Ray.

33

Ray's Last Dance

In any other case, after years of legal wrangling and maneuvering, the courts would have finally closed the door to Ray's antics to free himself. But somehow, in the matter of the *State of Tennessee* v. *James Earl Ray*, there always seems to be another proceeding under way before a new judge. Besides Pepper and his investigators, Herman and Billings, the Ray defense team for the past few years has also included a colorful Memphis lawyer, Wayne Chastain, who is a former journalist. With his shock of white hair and seersucker suits heavily stained with ink spots, he is a familiar sight shuffling around the criminal courthouse. Chastain has believed in a conspiracy in the case since the days when he covered it for the now defunct *Memphis Press-Scimitar.* Even prosecutors do not doubt his motivation, and the word used to describe him invariably is *decent.* When Chastain became sick in January 1997, Jack McNeil, a former local councilman, filled in for him. McNeil, in sharp contrast, is abrasive and a rabid conspiracy buff who can make even Oliver Stone seem staid.*

---

* McNeil refused to meet with me because of my book *Case Closed,* about the JFK murder. "Do you work for the CIA?" he asked over the telephone. Later, he went on to explain how Jack Ruby had been injected with cancer cells by the CIA, and how his cocounsel, Chastain, had also been injected with cancer. "I move around," he said. "I don't sleep in the same place all the time. I won't make it easy for them to find me."

While Ray's defense team was an eccentric assortment of courtroom talent, few expected it to successfully revive Ray's legal battle nearly three decades after the murder. But that is exactly what they accomplished in early 1997, due largely to a sympathetic judge, Joe Brown, who took charge of the case. He is the first black judge ever to have control of James Earl Ray's fate, and he waged a complex procedural battle in Memphis's highly political criminal courts system to have the Ray case assigned to him, and then keep it.*

Brown is one of the most outspoken judges on any U.S. bench, ABC's Ted Koppel, in a *Nightline* profile, said he is "foul-mouthed, [has] a lousy temper, and carries a gun—Joe Brown is a man on a mission."[1] A transplanted Californian, Brown relishes shaking up the Memphis establishment. He talks about running for mayor, while at the same time complaining bitterly about how the city's "secret powers" have conspired to ruin his career.[2] Brown dresses in an updated version of 1970s funk, even wearing self-designed judicial robes, one purple, another adorned with an African motif. He often boasts of his own intelligence: "Very few people on this planet have an IQ like me," he says. "I dumb things down a lot so people can understand."[3] And Brown has little patience for those who are not quick enough to keep up with his rapid delivery. In the fall of 1997, the flamboyant Brown developed his own syndicated legal show on television.

Pepper wisely decided to focus on a single issue before Brown—that the fatal .30-06 round that killed King did not come from the rifle bought by Ray. Early tests by the FBI in 1968 had proven inconclusive, since the gun in question is a model that does not leave distinctive ballistics markings on each cartridge fired. Instead, each bullet has different markings, and since there is no consistency, it is impossible to match any of the bullets ever fired from the gun. Now, Pepper suggested newer technology might settle the issue. There was virtually no risk in Pepper making the request. If, of course, tests eliminated the rifle as the murder weapon, Ray would likely be on his way to a new trial. If, as expected, the tests were inconclusive, then Ray was no worse off than he was before. And even if the tests matched the death slug to Ray's rifle, it did not ruin the defense that Ray had passed the murder weapon to Raoul the night before the murder. The rifle/ballistics issue was also the perfect one to present

---

* In September 1997, another Criminal Court judge, John Colton, appointed a special master to investigate Judge Brown's handling of the case, and the special master determined that Brown had left the files in "shambles." Judge Colton tried to move the case back to his own Division 3. Brown fought Colton in a nasty public dispute, and the Court of Appeals made both judges declare a truce. The case stayed with Brown.

to Judge Brown, an avid gun enthusiast who considers himself an expert marksman.*

What infuriated the prosecution about Brown was that he often seemed more of an advocate than a neutral observer. Brown has made no excuse for the apparent courtroom advocacy, believing, he said, that he was given the Ray case to ensure the truth was reached. In a July 1997 hearing concerning the test-firing of the rifle, Brown responded to an objection to one of his rulings by saying, "Dr. King is dead. In his grave. A national hero. A world hero. A national holiday named after him. And I'm not going to allow the vicissitudes of somebody's artful cross-examination to keep me, as the trier of fact, from getting to the bottom of this."

"No matter what happens in these motions by Ray," Brown told the author, "eventually I have to decide if enough evidence has been presented to grant him a new trial. No matter what happens with the test results on the rifle, that is only one factor to consider. I have to write findings of fact on this case, and I've been thinking about them for a long time. That is what makes everybody so nervous around here." He broke into a broad smile. "I get to control the fucking historical record."[4]

At court hearings, prosecutors seethed as Brown entertained the King family like celebrities in his chambers. "It is unlike anything I have ever seen in a courtroom," recalls John Campbell, the assistant district attorney general who has led the prosecution's effort on all the motions. "It is as though I am not just fighting the defense, but also the judge. Any other judge would have closed Ray and Pepper down by now. But Brown has been a lifesaver to them."[5]

Brown makes no effort to hide his feelings about the case, most unusual for a presiding judge. He told the author that, as far as he is concerned, Ray "was used in the conspiracy, to throw them off the track. That was his role. I'm sure of it. Somebody told him, 'You have one last task to do for your country.' 'We have Commies here,' they told him. Ray was a bigot. And he expected to be pardoned for doing his patriotic duty."[6]

One of the reasons Brown came to believe there was a wide-ranging conspiracy in the King case resulted from a visit to the assassination scene before the case was even assigned to him. "I know enough about guns to realize that

---

* In the court hearings over the testing issue, Brown frequently asked more questions of the experts than did either the defense or prosecution. In his chambers, he usually keeps several rifles, with large telescopic sights, leaning against the wall, and will gladly show visitors the guns and their special attributes. When he met the author, he told in hushed tones a bizarre story about semiautomatic weapons he claimed had been stolen from his house, with no sign of forced entry or a break-in. "Somebody powerful is trying to set me up," he said.

the shot that killed King came from more than three hundred yards away [Ray was less than seventy yards away]," he told the author. "It could have been from a higher location, by a professional shooter. I have shot deer and bears with a .30-06 from a hundred yards, and the bullet either goes through them or disintegrates. But in this case, we have a bullet in bad shape. That will tell you right there that it was fired from much farther than the state says. Hell, that gun [Ray's rifle] should be taken and shot from a hundred yards to see what it shoots like. No one has asked me for that test. Pepper doesn't even know what to ask for."[7]

The test that Pepper did ask for, in February 1997, was for the Ray rifle to be test-fired and those new bullets compared to the death slug under a high-powered scanning electron microscope, a device that did not exist for the FBI in 1968 or the House Select Committee on Assassinations in 1978. In March, Pepper added to the public pressure for such a test when he successfully convinced Dexter King to meet James Earl Ray in prison, television cameras rolling. King did so, endorsing Ray's innocence, and put the case back into the national headlines. At the same time that Pepper was pushing the ballistics issue with Brown, he made the rounds on the media circuit with Dexter King. Even Jerry Ray was trotted out for several shows on Black Entertainment Television and MSNBC. He always proclaimed his brother's innocence and sounded the alarm that if the process did not move along quickly, James would soon be dead from cirrhosis of the liver. "We're both victims," Dexter told Jerry. "I lost a father, and you lost a brother."[8] In April, Pepper made a public plea for help in arranging a liver transplant for Ray. By early May, Brown had conducted hearings and finally ordered a new round of ballistics tests, as requested by Pepper.

Tennessee lawyer Andrew Hall and Mark Lane (who temporarily returned to the case) started a clemency appeal later in the summer.

The May tests on the rifle were inconclusive, as had been the FBI's original testing. But Judge Brown sealed the results, and entertained motions by Pepper to retest the gun, using a cleaning process that Pepper contended would lead to a conclusive result, and the prosecution argued would damage the rifle barrel and render any test results worthless.

Developments in the case, which were moving along quickly in the spring and summer, suddenly seemed stalled on all fronts. The Department of Corrections refused to let Ray travel out of the state to be examined at a Pittsburgh medical facility that might consider giving him a liver transplant—the two facilities in Tennessee that specialize in such transplants had already rejected him due to his age and the poor aftercare he would get in prison.

In November 1997, Ray fired Jack McNeil, the Memphis counsel who had increasingly tried to dominate the defense's strategy. (Even without Pepper's approval, McNeil worked unsuccessfully to bring the information about Loyd Jowers before the local grand jury.) Mike Roberts, a local law professor who temporarily joined the Ray defense team, lasted only a few weeks before Ray dismissed him. Mark Lane left the case again after the clemency appeal failed. By year's close, few were still standing with Ray. There were, of course, William Pepper, Kenny Herman, John Billings, and, in the most surreal aspect, the King family.

As 1998 began, the request for retesting the rifle was still pending. Meanwhile, the prosecution had made its own motion for the judge to recuse himself because of his evident bias. On January 16, 1998, Brown refused to remove himself.

"We are laying low," Pepper told one reporter soon afterward. "The thirtieth anniversary of the assassination is coming up next spring. James will have his seventieth birthday right before that. We have solved the case. There is new evidence and witnesses. The truth will emerge by then."

The truth, elusive in many legal cases, has certainly suffered in thirty years of conjecture and confabulation in the assassination of Martin Luther King, Jr. Raoul. Shooters in the shrubbery. Two Mustangs. As time passes, new witnesses, increasing speculation, and blurred memories from those involved, further obfuscate the real history of April 4, 1968. Whether James Earl Ray ended up in the bathroom window of Bessie Brewer's rooming house as a tool of conspirators who promised him money, or for his own warped motivation fueled by racism and ego, he knows precisely what happened on the day Martin Luther King was killed.

Ray knew that King was at the Lorraine from either television or radio news on the night of April 3 or the front-page photograph in *The Commercial Appeal* on the morning of April 4. Since he did not know when he might get a shot at King, he ideally needed a place where he could unobtrusively stay, possibly for a few days. King was scheduled to be in Memphis for at least two days. As with many successful assassinations, luck played some role. For Ray, it was fortunate that King's favorite Memphis motel, the black-run Lorraine, was located on the edge of a seedy area frequented by transients and drunks. The witnesses to the day's events would be of poor quality.

A drive past the front of the Lorraine, along Mulberry Street, immediately suggested where Ray might try to set up the sniper's nest. King's room, 306, which had been mentioned in the local press coverage, was clearly visible on the second floor, overlooking the motel's parking lot and swimming pool, toward the street. On the other side of Mulberry was an eight-foot-high retaining wall. Eighty feet up a slight incline from that wall were several buildings that fronted along South Main Street, the next street over from Mulberry. The rear of some of those buildings had windows that faced the Lorraine.

The question that immediately confronted Ray was whether he could get access to any of those buildings. The one on the far right corner from the motel had three windows, one of which had an unobstructed view of King's room. That, however, turned out to be a furniture company. The next two buildings, in the middle of the block, were connected by a common stairway, and they comprised the two wings of a converted rooming house. The building that made up the left wing had its rear windows boarded over from the inside, but the one on the right had a promising view, with three windows overlooking the Lorraine. One of the windows, on the far right, was a half window, typically indicating a bathroom.

There was no other building for Ray to choose along that street. To the left of the rooming house was an empty lot that some people used for parking. The final building opposite the Lorraine, on the far left of the lot, was Fire Station No. 2.

Ray knew that in order to monitor the Lorraine, and therefore see when King was a clear target, he needed to rent a room that was in the wing without the boarded windows, as close as possible to the rear.

When he arrived at the rooming house between 3:00 and 3:30 P.M., he did not take any of his belongings in with him. It was possible that the only vacancy might not afford him the view he needed. When Bessie Brewer showed him the first room, number 8, it was twenty feet from her own office and was located in the boarded-up wing. He did not even step inside before rejecting it.[9]

Although he knew he wanted to be in the other wing, he might not have wanted to make a specific request for that location, something that would have been unusual and possibly memorable in such a cheap rooming house. He told Brewer that he did not need a stove and refrigerator (which were visible when the door was opened to the room he had rejected) and asked instead for a sleeping room.

Room 5B, where she next took him, was in the correct wing. It had a single window that faced directly onto the airway that separated the two wings of the rooming house. Ray did not walk into the room, but took it without any hesitation.*

Unsure at the time he rented the room whether his own window would afford a clear shot, he asked Mrs. Brewer where the communal bathroom was located. While any assassin would prefer to set up a sniper's nest in a private room, as opposed to a shared rest room, he had to decide which afforded the

---

* Some charge that there was only one room available for rent on the necessary side, raising the possibility that a conspiracy arranged for the room to be left empty. In fact, there were six rooms vacant at the rooming house, and three were on the "correct" side for the assassin.

best shot. Luckily for Ray, the bathroom was at the end of the hallway, right where he had spotted the half window when he had earlier canvassed the area. That meant it had one of the best views back to the Lorraine (the other two rear windows were in Room 6B, occupied by Charlie Stephens and Grace Walden).

While Brewer and Ray were standing in the hallway, Stephens came out of his room. Ray kept his head down, glancing away from Stephens, who did not get a very good look at him.

After paying for a week's rent, Ray finally went inside his room. He must have been disappointed when he discovered that in order to get a clear view of the Lorraine and King's room, he had to put his head slightly outside the window. That resolved any second thought about choosing between the bathroom and his room as the snipers nest. A quick trip to the bathroom, on the other hand, showed what an ideal location it was. Under the window was an old cast-iron tub. It was pushed against the wall, so that Ray could stand inside with his feet solidly placed on the broad bottom, lean against the wall for support, and have an unobstructed view across to the Lorraine. A small wire-mesh screen was at the bottom of the window.

Now he decided to take his car and drive until he found a shop that sold binoculars. While two hundred feet might be a good distance for a rifle shot made with a seven-power scope, it was too far for the unaided eye to clearly monitor the activity and easily recognize the individuals at the motel. Although he could have used the Redfield scope mounted on his Remington, it would have exposed him to view, since he would have had to stick the tip of the barrel out the window to get a clear view. It also would not have afforded him the same wide-ranging view as binoculars.

According to witnesses, Ray left about 4:00 P.M. to find the binoculars. It is very unlikely that he had yet brought anything into his room, as it had no doorknob and could only be locked from the outside with a padlock. He had not even asked Mrs. Brewer for the padlock. Ray had been around enough flophouses to know that if he left anything of value unattended in an unlocked room, it would likely not be there when he returned.

The witnesses at York Arms Company, where Ray bought the binoculars, confirm that he arrived about 4:00 P.M. or a little later.[10] The store was located just a few blocks from the rooming house. After rejecting two pairs of binoculars that were too expensive, Ray paid $41.55 for a pair of Bushnells. Those binoculars not only turned out to be ones Ray could afford, but they were seven-power, the same magnification as his Redfield scope. That meant Ray could get an accurate idea of how people would appear when viewed through the scope (it was set to its maximum seven-power range when found after the murder).

According to Frances Thompson, a worker at a company across the street from the rooming house, the Mustang returned about 4:30.[11] Ray's excursion for the binoculars had taken half an hour. But he had lost his parking space directly in front of Jim's Grill. He was now forced to park some sixty feet away, just beyond the Canipe Amusement Company. That was at the edge of an empty lot that separated the rooming house from the fire station. Losing the closer space must have bothered him. The first space afforded him a greater chance of getting the rifle into the rooming house without being spotted, and also a shorter distance to run when escaping from the rooming house to his car.

He did not immediately get out of the Mustang once he returned. It was critical that he pick the right moment to try and get the rifle into the rooming house. He did not want to be identified as the man seen carrying a long box into the place from which Martin Luther King was later shot. Moreover, some female workers at Seabrook Wallpaper Company across the street had finished a shift at 4:30. They were standing inside the showroom window, waiting for their husbands to pick them up. It is possible Ray saw them. They certainly noticed him. Elizabeth Copeland, a customer service representative, remembered that a man sat in the Mustang as though he were waiting for someone or something.[12] When Peggy Hurley, another worker, left work at 4:45 P.M., the same man was still sitting behind the steering wheel of the Mustang.[13] None of the women remembered him getting out of the car, which would indicate he waited, either by luck or by design, until the last of them had been picked up. What is known is that a few minutes past 5:00 P.M., the Mustang was empty.[14] In that fifteen-minute window between Peggy Hurley seeing him in the car and the two men seeing the Mustang empty as they entered Jim's Grill, Ray had found the right time to dash inside the rooming house.

He had wrapped an old green blanket around the rifle, which was in a cardboard box. He also carried a blue zippered bag. What Ray took upstairs to his room says a lot about his plans for the assassination.

In addition to the rifle, Ray had a box of cartridges; the first section only of that day's Memphis newspaper; the just-purchased binoculars; a box of Band-Aids; a bottle of aftershave; duckbill pliers and a tack hammer; two maps; a partial roll of toilet paper; a Gillette travel kit filled with a razor, shaving cream, deodorant, hair cream, and a razor blade in a dispenser; a small towel; a white handkerchief; a toothbrush and a tube of Colgate toothpaste; a seven-ounce can of Right Guard deodorant; a pair of black socks; a bottle of Bufferin; a tube of Brylcreem hair gel; three small bars of soap (Dial, Cashmere Bouquet, and Cameo); a tube of Head & Shoulders shampoo; a plastic bottle of Mennen Afta shave lotion; an elastic belt; a hairbrush; a can of Kiwi brown shoe polish; a can of Palmolive Rapid-Shave cream; some loose buttons and bobby pins; a brown paper bag with two cans of unopened Schlitz beer and a plastic six-pack carrier; a toothpick; a key; a metal ring; two coat hangers; and a portable radio.*

The soap, toilet paper, and hangers are evidence of someone accustomed to staying at flophouses, where hotel basics are never provided. But the wide range of toiletries indicates that Ray intended to stay there, at the very least overnight. It was 5:00 P.M. when he finally settled into his room. He had no idea if King was even at the Lorraine at that moment. Once nightfall came—in ninety minutes—he might not be able to get off a decent shot.

Defenders of Ray suggest that he might have taken all of those items into his room not because he intended to stay, but because he feared leaving them in the Mustang in a dicey area. However, Ray left several hundred dollars' worth of camera equipment in the Mustang, so he was clearly not concerned about having things stolen from the car.

Ray set about to rearrange Room 5B so he could easily monitor the Lorraine. He pushed away a wooden dresser that rested under the window ledge, and instead replaced it with a straight-back chair. Sitting in that chair, with the curtains pushed to one side and the window open three-quarters, he could lean slightly and watch the motel. He tuned his radio to a local station that would have provided news updates about King and his entourage, one of the biggest stories in Memphis.

Ray went into the bathroom a couple of times, without the gun, probably to get used to it as a sniper's nest. He might even have taken his binoculars with him, to see what a seven-power magnification looked like from that perch. However, it is unlikely that Ray was in there as much as his neighbors Willie Anschutz and Charlie Stephens later estimated to the police. Staying in the bathroom for an extended time would have unnecessarily called attention to him. And Ray would certainly not have remained there with the rifle—that would have been too much a risk—and he could just as easily monitor the

---

* That radio turned out to have Ray's Missouri State Penitentiary inmate number etched on the side, but Ray had scratched it out. Some conspiracists argue that Ray would never have left behind, after the assassination, a piece of evidence that so directly tied back to him. However, the author examined the radio, and the identification number is barely noticeable, almost requiring a magnifying glass to see. Ray effectively obliterated it by scratching over it. Moreover, that identification number, even if made out, could have referred to anything, including the owner's own filing system. There was no indicator it referred to a system maintained at the Missouri State Penitentiary. The radio and its number did not help the FBI identify Ray as the shooter. The FBI, in its original examination, did not even see the etched number. Only *after* the FBI had identified Ray from fingerprints, and realized that he had escaped in 1967 from the Missouri State Penitentiary, did they learn that the radio and its number were from there (MURKIN 2634, section 26).

motel from his own room. Since he might have to remain at the rooming house for a day or two, it is unlikely that he started off his stay locked in the bathroom.

King, in fact, had been at the Lorraine all day. Twice that late afternoon he had appeared, both times walking between his room and his brother's downstairs room, number 201. That required King to walk about ten feet along the balcony that ran along the second floor, then take an inside staircase to the first floor before proceeding about twenty feet along the edge of the parking lot to reach Room 201. When walking between both his room and the stairwell, and his brother's room and the stairwell, King was exposed to Ray. Even if Ray was watching at those times, King was visible only briefly and he was moving all the time. That ten- to twenty-second exposure would have afforded Ray little chance for a shot if he was just monitoring the motel from his room. Anyway, Ray had just settled into the rooming house. He was in no rush.

Shortly before six, with half an hour before darkness, King again emerged from his room and moved to the edge of the balcony. There he leaned with his elbows against the railing, and started talking to people gathered in the lower courtyard. King's friends and aides later differed in their estimates of how long he was on that balcony before the shot was fired. One of the shortest estimates was from the Reverend Billy Kyles, who thought King was there about six minutes, and the longest was from SCLC attorney Chauncey Eskridge, who estimated fifteen minutes.[15]

The considerable time that transpired from when King came onto the balcony until he was shot is the best evidence that Ray did not expect to get such an early opportunity. If Ray was sitting in the chair monitoring the motel, he would have seen King exit his room and stand at the edge of the balcony. He might have expected him to start walking at any second toward the stairwell, as he had earlier when going to his brother's room. Instead, King remained fixed on the balcony. Dusk was just starting to darken the sky.* And King was still there, not apparently in any rush to leave. Ray had to make a fast decision. Should he wait until he had figured out a schedule for King coming and going from the motel over the next couple of days, carefully choosing his time and then carrying out the assassination, or should he try to shoot him now? He realized that every trip he took to the bathroom with the gun increased his chance of detection. By the time he got there and set up, King might have left the balcony, and then he would have to risk bringing the gun back to his room.

---

* Ray probably did not know that his Redfield scope had its lenses treated with a chemical formula that not only prevented the fogging, distortion, and color halos that affected cheaper scopes, but also enhanced objects seen through the scope at dusk, when lighting conditions are just slightly reduced.

And what about his toiletries, his maps, the rest of his goods? King was still standing there. He was not walking from side to side. It was a dead-on shot. Ray could not hesitate any longer.

He grabbed for the box of Band-Aid sheer strips. He probably intended, as he did on other crimes, to use them over his fingertips to ensure he did not leave behind any prints. But he did not have the time.* Instead, he would have to wipe down anything he touched. He had not been in the room long enough to leave many prints, and when moving the furniture, he had likely used his handkerchief and towel so nothing was left behind.

Ray quickly threw almost all his goods into the zippered bag. In his rush, some items, such as the newspaper, two maps, the pliers, and toilet paper, fell into the blanket. He grabbed the zippered bag, the blanket, and boxed rifle, and quickly moved down the hallway into the bathroom. He left behind only the strap to the binocular case and the elastic belt he had brought up from the Mustang. Now in the bathroom, he locked the door behind him and glanced outside the window. King was still there. He took the rifle out of the box. In the cartridge box, probably using his handkerchief as a holder, he loaded a single bullet into the chamber. Now, rushing to get a shot off while King was an easy target, he did not have time to load the clip with extra bullets, or at least, not enough time to load it while ensuring his prints stayed off each one. One shot would have to do.

It must have been almost 6:00 P.M. when Ray finally stepped into the tub. He had to steady himself against the left wall as he used the tip of the gun barrel to push out the small wire-mesh screen at the bottom of the window. The police later found the screen in the backyard behind the rooming house, under the bathroom window. Ray was not the type to be burdened with a conscience that would have given him last moments of self-doubt, but a first murder, even for someone amoral like him, must have given him a tremendous rush of adrenaline. At the other end of the telescopic site was one of the country's key civil rights leaders.

Ray's excitement at this moment is best evidenced by the window itself. After knocking out the wire screen, he pushed the window up and shoved it so hard that it jammed. Now he only had a five-inch gap through which to shoot. He glanced outside again. Two hundred feet away he had a perfect view of King, still leaning slightly over the railing. He put the gun through the window's opening, and for the first time watched as King's head filled the scope's lens. With seven-power magnification, King seemed less than thirty feet away.

---

* When the police found the Band-Aids, it was a newly purchased box, containing twenty-one regular adhesive bandages and ten "junior" bandages, the same number advertised on the front of the container.

Ray's mind might have raced back to the advice he had picked up in the last week at several gun stores. The .30-06 would drop very little at this range. There was a slight crosswind (7 miles per hour), but he didn't have to compensate. During his practice rounds near Corinth, Mississippi, the gun had fired with a solid but not jarring kick. How easy it must have seemed then to hit fixed targets. Ray placed the crosshairs right in the middle of King's head, steadied himself as much as possible, and pulled the trigger.[16]

Ray must have seen King crash onto the balcony. He knew he had hit King, but just did not know how successful a shot it was. He jumped from the tub, quickly wiped the rifle to clean it of prints, and then threw it into the box. He grabbed his small bag and the blanket and wrapped the gun in the middle so it formed a single, long bundle. With his head down, he walked quickly out of the bathroom. He moved down the hallway at a fast pace, not a run. Two men came out of adjoining rooms. One said, "That sounded like a shot." Ray could not contain himself. "It was," he muttered as he passed, never once looking up.

There were two staircases Ray could have used to exit. It is likely he used the one between the two buildings, because in that way he avoided having to pass by rooms in the other wing, where still more tenants may have spilled into the hallway because of the noise.

Once outside, he turned left to walk to his Mustang. In less than fifty feet he could get the bundle of evidence into his car and safely away from the scene of the murder. No sooner had he started to walk briskly along the front of the rooming house, however, than he suddenly noticed the rear of two police cars. They were parked at the end of the block, in the driveway of the fire station, about 170 feet away from him, near Butler Avenue. (Ten minutes before the assassination, TACT 10 squad, consisting of three police cars with eleven men, had pulled up to the fire station for a rest break.) Ray had to make an instantaneous decision. Were policemen sitting in the cars? He could not see the inside of either of them, but by the time he got to the Mustang, he would be in plain view of whoever was there. Were there police already on the street and he hadn't yet seen them? If caught with the gun, he was finished. He dropped it, almost instinctively, against a storefront at 424 South Main Street, only a few doors from where he had exited the rooming house. The windows of the store, Canipe's, were dark. It seemed closed. The doorway in which he tossed the bundle was recessed from the street. Maybe no one would find it for a while.*

---

* "If he had not dropped the bundle there," John Campbell, an assistant district attorney general, told the author, "he might well have gotten away with the crime. It was that close to being a perfect assassination." Ray had indeed been careful inside the

In thirty seconds he was inside the Mustang and had flipped on the ignition and squealed away from the curb. The first policemen who arrived on the scene, about two to three minutes after the shooting, did not see Ray or the Mustang. He had managed to leave the scene literally seconds ahead of their arrival.

James Earl Ray was no longer a two-bit punk from the backwaters of Missouri. He had gambled on the big time and pulled it off. He pointed his car in the direction of Atlanta and drove straight into the history books.

Back in a ramshackle house in Missouri, Speedy talked to a reporter. He seemed unimpressed by all the publicity surrounding his now infamous son. Sure Jimmy might have killed King. He was always the smartest child. He knew that "niggers are behind all these troubles." He was the one who would have understood that King was going to be president if somebody did not stop him.

The more they talked about James, the more contemplative Speedy became. He seemed to stare almost at the horizon instead of the reporter. He shook his head, more to himself than to anyone else. Maybe Jimmy was just too ambitious for his own good, wanted to get too far away from his roots, become somebody he was not. "People try to get too much out of life," Speedy said, slowly pronouncing each word as though he were repeating the thought as it entered his head. "Sometimes I think Jimmy outsmarted himself. I can't figure out why Jimmy tried to compete with all them bigshots. Life don't amount to a shit anyway. Jimmy had too much nerve for his own good. He tried to go too far too fast."[17]

---

rooming house. None of his prints were in Room 5B or the bathroom. As for the bundle, his prints were found on the rifle, telescopic site, binoculars, newspaper, bottle of after-shave, and one of the beer cans. In an interview with *Playboy* in 1977, Ray suggested that the FBI "transferred my prints to some objects so they could use that as evidence." When the *Playboy* interviewer asked Ray, "To which objects do you think the FBI may have transferred prints?" Ray astonishingly replied, "The beer cans are the only thing I can think of. I believe my prints would have been on the gun. I seldom drink beer. I never buy it. I would have bought whiskey."

Epilogue

There is no doubt that James Earl Ray shot and killed Martin Luther King, Jr. The more puzzling questions are what motivated him, and whether he acted alone or as part of a conspiracy. As for motivation in something as complex as a political murder, the shooter is often driven by several different factors, with no single one predominating. For instance, when Oswald killed John Kennedy, his radical political beliefs were part of the reason he shot at the president, but his primary incentive appears to have been his desire for glory, the almost psychotic craving of a nobody to suddenly become someone. With Ray, there is some of that same yearning for fame and acknowledgment, at least among his criminal peers—as seen in his oft-stated belief, even wish, that the FBI would place him on its ten most-wanted list. Certainly killing King would accomplish that in an instant. Ray relished that newfound notoriety, even taking the risk, while on the run, of visiting a local bar in Toronto in order to watch the popular television program *The F.B.I.* on the night he was placed at the top of the Bureau's most-wanted list. After his arrest, he constantly asked the policemen assigned to guard him about the publicity over the case and how he was portrayed in the press.

But fame alone does not explain why Ray killed King. Another reason was likely his demeaning and dismissive view of blacks. There are prominent incidents in Ray's life—from his refusal to be transferred to an integrated honor farm while in prison, to his bar fights with black sailors while in Mexico, to his repeated attempts to flee to segregationist Rhodesia after killing King—that demonstrate that he is a committed racist. His racism alone would have made it easier for him to murder Martin Luther King, Jr. After all, to Ray he would only be killing a black man in the South. Racists like him would think he was heroic. King was a troublemaker, thought Ray, and no one worthwhile would miss him.

However, his desire for notoriety, even combined with his racism, does not provide a complete and satisfactory answer to why he went to Mrs. Brewer's rooming house on April 4, 1968. Since Ray was a career criminal, driven primarily by the desire to make money, it would seem that he had to believe there was a profit in killing King. Ray's love of quick money, mixed with the racism with which he was raised, was a combustible blend in the volatile political and social climate of the late 1960s.

That he was driven primarily by money does not necessarily mean that he was hired to commit the crime. He might well have learned about a bounty on King, especially the $50,000 offer from St. Louis, and thought he could collect it by committing the murder.

Although Ray had previously bragged to other convicts, and to his brothers, that he might one day kill King, he does not appear to have become serious about those threats until after his December 1967 trip to New Orleans. Following his return to Los Angeles, he took certain actions—having plastic surgery and sending out photos of himself that might create confusion in case of a large manhunt—that appear to be precautions a professional criminal would undertake in preparing for a major crime.

As for a conspiracy, there are several persuasive arguments against Ray's having been brought into an elaborate plot. The crime did not take place for another three and a half months after his visit to New Orleans, during which Ray returned to a leisurely lifestyle in Los Angeles; no plotter could afford to let him in on such a high-profile crime months in advance of the operation. Also, while some conspiracists have speculated that racist Southern businessmen contracted with the New Orleans mob to kill King, it would be an unprecedented assignment for organized crime. Professor Robert Blakey, the Select Committee's chief counsel, as well as the author of the key crime-fighting tool against the mob, RICO (Racketeer Influenced and Corrupt Organizations Act), told the author, "It would not at all be a characteristic of the mob. Except for the CIA/mob effort on Castro, I know of no single instance in which they ever took an assignment from outsiders to kill someone else. It's not what they do. They are a parasite on the body politic and they do not survive by killing the hand that feeds it. Marcello was clearly a racist, but he would not take the assignment because it was not what he did for business, and it involved far too many potential risks."

There is also the perplexing question of why anyone with a substantial contract on King would hire Ray, a person who had no reputation for killing, and had never demonstrated he had the capability or nerve to carry out such an assignment. A professional hit man would surely have been hired.

However, if the St. Louis offer of $50,000 to kill King became known to John and Jerry Ray—which, despite their adamant denials, appears possible—a plan to collect the bounty could have been set in motion. A New Orleans rendezvous could have been a chance for one of the brothers to pass the idea on to James. Fifty thousand dollars was a lot of money, and certainly worth considering, even if they were not ready to commit murder.

If there was ultimately a conspiracy behind King's death, a crude family plot seems more likely than a sophisticated operation involving the mafia or some government agency. That James Earl Ray has lived thirty years after the murder is persuasive evidence that professional conspirators were not involved, since if they had been, they would have disposed of him. They could never be safe so long as Ray lived, and he would have little incentive not to turn them in to authorities in order to win his own coveted freedom. However, if the conspirators included family members—a charge that all Ray's relatives have persistently denied—then he would have an incentive to stay silent. The special bond among the Rays would prevent James from turning in the only people he ever trusted.

The ultimate answers, of course, reside with Ray. He has not helped resolve the crime's mysteries but instead has relished adding confusion and controversy by maintaining steadfast silence on some matters while giving often changing stories about others. He obviously wants to take his secrets to the grave. But he has failed. Whether he acted with the foreknowledge or assistance of his brothers, or whether he was offered money before the murder or merely had heard about an offer and acted on his own, James Earl Ray is the reason that Martin Luther King, Jr., is dead. A four-time loser looking for a big score killed the dreamer, and put himself in the history books.

A Final Analysis

Author's Note Written for This Edition

On April 23, 1998, three weeks after the publication of the hardcover book, James Earl Ray died in a Tennessee prison of liver failure at the age of 70. There was no death bed confession, no indication he was burdened by his conscience and had decided to free the King family and many concerned Americans from the web of deceit he had spun over the decades. Rather, Ray passed defiantly, protesting to the very end that he was merely a patsy in a convoluted conspiracy led by someone he knew only by the name Raoul. Ray also died with the satisfaction that during the last year of his life he had pulled one of the grandest cons of his long criminal career—he had duped the King family into publicly endorsing his innocence.

There was never any question that the Kings had their hearts in the right place as they searched for absolute answers in the assassination. In the years following the murder, they had learned the shocking details of J. Edgar Hoover's obsessive war against Dr. King and were therefore legitimately suspicious that the government might have been involved in the killing. Into this setting entered Ray and his last lawyer, William Pepper, who presented the Kings with purported new witnesses and evidence, persuading them that the assassination was a massive plot that ran all the way up to Lyndon Johnson. This was a tragic turn of events since the Kings accepted the Ray team's evidence without aggressively investigating it.

Once convinced of a gigantic conspiracy, they dug in their heels, and did not want to consider other answers. Although I sent copies of this book to several family members, they refused to read it. They boycotted shows on which I appeared. King family associates attacked me publicly while also refusing to read the book. While this book covers most of Ray's "new" evidence in detail—and reveals it to be bogus—Coretta Scott King and her son, Dexter, instead asked President Clinton to establish a new, full inquiry into the case. To their disappointment, the Justice Department finally agreed to only a limited investigation.

While Ray's death prompted the Kings to accelerate their effort at obtaining a new murder inquiry, the Ray brothers—Jerry and John—fell back to old habits and started to think of ways to profit from the turn of events. Jerry (who alternately referred to me in widely distributed letters as an "FBI pimp" or a "slimeball," and once caused the police to be called at one of my book signings he disrupted in Memphis) bragged about an "explosive" book he intended to write. He also unsuccessfully lobbied the District Attorney General in Memphis to release to him the murder weapon and other personal items belonging to James, all of which could fetch high prices on the auction block. Although Jerry had spent some ten years working with the arch-racist and convicted church bomber, J.B. Stoner, and himself had written heatedly about "Nigger beasts," he continued his calculated campaign to become an ally of the Kings. Not only did he brag about Dexter King's embrace of him before James's death, but at the memorial service for James, Jerry sat next to Isaac Farris, Jr., a nephew of Dr. King who represented the King family. "They are not a dumb family," Jerry Ray told me. "They know what really happened."

As for John Ray, who had remained silent for years about the assassination, he announced four months after James's death that he would "solve the whole case" if the government gave him a "six-figure" payoff. Nobody took up his offer.

The results of the latest Justice Department investigation are not expected until sometime in 1999, and most observers, including this author, expect that none of the so-called new evidence will amount to anything substantive. This will leave the King family, and many others who share their opinions, unsatisfied.

However, if those convinced of a widespread plot are willing to approach this murder with an open mind, there can be closure. After thirty years, there is ample credible evidence to determine who shot Dr. King, and what the most likely reasons were for the murder. Two separate events took place in the late 1960s. On the one hand, the government waged an illegal war against Dr. King. Its purpose was to ruin his reputation and career and leave him without honor in his own community. At the same time, a racist named James Earl Ray, almost certainly motivated by the lure of big money, and possibly helped by a small conspiracy of like-minded bigots, moved toward killing King. I have little doubt that some government officials celebrated King's death and would have pinned a medal on Ray. But my investigation shows the government was not behind Ray.

While it may not have pulled the trigger, the government did however, by such outrageous conduct, create an atmosphere where racists thought it was safe to shoot a black leader in the South and think they could get away with it. To that extent, the government bears moral responsibility for the death of Dr. King. But the ultimate responsibility—for the sake of justice and history— must be placed squarely on the man with blood on his hands, James Earl Ray. To say otherwise, in light of the overwhelming evidence of his guilt, is to let Ray have the final laugh, and to mock the great memory of Dr. King.

Acknowledgments

This book involved much more extensive research than I originally envisioned, and since it was completed under a short deadline, I often put great demands on many people in procuring information. Most took time from their own hectic schedules to assist me, and this book would not have been possible without many of their efforts.

Professor David Garrow originally encouraged me to tackle this subject, and his unwavering commitment to an accurate historical record—evidenced so well in his prodigious work on Martin Luther King, Jr., and the civil rights movement—served as a model for this project.

In obtaining documents, I am indebted to Dr. Ed Frank and his excellent staff at the University of Memphis's Special Collection, with its superb Sanitation Strike Archives; Maritta Aspen and Tom Moutes of the Los Angeles Police Department, Records and Identification Division, for their diligent search to locate James Earl Ray's arrest records; Frank McEwen, supervisor at the St. Louis Police Records Department, who obtained a copy of Ray's files in record time; John White and Steven Niven, reference archivists at the Southern Historical Collection at the University of North Carolina at Chapel Hill, for their assistance in working through the George McMillan papers; N'Jeri Yasin and Kimberly Mac-Kall were outstanding in their support at the FBI reading room, and made an

otherwise onerous task—combing more than 50,000 pages related to the assassination—quite manageable; Tim Kniest, the public information officer at the
Missouri Department of Corrections, was always willing to track down arcane
information about the prison in which James Earl Ray served nearly seven years;
Jim Baggett of the Birmingham Library's historical collection found relevant files
on short notice; Linda Hanson, archivist at the Lyndon Baines Johnson Presidential Library, was, as on previous book projects, helpful in quickly procuring
relevant oral histories; Elizabeth Lockwood, of the Access and Freedom of Information staff at the National Archives, College Park, Maryland, facilitated the
task of reviewing several thousand pages of Justice Department documents on
the case; Rick Ewig, director, and Carol Bowers, archival specialist, of the American Heritage Center at the University of Wyoming, were always eager to follow
up on my many requests relating to the Clay Blair, Jr., papers; Elvis Brathwaite, of
Wide World Photos, as always, was instrumental in locating interesting pictures;
and Jeffrey Smith, curator and director of rare books and manuscripts at the Special Collections at Ohio State University, was ultimately able to provide little from
the William Bradford Huie papers, but it was not for lack of trying.

In obtaining information in other countries, I am grateful to Julie Kirsh, the
manager of the News Research division at the *Toronto Sun;* Alexandra Erskine,
archivist at London's *Daily Telegraph;* the Mexican ambassador to the United
States, the Honorable Jesús Silva-Herzog; and Peter Brighton of London's
Searchlight magazine.

The district attorney general's office in Memphis at times seemed like a second office. District Attorney General Bill Gibbons encouraged his staff to help
my wife, Trisha, and me, providing files and giving us unlimited entrée to those
we needed to interview. It is hard to overestimate the assistance they provided,
including access to the four-drawer cabinet consisting of the original case file
prepared by the prosecution for the 1968 murder trial that never took place.
Particularly stellar was Assistant District Attorney General John Campbell. As
the lead prosecutor for the past four years, he knows the case better than anyone in the office, and he saved me from heading down many fruitless paths of
inquiry. He patiently provided a clear understanding of the case's complexities.
Criminal investigator Mark Glankler shared the inside story of his own extensive work, and without his cooperation it would have been impossible to resolve
many of the recent issues raised by the Ray defense team. George King, the
chief of the Criminal Investigative Division, allowed Glankler and other investigators to provide their information on the record.

Those who know how the district attorney general's office operates know it
would not run very efficiently without Betty Krupicka, the executive assistant
to Bill Gibbons. She consistently went out of her way to ensure that we had
easy and constant access to the office and its information.

Even some who were retired from the office, such as former district attorney general John Pierotti, and Judges James Beasley and Robert Dwyer, were generous in taking time to reconstruct the behind-the-scenes details of the original investigation.

Early on, when searching for the papers of several authors who had written about the case, I stumbled across relatives or spouses who often turned into friends. Priscilla Johnson McMillan and Cecily McMillan, the first and second wives of the late George McMillan, not only were willing to search their houses and attics for documents, but always offered encouragement when needed; Dr. John Frank, the son of author Gerold Frank, agreeably answered my repeated requests to pick through his father's papers; and my greatest fortune was in finding Martha Huie, the wife of the late author William Bradford Huie. While she did not have any of her husband's papers, she turned into my most consistent pen pal in Memphis, regularly sending me clippings of every local article remotely related to the case. On our trips to Memphis, she and her family graciously received my wife and me, always providing us names of people to interview and introductions to others who were useful in procuring information. Her enthusiasm will always be fondly remembered.

Among journalists, Marc Perrusquia of *The Commercial Appeal* has led the coverage since 1993 with his insightful and solid reporting, and he was generous in providing me information and leads. Arthur Brice of *The Atlanta Journal-Constitution* also had a fine perception of the case's nuances, and our occasional conversations were helpful in providing clues to the latest twists and turns.

There are dozens of people who have taken the time to speak with me, but a few deserve special mention, including Judge Joe Brown and Judge John P. Colton, Jr., who have both overseen parts of Ray's recent legal maneuvering; N. E. Zachary, the former homicide chief of the Memphis police department; Lewis Garrison and Marvin Ballin, Memphis attorneys who represent individuals who figure in some of the latest controversies in the case; the Reverend Billy Kyles, one of Memphis's most prominent preachers, whose recollection of his work with Dr. King, and the days around the assassination, was of particular assistance; Dr. Jerry Francisco, the Memphis medical examiner, who carefully answered any questions I had regarding King's autopsy; Gene Stanley, a Knoxville attorney whose representation of a former client brought him into the periphery of the case, who was willing to spend the time necessary to resolve any outstanding questions; G. Robert Blakey, a Notre Dame professor and former chief counsel of the House Select Committee on Assassinations, who was generous in sharing his insights, and Jack Valenti, president of the Motion Picture Association of America, was kind enough to answer for the record some outrageous—and patently false—charges that had been made against him as part of the widening conspiracy theory spun by Ray's supporters.

Janet Mattick is a New York attorney at the Manhattan law firm of Reboul, MacMurray, Hewitt, Maynard & Kristol. She represents a man, referred to in this book as Raul Mirabal, who has been accused by James Earl Ray and his attorney and investigators as being the mastermind of the King assassination. After talking to me and reviewing some of my earlier work, Ms. Mattick felt comfortable enough to recommend to her client that he speak with me. Eventually he did—his first-ever interview on the record—and Ms. Mattick provided documentation supporting what he recounted. That interview was critical in resolving the truth or falsity of James Earl Ray's long-standing alibi in the murder.

Wayne Chastain, a former journalist turned lawyer, represented Ray for several years. Although he expected that he would disagree with my conclusions about his client's guilt, he nevertheless was generous with his time and extensive knowledge of the case. The same is true of two of Ray's investigators, Kenny Herman and John Billings, both of whom sincerely believe their client is innocent and are doing their best to free him. Herman repeatedly went out of his way to assist my research when in Memphis (and later by e-mail).

On the issue of whether the military was involved in a plot to kill King, I am grateful to the incredible help of retired major Rudi Gresham. Gresham was a one-person research team, and through his intervention I obtained the necessary military documents to resolve open issues. Several people agreed to be interviewed who were key to the story; special thanks are due to Deputy Colonel John Smith, information officer for the U.S. Army; Daniel Ellsberg; and a number of retired military officers: General William P. Yarborough; General Henry Cobb; Colonel Ian D.W. Sutherland; Colonel Harry Summers, Jr.; Colonel Lee Mize; Captain Billy Eidson; Jimmy Dean, the administrator of the Special Forces Association; and General Ray Davis.

Several people in Memphis went out of their way to assist me. Among those was William R. Key, the Criminal Court clerk for the Thirtieth Judicial District in Shelby County, Tennessee. He is responsible for storing and maintaining the case's physical evidence, and pursuant to an order from Judge John P. Colton, Jr., provided my wife and me access to all of the case's evidence, including the murder weapon. Nick Owens, in the clerk's office, was careful about balancing his duty to preserve the integrity of the evidence with allowing us the fullest possible review.

Ellis H. Chappell and Adam Feibelman reside in separate buildings that used to comprise the rooming house from which Ray fired the fatal shot. They did not slam their doors when my wife and I unexpectedly appeared one day, and they were gracious in letting us have unrestricted access to their homes on several occasions, for everything from taking photos and measurements to even observing the hotel from the sniper's nest with a replica of the rifle scope used by Ray.

Mohamad A. Hakimian and Rick Roberts helped convert a room at Memphis's wonderful Peabody Hotel into a virtual office, and the staff accommodated my many requests, from photocopying documents in the middle of the night to repeatedly securing a quiet corner of the bustling lobby for an interview.

Some private companies aided my research. I am especially thankful to Nancy Childs of Polaroid and Ken Johnson of Redfield Scopes. Herbert Koogle, of Koogle & Pouls Engineering in Albuquerque, New Mexico, provided background information regarding the survey of the murder scene his firm had undertaken in 1978 for the House Select Committee on Assassinations; Mark Christofferson of Guns & Things in Alberta, Canada, was incredibly patient in answering my many ballistics questions, and he is responsible for finding me a replica of Ray's rifle, even down to the same mounting brackets for the telescopic sight.

Steve Goldberg, Esq., Los Angeles, was always available with sagacious legal advice. Victor Kovner, Esq., was meticulous as usual in his vetting of the manuscript. Former FBI analyst Farris Rookstool and insurance investigator David Perry, both of Dallas, gladly handled offbeat requests I sent their way. Gus Russo was kind in sharing his extensive contacts. David Scott Weisblatt, fresh from college graduation, obtained public documents between his summer jobs. Former FBI special agent Buck Revell willingly located retired agents. Former agent Robert Fitzpatrick was instrumental in my understanding of the FBI's local surveillance of Martin Luther King in Memphis prior to the assassination. And Jerry Ray, James Earl Ray's brother, grudgingly provided a number of audiotapes that were part monologue about the case, part venomous insults against writers with whom he disagreed, and part showcase for Jerry's singing.

David Lifton, author of *Best Evidence*, about the JFK assassination, may seem an unlikely person to assist me, as we have diametrically different conclusions about that murder. However, after I called him to obtain an article he had coauthored in 1977 ("A Man He Calls Raoul," *New Times*), we struck up a relationship largely through e-mail. Eventually, he provided copies of much of his own voluminous research for that article. The fact that he had to retrieve it from a distant storage locker and copy it himself overnight while under his own deadline for a book about Lee Harvey Oswald, is especially appreciated. His material was useful, and I believe that while we will never concur about who killed JFK, we will surprise both our boosters and antagonists by our very near agreement on the King case.

I am lucky to count Fredric Dannen as my closest friend. He always finds time in the middle of his own journalism deadlines to read the first draft of my manuscripts. His critique is unsparing but inevitably right, making for a better book.

My new agent, Andrew Wylie, has shown me great attention and spent much time both negotiating the right contract for this book and in nurturing the project at all stages. At least for me, he lived up to his reputation as a consummate dealmaker.

As for my publishers, Random House, I am very pleased to have another book with them. Each project is like returning to visit a group of dear friends, and I greatly appreciate the unusual extent to which they allow me to participate in all stages of the publishing process. Harry Evans, the former publisher, had the foresight to sign this when no one else was thinking about a book on the King assassination. I could not ask for anyone better than Ann Godoff, publisher and editor in chief, to watch over its publication. And the support team within Random House is superb. Art director Andy Carpenter makes designing imaginative jackets seem effortless. Lesley Oelsner, Esq., made the legal review as painless as possible, ensuring the integrity of the manuscript. Editorial associate Barbé Hammer never tires of my many questions and requests. Fact checker Marina Harss did a thorough review of the manuscript. John McGhee was careful and comprehensive in his copy-editing. Amy Edelman managed the very tight schedule, pushing me gently along to complete the manuscript, without ever adding to the project's pressure. Beth Pearson, who has overseen the editorial production now on three of my books, has become a friend and trusted critic. The long hours she spends painstakingly reviewing the manuscript and her penchant for probing questions always result in a better book.

As on each book, I am greatly indebted to my good friend and editor, Robert Loomis. Bob is usually juggling a dozen books at any moment but still manages to spoil me with extraordinary time and care. He always maintains an unflappable demeanor, punctuated with his dry but often biting sense of humor, and his great interest in the subject, fine editing of the manuscript, and the constant debate in which he engages me are indispensable contributions. This book would not exist without his early enthusiasm and constant guidance.

Finally, I come to my family. My dear mother, Gloria, is my strongest booster, always giving me encouragement at some moment when I am low. Her support has paid dividends for decades.

And most of all, I pay tribute to my wife, my soul mate, Trisha. Once again, I have incurred a debt to her that I can never repay. Describing her role as researcher, interviewer, webmaster, photocopier, and unofficial editor only partly explains what she does. Trisha also provides unselfish love and nurturing, and her uncanny intuition and commitment to the truth guide me daily. I cannot imagine tackling these projects, all-consuming as they are, without her at my side. Since my name is on the book jacket, I get the credit, but this is very much a team effort, and *Killing the Dream* is as much hers as mine. I am blessed to have her as my partner.

Notes

Abbreviations Used for Frequently Occurring Citations

MURKIN: The volumes of files concerning the FBI's investigation of the murder of Martin Luther King, Jr., maintained at the FBI reading room, Washington, D.C.

MLK FBI: The volumes of files concerning the FBI's monitoring of Martin Luther King, Jr., maintained at the FBI reading room, Washington, D.C.

OPR FBI: The 20 boxes of files of the Department of Justice's Office of Professional Responsibility Task Force Review of the FBI's Security and Assassination Investigations of Martin Luther King, maintained at the National Archives, College Park, Maryland.

Sanitation Strike Archives: Files of the J. W. Brister Library, Monograph Series, The Memphis Multi-Media Archival Project, the 1968 Sanitation Workers' Strike, maintained at the Special Collections, McWhether Library, University of Memphis, Memphis, Tennessee.

Attorney General File: Documents maintained as the active case file on the assassination of Martin Luther King, Jr., in the office of the district attorney general, Memphis, Tennessee.

HSCA Rpt.: Report of the Select Committee on Assassinations of the U.S. House of Representatives, Ninety-Fifth Congress, 1979 (edition printed by Bantam Books).

HSCA vol.: The thirteen Martin Luther King, Jr., volumes of Hearing and Appendices of the House Select Committee on Assassinations, 1979, referred to by volume and page number (U.S. Government Printing House edition).

McMillan/Southern Historical Collection: The nine boxes of research papers of the late author George McMillan, maintained as collection 4271 at the Southern Historical Collection, Wilson Library, University of North Carolina.

20,000 Words: After Ray's arrest in June 1968, his first attorneys, Arthur Hanes, Sr., and Arthur Hanes, Jr., as well as his second attorney, Percy Foreman, entered into contracts with author William Bradford Huie. Under the arrangements, intended mostly to pay for Ray's legal costs, Ray provided written material to Huie covering the periods before and after the assassination. The materials Huie received have come to be known as the "20,000 Words." A complete set was published in 1979 as a volume of the House Select Committee on Assassinations report (vol. XII), and any reference to the 20,000 Words in this book refers to that published version.

A Note About the Use of George McMillan Archives

Author George McMillan began researching a book on the assassination of Martin Luther King, Jr., shortly after the 1968 murder, and worked on it for seven years. His book, *The Making of an Assassin*, was published by Little, Brown in 1976. During the research, he obtained more access to the Ray family than any other author or journalist. James was the only one who refused to talk to him. "Jimmy would never tell anybody anything about himself," Jerry Ray told McMillan. "It's been like that since he was a little boy." But Ray's father, sisters, and brothers all cooperated, with the most extensive help coming from Jerry, with whom McMillan talked frequently on the phone and also met several dozen times.

McMillan, as did other authors on the case, tried early on to make exclusive deals with the Rays so that he could write the "official" story. Jerry repeatedly made it clear that the Rays would not talk without some payment. "A book comes in with a lot of money," he told McMillan on one occasion, "and I'm only making $115 a week. I guess you know all of us are poor. We haven't a cent."

From 1969 to 1972, McMillan made various offers to the Rays, normally proposing a $4,000 to $5,000 payment to each, but a deal was never consummated. However, while the Rays stalled, refusing to give anybody exclusivity, they collected money from half a dozen writers. McMillan, while never getting the sole access he desired, nevertheless paid James's father $1,000, his sister Carol $1,000, $500 to his brother John, and more than $4,000 to Jerry. Yet McMillan's efforts were not in vain. The Ray family told him some explosive things, including that James shot King, that the family knew of his plans nearly a year before, and that Jerry had even received a telephone call the night before boasting of the next day's assassination.

However, after McMillan's book was published, the Ray family denounced it in unison. Jerry sued McMillan for $2.2 million for libel and fraudulent conversion of materials belonging to the Rays. (McMillan was the only author sued, but Jerry and John Ray talked about beating up other authors—William Bradford Huie and Clay Blair—whose books they did not like.) That lawsuit was dismissed since Jerry had earlier accepted $500 to sign a broad legal release for any claims he might have had against McMillan or his publisher. James Earl Ray also sued McMillan for libel but his case was dismissed when a judge determined he was "libel-proof." Notwithstanding the unsuccessful legal efforts, Jerry has said that he made everything up in order to fool McMillan—"There isn't one word of truth in his whole book," Jerry wrote to Little, Brown. The Rays' denunciation has cast some doubt on the value of the McMillan papers regarding the family's admissions.

However, the author and his wife, Trisha, were the first researchers to examine the entire McMillan collection since the family donated it to the Southern Historical Collection at the University of North Carolina. In the history that is laid out of the relationship between the Rays and McMillan, it is evident that McMillan did in fact gain an unprecedented level of trust with the family. Priscilla McMillan, then George's wife, and a renowned author in her own right (*Marina and Lee*, Harper & Row, 1977), told the author, "George had spent much of his life at the bottom, and therefore he really, really understood and liked the Rays. They picked up on that, that he was not talking down to them. He became a friend and they responded to it. Jerry actually wanted to live with us, to move in. He stayed with us once at a hotel, and was so sad to leave the next morning. He had finally found some feeling of family. And George liked him even though he knew Jerry was capable of shooting someone. He knew the Rays had a different idea of the truth and they could lie, but they didn't view it as lying. You just had to be very careful with what they told you and make sure you checked everything."

A careful review of the McMillan papers reveals that during the early years of his relationship with the Rays—when they trusted him completely—McMillan received their unfiltered feelings, opinions, and recollections. The Rays, especially Jerry, emphasized their friendship with the author, and being naive about how their words would eventually look in print, had remarkably frank discussions with him. As McMillan's research progressed, the Rays began suspecting he was not doing a book favorable to James. For instance, by mid-1970, the Rays had heard rumors that McMillan had consulted a number of psychiatrists as part of his research. As Jerry told McMillan in a June 1970 telephone conversation, James had "heard you were consulting shrinks and he knows that any book written with a shrink around is going to be a sex book because that is all those shrinks are interested in is sex." That marked the beginning of a nearly two-year period in which the family was warier in its dealings with McMillan—they were generally as open, but talked to him on fewer occasions.

By mid-1972, the family was turning against him. Some, like James's sister Carol, eventually asked the phone company to stop McMillan from calling her. She angrily told McMillan that he should expose the injustices done to her brothers and father, rather than go ahead and write a book about "somebody killing a nigger in Memphis."

However, Jerry, instead of cutting away from McMillan, maintained the relationship even past the publication, but his letters became belligerent. At one stage, he warned McMillan, "Do something for your country and come over to the Honest side, the American public isnt foolish as you Book writers think, Neither are the Black Savsges." Another time, Jerry told him, "I hate how you try to run the poor white down but on the other hand a Nigger cant do no wrong."

It is during this period that Jerry pulled pranks and told some lies, always trying to get paid for his new "information." For instance, he sent McMillan on a futile chase for a neo-Nazi—Rudolf Stroheim—that James had supposedly known in Germany. There was no such person. He did the same regarding another person who supposedly knew something about the case, a fictional character named Emmett Daniels. In 1975, Jerry sold Ray "family" pictures to McMillan: They turned out to be old photos of strangers the Rays had bought in an antique store.

Jerry Ray uses those demonstrably false examples to charge that everything else he told McMillan was also a lie. However, none of Jerry's lies took place before mid-1972, and most occurred in 1974 and 1975. Before then, Jerry's trust, as well as that of the rest of the Ray family, was intact and unchallenged. Their hesitation developed only midway through the research, and their full fury only after the publication of McMillan's book, in which James is identified as the lone assassin. Then, expectedly, they had to decide how to attack the book and distance themselves from their own integral assistance. Jerry also had good legal reasons to denounce the book and what he had told McMillan. If McMillan was accurate, then Jerry could be indicted for being part of the King assassination. "If this stuff was true," Jerry nervously told the *Chicago Sun-Times* after the book's publication, "if we were sitting around plotting murders, they'd get me for conspiracy."

The Rays denunciation of the McMillan book must also be seen in light of their subsequent belief that all book writers from major publishing companies were probably working for the government, and hence were doing books that, as James said, "were the only ones that convicted me." Jerry told a congressional committee, "McMillan is an FBI writer, a pro-FBI writer, and his wife is a CIA writer." John speculated that another writer on the case, Gerold Frank, was paid either by "the Wealthy East or the FBI." James himself complained about the "U.S. judicial system's operations, in league with dominant publishing companies in railroading innocent defendants."

Mark Lane, the conspiracy buff who was James Earl Ray's attorney before the House Select Committee during the late 1970s, joined in the attack. Lane contended that the evidence
for McMillan concocting some of his conversations with Jerry Ray is that "During several
conversations with Jerry Ray I noticed that although his manner was informal in general, he
referred to his brother almost invariably as James. Yet, in McMillan's book, all of the reconstructed conversations attributed to Jerry find him referring to his brother as Jimmy." But
Lane never examined the McMillan archive, including the many letters from family members
to McMillan—all of them from the late 1960s and early 1970s refer to Jimmy. Even in his first
arrest in Los Angeles, James gave the police his nickname as "Jimmy."

Every attempt has been made in this book to verify the information Jerry Ray and other
family members gave McMillan, and their statements given from 1968 to mid-1972 are
judged to be truthful. As for later remarks from the Rays, each is judged on its own merits and
is used only if it is confirmed by something the Rays independently told McMillan in the earlier period, or if the author obtained additional corroboration of its truthfulness.

Chapter 1: "I Am a Man"

1. The 1,300 strikers included 1,100 in sanitation and 230 in asphalt, sewers, and
drains.

2. The first attempt at unionization, in 1963, failed when the city simply fired several of
the key organizers. In 1966, the sanitation and sewer workers were awarded a charter—
Local 1733—by the American Federation of State, County and Municipal Employees.

3. James Lawson interview with David Yellin and Bill Thomas, July 1, 1968, "James
Lawson," Tape 1, WMC-TV Studio, Carton 22, Sanitation Strike Archives.

4. Ibid.

5. On June 21, 1964, James Chaney, a black teenager from Philadelphia, Mississippi, together with Andrew Goodman and Michael Schwerner, white students from New York City,
disappeared after an arrest for speeding. On August 4, their bullet-ridden bodies were discovered, buried in a nearby earthen dam.

6. Billy Kyles interview with author, August 2, 1997.

7. Ibid.

8. James Lawson interview with David Yellin and Bill Thomas, July 1, 1968, "James
Lawson," Tape 1, WMC-TV Studio, Carton 22, Sanitation Strike Archives.

9. Billy Kyles interview with author, August 2, 1997.

10. Testimony of Ralph Abernathy, August 14, 1978, HSCA vol. 1, p. 13.

11. During the first week of March, there seemed a possibility for a settlement. Some of
Loeb's closest friends had persuaded him to send a letter to Jesse Epps, setting forth the city's
maximum concessions. Although less than the workers wanted, it might have ended the
walkout. However, before the letter was sent, one of the local newspapers, *The Commercial Appeal*, ran a story with the headline "Loeb May Offer Compromise." Refusing to appear as
though he had buckled at all under the strikers' demands, Loeb did not send the letter, and
the strike remained a standoff.

12. James Lawson interview with David Yellin and Bill Thomas, July 1, 1968, "James
Lawson," Tape 1, WMC-TV Studio, Carton 22, Sanitation Strike Archives.

13. Gerold Frank, *An American Death* (New York: Doubleday & Co., 1972), p. 17.

14. Billy Kyles interview with author, August 2, 1997.

15. Frank, *An American Death*, pp. 17–18.

16. Jim Lawson interview with Joan Beifuss and David Yellin, July 8, 1970, "James Lawson," Tape 243, Series X, 1 of 2, Carton 1 of 2, 140, p. 5, Sanitation Strike Archives.

17. Billy Kyles interview with author, August 2, 1997.

18. James Lawson interview with David Yellin and Bill Thomas, July 1, 1968, "James
Lawson," Tape 1, WMC-TV Studio, Carton 22, Sanitation Strike Archives.

19. Jim Lawson interview with Joan Beifuss and David Yellin, July 8, 1970, "James Lawson," Tape 243, Series X, 1 of 2, Carton 1 of 2, 140, pp. 7–9, Sanitation Strike Archives.

20. Interview with Mrs. N. E. Zachary, June 13, 1997.

21. FBI statement of Clyde Manasco, April 18, 1968, MURKIN 3763–3872, section 46, p. 17, also statement of April 10, 1968, MURKIN 2323–2324, section 21, p. 136; see also, regarding physical description, statement of Quinton B. Davis, April 10, 1968, MURKIN 2323–2324, section 21, pp. 133–34.

22. FBI statement of Clyde Manasco, April 10, 1968, MURKIN 2323–2324, section 21, p. 136.

23. See, generally, FBI statement of Quinton B. Davis, April 18, 1968, MURKIN 3763–3872, section 46, p. 19; see also Davis statement, April 10, 1968, MURKIN 2323–2324, section 21, p. 132, and FBI statement of Clyde Manasco, April 8, 1968, MURKIN 2323–2324, section 21, p. 135.

24. FBI statement of Clyde Manasco, April 10, 1968, MURKIN 2323–2324, section 21, p. 137.

25. FBI statement of Quinton B. Davis, April 10, 1968, MURKIN 2323–2324, section 21, p. 133.

26. Ibid., p. 134—words quoted are the agent's summary of Davis's conclusion.

27. FBI statement of Clyde Manasco, April 10, 1968, MURKIN 2323–2324, section 21, p. 137.

Chapter 2: The Riot

1. Billy Kyles interview with author, August 2, 1997.

2. Ralph David Abernathy, *And the Walls Came Tumbling Down* (New York: Harper & Row, 1989), p. 417.

3. Ibid.

4. Jim Lawson interview with Joan Beifuss and David Yellin, July 8, 1970, "James Lawson," Tape 244, Series X, 2 of 2, Carton 2 of 2, 141, pp. 9–10, Sanitation Strike Archives.

5. Billy Kyles interview with author, August 2, 1997.

6. Abernathy, *And the Walls Came Tumbling Down*, p. 417.

7. Billy Kyles interview with author, August 2, 1997.

8. Jim Lawson interview with Joan Beifuss and David Yellin, July 8, 1970, "James Lawson," Tape 244, Series X, 2 of 2, Carton 2 of 2, 141, p. 15, Sanitation Strike Archives.

9. Abernathy, *And the Walls Came Tumbling Down*, p. 418.

10. Ibid., pp. 418–19.

11. "Guard Keeps Memphis Quiet; King Vows Another March," *The Atlanta Constitution*, March 30, 1968, p. A3.

12. "Guard and Police Keep Edgy Memphis Quiet," *The Atlanta Constitution*, March 29, 1968, pp. A1, A16.

13. Abernathy, *And the Walls Came Tumbling Down*, p. 419.

14. Billy Kyles interview with author, August 2, 1997.

15. David J. Garrow, *Bearing the Cross: Martin Luther King, Jr., and the Southern Christian Leadership Conference* (New York: William Morrow and Company, 1986), pp. 611–12.

16. Andrew Young quoted by David Nordan, "King, Aides Map Strategy; His Leadership Under Study," *The Atlanta Constitution*, March 31, 1968, p. 1.

17. Jim Lawson interview with Joan Beifuss and David Yellin, July 8, 1970, "James Lawson," Tape 244, Series X, 2 of 2, Carton 2 of 2, 141, pp. 37–38, Sanitation Strike Archives.

18. Ibid., p. 40.

19. Abernathy, *And the Walls Came Tumbling Down*, p. 422.

20. Steve Kopp interviewed by the FBI, April 8, 1968, MURKIN 2323–2324, section 21, pp. 143–44.

21. Ibid., pp. 141–42.

22. Ibid., p. 141.

23. Ibid., p. 143; Frank, *An American Death*, p. 35.

24. John Webster DeShazo interviewed by the FBI, April 7, 1968, MURKIN 2323–2324, section 21, p. 39.

25. See generally Donald F. Wood statement to the FBI, April 5, 1968, MURKIN 2076–2150, section 18, pp. 113–14.

26. John Webster DeShazo interviewed by the FBI, April 7, 1968, MURKIN 2323–2324, section 21, p. 40.

27. Ibid., p. 39.

28. Photocopy of Aeromarine Supply Co. Invoice 2251A, MURKIN 2323–2324, section 21, p. 35.

29. Donald F. Wood statement to the FBI, April 5, 1968, MURKIN 2076–2150, section 18, p. 114.

30. Ibid., p. 115.

Chapter 3: "Nobody's Going to Kill You, Martin"

1. Abernathy, *And the Walls Came Tumbling Down*, p. 423.

2. See generally Garrow, *Bearing the Cross*, pp. 615–16.

3. Ibid.; Abernathy, *And the Walls Came Tumbling Down*, p. 425.

4. Abernathy, *And the Walls Came Tumbling Down*, p. 425; see also testimony of Ralph Abernathy, August 14, 1978, HSCA vol. 1, p. 18.

5. Testimony of Ralph Abernathy, August 14, 1978, HSCA vol. 1, p. 18.

6. Abernathy, *And the Walls Came Tumbling Down*, p. 427.

7. Garrow, *Bearing the Cross*, p. 618.

8. Abernathy, *And the Walls Came Tumbling Down*, pp. 427–28.

9. Ibid., p. 428.

10. Statement of Annie Estelle Peters to the FBI, April 16, 1968, MURKIN 2323–2324, section 21, p. 240.

11. Statement of Jimmie Garner, April 14 and 15, 1968, MURKIN 2323–2324, section 21, pp. 247–52.

12. William Bradford Huie, the writer who struck a financial arrangement with Ray and his first lawyers, Arthur Hanes, Sr., and Arthur Hanes, Jr., for the exclusive story, reported that Ray told the Haneses that he had test-fired the rifle near Corinth, Mississippi, which could be reached on the road from Atlanta (William Bradford Huie interviewed by House Select Committee investigators, April 21, 1978, HSCA vol. VII, p. 441); see also Frank, *An American Death*, p. 38, and George McMillan, *The Making of an Assassin* (Boston: Little Brown & Co., 1976), pp. 297–98. Note: Ray denies that he stopped along the road to take the practice shots, although that is the reasonable explanation as to why both boxes of ammo he says he bought were mostly empty before the assassination shot was ever fired. Ray has a much more convoluted explanation for what he did with the rifle, and it is discussed in detail in Chapter 25. Also, some conspiracists suggest that a couple of dozen shots are not enough to adjust the scope. Yet firearms experts, as well as Remington and Redfield representatives, told the author that it was often possible to do a proper adjustment with as few as six to eight shots.

Chapter 4: "I've Been to the Mountaintop"

1. Letter to N. P. Huston, chief of the Criminal Investigative Division for the Memphis Police, from Don H. Smith, re: Detail with Dr. Martin Luther King, Jr., dated April 5, 1968, MLK Exhibit F-187, HSCA vol. IV, pp. 257–58.

2. Testimony of Frank Holloman, chief of Memphis Police, November 10, 1978, HSCA vol. IV, pp. 254–55.

3. Testimony of Ralph Abernathy, August 14, 1997, HSCA vol. 1, pp. 32–33; Billy Kyles interviewed by author, August 2, 1997; Walter Bailey interviewed by Bill Thomas and Gwen Kyles, July 10, 1968, Tape 22, Series 1 of 1, Sanitation Strike Archives.

4. Abernathy, *And the Walls Came Tumbling Down*, p. 429.

5. Frank, *An American Death*, p. 50.

6. Jim Lawson interview with Joan Beifuss and David Yellin, July 8, 1970, "James Lawson," Tape 244, Series VIII, 2 of 2, Carton 22, 137, Sanitation Strike Archives.

7. Martin Luther King, Jr., *I've Been to the Mountaintop* (San Francisco: Harper San Francisco, 1995).

8. Abernathy, *And the Walls Came Tumbling Down*, p. 433.

9. Jim Lawson interview with Joan Beifuss and David Yellin, July 8, 1970, "James Lawson," Tape 244, Series VIII, tape 2 of 2, Carton 22, 137, Sanitation Strike Archives.

10. Billy Kyles interviewed by author, August 2, 1997.

11. "Oliver Rexall Drug Store," FBI summary information, includes interviews with Peggy Burns, store clerk, April 4 and 11, 1968, MURKIN 2322, section 20, pp. 134–38, and April 19, 1968, MURKIN 2634, section 26, p. 19.

12. FBI interview with Peggy Burns, store clerk, April 11, 1968, MURKIN 2322, section 20, p. 138.

13. Huie, *He Slew the Dreamer*, p. 117.

14. FBI interview with Ivan B. Webb, April 11, 1968, MURKIN 2322, section 20, p. 146; also see FBI summary in MURKIN 621–750, section 6, pp. 42–43.

15. Frank, *An American Death*, p. 38.

Chapter 5: Mrs. Brewer's Rooming House

1. Abernathy, *And The Walls Came Tumbling Down*, p. 437.

2. Testimony of Ralph Abernathy, August 14, 1978, HSCA vol. 1, p. 19.

3. Andrew Young quoted in Garrow, *Bearing the Cross*, p. 623.

4. Bob Fitzpatrick, retired FBI agent, interviewed by author, July 21, 1997. See Marc Perrusquia, "King Scrutiny a Myth, Say Agents Here in '68," *The Commercial Appeal*, November 30, 1997, p. A1. For further discussion about the military-intelligence role in the surveillance of King, see Chapter 32.

5. General William Yarborough interviewed by author, July 17, 1997.

6. Bessie Brewer interviewed by the FBI, April 9, 1968, MURKIN ME, Sub. D, section 1, p. 136.

7. Ibid.

8. Ibid.

9. Charlie Quitman Stephens interviewed by the FBI, April 5, 1968, MURKIN 2322, section 20, p. 32.

10. Frank, *An American Death*, p. 60.

11. For descriptions of each of the tenants and their problems see FBI report summary information, including interview with Bessie Brewer, April 10, 1968, MURKIN 2322, section 20, pp. 26–28; also William Charles Anschutz interviewed by the FBI, April 5, 1968, MURKIN 2322, section 20, p. 30.

12. All conversations between Willard and Carpenter recounted from Ralph Meredith Carpenter, April 5, 1968, MURKIN ME Sub D, section 1, pp. 110–11.

13. Elizabeth Copeland interviewed by the FBI, April 5, 1968, MURKIN ME, Sub. D, section 1, p. 18.

14. Frances B. Thompson interviewed by the FBI, April 5, 1968, MURKIN ME, Sub. D, section 1, p. 19.

15. Peggy Jane Hurley interviewed by the FBI, April 5, 1968, MURKIN ME, Sub. D, section 1, p. 3.

16. Charles Hardy Hurley interviewed by the FBI, April 5, 1968, MURKIN ME, Sub. D, section 1, p. 4.

17. FBI statements of Kenneth W. Foster, April 12, 1968, and William Zenie (Bill) Reed, April 13, 1968, MURKIN ME, Sub D, section 1, pp. 185–86, 197–98.

18. Charlie Quitman Stephens interviewed by the FBI, April 5, 1968, MURKIN 2322, section 20, p. 32.

19. Ibid., p. 33; William Charles Anschutz interviewed by the FBI, April 5, 1968, MURKIN ME, Sub. D, section 1, p. 14.

Chapter 6: The Assassination

1. Abernathy, *And the Walls Came Tumbling Down*, p. 438.

2. Testimony of Ralph Abernathy, August 14, 1978, HSCA vol. 1, p. 19.

3. Billy Kyles interview with David Yellin, Joan Beifuss, and Bill Thomas, June 12, 1968, Tape 258, Series 1, 1 of 2, 124, Sanitation Strike Archives; see also FBI interview with Kyles on April 23, 1968, MURKIN 2634, section 26, pp. 40–47. Memphis police surveillance reports list Kyles as knocking on the door at 5:50 P.M., and calling King outside. However, it appears that Kyles actually had a conversation with King at the room earlier and it was not listed by the surveillance team since that was the point at which Detective Redditt was being replaced because of the death threat that had been received on him. In his book *Orders to Kill*, William Pepper raises the strong inference that Kyles might have been an FBI informant. "It's insulting and degrading," Kyles told the author about Pepper's accusation. "It casts an aspersion over my forty years of civil rights activism. I saw how Pepper operates when he did the movie on Ray [a 1993 HBO mock trial of James Earl Ray]. He altered my testimony there. I saw what happened that night, but they wanted to change everything to get the verdict they wanted [Ray was acquitted]. I thought of suing Pepper over what he said, but I was counseled to leave it alone. 'Don't help the man sell his book,' I was told, so I left him alone."

4. Banter among Kyles, Abernathy, and King recounted in Billy Kyles interview with David Yellin, Joan Beifuss, and Bill Thomas, June 12, 1968, Tape 258, Series 1, 1 of 2, 124, Sanitation Strike Archives.

5. Billy Kyles interviewed by author, August 2, 1997.

6. National Weather Service archives reported the sun would have set at 6:24 P.M. on April 4, 1968, in Memphis, TN.

7. Abernathy, *And the Walls Came Tumbling Down*, p. 441.

8. Autopsy findings, MURKIN 2322, section 20, pp. 183–94.

9. FBI interview with George W. Loenneke, April 13, 1968, MURKIN ME, Sub. D, section 1, pp. 88–89.

10. See generally "No. 2 Engine House, Memphis Fire Department, 474 South Main Street, Memphis, Tennessee," MURKIN 2322, section 20, pp. 88–114.

11. FBI interview with William Charles Anschutz, April 5, 1968, MURKIN ME, Sub. D, section 1, p. 14.

12. FBI interview with Charles Stephens, April 5, 1968, MURKIN ME, Sub. D, section 1, p. 20.

13. FBI interview with Guy Warren Canipe, Jr., April 5, 1968, MURKIN ME, Sub. D, section 1, pp. 121–22; as for Finley's identification of the Mustang, see FBI interview with Bernell Finley, MURKIN ME, Sub. D, section 1, p. 118, and MURKIN 126–250, section 2, p. 231; Julius Graham, the other customer on April 4 at Canipe's, also remembered the car "screeching" away—see FBI interview with Julius Graham, April 5, 1968, MURKIN ME, Sub. D, section 1, p. 114.

14. FBI interview with Guy Warren Canipe, Jr., April 5, 1968, MURKIN ME, Sub. D, section 1, p. 122; see interview with James Earl Ray by House Select Committee investigators, May 3, 1977, HSCA vol. X, pp. 310–11, where Ray discusses that the blanket is likely his, one that he used to take into flophouses at which he stayed.

Chapter 7: The Hunt

1. Interview with N. E. Zachary, June 13, 1997.

2. Ibid.

3. Affidavit of Frank Kallaher with attached transcripts of April 4, 1968, Memphis police radio broadcasts, MLK Exhibit F-195, HSCA vol. IV, p. 290.

4. Ibid., p. 291.

5. Ibid., p. 293.

6. Ibid., p. 288.

7. A former police official in the Memphis force told the author that even if there had been an all-points bulletin for other states, he is not sure it would have helped. "Hell, do you know how much trouble King caused in those other states? I wouldn't be surprised if some of those state troopers had gotten word of the white Mustang, they would have just waved him right through, might have even thought of giving him an escort."

8. Frank, *An American Death*, p. 126.

9. Memo to Cartha DeLoach from Alex Rosen, April 12, 1968, MURKIN 1051–1175, section 9, pp. 128–29; see "Laundry Marks," 3-by-5-inch index card file, Mrs. Lucy Pinela, remarks taken by Special Agent Ross Kahl, Attorney General File.

10. Memo to Cartha DeLoach from Alex Rosen, April 12, 1968, MURKIN 1051–1175, section 9, p. 128; "Pliers, Amusement Company," 3-by-5-inch index card file, Thomas M. Ware, remarks taken by Special Agent Hearn Hubbard, Attorney General File.

11. See, generally, FBI report on Mustang, how it was found, and what was found in it, MURKIN 2323–2324, section 21, pp. 201–17.

12. Martin Waldron, "Mystery Deepens in Dr. King Inquiry," *The New York Times*, April 13, 1968.

13. See FBI Laboratory Report, April 18, 1968, MURKIN 751–900, section 8, pp. 65–70.

14. FBI interview with Peter Cherpes, April 10, 1968, MURKIN 2323–2324, section 21.

15. See, generally, FBI interview with William D. Paisley, Sr., April 9, 1968, MURKIN 2323–2324, section 21, and FBI interview with William David Paisley, Jr., April 9, 1968, MURKIN 2323–2324, section 21.

16. Teletype to Director from Los Angeles, April 13, 1968, covering interview with Mrs. Frank (Margarita) Powers, MURKIN 621–750, section 6, p. 87; also FBI interview with Margarita Powers, April 12, 1968, MURKIN 2325, section 22, pp. 59–61.

17. FBI interview with Robert Kelly, April 12, 1968, MURKIN 2325, section 22, p. 110.

18. FBI interview with Allan O. Thompson, April 12, 1968, MURKIN 2325, section 22, p. 106.

19. See, generally, FBI Laboratory Report, April 22, 1968, MURKIN 751–900, section 8, pp. 61–70.

20. FBI interview with Rodney Arvidson, owner of the National Dance Studio, April 13, 1968, MURKIN 1051–1175, section 9, p. 279.

21. "Investigation at International School of Bartending, Los Angeles, Attended by Galt from January 19, 1968 to March 2, 1968," MURKIN 2325, section 22, pp. 135–36.

22. FBI report on the money order, April 26, 1968, MURKIN 2151–2321, section 19, pp. 179–80; also MURKIN 3221–3332, section 33, p. 227, and MURKIN 3763–3872, section 46, pp. 215–16.

23. FBI photo lineup with Jimmie Garner on April 17, 1968, MURKIN 2323–2324, section 21, pp. 259–61.

24. See FBI Laboratory Reports, April 17 and 19, 1968, MURKIN 751–900, section 8.

25. Press release issued on behalf of Ramsey Clark, April 17, 1968, MURKIN 1576–1730, section 13, pp. 284–87; Evert Clark, "F.B.I. Accuses Galt of Conspiracy in Dr. King Slaying," *The New York Times*, April 18, 1968, p. 1.

26. See MURKIN 1301–1421, section 11, p. 183.

27. Fred P. Graham, "F.B.I. Says 'Galt' Is an Escaped Convict," *The New York Times*, April 20, 1968, pp. A1, 31.

28. Memo to Cartha DeLoach from Alex Rosen, June 4, 1968, MURKIN 4251–4350, section 54, p. 90.

29. FBI interview with John Larry Ray, April 22, 1968, HSCA vol. VIII, pp. 34–35; see also MURKIN 3333, section 34, p. 280.

30. Jerry Ray quoted by informant in Airtel to Director from SAC, Newark, June 11, 1968, MURKIN 4576–4663, section 59, p. 41. The informant was actually Marjorie Fetters, someone Jerry knew. (Jerry Ray tapes to author, October 22, 1997, December 26, 1997).

Chapter 8: "I Feel So Trapped"

1. Thomas Talburt, "King's Assassin May Be Dead," *The Commercial Appeal*, June 8, 1968.

2. Radio and TV reports made for Bantam Books, transcript of *The Tonight Show*, April 29, 1968, Clay Blair collection, University of Wyoming.

3. See, generally, "Assassination of Martin Luther King, Jr.," to Attorney General from FBI Director, May 27, 1968, MURKIN 3901–3986, section 48, pp. 75–76; memo to Alex Rosen from McGowan, May 12, 1968, MURKIN 3221–3332, section 33, pp. 210–11.

4. See memo to Cartha DeLoach from Alex Rosen, May 20, 1968, MURKIN 3628–3761, section 44, pp. 203–8.

5. "King Associate Puzzled," *The New York Times*, April 13, 1968; Martin Waldron, "Fading Clues Raise Question of Conspiracy," *The New York Times*, April 21, 1968.

6. Peter Kihss, "Photos Cited by Research Group in Kennedy Death," *The New York Times*, May 1968.

7. See General Investigative Division memo of June 7, 1968, MURKIN 4442–4500, section 57, p. 43; of the 270,000, 218,000 were new and over 46,000 were renewals.

8. See, generally, memo to Cartha DeLoach from Alex Rosen, June 4, 1968, MURKIN 4144–4250, section 53, pp. 212–13.

9. See cablegram of June 2, 1968, MURKIN 4061–4142, section 51, p. 174.

10. Memo to Alex Rosen from McGowan, June 2, 1968, MURKIN 4061–4142, section 51, pp. 171–73.

11. Statement of Kenneth Leonard Human, June 11, 1968, in folder "Scotland Yard," p. 1234, Attorney General File.

12. Passport of Ramon George Sneyd issued in Lisbon, Portugal, MLK Exhibit F-237, HSCA vol. V, p. 24.

13. Statement of Kenneth Leonard Human, op. cit., p. 1234.

14. Canceled passport of Ramon George Sneya issued in Ottawa, Canada, MLK Exhibit F-235, HSCA vol. V, p. 18.

15. Letter of Philip Birch to author, October 18, 1997.

16. "All Ports Warning Where Special Branch Officers Are in Attendance," in folder "Scotland Yard," p. 1264, Attorney General File; see also Metropolitan Police Memorandum, Flying Squad, to Detective Chief Superintendent from K. Thompson, July 22, 1968, p. 2, Attorney General File.

17. Philip Birch quoted by Brian Park, "The Day Sergeant Birch Spotted a Face in the Crowd," London *Daily Express*, June 11, 1968.

18. Letter of Philip Birch to author, October 18, 1997.

19. Besides the .38-caliber revolver, a wide assortment of items was found either on Ray or in his luggage. Most were toiletries and clothes, but there was also his Polaroid 220 camera, a pamphlet on gun silencers, a portable radio, a dictionary, maps of London and Portugal, a 1967 almanac, a book on Rhodesia, several paperback books on hypnosis, a paperback novel, *The Ninth Directive*, and £51 in British money.

20. Letter of Philip Birch to author, October 18, 1997.

21. Statement of Philip Birch, June 10, 1968, in folder "Scotland Yard," p. 1233, Attorney General File.

22. "Property in Respect of Ramon George Sneyd," in folder "Scotland Yard," pp. 1272–74, Attorney General File; see also FBI memo to Director from Legat, London, June 9, 1968, MURKIN 4576–4663, section 59, pp. 27–29; letter of Philip Birch to author, October 18, 1997.

23. Metropolitan Police Memorandum, Flying Squad, to Detective Chief Superintendent from K. Thompson, July 22, 1968, in folder "Scotland Yard," p. 4, Attorney General File.

24. Conversation between Sneyd and Butler recounted in the Statement of Thomas Butler, June 10, 1968, in folder "Scotland Yard," pp. 1237–38; see also Statement of Detective Chief Inspector Kenneth Thompson, June 10, 1968, in folder "Scotland Yard," pp. 1239–41, Attorney General File.

25. Letter of Philip Birch to author, October 18, 1997. Note that Birch contests Ray's version, published in his book *Who Killed Martin Luther King?*, in which he stated that the British police forced him to have fingerprints taken while at Heathrow. "That is not the case," writes Birch. "No attempt was made for his fingerprints to be taken whilst there and was not even considered."

26. Ibid.; Butler statement, p. 1238, Thompson statement, p. 1240; see Metropolitan Police Memorandum, Flying Squad, to Detective Chief Superintendent from K. Thompson, July 22, 1968, in folder "Scotland Yard," p. 5, Attorney General File; Statement of Kenneth Thompson, July 31, 1978, to Edward Evans, Chief Investigator, MLK Exhibit F-240, HSCP vol. V, p. 37; see also FBI memo to Cartha DeLoach from Alex Rosen, June 21, 1968, MURKIN 4576–4663, section 59, pp. 197–98; "Oral Statements of James Earl Ray, alias Ramon George Sneyd," file 4, Attorney General File.

Chapter 9: Story for Sale

1. Frank, *An American Death*, p. 203.

2. See, generally, UPI report of June 27, 1968, quoting Dr. Edward Fields, the then secretary of the Legal Aid Fund and president of the National States Rights Party, announcing, "We have offered to defend Ray free of charge, pay all legal costs, attorney fees, court costs and cost of appeals, if there are any, and bond." When told by reporters that Hanes was Ray's evident choice, Fields said that Hanes was "a personal friend of mine and would be a good attorney."

3. Frank, *An American Death*, p. 204.

4. Actually, Birmingham had an unusual system in which voters elected three city commissioners, and one of those commissioners wore the honorary title of "mayor." So when Bull Connor brutally broke up the civil rights marches in the city, Hanes had been the mayor.

5. William Bradford Huie personally knew Hanes and wrote, "The mayor differed from Bull, not in attitudes but in being more literate and not saying 'nigger' in public."

6. Testimony of James Earl Ray, HSCA vol. III, pp. 256, 260.

7. Letter to Arthur Hanes, Sr., addressed to the Birmingham Bar Association, from R. G. Sneyd, MLK Exhibit F-94, HSCA vol. III, pp. 258–59.

8. See memo to Cartha DeLoach from Alex Rosen, June 17, 1968, MURKIN 4501–4575, section 58, p. 5.

9. William Bradford Huie interviewed by House Select Committee investigators, April 21, 1978, HSCA vol. VII, p. 441.

10. William Bradford Huie interviewed by Bob Ward, "William Bradford Huie Paid for Their Sins," *Writer's Digest*, September 1974, p. 21, David S. Lifton Archives, Los Angeles.

11. Arthur Hanes, Sr., quoted in Huie, *He Slew the Dreamer*, p. 153.

12. Ibid., p. 154.

13. Airtel to Director from Legat, London, June 24, 1968, MURKIN 4697–4759, section 61, p. 135.

14. See, generally, "Ray Extradition Faces Hurdles," *The Washington Daily News*, June 15, 1968.

15. See, generally, memo to Cartha DeLoach from Alex Rosen, June 15, 1968, MURKIN 4501–4575, section 58, p. 173.

16. Affidavit of Robert A. Frazier, June 10, 1968, p. 34, part of 193-page Extradition File of James Earl Ray, available from the Department of Justice via a Freedom of Information request; the author's research copy was from the David S. Lifton Archives, Los Angeles.

17. Testimony of Alexander Eist, November 9, 1978, HSCA vol. IV, pp. 18–19.

18. Ibid., p. 20.

19. Ibid., p. 21.

20. Ibid.

21. Ibid., p. 22.

22. Memo to Cartha DeLoach from Alex Rosen, June 28, 1968, MURKIN 4697–4759, section 61, p. 166; memo to DeLoach from Rosen, July 2, 1968, MURKIN 4761–4830, section 63, pp. 103–4.

23. Alvin Schuster, "Ray Tells Court He Is Not Guilty in Dr. King Death," *The New York Times*, June 28, 1968, pp. A1, 25.

24. Testimony of James Earl Ray, *James Earl Ray v. James H. Rose, Warden*, Civil Action No. C-74-166, U.S. District Court for the Western District of Tennessee, October 25, 1974, p. 736, Box 13, OPR FBI.

25. Ray said that Hanes told him "we needed considerable funds" to defend the case—testimony of James Earl Ray, *James Earl Ray v. James H. Rose, Warden*, Civil Action No. C-74-166, U.S. District Court for the Western District of Tennessee, October 25, 1974, p. 739, Box 13, OPR FBI; see also reproduction of July 5, 1968, agreement between Hanes and Ray in Huie, *He Slew the Dreamer*, pp. 154–55; see "An Analysis of the Guilty Plea Entered by James Earl Ray; Criminal Court of Shelby County, Tenn., on March 10, 1969," Supplementary Staff Report of the Select Committee on Assassinations, March 1979, HSCA vol. XIII, p. 223.

26. UPI report of July 5, 1968, quoting Arthur Hanes, Sr.

27. Arthur Hanes, Sr., quoted in Huie, *He Slew the Dreamer*, pp. 157–8.

28. See, generally, Huie-Ray-Hanes contracts dated July 8, 1968, and follow-up agreement by Huie to Hanes dated July 8, 1968, and letter agreement between Hanes and Ray, Attorney General File; also maintained as MLK Document 110116 by the House Select Committee. See also "An Analysis of the Guilty Plea Entered by James Earl Ray; Criminal Court of Shelby County, Tenn., on March 10, 1969," Supplementary Staff Report of the Select Committee on Assassinations, March 1979, HSCA vol. XIII, p. 223; also, regarding Hanes's desire to reach such an agreement to ensure his legal fee was paid, see HSCA Rpt., p. 413.

29. See, generally, William Bradford Huie interviewed by House Select Committee investigators, April 21, 1978, HSCA vol. VII, p. 442.

30. "Lawyer Says Ray Gave Him Names," *The New York Times*, July 7, 1968, p. 1.

31. For those involved in the transfer, see memo to Cartha DeLoach from Alex Rosen, July 19, 1968, MURKIN 4901–4982, section 66, pp. 19–22.

32. Memo for Tolson, et al., from Hoover, July 16, 1968, MURKIN 4847–4900, section 65, pp. 1–2, 21.

33. For general concern over Ray's security and the discussion and planning that went into moving him, see, for example, memo to Cartha DeLoach from Rosen, June 21, 1968, MURKIN 4576–4663, section 59, pp. 195–96; MURKIN 4501–4575, section 58, pp. 31,

65; also memo to McGowan from Rosen, July 18, 1968, MURKIN 4901–4982, section 66, pp. 73–76.

34. See memo to Cartha DeLoach from Alex Rosen, June 13, 1968, MURKIN 4442–4500, section 57, pp. 134–35.

35. See generally "Custody Log, James Earl Ray, July 19, 1968, Aboard USAF Plane C135," MURKIN 4901–4982, section 66, pp. 178–81.

36. See memo to the Attorney General from the FBI Director, July 15, 1968, MURKIN 4831–4846, section 64, pp. 98–99.

37. Anthony Lewis, "The Ray Case: Round One: The Battle Over Extradition," *The New York Times*, July 7, 1968.

Chapter 10: Enter Raoul

1. Arthur Hanes, Sr., quoted in "Prisoner Charges Ray Favoritism," *The Memphis Press-Scimitar*, September 17, 1968, pp. 1, 5.

2. Memo to Pollak from Director, FBI, June 14, 1968, MURKIN 4501–4575, section 58, p. 35.

3. Frank, *An American Death*, p. 236.

4. Ibid.; William Bradford Huie, "I Had Been in Trouble Most My Life, in Jail Most of It," *Look*, November 12, 1968, p. 104.

5. Ibid., p. 112.

6. William Bradford Huie, "I Got Involved Gradually, and I Didn't Know Anybody Was to Be Murdered," *Look*, November 26, 1968, p. 87.

Chapter 11: Hiding the Truth

1. Testimony of James Earl Ray, *James Earl Ray* v. *James H. Rose, Warden*, Civil Action No. C-74-166, U.S. District Court for the Western District of Tennessee, October 25, 1974, p. 773, Box 13, OPR FBI. The *Ray* v. *Foreman* lawsuit was filed by Ray after his guilty plea against Foreman, Huie, and Hanes, and it charged them with violating Ray's constitutional rights and tried unsuccessfully to enjoin the publication of Huie's book. *Ray* v. *Rose* was Ray's subsequently unsuccessful habeas corpus action, which involved many of the same issues. Memo to Cartha DeLoach from Alex Rosen, November 13, 1968, MURKIN 5351–5396, section 73, pp. 70–72; memo to Director from Stephen Pollak, November 7, 1968, MURKIN 5351–5396, section 73, pp. 110–11.

2. Criminal Court, Shelby County, Order on Sequestration of Witnesses, MURKIN 5351–5396, section 73, p. 17; "Ray Article May Bring Court Action," *The Memphis Press-Scimitar*, October 29, 1968, p. 19.

3. Testimony of James Earl Ray, *James Earl Ray* v. *James H. Rose, Warden*, Civil Action No. C-74-166, U.S. District Court for the Western District of Tennessee, October 25, 1974, p. 774, Box 13, OPR FBI.

4. Martin Waldron, "A Klan Organizer Made Visit to Ray," *The New York Times*, October 3, 1968.

5. Testimony of James Earl Ray, *James Earl Ray* v. *James H. Rose, Warden*, Civil Action No. C-74-166, U.S. District Court for the Western District of Tennessee, October 25, 1974, p. 776, Box 13, OPR FBI.

6. See, generally, interest of John Ray, memo to Cartha DeLoach, MURKIN 4501–4575, section 58, p. 172; also Jerry Ray in HSCA Rpt., and interviews with George McMillan in McMillan/Southern Historical Collection.

7. Jerry Ray quoted by Mark Lane in *Murder in Memphis: The FBI and the Assassination of Martin Luther King* (New York: Thunder's Mouth Press, 1993), p. 195.

8. See Foreman on *The Dick Cavett Show*, Box 5, Trial One, Letter and Memos, 1968–69, McMillan/Southern Historical Collection.

9. Testimony of James Earl Ray, *James Earl Ray* v. *James H. Rose, Warden*, Civil Action No. C-74-166, U.S. District Court for the Western District of Tennessee, October 25, 1974, p. 777, Box 13, OPR FBI.

10. Percy Foreman quoted by William Bradford Huie, *He Slew the Dreamer*, p. 191.

11. Ibid.

12. Huie, *He Slew the Dreamer*, p. 193.

13. Arthur Hanes, Sr., and Arthur Hanes, Jr., quoted by Mark Lane in *Murder in Memphis*, p. 200.

14. Testimony of James Earl Ray, *James Earl Ray* v. *James H. Rose, Warden*, Civil Action No. C-74-166, U.S. District Court for the Western District of Tennessee, October 25, 1974, p. 786, Box 13, OPR FBI.

15. Deposition of Percy Foreman, *Ray* v. *Foreman*, April 3, 1974; See also *Ray* v. *Foreman* deposition, HSCA vol. V, pp. 162–64, and HSCA Rpt., p. 413.

16. HSCA Rpt., p. 413, citing outside contact report with Thomas E. Smith, December 8, 1978, MLK Document 20079.

17. Deposition of Percy Foreman, April 3, 1974, *U.S.* v. *Rose*, reprinted in HSCA vol. V, pp. 178–82.

18. HSCA Rpt., p. 415.

19. Testimony of James Earl Ray, *James Earl Ray* v. *James H. Rose, Warden*, Civil Action No. C-74-166, U.S. District Court for the Western District of Tennessee, October 29, 1974, pp. 818–19, Box 13, OPR FBI; James Earl Ray interview in *Playboy*, September 1977, p. 79.

20. HSCA Rpt., pp. 413–15.

21. Testimony of James Earl Ray, *James Earl Ray* v. *James H. Rose, Warden*, Civil Action C-74-166, In the U.S. District Court for the Western District of Tennessee, October 29, 1974, pp. 814–15, Box 13, OPR FBI.

22. Agreement, February 3, 1969, attached as an exhibit to *James Earl Ray* v. *James H. Rose, Warden*, Civil Action No. C-74-166, U.S. District Court for the Western District of Tennessee, October 25, 1974, Box 13, OPR FBI.

23. Huie, *He Slew the Dreamer*, p. 193.

24. Ibid., p. 194; testimony of James Earl Ray, *James Earl Ray* v. *James H. Rose, Warden*, Civil Action No. C-74-166, U.S. District Court for the Western District of Tennessee, October 25, 1974, p. 815–16, Box 13, OPR FBI.

25. James Earl Ray, *Who Killed Martin Luther King?: The True Story by the Alleged Assassin* (Washington, D.C.: National Press Books, 1992), pp. 123–24, 128.

26. Testimony of James Earl Ray, *James Earl Ray* v. *James H. Rose, Warden*, Civil Action No. C-74-166, U.S. District Court for the Western District of Tennessee, October 29, 1974, p. 819, Box 13, OPR FBI.

27. Trial Exhibit 47, *James Earl Ray* v. *James H. Rose, Warden*, Civil Action No. C-74-166, U.S. District Court for the Western District of Tennessee, October 29, 1974, reproduced on pp. 821–22, Box 13, OPR FBI.

28. Testimony of James Earl Ray, *James Earl Ray* v. *James H. Rose, Warden*, Civil Action No. C-74-166, U.S. District Court for the Western District of Tennessee, October 29, 1974, p. 828, Box 13, OPR FBI.

29. Ibid., pp. 826–29, 832.

30. Ibid., p. 831.

31. See Exhibit 41, displayed at *James Earl Ray* v. *James H. Rose, Warden*, Civil Action No. C-74-166, U.S. District Court for the Western District of Tennessee, Box 13, OPR FBI.

32. Testimony of James Earl Ray, *James Earl Ray* v. *James H. Rose, Warden*, Civil Action No. C-74-166, U.S. District Court for the Western District of Tennessee, October 29, 1974, p. 841, Box 13, OPR FBI.

33. Ibid., p. 852.

34. Ibid., pp. 853–54.

35. See Exhibits 11A and 11B in *James Earl Ray* v. *James H. Rose, Warden*, Civil Action No. C-74-166, U.S. District Court for the Western District of Tennessee, Box 13, OPR FBI.

36. See Exhibit 8, *James Earl Ray* v. *James H. Rose, Warden*, Civil Action No. C-74-166, U.S. District Court for the Western District of Tennessee, Box 13, OPR FBI.

37. Testimony of James Earl Ray, *James Earl Ray* v. *James H. Rose, Warden*, Civil Action No. C-74-166, U.S. District Court for the Western District of Tennessee, October 29, 1974, p. 865, Box 13, OPR FBI.

38. See Martin Waldron, "Ray Is Reported Planning to Plead Guilty Monday," *The New York Times*, March 8, 1969, p. 1.

39. "Judge Says Bevel Can't Defend Ray," *The New York Times*, January 25, 1969.

40. "Conspiracy Is Seen," *The New York Times*, March 10, 11, 1968, p. A16.

41. James Chisum, "Probers Stand Pat," *The Commercial Appeal*, April 5, 1993, p. 1.

Chapter 12: Little Dixie

1. James Earl Ray, *Tennessee Waltz: The Making of a Political Prisoner* (St. Andrews, TN: St. Andrews Press, 1987), p. 2.

2. Biographical summary data, Biographical Data on JER folder, Box 3—Biographical Data on JER and Family, McMillan/Southern Historical Collection.

3. Letter from William Maher to George McMillan, April 14, 1972, Maher folder, Box 1—Correspondence Related to Book Research—Research Files on Ewing, McMillan/Southern Historical Collection.

4. Earl Ray quoted in handwritten notes taken by Clay Blair, Jr., maintained as collection 8259 at the American Heritage Center, University of Wyoming.

5. List of jobs taken by George Ray listed in Blair notes, ibid.; see also interview with George Ray by George McMillan, March 20, 1969, Jerry Raynes folder, Box 1—Correspondence Related to Book Research—Research Files on Ewing, McMillan/Southern Historical Collection.

6. George Ray quoted by George McMillan, *The Making of an Assassin* (New York: Little Brown and Co., 1976), p. 18.

7. Ibid., pp. 17–18.

8. Interview with William Maher by George McMillan, January 7, 1969, Maher folder, Box 1—Correspondence Related to Book Research—Research Files on Ewing, McMillan/Southern Historical Collection.

9. Ibid.; McMillan, *The Making of an Assassin*, p. 16.

10. FBI documents "Earl Everett Ray," undated, MURKIN 3987, section 49, pp. 80–83; see also Teletype to FBI Director from Buffalo SAC, April 26, 1968, MURKIN 2151–2321, section 19, pp. 289–90; also Investigation Summary, MURKIN 4441, section 56, p. 90.

11. George Ray interviewed by George McMillan, Jerry Raynes folder, p. 14, Box 1—Correspondence Related to Book Research—Research Files on Ewing; also interview with George Ray by George McMillan, March 20, 1969, Jerry Raynes folder, Box 1—Correspondence Related to Book Research—Research Files on Ewing; and interview with George Ray, October 17, 1969, no folder, McMillan/Southern Historical Collection; see also McMillan, *The Making of an Assassin*, p. 15.

12. See letter of John Ray, April 4, 1972, "Ray, Lucille Maher" folder, Box 1—Correspondence Related to Book Research—Research Files on Ewing; also interview with George Ray by George McMillan, March 20, 1969, Jerry Raynes folder, Box 1—Correspondence Related to Book Research—Research Files on Ewing, McMillan/Southern Historical Collection.

13. Findings of the Select Committee of the House of Representatives on the Assassination of Martin Luther King, Jr., HSCA Rpt., 1979, p. 287.

14. George Ray quoted in McMillan, *The Making of an Assassin*, pp. 31–32.

15. William Maher quote in McMillan, *The Making of an Assassin*, pp. 32–33.

16. Interview with George Ray by George McMillan, March 20, 1969, Jerry Raynes folder, Box 1—Correspondence Related to Book Research—Research Files on Ewing, McMillan/Southern Historical Collection; see McMillan, *The Making of an Assassin*, p. 34.

17. FBI document titled "Re James Earl Ray Neighborhood," undated, MURKIN 3333, section 34, p. 91; James Earl Ray, *Tennessee Waltz*, p. 3.

18. See, generally, interview with Mr. and Mrs. Virgil Graves by George McMillan, September 12, 1968, no folder, Box 1—Correspondence Related to Book Research—Research Files on Ewing, McMillan/Southern Historical Collection.

19. James Earl Ray, *Who Killed Martin Luther King?*, p. 18.

20. Interview with Jerry Ray by George McMillan, October 16, 1969, no folder, Box 1—Correspondence Related to Book Research—Research Files on Ewing, McMillan/Southern Historical Collection.

21. James Earl Ray, *Tennessee Waltz*, p. 1.

22. Interview with John Sperry by George McMillan, no date, Ewing Interviews Alphabetical folder, Box 1—Correspondence Related to Book Research—Research Files on Ewing, McMillan/Southern Historical Collection; see also McMillan, *The Making of an Assassin*, pp. 36, 39.

23. See, generally, interview with Winifred Wood and Frances Delaney by George McMillan, March 14, 1971, Ewing Interviews Alphabetical folder, Box 1—Correspondence Related to Book Research—Research Files on Ewing; also interview with Jerry Ray by George McMillan, April 1, 1972, Jerry Ray Interviews 1969–1975, Box 5—Trial and Post-Trial Materials, McMillan/Southern Historical Collection.

24. Reference to "Little Dixie" from La Grange newspaper quoted in handwritten notes taken by Clay Blair, Jr., op. cit.

25. Interview with Robert Brown by George McMillan, undated, no folder, Box 1—Correspondence Related to Book Research—Research Files on Ewing, McMillan/Southern Historical Collection.

26. Letter from Charles Baldwin, county supervisor of the U.S. Department of Agriculture, to George McMillan, October 28, 1968, Ewing Interviews Alphabetical folder, Box 1—Correspondence Related to Book Research—Research Files on Ewing, McMillan/Southern Historical Collection.

27. George Ray interviewed by George McMillan, Jerry Raynes folder, p. 12, Box 1—Correspondence Related to Book Research—Research Files on Ewing, McMillan/Southern Historical Collection.

28. Interview with Jerry Ray by George McMillan, sometime in mid-April 1969, Jerry Ray Phone Conversations folder, Box 5—Trial and Post-Trial Materials, McMillan/Southern Historical Collection.

29. Interview with Jerry Ray by George McMillan, January 8 and 9, 1972, Jerry Ray Interviews 1969–1975 folder, Box 5—Trial and Post-Trial Materials, McMillan/Southern Historical Collection.

30. See, generally, interview with George Ray by George McMillan, March 20, 1969, Jerry Raynes folder, Box 1—Correspondence Related to Book Research—Research Files on Ewing, McMillan/Southern Historical Collection.

31. Letter from William Maher to George McMillan, July 11, 1970, Maher folder, Box 1—Correspondence Related to Book Research—Research Files on Ewing; see also interview with Jerry Ray by George McMillan, Memorial Day, no year, and interview with Jerry Ray, January 8–9, 1972, Jerry Ray Interviews 1969–1975 folder, Box 5—Trial and Post-Trial Materials, McMillan/Southern Historical Collection.

32. Interview with George Ray by George McMillan, October 17, 1969, no folder, Box 1—Correspondence Related to Book Research—Research Files on Ewing, McMillan/Southern Historical Collection.

33. Interview with George Ray by George McMillan, March 20, 1969, Jerry Raynes folder, Box 1—Correspondence Related to Book Research—Research Files on Ewing, McMillan/Southern Historical Collection; George Ray quoted in McMillan, *The Making of an Assassin*, p. 48.

34. "James Earl Ray Neighborhood," FBI St. Louis file, Attorney General File, p. 82.

35. Interview with Mr. and Mrs. Virgil Graves by George McMillan, September 12, 1968, no folder, Box 1—Correspondence Related to Book Research—Research Files on Ewing; and interviews with Robert Hunter, Juvenile Judge, September 9, 1968, and Genevieve Trevilla, September 7, 1968, by George McMillan, Ray Family Chronology folder, Box 3—Biographical Data on JER and Family, McMillan/Southern Historical Collection; McMillan, *The Making of an Assassin*, p. 49.

36. Interview with Mr. and Mrs. Virgil Graves by George McMillan, September 12, 1968, no folder, Box 1—Correspondence Related to Book Research—Research Files on Ewing, McMillan/Southern Historical Collection.

37. George Ray quoted in McMillan, *The Making of an Assassin*, p. 50.

38. See letter of John Ray, April 4, 1972, "Ray, Lucille Maher" folder, Box 1—Correspondence Related to Book Research—Research Files on Ewing; and Jerry Ray interview by George McMillan, September 27, 1971, Jerry Ray Interviews 1969–1975, Box 5—Trial and Post-Trial Materials, McMillan/Southern Historical Collection.

39. Interview with Carol Ray Pepper by George McMillan, Carol Ray Pepper folder, Box 1—Correspondence Related to Book Research—Research Files on Ewing; also Jerry Raynes folder, pp. 10, 25, Box 1—Correspondence Related to Book Research—Research Files on Ewing, and interview with George Ray, October 17, 1969, no folder, McMillan/Southern Historical Collection.

40. George Ray interviewed by George McMillan, Jerry Raynes folder, pp. 13, 20, 26, Box 1—Correspondence Related to Book Research—Research Files on Ewing, McMillan/Southern Historical Collection.

41. Interview with Jerry Ball by George McMillan, March 13, 1971, no folder, Box 1—Correspondence Related to Book Research—Research Files on Ewing, McMillan/Southern Historical Collection; McMillan, *The Making of an Assassin*, pp. 68–69; see also James Earl Ray, *Who Killed Martin Luther King?*, p. 18.

42. George Ray interviewed by George McMillan, Jerry Raynes folder, p. 11, Box 1—Correspondence Related to Book Research—Research Files on Ewing, McMillan/Southern Historical Collection; see also *The Making of an Assassin*, p. 71.

43. Interview with Richard Hadfield by George McMillan, March 13, 1971, Quincy Interviews folder, Box 2—Research Files on Alton and Quincy, McMillan/Southern Historical Collection.

44. FBI document titled "James Earl Ray School Records," undated, MURKIN 3333, section 34, p. 92.

45. See, generally, for James's sensitivity about the clothes he wore, interview with Jerry Ray by George McMillan, October 16, 1969, no folder, Box 1—Correspondence Related to Book Research—Research Files on Ewing; see also letter of Merle Wenneker to George McMillan, November 12, 1968, no folder, Box 1—Correspondence Related to Book Research—Research Files on Ewing, McMillan/Southern Historical Collection.

46. Interview with Robert Brown by George McMillan, undated, no folder; see also interview with Carlisle Washburn by George McMillan, undated, no folder, Box 1—Correspondence Related to Book Research—Research Files on Ewing, and interview with Richard Hadfield by George McMillan, March 13, 1971, Quincy Interviews folder, Box 2—Research Files on Alton and Quincy, McMillan/Southern Historical Collection.

47. McMillan, *The Making of an Assassin*, pp. 54–55.

48. Note by Merle C. Wenneker to George McMillan, undated, no folder but with general papers, Box 1—Correspondence Related to Book Research—Research Files on Ewing, McMillan/Southern Historical Collection.

49. McMillan, *The Making of an Assassin*, p. 61; see, generally, interview with Gerald Hobbs by George McMillan, March 14 (no year), Ewing Interview Alphabetical folder, Box 1—Correspondence Related to Book Research—Research Files on Ewing, McMillan/Southern Historical Collection.

50. Interview with Robert Brown by George McMillan, undated, no folder, Box 1—Correspondence Related to Book Research—Research Files on Ewing, McMillan/Southern Historical Collection; see also Clay Blair, Jr., *The Strange Case of James Earl Ray: The Man Who Murdered Martin Luther King* (New York: Bantam Books, 1969), pp. 29–30.

51. Note by Merle C. Wenneker to George McMillan, undated, no folder but with general papers, Box 1—Correspondence Related to Book Research—Research Files on Ewing, McMillan/Southern Historical Collection.

52. See, generally, interview with George Ray by George McMillan, March 20, 1969, Jerry Raynes folder, Box 1—Correspondence Related to Book Research—Research Files on Ewing, McMillan/Southern Historical Collection.

53. Interview with Jerry Ray by George McMillan, October 16, 1969, no folder, Box 1—Correspondence Related to Book Research—Research Files on Ewing, McMillan/Southern Historical Collection.

54. McMillan, *The Making of an Assassin*, pp. 60–61.

55. FBI teletype to Director from Springfield, April 24, 1968, MURKIN 1991–2075, section 17, p. 146; see also interview with George Ray by George McMillan, March 20, 1969, no folder, Box 1—Correspondence Related to Book Research—Research Files on Ewing, McMillan/Southern Historical Collection.

56. Interview with Robert Brown by George McMillan, undated, no folder, Box 1—Correspondence Related to Book Research—Research Files on Ewing, McMillan/Southern Historical Collection.

57. James Earl Ray, *Who Killed Martin Luther King?*, p. 18.

58. FBI interview with George Ray, April 23, 1968, MURKIN 3333, section 34, pp. 228–29.

59. FBI Document "Summary: Family of James Earl Ray," undated, MURKIN 3987, section 49, p. 34; statement of Ruby Carpenter to the FBI, summary contained in teletype to Director from Springfield, April 24, 1968, MURKIN 1991–2075, section 17, p. 147; James Earl Ray, *Who Killed Martin Luther King?*, p. 18; see, generally, narration of James Wolf, Deputy Chief Counsel, HSCA vol. VIII, pp. 1–13.

60. Carol Ray Pepper interviewed by George McMillan, July 17, 1969, Carol Ray Pepper folder, Box 1—Correspondence Related to Book Research—Research Files on Ewing; see also interview with Jerry Ray by George McMillan, October 16, 1969, no folder, Box 1—Correspondence Related to Book Research—Research Files on Ewing, McMillan/Southern Historical Collection.

61. George Ray interviewed by George McMillan, March (no year), Jerry Raynes folder, p. 5, Box 1—Correspondence Related to Book Research—Research Files on Ewing, McMillan/Southern Historical Collection.

62. Interview with Carlisle Washburn by George McMillan, undated, no folder, Box 1—Correspondence Related to Book Research—Research Files on Ewing, McMillan/Southern Historical Collection.

63. McMillan, *The Making of an Assassin*, p. 63.

64. Mike O'Brien quoted in Gerold Frank, *An American Death*, p. 287.

65. FBI document titled "Re: Ray Background: Education," undated, MURKIN 4760, section 62, p. 51.

66. Interview with Robert Brown by George McMillan, undated, no folder; see also interview with George Ray by George McMillan, March 20, 1969, Jerry Raynes folder, Box 1—Correspondence Related to Book Research—Research Files on Ewing, McMillan/Southern Historical Collection.

67. Interview with Carlisle Washburn by George McMillan, undated, no folder, Box 1—Correspondence Related to Book Research—Research Files on Ewing, McMillan/Southern Historical Collection; see also *The Making of an Assassin*, p. 63.

68. Jerry Ray quoted in McMillan, *The Making of an Assassin*, p. 64.

69. John Ray quoted in ibid., p. 77.

70. Jerry Ball quoted in ibid., p. 65.

71. Charles Peacock quoted in biographical summary data, Biographical Data on JER folder, Box 3—Biographical Data on JER and Family, McMillan/Southern Historical Collection.

72. Jerry Ray interviewed by George McMillan, September 25, 1971, Jerry Ray Interviews 1969–1975 folder, Box 5—Trial and Post-Trial Materials, McMillan/Southern Historical Collection.

73. Jerry Ray interview by George McMillan, February 12, 1969, Jerry Ray Interviews 1969–1975 folder, Box 5—Trial and Post-Trial Materials, McMillan/Southern Historical Collection.

74. Jerry Ray interviewed by George McMillan, September 25, 1971, Jerry Ray Interviews 1969–1975 folder, Box 5—Trial and Post-Trial Materials, McMillan/Southern Historical Collection.

75. McMillan, *The Making of an Assassin*, p. 79.

76. Letter from Virgil Graves to Mrs. West (no first name), August 24, 1968, no folder, Box 1—Correspondence Related to Book Research—Research Files on Ewing, McMillan/Southern Historical Collection.

77. Interview with Virgil Graves by George McMillan, September 12, 1968, no folder, Box 1—Correspondence Related to Book Research—Research Files on Ewing, McMillan/Southern Historical Collection.

78. Virgil Graves quoted in William A. McWhirter, "A Character Shaped by a Mean Life," *Life*, May 3, 1968, p. 23.

79. Interview with Virgil Graves by George McMillan, September 12, 1968, no folder, Box 1—Correspondence Related to Book Research—Research Files on Ewing, McMillan/Southern Historical Collection; McMillan, *The Making of an Assassin*, p. 82.

80. McMillan, *The Making of an Assassin*, p. 82.

81. John Ray quoted in ibid., p. 84.

82. Interview with Jerry Ray by George McMillan, January 8 and 9, 1972, Jerry Ray Interviews 1969–1975 folder, Box 5—Trial and Post-Trial Materials, McMillan/Southern Historical Collection.

83. Letter from Terry Rife to George McMillan, March 22, 1972, Interviews and Correspondence—Rife, Walter, folder, Box 1—Correspondence Related to Book Research—Research Files on Ewing, McMillan/Southern Historical Collection.

84. James Earl Ray, *Who Killed Martin Luther King?*, pp. 18–19; see also Jerry Ray interviewed by George McMillan, September 25, 1971, Jerry Ray Interviews 1969–1975 folder, Box 5—Trial and Post-Trial Materials, McMillan/Southern Historical Collection.

85. Interview with Mary Hagen by George McMillan, September 8, 1968, Alton folder; see also Mike Hilfrink, "Quincy's High Suicide Rate Alarms Officials," *The Herald-Whig*, July 31, 1968, Quincy Interview folder, Box 2—Research Files on Alton and Quincy, McMillan/Southern Historical Collection.

86. See, generally, "Neighborhood Analyses," Project Head Start, Quincy, Illinois, March 1967, Alton folder, Box 2—Research Files on Alton and Quincy; "Historical Sketches of Quincy, the First 100 Years" by Carl Landrum, Quincy, Illinois, Alton folder, Box 2—Research Files on Alton and Quincy, McMillan/Southern Historical Collection; also McMillan, *The Making of an Assassin*, p. 90.

87. James Earl Ray, *Who Killed Martin Luther King?*, p. 19; see also FBI interview with George Parsons, April 20, 1968, "Family of James Earl Ray," Attorney General File, p. 2754.

88. James Earl Ray, *Who Killed Martin Luther King?*, p. 21.

89. Ibid., p. 20.

90. James Earl Ray, *Tennessee Waltz*, p. 4.

91. George Ray interviewed by George McMillan, March (no year), Jerry Raynes folder, p. 2, Box 1—Correspondence Related to Book Research—Research Files on Ewing, McMillan/Southern Historical Collection.

92. John Ray quoted in McMillan, *The Making of an Assassin*, pp. 87–88.

93. FBI interview with Walter Terry Rife, April 19, 1968, File SI 44-561, MURKIN 3987, section 49, p. 105; see also letter from Terry Rife to George McMillan, March 22, 1972, Interviews and Correspondence—Rife, Walter, folder, Box 1—Correspondence Related to Book Research—Research Files on Ewing, McMillan/Southern Historical Collection.

94. FBI document "Associates of James Earl Ray," interview with Walter Rife, April 23, 1968, MURKIN 3987, section 49, p. 95; see also interview with Walter Rife by George McMillan, Part II, undated, Interviews and Correspondence—Rife, Walter, folder, pp. 23–24, 27, Box 1—Correspondence Related to Book Research—Research Files on Ewing, McMillan/Southern Historical Collection.

95. Interview with Walter Rife by George McMillan, Part II, undated, Interviews and Correspondence—Rife, Walter, folder, p. 24, Box 1—Correspondence Related to Book Research—Research Files on Ewing, McMillan/Southern Historical Collection; see also McMillan, *The Making of an Assassin*, p. 87.

96. FBI document "Associates of James Earl Ray," interview with Walter Rife, April 23, 1968, MURKIN 3987, section 49, p. 104.

97. Ibid., pp. 104–6.

98. Interview with Walter Rife by George McMillan, Part I, September 9, 1968, Interviews and Correspondence—Rife, Walter, folder, p. 8, Box 1—Correspondence Related to Book Research—Research Files on Ewing, McMillan/Southern Historical Collection; Walter Rife quoted in McMillan, *The Making of an Assassin*, pp. 87, 146.

99. Walter Rife quoted in McMillan, *The Making of an Assassin*, p. 87.

100. James Early Ray, *Tennessee Waltz*, p. 6.

101. James Earl Ray, *Who Killed Martin Luther King?*, p. 21.

102. Interview with Walter Rife by George McMillan, Part II, undated, Interviews and Correspondence—Rife, Walter, folder, Box 1—Correspondence Related to Book Research—Research Files on Ewing, McMillan/Southern Historical Collection; McMillan, *The Making of an Assassin*, p. 87.

103. John Ray quoted in McMillan, *The Making of an Assassin*, p. 96.

Chapter 13: "Hitler Politics"

1. Statement by Mary Maher, 1968, taken by State Attorney's Office, Edwardsville, Illinois, reported in biographical summary data, Biographical Data on JER folder, Box 3—Biographical Data on JER and Family, McMillan/Southern Historical Collection.

2. Eric Duncan quoted in McMillan, *The Making of an Assassin*, p. 101.

3. Ibid., pp. 100–102.

4. Boob Roberts quoted in McMillan, *The Making of an Assassin*, p. 101; see also "Memo to Myself, by George McMillan: Ray at the Hartford Tannery," Alton folder, Box 2—Research Files on Alton and Quincy, McMillan/Southern Historical Collection.

5. Eric Duncan quoted in McMillan, *The Making of an Assassin*, p. 101; see also "Memo to Myself, by George McMillan: Ray at the Hartford Tannery," Alton folder, Box 2—Research Files on Alton and Quincy, McMillan/Southern Historical Collection.

6. McMillan, *The Making of an Assassin*, p. 101.

7. FBI interview with William E. Maher, April 22, 1968, MURKIN 1731–1820, section 14, p. 57, and MURKIN 2076–2150, section 18, p. 199; see also interview with Jerry Ray by George McMillan, September 27, 1971, Jerry Ray Interviews 1969–1975, Box 5—Trial and Post-Trial Materials, and interview with Ande Yakstis, *Alton Telegraph* reporter, by George

McMillan, August 15, 1968, Alton folder, Box 2—Research Files on Alton and Quincy, McMillan/Southern Historical Collection.

8. Interview with Jerry Ray by George McMillan, April 1, 1972, Jerry Ray Interviews 1969–1975, Box 5—Trial and Post-Trial Materials, McMillan/Southern Historical Collection; McMillan, *The Making of an Assassin*, p. 106.

9. Unidentified sister quoted by Clay Blair, Jr., *The Strange Case of James Earl Ray*, p. 36.

10. Interview with Jerry Ray by George McMillan, May 29, 1972, Jerry Ray Interviews 1969–1975, Box 5—Trial and Post-Trial Materials, McMillan/Southern Historical Collection.

11. Interview with Jerry Ray by George McMillan, October 16, 1969, no folder, Box 1—Correspondence Related to Book Research—Research Files on Ewing, McMillan/Southern Historical Collection; see also McMillan, *The Making of an Assassin*, p. 99, and Clay Blair, *The Strange Case of James Earl Ray*, p. 33.

12. James Earl Ray, *Tennessee Waltz*, p. 6.

13. Letter from the Department of the Army to George McMillan, June 10, 1970, Army folder, Box 3—Biographical Data on JER and Family; see also John Ray quoted by Jerry Lipson, "Ray's Road to Jail Began in Army," *Chicago Daily News*, undated, p. 1, Box 1—Correspondence Related to Book Research—Research Files on Ewing, McMillan/Southern Historical Collection.

14. Interview with Carol Ray Pepper by George McMillan, undated, Carol Ray Pepper folder, Box 1—Correspondence Related to Book Research—Research Files on Ewing, McMillan/Southern Historical Collection; see also McMillan, *The Making of an Assassin*, p. 104.

15. George Ray interviewed by George McMillan, Jerry Raynes folder, p. 23, Box 1—Correspondence Related to Book Research—Research Files on Ewing, McMillan/Southern Historical Collection.

16. Ibid., p. 11; see also *The Making of an Assassin*, p. 105, and Frank, *An American Death*, p. 403.

17. Interview with Jerry Ray by George McMillan, January 8 and 9, 1972, Jerry Ray Interviews 1969–1975, Box 5—Trial and Post-Trial Materials, McMillan/Southern Historical Collection; McMillan, *The Making of an Assassin*, p. 106.

18. Letter from William Maher to George McMillan, February 3, 1969, Maher folder, Box 1—Correspondence Related to Book Research—Research Files on Ewing, McMillan/Southern Historical Collection.

19. James Earl Ray, *Tennessee Waltz*, p. 7.

20. Official Statement of Military Service of James Earl Ray, 16 163 129, Department of the Army; FBI document "Re: James Earl Ray Background," FBI—St. Louis file, prepared by Special Agent Harold R. Dobson, serials 3407–3791, Attorney General File, p. 88. Note: Ray's full military record has never been released because, pursuant to the Freedom of Information Act, James Earl Ray would have to sign a release for any person besides himself to obtain it. It is not clear that the Army can find his file, even if Ray were to ask for it. As of 1975, an Army spokesman informed author George McMillan that "the Army has been unsuccessful in all attempts to locate Ray's military personnel records." Since the records were provided to the FBI as part of their postassassination inquiry, Army officials have suggested the file may not have been returned. The Bureau claims it does not have it. However, a fairly detailed portrait of Ray's service can be reconstructed, since the Army has released some summary documents, Ray has commented on it in his own books and interviews, and the archives of other authors have provided background research on particular issues, including his Army medical records.

21. "Short Report on Wesermuende/Bremerhaven 1945/47," p. 1, Army folder, Box 3—Biographical Data on JER and Family, McMillan/Southern Historical Collection.

22. Ibid.; see also letter from Arthur Zigouras to George McMillan, undated, p. 1, Army folder, Box 3—Biographical Data on JER and Family, McMillan/Southern Historical Collection.

23. Letter from Arthur Zigouras to George McMillan, undated, p. 1, Army folder, Box 3—Biographical Data on JER and Family, McMillan/Southern Historical Collection.

24. James Earl Ray, *Tennessee Waltz*, p. 7.

25. "Short Report on Wesermuende/Bremerhaven 1945/47," p. 1, Army folder, Box 3—Biographical Data on JER and Family, McMillan/Southern Historical Collection.

26. Ibid.; see also "Memo: Black Market Operations in Germany," from Oliver J. Fredericksen, *The American Military Occupation of Germany, 1945–1953*, Historical Division, Headquarters, United States Army, 1953, two pages, Army folder; also letter from Arthur Zigouras to George McMillan, undated, pp. 1, 4, Army folder, Box 3—Biographical Data on JER and Family, McMillan/Southern Historical Collection.

27. McMillan, *The Making of an Assassin*, p. 105.

28. Interview with Jerry Ray by George McMillan, April 1, 1972, Jerry Ray Interviews 1969–1975, Box 5—Trial and Post-Trial Materials; see also interview with Jerry Ray by George McMillan, May 29 (no year), Jerry Ray Interviews 1969–1975, Box 5—Trial and Post-Trial Materials; see also John Ray quoted by Jerry Lipson, "Ray's Road to Jail Began in Army," *Chicago Daily News*, undated, p. 1, Box 1—Correspondence Related to Book Research—Research Files on Ewing; also memorandum to file by George McMillan, summarizing Clay Blair's conversation with Mabel Fuller, July 3, 1969, Army folder, Box 3—Biographical Data on JER and Family, McMillan/Southern Historical Collection; see also McMillan, *The Making of an Assassin*, p. 108.

29. Extracts from the 382nd Military Police Battalion, report on 1,744 women detained as "Venereal Disease Suspects," Chapter 11 file within Army—1946–48 folder, Box 3—Biographical Data on JER and Family, McMillan/Southern Historical Collection.

30. Interview with Stow Symon, Supervising Sociologist at Pontiac Branch, Illinois State Prison, by George McMillan, September 13, 1968, Pontiac folder, Box 3—Biographical Data on JER and Family, McMillan/Southern Historical Collection.

31. Interview with Jerry Ray by George McMillan, April 1, 1972, Jerry Ray Interviews 1969–1975, Box 5—Trial and Post-Trial Materials, McMillan/Southern Historical Collection.

32. Letter from Arthur Zigouras to George McMillan, undated, p. 3, Army folder, Box 3—Biographical Data on JER and Family, McMillan/Southern Historical Collection.

33. Interview with Jerry Ray by George McMillan, January 8 and 9, 1972, Jerry Ray Interviews 1969–1975, Box 5—Trial and Post-Trial Materials, McMillan/Southern Historical Collection.

34. FBI memo to the Director from St. Louis, includes agents' interview with John Ray, May 2, 1968, MURKIN 2926–3030, section 30, p. 45, and MURKIN 3333, section 34, p. 294; see also interview with Jerry Ray by George McMillan, June 26, 1972, Jerry Ray Interviews 1969–1975, Box 5—Trial and Post-Trial Materials, McMillan/Southern Historical Collection.

35. James Earl Ray quoted in Frank, *An American Death*, p. 289.

36. James Earl Ray, 20,000 Words, HSCA vol. XII, pp. 38, 149.

37. Investigation conducted by St. Louis FBI, MURKIN x–125, section 1, p. 24; see also Headquarters, 16th Infantry Regiment, Special Court Martial, November 18, 1948, Army folder, Box 3—Biographical Data on JER and Family, McMillan/Southern Historical Collection.

38. FBI document "Re: Ray Background—Army Service Record," FBI St. Louis file op. cit., Attorney General File, p. 86.

39. Headquarters, 16th Infantry Regiment, Special Court-Martial, November 18, 1948, Army folder, Box 3—Biographical Data on JER and Family, McMillan/Southern Historical Collection; see also FBI document "Re: Ray Background—Army Service Record," FBI St. Louis file, op. cit., Attorney General File, p. 86.

40. Headquarters, 16th Infantry Regiment, Special Court-Martial, December 10, 1948, Army folder, Box 3—Biographical Data on JER and Family, McMillan/Southern Historical Collection.

41. John Ray quoted in McMillan, *The Making of an Assassin*, p. 112.

42. FBI document "Re: Ray Background—Army Service Record," FBI St. Louis file, op. cit., Attorney General File, p. 86; see also MURKIN x–125, section 1, p. 24; and biographical

summary data, Biographical Data on JER folder, Box 3—Biographical Data on JER and Family, McMillan/Southern Historical Collection.

43. James Earl Ray, *Who Killed Martin Luther King?*, p. 23.

44. See, generally, discussion of employment by Ray in MURKIN 3987, section 49, and FBI St. Louis file, Attorney General File.

45. Interview with Genevieve Trevilla by George McMillan, September 7, 1968, Ray Family Chronology folder, Box 3—Biographical Data on JER and Family, McMillan/Southern Historical Collection.

46. FBI document "Re: Suzan Jane Ryan Donian—Subject's Sister," MURKIN 3334-3335, section 35, p. 95.

47. See, generally, interview with Carol Ray Pepper by George McMillan, undated, Carol Ray Pepper folder, Box 1—Correspondence Related to Book Research—Research Files on Ewing; see also interview with Loren E. Schnack by George McMillan, September 6, 1968, in which Schnack says Melba Ray's IQ is 90, Ray Family Chronology folder, Box 3—Biographical Data on JER and Family, McMillan/Southern Historical Collection.

48. See, generally, George Ray interviewed by George McMillan, Jerry Raynes folder, p. 23, Box 1—Correspondence Related to Book Research—Research Files on Ewing, McMillan/Southern Historical Collection.

49. Interview with Jerry Ray by George McMillan, September 27, 1971, Jerry Ray Interviews 1969–1975, Box 5—Trial and Post-Trial Materials; see also interview with Jerry Ray by George McMillan, Memorial Day, no year, Jerry Ray Interviews 1969–1975, McMillan/Southern Historical Collection; see also McMillan, *The Making of an Assassin*, p. 117.

50. Interview with Eda Jansen, Police Matron in Quincy, by George McMillan, Pontiac file, Box 3—Biographical Data on JER and Family, McMillan/Southern Historical Collection; McMillan, *The Making of an Assassin*, p. 126.

51. Jerry Ray interview by George McMillan, September 27, 1971, Jerry Ray Interviews 1969–1975, Box 5—Trial and Post-Trial Materials, McMillan/Southern Historical Collection.

52. Ibid; McMillan, *The Making of an Assassin*, p. 117.

53. Certificate of Plea of Guilty, *People of the State of Illinois* v. *Earl Ray*, Chancery Case No. 4775, September 21, 1948, Box 3—Biographical Data on JER and Family, McMillan/Southern Historical Collection; see also FBI document "Earl Everett Ray," Springfield, FBI, William Robert III, vol. XIX, Attorney General File, p. 2802.

54. Biographical summary data, Biographical Data on JER folder, Box 3—Biographical Data on JER and Family, McMillan/Southern Historical Collection; see also Frank, *An American Death*, p. 177.

55. Blair, *The Strange Case of James Earl Ray*, p. 37.

56. McMillan, *The Making of an Assassin*, p. 133.

57. Interview with Jerry Ray by George McMillan, April 2, 1971, Jerry Ray Interviews 1969–1975, Box 5—Trial and Post-Trial Materials, McMillan/Southern Historical Collection.

58. Blair, *The Strange Case of James Earl Ray*, p. 38.

59. Letter from William Maher to George McMillan, September 6, 1968, Box 1—Correspondence Related to Book Research—Research Files on Ewing, McMillan/Southern Historical Collection.

60. FBI document "James Earl Ray—Veterans Administration," FBI St. Louis file, op. cit., Attorney General File, p. 89; see also FBI document "Re: Veterans Administration Records," MURKIN 3334–3335, section 35, pp. 114–15, and biographical summary data, Biographical Data on JER folder, Box 3—Biographical Data on JER and Family, McMillan/Southern Historical Collection.

61. James Earl Ray, *Who Killed Martin Luther King?*, p. 24.

62. James Earl Ray, *Tennessee Waltz*, p. 9.

63. Ibid.

64. Ibid.

65. James Earl Ray, *Who Killed Martin Luther King?*, p. 25.

66. James Earl Ray, *Tennessee Waltz*, p. 10.

67. Ibid.

68. James Earl Ray, *Who Killed Martin Luther King?*, p. 25.

69. Police Department Arrest Report, 24 Summary Sheet, Records and Identification Division, Los Angeles Police Department.

70. Ibid.

71. Ibid.

72. Ray's statement is reproduced in its entirety in Blair, *The Strange Case of James Earl Ray*, p. 40.

73. James Earl Ray, *Tennessee Waltz*, p. 10.

74. Probation report details listed in Blair, *The Strange Case of James Earl Ray*, pp. 40–41.

75. Reprinted in Blair, *The Strange Case of James Earl Ray*, p. 41; see also biographical summary data, Biographical Data on JER folder, Box 3—Biographical Data on JER and Family, McMillan/Southern Historical Collection.

76. James Earl Ray, *Tennessee Waltz*, p. 10.

77. Ibid., p. 11.

78. Ibid.

79. Ibid.

Chapter 14: The Red Top Caper

1. As for the roll of coins being from the Chinese restaurant theft, see James Earl Ray, *Who Killed Martin Luther King?*, p. 27; as for the arrest itself, see FBI teletype to Director from Omaha, April 10, 1968, MURKIN 1301–1421, section 11, p. 228.

2. FBI teletype to Director from Omaha, April 10, 1968, MURKIN 1301–1421, section 11, p. 229.

3. James Earl Ray, *Who Killed Martin Luther King?*, p. 27.

4. FBI teletype to Director from Omaha, April 10, 1968, MURKIN 1301–1421, section 11, pp. 229–30.

5. James Earl Ray, *Who Killed Martin Luther King?*, p. 27.

6. Jerry Ray quoted in McMillan, *The Making of an Assassin*, p. 118.

7. FBI document "Family of James Earl Ray," Springfield, FBI, William Robert III, vol. XIX, Attorney General File, p. 2760.

8. Certificate of Evidence, *People of the State of Illinois* v. *Jerry Ryan*, Criminal Case No. 5051, February 11, 1954, Ray Family Chronology folder, p. 3, Box 3—Biographical Data on JER and Family, McMillan/Southern Historical Collection.

9. Unidentified probation officer quoted in Blair, *The Strange Case of James Earl Ray*, p. 43.

10. James Earl Ray, *Who Killed Martin Luther King?*, p. 28.

11. Arvey cannot find the work record for Ray's employment, but believes he was in the envelope division; see, generally, Blair, *The Strange Case of James Earl Ray*, p. 43.

12. McMillan, *The Making of an Assassin*, p. 137.

13. Blair, *The Strange Case of James Earl Ray*, p. 43.

14. Arrest information gathered by the Chicago police subsequent to Ray's arrest in May 1952, under listing "Previous Record," MURKIN 3334–3335, section 35, p. 103, see also U.S. District Court, Western District of Missouri, Presentence Report, April 26, 1955, Kansas City file, Attorney General File, p. 1048.

15. Blair, *The Strange Case of James Earl Ray*, p. 44.

16. FBI document "Re: Previous Employment," MURKIN 3334–3335, section 35, p. 114.

17. James Earl Ray, *Who Killed Martin Luther King?*, p. 28.

18. Robert Everhart quoted in Blair, *The Strange Case of James Earl Ray*, p. 46.

19. James Earl Ray, *Who Killed Martin Luther King?*, p. 28.

20. Robert Everhart quoted in Blair, *The Strange Case of James Earl Ray*, p. 46.

21. FBI interview with Captain George Green, May 2, 1968, MURKIN 3334–3335, section 35, p. 111.

22. Ibid.

23. Ray and Everhart quoted in Blair, *The Strange Case of James Earl Ray*, p. 47; see also biographical summary data, Biographical Data on JER folder, Box 3—Biographical Data on JER and Family, McMillan/Southern Historical Collection.

24. James Earl Ray, *Who Killed Martin Luther King?*, p. 29.

25. FBI report "Re: Cook County Hospital Records," MURKIN 3334–3335, section 35, p. 113.

26. Interview with Jerry Ray by George McMillan, January 8 and 9, 1972, Jerry Ray Interviews 1969–1975, Box 5—Trial and Post-Trial Materials, McMillan/Southern Historical Collection.

27. Jerry Ray quoted in McMillan, *The Making of an Assassin*, p. 130.

28. James Earl Ray, *Who Killed Martin Luther King?*, p. 28.

29. Blair, *The Strange Case of James Earl Ray*, p. 48.

30. Department of Public Safety, Division of the Criminologist, Classification Report, dated June 30, 1957, 1 page, MURKIN 3334–3335, section 35, p. 107; see also Department of Public Safety, Division of the Criminologist, "Professional Summary," July 19, 1955, MURKIN 3334–3335, section 35, p. 108.

31. Department of Public Safety, Division of the Criminologist, Classification Report, dated June 30, 1957, 1 page, MURKIN 3334–3335, section 35, p. 107.

32. Ibid.

33. Ibid., p. 109; see also Parole Progress Report, dated April 9, 1953, MURKIN 3334–3335, section 35, p. 110.

34. Ray was identified as a model prisoner in a later FBI summary, MURKIN 3987, section 49, p. 148; Blair, *The Strange Case of James Earl Ray*, p. 49.

35. James Earl Ray, *Tennessee Waltz*, p. 15.

36. Unidentified psychologist quoted in McMillan, *The Making of an Assassin*, p. 141.

37. State of Illinois, Department of Public Safety, Division of the Criminologist, Parole Progress Report, MURKIN 3334–3335, section 35, p. 110.

38. Ibid.

39. Ibid.

40. Ibid., p. 109.

41. Ibid.

42. See Certificate of Evidence, Criminal Case Nos. 5007 & 5008, *People of the State of Illinois* v. *John Ryan alias John Ray*, May 19, 1953, and attached transcript of proceedings for June 1, 1953, Ray Family Chronology folder, Box 3—Biographical Data on JER and Family, McMillan/Southern Historical Collection.

43. Ibid.

44. FBI document "Family of James Earl Ray," Springfield, FBI, William Robert III, vol. XIX, Attorney General File, p. 2766.

45. Certificate of Evidence, *People of the State of Illinois* v. *Jerry Ryan*, Criminal Case No. 5051, February 11, 1954, Ray Family Chronology folder, Box 3—Biographical Data on JER and Family, McMillan/Southern Historical Collection.

46. Interview with Robert Hunter, Juvenile Judge, by George McMillan, September 9, 1968, Box 3—Biographical Data on JER and Family, McMillan/Southern Historical Collection.

47. Interview with Genevieve Trevilla by George McMillan, September 7, 1968, Ray Family Chronology folder, Box 3—Biographical Data on JER and Family, McMillan/Southern Historical Collection.

48. FBI document "Family of James Earl Ray," Springfield, FBI, William Robert III, vol. XIX, Attorney General File, p. 2758.

49. Ibid.

50. Interview with Jerry Ray by George McMillan, October 16, 1969, no folder, Box 1—Correspondence Related to Book Research—Research Files on Ewing, McMillan/Southern Historical Collection.

51. Interview with Robert Hunter, Juvenile Judge, by George McMillan, September 9, 1968; see also interview with Genevieve Trevilla by George McMillan, September 7, 1968, Ray Family Chronology folder, Box 3—Biographical Data on JER and Family, McMillan/Southern Historical Collection.

52. FBI document "Family of James Earl Ray," Springfield, FBI, William Robert III, vol. XIX, Attorney General File, p. 2758.

53. Ibid., p. 2764.

54. Ibid., p. 2758; undated interview with Carol Ray Pepper by George McMillan, Carol Ray Pepper folder, Box 1—Correspondence Related to Book Research—Research Files on Ewing, McMillan/Southern Historical Collection.

55. FBI document "Family of James Earl Ray," Springfield, FBI, William Robert III, vol. XIX, Attorney General File, p. 2763; see also Carol Ray Pepper's statement, "I'm not belligerent," to George McMillan in telephone interview of April 17, 1969, Carol Ray Pepper folder, Box 1—Correspondence Related to Book Research—Research Files on Ewing, McMillan Archives at the Southern Historical Collection.

56. Letter of William Maher to George McMillan, February 3, 1969, Maher folder, Box 1—Correspondence Related to Book Research—Research Files on Ewing; also, see interview with Maher by McMillan, undated, Maher folder, Box 1—Correspondence Related to Book Research—Research Files on Ewing, and interview with Ande Yakstis, *Alton Telegraph* reporter, by George McMillan, August 15, 1968, Alton folder, Box 2—Research Files on Alton and Quincy, McMillan/Southern Historical Collection.

57. James Earl Ray, *Who Killed Martin Luther King?*, p. 30.

58. Harold Riggins quoted in biographical summary data, Biographical Data on JER folder, Box 3—Biographical Data on JER and Family, McMillan/Southern Historical Collection.

59. Andrew Biro quoted in Blair, *The Strange Case of James Earl Ray*, p. 54.

60. James Earl Ray, *Who Killed Martin Luther King?*, p. 30.

61. Harold Riggins quoted in Frank, *An American Death*, p. 293.

62. James Earl Ray, *Who Killed Martin Luther King?*, p. 30.

63. Interview with Walter Rife by George McMillan, Part II, undated, Interviews and Correspondence—Rife, Walter, folder, p. 20, Box 1—Correspondence Related to Book Research—Research Files on Ewing, McMillan/Southern Historical Collection.

64. Ibid.

65. Ibid.; see also Walter Rife quoted in McMillan, *The Making of an Assassin*, p. 147.

66. Interview with Walter Rife by George McMillan, Part I, September 9, 1968, Interviews and Correspondence—Rife, Walter, folder, p. 5, and interview with Rife, Part II, undated, Box 1—Correspondence Related to Book Research—Research Files on Ewing, McMillan/Southern Historical Collection.

67. Clipping "Quincyan Calls Ray Prejudiced," April 25, 1968, Quincy Interviews folder, Box 2—Research Files on Alton and Quincy, McMillan/Southern Historical Collection.

68. FBI document "Associates of James Earl Ray," interview with Walter Rife, April 23, 1968, MURKIN 3987, section 49, p. 108; see also interview with Walter Rife by George McMillan, Part II, undated, Interviews and Correspondence—Rife, Walter folder, pp. 12–13, 29, 32, Box 1—Correspondence Related to Book Research—Research Files on Ewing, McMillan/Southern Historical Collection; Walter Rife quoted in McMillan, *The Making of an Assassin*, pp. 146–47; see also Memo to FBI Director from SAC, Springfield, MO, April 25, 1968, MURKIN 1991–2075, section 17, p. 72.

69. Interview with Walter Rife by George McMillan, Part I, September 9, 1968, Interviews and Correspondence—Rife, Walter, folder, p. 5, Box 1—Correspondence Related to Book Research—Research Files on Ewing, McMillan/Southern Historical Collection.

70. Interview with Walter Rife by George McMillan, Part II, undated, Interviews and Correspondence—Rife, Walter, folder, pp. 13–14, 32, Box 1—Correspondence Related to Book Research—Research Files on Ewing, McMillan/Southern Historical Collection.

Chapter 15: "A Menace to Society"

1. Interview with Walter Rife by George McMillan, Part I, September 9, 1968, Interviews and Correspondence—Rife, Walter, folder, p. 6, Box 1—Correspondence Related to Book Research—Research Files on Ewing, McMillan/Southern Historical Collection.

2. FBI document "Re: Burglary of United States Post Office, Kellerville, Illinois, March 7, 1955," MURKIN 3334–3335, section 35, p. 134; see also FBI interview with Walter Rife, MURKIN 3987, section 49, p. 107; see also interview with Walter Rife by George McMillan, Part II, undated, Interviews and Correspondence—Rife, Walter, folder, pp. 15–18, Box 1—Correspondence Related to Book Research—Research Files on Ewing, McMillan/Southern Historical Collection.

3. Interview with Walter Rife by George McMillan, Part I, September 9, 1968, Interviews and Correspondence—Rife, Walter, folder, p. 5, Box 1—Correspondence Related to Book Research—Research Files on Ewing, McMillan/Southern Historical Collection; McMillan, *The Making of an Assassin*, p. 144.

4. U.S. District Court, Western District of Missouri, Presentence Report, April 26, 1955, Kansas City file, Attorney General File, p. 1047.

5. Of twenty-seven money orders passed by the duo, Rife was responsible for fifteen and Ray for the other twelve. Detailed breakdown of each money order passed, and the locations, contained in U.S. District Court, Western District of Missouri, Presentence Report, April 26, 1955, Kansas City file, Attorney General File, pp. 1046–47.

6. Walter Rife quoted in Blair, *The Strange Case of James Earl Ray*, p. 58; see also interview with Walter Rife by George McMillan, Part I, September 9, 1968, Interviews and Correspondence—Rife, Walter, folder, p. 9, Box 1—Correspondence Related to Book Research—Research Files on Ewing, McMillan/Southern Historical Collection.

7. Walter Rife quoted in Blair, *The Strange Case of James Earl Ray*, p. 58.

8. Interview with Walter Rife by George McMillan, Part I, September 9, 1968, Interviews and Correspondence—Rife, Walter, folder, p. 10, Box 1—Correspondence Related to Book Research—Research Files on Ewing, McMillan/Southern Historical Collection.

9. Ibid., pp. 6–9.

10. Walter Rife quoted in Blair, *The Strange Case of James Earl Ray*, p. 59.

11. Ibid.

12. James Earl Ray, *Tennessee Waltz*, p. 16.

13. Interview with Walter Rife by George McMillan, Part I, September 9, 1968, Interviews and Correspondence—Rife, Walter, folder, p. 9, Box 1—Correspondence Related to Book Research—Research Files on Ewing, McMillan/Southern Historical Collection; McMillan, *The Making of an Assassin*, p. 147.

14. U.S. District Court, Western District of Missouri, Presentence Report, April 26, 1955, Kansas City file, Attorney General File, p. 1045.

15. Lynn Chaffee quoted in Blair, *The Strange Case of James Earl Ray*, p. 60.

16. U.S. District Court, Western District of Missouri, Presentence Report, April 26, 1955, Kansas City file, Attorney General File, p. 1045.

17. Walter Rife quoted in Blair, *The Strange Case of James Earl Ray*, p. 60; see also interview with Walter Rife by George McMillan, Part I, September 9, 1968, Interviews and Correspondence—Rife, Walter, folder, p. 6, Box 1—Correspondence Related to Book Research—Research Files on Ewing, McMillan/Southern Historical Collection.

18. U.S. District Court, Western District of Missouri, Presentence Report, April 26, 1955, Kansas City file, Attorney General File, p. 1046; see, generally, FBI document "Re: Bur-

glary of United States Post Office, Kellerville, Illinois, March 7, 1955," MURKIN 3334–3335, section 35, p. 133.

19. McMillan, *The Making of an Assassin*, p. 148.

20. FBI interview with Walter Rife, MURKIN 3987, section 49, p. 107.

21. Ibid.; FBI teletype to Director from SAC, Springfield, April 25, 1968, MURKIN 1991–2075, section 17, p. 71; see also Blair, *The Strange Case of James Earl Ray*, p. 59.

22. FBI document "James Earl Ray, Post Office Arrest—1955, At St. Louis, Missouri," MURKIN 3333, section 34, p. 102; see also U.S. District Court, Western District of Missouri, Presentence Report, April 26, 1955, Kansas City file, Attorney General File, p. 1045.

23. James Earl Ray, *Tennessee Waltz*, p. 17.

24. U.S. District Court, Western District of Missouri, Presentence Report, April 26, 1955, Kansas City file, Attorney General File, p. 1051.

25. Walter Rife quoted in Blair, *The Strange Case of James Earl Ray*, p. 62.

26. James Earl Ray, *Who Killed Martin Luther King?*, pp. 32–33.

27. Ibid.

28. Ibid., p. 34.

29. McMillan, *The Making of an Assassin*, p. 151.

30. U.S. Department of Justice, Bureau of Prisons, United States Penitentiary, Leavenworth, Kansas, Special Progress Report, October 9, 1956, Kansas City file, Attorney General File, p. 1065.

31. Ibid.

32. James Earl Ray, *Who Killed Martin Luther King?*, p. 35.

33. Interview with Walter Rife by George McMillan, Part I, September 9, 1968, Interviews and Correspondence—Rife, Walter, folder, p. 5, Box 1—Correspondence Related to Book Research—Research Files on Ewing, McMillan/Southern Historical Collection; McMillan, *The Making of an Assassin*, p. 150.

34. FBI document summarizing prison records at Menard Prison, Springfield FBI, vol. XIX, Attorney General File, p. 2787; see also MURKIN 3503, section 39, p. 105.

35. U.S. Department of Justice, Bureau of Prisons, United States Penitentiary, Leavenworth, Kansas, "Release Progress Report," April 1958, Kansas City FBI file, Attorney General File, p. 1064; see also summary of Ramsey Clark interview, Box 1—Correspondence Related to Book Research—Research Files on Ewing, "The Crime" folder, McMillan/Southern Historical Collection.

36. Interview with Walter Rife by George McMillan, Part II, undated, Interviews and Correspondence—Rife, Walter, folder, p. 20, Box 1—Correspondence Related to Book Research—Research Files on Ewing; see also interview with Thomas Maples by George McMillan, September 12, 1968, Box 2—Research Files on Alton and Quincy, McMillan/Southern Historical Collection.

37. U.S. Department of Justice, Bureau of Prisons, United States Penitentiary, Leavenworth, Kansas, "Release Progress Report," April 1958, Kansas City FBI file, Attorney General File, p. 1064.

Chapter 16: A Professional Criminal

1. James Earl Ray, *Who Killed Martin Luther King?*, pp. 36–37.

2. Ibid., p. 37.

3. See, generally, "The Soulard Area—Report on Research into *Adaptations by Urban White Families to Poverty*" conducted under contract with the Office of Economic Opportunity—Contract OE-1241, The Social Science Institute, Washington University, August 15, 1968, Box 1—Correspondence Related to Book Research—Research Files on Ewing, McMillan/Southern Historical Collection.

4. See, generally, FBI summary of Ray family status, MURKIN 3333, section 34, p. 109.

5. James Earl Ray, *Who Killed Martin Luther King?*, p. 37.

6. Ibid.

7. FBI summary document, MURKIN 3333, section 34, p. 109.

8. Ibid., p. 110.

9. James Earl Ray, *Who Killed Martin Luther King?*, p. 37.

10. James Earl Ray, *Tennessee Waltz*, p. 20.

11. Ibid.

12. Ibid.

13. Ibid., p. 21.

14. FBI interview with Cecil Clayton Lillibridge, April 29, 1968, Kansas City file, Attorney General File, pp. 999–1001.

15. FBI interview with James Loama Owens, May 16, 1968, St. Louis file, Harold R. Dobson, Attorney General File, p. 2961.

16. James Earl Ray, *Tennessee Waltz*, p. 21.

17. Ibid.

18. Ibid., p. 21.

19. Interview with James Earl Ray, December 2, 1977, HSCA vol. XI, pp. 406–8.

20. James Earl Ray, *Who Killed Martin Luther King?*, p. 40.

21. Certified copy of the Certificate of Death of Earl Everet (*sic*) Ray, New York State Department of Health, Office of Vital Statistics, District Number 1401, Registered Number 2675, maintained on file in Buffalo, New York.

22. FBI interview with James Loama Owens, May 16, 1968, St. Louis file, Harold R. Dobson, Attorney General File, p. 2955.

23. Jerry Ray interview by George McMillan, September 27, 1971, Jerry Ray Interviews 1969–1975, Box 5—Trial and Post-Trial Materials, McMillan/Southern Historical Collection.

24. FBI summary report on John Eugene Gawron, MURKIN 4143, section 52, p. 89.

25. Ibid., p. 90.

26. Ibid., p. 89.

27. FBI document "Joseph Elmer 'Blackie' Austin," MURKIN 3987, section 49, pp. 111–17; also, same file, unredacted, Springfield file, Attorney General File, p. 2832.

28. FBI document "Joseph Elmer 'Blackie' Austin," Springfield file, Attorney General File, p. 2837.

29. FBI interview with James Loama Owens, May 16, 1968, St. Louis file, Harold R. Dobson, Attorney General File, p. 2953; see also U.S. Department of Justice rap sheet for James Owens, St. Louis file, Harold R. Dobson, Attorney General File, pp. 2969–71.

30. FBI interview with James Loama Owens, May 16, 1968, St. Louis file, Harold R. Dobson, Attorney General File, p. 2953.

31. Interview with Ande Yakstis, *Alton Telegraph* reporter, by George McMillan, August 15, 1968, Alton folder, Box 2—Research Files on Alton and Quincy, McMillan/Southern Historical Collection.

32. FBI interview with James Loama Owens, May 16, 1968, St. Louis file, Harold R. Dobson, Attorney General File, p. 2961—language quoted in this instance is the agents' summary of what Owens said; see also, regarding Ray's reading habits, ibid., p. 2966.

33. Ibid., pp. 2954, 2956.

34. Ibid., p. 2954.

35. Ibid., pp. 2954–55.

36. See the Report of the Metropolitan Police Department, City of St. Louis, Complaint Number 146,048, July 11, 1959, pp. 1–4, Bureau of Records, St. Louis Police Department; Blair, *The Strange Case of James Earl Ray*, p. 65.

37. Report of the Metropolitan Police Department, City of St. Louis, Complaint Number 146,048, July 11, 1959, p. 2, Bureau of Records, St. Louis Police Department.

38. Blair, *The Strange Case of James Earl Ray*, p. 65.

39. Report of the Metropolitan Police Department, City of St. Louis, Complaint Number 169,866, July 11, 1959, pp. 1–3, Bureau of Records, St. Louis Police Department; Commitment Report of James Earl Ray, Missouri State Penitentiary, January 6, 1959, Prison Records up to August 15, 1973, folder, p. 2, Box 6—Trial and Post Trial Materials, Behavior Studies, Newspaper Clippings, McMillan/Southern Historical Collection.

40. Biographical summary data, Biographical Data on JER folder, Box 3—Biographical Data on JER and Family, McMillan/Southern Historical Collection.

41. Commitment Report of James Earl Ray, Missouri State Penitentiary, January 6, 1959, Prison Records up to August 15, 1973, folder, p. 2, Box 6—Trial and Post Trial Materials, Behavior Studies, Newspaper Clippings, McMillan/Southern Historical Collection.

42. Ibid.

43. Blair, *The Strange Case of James Earl Ray*, p. 68.

44. FBI Statement of James Loama Owens, May 16, 1968, St. Louis file, Harold R. Dobson, Attorney General File, p. 2957.

45. Ibid.

46. Ibid.

47. Report of the Metropolitan Police Department, City of St. Louis, Complaint Number 222,015, October 10, 1959, pp. 1–11, plus a three-page supplementary statement by James Owens, and Supplementary Report dated October 12, 1959, Complaint Number 223,556, pp. 1–3, Bureau of Records, St. Louis Police Department.

48. Commitment Report of James Earl Ray, Missouri State Penitentiary, January 6, 1959, Prison Records up to August 15, 1973, folder, Box 6—Trial and Post Trial Materials, Behavior Studies, Newspaper Clippings, McMillan/Southern Historical Collection.

49. Report of the Metropolitan Police Department, City of St. Louis, Complaint Number 222,015, October 10, 1959, pp. 1–11, plus a three-page supplementary statement by James Owens, and Supplementary Report dated October 12, 1959, Complaint Number 223,556, pp. 1–3, Bureau of Records, St. Louis Police Department; Commitment Report of James Earl Ray, Missouri State Penitentiary, January 6, 1959, Prison Records up to August 15, 1973 folder, Box 6—Trial and Post Trial Materials, Behavior Studies, Newspaper Clippings, McMillan/Southern Historical Collection; see also FBI document "James Earl Ray—Arrest—1959," MURKIN 3333, section 34, pp. 118, 121.

50. FBI document "James Earl Ray—Arrest—1959," MURKIN 3333, section 34, p. 119.

51. Ibid.

52. Report of the Metropolitan Police Department, City of St. Louis, Complaint Number 222,015, October 10, 1959, pp. 1–11, plus a three-page supplementary statement by James Owens, and Supplementary Report dated October 12, 1959, Complaint Number 223,556, pp. 1–3, Bureau of Records, St. Louis Police Department; Commitment Report of James Earl Ray, Missouri State Penitentiary, January 6, 1959, Prison Records up to August 15, 1973, folder, Box 6—Trial and Post Trial Materials, Behavior Studies, Newspaper Clippings, McMillan/Southern Historical Collection; see also FBI document "James Earl Ray—Arrest—1959," MURKIN 3333, section 34, p. 119.

53. Report of the Metropolitan Police Department, City of St. Louis, Complaint Number 222,015, October 10, 1959, pp. 1–11, plus a three-page supplementary statement by James Owens, and Supplementary Report dated October 12, 1959, Complaint Number 223,556, pp. 1–3, Bureau of Records, St. Louis Police Department; FBI document "James Earl Ray—Arrest—1959," MURKIN 3333, section 34, p. 119.

54. Report of the Metropolitan Police Department, City of St. Louis, Complaint Number 222,015, October 10, 1959, pp. 1–11, plus a three-page supplementary statement by James Owens, and Supplementary Report dated October 12, 1959, Complaint Number 223,556, pp. 1–3, Bureau of Records, St. Louis Police Department; Commitment Report of James Earl Ray, Missouri State Penitentiary, January 6, 1959, Prison Records up to August 15, 1973, folder, p. 2, Box 6—Trial and Post Trial Materials, Behavior Studies, Newspaper Clippings,

McMillan/Southern Historical Collection; see also FBI document "James Earl Ray—Arrest—1959," MURKIN 3333, section 34, p. 120.

55. FBI document "James Earl Ray—Arrest—1959," MURKIN 3333, section 34, p. 120, see also Commitment Report of James Earl Ray, Missouri State Penitentiary, January 6, 1959, Prison Records up to August 15, 1973, folder, p. 2, Box 6—Trial and Post Trial Materials, Behavior Studies, Newspaper Clippings, McMillan/Southern Historical Collection.

56. Blair, *The Strange Case of James Earl Ray*, p. 73.

57. Report of the Metropolitan Police Department, City of St. Louis, Complaint Number 222,015, October 10, 1959, pp. 1–11, plus a three-page supplementary statement by James Owens, and Supplementary Report dated October 12, 1959, Complaint Number 223,556, pp. 1–3, Bureau of Records, St. Louis Police Department.

58. FBI document "James Earl Ray—Arrest—1959," MURKIN 3333, section 34, p. 120.

59. Commitment Report of James Earl Ray, Missouri State Penitentiary, January 6, 1959, Prison Records up to August 15, 1973, folder, pp. 1–2, Box 6—Trial and Post Trial Materials, Behavior Studies, Newspaper Clippings, McMillan/Southern Historical Collection; see also Blair, *The Strange Case of James Earl Ray*, p. 73.

60. Commitment Report of James Earl Ray, Missouri State Penitentiary, January 6, 1959, Prison Records up to August 15, 1973, folder, p. 2, Box 6—Trial and Post Trial Materials, Behavior Studies, Newspaper Clippings, McMillan/Southern Historical Collection.

61. Ibid.

62. Report of the Metropolitan Police Department, City of St. Louis, Complaint Number 222,015, October 10, 1959, pp. 1–11, plus a three-page supplementary statement by James Owens, and Supplementary Report dated October 12, 1959, Complaint Number 223,556, pp. 1–3, Bureau of Records, St. Louis Police Department.

63. Biographical summary data, Biographical Data on JER folder, Box 3—Biographical Data on JER and Family, McMillan/Southern Historical Collection; see also Blair, *The Strange Case of James Earl Ray*, pp. 74–75.

64. Richard Schreiber quoted in Blair, *The Strange Case of James Earl Ray*, p. 77.

65. Ibid.

66. FBI statement of James Loama Owens, May 16, 1968, St. Louis file, Harold R. Dobson, Attorney General File, p. 2957.

Chapter 17: "A Natural Hustler"

1. "The Jefftown Journal—Historical Edition," compiled and researched by the Jefftown Journal Staff, edited by James Caffey, summer 1972, p. 24, Chapter XV folder, Box 4—Research Materials by Chapter—Files on: Motive, Drugs, Poverty, McMillan/Southern Historical Collection; McMillan, *The Making of an Assassin*, p. 164.

2. In the 1980s, Missouri changed the name to the Jefferson City Correctional Center.

3. Interview with Tim Kniest, September 17, 1997.

4. "The Jefftown Journal—Historical Edition," compiled and researched by the Jefftown Journal Staff, edited by James Caffey, summer 1972, p. 31, Chapter XV folder, Box 4—Research Materials by Chapter—Files on: Motive, Drugs, Poverty, McMillan/Southern Historical Collection.

5. Ibid.

6. McMillan, *The Making of an Assassin*, p. 166.

7. "The Jefftown Journal—Historical Edition," compiled and researched by the Jefftown Journal Staff, edited by James Caffey, summer 1972, p. 31, Chapter XV folder, Box 4—Research Materials by Chapter—Files on: Motive, Drugs, Poverty, McMillan/Southern Historical Collection; see also McMillan, *The Making of an Assassin*, pp. 166–67.

8. McMillan, *The Making of an Assassin*, p. 166–67.

9. Ibid., p. 164.

10. "The Jefftown Journal—Historical Edition," compiled and researched by the Jefftown Journal Staff, edited by James Caffey, summer 1972, p. 31, Chapter XV folder, Box 4—Research Materials by Chapter—Files on: Motive, Drugs, Poverty, McMillan/Southern Historical Collection.

11. Ibid., p. 32.

12. Ibid.

13. James Earl Ray, *Who Killed Martin Luther King?*, p. 42; see also statement of Earnest, under Mo Pen heading, Episode Card Index, Attorney General File, and FBI interview with Danton Steele, MURKIN 4441, section 56, p. 29.

14. McMillan, *The Making of an Assassin*, p. 170.

15. James Earl Ray, *Who Killed Martin Luther King?*, p. 42.

16. Ibid.

17. Blair, *The Strange Case of James Earl Ray*, p. 82.

18. James Earl Ray, *Who Killed Martin Luther King?*, p. 45.

19. Ibid.

20. Ibid., p. 46.

21. Ibid.

22. Ibid.

23. Ibid., pp. 46–47.

24. Ibid., p. 47.

25. Ibid.

26. Ibid.

27. Ibid., p. 48.

28. Ibid.

29. Ibid.

30. There are several hundred FBI interviews and reinterviews of nearly one hundred inmates who served with Ray at the prison. Almost all were conducted by special agents in April and May 1968, after King was assassinated but before Ray was captured in London. At the time, the FBI was not only interested in determining whether Ray was capable of killing King, but also whether any of his former prison mates would have leads about where he might hide as a fugitive.

His fellow inmates present two different and incompatible portraits of Ray, only one of which, of course, can be accurate. One person is quiet, not involved in any of the prison's rackets, not a drug abuser, and without any racial prejudice. The other Ray is a sometimes violent inmate, a successful prison smuggler, an amphetamine abuser, and also an avowed racist who occasionally threatened King's life. Weighing this testimony for credibility and seeking corroboration is no easy task when some convicts have little hesitation to lie if it is in their best interest. Furthermore, the FBI, in its files about the assassination maintained at the Bureau's reading room in Washington, D.C., has blacked out the prisoner's names. Without the names, it is not possible to determine how long each witness knew Ray, or even if, say, he was telling the truth when he claimed to have been a cellmate or to have worked with him in the bakery. Also, since the FBI sometimes conducted multiple interviews of the same inmate, it is also impossible to determine whether only one person was repeating an accusation about something—such as Ray's purported drug dealing—or if the numerous statements are actually from different inmates, thereby providing some independent corroboration.

But a breakthrough came in mid-1997 when the author obtained access to the original investigatory file prepared by the state of Tennessee for its criminal case against Ray. That attorney general's file fills a deep, four-drawer cabinet and was never used once Ray pleaded guilty. However, it not only contains an enormous amount of original documentation about the case, but also many of the FBI interviews with Ray's fellow inmates. None of the papers in the attorney general's file has any redactions. This allowed matching of the sanitized FBI files against the uncensored information in the attorney general's papers and thereby identification of most of the inmates in the FBI documents.

Once the identities were known, it was evident that many of those who claimed Ray was merely a passive prisoner with no racial hatred were themselves often accused of having been Ray's drug suppliers or prison protectors. Their denials that Ray was involved in the rackets or a drug user must be viewed in light of the difficulty such an admission would have caused for them. Moreover, although some may not have been close to Ray or felt any loyalty to him, as with many convicts there was a general dislike for the FBI and an overall unwillingness to cooperate with federal agents for fear of appearing to be informers. This is especially true since Ray was still on the run at the time of the interviews. Almost all the prisoners interviewed by the FBI were white and many were themselves racist. In the wake of the King assassination—something many of them publicly applauded—they would not help the federal government make a case against a former cellmate. Therefore, one must be open to the possibility that many of the statements portraying a kind and gentle Ray are questionable.

On the other hand, those inmates who gave the FBI often detailed accounts of Ray's involvement in prison rackets, his drug abuse, and his racism had little reason to lie—the files do not indicate that the government offered reduced sentences, deals, or improved conditions for cooperation (though a prisoner might have personally benefited if he had information that led to Ray's capture, and volunteered that). With the exception of one prisoner, none of them later tried to sell their information or profit from it. Moreover, some who spoke frankly about Ray's drug problems and bigotry had been released from prison by the time they spoke to the FBI, so they did not even have to cooperate with the agents if they did not want to. Quite a few considered themselves friends of Ray's and spoke only reluctantly about his prison tenure.

Therefore, Ray's racism and drug problems, highlighted by several dozen inmates, are probably underplayed by other inmates who disliked the FBI, sought to protect themselves, or wanted to assist Ray. One inmate, Robert Hess, was typical of many when he told FBI agents, "I remember Jim Ray but I don't know anything about him now and if I did know anything I wouldn't tell any representative of law enforcement."

31. Letter to Warden Swenson from ex–Ray colleague, name withheld, MURKIN 2151–2321, section 19, pp. 64–68.

32. See FBI interviews with Orlan Eugene Rose, Billy Edward Miles, and Jimmy Z. Bradley, all conducted on April 22, 1968, Kansas City FBI file 44-760; also FBI interview with Howard Nunn, May 9, 1968, and with Julius Maurice Block, April 30, 1968, and with Sterling Junior Hill, May 1, 1968, and Robert A. Hess, April 24, 1968, Attorney General File.

33. FBI interview with William E. Russell, June 7, 1968, St. Louis FBI 44-775, Harold R. Dobson, Attorney General File; see also FBI interview with Russell, MURKIN 4760, section 62, p. 144.

34. FBI investigation, MURKIN 4441, section 56, p. 8; see also Airtel to Director from SAC, Cleveland, April 23, 1968, MURKIN 1901–1990, section 16, p. 132; see also Airtel to Director from SAC, Birmingham, May 23, 1968, MURKIN 4251–4350, section 54, p. 121.

35. McMillan, *The Making of an Assassin*, p. 206.

36. Ibid., p. 197.

37. Ibid., p. 198.

38. See, generally, FBI interview with John L. Menard, May 17, 1968, MURKIN 4441, section 56, p. 23, and interview with unidentified prisoner (name redacted), MURKIN 4441, section 56, p. 37.

39. McMillan, *The Making of an Assassin*, p. 198.

40. James Earl Ray, *Tennessee Waltz*, p. 39.

41. Jerry Ray interviewed by George McMillan, July 12, 1975, Box 5—Trial and Post-Trial Materials, McMillan/Southern Historical Collection.

42. McMillan, *The Making of an Assassin*, pp. 198–99.

43. Raymond Curtis interviewed by George McMillan, January 27, 1969, pp. 2a–2b, Interview Curtis Raymond folder, Box 1—Correspondence Related to Book Research—Re-

search Files on Ewing, McMillan/Southern Historical Collection; McMillan, *The Making of an Assassin,* p. 179; as for Curtis and Ray spending time together in Jeff City, see statement of unidentified inmate (name redacted) in teletype to Director from Kansas City, MURKIN 2441–2552, section 24, p. 31.

44. Neil Aeby information listed under Mo Pen, 3-by-5 Episode Card Index, Attorney General File.

45. Raymond Curtis interviewed by George McMillan, January 27, 1969, p. 2b, Interview Curtis Raymond folder, Box 1—Correspondence Related to Book Research—Research Files on Ewing, McMillan/Southern Historical Collection; McMillan, *The Making of an Assassin,* p. 182; see also interview with Malik Hakim, McMillan, pp. 185–89.

46. Raymond Curtis interviewed by George McMillan, January 27, 1969, pp. 2b, 21, Interview Curtis Raymond folder, Box 1—Correspondence Related to Book Research—Research Files on Ewing, McMillan/Southern Historical Collection.

47. FBI interview with Cecil Clayton Lillibridge, April 29, 1968, Kansas City file 44-760, Attorney General File.

48. FBI interview with James Loama Owens, May 16, 1968, St. Louis 44-775, Harold R. Dobson, Attorney General File; see also MURKIN 4760, section 62, p. 65, and MURKIN 3628–3761, section 44, p. 54.

49. See Kenneth Lee Wade interviewed by FBI agents Dale Norton and Michael Geary, May 17, 1968, San Francisco file 173-65, Attorney General File; Paul Alvin, Lail information at Mo Pen, 3-by-5 Episode Card Index, Attorney General File.

50. HSCA Rpt., pp. 427–28.

51. Richard L. Menard interviewed by FBI agent Roy Humphreys, May 17, 1968, Kansas City file 44-760, Attorney General File; see also Richard L. Menard information in Mo Pen, 3-by-5 Episode Card Index, Attorney General File.

52. John Ray statement to the FBI, MURKIN 4143, section 52, p. 43; see also John Ray statement in MURKIN 4760, section 62, pp. 193, 195, summarized in teletype of May 16, 1968, MURKIN 3628–3761, section 44, p. 59; also, since the FBI interviews with Ray's prison mates are redacted for privacy purposes, none of the prisoners' names appear in the documents. However, the author was able to identify many since the smaller collection of FBI interviews maintained at the Attorney General File in Memphis are not redacted. However, in some instances, it was not possible to identify a prisoner. For instance, there are unidentified Jeff City prisoners who also talk about Ray's narcotic dealings in MURKIN 2151–2321, section 19, p. 23; MURKIN 3503, section 39, p. 27; MURKIN 4760, section 62, p. 33; MURKIN 2441–2552, section 24, p. 195; and also separate interview in same file at pp. 199–200; also MURKIN 4143, section 52, p. 57; memo to Cartha DeLoach, April 22, 1968, MURKIN 1731–1820, section 14, p. 173; Airtel to Director from SAC, San Francisco, May 5, 1968, MURKIN 3336–3418, section 36, p. 117, and MURKIN 1901–1990, section 16, pp. 148–49.

53. FBI interview with Billy Edward Miles, April 22, 1968, Kansas City FBI file 44-760; see also informant information about Ray and the prison lottery, Mo Pen, 3-by-5 Episode Card Index, Attorney General File.

54. FBI interview with William Robert Turner, April 24, 1968, Kansas City file 44-760, Attorney General File; also MURKIN 3503, section 39, p. 72.

55. McMillan, *The Making of an Assassin,* p. 241.

56. Interview with James Earl Ray in *Playboy,* September 1977, p. 82.

57. James Earl Ray interviewed by Dan Rather, March 9, 1977, HSCA vol. 1, pp. 324–25.

58. FBI interview with James (Jimmy) H. Carpenter, May 12, 1968, St. Louis FBI 44-775, Harold R. Dobson, Attorney General File.

59. FBI interview with Walter E. Nolan, May 20, 1968, St. Louis FBI 44-775, Harold R. Dobson, Attorney General File; Joseph Frank Guinan and Harry Sero, information listed under Mo Pen, 3-by-5 Episode Card Index, Attorney General File.

60. FBI interview with Jimmy Bradley, April 22, 1968, Kansas City FBI file 44-760, Attorney General File; see also MURKIN 2151–2321, section 19, pp. 28–30, MURKIN 3503,

section 39, pp. 30–31; see also statement from unidentified inmates (names redacted) in MURKIN 2751–2925, section 29, p. 21, and MURKIN 2326–2440, section 23, pp. 246–47.

61. FBI interview with Orlan Eugene Rose, April 24, 1968, MURKIN 2151–2321, section 19, pp. 61–63; MURKIN 3503, section 39, p. 33.

62. Lewis Raymond Dowda information listed under Mo Pen, 3-by-5 Episode Card Index, Attorney General File. Also, the FBI MURKIN files contain Jeff City inmates who talk extensively about Ray's drug use at the prison, but the inmates' names are redacted for privacy—among those are MURKIN 3503, section 33, p. 42, and MURKIN 4760, section 62, p. 139.

63. Airtel to Director from SAC Cleveland, April 23, 1968, MURKIN 1901–1990, section 16, p. 131.

64. Memorandum to Cartha DeLoach from Alex Rosen, May 1, 1968, MURKIN 3131–3220, section 32, p. 168; see also statements of unidentified inmates, listed in FBI teletype to Director from Jacksonville, April 29, 1968, MURKIN 2441–2552, section 24, pp. 199–200, and Airtel to Director from SAC Cleveland, April 23, 1968, MURKIN 1901–1990, section 16, p. 132, and FBI summary investigative information contained in MURKIN 4143, section 52, p. 50.

65. FBI interview with Sterling Junior Hill, May 1, 1968, Kansas City file 44-760, Attorney General File.

66. James Earl Ray, *Tennessee Waltz*, p. 31.

67. FBI interview with James Edward "Ted" Richardson, May 6, 1968, St. Louis 44-775 folder, Attorney General File; see also Richardson interview (redacted) at MURKIN 3333, section 34, p. 171.

68. See, generally, FBI interview with Jimmy Bradley, April 22, 1968, Kansas City FBI file 44-760, Attorney General File; see also memo to Cartha DeLoach from Alex Rosen, May 1, 1968, MURKIN 3131–3220, section 32, p. 169.

69. FBI interview with Cecil Clayton Lillibridge, April 29, 1968, Kansas City file 44-760, Attorney General File.

70. Carl M. Craig information listed under Mo Pen, 3-by-5 Episode Card Index, Attorney General File; see also Airtel to Director from SAC, Kansas City, April 26, 1968, MURKIN 2441–2552, section 24, p. 147.

71. FBI interview with Cecil Clayton Lillibridge, April 29, 1968, Kansas City file 44-760, Attorney General File.

72. FBI Case Report and Summary, 5/6/68–6/12/68, MURKIN 4441, section 56, p. 6.

73. James Earl Ray notes on the envelope of a letter addressed to him, from Guy M. Sone, Clerk of the Circuit Court of Cole County, FBI laboratory marking 44-38861 JK K211.

74. Jerry Ray interview by George McMillan, May 31, 1972, Jerry Ray Interviews 1969–1975, Box 5—Trial and Post-Trial Materials, McMillan/Southern Historical Collection.

75. Letter to Rep. Thomas Curtis from James Earl Ray, June 14, 1965.

76. Ibid.

77. The inmate statements are again contradictory, but those who pinpoint a bias often describe actions by Ray that corroborate their view. Also, in a mostly segregated prison in the 1960s, where the white inmates came largely from poor and rough backgrounds not that dissimilar to Ray's family, it would not be surprising to find that a majority of inmates harbored racist views. In this sense, James Earl Ray was not an exception. If anything, bigotry was ideally suited to the mean atmosphere in Jeff City, and if expressed by Ray it was likely another reason that most inmates considered him one of the gang, not an unusual or objectionable character. This, of course, helps to explain why prisoners who spoke to the FBI were split over the question of whether Ray was a bigot: Some clearly found that since Ray's views were like their own—racist—they were not objectionable. Therefore, many of the statements portraying Ray as devoid of racial bias probably underplay his resentment toward blacks.

78. Jerry Ray interviewed by George McMillan, May 10, 1970, Jerry Ray Interviews 1969–1975, Box 5—Trial and Post-Trial Materials, McMillan/Southern Historical Collection.

79. HSCA report on interview with William Bradford Huie, April 10, 1978, HSCA vol. VIII, p. 44.

80. FBI interview with Julius Maurice Block, April 30, 1968, Kansas City file 44-760, MURKIN 3503, section 39, p. 60; see also Billy Bob information listed under Mo Pen, 3-by-5 Episode Card Index, Attorney General File, and interview with unidentified inmate (name redacted) contained in teletype to Director from Kansas City, April 23, 1968, MURKIN 1991–2075, section 17, p. 21.

81. Interview with James W. Brown listed under Mo Pen, 3-by-5 Episode Card Index, Attorney General File; see also HSCA vol. XIII, p. 246, and FBI interview with James Wilson Brown, April 30, 1968, Birmingham Field Office; see also FBI interview with Brown, April 30, 1968, MURKIN 3763–3872, section 46, p. 29, and FBI summary document MURKIN 2674–2750, section 28, p. 178.

82. Glenn Jefferson Buckley information listed under Mo Pen, 3-by-5 Episode Card Index, Attorney General File.

83. Harry Sero interview by FBI, April 26, 1968, MURKIN Memphis field office 44-1987, Subs. D, vol. 1, p. 210.

84. FBI interview with Cecil Clayton Lillibridge, April 29, 1968, Kansas City file 44-760, Attorney General File.

85. FBI interview with Paul Bridgeman, contained in teletype to Director from Minneapolis, June 7, 1968, MURKIN 4251–4350, section 54, p. 158.

86. Ibid.

87. Teletype to Director from St. Louis, May 9, 1968, MURKIN 3221–3332, section 33, p. 181.

88. FBI interview with Cecil Clayton Lillibridge, April 29, 1968, Kansas City file 44-760, MURKIN 3503, section 39, pp. 61–64; also 3-by-5 Episode Index Card file under Cecil Clayton Lillibridge, Attorney General File; see, generally, MURKIN 2553–2633, section 25, p. 109.

89. FBI interview with Cecil Clayton Lillibridge, April 29, 1968, Kansas City file 44-760, Attorney General File.

90. Harry Sero information listed in Episode Card Index, Mo Pen heading, Special Agent Hester, Episode Card Index, Attorney General File; see also FBI interview with Sero, April 26, 1968, MURKIN Memphis field office 44-1987, Sub D, vol. 1, pp. 209–10, and memo to Cartha DeLoach from Alex Rosen, April 26, 1968, MURKIN 2151–2321, section 19, pp. 131–32.

91. Lewis Raymond Dowda information listed under Mo Pen, 3-by-5 Episode Card Index; see also James W. Brown and Raymond Curtis, same index, Attorney General File; see also statement of unidentified inmate (redacted name), April 24, 1968, MURKIN 2326–2440, section 23, pp. 245–46.

92. James W. Brown information listed under Mo Pen, 3-by-5 Episode Card Index, Attorney General File; see also HSCA vol. XIII, p. 246, and FBI interview with James Wilson Brown, April 30, 1968, Birmingham Field Office; Also FBI interview with Brown of April 30, 1968, MURKIN 3763–3872, section 46, p. 29, and FBI teletype to SACs, from Director, May 2, 1968, MURKIN 2674–2750, section 28, pp. 180–81.

93. Johnny Valenti information under Mo Pen heading, Episode Index Card file—see also cards for Chester Ealey and "Nonnie" Eden; see also FBI interview with Johnny Valenti, May 11, 1968, St. Louis field office 44-775, Attorney General File.

94. FBI interview with Thomas Britton (name is redacted in FBI copy), contained in teletype to Director from Birmingham, May 7, 1968, MURKIN 3131–3220, section 32, p. 86, and also in MURKIN 3221–3332, section 33, p. 20.

95. FBI interview with Thomas Britton, May 7, 1968, MURKIN 3131–3220, vol. 1, section 35, Memphis Field Office; see also HSCA vol. XIII, p. 246.

96. Ibid.; see also interview in MURKIN 3763–3872, section 46, pp. 36–42, and memo to Cartha DeLoach, May 9, 1968, MURKIN 3419–3440, section 37, p. 69.

97. See, generally, Lee Bercia information listed under Mo Pen, Special Agent Ayers, Episode Card Index, Attorney General File; see also FBI Kansas City Field Office investigative report, MURKIN 4441, section 56, p. 19.

98. FBI teletype to Director from Miami, April 26, 1968, MURKIN 2151–2321, section 19, p. 226; see also statements of unidentified Jeff City inmate (name redacted), MURKIN 3503, section 39, p. 119, MURKIN 2326–2440, section 23, p. 245, and MURKIN 4143, section 52, p. 55, citing inmate who says Ray was "close with the one that did it."

99. See FBI Airtel to Director from SAC, Jackson, May 15, 1968, MURKIN 3901–3986, section 48, pp. 126–33; Airtel to Director from SAC Dallas, May 1, 1968, MURKIN 2926–3030, section 30, pp. 18–19; see also MURKIN 5101, section 69, FBI summary investigation, pp. 173–75; see, generally, memo from McGowan to Alex Rosen, April 24, 1968, MURKIN 2635–2673, section 27, pp. 29–38.

100. See, generally, FBI interview with Thomas Britton, MURKIN 3763–3872, section 46, pp. 36–42, and HSCA vol. XIII, p. 246; FBI memorandum from W. A. Branigan to W. C. Sullivan, June 14, 1968, MURKIN 4664–4696, section 60, p. 47; also statement of Orville Ernest Gann, May 6, 1968, St. Louis field office file 44-775, and statement of James (Jimmy) H. Carpenter, May 12, 1968, St. Louis field office file 44-775, Attorney General File. Also, there was even a suggestion that Ray was a member of Cooley's Organization—see FBI interview with Thomas Britton, MURKIN 3763–3872, section 46, p. 40; and HSCA vol. XIII, p. 246.

101. HSCA Rpt., p. 470.

102. Testimony of Russell George Byers, November 29, 1978, HSCA vol. VII, pp. 181, 188.

103. Ibid., p. 189.

104. Ibid., p. 245.

105. Ibid., pp. 182–183, 191.

106. Testimony of Murray L. Randall, November 29, 1978, HSCA vol. VII, pp. 208, 214, and testimony of Lawrence Weenick, November 29, 1978, HSCA vol. VII, p. 241.

107. HSCA Rpt., p. 472.

108. Testimony of Edward Evans, Chief Investigator, HSCA vol. VII, p. 250.

109. HSCA Rpt., pp. 476–77.

110. Ibid., p. 480.

111. Testimony of Russell George Byers, November 29, 1978, HSCA vol. VII, pp. 184, 197.

112. FBI interview with James Edward "Ted" Richardson, May 6, 1968, St. Louis field office file 44-775, Attorney General File; see also Richardson interview (redacted) at MURKIN 3333, section 34, p. 171.

113. James Earl Ray, Who Killed Martin Luther King?, p. 53.

114. Ibid., p. 54.

115. Testimony of Russell George Byers, November 29, 1978, HSCA vol. VII, p. 185.

116. Testimony of Edward Evans, Chief Investigator, HSCA vol. VII, p. 295; see also HSCA Rpt., p. 481.

117. HSCA Rpt., p. 481.

118. Ibid.

119. Ibid., p. 480.

120. FBI interview with Donald Lee Mitchell, September 30, 1968, MURKIN 44-1854, Miami Field Office; see also HSCA vol. XIII, p. 248.

Chapter 18: Breakout

1. "Pre-Parole Progress Report," October 8, 1965, Chronological Data Sheet, Summary Sheet by Carl White, Attorney General File.

2. Ibid.

3. Chronological Data Sheet on James Earl Ray's time at Missouri State Penitentiary, describing October 1, 1963, parole denial, Attorney General File.

4. James Earl Ray, Tennessee Waltz, p. 32.

5. See, generally, Harold Swenson memo of April 24, 1968, regarding cell assignments for James Earl Ray, Kansas City field office 44-760, Attorney General File.

6. James Earl Ray, Who Killed Martin Luther King?, p. 50.

7. Ibid.

8. James Earl Ray, *Tennessee Waltz*, p. 33; see also certificate from Fulton State Hospital re: James Earl Ray, October 24, 1966, two pages, Attorney General File.

9. Certificate from Fulton State Hospital re: James Earl Ray, October 24, 1966, two pages, Attorney General File.

10. James Earl Ray, *Who Killed Martin Luther King?*, p. 51.

11. James Earl Ray, *Tennessee Waltz*, p. 35.

12. James Earl Ray, *Who Killed Martin Luther King?*, p. 52.

13. James Earl Ray, *Tennessee Waltz*, pp. 35–36.

14. Ibid., p. 36.

15. James Earl Ray, *Who Killed Martin Luther King?*, p. 53.

16. Certificate from Fulton State Hospital re: James Earl Ray, October 24, 1966, two pages, Attorney General File.

17. Letter to Board of Probation and Parole from Dr. Henry V. Guhleman, December 20, 1968, two pages, Attorney General File.

18. Ibid.

19. Ibid.

20. Ibid.

21. James Earl Ray, *Tennessee Waltz*, p. 37.

22. Ibid., p. 38.

23. FBI interview with Everett Wayne Cox, April 24, 1968, contained in teletype to Director from Oklahoma City, MURKIN 1901–1990, section 16, p. 154.

24. See, generally, FBI interview with unidentified inmate (name redacted), MURKIN 2151–2321, section 19, p. 165.

25. FBI interview with George Ben Edmundson, April 25, 1968, MURKIN 3503, section 39, p. 52; see also summary of Edmundson interviews, MURKIN 3503, section 39, pp. 5–6.

26. Ibid., pp. 52–53.

27. Interview with James Earl Ray, December 2, 1977, HSCA vol. XI, p. 352; James Earl Ray, 20,000 Words, HSCA vol. XII, pp. 121–22; see also Frank, *An American Death*, p. 236.

28. FBI interview with unidentified inmate (name redacted), MURKIN 3873–3900, section 47, p. 145; see also MURKIN 4441, section 56, p. 5.

29. Ibid.; see also MURKIN 4441, section 56, p. 5.

30. FBI interview with unidentified inmate (name redacted), MURKIN 3873–3900, section 47, p. 144; see also MURKIN 4441, section 56, p. 4.

31. Ibid.; see also MURKIN 4441, section 56, p. 6.

32. James Earl Ray, *Tennessee Waltz*, p. 40.

33. Statement of James Wolf, Deputy Chief Counsel, HSCA vol. VIII, p. 2; letter to Stephen J. Pollak, Assistant Attorney General, from FBI Director, June 17, 1968, Attorney General File; see also April 29, 1968, teletype from FBI Memphis to Director, MURKIN 2441–2552, section 24, p. 83, and statement of Warden Harold Swenson, MURKIN 3503, section 39, p. 8.

34. Statement of James Wolf, Deputy Chief Counsel, HSCA vol. VIII, p. 6.

35. HSCA Rpt., p. 444.

36. Ibid., p. 439; John Ray quoted in *St. Louis Post-Dispatch*, June 9, 1968.

37. FBI interview with John Larry Ray, April 22, 1968, HSCA vol. VIII, p. 33, and also in MURKIN 3333, section 34, p. 271; see also FBI teletype to Director from St. Louis, April 26, 1968, MURKIN 2151–2321, section 19, pp. 232–33.

38. FBI teletype to Bureau from St. Louis, April 26, 1968, MURKIN 2151–2321, section 19, pp. 205–6.

39. Testimony of John Ray, HSCA vol. VIII, p. 57.

40. Ibid., p. 60; statement of James Earl Ray, MLK Exhibit F-635, HSCA vol. VIII, p. 58; see also James Earl Ray interview, December 2, 1977, HSCA vol. XI, pp. 309, 312–13; compi-

lation of the statements of James Earl Ray, Staff Report of the Select Committee on Assassinations, U.S. House of Representatives, 95th Congress, Second Session, August 18, 1978, p. 3.

41. Testimony of John Ray, HSCA vol. VIII, P. 60.

42. HSCA interview with Walter Rife, February 7, 1978, MLK Exhibit F-640, HSCA vol. VIII, pp. 64–65.

43. Testimony of John Ray, HSCA vol. VIII, p. 66.

44. HSCA Rpt., p. 442.

45. James Earl Ray, 20,000 Words, HSCA vol. XII; see also Huie, *He Slew the Dreamer,* pp. 17, 19.

46. William Bradford Huie, "I Had Been in Trouble All My Life, in Jail Most of It," *Look,* November 12, 1968, pp. 97, 99.

47. HSCA interview with James Earl Ray, December 2, 1977, HSCA vol. XI, pp. 229–32 and 246–60; Huie, *He Slew the Dreamer,* p. 19.

48. See statement of unidentified inmate (name redacted), MURKIN 4760, section 62, p. 34.

49. See, generally, FBI interview with unidentified inmate (name redacted), MURKIN 3503, section 39, p. 59; see also statement of Stephan I. Kral, April 26, 1968, MURKIN 3503, section 39, p. 19.

50. James Earl Ray, *Tennessee Waltz,* p. 40; see also interview with James Earl Ray, December 2, 1977, HSCA vol. XI, p. 254.

51. James Earl Ray, *Tennessee Waltz,* p. 40; see also interview with James Earl Ray, December 2, 1977, HSCA vol. XI, p. 271.

52. James Earl Ray, *Tennessee Waltz,* pp. 40–41.

53. James Earl Ray, 20,000 Words, HSCA vol. XII.

54. Statement of Stephan I. Kral, April 26, 1968, MURKIN 2326–2440, section 23, p. 79.

55. Statement of Alfred Burkhardt, April 26, 1968, MURKIN 2326–2440, section 23, p. 78; see also interview with James Earl Ray, December 2, 1977, HSCA vol. XI, p. 232.

56. Ibid.; statement of Alfred Burkhardt, April 26, 1968, MURKIN 2326–2440, section 23, p. 78.

57. James Earl Ray, *Tennessee Waltz,* p. 41; see also interview with James Earl Ray, December 2, 1977, HSCA vol. XI, pp. 270, 272–73.

58. Inter-Office Communication of the Department of Corrections to M. J. Elliott, Associate Warden, from Captain Danton Steele, May 3, 1967, MURKIN 3503, section 39, p. 9.

59. FBI summary document, Kansas City field office, MURKIN x–125, section 1, p. 8.

60. FBI interview with unidentified inmate (name redacted), MURKIN 3503, section 39, p. 14.

61. Statement of Major Bernard Poiry, April 23, 1968, MURKIN 3503, section 39, p. 15.

Chapter 19: Indian Trail

1. James Earl Ray, 20,000 Words, HSCA vol. XII, pp. 108–9.

2. Interview with James Earl Ray, December 2, 1977, HSCA vol. XI, p. 314.

3. James Earl Ray, 20,000 Words, HSCA vol. XII, p. 110; see also interview with James Earl Ray, December 2, 1977, HSCA vol. XI, pp. 323–24.

4. James Earl Ray, 20,000 Words, HSCA vol. XII, p. 113; see interview of James Earl Ray with the House Select Committee investigators, HSCA vol. IX, pp. 263–64, and Huie, *He Slew the Dreamer,* p. 21.

5. James Earl Ray, 20,000 Words, HSCA vol. XII, p. 73.

6. Huie, *He Slew the Dreamer,* p. 22.

7. Ibid.

8. Mr. and Mrs. Donnelly quoted in Huie, *He Slew the Dreamer,* p. 22.

9. MURKIN summary on Jerry William Ray, file 3334–3335, section 35, pp. 56, 58.

10. See, generally, interview with Clara Klingeman by William Bradford Huie, *He Slew the Dreamer*, p. 23.

11. "Six Week Report on Work Habits," listed by Huie, *He Slew the Dreamer*, p. 26.

12. Gertrude Struve Paulus interviewed by Huie, *He Slew the Dreamer*, p. 25.

13. James Earl Ray quoted by Huie, *He Slew the Dreamer*, p. 27.

14. James Earl Ray, 20,000 Words, HSCA vol. XII, p. 139.

15. Ibid., pp. 99, 134; see also James Earl Ray quoted in Compilation of the Statements of James Earl Ray, Staff Report of the Select Committee on Assassinations, U.S. House of Representatives, 95th Congress, Second Session, August 18, 1978, p. 6.

16. Interview with James Earl Ray, December 2, 1977, HSCA vol. XI, pp. 355–56; James Earl Ray quoted in Compilation of the Statements of James Earl Ray, Staff Report of the Select Committee on Assassinations, U.S. House of Representatives, 95th Congress, Second Session, August 18, 1978, p. 8.

17. James Earl Ray quoted in Compilation of the Statements of James Earl Ray, Staff Report of the Select Committee on Assassinations, U.S. House of Representatives, 95th Congress, Second Session, August 18, 1978, p. 8.

18. James Earl Ray quoted by Huie, *He Slew the Dreamer*, p. 29.

19. Huie, *He Slew the Dreamer*, p. 26; FBI interview with Harvey Klingeman and Clara Klingeman, August 23, 1968, Chicago folder, p. 2513, Attorney General File.

20. FBI interview with Harvey Klingeman and Clara Klingeman, August 23, 1968, Chicago folder, p. 2510, Attorney General File.

21. Art Petacque, "FBI Tries to Tag Voices in Ray Case," *The Commercial Appeal*, Memphis, October 25, 1968, p. 1.

22. Frank, *An American Death*, p. 300; interview with James Earl Ray by House Select Committee investigators, HSCA vol. IX, p. 269; see also James Earl Ray quoted in Compilation of the Statements of James Earl Ray, Staff Report of the Select Committee on Assassinations, U.S. House of Representatives, 95th Congress, Second Session, August 18, 1978, p. 8.

23. Testimony of Jerry Ray, November 29, 1978, HSCA vol. VII, pp. 407–8.

24. Jerry Ray interviewed by George McMillan, June 27, 1972, Jerry Ray Interviews 1969–1975, Box 5—Trial and Post-Trial Materials, McMillan/Southern Historical Collection.

25. McMillan, *The Making of an Assassin*, p. 239.

26. Ibid., p. 240.

27. Jerry Ray interviewed by George McMillan, May 10, 1970, p. 2; May 31, 1972, p. 2; and February 23, 1975, and July 7, 1975, Jerry Ray Interviews 1969–1975, Box 5—Trial and Post-Trial Materials, McMillan/Southern Historical Collection.

28. Interview with James Earl Ray, December 2, 1977, HSCA vol. XI, p. 351; Huie, *He Slew the Dreamer*, p. 28.

29. FBI Airtel to Director from SAC, Memphis, August 26, 1968, MURKIN 5101, section 69, p. 170.

30. Order Conferring Immunity Upon and Compelling Testimony of Gerald (Jerry) William Ray, MLK Exhibit F-589, HSCA vol. VII, pp. 392–93.

31. Testimony of Jerry Ray, November 29, 1978, HSCA vol. VII, p. 391.

32. Ibid., p. 395.

33. Ibid., p. 515.

34. FBI interview with Harvey Klingeman and Clara Klingeman, August 23, 1968, Chicago folder, p. 2509, Attorney General File.

35. Interview with James Earl Ray, December 2, 1977, HSCA vol. XI, pp. 364–65.

36. James Earl Ray, 20,000 Words, HSCA vol. XII, p. 138.

37. FBI statement of James (Jimmy) H. Carpenter, May 14, 1968, St. Louis Folder, Attorney General File; also same interview listed with name redacted in MURKIN 4760, section 62, pp. 98–101.

38. James Earl Ray, 20,000 Words, HSCA vol. XII, pp. 73, 105; see interview with James Earl Ray by House Select Committee investigators, HSCA vol. IX, p. 271, and vol. XI, p. 371,

and James Earl Ray in Compilation of the Statements of James Earl Ray, Staff Report of the Select Committee on Assassinations, U.S. House of Representatives, 95th Congress, Second Session, August 18, 1978, p. 10.

39. Interview with James Earl Ray, December 2, 1977, HSCA vol. XI, p. 378, also statement in vol. 1, p. 93; Jerry Ray interviewed by George McMillan, May 30, 1972, Jerry Ray Interviews 1969–1975, Box 5—Trial and Post-Trial Materials, McMillan/Southern Historical Collection McMillan; McMillan, *The Making of an Assassin*, p. 245; see also Compilation of the Statements of James Earl Ray, Staff Report of the Select Committee on Assassinations, U.S. House of Representatives, 95th Congress, Second Session, August 18, 1978, pp. 6, 11; also James Earl Ray, 20,000 Words, HSCA vol. XII, p. 120. As for John Ray occasionally living with Gawron, see FBI interview with John Larry Ray, May 23, 1968, MURKIN 4760, section 62, p. 192. For Gawron seeing James Earl Ray in the summer of 1967, see interview with James Earl Ray, December 2, 1977, HSCA vol. XI, p. 340, plus citations in following note.

39. See statement of Jerry Ray reported in FBI Airtel, June 11, 1968, to Director from SAC, Newark, MURKIN 4576–4663, section 59, p. 40; Jerry Ray interviewed by George McMillan, May 30, 1972, Jerry Ray Interviews 1969–1975, Box 5—Trial and Post-Trial Materials, McMillan/Southern Historical Collection; also see interview with James Earl Ray, December 2, 1977, HSCA vol. XI, pp. 352–53; McMillan, *The Making of an Assassin*, p. 245.

40. Memo to Cartha DeLoach from Alex Rosen, May 16, 1968, MURKIN 3628–3761, section 44, p. 60; see also FBI interview with John Larry Ray, May 23, 1968, MURKIN 4760, section 62, p. 189.

41. James Earl Ray, 20,000 Words, HSCA vol. XII, pp. 98–99; interview with James Earl Ray by House Select Committee investigators, HSCA vol. IX, pp. 265–66, and Huie, *He Slew the Dreamer*, p. 29; see also Frank, *An American Death*, p. 300.

42. Mrs. Donnelly quoted by Huie, *He Slew the Dreamer*, p. 22.

43. Narration of James Wolf, Esq., December 1, 1978, HSCA vol. VIII, p. 10.

44. Ibid., pp. 10–28, including MLK Exhibit F-662, August 13, 1978, interview with James Rogers, and MLK Exhibit F-663, June 18, 1978, interview with Ronald Siebelt Goldenstein, and MLK Exhibit F-664, April 25, 1978, interview with Clarence Haynes; see also HSCA vol. VIII, pp. 507–36.

45. HSCA vol. VIII, pp. 126, 132, 139, 184–85, 230–31, 237, 247, 248, 255, 272, and 334.

46. See, generally, FBI Airtel to Director from SAC, Springfield, August 24, 1968, MURKIN 5101, section 69, pp. 24–26.

47. Narration of James Wolf, Esq., December 1, 1978, HSCA vol. VIII, p. 9.

48. Ibid., p. 13.

49. Interview with James Earl Ray, December 2, 1977, HSCA vol. XI, pp. 376–77, 388; James Earl Ray, *Who Killed Martin Luther King?*, p. 60; narration of James Wolf, Esq., December 1, 1978, HSCA vol. VIII, p. 12; see also Huie, *He Slew the Dreamer*, pp. 31–32, and James Earl Ray, 20,000 Words, HSCA vol. XII, p. 100.

50. Narration of James Wolf, Esq., December 1, 1978, HSCA vol. VIII, pp. 12–13; see also FBI interview with Mr. A. G. Arb, vice president of Jefferson-Gravois Bank, May 15, 1968, FBI St. Louis 44-775, Attorney General File, p. 3109.

51. FBI statement of John Ray, May 18, 1968, MURKIN 4760, section 62, pp. 194–95, 198.

52. Testimony of John Ray, December 1, 1978, HSCA vol. VIII, p. 69, Testimony of Jerry Ray, HSCA vol. VII; James Earl Ray, *Who Killed Martin Luther King?*, p. 216.

Chapter 20: Gray Rocks

1. James Earl Ray, *Who Killed Martin Luther King?*, p. 60.

2. FBI teletype to Director from Legat, Ottawa, April 25, 1968, MURKIN 2151–2321, section 19, p. 92; see also Huie, *He Slew the Dreamer*, p. 35.

3. Interview with James Earl Ray by House Select Committee investigators, HSCA vol. IX, p. 286; also, author interview with Josephine Galt, October 9, 1997.

4. Jay Walz, "Three Whose Names Ray Used Resemble Him," *The New York Times*, June 12, 1968, p. 1.

5. James Earl Ray, 20,000 Words, HSCA vol. XII, p. 141; Compilation of the Statements of James Earl Ray, Staff Report of the Select Committee on Assassinations, U.S. House of Representatives, 95th Congress, Second Session, August 18, 1978, p. 13; interview with James Earl Ray by the House Select Committee investigators, March 28, 1977, HSCA vol. IX, pp. 282, 343; interview with James Earl Ray by the House Select Committee investigators, March 28, 1977, HSCA vol. IX, p. 282.

6. Interview with James Earl Ray by the House Select Committee investigators, March 28, 1977, HSCA vol. IX, p. 283; interview with James Earl Ray, December 2, 1977, HSCA vol. XI, p. 422; Compilation of the Statements of James Earl Ray, Staff Report of the Select Committee on Assassinations, U.S. House of Representatives, 95th Congress, Second Session, August 18, 1978, p. 13.

7. Interview with James Earl Ray by the House Select Committee investigators, March 28, 1977, HSCA vol. IX, p. 284.

8. See memo from M. A. Jones to Bishop, Re: Books by Ian Fleming, May 3, 1968, MURKIN 3131–3220, section 32, pp. 42–72.

9. Interview with James Earl Ray by the House Select Committee investigators, March 28, 1977, HSCA vol. IX, pp. 281, 344.

10. Blair, *The Strange Case of James Earl Ray*, p. 187.

11. Huie, *He Slew the Dreamer*, p. 35; also Huie, "James Earl Ray and the Conspiracy to Kill Martin Luther King," *Look*, November 12, 1968.

12. Interview with James Earl Ray by the House Select Committee investigators, March 28, 1977, HSCA vol. IX, p. 281, and vol. XI, p. 420; Compilation of the Statements of James Earl Ray, Staff Report of the Select Committee on Assassinations, U.S. House of Representatives, 95th Congress, Second Session, August 18, 1978, p. 13.

13. James Earl Ray, 20,000 Words, HSCA vol. XII, pp. 104, 118, 121; see also Huie, *He Slew the Dreamer*, p. 35. The FBI could not find any motel at which Ray spent that night, raising questions as to whether he lied. A review of Ray's three-day trip from St. Louis to Montreal, however, confirms it is likely he did stop in Toronto before he used the Galt name. By his own account, he drove from St. Louis to Indianapolis on July 15, a four-hour, 250-mile drive. He spent the night there—"I slept beside the road." Two nights later, July 17, he was traced to Dorion, a small town outside Montreal. The question is whether he stayed in Toronto on the night of July 16. During that day, he drove to Canada, and there was heavy traffic since Montreal was hosting Expo '67, a popular fair. Although his final goal was Montreal, it was too far for a single day's journey, more than eight hundred miles from Indianapolis, fifteen to seventeen hours under normal driving conditions. Ray first drove to Detroit, and the only route from there to Montreal was Highway 401, which passes directly past Toronto. By the time Ray reached Toronto on the sixteenth, he would already have been driving close to ten hours. Ray would have considered stopping in a large city such as Toronto a safe choice for a fugitive, since "you could get lost quite a bit easier." Laying over there would have left him only another six-hour trip the following day to Dorion.

14. For Ray sleeping in his car while he traveled to Montreal, see interview with James Earl Ray, December 2, 1977, HSCA vol. XI, pp. 372, 405; see James Earl Ray, 20,000 Words, HSCA vol. XII, p. 97.

15. Author's review of 1966 and 1967 telephone books for Toronto, Bell Telephone Company of Canada; author's review of telephone books for Toronto for 1967 and 1968, and conversation with research librarians at Toronto Research Library.

16. Testimony of James Earl Ray in the HBO mock trial of the *State of Tennessee v. Ray*, April 4, 1993.

17. October 12, 1997, audiotape made by Jerry Ray and sent to author (Tape 3 in a series of 7, as of February 1998). Jerry Ray, who sent the author audiotapes with answers to written questions, said he would not answer everything asked since he intended to write his own book if James died before him. "Some things I keep quiet so I can write that book," Jerry says. "But it will be a shocking book, and there will be things that no one ever knew about. I can't go into details right now about it."

18. Interview with James Earl Ray, December 2, 1977, HSCA vol. XI, p. 359.

19. James Earl Ray, 20,000 Words, HSCA vol. XII, p. 123; see also interview with James Earl Ray, December 2, 1977, HSCA vol. XI, pp. 408–9.

20. James Earl Ray, 20,000 Words, HSCA vol. XII, pp. 123–24, see also interview with James Earl Ray by House Select Committee investigators, HSCA vol. IX, pp. 353–54.

21. James Earl Ray, 20,000 Words, HSCA vol. XII, p. 124; Interview with James Earl Ray, December 2, 1977, HSCA vol. XI, pp. 409–10, and interview of September 29, 1977, vol. X, pp. 398–99.

22. James Earl Ray, 20,000 Words, HSCA vol. XII, pp. 65–66.

23. Ibid., pp. 85, 130; see also interview with James Earl Ray by House Select Committee investigators, April 14, 1977, HSCA vol. IX, pp. 401, 409–10.

24. Frank, *An American Death*, p. 300; see also FBI review document, Canada investigation, Attorney General File.

25. Frank, *An American Death*, p. 301; see also FBI report on the money order, April 26, 1968, MURKIN 2151–2321, section 19, pp. 179–80; also MURKIN 3221–3332, section 33, p. 227, MURKIN 3763–3872, section 46, pp. 215–16.

26. James Earl Ray interviewed by House Select Committee investigators, April 14, 1977, HSCA vol. IX, p. 422.

27. James Earl Ray, *Who Killed Martin Luther King?*, p. 80.

28. James Earl Ray quoted by William Bradford Huie in *Look*, November 12, 1968, p. 104.

29. Interview with James Earl Ray by House Select Committee investigators, HSCA vol. IX, p. 349, and vol. XI, p. 352; see also James Earl Ray interviewed by Dan Rather, March 9, 1977, HSCA vol. 1, p. 175.

30. Interview with James Earl Ray, December 2, 1977, HSCA vol. XI, p. 417; James Earl Ray quoted by William Bradford Huie in *Look*, November 12, 1968, p. 104; see also Huie, *He Slew the Dreamer*, p. 35.

31. Huie, *He Slew the Dreamer*, p. 35.

32. Interview with James Earl Ray by House Select Committee investigators, HSCA vol. XI, pp. 434–35; James Earl Ray, 20,000 Words, HSCA vol. XII, p. 167.

33. James Earl Ray interviewed by Dan Rather, March 9, 1977, HSCA vol. 1, p. 227; James Earl Ray, 20,000 Words, HSCA vol. XII, p. 168; see also HSCA vol. III, p. 177, and vol. XI, pp. 431–33.

34. Interview with James Earl Ray by House Select Committee investigators, HSCA vol. XI, p. 432.

35. James Earl Ray quoted by William Bradford Huie in *Look*, November 12, 1968, p. 104.

36. James Earl Ray quoted in HSCA vol. III, p. 178; also James Earl Ray, 20,000 Words, HSCA vol. XII, p. 170.

37. See, generally, Huie, *He Slew the Dreamer*, p. 40.

38. See travel brochure on Gray Rocks Inn, Chapter 24 Research, Notes, Drafts, Etc. folder, Box 8—Book Manuscript, McMillan/Southern Historical Collection.

39. James Earl Ray interview by House Select Committee, December 2, 1977, HSCA vol. XI, pp. 429–30.

40. James Earl Ray, *Who Killed Martin Luther King?*, p. 64.

41. James Earl Ray, 20,000 Words, HSCA vol. XII, p. 103.

42. Claire Keating quoted by Huie, *He Slew the Dreamer*, p. 42. Note that in the Huie book she is not identified by name, but described only as the woman Ray met at Gray Rocks.

43. Ibid., p. 43.

44. Ibid.

45. Ibid., p. 45.

46. Ibid. p. 43; see also Keating statement to the Royal Canadian Mounted Police, MURKIN 5451–5505, section 75, p. 203; same file also in possession of Attorney General, Memphis.

47. See, generally, HSCA vol. VII, p. 313.

48. Claire Keating quoted by Huie, *He Slew the Dreamer*, p. 45.

49. Ibid.

50. Ibid.

51. James Earl Ray, 20,000 Words, HSCA vol. XII, p. 128.

52. James Earl Ray quoted in HSCA vol. III, pp. 180–81; also 20,000 Words, HSCA vol. XII.

53. James Earl Ray quoted in HSCA vol. III, p. 181.

54. HSCA vol. VII, MLK Exhibit 607, James Earl Ray Transactions in Canada with "Raoul"; with his brothers, p. 313; see also Keating statement to the Royal Canadian Mounted Police, MURKIN 5451–5505, section 75, p. 204.

55. Claire Keating quoted by Huie, *He Slew the Dreamer*, p. 46.

56. James Earl Ray, *Who Killed Martin Luther King?*, p. 66.

57. MURKIN 5451–5505, section 75, p. 203.

58. MURKIN 4697–4759, section 61, p. 96.

59. James Earl Ray, *Who Killed Martin Luther King?*, p. 66.

60. Interview with James Earl Ray by House Select Committee investigators, April 14, 1977, HSCA vol. IX, p. 401; see also James Earl Ray interviewed by Dan Rather, March 9, 1977, HSCA vol. I, p. 179.

61. James Earl Ray, 20,000 Words, HSCA vol. XII, p. 129.

62. Interview with James Earl Ray by House Select Committee investigators, April 14, 1977, HSCA vol. IX, pp. 401–6.

63. James Earl Ray, 20,000 Words, HSCA vol. XII, p. 130.

64. Interview with James Earl Ray by House Select Committee investigators, April 14, 1977, HSCA vol. IX, pp. 402–3.

65. Ibid., pp. 407–8.

66. James Earl Ray, 20,000 Words, HSCA vol. XII, p. 131.

67. Ibid.

68. James Earl Ray statement in HSCA vol. III, p. 183; James Earl Ray interviewed by Dan Rather, March 9, 1977, HSCA vol. I, p. 180.

69. James Earl Ray, 20,000 Words, HSCA vol. XII, p. 132.

70. Ibid.

71. James Earl Ray interviewed by House Select Committee investigators, April 14, 1977, HSCA vol. IX, p. 415.

72. James Earl Ray, *Who Killed Martin Luther King?*, p. 64.

73. James Earl Ray interviewed by House Select Committee investigators, December 2, 1977, HSCA vol. XI, pp. 434–35.

74. Interview with Jerry Ray by George McMillan, May 30, 1972, Jerry Ray Interviews 1969–1975, Box 5—Trial and Post-Trial Materials, McMillan/Southern Historical Collection.

75. James Earl Ray interviewed by House Select Committee investigators, April 14, 1977, HSCA vol. IX, p. 414.

76. Ibid.

77. See, generally, Jeff Cohen and David S. Lifton, "A Man He Calls Raoul," *New Times*, April 1, 1977.

78. See interview with Jerry Ray by George McMillan, July 12, 1975, and May 30, 1972, Jerry Ray Interviews 1969–1975, Box 5—Trial and Post-Trial Materials, McMillan/Southern Historical Collection.

79. Interview with Jerry Ray by George McMillan, July 12, 1975, and May 30, 1972, Jerry Ray interviews 1969–1975, Box 5—Trial and Post-Trial Materials, McMillan/Southern Historical Collection; see also McMillan, *The Making of an Assassin*, p. 258–59.

80. McMillan, *The Making of an Assassin*, p. 259.

81. James Earl Ray, *Who Killed Martin Luther King?*, p. 69.

Chapter 21: Wallace Country

1. James Earl Ray, 20,000 Words, HSCA vol. XII, p. 14; Huie, *He Slew the Dreamer*, p. 53.

2. James Earl Ray, *Who Killed Martin Luther King?*, p. 69.

3. Ibid.

4. Huie, *He Slew the Dreamer*, p. 53; see also Blair, *The Strange Case of James Earl Ray*, p. 116.

5. FBI interview with Peter Cherpes, April 10, 1968, MURKIN 2323–2324, section 21, p. 85.

6. James Earl Ray, *Who Killed Martin Luther King?*, p. 70.

7. Peter Cherpes quoted in Blair, *The Strange Case of James Earl Ray*, pp. 116–17.

8. Peter Cherpes quoted in Huie, *He Slew the Dreamer*, p. 57.

9. Peter Cherpes quoted in Blair, *The Strange Case of James Earl Ray*, p. 117.

10. FBI interview with Herbert Kelly, April 10, 1968, and with Peter Cherpes, April 11, 1968, MURKIN 2323–2324, section 21, pp. 84, 89.

11. See, generally, FBI interview with Lawrence Chancelor Howell, April 19, 1968, MURKIN ME, Sub. D, section 1, pp. 211–12; FBI interview with D. T. Green, April 10, 1968; interview with Charles Jackson Davis, April 10, 1968; interview with Percy Strickland, April 8, 1968, MURKIN 2323–2324, section 21, pp. 93–95; interview with Mrs. O. L. Black, April 12, 1968; interview with James E. Weldon and Tammy Lorraine Weldon, April 12, 1968; interview with Thomas D. Franklin, April 12, 1968, MURKIN 2634, section 26, pp. 120–21.

12. FBI interview with Peter Cherpes, April 18, 1968, MURKIN 3763–3872, section 46, p. 43.

13. Photocopy of Birmingham Trust National card agreement for Galt and safe deposit box, August 28, 1967, MURKIN 2323–2324, section 21, pp. 103–4.

14. FBI interview with William D. Paisley, Sr., April 9, 1968, MURKIN 2323–2324, section 21, p. 67.

15. Huie, *He Slew the Dreamer*, p. 54.

16. James Earl Ray interviewed by House Select Committee investigators, April 14, 1977, HSCA vol. IX, p. 430.

17. FBI interview with William D. Paisley, Sr., April 9, 1968, MURKIN 2323–2324, section 21, p. 67.

18. William Paisley quoted in Blair, *The Strange Case of James Earl Ray*, p. 117; see also FBI interview with William David Paisley, Jr., April 9, 1968, MURKIN 2323–2324, section 21, p. 71.

19. FBI interview with William D. Paisley, Sr., included in Airtel of April 9, 1968, MURKIN 251–375, section 3, p. 93.

20. FBI interview with Mrs. William D. Paisley, Sr., April 9, 1968, MURKIN 2323–2324, section 21, p. 73.

21. FBI interview with William D. Paisley, Sr., April 9, 1968, MURKIN 2323–2324, section 21, p. 68.

22. FBI interview with William David Paisley, Jr., April 9, 1968, MURKIN 2323–2324, section 21, p. 71.

23. FBI interview with William D. Paisley, Sr., April 9, 1968, MURKIN 2323–2324, section 21, p. 67.

24. William Paisley quoted in Huie, *He Slew the Dreamer*, p. 55.

25. FBI interview with William D. Paisley, Sr., April 9, 1968, MURKIN 2323–2324, section 21, p. 67.

26. FBI interviews with Peter Cherpes, April 10 and 11, 1968, MURKIN 2323–2324, section 21, pp. 86–87.

27. FBI summary information, April 9, 1968, MURKIN 2326–2440, section 23, p. 2.

28. See FBI documents of April 16, 1968, regarding Galt's purchase of a bank draft for the equipment, MURKIN 3763–3872, section 46, pp. 21–22.

29. Memo to Trotter from Latona, "Latent Print on Coupon Identical James Earl Ray," May 8, 1968, MURKIN 3031–3130, section 31, p. 186; see also Airtel to FBI Director from SAC, New York, May 4, 1968, MURKIN 3031–3130, section 31, pp. 20–23.

30. James Earl Ray, Who Killed Martin Luther King?, p. 70. The spelling "Starlite," as used here, is the spelling used by the House Select Committee on Assassinations, though some authors have spelled it "Starlight."

31. Ibid., p. 71.

32. James Earl Ray interviewed by House Select Committee investigators, April 14, 1977, HSCA vol. IX, p. 443.

33. James Earl Ray, 20,000 Words, HSCA vol. XII, pp. 15, 77.

34. Ibid., p. 15.

35. See, generally, McMillan, The Making of an Assassin, p. 261.

36. James Earl Ray, 20,000 Words, HSCA vol. XII, p. 15.

37. Ibid., p. 16.

38. Huie, He Slew the Dreamer, p. 60.

39. Ibid., p. 61.

40. McMillan, The Making of an Assassin, p. 263.

41. "Chronological Listing of Known Activities of James Earl Ray Since His Escape and Laboratory Examination of Evidence Attendant Thereto," MURKIN 4143, section 52, p. 10.

42. James Earl Ray interviewed by House Select Committee investigators, April 14, 1977, HSCA vol. IX, p. 453.

43. Continental Dance Club Studios enrollment agreement signed by Eric Galt, MURKIN 2323–2324, section 21, p. 122.

44. James Earl Ray, 20,000 Words, HSCA vol. XII, p. 15.

45. Huie, He Slew the Dreamer, p. 62; see also FBI interview of J. D. (Elizabeth) Weeks, April 17, 1968, MURKIN 3763–3872, section 46, pp. 26–28.

46. FBI interview with Doris Ladner, April 15, 1968, MURKIN 2323–2324, section 21, pp. 124–25.

47. James Earl Ray, 20,000 Words, HSCA vol. XII, p. 16.

48. Ibid.

49. Compilation of the Statements of James Earl Ray, Staff Report of the Select Committee on Assassinations, U.S. House of Representatives, 95th Congress, Second Session, August 18, 1978, p. 28.

50. Huie, He Slew the Dreamer, p. 61.

51. Memo to Trotter from Latona, "Latent Print on Coupon Identical James Earl Ray," May 8, 1968, MURKIN 3031–3130, section 31, p. 186; see also Airtel to FBI Director from SAC New York, May 4, 1968, MURKIN 3031–3130, section 31, pp. 20–23.

52. FBI teletype to Director from Birmingham, June 12, 1968, MURKIN 4351–4440, section 55, p. 152.

53. Ibid., p. 154.

54. FBI summary sheet, MURKIN 4351–4440, section 55, p. 147.

55. FBI summary document, "Purchase of 1966 White Mustang Two-Door by Eric S. Galt, 2608 Highland Avenue, from Owner, William D. Paisley, on August 29 and 30, 1967," April 9, 1968, MURKIN 2323–2324, section 21, p. 66.

56. James Earl Ray, 20,000 Words, HSCA vol. XII, p. 78.

57. James Earl Ray interviewed by House Select Committee investigators, April 14, 1977, HSCA vol. IX, p. 462.

58. Ibid., p. 459.

59. James Earl Ray, 20,000 Words, HSCA vol. XII, pp. 82, 84.

60. FBI summary report, April 12, 1968, MURKIN 2323–2324, section 21, pp. 6–7.

61. Marlin Myers interviewed by FBI, April 12, 1968, MURKIN 2323, section 21, p. 117.

62. FBI interview with Peter Cherpes, April 8, 1968, MURKIN 2323–2324, section 21, p. 82.

63. As for the Confederate sticker, see FBI interview with William David Paisley, Jr., April 9, 1968, MURKIN 2323–2324, section 21, p. 70.

64. James Earl Ray, *Who Killed Martin Luther King?*, p. 73.

Chapter 22: Mexican Holiday

1. James Earl Ray quoted in Huie, *He Slew the Dreamer*, p. 66.

2. James Earl Ray quoted in Compilation of the Statements of James Earl Ray, Staff Report of the Select Committee on Assassinations, U.S. House of Representatives, 95th Congress, Second Session, August 18, 1978, p. 28.

3. Ibid.

4. Ray was issued tourist card number 7475449, listing his permanent address as the Birmingham rooming house at 2608 Highland. See, generally, FBI summary document about Ray in Mexico, MURKIN 5101, section 69, p. 147.

5. James Earl Ray, 20,000 Words, HSCA vol. XII, p. 1834.

6. James Earl Ray interviewed by Dan Rather, March 9, 1977, HSCA vol. 1, p. 185.

7. James Earl Ray, 20,000 Words, HSCA vol. XII, p. 183; see also Compilation of the Statements of James Earl Ray, Staff Report of the Select Committee on Assassinations, U.S. House of Representatives, 95th Congress, Second Session, August 18, 1978, pp. 31–32.

8. James Earl Ray, 20,000 Words, HSCA vol. XII, p. 184; see also Compilation of the Statements of James Earl Ray, Staff Report of the Select Committee on Assassinations, U.S. House of Representatives, 95th Congress, Second Session, August 18, 1978, p. 32.

9. Huie, *He Slew the Dreamer*, p. 67; see also James Earl Ray, 20,000 Words, HSCA vol. XII, p. 184.

10. Compilation of the Statements of James Earl Ray, Staff Report of the Select Committee on Assassinations, U.S. House of Representatives, 95th Congress, Second Session, August 18, 1978, p. 32.

11. FBI interview with Cecil Clayton Lillibridge, April 29, 1968, Kansas City file, Attorney General File, pp. 999–1001.

12. James Earl Ray quoted in Compilation of the Statements of James Earl Ray, Staff Report of the Select Committee on Assassinations, U.S. House of Representatives, 95th Congress, Second Session, August 18, 1978, p. 33.

13. Huie, *He Slew the Dreamer*, p. 70.

14. James Earl Ray, 20,000 Words, HSCA vol. XII, p. 185; see also Huie, *He Slew the Dreamer*, p. 69.

15. Ibid.

16. FBI summary document about Ray in Mexico, interview with Elpidio Velazquez, MURKIN 5101, section 69, p. 172.

17. FBI summary document about Ray in Mexico, interview with Dr. Oscar Gomez Palofox, MURKIN 5101, section 69, p. 155.

18. Huie, *He Slew the Dreamer*, pp. 71–72.

19. James Earl Ray, 20,000 Words, HSCA vol. XII, p. 185; see also Huie, *He Slew the Dreamer*, p. 69.

20. Ibid. James Earl Ray, 20,000 Words, HSCA vol. XII, pp. 49, 186; see also Huie, *He Slew the Dreamer,* p. 70.

21. James Earl Ray, 20,000 Words, HSCA vol. XII, p. 186; see also Huie, *He Slew the Dreamer,* p. 70.

22. James Earl Ray, *Tennessee Waltz,* p. 59; see also FBI summary document about Ray in Mexico, interview with Rodimir Biscara, MURKIN 5101, section 69, pp. 154–55.

23. James Earl Ray, 20,000 Words, HSCA vol. XII, p. 186; see also Huie, *He Slew the Dreamer,* p. 70.

24. Huie, *He Slew the Dreamer,* pp. 73–74.

25. FBI summary information about James Earl Ray's time in Mexico during October and November 1967, July 24, 1968, MLK Exhibit F-172, HSCA vol. IV, pp. 156–57.

26. Manuela Aguirre Medrano interviewed by House Select Committee investigators, June 5, 1978, MLK Exhibit F-173, HSCA vol. IV, p. 179.

27. See, generally, description set forth by Huie, *He Slew the Dreamer,* p. 72.

28. FBI summary document about Ray in Mexico, interview with Leopoldo Cisneros, MURKIN 5101, section 69, p. 162.

29. Manuela Aguirre Medrano interview summarized in FBI information about James Earl Ray's time in Mexico during October and November 1967, July 24, 1968, MLK Exhibit F-172, HSCA vol. IV, p. 157; see also FBI summary document about Ray in Mexico, interview with Rodimir Biscara, MURKIN 5101, section 69, p. 155.

30. See, generally, Manuela Aguirre Medrano interviewed by House Select Committee investigators, June 5, 1978, MLK Exhibit F-173, HSCA vol. IV, pp. 185–86.

31. Huie, *He Slew the Dreamer,* p. 73. Note: Huie referred to the bartender as Oscar Mendiola, and it is not clear if Biscara gave Huie a false name, or if Huie identified the wrong person; see also FBI summary document about Ray in Mexico, interview with Jose Manuel Guzman Garcia and Eleno Guzman Garcia, MURKIN 5101, section 69, p. 155.

32. FBI summary document about Ray in Mexico, interview with Jose Manuel Guzman Garcia, MURKIN 5101, section 69, p. 155.

33. Irma Morales in Index Card File, Attorney General File.

34. Manuela Aguirre Medrano interview summarized in FBI information about James Earl Ray's time in Mexico during October and November 1967, July 24, 1968, MLK Exhibit F-172, HSCA vol. IV, p. 157.

35. Ibid., p. 159.

36. Ibid., p. 158; see also teletype to Director from Legat Mexico, April 23, 1968, MURKIN 1991–2075, section 17, pp. 162–63.

37. Manuela Aguirre Medrano interviewed by House Select Committee investigators, June 5, 1978, MLK Exhibit F-173, HSCA vol. IV, p. 174.

38. Ibid.

39. Ibid.; Manuela Aguirre Medrano interview summarized in FBI information about James Earl Ray's time in Mexico during October and November 1967, July 24, 1968, MLK Exhibit F-172, HSCA vol. IV, p. 159.

40. Manuela Aguirre Medrano interviewed by House Select Committee investigators, June 5, 1978, MLK Exhibit F-173, HSCA vol. IV, p. 183.

41. Manuela Aguirre Medrano interview summarized in FBI information about James Earl Ray's time in Mexico during October and November 1967, July 24, 1968, MLK Exhibit F-172, HSCA vol. IV, pp. 157, 159; see FBI summary document about Ray in Mexico, MURKIN 5101, section 69, pp. 7, 8.

42. FBI summary document about Ray in Mexico, MURKIN 5101, section 69, pp. 7–8.

43. Huie referred to this woman as Nina, but it is not known if he had the name wrong, or if he merely used that name to disguise her real identity. FBI summary document about Ray in Mexico, interview with Rodolfo Gonzalez, MURKIN 5101, section 69, p. 155.

44. FBI summary document about Ray in Mexico, interview with Elisa Arellano Torres, MURKIN 5101, section 69, p. 157.

45. FBI summary document about Ray in Mexico, interview with Mr. and Mrs. Salvador Meza, MURKIN 5101, section 69, p. 156.

46. George McMillan, *The Making of an Assassin*, p. 269.

47. FBI summary document about Ray in Mexico, interview with Elisa Arellano Torres, MURKIN 5101, section 69, p. 158.

48. James Earl Ray, 20,000 Words, HSCA vol. XII, p. 187.

49. See, generally, James Earl Ray, 20,000 Words, HSCA vol. XII, pp. 37, 41.

50. Ibid., p. 187.

51. Ibid., p. 35.

52. FBI summary document, quoting interview with Hotel Rio clerk Roberto Wong, about Ray in Mexico, MURKIN 5101, section 69, p. 149; see also interview with Luis Garcia contained in FBI summary document about Ray in Mexico, MURKIN 5101, section 69, pp. 152–53.

53. Huie, *He Slew the Dreamer*, pp. 74–75; see Memo to Cartha DeLoach from Alex Rosen, April 17, 1968, MURKIN 1576–1730, section 13, p. 289.

54. James Earl Ray, 20,000 Words, HSCA vol. XII, p. 35.

55. Manuela Aguirre Medrano interview summarized in FBI information about James Earl Ray's time in Mexico during October and November 1967, July 24, 1968, MLK Exhibit F-172, HSCA vol. IV, p. 159; see also FBI teletype to Director from Legat Mexico City, April 25, 1968, MURKIN 2151–2321, section 19, p. 100, and memo to Cartha DeLoach from Alex Rosen, April 26, 1968, MURKIN 2151–2321, section 19, p. 130.

56. See, generally, FBI summary document about Ray in Mexico, interview with Jose Manuel Guzman Garcia, MURKIN 5101, section 69, p. 155.

57. FBI summary document about Ray in Mexico, interview with Elisa Arellano Torres, MURKIN 5101, section 69, p. 157.

58. FBI summary document about Ray in Mexico, interview with Manuela Aguirre Medrano, MURKIN 5101, section 69, p. 161; see also "Arcella Gonzales" index card file, Attorney General File.

59. FBI summary document about Ray in Mexico, interviews with Juan Manuel Fregoso Gutierrez and Genova Curiel de Fregoso, MURKIN 5101, section 69, pp. 164–66.

60. James Earl Ray interviewed by House Select Committee investigators, April 14, 1977, HSCA vol. IX, p. 482; Compilation of the Statements of James Earl Ray, Staff Report of the Select Committee on Assassinations, U.S. House of Representatives, 95th Congress, Second Session, August 18, 1978, p. 34; see also James Earl Ray, *Tennessee Waltz*, pp. 58–59.

61. James Earl Ray, *Tennessee Waltz*, p. 59.

62. James Earl Ray interviewed by House Select Committee investigators, April 14, 1977, HSCA vol. IX, p. 488.

63. See FBI summary document about Ray in Mexico, interview with Rodolfo Gonzalez, MURKIN 5101, section 69, p. 156; also interview with Francisco Perez Gomez, p. 156.

64. FBI summary document about Ray in Mexico, interview with Elisa Arellano Torres, MURKIN 5101, section 69, p. 157.

65. Manuela Aguirre Medrano interviewed by House Select Committee investigators, June 5, 1978, MLK Exhibit F-173, HSCA vol. IV, p. 185.

66. Compilation of the Statements of James Earl Ray, Staff Report of the Select Committee on Assassinations, U.S. House of Representatives, 95th Congress, Second Session, August 18, 1978, p. 34.

67. James Earl Ray, *Tennessee Waltz*, p. 60.

68. Compilation of the Statements of James Earl Ray, Staff Report of the Select Committee on Assassinations, U.S. House of Representatives, 95th Congress, Second Session, August 18, 1978, pp. 34–35.

69. Rosenson was actually prosecuted for violating 18 U.S.C. 1407, traveling outside the United States without registering as a convicted felon (*U.S. v. Randolph Erwin Rosenson,*

Crim. Doc. 382561966, Division 6, U.S. District Court, Eastern District of Louisiana, HSCA Rpt., p. 516.

70. HSCA conclusion based on the interview of Charlie Stein, March 22, 1978, as well as the outside contact report with George Pittman, January 25, 1978; HSCA Rpt., p. 516.

71. HSCA Rpt., p. 516, based on the executive-session interview with Randy Rosenson, November 29, 1977.

72. Ibid., based on the bank records from the Birmingham Trust National Bank.

73. Ibid., based on executive-session interview with Randy Rosenson, November 29, 1977.

74. HSCA Rpt., pp. 516–17.

75. Interview with Gene Stanley, July 10, 1997.

76. Interview with Gene Stanley, July 30, 1997.

23: Dancing in Los Angeles

1. Teletype to Director from Los Angeles, April 13, 1968, covering interview with Mrs. Frank (Margarita) Powers, MURKIN 621–750, section 6, p. 87; also FBI interview with Margarita Powers, April 12, 1968, MURKIN 2325, section 22, pp. 59–61.

2. "Chronological Listing of Known Activities of James Earl Ray Since His Escape and Laboratory Examination of Evidence Attendant Thereto," MURKIN 4143, section 52, p. 18.

3. FBI interview with Mrs. Ronald G. McIntire, April 14, 1968, MURKIN 1051–1175, section 9, p. 243; Index Card File, "Mrs. Ronald G. McIntire," filed under "Los Angeles—Phone Records," Attorney General File. Ms. McIntire had placed an ad in the newspaper in November to sell her Montgomery-Ward console TV (trade name, Airline). Ray bought it for $90 cash, and took it himself in his Mustang.

4. James Earl Ray testimony in Compilation of the Statements of James Earl Ray, Staff Report of the Select Committee on Assassinations, U.S. House of Representatives, 95th Congress, Second Session, August 18, 1978, p. 48.

5. Garrow, Bearing the Cross, p. 579.

6. Ibid.

7. Ibid., p. 583.

8. FBI interview with Mark Freeman, April 19, 1968, Los Angeles Field Office, Attorney General File.

9. James Earl Ray interviewed by House Select Committee investigators, April 14, 1977, HSCA vol. IX, p. 499.

10. McMillan, The Making of an Assassin, p. 273.

11. "Chronological Listing of Known Activities of James Earl Ray Since His Escape and Laboratory Examination of Evidence Attendant Thereto," MURKIN 4143, section 52, p. 18; see McMillan, The Making of an Assassin, p. 274.

12. FBI interview with Mark Freeman, April 19, 1968, Los Angeles Field Office, Attorney General File.

13. James Earl Ray, 20,000 Words, HSCA vol. XII, pp. 32, 86, 201.

14. Mark Freeman interviewed by George McMillan, January 18, 1975, "Hypnosis, Pills, Headaches, etc.," folder, Box 9—as listed through P4 of Index, and Newspaper Clippings, McMillan/Southern Historical Collection; also McMillan, The Making of an Assassin, p. 275.

15. Dr. Mark O. Freeman interviewed by Special Agent Benjamin, Index Card File (L.A. Return), Attorney General File.

16. McMillan, The Making of an Assassin, p. 275.

17. FBI interview with Mark Freeman, April 19, 1968, Los Angeles Field Office, Attorney General File.

18. James Earl Ray, 20,000 Words, HSCA vol. XII, p. 29.

19. James Earl Ray interviewed by House Select Committee investigators, April 14, 1977, HSCA vol. IX, p. 491.

20. Ibid.

21. James Earl Ray, 20,000 Words, HSCA vol. XII, p. 31; see Index Card File, "Los Angeles—Phone Records," Attorney General File index 2; see also James Earl Ray quoted in Compilation of the Statements of James Earl Ray, Staff Report of the Select Committee on Assassinations, U.S. House of Representatives, 95th Congress, Second Session, August 18, 1978, p. 38.

22. FBI interview with Rodney Arvidson, owner of the National Dance Studio, April 13, 1968, MURKIN 1051–1175, section 9, p. 279.

23. Ibid., p. 280.

24. James Earl Ray, 20,000 Words, HSCA vol. XII, p. 29.

25. Frank, *An American Death*, p. 306.

26. FBI interview with Marie Martin, April 13, 1968, MURKIN 2325, section 22, p. 158.

27. Teletype to Director from Los Angeles, April 15, 1968, includes interview with Marie (listed in document incorrectly as Maria) Martin, MURKIN 751–900, section 8, p. 198; see also Frank, *An American Death*, p. 162.

28. Teletype to Director from Los Angeles, April 15, 1968, includes interviews with Marie (listed in document incorrectly as Maria) Martin and Rita Stein, MURKIN 751–900, section 8, pp. 198, 203.

29. FBI interview with Marie Martin, April 13, 1968, MURKIN 2325, section 22, p. 158.

30. James Earl Ray interview by House Select Committee investigators, April 29, 1977, HSCA vol. X, p. 47.

31. Teletype to Director from Los Angeles, April 15, 1968, includes interview with Marie (listed in document incorrectly as Maria) Martin, MURKIN 751–900, section 8, p. 196.

32. FBI summary information about interview with Marie Martin in MURKIN 4143, section 52, p. 82; also teletype to Director from Los Angeles, summarizing another interview with Marie Martin, MURKIN 3441–3502, section 38, p. 83.

33. Teletype to Director from Los Angeles, April 25, 1968, MURKIN 2151–2321, section 19, p. 252.

34. Teletype to Director from Los Angeles, April 25, 1968, including interview with Rita Stein, MURKIN 1991–2075, section 17, p. 156.

35. As for the fact that she asked the question in a joking manner, see FBI interview with Marie Martin, April 13, 1968, MURKIN 1051–1175, section 9, p. 263.

36. Conversation recounted from Frank, *An American Death*, pp. 163–64; generally, teletype to Director from Los Angeles, April 15, 1968, includes interviews with Marie (listed in document incorrectly as Maria) Martin and Rita Stein, MURKIN 751–900, section 8, pp. 195–203; also FBI interview with Rita Stein, April 13, 1968, MURKIN 1051–1175, section 9, p. 270, as well as reinterview with Rita Stein, MURKIN 2751–2925, section 29, p. 234.

37. FBI interview with Stein's mother (name redacted), April 27, 1968, MURKIN 3762, section 45, p. 43.

38. See, generally, "Analysis of James Earl Ray's Trip to New Orleans, December 15–December 21, 1967," Supplementary Staff Report of the Select Committee on Assassinations, HSCA vol. XIII, pp. 270–71; for Stein's quirkiness, belief in UFOs, conversations with inanimate objects, and the like, see FBI interview with his mother (name redacted), April 27, 1968, MURKIN 3762, section 45, p. 43; as for his belief in "Cosmic Philosophy" and his renunciation of material wealth, see FBI interview with Anthony Charles DeCarvelho, April 26, 1968, New Orleans field office 157-10673, Attorney General File, p. 2155.

39. "Analysis of James Earl Ray's Trip to New Orleans, December 15–December 21, 1967," Supplementary Staff Report of the Select Committee on Assassinations, HSCA vol. XIII, pp. 268–69; teletype to Director from Los Angeles, April 25, 1968, MURKIN 2151–2321, section 19, p. 252; see also McMillan, *The Making of an Assassin*, p. 279.

40. Frank, *An American Death*, p. 165.

41. James Earl Ray, *Who Killed Martin Luther King?*, p. 80.

42. FBI interview with Charles Stein, May 2, 1968, Los Angeles Field Office, Attorney General File.

43. James Earl Ray, *Tennessee Waltz*, p. 62.

44. See, generally, teletype to Director from Los Angeles, April 15, 1968, including interview with Marie (listed in document incorrectly as Maria) Martin, MURKIN 751–900, section 8, p. 197; also memo to Cartha DeLoach from Alex Rosen, April 16, 1968, MURKIN 1576–1730, section 13, p. 280; and FBI interview with Charles Stein, April 14, 1968, MURKIN 2325, section 22, p. 163; FBI interview with Marie Martin, April 14, 1968, Los Angeles Field Office, Attorney General File.

45. Frank, *An American Death*, p. 165.

46. Ibid.; James Earl Ray, 20,000 Words, HSCA vol. XII, pp. 29, 51.

47. William Bradford Huie, "I Got Involved Gradually, and I Didn't Know Anybody Was to be Murdered," *Look*, November 26, 1968, p. 92, maintained at MURKIN 5351–5396, section 73, p. 64.

48. James Earl Ray quoted in Compilation of the Statements of James Earl Ray, Staff Report of the Select Committee on Assassinations, U.S. House of Representatives, 95th Congress, Second Session, August 18, 1978, p. 43.

49. FBI interview with Mark Freeman, April 19, 1968, Los Angeles Field Office, Attorney General File; "Chronological Listing of Known Activities of James Earl Ray Since His Escape and Laboratory Examination of Evidence Attendant Thereto," MURKIN 4143, section 52, p. 18; see HSCA Rpt. quoting Dr. Mark Freeman's FBI interview, p. 460.

50. FBI interview with Marie Martin, April 13, 1968, MURKIN 2325, section 22, p. 158.

51. Charles Stein summarized in "Analysis of James Earl Ray's Trip to New Orleans, December 15–December 21, 1967," Supplementary Staff Report of the Select Committee on Assassinations, HSCA vol. XIII, p. 272; teletype to Director from Los Angeles, April 15, 1968, including interview with Marie (listed in document incorrectly as Maria) Martin, MURKIN 751–900, section 8, p. 197, as well as FBI summary document, MURKIN 4143, section 52, p. 81; see also FBI interview with Marie Martin, April 13, 1968, MURKIN 2325, section 22, p. 158; also, as to last-minute nature of Ray's condition, see FBI reinterview with Rita Stein, MURKIN 2751–2925, section 29, p. 235, and FBI interviews with Charles Stein, April 13 and May 2, 1968, Los Angeles Field Office, Attorney General File.

52. FBI interview with Charles Stein, April 13, 1968, MURKIN 2325, section 22, p. 150.

53. Frank, *An American Death*, p. 165.

54. James Earl Ray, 20,000 Words, HSCA vol. XII, p. 95.

55. Compilation of the Statements of James Earl Ray, Staff Report of the Select Committee on Assassinations, U.S. House of Representatives, 95th Congress, Second Session, August 18, 1978, p. 44.

56. FBI interview with Charles Stein, April 13, 1968, MURKIN 1051–1175, section 9, p. 266, and also April 13, 1968, MURKIN 2325, section 22, p. 150; FBI interview with Charles Stein, May 2, 1968, Los Angeles Field Office, Attorney General File; see also FBI interview with Rita Stein, April 13, 1968, MURKIN 1051–1175, section 9, p. 270, and MURKIN 751–900, section 8, p. 201.

57. See, generally, James Earl Ray testimony in Compilation of the Statements of James Earl Ray, Staff Report of the Select Committee on Assassinations, U.S. House of Representatives, 95th Congress, Second Session, August 18, 1978, pp. 44–45; teletype to Director from Los Angeles, April 15, 1968, including interview with Rita Stein, MURKIN 751–900, section 8, p. 201; and see Marie Martin interview in MURKIN 1051–1175, section 9, p. 269. See also Ray's version of the event in HSCA vol. X, pp. 49–52.

58. James Earl Ray, *Who Killed Martin Luther King?*, p. 82.

59. FBI interview with Charles Stein, April 14, 1968, MURKIN 2325, section 22, pp. 167–68.

60. Teletype to Director from Los Angeles, April 15, 1968, containing interview with Charles Stein, MURKIN 751–900, section 8, pp. 236–37; also FBI interview with Stein, April 14, 1968, MURKIN 2325, section 22, p. 167.

61. See summary of Charles Stein testimony at "Analysis of James Earl Ray's Trip to New Orleans, December 15–December 21, 1967," Supplementary Staff Report of the Select Committee on Assassinations, HSCA vol. XIII, p. 272; also summary of interview with Charles Stein by FBI, MURKIN 4143, section 52, p. 87; also Frank, *An American Death*, p. 166.

62. FBI interview with Charles Stein, April 13, 1968, MURKIN 1051–1175, section 9, p. 266. At one point, Stein told the FBI that Ray stopped half a dozen times at phone booths, and another time said it was only once—see, generally, MURKIN 2751–2925, section 29, p. 231.

63. See Charles Stein testimony at "Analysis of James Earl Ray's Trip to New Orleans, December 15–December 21, 1967," Supplementary Staff Report of the Select Committee on Assassinations, HSCA vol. XIII, p. 272; also James Earl Ray testimony in Compilation of the Statements of James Earl Ray, Staff Report of the Select Committee on Assassinations, U.S. House of Representatives, 95th Congress, Second Session, August 18, 1978, p. 45; see also James Earl Ray, 20,000 Words, HSCA vol. XII, p. 45.

64. James Earl Ray, 20,000 Words, HSCA vol. XII, p. 45; James Earl Ray testimony in Compilation of the Statements of James Earl Ray, Staff Report of the Select Committee on Assassinations, U.S. House of Representatives, 95th Congress, Second Session, August 18, 1978, p. 45; see James Earl Ray interview by Select Committee investigators, April 29, 1977, HSCA vol. X, p. 57.

65. Teletype to Director from Los Angeles, April 15, 1968, including interview with Marie (listed in document incorrectly as Maria) Martin, MURKIN 751–900, section 8, p. 197; Frank, *An American Death*, p. 167.

66. FBI interview with Charles Stein, April 13, 1968, MURKIN 1051–1175, section 9, p. 268, and MURKIN 2325, section 22, p. 152.

67. FBI interview with Charles Stein, April 14, 1968, MURKIN 2325, section 22, p. 164; FBI interview with Charles Stein, May 2, 1968, Los Angeles Field Office, Attorney General File.

68. FBI interviews with Charles Stein, April 13, 1968, MURKIN 1051–1175, section 9, p. 267; April 13, 1968, MURKIN 2325, section 22, p. 151; and April 14, 1968, MURKIN 2325, section 22, p. 164.

69. FBI interview with Charles Stein, in May 5, 1968, teletype, MURKIN 2751–2925, section 29, p. 232; FBI interview with Charles Stein, May 2, 1968, Los Angeles Field Office, Attorney General File.

70. FBI interview with Charles Stein, April 13, 1968, MURKIN 1051–1175, section 9, p. 267.

71. FBI interview with Bryan Dupepe, owner/manager of Provincial Motel, April 14, 1968, MURKIN 2635–2673, section 27, p. 125.

72. Teletype to Director from New Orleans, April 25, 1968, summarizing an interview with Charles Stein, MURKIN 2151–2321, section 19, p. 34; FBI interview with Marie Lee (name redacted), April 25, 1968, MURKIN 3762, section 45, pp. 32, and May 1, 1968, interview reported on p. 64 of same file; see Frank, *An American Death*, p. 168.

73. Teletype to Director from New Orleans, April 14, 1968, summarizing an interview with Dupepe, owner/manager of the Provincial Motel, MURKIN 1176–1300, section 10, pp. 46–47.

74. Huie, *He Slew the Dreamer*, pp. 78–79.

75. Ibid., p. 98.

76. James Earl Ray testimony in Compilation of the Statements of James Earl Ray, Staff Report of the Select Committee on Assassinations, U.S. House of Representatives, 95th Congress, Second Session, August 18, 1978, p. 47.

77. Huie, *He Slew the Dreamer*, p. 98.

78. Ibid., p. 79.

79. James Earl Ray testimony in Compilation of the Statements of James Earl Ray, Staff Report of the Select Committee on Assassinations, U.S. House of Representatives, 95th Congress, Second Session, August 18, 1978, p. 47.

80. Huie, "I Got Involved Gradually and I Didn't Know Anyone Was to be Murdered," *Look*, November 26, 1968, p. 92; filed in MURKIN 5351–5396, section 73, p. 64.

81. James Earl Ray testimony in Compilation of the Statements of James Earl Ray, Staff Report of the Select Committee on Assassinations, U.S. House of Representatives, 95th Congress, Second Session, August 18, 1978, p. 46.

82. Memo to Cartha DeLoach from Alex Rosen, April 17, 1968, including interview with Sharon Rhodes, MURKIN 1576–1730, section 13, pp. 289–90.

83. HSCA vol. VII, p. 317.

84. HSCA Rpt., p. 461.

85. "Re: Ray's Relative John Larry Ray, at St. Louis Missouri," St. Louis FBI field office, Attorney General File, p. 3722.

86. See, generally, "Re: Ray's Relative John Larry Ray, at St. Louis Missouri," St. Louis FBI field office, Attorney General File, pp. 3722–23.

87. Testimony of John Ray, December 1, 1978, HSCA vol. VIII, pp. 587, 592.

88. Testimony of Edward Evans, Chief Investigator, HSCA vol. VII, p. 310.

89. For information about how Carol Pepper registered and paid for the liquor license under her name, but how John then operated the tavern, see, generally, "Grapevine Tavern," FBI summary information report, MURKIN 3333, section 34, pp. 290–95.

90. Testimony of John Ray, December 1, 1978, HSCA vol. VIII, pp. 587–89; HSCA Rpt., p. 483.

91. HSCA Rpt., p. 483.

92. See, generally, testimony of Edward Evans, chief investigator, HSCA vol. VII, pp. 296–98.

93. See, generally, HSCA vol. VII, pp. 297–302.

94. Testimony of John Ray, December 1, 1978, HSCA vol. VIII, pp. 35–36.

95. Ibid., pp. 32, 597.

96. HSCA vol. VII, pp. 295–96.

97. Testimony of Edward Evans, Chief Investigator, HSCA vol. VII, p. 309.

98. See, generally, FBI interview with Naomi Regazzi, May 21, 1968, St. Louis file 44-775, Attorney General File, p. 3111.

99. FBI interview with Charles Stein, April 13, 1968, MURKIN 1051–1175, section 9, p. 268; teletype to Director from Los Angeles, April 25, 1968, MURKIN 1991–2075, section 17, p. 156.

100. Teletype to Director from Los Angeles, April 25, 1968, MURKIN 1991–2075, section 17, p. 156.

101. "Chronological Listing of Known Activities of James Earl Ray Since His Escape and Laboratory Examination of Evidence Attendant Thereto," MURKIN 4143, section 52, p. 20.

102. FBI interview with Rita Stein, contained in teletype to Director from Los Angeles, April 25, 1968, MURKIN 1991–2075, section 17, p. 156.

103. Huie, *He Slew the Dreamer*, p. 82.

24: The Swingers Club

1. Ray letter to American–Southern African Council reprinted in HSCA vol. XIII, p. 252.

2. "Chronological Listing of Known Activities of James Earl Ray Since His Escape and Laboratory Examination of Evidence Attendant Thereto," MURKIN 4143, section 52, p. 22.

3. Frank, *An American Death*, p. 180.

4. HSCA vol. XIII citing FBI Airtel to Director from Los Angeles, May 10, 1968, LA MURKIN 44–1574, serial 1236, p. 252.

5. James Earl Ray, 20,000 Words, HSCA vol. XII, p. 204.

6. James Earl Ray quoted by Huie, *He Slew the Dreamer,* p. 82.

7. James Earl Ray, 20,000 Words, HSCA vol. XII, p. 85.

8. Xavier von Koss interviewed by Huie, reported in *He Slew the Dreamer,* pp. 92–93.

9. Ibid.

10. FBI interview with Andreas Jorgensen, dance instructor, April 13, 1968, MURKIN 1051–1175, section 9, p. 275; see also interview with Rodney Arvidson, owner of National Dance Studio, same file, p. 277.

11. FBI interview with Rodney Arvidson, owner of National Dance Studio, April 13, 1968, MURKIN 1051–1175, section 9, pp. 276–77.

12. FBI interview with Cathryn Norton, dance instructor, April 13, 1968, MURKIN 1051–1175, section 9, p. 272.

13. See, generally, teletype to all Continental Offices from Director, MURKIN 621–750, section 6, pp. 216–18.

14. "Investigation at International School of Bartending, Los Angeles, Attended by Galt from January 19, 1968, to March 2, 1968," MURKIN 2325, section 22, pp. 135–36.

15. Ibid., p. 136.

16. See Compilation of the Statements of James Earl Ray, Staff Report of the Select Committee on Assassinations, U.S. House of Representatives, 95th Congress, Second Session, August 18, 1978, p. 38.

17. Memo to Cartha DeLoach from Alex Rosen, April 17, 1968, including interview with Richard Gonzalez, MURKIN 1576–1730, section 13, p. 289; see also teletype to Director from Los Angeles, including interview with Donald Jacobs, April 15, 1968, MURKIN 751–900, section 8, p. 238.

18. FBI interview with Robert Kelly, April 12, 1968, MURKIN 2325, section 22, p. 110.

19. Dennis LeMaster interviewed by House Select Committee investigators, March 10, 1978, MLK Exhibit F-171, p. 144.

20. Memo to Cartha DeLoach from Alex Rosen, April 12, 1968, MURKIN 1051–1175, section 9, p. 130; see also "Chronological Listing of Known Activities of James Earl Ray Since His Escape and Laboratory Examination of Evidence Attendant Thereto," MURKIN 4143, section 52, p. 24.

21. James Earl Ray, 20,000 Words, HSCA vol. XII, p. 86.

22. See FBI interview with Robert Harold Gray, April 16, 1968, MURKIN 2325, section 22, p. 109; also H. Harold Robert interviewed by Special Agent Benjamin Moorehead, Index Card File under "L.A.—St. Francis," Attorney General File.

23. HSCA vol. XIII, p. 253, citing an FBI interview with Ronald Hewitson; see letter reproduced in HSCA vol. IV, p. 116.

24. "Chronological Listing of Known Activities of James Earl Ray Since His Escape and Laboratory Examination of Evidence Attendant Thereto," MURKIN 4143, section 52, p. 25.

25. See Airtel to Director from SAC Los Angeles, May 10, 1968, Re: The Local Swinger, P.O. Box 3802, Downey, California, MURKIN 3334–3335, section 35, pp. 1–2; "Chronological Listing of Known Activities of James Earl Ray Since His Escape and Laboratory Examination of Evidence Attendant Thereto," MURKIN 4143, section 52, p. 25.

26. James Earl Ray, 20,000 Words, HSCA vol. XII, p. 40.

27. "Chronological Listing of Known Activities of James Earl Ray Since His Escape and Laboratory Examination of Evidence Attendant Thereto," MURKIN 4143, section 52, p. 27.

28. Teletype to Director from Los Angeles, April 26, 1968, MURKIN 2151–2321, section 19, pp. 313–14; teletype to Director from Atlanta, April 26, 1968, MURKIN 2151–2321, section 19, pp. 334–36; see also teletype on p. 247 of same MURKIN section; "Chronological Listing of Known Activities of James Earl Ray Since His Escape and Laboratory Examination of Evidence Attendant Thereto," MURKIN 4143, section 52, p. 28.

29. James Earl Ray, 20,000 Words, HSCA vol. XII, p. 37.

30. Ibid.

31. FBI interview with Dr. Russell Hadley, October 2, 1968, Los Angeles Field Office, Attorney General File.

32. James Earl Ray, 20,000 Words, HSCA vol. XII, p. 40.

33. Ibid., p. 41.

34. Ibid.

35. James Earl Ray, *Who Killed Martin Luther King?*, p. 84.

36. James Earl Ray to Huie, quoted in McMillan, *The Making of an Assassin*, pp. 281–82.

37. James Earl Ray, *Who Killed Martin Luther King?*, p. 83.

38. FBI interview with Bo Del Monte, April 22, 1968, MLK Exhibit F-168, reprinted in HSCA vol. IV, p. 122.

39. FBI interview with James E. Morrison, April 22, 1968, MLK Exhibit F-169, reprinted in HSCA vol. IV, p. 123.

40. Leonard Scott Delmonte (a.k.a. Bo Del Monte), interviewed by House Select Committee investigators, February 10, 1978, MLK Exhibit F-170, pp. 131–33.

41. Ibid., p. 136.

42. Dennis LeMaster interviewed by House Select Committee investigators, March 10, 1978, MLK Exhibit F-171, p. 145.

43. "Puzzlers in Ray Case Include Who Received Duplicate Driver's License in His Absence," *The New York Times*, March 11, 1969, p. 17.

44. Ibid.

45. Huie, *He Slew the Dreamer*, p. 88.

46. James Earl Ray interviewed by the House Select Committee investigators, April 29, 1977, HSCA vol. X, p. 80.

47. FBI summary interview with Tomas Lau, contained in teletype to Director from Los Angeles, April 15, 1968, MURKIN 751–900, section 8, p. 238; see also Lau interview in MURKIN 2325, section 22, p. 137.

48. FBI interview with Marie Martin, MURKIN 4143, section 52, p. 82.

49. Teletype to Director from Los Angeles, May 14, 1968, including interview with Marie Martin, MURKIN 3441–3502, section 38, p. 83.

50. See MLK Exhibit F-52, HSCA vol. II, pp. 50–51; FBI interview with Allan O. Thompson, April 12, 1968, MURKIN 2325, section 22, p. 106.

25: Memphis Bound

1. James Earl Ray quoted in Compilation of the Statements of James Earl Ray, Staff Report of the Select Committee on Assassinations, U.S. House of Representatives, 95th Congress, Second Session, August 18, 1978, p. 208.

2. In the 20,000 Words, Ray said he was told to meet Raoul in Birmingham in two days, but it had taken him three to reach only New Orleans.

3. FBI summary sheet, New Orleans field office, MURKIN 3762, section 45, p. 48; see, generally, MURKIN 2151–2321, section 19, p. 36. The date of March 21 was selected as the precise day for Ray's drop-off, because all the Stein family could remember was that on the day he arrived it was windy and raining that night. The FBI's check with the U.S. Weather Bureau indicated that it rained heavily in New Orleans only on the day and evening of March 21 and the early morning of March 22. This was the only rainfall recorded during the period March 17 to March 24 (MURKIN 2151–2321, section 19, pp. 36, 38, 131).

4. FBI summary report of Ray chronology, MURKIN 4143, section 52, p. 34.

5. Huie, *He Slew the Dreamer*, p. 108.

6. FBI summary report of Ray chronology, MURKIN 4143, section 52, p. 34.

7. Note that in the 20,000 Words, Ray says he exchanged $200 to $300. Before the House Select Committee, however, he said it was $700 in Canadian currency—see HSCA vol. XII; see Compilation of the Statements of James Earl Ray, Staff Report of the Select Commit-

tee on Assassinations, U.S. House of Representatives, 95th Congress, Second Session, August 18, 1978, at HSCA vol. III, p. 213.

8. Huie, *He Slew the Dreamer,* p. 110.

9. Ibid.

10. Ibid.

11. James Earl Ray, 20,000 Words, HSCA vol. XII, p.

12. Ibid.

13. James Earl Ray interview with Select Committee Investigators, HSCA vol. II; see Compilation of the Statements of James Earl Ray, Staff Report of the Select Committee on Assassinations, U.S. House of Representatives, 95th Congress, Second Session, August 18, 1978, at HSCA vol. III, p. 213.

14. James Earl Ray interview with Select Committee Investigators, HSCA vol. IV; see Compilation of the Statements of James Earl Ray, Staff Report of the Select Committee on Assassinations, U.S. House of Representatives, 95th Congress, Second Session, August 18, 1978, at HSCA vol. III, p. 213.

15. James Earl Ray interview with Select Committee Investigators, HSCA vol. V; see Compilation of the Statements of James Earl Ray, Staff Report of the Select Committee on Assassinations, U.S. House of Representatives, 95th Congress, Second Session, August 18, 1978, at HSCA vol. III, p. 213.

16. FBI statement of Clyde Manasco, statement of April 10, 1968, MURKIN 2323–2324, section 21, pp. 131–32.

17. See, generally, FBI statement of Quinton B. Davis, April 18, 1968, MURKIN 3763–3872, section 46, p. 19; see also Davis statement, April 10, 1968, MURKIN 2323–2324, section 21, p. 132, and FBI statement of Clyde Manasco, April 8, 1968, MURKIN 2323–2324, section 21, p. 135.

18. FBI summary report of Ray chronology, MURKIN 4143, section 52, p. 32.

19. See MLK Exhibit F-52, Change of Address Order submitted by Eric S. Galt to the Hollywood, California, post office, HSCA vol. II, pp. 50–51; see also interview with James Earl Ray by House Select Committee investigators, March 28, 1977, HSCA vol. IX, p. 225, in which Ray says that while he "really didn't know," he expected to be in Atlanta "three weeks or something."

20. Steve Kopp interviewed by the FBI, April 8, 1968, MURKIN 2323–2324, section 21, p. 141.

21. See, generally, Donald F. Wood statement to the FBI, April 5, 1968, MURKIN 2076–2150, section 18, pp. 113–14; see also House Select Committee interview with James Earl Ray, April 29, 1977, HSCA vol. X, p. 154.

22. Photocopy of Aeromarine Supply Co. Invoice 2251A, MURKIN 2323–2324, section 21, p. 35.

23. Testimony of James Earl Ray, August 17, 1978, HSCA vol. II, pp. 10, 40–41; see also Ray interview by Select Committee investigators, HSCA vol. X, pp. 230, 243.

24. Donald F. Wood statement to the FBI, April 5, 1968, MURKIN 2076–2150, section 18, p. 114.

25. James Earl Ray, 20,000 Words, HSCA vol. XII.

26. Compilation of the Statements of James Earl Ray, Staff Report of the Select Committee on Assassinations, U.S. House of Representatives, 95th Congress, Second Session, August 18, 1978, reported in HSCA vol. III, p. 218; see also James Earl Ray, 20,000 Words, HSCA vol. XII, p. 54.

27. James Earl Ray, 20,000 Words, HSCA vol. XII, p. 54.

28. James Earl Ray testimony, HSCA vol. II, p. 15; Compilation of the Statements of James Earl Ray, Staff Report of the Select Committee on Assassinations, U.S. House of Representatives, 95th Congress, Second Session, August 18, 1978, reported in HSCA vol. III, ftnt. 4, p. 220.

29. Compilation of the Statements of James Earl Ray, Staff Report of the Select Committee on Assassinations, U.S. House of Representatives, 95th Congress, Second Session, August 18, 1978, reported in HSCA vol. III, ftnt. 15, p. 221.

30. James Earl Ray testimony, HSCA vol. II, p. 12.

31. Statement of Annie Estelle Peters to the FBI, April 16, 1968, MURKIN 2323–2324, section 21, p. 240.

32. James Earl Ray, 20,000 Words, HSCA vol. XII, p. 22.

33. Testimony of James Earl Ray, HSCA vol. II, pp. 64–65, 88.

34. James Earl Ray interviewed by Dan Rather, March 9, 1977, HSCA vol. I, p. 197.

35. Huie, *He Slew the Dreamer,* p. 115.

36. Ibid.

37. Ibid., p. 116.

38. James Earl Ray, 20,000 Words, HSCA vol. XII, p. 55.

39. Testimony of James Earl Ray, HSCA vol. II, p. 63.

40. Ibid., pp. 63–64; James Earl Ray interviewed by the House Select Committee, March 28, 1977, HSCA vol. IX, p. 13.

41. Testimony of James Earl Ray, HSCA vol. II, p. 61; James Earl Ray interviewed by the House Select Committee, March 28, 1977, HSCA vol. IX, p. 13.

42. See MLK Exhibit F-59, Piedmont Laundry receipt of April 1, 1968, in HSCA vol. II, p. 65.

43. Peters had Thursdays off, but was there on Friday, April 1, when Ray brought in the laundry. She was also off on April 4, the day King was killed, but was back at work on April 5, the day Ray returned to get his laundry. Testimony of James Earl Ray, HSCA vol. II, p. 66; see MLK Exhibit F-60, interview with Annie Estelle Peters, September 27, 1977, HSCA vol. II, pp. 70–85.

44. Testimony of James Earl Ray, HSCA vol. II, p. 67.

45. Mark Lane before the House Select Committee on Assassinations, August 17, 1978, HSCA vol. II, pp. 3, 68.

46. Testimony of James Earl Ray, HSCA vol. II, p. 89.

47. Testimony of Annie Estelle Peters, August 18, 1978, p. 509.

48. See partial MLK Exhibit F-106, Piedmont Laundry Counterlist, in HSCA vol. II, p. 91; for full exhibit see HSCA vol. III, pp. 308–505.

49. Testimony of James Earl Ray, HSCA vol. II, p. 94.

26: The Alibi

1. "Oliver Rexall Drug Store," FBI summary information, includes interviews with Peggy Burns, store clerk, April 4 and 11, 1968, MURKIN 2322, section 20, pp. 134–38, and April 19, 1968, interview, MURKIN 2634, section 26, p. 19.

2. Huie, *He Slew the Dreamer,* p. 117.

3. Frank, *An American Death,* p. 38; see also unpublished reporters' notes from *The Memphis Press-Scimitar,* maintained at Sanitation Strike Archives, listing an interview with Webb in which he told the unidentified reporter, "His car was there all night, and there was a light in his room all night."

4. Testimony of James Earl Ray, HSCA vol. II.

5. James Earl Ray quoted in Compilation of the Statements of James Earl Ray, Staff Report of the Select Committee on Assassinations, U.S. House of Representatives, 95th Congress, Second Session, August 18, 1978, p. 69.

6. Testimony of James Earl Ray, HSCA vol. I, p. 101; James Earl Ray quoted in Compilation of the Statements of James Earl Ray, Staff Report of the Select Committee on Assassinations, U.S. House of Representatives, 95th Congress, Second Session, August 18, 1978, p. 73.

7. James Earl Ray interviewed by the House Select Committee, May 3, 1977, HSCA vol. X, p. 322.

8. See also James Earl Ray quoted in Compilation of the Statements of James Earl Ray, Staff Report of the Select Committee on Assassinations, U.S. House of Representatives, 95th Congress, Second Session, August 18, 1978, p. 70.

9. Testimony of James Earl Ray, HSCA vol. I, p. 101.

10. Ibid., p. 354.

11. Testimony of James Earl Ray, Compilation of the Statements of James Earl Ray, Staff Report of the Select Committee on Assassinations, U.S. House of Representatives, 95th Congress, Second Session, August 18, 1978, p. 73; in his testimony before the committee, reported in HSCA vol. III, p. 255, Ray was asked, "Mr. Ray, you have previously stated that you had no knowledge at the time of your trip to Memphis, of the activities of Dr. Martin Luther King; is that correct?" Ray: "That is correct."

12. James Earl Ray interviewed by the House Select Committee, March 28, 1977, HSCA vol. IX, pp. 14, 105; also May 3, 1977, HSCA vol. X, p. 293; also, Ray said he saw two men stare at him in a strange way when he was in Jim's Grill; one of them was "dark and somewhat swarthy," Ray said, and he suggested to the Select Committee that it might be Walter Alfred "Jack" Youngblood, a person who claimed to have worked at times with U.S. intelligence. Ray's attorneys had developed Youngblood as a possible suspect as Raoul, and Ray, after being shown some pictures of the real Youngblood by his defense team, suddenly "remembered" it looked like a man he claimed to have seen at Jim's. The problem for Ray is not only that there is no evidence that Youngblood was even in Memphis that day, but there is also no evidence that Ray was ever in Jim's Grill. None of the witnesses in that restaurant, later interviewed by the police, ever saw anyone who looked like Ray in there at any time on the day of the assassination.

13. James Earl Ray interviewed by the House Select Committee, March 28, 1977, HSCA vol. IX, p. 70.

14. Huie, He Slew the Dreamer, p. 167.

15. Ibid.

16. Ibid.; see James Earl Ray interviewed by the House Select Committee, March 28, 1977, HSCA vol. IX, p. 63.

17. James Earl Ray interviewed by the House Select Committee, March 28, 1977, HSCA vol. IX, pp. 19, 74; also Ray interviewed by Dan Rather, March 9, 1977, HSCA vol. I, p. 212.

18. James Earl Ray interviewed by the House Select Committee, March 28, 1977, HSCA vol. IX, p. 16.

19. Ibid., pp. 16–18, 97–98; see also Compilation of the Statements of James Earl Ray, Staff Report of the Select Committee on Assassinations, U.S. House of Representatives, 95th Congress, Second Session, August 18, 1978, pp. 78–79; see James Earl Ray interviewed by the House Select Committee, May 3, 1977, HSCA vol. X, p. 319.

20. James Earl Ray interviewed by the House Select Committee, March 28, 1977, HSCA vol. IX, pp. 19–20; see, generally, Ray interviewed by the House Select Committee, May 3, 1977, HSCA vol. X, p. 337.

21. Huie, He Slew the Dreamer, p. 3.

22. James Earl Ray interviewed by Dan Rather, March 9, 1977, HSCA vol. 1, p. 349.

23. James Earl Ray testimony, HSCA vol. I, p. 351.

24. See, generally, James Earl Ray interviewed by House Select Committee investigators, May 3, 1977, HSCA vol. X, pp. 345–46.

25. James Earl Ray interviewed by Dan Rather, March 9, 1977, HSCA vol. 1, p. 213.

26. James Earl Ray testimony, HSCA vol. II, pp. 106–7.

27. Ibid., p. 107.

28. Ibid., pp. 107–8.

29. Mark Lane, "The Assassination of Dr. Martin Luther King, Jr.—Was James Earl Ray a Patsy?" Hustler, November 1978, republished in HSCA vol. V, pp. 393–98.

30. Grace Walden quoted by Lane, "The Assassination of Dr. Martin Luther King, Jr.," *Hustler,* November 1978, republished in HSCA vol. V, p. 394.

31. *National Enquirer,* October 11, 1977, p. 32.

32. Mark Lane quoted in HSCA vol. II, pp. 108–9.

33. Dean Cowden quoted in *National Enquirer,* October 11, 1977, p. 32.

34. Thomas Wilson quoted in *National Enquirer,* October 11, 1977, p. 32.

35. Narration of Robert Blakey, HSCA vol. V, p. 452.

36. Ibid., pp. 452–53; see also MLK Exhibits F-321 and F-322, statements of Memphis police officers James Simpson and Michael Dougherty, HSCA vol. V, pp. 454–58.

37. See MLK Exhibit F-327, affidavit of Dr. Sidney Vick, November 7, 1978, HSCA vol. V, pp. 516–18; Commitment Proceedings, pp. 519–20; narration of Robert Blakey, p. 515.

38. See testimony of Dr. Jack C. Neale III, November 14, 1978, HSCA vol. V, p. 577; also testimony of Dr. James H. Druff, November 14, 1978, HSCA vol. V, pp. 556–58, 568; also MLK Exhibit F-339, report of Dr. Roger Peele, assistant superintendent of St. Elizabeth's Hospital, Washington, D.C., Re: Grace Walden, November 7, 1978, HSCA vol. V, pp. 613–20.

39. Testimony of Dr. James H. Druff, November 14, 1978, HSCA vol. V, p. 568.

40. Grace Walden, quoted on the NBC *Today* show, August 15, 1978, transcript reproduced at HSCA vol. V, pp. 622–25.

41. HSCA vol. V, p. 573; as for the height description, see Mark Lane, *Code Name "Zorro,"* p. 198.

42. Memphis police interview with Grace Hays Stephens (née Walden), April 4, 1968, one page, James Earl Ray Supplements, 1968 Homicide, Attorney General File.

43. FBI interview with Grace Walden, April 5, 1968, MURKIN ME, Sub. D, section 1, p. 5; see also FBI interview with Walden, April 24, reprinted in HSCA vol. V, p. 425.

44. See, generally, affidavit of Robert Williams, November 3, 1978, MLK Exhibit F-317, HSCA vol. V, pp. 427–28; also affidavit of William Herrington, November 3, 1978, MLK Exhibit F-318, HSCA vol. V, pp. 430–31.

45. See affidavit of John R. Jacobs, November 6, 1978, MLK Exhibit F-319, HSCA vol. V, pp. 434–35; narration of Robert Blakey, HSCA vol. V, p. 437.

46. HSCA vol. V, p. 444.

47. Lane, *Code Name "Zorro,"* p. 358.

48. Testimony of Dean Cowden, August 18, 1978, HSCA vol. III, p. 515; see also affidavit of Coy Dean Cowden, August 15, 1978, MLK Exhibit F-119, HSCA vol. III, pp. 535–38; and affidavit of Collie Cowden Marshall, August 14, 1978, MLK Exhibit F-120, HSCA vol. III, pp. 540–42.

49. Testimony of Dean Cowden, August 18, 1978, HSCA vol. III, p. 517.

50. Ibid., p. 545.

51. Ibid., p. 534.

52. See testimony of Ernestine Johnson, House Select Committee investigator, HSCA vol. V, pp. 547–49.

53. Testimony of Larce E. McFall and Phillip McFall, August 18, 1978, and affidavit of Phillip McFall, August 15, 1978, HSCA vol. III, pp. 550–58.

54. James R. Reid, "Willie Green Tells Again of April 4," *The Memphis Press-Scimitar,* May 5, 1977, Sanitation Strike Archives.

55. Internal notes by *Memphis Press-Scimitar* reporters, James Earl Ray file, 5700, Sanitation Strike Archives.

56. The reporter, James Reid, evidently reported the story accurately, with his one error during the rush of deadline stories that followed in the wake of the King assassination being that he reported Green saw the suspect after the killing, rather than before. Of course, it was a critical mistake that allowed the issue to simmer for three decades.

27: On the Run

1. Testimony of James Earl Ray, HSCA vol. II, p. 106.
2. Ibid.
3. Ibid.
4. See, generally, James Earl Ray interviewed by House Select Committee investigators, March 28, 1977, HSCA vol. IX, p. 237.
5. Ibid., pp. 240–41.
6. Ibid., p. 241.
7. James Earl Ray interviewed by House Select Committee investigators, May 3, 1977, HSCA vol. X, p. 349.
8. Compilation of the Statements of James Earl Ray, Staff Report of the Select Committee on Assassinations, U.S. House of Representatives, 95th Congress, Second Session, August 18, 1978, pp. 85–87.
9. Testimony of James Earl Ray, HSCA vol. II, pp. 106, 111; see also Compilation of the Statements of James Earl Ray, Staff Report of the Select Committee on Assassinations, U.S. House of Representatives, 95th Congress, Second Session, August 18, 1978, ftnt. 2, p. 86.
10. Testimony of James Earl Ray, HSCA vol. II, p. 111; see also James Earl Ray interviewed by House Select Committee investigators, March 28, 1977, HSCA vol. IX, pp. 232–33.
11. Testimony of James Earl Ray, HSCA vol. II, p. 112; Compilation of the Statements of James Earl Ray, Staff Report of the Select Committee on Assassinations, U.S. House of Representatives, 95th Congress, Second Session, August 18, 1978, p. 88.
12. Testimony of James Earl Ray, HSCA vol. II, p. 112; James Earl Ray interviewed by House Select Committee investigators, March 28, 1977, HSCA vol. IX, p. 233; see also James Earl Ray interviewed by House Select Committee investigators, May 3, 1977, HSCA vol. X, p. 351.
13. James Earl Ray interviewed by House Select Committee investigators, March 28, 1977, HSCA vol. IX, p. 235.
14. Testimony of James Earl Ray, HSCA vol. II, p. 44.
15. Ibid.; James Earl Ray interviewed by House Select Committee investigators, March 28, 1977, HSCA vol. IX, p. 227.
16. Testimony of James Earl Ray, HSCA vol. II, p. 112.
17. James Earl Ray interviewed by House Select Committee investigators, March 28, 1977, HSCA vol. IX, p. 228.
18. Ibid., p. 230.
19. Compilation of the Statements of James Earl Ray, Staff Report of the Select Committee on Assassinations, U.S. House of Representatives, 95th Congress, Second Session, August 18, 1978, p. 89.
20. James Earl Ray interviewed by House Select Committee investigators, March 28, 1977, HSCA vol. IX, pp. 229, 231.
21. Testimony of Annie Estelle Peters, August 18, 1978, HSCA vol. III, p. 511.
22. Annie Estelle Peters interviewed by House Select Committee investigators, September 27, 1977, MLK Exhibit F-60, HSCA vol. II, p. 72.
23. James Earl Ray interviewed by House Select Committee investigators, May 3, 1977, HSCA vol. X, p. 353.
24. James Earl Ray, 20,000 Words, HSCA vol. XII, p. 91; James Earl Ray interviewed by House Select Committee investigators, May 3, 1977, HSCA vol. X, pp. 353–54.
25. See James Earl Ray interviewed by House Select Committee investigators, November 14, 1977, pp. 17–19.
26. James Earl Ray, 20,000 Words, HSCA vol. XII, p. 91; James Earl Ray interviewed by House Select Committee investigators, May 3, 1977, HSCA vol. X, p. 353.

27. James Earl Ray, 20,000 Words, HSCA vol. XII, p. 91.

28. See, generally, MURKIN 4351, section 55, p. 25, memo regarding ethnic mix of the neighborhood into which Ray moved.

29. "Felinska Szpakowska," 3-by-5 index card in Episode Card Index, filed under "Toronto," Attorney General File; also MURKIN 4442–4500, section 57, p. 60.

30. James Earl Ray, 20,000 Words, HSCA vol. XII, p. 24.

31. FBI document summarizing Ray in Toronto, April 8, 1968–May 6, 1968, MURKIN 4442–4500, section 57, p. 60.

32. See, generally, James Earl Ray interviewed by House Select Committee investigators, May 3, 1977, HSCA vol. X, pp. 354–55; also Frank, An American Death, p. 312.

33. See Gregory Jaynes, "Ray Mystery Deepens on Possible Contacts with Two Other Men," The Commercial Appeal, June 10, 1968, p. 1.

34. See, generally, James Earl Ray in Compilation of the Statements of James Earl Ray, Staff Report of the Select Committee on Assassinations, U.S. House of Representatives, 95th Congress, Second Session, August 18, 1978, p. 94; also James Earl Ray interviewed by House Select Committee investigators, HSCA vol. XI, pp. 24–25.

35. James Earl Ray interviewed by House Select Committee investigators, May 3, 1977, HSCA vol. X, pp. 357–59, and Ray interviewed November 14, 1977, HSCA vol. XI, pp. 27, 40.

36. James Earl Ray interviewed by House Select Committee investigators, May 3, 1977, HSCA vol. X, p. 357.

37. MLK Exhibit F-233, HSCA vol. V, p. 15; see also FBI document summarizing Ray in Toronto, April 8, 1968–May 6, 1968, MURKIN 4442–4500, section 57, p. 60. Note: The House Select Committee on Assassinations, in its reports, spells the name as both Bridgman and Bridgeman. Ray's letters requesting a copy of the birth certificate list Bridgman, and that is the preferred spelling used in the text.

38. James Earl Ray, 20,000 Words, HSCA vol. XII, p. 24.

39. FBI document summarizing Ray in Toronto, April 8, 1968–May 6, 1968, MURKIN 4442–4500, section 57, p. 61.

40. Frank, An American Death, pp. 312–13; see also Gregory Jaynes, "Ray Mystery Deepens on Possible Contacts with Two Other Men," The Commercial Appeal, June 10, 1968, p. 1.

41. FBI document summarizing Ray in Toronto, April 8, 1968–May 6, 1968, MURKIN 4442–4500, section 57, p. 61; James Earl Ray interviewed by House Select Committee investigators, November 14, 1977, 1977, HSCA vol. XI, p. 27.

42. James Earl Ray interviewed by House Select Committee investigators, May 3, 1977, HSCA vol. X, p. 357.

43. Martin Waldron, "Alabamian Named in Dr. King Inquiry," The New York Times, April 12, 1968, p. 1.

44. James Earl Ray interviewed by House Select Committee investigators, May 3, 1977, HSCA vol. X, p. 356.

45. James Earl Ray, 20,000 Words, HSCA vol. XII, p. 24.

46. Huie, He Slew the Dreamer, p. 128.

47. James Earl Ray interviewed by House Select Committee investigators, November 14, 1977, HSCA vol. XI, p. 12.

48. James Earl Ray interviewed by House Select Committee investigators, March 22, 1977, HSCA vol. IX, p. 425.

49. James Earl Ray interviewed by House Select Committee investigators, November 14, 1977, HSCA vol. XI, p. 12.

50. James Earl Ray interviewed by House Select Committee investigators, March 22, 1977, HSCA vol. IX, p. 425.

51. Ibid., pp. 425–26; James Earl Ray interviewed by House Select Committee investigators, November 14, 1977, HSCA vol. XI, p. 32.

52. See James Earl Ray interviewed by House Select Committee investigators, HSCA vol. IX, p. 512.

53. FBI summary of Ray in Canada, MURKIN 4442–4500, section 57, p. 61.

54. Ibid., p. 62.

55. See James Earl Ray interviewed by House Select Committee investigators, November 14, 1977, HSCA vol. XI, p. 38; HSCA vol. V, p. 16.

56. Lillian Spencer quoted by Huie, *He Slew the Dreamer*, p. 130; see also FBI summary of Ray in Canada, MURKIN 4442–4500, section 57, p. 62.

57. FBI summary of Ray in Canada, MURKIN 4442–4500, section 57, p. 62; HSCA vol. V, p. 20.

58. MLK Exhibit F-234, a reproduction of the Statutory Declaration in Lieu of Guarantor, HSCA vol. V, p. 17.

59. HSCA vol. V, p. 16.

60. Evert Clark, "F.B.I. Accuses Galt of a Conspiracy in Dr. King Slaying," *The New York Times*, April 18, 1968, p. 1.

61. Memo to Cartha DeLoach from Alex Rosen, June 5, 1968, MURKIN 4144–4250, section 53, p. 227.

62. Mrs. Szpakowska recounted in Frank, *An American Death*, p. 315.

63. See spot announcement for FBI, MURKIN 1576–1730, section 13, p. 327; see also Huie, *He Slew the Dreamer*, p. 134.

64. Huie, *He Slew the Dreamer*, pp. 134–35.

65. James Earl Ray interviewed by House Select Committee investigators, May 3, 1977, HSCA vol. X, p. 360.

66. James Earl Ray, 20,000 Words, HSCA vol. XII, p. 25.

67. Ibid., p. 26.

68. FBI summary information about Sun Fung Loo, MURKIN 4442–4500, section 57, p. 64; see also teletype to Director from Buffalo, June 6, 1968, MURKIN 4351–4440, section 55, p. 24.

69. HSCA vol. V, p. 18; see also memo to Stephen J. Pollack, June 13, 1968, MURKIN 4351–4440, section 55, p. 144.

70. Teletype to Director from Buffalo, June 6, 1968, MURKIN 4251–4350, section 54, p. 142; Lillian Spencer, 3-by-5 index card, Episode Index, Toronto, Attorney General File.

71. James Earl Ray, 20,000 Words, HSCA vol. XII, p. 26; James Earl Ray interviewed by House Select Committee investigators, May 3, 1977, HSCA vol. X, p. 361.

72. James Earl Ray, 20,000 Words, HSCA vol. XII, p. 26.

73. Teletype to Director from Buffalo, June 6, 1968, MURKIN 4251–4350, section 54, pp. 141–42; also memo to Cartha DeLoach from Alex Rosen, June 5, 1968, MURKIN 4144–4250, section 53, p. 227; Frank, *An American Death*, p. 316.

74. James Earl Ray, 20,000 Words, HSCA vol. XII, p. 27.

75. U.S. Department of Justice, Re: James Earl Ray, June 13, 1968, MURKIN 4576–4663, section 59, p. 116.

76. James Earl Ray interviewed by House Select Committee investigators, May 3, 1977, HSCA vol. X, p. 362; also U.S. Department of Justice, Re: James Earl Ray, June 13, 1968, MURKIN 4576–4663, section 59, p. 117; FBI summary information on Portugal and James Earl Ray, MURKIN 5451–5505, section 75, p. 257.

77. James Earl Ray interviewed by House Select Committee investigators, May 3, 1977, HSCA vol. X, p. 362.

78. U.S. Department of Justice, Re: James Earl Ray, June 13, 1968, contains summary of information provided by Gentil Soares, MURKIN 4576–4663, section 59, p. 116; see also memo to Alex Rosen from McGowan, June 13, 1968, MURKIN 4501–4575, section 58, p. 32.

79. U.S. Department of Justice, Re: James Earl Ray, June 13, 1968, contains summary of information provided by Gloria Sausa Riseiro, MURKIN 4576–4663, section 59, p. 120; Frank, *An American Death*, p. 317.

80. U.S. Department of Justice, Re: James Earl Ray, June 13, 1968, MURKIN 4576–4663, section 59, p. 120.

81. James Earl Ray, 20,000 Words, HSCA vol. XII, p. 27; see also HSCA vol. V, p. 23; see also James Earl Ray interviewed by House Select Committee investigators, May 3, 1977, HSCA vol. X, p. 363.

82. U.S. Department of Justice, Re: James Earl Ray, June 13, 1968, MURKIN 4576–4663, section 59, p. 121.

83. Teletype to Director from Legat, June 29, 1968, MURKIN 4697–4759, section 61, p. 169; see also U.S. Department of Justice, July 1, 1968, Re: James Earl Ray, MURKIN 4697–4759, section 61, pp. 183–84.

84. Teletype to Director from Legat, June 29, 1968, MURKIN 4697–4759, section 61, pp. 169–70; see also U.S. Department of Justice, July 1, 1968, Re: James Earl Ray, MURKIN 4697–4759, section 61, p. 184.

85. See, generally, U.S. Department of Justice, Re: James Earl Ray, June 13, 1968, MURKIN 4576–4663, section 59, pp. 121–22.

86. HSCA vol. V, p. 25.

87. Manuela Lopes quoted in Airtel to Director from Legat, London, June 9, 1968, MURKIN 4501–4575, section 58, p. 70 (in the Airtel her first name is redacted).

88. FBI summary information on Portugal and James Earl Ray, MURKIN 5451–5505, section 75, p. 257.

89. Ibid., p. 258.

90. U.S. Department of Justice, Re: James Earl Ray, June 13, 1968, MURKIN 4576–4663, section 59, pp. 117–18.

91. Airtel to Director from Legat, London, June 9, 1968, MURKIN 4501–4575, section 58, p. 70; HSCA vol. V, p. 23.

92. MLK Exhibit F-240, July 31, 1978, statement of Kenneth Thompson, HSCA vol. V, p. 39; HSCA vol. V, p. 25.

93. Ian Colvin 3-by-5 index card, 1 of 1, Episode Card File, London, Attorney General File.

94. Ian Colvin, "Dr. King Suspect Here 3 Weeks; Mystery Calls to Join Mercenaries," Daily Telegraph (London), June 10, 1968, p. 1.

95. Ibid.

96. See, generally, James Earl Ray interviewed by House Select Committee investigators, May 3, 1977, HSCA vol. X, p. 368; also MLK Exhibit F-240, July 31, 1978, statement of Kenneth Thompson, HSCA vol. V, p. 39; HSCA vol. V, p. 42; see also Episode Card File, London, Attorney General File.

97. MLK Exhibit F-240, July 31, 1978, statement of Kenneth Thompson, HSCA vol. V, p. 39; HSCA vol. V, p. 43.

98. Colvin, "Dr. King Suspect Here 3 Weeks," p. 1.

99. Ian Colvin 3-by-5 index card, 2 of 2, Episode Card File, London, Attorney General File; Colvin, "Dr. King Suspect Here 3 Weeks," p. 1.

100. FBI summary sheet, MURKIN 4351–4440, section 55, p. 148.

101. MLK Exhibit F-240, July 31, 1978, statement of Kenneth Thompson, HSCA vol. V, p. 39; Airtel of July 11, 1968, MURKIN 4901–4982, section 66, p. 45; HSCA vol. V, p. 39; see also Janet Elizabeth Nassau, 3-by-5 index card, Episode Card Index, Attorney General File.

102. MLK Exhibit F-66, HSCA vol. V, p. 58.

103. See MLK Exhibit F-240, July 31, 1978, statement of Kenneth Thompson, and MLK Exhibit F-241, August 1, 1978, statement of John George Batchelor, and August 1, 1978, statement of Peter Arthur Elliott, HSCA vol. V, pp. 34–57; see MURKIN 4697–4759, section 61, p. 118.

104. Huie, He Slew the Dreamer, p. 136.

105. Anna Thomas quoted in Huie, He Slew the Dreamer, pp. 140–41.

106. Anna Elizabette Thomas, 3-by-5 index card, 1 of 2, Episode Card Index, Attorney General File.

107. MLK Exhibit F-240, July 31, 1978, statement of Kenneth Thompson, HSCA vol. V, p. 39; HSCA vol. V, p. 45.

108. Anna Thomas quoted in Huie, *He Slew the Dreamer,* p. 141; see also MLK Exhibit F-240, July 31, 1978, statement of Kenneth Thompson, HSCA vol. V, p. 39; HSCA vol. V, p. 41; Anna Elizabette Thomas, 3-by-5 index card, 2 of 2, Episode Card Index, Attorney General File.

109. HSCA vol. V, p. 59.

110. Anna Thomas quoted in Huie, *He Slew the Dreamer,* p. 141.

111. Anna Elizabette Thomas, 3-by-5 index card, 2 of 2, Episode Card Index, Attorney General File.

28: "The Legal Truth"

1. Ian McDonald, "Conspiracy Suspicions in King Case," *Daily Telegraph,* June 5, 1971.

2. William Bradford Huie, "Why James Earl Ray Murdered Dr. King," *Look,* April 1969.

3. Publicity release of *The Greatest Police Fraud Ever: The James Earl Ray Hoax* by Joachim Joesten, MURKIN 5451–5505, section 75, pp. 175–78.

4. Harold Weisberg, *Frame-Up* (New York: Outerbridge & Dienstfrey, 1969).

5. One of the best discussions of J. B. Stoner, his views, actions, and reprehensible behavior is covered by Melissa Fay Greene, *The Temple Bombing* (New York: Addison-Wesley, 1996); as for Stoner's replacement as Ray's lawyer, see "Rightist Is Hired as Ray's Lawyer," *The New York Times,* March 21, 1969.

6. Testimony of Jerry Ray, November 30, 1978, HSCA vol. VII, p. 328.

7. Frank, *An American Death,* p. 402n.

8. MLK Exhibit F-594, letter from Jerry Ray to two radio talk-show hosts, Mickey and Teddy on Ring Radio (undated but written during Stoner's 1972 campaign for U.S. Senator), on official Stoner campaign stationery. The letter provides rather strong evidence of Jerry Ray's deep-seated racial hatred. It reads in its entirety:

I guess you could call this a fan letter as i usually wouldn't waste my time writing to a couple of Jew Devils, but been you two are in mourning for them Eleven Jews that got done in by the Arabs in Munich then i figured that i owed you a letter.

The only reason the Jews has so much power is on account of there money but eventually the Jews push there luck a little to far, as i am sure you know the Jews has been run out of every country they have ever been in and they will eventually will be run out of the U.S. it might take another 50 or 75 years but the Jews are like the Nigger beast, give them a rope and they will hang themselves.

I am sure when history is written my Brother James Ray, and the Hon. Gov. George Wallace will be Heroes alongside of JB Stoner.

Continued success with your show as you awaken people to the facts of the Jews.

The Jews are behind Women Liberation, Since the NAACP was founded by a Jew has always been the head of it, that Mangy Jew Devil Kivie Kaplan is presently President of the NAACP. I forgot to mention that Sirhan Sirhan will also down in history as a hero, although Robert Kennedy wasnt a Jew but he is worse he sold the Arabs out for the Jew dollar.

Robert Kennedy was worse than a Jew if that's possible, he framed up on Hoffa, and sold the Arabs out so i celebrated when he joined the rest of his kind in hell.

I hope you still have your Skull caps on, you might just as well as keep them on as i believe the Arabs will stop at Eleven. Continued success and i hope you stay on [the air] indefinitely.

[signed] Your Fan, Jerry Ray.

Before the House Select Committee, Jerry said the letter was "a joke."

9. J. B. Stoner quoted in "Ray Lawyer Tells Who Killed King," *The Memphis Press-Scimitar,* August 9, 1969.

10. MLK Exhibit F-614, HSCA vol. VII, p. 453.

11. "At Ray's Request, a Brother Is Barred as Prison Visitor," *The New York Times*, September 5, 1969.

12. Testimony of Jerry Ray, November 30, 1978, HSCA vol. VII, pp. 453–56.

13. "James Earl Ray's Brother Persecuted," by Jerry Ray, untitled journal, Jerry Ray file, Miscellaneous folder, Box 5, McMillan/Southern Historical Collection.

14. For their first application for a new trial, see "A Retrial for Ray Asked in Memphis by New Lawyers," *The New York Times*, April 8, 1969.

15. Martin Waldron, "Ray Fails in Move for Second Trial," *The New York Times*, May 27, 1969, p. 1; in an unusually personal note for coverage in the *Times*, Waldron called Ray "the pudgy 41-year-old convict," noting that Ray's weight "has risen from 170 to almost 190 in two months."

16. "Tennessee Court Bars Ray's Plea for New Trial," *The New York Times*, January 9, 1970.

17. "Ray Says Lawyer Promised Pardon After Guilty Plea," *The New York Times*, May 9, 1970.

18. "Ray Loses Bid to Block Publication of Huie Book," *The New York Times*, December 2, 1969.

19. U.S. Circuit Court of Appeals, *Ray v. Foreman*, April 29, 1971, 441 Federal Reporter 2d, 1266.

20. James Earl Ray, *Who Killed Martin Luther King?*, p. 143.

21. Ibid., pp. 146–47.

22. "Ray's Lawyers Open Bid for a New Trial," *The New York Times*, December 5, 1972.

23. *Ray v. Rose*, Civil Action No. C-74-166, U.S. District Court for the Western District of Tennessee.

24. Memorandum Decision, *Ray v. Rose*, 373 F. Supp. 687 (1973).

25. *Ray v. Rose*, 491 S. 2d 285 (1974); see also "Ray's Guilty Plea in Dr. King's Death Will Be Reviewed," *The New York Times*, January 30, 1974.

26. *Ray v. Rose*, 417 U.S. 936 (1974).

27. See, generally, Orville Hancock and Kay Pittman Black, "High Court Clears Way for Ray to Change Plea," *The Memphis Press-Scimitar*, June 3, 1974, p. 1; also *Daily Telegraph* (London), "Dr. King Case Likely to Be Reopened," June 4, 1974, in which the correspondent reported that the King assassination "is almost certain to be reopened." Those reactions were not atypical for many reporters covering the case.

28. Memorandum Decision, Civil Action No. C-74-166, U.S. District Court for the Western District of Tennessee.

29. U.S. Court of Appeals, No. 75-1795, filed May 10, 1976, 535 F2d 966.

30. Testimony of William C. Sullivan, November 1, 1975, Senate Select Committee to Study Governmental Operations with Respect to Intelligence Activities.

31. Senate Report No. 94-775, Final Report of the Select Committee to Study Governmental Operations with Respect to Intelligence Activities, Book II, p. 11.

32. Report of the Department of Justice Task Force to Review the FBI Martin Luther King, Jr., Security and Assassination Investigations, January 11, 1977, p. 97.

33. James Earl Ray, *Who Killed Martin Luther King?*, p. 205.

34. *Playboy*, September 1977, sidebar, "James Earl Ray's Lie-Detector Test," p. 71.

35. *Playboy*, September 1977, p. 176.

36. James Earl Ray, *Who Killed Martin Luther King?*, pp. 171–72.

37. Mark Lane and Dick Gregory, *Code Name "Zorro."* Zorro, Spanish for fox, was the code name the FBI assigned to Martin Luther King, Jr.

38. Ray, *Who Killed Martin Luther King?*, p. 178.

39. Interview with Chris Gugas, November 12, 1995; author's review of his seven-page curriculum vitae.

40. James Earl Ray quoted by Chris Gugas, *The Silent Witness: A Polygraphist's Casebook* (Englewood Cliffs, N.J.: Prentice Hall, 1979), p. 228.

41. Ibid., p. 233.

42. Ibid., p. 237.

43. HSCA Rpt., p. 557, fn. 16.

44. HSCA Rpt., p. 4.

45. Ibid.

46. James Earl Ray quoted in "Ray Calls Panel Finds Hoax," *The Commercial Appeal*, January 15, 1979, p. 3.

47. "Ray Loses New Trial Bid," *The Commercial Appeal*, June 23, 1979.

48. "Ray Suit Dismissed," *The Commercial Appeal*, February 9, 1980.

49. "Ray Files Libel Suit in Federal Court," *The Commercial Appeal*, July 2, 1980; "Libel Suit Ruling Favors Rep. Ford," *The Commercial Appeal*, February 20, 1981.

50. "Ray Given Rebuff," *The Commercial Appeal*, June 20, 1980.

51. The Tennessee Bureau of Investigation and many newspapers originally reported the spelling as Alkabulan. According to Ron Bishop, an administrative assistant in the Corrections Department, it is actually Alke-bulan. Ray, in *Who Killed Martin Luther King?*, spells it Alke-Bulan. However, the author has chosen the spelling listed in the charter of the organization, Alkebu-lan.

52. James W. Brosnan, "Ray Attack Aimed at Publicity, Not at Murder, Officials Agree," *The Commercial Appeal*, June 6, 1981.

53. Ibid.

54. "Ray Says Polygraph Test Was Rigged, Files Suit," *The Commercial Appeal*, March 30, 1982.

55. Tom Madden, "Ray Files Suit; Seeks 'Day in Court,' " *The Commercial Appeal*, May 18, 1982.

56. "Panel Denies Ray Parole Hearing," *The Commercial Appeal*, May 28, 1982.

29: The Mock Trial

1. William Pepper, *Orders to Kill: The Truth Behind the Murder of Martin Luther King* (New York: Carroll & Graf, 1995), pp. 148–50.

2. Ibid, p. 149.

3. Ibid, p. 150.

4. Interview with Ken Herman, August 6, 1997.

5. Pepper, *Orders to Kill*, p. 161.

6. HSCA Rpt., p. 515.

7. Pepper, *Orders to Kill*, pp. 179–80.

8. Interview with John Billings, August 7, 1997.

9. Interview with Ken Herman, August 6, 1997.

10. Ibid.

11. Pepper, *Orders to Kill*, p. 262.

12. "Death Scene of Dr. King is Changed," *The Memphis Press-Scimitar*, August 7, 1968. Reported in the article, in part, is, "If the jury in the James Earl Ray trial should be shown the scene of the slaying, the view will be different from what the killer saw. A heavy growth of trees behind the rooming house at 422½ S. Main, from which an assassin shot Dr. Martin Luther King Jr., has been cut down. The nearly 10-foot high embankment which had trees and growth has been stripped, with only tree stumps remaining to show what the scene was like that April evening. . . . A clerk at the Lorraine said the trees were cut down last week." The area around the crime scene was largely unkempt before the August pruning. It is possible, however, that city crews were dispatched to the area immediately after the murder to remove some of the overgrowth that might otherwise have hindered investigators who were

carefully searching the area. However, if such work took place, it was obviously not even considered a large enough assignment to list in the city records, and certainly was not like the major cutting and clear-up that was charged by Pepper and others.

13. Interview with John Billings, August 7, 1997.
14. Pepper, *Orders to Kill*, p. 308.
15. Interview with Jack Saltman, July 14, 1997.
16. Interview with John Billings, August 7, 1997.
17. Interview with Ken Herman, August 6, 1997.

30: The Confession

1. *Prime Time Live*, December 16, 1993.
2. Interview with Lewis Garrison, June 12, 1997.
3. John Billings quoted by Marc Perrusquia, "Pierotti Calls Claim of Plot in King Assassination 'A Sham,'" *The Commercial Appeal*, December 12, 1993, p. A1.
4. Interview with Ken Herman, August 6, 1997.
5. Ibid.
6. Ibid.
7. Ibid.
8. Ibid.
9. Supplement Ent #12, Martin Luther King, Jr., MC, 39, Homicide No. 3367, "Re: Interview of Customers in Jim's Grill, 418 S. Main on April 4, 1968," p. 1612, Attorney General File.
10. FBI Statement of Loyd Jowers, April 5, 1968, MURKIN ME Sub. D, section 1, p. 179.
11. Statement of Loyd Jowers, April 7, 1968, questioned by Lt. J. D. Hamby, National Archives Box 13, folder 34, p. 1435, OPR FBI.
12. Interview with Loyd Jowers by George R. King and John Getz, investigation for Mr. Stanton, February 6, 1969, Attorney General File.
13. Supplement Ent #12, Martin Luther King, Jr., MC, 39, Homicide No. 3367, "Re: Interview of Customers in Jim's Grill, 418 S. Main on April 4, 1968," p. 1612, Attorney General File.
14. Statement of Loyd Jowers, April 7, 1968, questioned by Lt. J. D. Hamby, National Archives Box 13, folder 34, p. 1438, OPR FBI.
15. Pepper, *Orders to Kill*, p. 100.
16. FBI statement of Loyd Jowers, April 5, 1968, MURKIN ME Sub. D, section 1, p. 179.
17. Interview with Loyd Jowers by George R. King and John Getz, investigation for Mr. Stanton, February 6, 1969, Attorney General File.
18. Pepper, *Orders to Kill*, p. 101.
19. Ibid.
20. Ibid., p. 102.
21. Memphis Police Department, Criminal Investigation Division, April 5, 1968, R&I Offense Number, 391-825, Attorney General File.
22. Memo of February 12, 1969, interview with Betty Spates, John Carlisle and Clyde Venson as investigators.
23. Weisberg, *Martin Luther King: The Assassination*, pp. 184, 273; Lane, *Code Name "Zorro,"* p. 167.
24. *Ray v. Rose*, October 23, 1974.
25. Interview with Mark Glankler, August 8, 1997.
26. Willie Akins, a Jowers associate, told *The Tennessean* on December 15, 1993, that Jowers had confided to him that he hired a mentally "slow" black laborer, Frank Holt, to shoot King from the bushes behind Jim's Grill.
27. FBI interview with Frank Holt, April 17, 1968, Attorney General File.
28. See, generally, Pepper, *Orders to Kill*, pp. 319–20.

29. *The Tennessean* arranged to have the polygraph given to Holt on December 18, 1993, and he passed completely on all key questions.

30. Marc Perrusquia, "Loyd Jowers: A Chronology of Statements," *The Commercial Appeal*, April 4, 1997, p. A10.

31. Pepper, *Orders to Kill*, p. 320.

32. Interview with Lewis Garrison, June 12, 1997.

33. Pepper, *Orders to Kill*, p. 321.

34. Affidavit of Betty Spates, March 8, 1994, Exhibit 37, p. 3; *Ray v. Dutton, Warden*, Criminal Courts, Shelby County.

35. Pepper, *Orders to Kill*, p. 341.

36. Interview with Wayne Chastain, August 4, 1997.

37. Affidavit of Betty Spates, March 8, 1994, Exhibit 37, pp. 3–4, *Ray v. Dutton, Warden*, Criminal Courts, Shelby County.

38. Review of Attorney General File; interview with John Campbell, April 12, 1997; statement of Alta Washington in *The Tennessean*, 1994; statement of Betty Spates, January 25, 1994, to Glankler and Simmons, p. 4; statement of Bobbie Jean Smith Balfour given to criminal investigators Mark Glankler, with the district attorney general, and John Simmons, with the Tennessee Bureau of Investigations, January 18, 1994, p. 12; transcript of telephone conversation between Bobbie Jean Smith Balfour and Betty Spates, January 21, 1994, copy provided by the district attorney general's office, pp. 4–5.

39. Statement of Loyd Jowers to Memphis Police, April 7, 1968, p. 3, Attorney General File.

40. The Spates statement, as of the time of this writing, December 1997, has not been released publicly, but a copy was provided to the author by the district attorney general's office.

41. Statement of Betty Spates Eldridge given to criminal investigators Mark Glankler, with the district attorney general, and John Simmons, with the Tennessee Bureau of Investigations, January 25, 1994, p. 6.

42. Ibid., p. 7.

43. Ibid., pp. 5–8; interview with Mark Glankler, August 8, 1997.

44. Statement of Betty Spates Eldridge given to criminal investigators Mark Glankler, with the district attorney general, and John Simmons, with the Tennessee Bureau of Investigations, January 25, 1994, p. 12.

45. Ibid., p. 12.

46. Ibid., pp. 13, 23.

47. Pepper, *Orders to Kill*, p. 342.

48. Ibid.

49. Statement of Bobbie Jean Smith Balfour given to criminal investigators Mark Glankler, with the district attorney general, and John Simmons, with the Tennessee Bureau of Investigations, January 18, 1994, p. 5; copy of statement made available to author by the district attorney general's office.

50. Ibid., p. 7.

51. Ibid., pp. 8–9.

52. Transcript of telephone conversation between Bobbie Jean Smith Balfour and Betty Spates, January 21, 1994, copy provided by the district attorney general's office, pp. 4–5.

53. Ibid., p. 9.

54. Ibid., p. 19.

55. Ibid., p. 8.

56. Ibid., p. 18.

57. Departmental Communication, April 12, 1968, prepared by N. E. Zachary, chief of homicide, Memphis Police, Re: Rev. Martin Luther King Murder, Box 13, p. 3333, OPR FBI.

58. HSCA Rpt., p. 507.

59. Departmental Communication, April 12, 1968, prepared by N. E. Zachary, chief of homicide, Memphis Police, Re: Rev. Martin Luther King Murder, Box 13, p. 3333, OPR FBI.

60. See memo to the Attorney General from the Director, April 25, 1968, MURKIN 2076–2150, section 18, pp. 85–86.

61. See, generally, Departmental Communication, April 26, 1968, prepared by N. E. Zachary, chief of homicide, Memphis Police, Re: Memo Number 145, Box 13, p. 3385, OPR FBI; FBI interview with Frank Camilla Liberto, April 19, 1968, MURKIN ME Sub. D, section 3, pp. 37–39; FBI interview with James William Latch, April 19, 1968, MURKIN ME Sub. D, section 3, pp. 40–41.

62. Interview with N. E. Zachary, June 13, 1997.

63. HSCA Rpt., p. 506.

64. Memo to Attorney General from Director, April 20, 1968, MURKIN 44-38861-1816; also staff summary of John McFerren interview, March 12, 1977, HSCA, MLK document 260200; see also FBI interview with John McFerren, April 18, 1968, MURKIN ME Sub. D, section 3, p. 50.

65. Memorandum of interview with John McFerren, Somerville, Tennessee, July 9, 1976, Box 13, OPR FBI.

66. Ibid.; see also FBI interview with John McFerren, April 8, 1968, MURKIN ME Sub. D, section 1, p. 36.

67. John McFerren interview, March 12, 1977, HSCA, MLK document 260200; see also FBI interview with John McFerren, April 8, 1968, MURKIN ME Sub. D, section 1, p. 37; see also MURKIN 2076–2150, section 18, pp. 77, 80.

68. John McFerren interview, March 12, 1977, HSCA, MLK document 260200.

69. FBI interview with John McFerren, April 18, 1968, MURKIN ME Sub. D, section 3, p. 51.

70. Memo to Cartha DeLoach from Alex Rosen, April 22, 1968, MURKIN 2076–2150, section 18, p. 76; see also memo to DeLoach from Rosen, April 20, 1968, MURKIN 1731–1820, section 14, pp. 183–84.

71. FBI interview with John McFerren, April 18, 1968, MURKIN ME Sub. D, section 3, p. 52.

72. Memorandum of interview with John McFerren, Somerville, Tennessee, July 9, 1976, Box 13, OPR FBI.

73. Ibid.

74. Interview with David Kaywood, June 12, 1997.

75. Memorandum of interview with John McFerren, Somerville, Tennessee, July 9, 1976, Box 13, OPR FBI.

76. See generally memorandum of telephone call from John McFerren, November 16, 1976, by James Walker, attorney at Department of Justice, Box 13, OPR FBI.

77. HSCA Rpt., pp. 507–8.

78. See statement reproduced in Lane, Code Name "Zorro," pp. 166–67.

79. James McCraw statement, October 24, 1992, Ray v. Jowers, et al. In August 1994, Pepper filed a $46-million civil lawsuit against Jowers.

80. Memo to Mssrs. Dwyer, Beasley, and Carlisle Re: James Murphy McCraw, also known as James N. McGraw, November 8, 1968, with attached documents, Attorney General File.

81. Interview with Jim Beasley, August 8, 1997.

82. Interview with Mark Glankler, August 8, 1997.

83. Interview with Robert Ferguson, October 1, 1997.

84. Interview with Lewis Garrison, June 12, 1997.

85. Ibid.

86. Ibid.

87. Statement of Loyd Jowers, April 7, 1968, Memphis police department, Box 12, Folder 34, p. 1435, OPR FBI.

88. FBI statement of Harold E. Parker, April 15, 1968, MURKIN ME Sub. D, section 1, pp. 91–92.

89. Dexter King quoted by Arthur Brice, "Ray Lawyer Points to Statements About Hit Man," *Atlanta Journal-Constitution,* September 21, 1997, p. A15.

90. Interview with John Campbell, October 10, 1977.

31: Exit Raoul

1. Dexter King quoted in "Dexter King Says 'Raoul' Has Been Found," *San Francisco Chronicle,* April 7, 1997, p. A7.

2. Interview with Lewis Garrison, June 12, 1997.

3. Interview with Ken Herman, August 6, 1997.

4. Interviews with Ken Herman, August 6 and 7, 1997.

5. William Pepper, *Orders to Kill,* pp. 373–77.

6. Interview with Ken Herman, August 6, 1997.

7. Interview with Jack Saltman, July 14, 1997.

8. Interviews with Ken Herman, August 6, 1997, and Jack Saltman, July 14, 1997.

9. Interview with Ken Herman, August 6, 1997.

10. Ibid.

11. Interview with Jack Saltman, July 14, 1997.

12. Interview with Ken Herman, August 6, 1997.

13. Ibid.

14. Ibid.

15. Interview with Jack Saltman, July 14, 1997.

16. Interview with John Billings, August 7, 1997.

17. Interview with Ken Herman, August 6, 1997.

18. Interview with Jack Saltman, July 14, 1997.

19. Interviews with Ken Herman, August 6, 1997, and John Billings, August 7, 1997.

20. Interview with Ken Herman, August 6, 1997.

21. Ibid.

22. Interview with Jack Saltman, July 14, 1997.

23. Interviews with Ken Herman, August 6, 1997, and Jack Saltman, July 14, 1997.

24. Interview with Jack Saltman, July 14, 1997.

25. James Earl Ray interviewed by *Playboy,* September 1977, p. 79.

26. HSCA Rpt., pp. 510–11.

27. Ibid., pp. 514–15; see also Melanson, *The Murkin Conspiracy,* pp. 46–49.

28. HSCA Rpt., pp. 511–12.

29. Interview with Ken Herman, August 6, 1997.

30. Interview with Jack Saltman, July 14, 1997; confirmed by interview with John Billings, August 7, 1997.

31. Marc Perrusquia, "Who Killed King? 'I'm Innocent,' Insists Raoul," *The Commercial Appeal,* January 26, 1997, p. A1.

32. Interview with Jack Saltman, July 14, 1997.

33. William Pepper quoted by Christopher Sullivan, "Martin Luther King's Murder Shrouded In Conspiracy Theories," *Los Angeles Times,* January 21, 1996, Bulldog Edition, p. A1.

34. William Pepper, *Orders to Kill,* pp. 343–44.

35. Interview with John Campbell, October 30, 1997.

36. Ibid.; also interview with Mark Glankler, August 8, 1997.

37. Interview with Mark Glankler, August 8, 1997.

38. Interview with Raul, October 29, 1997.

39. Ibid.

40. Interview with Mark Glankler, August 8, 1997.

41. Ibid.

42. The following section of disclosures about Raul Mirabal is based upon investigative work by Mark Glankler, and confirmed independently by the author through his own interview with Raul, and review of documentation including work records, interviews with colleagues, and pension contributions. The district attorney general in Memphis maintains copies of those records.

43. Interview with Raul, October 29, 1997.

44. Author's review of Raul Mirabal's work records, made available by Janet Mattick, Esq.

45. Interview with Jack Saltman, July 14, 1997.

46. Interview with John Billings, August 7, 1997.

47. Interview with Raul, October 29, 1997.

48. Ibid.; interview with Ken Herman, August 6, 1997.

49. Interview with Raul's daughter, October 29, 1997.

50. Interview with Raul, October 29, 1997.

51. Ibid.

52. Interview with Janet Mattick, October 29, 1997.

53. Interview with Ed McDonald, October 29, 1997.

54. Interview with Raul's daughter, October 29, 1997.

55. Interview with Janet Mattick, October 29, 1997.

56. Interview with Raul, October 29, 1997.

57. Ibid.

58. Interview with Ken Herman, August 6, 1997.

59. Interview with Jack Saltman, July 14, 1997.

60. Ibid.

61. Interview with John Campbell, August 5, 1997.

62. Interview with John Pierotti, June 16, 1997.

63. Pepper, *Orders to Kill*, p. 373.

64. Interview with John Campbell, October 30, 1997.

65. Interview and review of file with John Campbell, October 30, 1997.

66. Interview with Jack Saltman, July 14, 1997.

67. Interview with Ken Herman, August 6, 1997.

68. Ibid.; also interview with John Billings, August 7, 1997.

69. Interview with John Billings, August 7, 1997.

70. Interview with Ken Herman, August 6, 1997.

71. E-mail from John Campbell to author, October 24, 1997.

72. Interview with John Billings, August 7, 1997.

73. Interview with Jack Saltman, July 14, 1997.

74. Interview with April Ferguson, August 19, 1997.

75. Interview with Gene Stanley, July 30, 1997.

76. Interview with Sid Carthew, October 30, 1997.

77. "BNP Organiser Emerges as Witness for Killer of Martin Luther King," *Searchlight*, January 1996.

78. Ibid.; see also "Pepper's Theory Sneezed At," *Searchlight*, 1997.

79. Interview with Ken Herman, August 6, 1997.

32: Military Hoax

1. See William Pepper, *Orders to Kill*, pp. 462–95.

2. Steve Tompkins, "Army Feared King, Secretly Watched Him," *The Commercial Appeal*, March 21, 1993, p. A1.

3. See John Branston, "Double Exposure," *The Memphis Flyer*, July 17–23, 1997, p. 15; also Pepper, *Orders to Kill*, p. 411.

4. Interview with Rudi Gresham, June 30, 1997.

5. Interview with Rudi Gresham, July 16, 1997.

6. Interview with Rudi Gresham, June 30, 1997.

7. Pepper, *Orders to Kill*, pp. 418–19.

8. Interview with Rudi Gresham, June 30, 1997.

9. Letter from Ola L. Mize to Rudi Gresham, September 29, 1995.

10. Interview with Rudi Gresham, June 30, 1997; interview with Lee Mize, July 17, 1997; also, three-page letter, Lee Mize to Rudi Gresham, September 29, 1995.

11. Pepper, *Orders to Kill*, pp. 420, 475.

12. Ibid., p. 420.

13. Ibid., pp. 428, 485.

14. Interview with Rudi Gresham, June 30, 1997; interview with Ian Sutherland, July 17, 1997.

15. Pepper, *Orders to Kill*, p. 418.

16. Interview with Rudi Gresham, June 30, 1997; also review of transfer file sheets, at home of Rudi Gresham, for 1967 and 1968.

17. Pepper, *Orders to Kill*, photo section.

18. Interview with Daniel Ellsberg, July 17, 1997.

19. Daniel Ellsberg, Memo for the Record, November 8, 1996, p. 1 of 2.

20. Interview with Daniel Ellsberg, July 17, 1997; see also Daniel Ellsberg, Memo for the Record, November 8, 1996, p. 1 of 2.

21. Interview with Daniel Ellsberg, July 17, 1997.

22. Interview with Rudi Gresham, June 30, 1997.

23. Interview with Rudi Gresham, July 16, 1997.

24. Interview with Henry Cobb, July 17, 1997.

25. Ibid.

26. Interview with Rudi Gresham, June 30, 1997.

27. See, generally, letter from the adjutant general to Major General (ret.) Henry Cobb, June 3, 1997.

28. Pepper, *Orders to Kill*, pp. 428–30.

29. See Morning Reports, 20th SFG, Jackson, Mississippi, April 1968.

30. Interview with Rudi Gresham, June 30, 1997. The 20th was actually switched from the 5th Rangers Group in 1959. There was a 5th Special Forces in 1960. Under an order of April 28, 1961, groups were established, such as 177, 178, 179. The group 184, part of the original 5th Rangers team, existed for one year. Coincidentally, Ian Sutherland was on the roster as the executive officer of the 184 unit. See, generally, Extract, Office of the Adjutant General, New Orleans, Special Orders, Number 131, July 19, 1960, and Number 74, April 28, 1961.

31. Conversation recounted by interviews with Rudi Gresham, July 16, 1997, and Billy Eidson, July 17, 1997.

32. Interview with Billy Eidson, July 17, 1997.

33. Interview with Rudi Gresham, July 16, 1997.

34. Interview with Billy Eidson, July 17, 1997.

35. Interviews with Rudi Gresham, June 30, 1997, and Ray Davis ("It was ridiculous when I examined it") and Harry Summers, Jr. ("A fake and not a very good one at that"), July 17, 1997.

36. Interview with Jimmy Dean, July 16, 1997.

37. William Pepper, *Turning Point*, ABC, June 19, 1997.

38. Interview with Billy Eidson, July 17, 1997.

39. Interview with Rudi Gresham, July 16, 1997; interviews with Billy Eidson, Lee Mize, and Henry Cobb, July 17, 1997.

40. Interview with Rudi Gresham, June 30, 1997.

41. Interview with Rudi Gresham, July 16, 1997; see also Marc Perrusquia, "Phony, Say Experts, of Claims by Ray's Lawyer of King Plot," *The Commercial Appeal*, June 28, 1997, p. B1.

42. Ibid.

43. Steve Tompkins quoted by John Branston, "Double Exposure," *The Memphis Flyer,* July 17–23, 1997, p. 16; interview with Rudi Gresham, June 30, 1997; interview with Steve Tompkins, August 20, 1997.

44. Conversation with Marc Perrusquia, July 24, 1997.

45. Marc Perrusquia, "Conspiracy Theories Run into Contradictions," published on November 30, 1997, on *The Commercial Appeal* Internet site.

33: Ray's Last Dance

1. ABC *Nightline,* April 3, 1977, transcript 87040301-j07.

2. Interview with Judge Joe Brown, August 3, 1997.

3. Ibid.

4. Ibid.

5. Interview with John Campbell, August 4, 1997.

6. Interview with Judge Joe Brown, August 3, 1997.

7. Ibid.

8. Jerry Ray quoted by Dwight Lewis, "Ray Brother Wants It Known: He Had No Part in Killing," *The Tennessean,* January 4, 1998, p. 20.

9. FBI interviews with Bessie Brewer, April 10, 1968, MURKIN 2322, section 20, pp. 26–28, and MURKIN ME, Sub. D, section 1.

10. FBI statement of Ralph Meredith Carpenter, April 5, 1968, MURKIN ME Sub. D, section 1, pp. 110–11.

11. Frances B. Thompson interviewed by the FBI, April 5, 1968, MURKIN ME, Sub. D, section 1, p. 19.

12. Elizabeth Copeland interviewed by the FBI, April 5, 1968, MURKIN ME, Sub. D, section 1, p. 18.

13. Charles Hardy Hurley interviewed by the FBI, April 5, 1968, MURKIN ME, Sub. D, section 1, p. 4.

14. FBI statements of Kenneth W. Foster, April 12, 1968, and William Zenie (Bill) Reed, April 13, 1968, MURKIN ME, Sub. D, section 1, pp. 185–86, 197–98.

15. Billy Kyles and Chauncey Eskridge, both in their FBI interviews, based their time estimates on when they remember King going onto the balcony. Since King was shot at 6:01, the time he went outside starts the clock. Kyles, who was visiting King, said they broke up at 5:55, but Eskridge was certain that King stepped into full view as early as 5:45.

16. Later the police cut away part of the windowsill, suspecting a small indentation may have been made by the rifle resting there. The author spoke to Robert Frazier, the FBI expert who examined the sill in 1968, and he said the sill consisted of "decomposed wood, and when it was pressed down it receives the imprint of the polishing mark of the rifle. It could have been made by light contact with the type of barrel of the Remington rifle." But Frazier admitted that there was not "sufficient detail" to make a comparison. "If it was from the rifle," he says, "the rifle just glanced or tapped it. It was not deep enough for the rifle to have rested on it."

17. "Trip to Quincy, Illinois, 10/15 thru 10/17/69," notes made October 20, 1969, by George McMillan, no folder, Box 1—Correspondence Related to Book Research, Research Files on Ewing, McMillan/Southern Historical Collection.

Bibliography

Books

Instances in which a second edition is listed refer to the paperback used by the author for research.

Abernathy, Ralph David. *And the Walls Came Tumbling Down.* New York: Harper & Row, 1989.

Beifuss, Joan Turner. *At the River I Stand: Memphis, the 1968 Strike, and Martin Luther King.* Memphis: B & W Books, 1985.

Bishop, Jim. *The Days of Martin Luther King, Jr.* New York: G. P. Putnam's Sons, 1971.

Blair, Clay, Jr. *The Strange Case of James Earl Ray: The Man Who Murdered Martin Luther King.* New York: Bantam Books, 1969.

Clarke, James W. *American Assassins: The Darker Side of Politics.* Princeton, N.J.: Princeton University Press, 1982.

Dorman, Michael. *King of the Courtroom: Percy Foreman for the Defense.* New York: Delacorte Press, 1969.

Frank, Gerold. *An American Death: The True Story of the Assassination of Dr. Martin Luther King, Jr., and the Greatest Manhunt of Our Time.* Garden City, N.Y.: Doubleday & Co., 1972.

Friedly, Michael, and David Gallen. *Martin Luther King, Jr.: The FBI File.* New York: Carroll & Graf, 1993.

Garrow, David J. *The FBI and Martin Luther King, Jr.: From "Solo" to Memphis.* New York: W. W. Norton & Company, 1981.

———. *Bearing the Cross: Martin Luther King, Jr., and the Southern Christian Leadership Conference.* New York: William Morrow and Co., 1986.

Goode, Stephen. *Assassination! Kennedy, King, Kennedy.* New York: Franklin Watts, 1979.

Greene, Melissa Fay. *The Temple Bombing.* Reading, Mass.: Addison-Wesley Publishing, 1996.

Gugas, Chris. *The Silent Witness: A Polygraphist's Casebook.* Englewood Cliffs, N.J.: Prentice-Hall, 1979.

Huie, William Bradford. *He Slew the Dreamer: My Search, with James Earl Ray, for the Truth About the Murder of Martin Luther King.* New York: Delacorte Press, 1970.

King, Coretta Scott. *My Life with Martin Luther King, Jr.* New York: Holt, Rinehart and Winston, 1969.

Lane, Mark, and Dick Gregory. *Code Name "Zorro": The Murder of Martin Luther King, Jr.* Englewood Cliffs, N.J.: Prentice-Hall, 1977.

Leek, Sybil, and Bert R. Sugar. *The Assassination Chain.* New York: Corwin Books, 1976.

Linedecker, Clifford L. *Prison Groupies.* New York: Windsor Publishing Corp., 1993.

Lomax, Louis E. *To Kill a Black Man.* Los Angeles: Holloway House, 1968.

McMillan, George. *The Making of an Assassin: The Life of James Earl Ray.* Boston: Little, Brown and Co., 1976.

Melanson, Philip H. *The Murkin Conspiracy: An Investigation into the Assassination of Dr. Martin Luther King, Jr.* New York: Praeger, 1989.

O'Reilly, Kenneth. *"Racial Matters": The FBI's Secret File on Black America, 1960–1972.* New York: The Free Press, 1989.

Pepper, William F. *Orders to Kill: The Truth Behind the Murder of Martin Luther King.* New York: Carroll & Graf, 1995.

Peterson, John J. *Into the Cauldron.* Clinton, Md.: Clavier House Publishing, 1973.

Ray, James Earl. *Tennessee Waltz: The Making of a Political Prisoner.* St. Andrews, Tenn.: Saint Andrew's Press, 1987.

———. *Who Killed Martin Luther King? The True Story by the Alleged Assassin.* Washington, D.C.: National Press Books, 1992.

Rowan, Carl T. *Breaking the Barriers: A Memoir.* Boston: Little, Brown and Co., 1991.

Seigenthaler, John (with contributors James Squires, John Hemphill, and Frank Ritter). *A Search for Justice.* Nashville, Tenn.: Aurora Publishers, 1971.

Select Committee on Assassinations, U.S. House of Representatives. *The Final Assassinations Report.* New York: Bantam, 1979.

Sparrow, Gerald. *The Great Assassins.* New York: Arco Publishing Co., 1969.

Staff Report to the National Commission on the Causes and Prevention of Violence (prepared by James F. Kirkham, Sheldon Levy, and William J. Crotty). *Assassination and Political Violence.* New York: Praeger Publishers, 1970.

Weisberg, Harold. *Martin Luther King: The Assassination.* New York: Carroll & Graf, 1993 (reprint of Weisberg's 1969 *Frame-Up*).

Young, Andrew. *A Way out of No Way: The Spiritual Memoirs of Andrew Young.* Nashville, Tenn.: Thomas Nelson Publishers, 1994.

Selected Articles and Periodicals

Auchmutey, Jim. "William Pepper: Lawyer Convinced King Family of Ray's Innocence." *The Atlanta Journal-Constitution,* July 11, 1997.

Billen, Andrew. "I Hired Martin Luther King's Killer, Says Memphis Businessman." *The Observer* (London), December 12, 1993.

Baker, Jackson. " 'Nearer to the Heart's Desire': Aided by an Unconventional Judge, the MLK Conspiracy Theorists Make Legal Headway." *The Memphis Flyer,* July 17–23, 1997.

Berg, Marsha Vande. "Ray: 'I'm Innocent, But . . .' " *The Tennessean,* May 29, 1977.

Black, Kay Pittman. "Attorneys to Bring Varied Backgrounds to Ray Hearing." *The Memphis Press-Scimitar,* June 20, 1974.

————, with Tom Jones. "Doctor Says Ray Told Him 'Others' Involved." *The Memphis Press-Scimitar,* October 23, 1974.

Branston, John. "Double Exposure: How a Reporter's 'Scoop' in the King Assassination Turned into a Prime-time Embarrassment." *The Memphis Flyer,* July 17–23, 1997.

Brice, Arthur. "James Earl Ray: Putting the King Case to Rest: Side Issues Complicate Search for Truth." *The Atlanta Journal-Constitution,* September 14, 1997.

————. "James Earl Ray Supporters Are Pinning Their Hopes on Loyd Jowers, an Elderly Fugitive Who Says He Hired the Assassin Who Killed Martin Luther King, Jr., but Finding Him May Be . . . A Shot in the Dark." *The Atlanta Journal-Constitution,* October 26, 1997.

Canellos, Peter S. "United by Doubt; King, Ray Camps Share Belief in Assassination Conspiracy." *The Boston Globe,* January 12, 1977.

Chappell, Kevin. "The Question That Won't Go Away: Who Killed King?" *Ebony,* May 1997.

"Chronicle of Ray's Whereabouts, from the Time He Fled." *The New York Times,* November 18, 1968.

Cohen, Jeff. "Who Killed Martin Luther King? The Framing of James Earl Ray." *The Fifth Estate,* vol. 9, no. 23, October 31–November 6, 1974.

————. "King Conspiracy Cover-Up Begins to Crack." *The Fifth Estate,* vol. 9, November 1974.

————. "The Secret Team Behind a Decade of Assassinations." *The Fifth Estate,* vol. 9, no. 26, November 21–27, 1974.

————, with David Lifton. "A Man He Calls Raoul." *New Times,* April 1, 1977.

Edginton, John, and John Sergeant. "The Murder of Martin Luther King, Jr." *Covert Action,* Summer 1990.

Gavzer, Bernard. "The Strange Case of James Earl Ray." *AP Newsfeatures,* January 19, 1969.

Hammer, Richard. "Clues to Man of Mystery." *The New York Times,* June 16, 1968.

Harrison, Eric. "The Killing of Dr. King Revisited." *Los Angeles Times,* September 24, 1994.

————. "Ray's Ill Health Gives Urgency to King Assassination Doubts for the Record." *Los Angeles Times,* January 5, 1997.

Howitt, Frank. "Killer or Decoy? This Crook Who Gave Up Too Easily." *Daily Telegraph* (London), July 31, 1968.

Huie, William Bradford. "The Story of James Earl Ray and the Plot to Assassinate Martin Luther King: 'I Had Been in Trouble All My Life, in Jail Most of It.' " *Look,* November 22, 1968.

————. "I Got Involved Gradually, and I Didn't Know Anybody Was to Be Murdered." *Look,* November 26, 1968.

————. "Why James Earl Ray Murdered Dr. King." *Look,* April 1969.

King, Coretta Scott. "Tragedy in Memphis." *Life,* September 19, 1969.

Lewis, Dwight, and Sheila Wissner. "Ray Smart Enough to Mastermind; Convicted Killer's File Shows a Fairly High IQ and Long List of Escape Attempts." *The Tennessean,* February 23, 1997.

Lollar, Michael. "Ray's 'Boxed-In' Feeling Forced Plea of Guilty, Brother Recalls in Trial." *The Commercial Appeal,* October 25, 1974.

McKinley, James. "Interview with James Earl Ray." *Playboy,* September 1977.

McKnight, Gerald D. "The 1968 Memphis Sanitation Strike and the FBI: A Case Study in Urban Surveillance." *South Atlantic Quarterly* 83, Spring 1984.

McWhirter, William A. "The Story of the Accused Killer of Dr. King: A Character Shaped by a Mean Life." *Life,* May 3, 1968.

O'Neil, Paul. "Ray, Sirhan—What Possessed Them?" *Life,* June 21, 1968.

Perrusquia, Marc. "Jowers Link Rejected, King Records Show." *The Commercial Appeal,* December 24, 1993.

————. "Conspiracy Theories Pile Up as Hearing on Ray Trial Nears." *The Commercial Appeal,* April 4, 1994.

————. "Who Killed King? 'I'm Innocent,' Insists Ray's Raoul." *The Commercial Appeal,* January 26, 1997.

———. "King Bullet Controversy Is a Misfire." *The Commercial Appeal*, February 16, 1997.

———. "Frail Ray Clings to King Story; Picks Photo of 'Raoul' Who He Says Framed Him." *The Commercial Appeal*, March 25, 1997.

———. "Whether for Truth or Profit, Ray's Lawyer Is a Driven Man." *The Commercial Appeal*, May 4, 1997.

———. "Emotions Mount as Ray Case Plods On: Is Bickering or Law the Focus?" *The Commercial Appeal*, August 17, 1997.

———. "King Security a Myth, Say Agents Here in '68; Army Intelligence Was Worried About Riots, They Recall." *The Commercial Appeal*, November 30, 1997.

Rosenbaum, Ron. "James Earl Ray and the Return of the Assassination Buff." *The Village Voice*, November 14, 1974.

Saunders, Julian. "Re-Examining the King Files." *The Ethnic NewsWatch*, January 31, 1994.

Shaw, Bynum. "Are You Sure Who Killed Martin Luther King?" *Esquire*, March 1972.

Smith, Warren, and Renfro T. Hays, "Sensational Evidence that James Earl Ray Did Not Kill Rev. Martin Luther King!" *Saga*, October 1969.

Sullivan, Christopher. "Martin Luther King's Murder Shrouded in Conspiracy Theories, Mystery." *Los Angeles Times*, January 21, 1996.

Timms, Ed. "Searching for Answers; Questions About King Assassination Persist as Ray Seeks Trial." *The Dallas Morning News*, March 2, 1997.

Tompkins, Stephen G. "Army Feared King, Secretly Watched Him; Spying on Blacks Started 75 Years Ago." *The Commercial Appeal*, March 21, 1993.

Waldron, Martin. "Ray Admits Guilt in Dr. King Death, Suggests a Plot." *The New York Times*, March 11, 1968.

———. "Ray's Arrest Ends Hunt That Began with His Escape from Missouri Prison in April of '67." *The New York Times*, June 9, 1968.

Walz, Jay. "3 Whose Names Ray Used Resemble Him." *The New York Times*, June 12, 1968.

Yellin, Emily. "Two Detectives Raising Fresh Doubts over Dr. King's Murder." *The New York Times*, November 23, 1997.

Selected Television Transcripts

"American Assassins." *CBS Reports* with Dan Rather, Part III, April 1976.

"Judge Joe Brown." *Nightline*, ABC News, April 3, 1997.

"The Death of Martin Luther King." CBS, 1968.

"Should James Earl Ray Have a New Trial?" *Nightline*, ABC News, February 20, 1997.

"Who Killed Martin Luther King?" BBC, John Edginton, producer, Otmoor Productions, 1993.

"Who Shot Martin Luther King, Jr.?" *Turning Point*, ABC News, June 19, 1997.

Papers and Archival Collections

Birmingham Police Department Surveillance files, Department of Archives and Manuscripts, Birmingham Public Library, Birmingham, Alabama.

Clay Blair, Jr., Papers, Collection 8259, American Heritage Center, University of Wyoming.

George McMillan Papers, Southern Historical Collection, Wilson Library, University of North Carolina at Chapel Hill.

Judge Robert M. McRae Papers, James Earl Ray Trial Records, Special Collections Department, McWhether Library, University of Memphis, Memphis, Tennessee.

Memphis Multi-Media Archival Project, the 1968 Sanitation Workers' Strike, J. W. Brister Library, Monograph Series, maintained at the Special Collections, McWhether Library, University of Memphis, Memphis, Tennessee.
Oral Histories relating to Martin Luther King, Jr., Lyndon B. Johnson Presidential Library, Austin, Texas.
William Bradford Huie Papers, University Library, Ohio State University.

Government Collections and Documents

District Attorney General, active case file on the assassination of Martin Luther King, Jr., Memphis, Tennessee.
FBI documents on the Bureau's investigation of the murder of Martin Luther King, MURKIN file, start at file number 44-1987-D; documents on Martin Luther King, Jr., start at file number 100-106670; documents on the Memphis Sanitation Strike start at file number 157-9146; all maintained at the FBI Reading Room, Washington, D.C.
Los Angeles Police Department, James Earl Ray file number 647-422, Records and Identification Bureau, Los Angeles, California.
Metropolitan Police Department, City of St. Louis, Police Reports on James Earl Ray, numbers 222014, 221989, 146048, 169866, 222015, 6094849, 223556, and 276643, Records Section, St. Louis, Missouri.
U.S. Department of Justice's Office of Professional Responsibility Task Force Review of the FBI's Security and Assassination Investigations of Martin Luther King, maintained at the National Archives, College Park, Maryland.

Government Publications

Compilation of the Statements of James Earl Ray, Staff Report of the Select Committee on Assassinations, U.S. House of Representatives, Ninety-fifth Congress, Second Session, U.S. Government Printing Office, Washington, D.C., August 18, 1978.
Report of the Department of Justice, Task Force to Review the FBI Martin Luther King, Jr., Security and Assassination Investigations, January 11, 1977.
Report of the House Select Committee on Assassinations, U.S. House of Representatives, Ninety-fifth Congress, Second Session, "Investigation into the Assassination of Martin Luther King, Jr.," plus Evidentiary Volumes I through XIII, U.S. Government Printing Office, Washington, D.C., 1979.

Selected Trial Transcripts and Proceedings

Extradition Proceedings, *United States of America* v. *James Earl Ray*, Justice Department file of 192 pages.
James Earl Ray v. *J. H. Rose, Warden*, Civil Action 74-166, U.S. District Court, Western District of Tennessee, 1974.
James Earl Ray v. *Michael Dutton, Warden*, in the Criminal Court of Shelby County, Tennessee, Habeas Corpus Petition, 1994.

James Earl Ray v. *Percy Foreman*, U.S. District Court, Western District of Tennessee, 1969.

James Earl Ray v. *State of Tennessee*, P-12454, in the Criminal Courts of Tennessee for the 30th Judicial District, Division IX, 1997.

James Earl Ray v. *Time Inc., et al.*, Civil Action No. C-76-274, U.S. District Court, Western District of Tennessee, 1976.

State of Tennessee v. *James Earl Ray*, in the Criminal Court of Shelby County, Division III, Tennessee, 1969.

Interviews conducted by the author and unpublished government and private documents reviewed for the book are cited as they appear in Notes, starting at page 343.

Index